PSYCHOLOGICAL

FOUNDATIONS

OF EDUCATION

From Devaney

NEW YORK · CHICAGO · SAN FRANCISCO · TORONTO · LONDON

PSYCHOLOGICAL FOUNDATIONS OF EDUCATION

MORRIS E. ESON
State University of New York at Albany

HOLT, RINEHART AND WINSTON, INC.

To all those who have made my life meaningful and significant, particularly to Joy and to Charles, Elizabeth, Marc, and Jud.

90123 22 98765

PREFACE

It is the author's belief that the first course in educational psychology, which this text has been written to serve, should demonstrate to the student how the concepts and the ways of thinking of psychology apply to school and classroom practice and how they can contribute to an understanding of the accepted aims of education. There are several approaches open to an author of a text in educational psychology in attempting to achieve this end. He can adopt consistently the view of one particular school of thought in psychology—the psychoanalytic, the associationist, the Gestalt, or the phenomenological—and he can describe how the particular point of view would deal with different practical problems in education. This approach has the virtue of being consistent but it fails because no single school of psychological thought alone is comprehensive enough to cover the wide range of problems that a teacher faces in the classroom. Yet, each psychological school or system can contribute something to the clarification of particular questions. In this book the author has attempted to bring to bear on the consideration of each educational problem that psychological point of view that promises to shed the greatest light on it. The author believes that this selective application of the points of view of several schools of psychology, while perhaps lacking in theoretical consistency, promises greater functional effectiveness and less distortion of reality.

In addition to the theorizing and experimentation that are generated within the framework of a single school of thought, much of the advance in modern psychology has taken place in special-interest and problem-oriented categories. Of the many special interests of psychologists, five have special relevance to educational psychology: the psychology of personality, the psychology of learning and problem-solving, developmental psychology, differential psychology or the understanding of individual differences, and social psychology. These are not to be viewed as separate and distinct categories, for they are closely intertwined and interrelated and together serve to make up the content of a meaningful educational psychology. The manner in which these special interests are related to the various aims of education is described in Chapter 1. The last chapter presents an integration of the various points of view and special interests of psychology and emphasizes the one consistent guiding principle of the book, namely, that the student in the classroom, no less than the teacher or the psychologist, is striving to realize his potential for growth and is striving to give meaning and significance to his existence and to his environment.

There are many ways in which the concepts of psychology may be made real to students. Theoretical discussion with persuasive logic is most effective for some. For others evidence derived from carefully controlled experiments persuades most readily. For still others careful analysis of an actual situation or case clarifies most fully. The author has found each of these avenues useful in helping students understand particular concepts. Each appears as a part of the exposition in this textbook.

The theoretical discussions, as well as the controlled research reports, have been drawn from many sources. The author has tried to convey the sense of each of these without distortion, but insofar as possible the student should read the complete reports. Many of these are to be found in the books of readings in educational psychology that are listed at the end of this volume and cross-referenced to each of its chapters.

The case material and the situational descriptions, designed to show how the psychological concepts can be seen to operate in concrete, living and dynamic situations come from several sources. Some are based upon the author's own experiences, some upon reports by other writers, and many upon the experiences of students who, in courses in educational psychology, mental hygiene, and adolescent psychology, have worked with the author in trying to understand better the educational process and human development.

The author is very much indebted to many of his teachers who introduced him to the pleasures of the study of psychology, particularly Mandel Sherman, Robert J. Havighurst, and the late David P. Boder. He is also grateful for the considerable help given him by Philip Jackson who read the entire manuscript, and whose constructive criticism was most useful. Morris Berger, a former student, a colleague, and a friend has been an invaluable source of help in each of these roles as he listened, criticized, and reacted, to early and late developments of most of the ideas in the book. It is with sorrow that the author expresses his gratitude to Elton Nelson who, shortly after the initial planning of the book, which was to have been a joint venture, was killed in a plane crash.

For specific assistance in getting the manuscript ready for the printer, the author wishes to thank Frances Smith, Judy Mohr, Barbara Cardell, Judy Simmons, Leona Griffin, and Mary O'Neil.

ALBANY, NEW YORK   MORRIS E. ESON

FEBRUARY 1964

CONTENTS

PART 1

PSYCHOLOGICAL PRINCIPLES AND EDUCATION

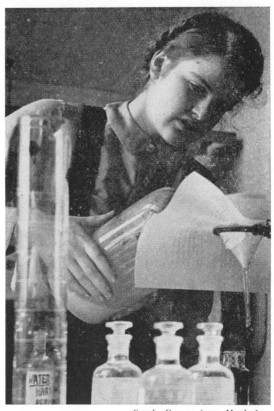

CHAPTER 1

THE ROLE OF
PSYCHOLOGY
IN EDUCATION

The maintenance and the advancement of any social order depend on the effectiveness of its institutions. The existence and the well-being of our own complex society depend on the integrity of our judicial system, legislative process, governmental operations, commercial enterprise, technological progress, artistic and cultural development, and a host of interrelated social and economic processes. The educational system is a keystone to the whole social structure, for only as it functions properly can all the others continue to serve the needs of the society. In many of those nations that have achieved independence without possessing an established system of education, the most crucial problems have arisen from the basic weakness of the social institutions resulting from the lack of an educated citizenry. The effectiveness of the educative process lies at the very heart of the social system. In fact, the effectiveness of the educative process reflects back on the schools themselves, determining the kinds of teachers who serve in the schools and the willingness and the understanding of the public in supporting the schools.

An educational system consists of many parts. It includes such items as textbooks, curricula, libraries, promotion policies, buildings, finances, but all of these are intended to serve but one purpose, namely, that of facilitating the optimal growth and development of the students. It is the human factor that is central to the educative process. Educational psychology is the systematic study of the development of the individual within the educational setting and of those conditions that favor the student's development into a responsible citizen, a sensitive human, and a productive, creative person.

THE APPLICATIONS OF PSYCHOLOGY TO EDUCATION

Our contemporary society pretends to make widespread use of psychology in meeting its problems. Many of these pretensions are based, unfortunately, on a view of psychology as a method of gaining power and control over others and as a technique for manipulation. This view of psychology, when carefully examined, turns out to be common sense misapplied for personal gain. When it is suggested that psychology can be of value in the analysis and determination of proper educational practice, this uncritical view of the science of psychology is not referred to, but rather the kind of psychology that is both empirical and systematic. Empirical means that our knowledge is based on experiment and careful observation, and systematic means that the facts and principles of psychology are ordered and arranged so that the whole system illuminates each of the separate parts. At the same time it should be recognized that educational practice is the kind of activity that must often proceed in advance of the development of sound scientific, psychological principles. In his *Talks to Teachers* (1902), William James, who did much to lay the foundations for our present-day empirical systematic psychology, noted the limitations of the applications of psychology to education in the following statement,

> I say moreover that you make a great, a very great mistake, if you think that psychology, being the science of the mind's laws, is something from which you can deduce definite programmes and schemes and methods of instruction for immediate schoolroom use. Psychology is a science and teaching is an art; and sciences never generate art directly out of themselves. An intermediary inventive mind must make the application, by using its originality.
>
> To know psychology, therefore, is absolutely no guarantee that we shall be good teachers. To advance to that result, we must have an additional endowment altogether, a happy tact and ingenuity to tell us what definite things to say and do when the pupil is before us. That ingenuity in meeting and pursuing the pupil, that tact for the concrete situation, though they are the alpha and omega of the teacher's art, are things to which psychology cannot help us in the least (pages 7-9).

Although a knowledge of psychology provides "no guarantee that we shall be good teachers," the inclusion of the study of educational psychology in a program of teacher education can be justified on the reasonable assumption that without it the teacher is less likely to be competent to perform his task. The relationship of psychology to education may be viewed as analogous to that of physiology to medicine or physics to engineering. The study of these basic disciplines provides no guarantee that the person will be a good physician or a good engineer, but the lack of such knowledge would be considered a serious deficiency. In truth, no single science has more profoundly influenced educational thought and practice during the past six or seven decades than that of psychology. The growth of psychology as a science has provided a framework for the educator in which to view the learner and the learning process. On the other hand, the educational setting has provided a field laboratory for the psychologist in which to test his hypotheses. This latter development has occurred to only a limited degree but we have reason to expect that in the future, more and more classroom-centered psychological research will be done. As psychology has pursued its special interests it has served to clarify the aims of education and has provided a framework for the examination of educational methods.

THE SPECIAL INTERESTS OF PSYCHOLOGY AND THE AIMS OF EDUCATION

Psychology has developed into a broad and diversified field. From its earliest beginnings, as that branch of philosophy that concerned itself with the nature of man and his reality, it has grown into an independent, varied discipline with a large number of special interests ranging all the way from the function of the single nerve cell to the problem of international disarmament. The *Psychological Abstracts,* a publication of the American Psychological Association that provides brief digests of articles of interest to psychologists, uses the following eleven-category classification (the subtopics are selected from the many that appear under each category):

1. General
    (a) History and systems
    (b) Professional aspects of psychology
2. Human experimental psychology
    (a) Vision
    (b) Motivation and emotion
    (c) Learning and memory
    (d) Problem solving and thinking
3. Physiological psychology
    (a) Brain lesions
    (b) Genetics and inheritance
4. Animal psychology
    (a) Reflexes and instinctive behavior
    (b) Sensory processes

5. Developmental psychology
   (a) Infancy
   (b) Childhood
   (c) Adolescence
6. Social psychology
   (a) Cultural factors
   (b) Status and class differences
   (c) Group processes
7. Personality and abilities
   (a) Intelligence
   (b) Personality measurement
   (c) Psychoanalytic theory
8. Therapy, guidance, and mental health
   (a) Psychotherapy
   (b) Case studies and casework
9. Abnormal psychology
   (a) Speech disorders
   (b) Crime and delinquency
   (c) Psychosomatics
10. Educational psychology
    (a) School and classroom learning
    (b) Learning and instructional aids
    (c) Interests, attitudes, and adjustment
    (d) Educational guidance
    (e) Educational measurement
11. Industrial and military psychology
    (a) Selection, placement, and appraisal
    (b) Work environment and performance

Most of these categories are directly or indirectly related to each other and provide the psychological background for school practice. Findings and principles derived in one category generally have implications in another. Thus, for example, Skinner's (1938) work with animal learning (Category 4) has led to a revival of an instrument developed by Pressey (1926) for educational measurement (Category 10d) and its application to programmed instruction and the so-called teaching machine. The study of aphasia, the loss of ability to use or understand language (Category 9a) due to brain disease or injury (Category 3a), has provided a basis for the understanding of language development (Category 5), which has been put to use in classroom teaching, in remedial reading, and in speech instruction (Category 10). The findings in industrial psychology in the area of work environment and performance (Category 11b) have provided a basis for modifying school building design. The illustrations of the interrelationships of the various categories could be multiplied many times.

A comprehensive educational psychology will synthesize most of the areas of psychological endeavor into a functional whole with a focus on the learner in the classroom. In the organization of this text some of the above mentioned categories have been regrouped and five general areas of psychology that are closely related to educational aims and methods have been used. These five areas are as follows: (1) psychodynamics and the psychology of personality, (2) the psychology of learning, problem solving, and thinking, (3) developmental psychology, (4) differential psychology or the study of individual differences, and (5) social psychology. Each of these is described and its relevance to educational aims as well as its place in the total design of this book is shown.

Psychodynamics and the Psychology of Personality

Educational psychology is the study of those conditions that favor the student's development into a responsible citizen, a sensitive human, and a productive and creative person. This statement involves a commitment to the proposition that education is an integral part of the development of the total personality. The meaning of this proposition hinges on the term personality. This does not mean a simple manipulation of individuals so that they might increase their social effectiveness. Although there might be a limited place in the school for teaching young people the social graces, how to dress properly, and how to groom themselves so that they might create a proper impression on others, this impression or social-stimulus value of the individual is not the meaning of personality as used here. Allport's (1961) definition coincides with the point of view held in this text, *personality is the dynamic organization within the individual of those psychophysical systems that determine his characteristic behavior and thought* (page 28).

There are a number of assumptions underlying this definition of personality. The determinants of the characteristic behavior and thought of an individual are multiple and varied, yet organized. This assumption of organization stems from a view that "living organisms tend to preserve a state of maximal *integration,* or internal consistency" (Mowrer and Kluckhohn, 1944). A further assumption underlying this dynamic view of personality is that the determinants of the individual's behavior and thought can best be understood when viewed as arising at least in part from within the individual. This assumption also views the growing individual as innately compelled to achieve higher and higher levels of integration, to strive toward "an individual style of life that is self-aware, self-critical, and self-enhancing" (Allport, 1955), and to realize his human potentialities. A third assumption of this dynamic view is that any segment of behavior can be meaningful only when it is understood within the context of the individual's total life situation as he perceives it.

The intention throughout this book is to make this psychodynamic point of view concrete and real. Truly effective education of the kind that has an impact on the student, must view the student as a dynamic, unique personality. This theme is developed in some detail in the next chapter and appears again and again throughout the book. The psychodynamic point of view plays a major role in Chapter 2 (Determinants of Behavior), Chapter 6 (Teaching for Values), Chapter 11 (Emotional Factors), and Chapters 15, and 16, which consider the teacher-pupil interaction and the teacher as a person.

The Psychology of Learning, Problem-Solving, Thinking, and Creativity

The one aim of education that has remained central through the centuries and through many structural and procedural changes, has been the development of the student's rational powers. Although the schools have served the various needs of the society in teaching for citizenship, vocational skills, moral character, and the like, it has been recognized that it is the person who has become able to use his rational powers "Who can bring all valid purposes into an integrated whole" (Educational Policies Commission, 1961). These rational powers consist of the acquisition and retention of the fixed meanings of the cultural environment, the organization of these into generalizations, the application of these generalizations to the solution of new problems, and the use of a cultivated imagination in creating new intellectual and esthetic challenges.

Bruner (1960), reporting on a conference of scientists, scholars, and educators concerned with the improvement of science education, points out that American psychology was for a long time "involved with the precise details of learning in highly simplified short-term situations and thereby lost much of its contact with the long-term educational effects of learning." He points out also that educational psychologists were largely interested in measurement of aptitude and achievement and to a lesser extent in the motivational and social aspects of classroom learning, and very little, if at all, in the correspondence between effective learning and thinking to the structure of the subject matter to be learned. This distribution of interest has been rapidly shifting and a great deal of effort is currently being directed toward the application of principles of psychology in the area of learning and thinking, to the improvement of instructional procedures. The content of recent issues of the *Journal of Educational Psychology*, the *Journal of Genetic Psychology*, *Child Development*, and others, reflects this shift in emphasis. The interest in programmed instruction, in the growth of logical thinking, and in creativity are all reflections of the psychologist's interest in rational powers.

A genuine interest in psychology as the foundation of our educational programs is the mark of a professionally competent teacher (Rivlin, 1953). This means that the teacher views psychology as one of the academic areas for the development of his own rational powers. It means further that psychology as a basic discipline will provide the teacher with a technical vocabulary with which he can better describe the events in the classroom and communicate about such events with colleagues. Such concepts as reinforcement, intelligence, psychosomatic disorder, massed versus distributed practice, phenomenal self, developmental task, are but a few of the many used in educational psychology, which when properly and accurately understood by the teacher should contribute to increased teaching effectiveness. The psychological generalizations that the student will learn about must be applied, insofar as possible, to the solution of educational problems. In order to prime this process of application, a large number of examples have been introduced in the text. It is also hoped that as a result of the study of psychology, the teacher will come to view the classroom learning process as a proper focus for creative and imaginative undertakings.

A great deal of emphasis has been placed on the psychology of learning in this book. Chapter 3 is devoted to a discussion of how fixed meanings are acquired; Chapter 4 to the development of understanding, thinking, and creativity; Chapter 5 to the fostering of application or transfer of training; Chapter 6 extends the concept of transfer into the realm of values and personality; Chapter 7 (the first chapter in Part 2) considers the management of learning; and Chapter 10 (the first chapter in Part 3) takes up individual differences in intelligence or the ways in which children differ in their use of these rational powers.

Developmental Psychology

Every statement of educational aims will imply that certain kinds of educational experiences are preferable in that they are presumed to produce certain desirable outcomes. These aims can be valid only if they are consistent with sound developmental theory. Throughout this text existing or proposed educational practice is examined in the light of the developmental process as it is understood today. Development has been variously described depending on the writer's particular interest and the selection of a particular aspect or phase of the process. (See Harris, 1957.) Essentially, the concept refers to the over-all pattern of change that results from maturational forces interacting with a multifaceted environment. Two descriptions of development and their relevance to educational aims illustrate this.

The first of these two descriptions is that of Anderson (1949). He analyzes what he calls the *enlargement of the life space,* or the achievement of independence and self-control. His analysis, which is based on the contrast of the infant and the adult, views development as proceeding along five interrelated lines. Each of these suggests a developmental aim of education. (1) He points out that development results in an increase in *sensitivity.* As the individual develops he becomes more sensitive to different kinds of stimulation, he senses differences in stimuli and is able to organize stimuli into patterns. Education that capitalizes on this developmental trend will make the student more fully aware of his world. It will help him make distinctions and see organization in his world. In brief it will increase his sensitivity and thereby give impetus to this aspect of development. (2) Anderson states that with development we witness "an enormous increase in the range, variety, and character of the reactions of the individual." This change in *performance* makes the individual more competent. A second aim of education, consistent with this developmental trend, is that of encouraging the growth of competence. (3) A third trend in development is the change in *level of function.* As the child grows older he becomes capable of functioning at levels of greater and greater complexity. He becomes more able to solve problems demanding more refined and complex sensing, more complex performance patterns and the use of symbolic processes. This developmental trend and the others as well do not occur spontaneously; they must be nurtured. The aim of the school would be to nurture increasing complexity of function. This would be achieved by providing challenging, though not disturbing, experiences. (4) Another facet of human development is that of growth in the temporal dimension. With the development of *memory* and *anticipation,* the person expands his life space backward into the past and forward into the future. This developmental gradient would suggest that the educational program would concern itself with making the student aware of his relationship to humanity and to his social group and expanding his life space by developing an historical awareness and building a future-oriented attitude upon this. (5) Anderson suggests that development brings with it *control* and *freedom.* "Progress from birth to maturity brings an increase in control over internal impulses and more control over external objects. Both make for greater effectiveness in the individual." Greater control brings with it greater independence. The aim of education is to teach control over the self and the environment so that the person can become free. "Good parents, good schools, and good communities facilitate this movement by creating opportunities for children to become independent and self-reliant."

In another context, Anderson (1957) describes the dynamics of development and he points out that the human system differs from other living systems in one fundamental respect, namely, that of *symbolization*. Much of what occurs in the five developmental trends just discussed takes place in and through the process of symbolization: "Pervading the whole and facilitating all the factors involved in development is the symbolic process by means of which the range of communication, control, and direction, as well as the emergence of new properties, is enormously increased" (page 45). A more elaborate statement of the significant role of language in the total development is presented by Church (1961). This would indicate that when education fosters the growth of the symbolic processes it thereby fosters all other facets of growth.

Another useful description of the developmental process and its relationship to educational objectives and procedures is that provided by Havighurst (1953). He sees human development as consisting of a series of learning tasks, which he calls developmental tasks. He defines this concept as follows: "A developmental task is a task which arises at or about a certain period in the life of the individual, successful achievement of which leads to his happiness and to success with later tasks, while failure leads to unhappiness in the individual, disapproval by the society, and difficulty with later tasks" (page 2).

Havighurst points out that any particular developmental task becomes appropriate for an individual when one or more of the following have occurred: (1) physical maturation has reached a point sufficient to endow the person with the physical resources necessary for the task, (2) the society expects certain behavior forms, (3) the personal values, aspirations, and psychological competence of the individual make it possible or necessary for the individual to enter into an activity.

The concept of the developmental task is helpful in thinking about the process of education for two reasons.

> First, it helps in discovering and stating the purposes of education in the schools. Education may be conceived as the effort of the society, through the school, to help the individual achieve certain of his developmental tasks.
>
> The second use of the concept is in the timing of educational efforts. When the body is ripe, and the society requires, and the self is ready to achieve a certain task, the teachable moment has come. Efforts at teaching which would have been largely wasted if they had come earlier, give gratifying results when they come at the *teachable moment,* when the task should be learned (Havighurst 1953, page 5).

Two of Havighurst's lists of developmental tasks follow. For a detailed discussion of the relationship of these tasks to educational aims and procedures, the reader is referred to Havighurst.

The Developmental Tasks of Middle Childhood

1. Learning physical skills necessary for ordinary games
2. Building wholesome attitudes toward oneself as a growing organism
3. Learning to get along with age-mates
4. Learning an appropriate masculine or feminine role
5. Developing fundamental skills in reading, writing, and calculating
6. Developing concepts necessary for everyday living
7. Developing conscience, morality and a scale of values
8. Achieving personal independence
9. Developing attitudes toward social groups and institutions

The Developmental Tasks of Adolescence

1. Achieving new and more mature relations with age-mates of both sexes
2. Achieving a masculine or feminine social role
3. Accepting one's physique and using the body effectively
4. Achieving assurance of economic independence
5. Achieving emotional independence of parents and other adults
6. Selecting and preparing for an occupation
7. Preparing for marriage and family life
8. Developing intellectual skills and concepts necessary for civic competence
9. Desiring and achieving socially responsible behavior
10. Acquiring a set of values and an ethical system as a guide to behavior

It is important for the teacher to adopt a developmental point of view that will enable him to consider behavior in terms of its history and its possible future course. Some behaviors that would ordinarily be ignored take on a new significance when viewed developmentally; others that would be exaggerated in importance are more readily seen as a natural part of the child's developmental pattern. The principles derived from developmental psychology, like those just presented as well as others such as Erikson (1950), Gesell (1954), Jersild (1960), Piaget, and Plant (1950), form a backdrop for much of the discussion in this book. They also form a basis for much of what is explicitly or implicitly the valid aims of education.

Differential Psychology or the Study of Individual Differences

One of the oft stated aims of education in our society is the fullest development of each individual child. Underlying this aim is the awareness that children differ widely in abilities and interests and that educational experiences must be diversified so that each child may obtain the greatest benefits from his schooling. This task grows more and more complicated as the schools serve ever increasing numbers of children and as they guide them into productive adult roles in a quickly changing technological world. Much is being accomplished in this regard as a result of the significant contributions of the field of educational and psychological measurement. A consideration of the general nature of these contributions follows.

The awareness of the existence of individual differences has had a long history. Plato in his *Republic* refers not only to the differences in men in what he considered natural endowments, but he also contends that in the ideal state men should be assigned to the various occupations for which their endowments fitted them. However, not much could be done practically about human differences until some valid and reliable means for identifying these differences had been developed. This did not occur until in our own century men like Binet and Simon in France developed a scale for assessing the intelligence of school-age children and others like Karl Pearson and R. A. Fisher in Great Britain had developed the statistical techniques required in test development. It is also interesting to note that Thorndike (1921) devotes more than half of the third volume of his monumental three volume *Educational Psychology* to the topic of individual differences.

It is not realistic to expect that every teacher will become an expert in measurement and statistics. However, it is important that the teacher realizes the significance and the implications of measurement psychology as well as its limitations. The study of this area of psychology will help the teacher examine his own assumptions about individual differences as well as those assumptions that lie behind a number of educational procedures such as grouping, promotion, and the like.

An effective statement of educational objectives will imply some method of determining to what extent these objectives have been met. This is one of the tasks of psychological measurement. Psychology, being an empirical science, teaches us that we must rely on evidence to support a particular educational practice. We cannot argue for a position out of intuition, some arbitrary opinion, or sheer logic. Psychological research has often shown that "logic in educational practice works in every case, except where it doesn't." Although there is much yet to be done in the development of measurement instruments, the contribution of this branch of psychology to research in education and to the formulation of educational aims has been considerable. The contribution of measurement psychology to the teacher's understanding of the individual child has been somewhat less impressive. This has been so partly because teachers have wrongly assumed that a human characteristic that can be described in a specific score is nothing more than that score and that a measured characteristic is more significant educationally than others that cannot be described quantitatively. Another limitation of measurement in psychology arises from the "bias of traditional psychology which looks at human beings as units that can be studied independently of their social surroundings" (Sanford, 1962). The teacher is well advised to keep a balanced view of the student by blending the understandings of the psychodynamics of behavior and those of measurement psychology.

This book attempts to maintain such a balance. In Part 2 some attention is given to questions involving individual differences and Chapter 9 considers the topic of evaluation generally. Part 3 is devoted in its entirety to the psychology of individual differences, their sources and how they can be influenced. However, a child cannot be measured, catalogued, and packaged, as it sometimes appears when the study of measurement is given a higher priority than the study of the child.

There is no conflict whatsoever between the concern for individual enhancement of the kind considered here and the integration of the individual as a member of the group. In many ways these are one and the same thing. Sanford (1962), in considering the objectives of higher education, provides a view of this relationship that is applicable to all levels of education: "The developed individual, according to this view, is adequately adapted to his environment and able to utilize culture in the interests of his basic needs; more than this he can criticize and help to improve society and, through creative activity, help to advance the civilization and to enlarge the culture" (page 35).

Social Psychology

Human beings acquire their human qualities in large part as a result of social interaction. It is through this interaction with others that the raw impulses and the multivariate potentialities of the child are shaped to the values, ideals, and action patterns of the society into which he is born. This process is called socialization. The extent to which the school should become involved in this socialization process has been a controversial issue. Some have argued that the aim of education should be largely to train children in cooperative and mutually helpful living; to help them become socially effective human beings in a democratic society. Some have extended this point of view and have developed statements of educational aims as being almost wholly those of life adjustment. The curriculum proposals that arise from such aims are open to ridicule because they have ignored the cognitive and other developmental aims of education. On the other hand, there are those who would deny that the school has any responsibility for deliberately participating in the socialization process and would limit the purpose of the school to intellectual development through disciplined manipulation of symbols.

Each society creates the agencies for socializing its young. These agencies serve in general to prepare the oncoming generation so that the values and the commitments of the adult society will be perpetuated. In our own society many agencies, such as the family, the church, the settlement house, 4-H clubs, scouts, and the like, take part in this endeavor on a more or less voluntary basis. The school, however, is the most deliberate and an almost universal instrument for the transmission of our democratic values and the American way of life. The task of the school becomes then to accomplish this without neglecting its other responsibilities. As Dewey (1931) states, "The motto must be: 'Learn to *act* with and for others while you learn to *think* and to judge for yourself.'"

Social psychology, which is the study of the individual in the group and in society as well as the study of the group and the society itself, contributes to our understanding of the social aims of education and their accomplishment in a number of different ways. Social psychology deals with attitude formation and change. This branch of psychology is involved when such matters as the growth of moral judgment, delinquency, and prejudice are examined in Chapter 6. Because instruction in school takes place in a group setting, it is important for the teacher to be able to describe the group structure and its effects upon the individual. Matters such as social acceptance, sociometry, and the use of sociodrama to foster proper socialization are discussed in Chapter 8. The child's family significantly influences the development of the social aspect of his personality. It is through the family that society mediates much of its value system. The teacher must understand how this influence operates so that he can view with proper perspective the growth of individual children in his class. It is in the home that the child is exposed to the influence of TV and the kind of parent-child relationships that exist will determine whether this influence will be detrimental. Questions bearing on these topics are taken up in Chapter 13. A similar discussion of the teacher-pupil interaction is presented in Chapter 15. One chapter is devoted to an important social-psychological issue, the influences of social class. In Chapter 14 there is a consideration of the values fostered in the various socioeconomic groups of our society, the problems of measuring school achievement in the lower classes, and the role of the school as an institution in a class-structured society.

THE ORGANIZATION OF THE BOOK

Although this text attempts to synthesize the five general areas of psychology that we have just discussed, these areas themselves do not provide a framework for a systematic presentation of those ideas that should be included in an educational psychology text. The organization of this text is based on the following set of teaching premises.

The first teaching premise is that learning takes place most efficiently when an interested student obtains a general, over-all view of the subject matter that he is trying to understand and master. A second premise is that the student reads more intelligently and participates more actively in the learning process when he is aware of the underlying assumptions of the discussion. Once the assumptions are understood and the general ideas of the subject are delineated, then the details can be presented to clarify and elaborate the general ideas. The best learning takes place when the student is constantly made aware of the significance and the application of the ideas or principles. To complete the learning process the student should have an opportunity to reintegrate these ideas around some central theme and, if possible, to personalize them.

This, then, is the reasoning behind the four parts of the book. The basic assumptions and the broad generalizations are presented in Part 1. This first chapter gives the broad outline of the book as a whole. The next chapter presents the writer's view of human nature and the determinants of behavior. These first two chapters serve to present the basic assumptions that are the foundations of the later discussion. Because the study of educational psychology should, in our estimation, enable the teacher to guide the *learning* of his students, an understanding of this complex and varied process is most essential. Accordingly, the next three chapters of Part 1 are devoted to this topic. Chapter 3 describes how children acquire the fixed meanings of the environment such as the names of concepts, a technical vocabulary, spelling, and the like. Chapter 4 takes up the topic of the development of understanding and problem-solving ability, which is another kind of learning. Chapter 5 considers the question of how both of these kinds of learning are applied to novel situations. This application of previous learning is called transfer of training. This first part is concluded with Chapter 6 on the teaching for values. In a sense this chapter should serve to reintegrate the ideas presented in all of Part 1 and should to a certain extent personalize a number of important issues for the teacher.

The second part of the book shows how the broad general principles presented in Part 1 can be applied to a variety of instructional problems and practices, such as the planning of instruction within the class, assigning homework, classification and grouping of students. These are some of the topics taken up in Chapter 7. Chapter 8 is devoted to the topic of managing the classroom group in order to insure maximum learning and optimum personality development. Part 2 is concluded with a chapter on the purposes and procedures of evaluation (Chapter 9) that should serve to integrate the content of the preceding eight chapters.

As pointed out above, an important aim of education in our society is the fullest development of each individual child. In order to accomplish this aim the teacher must have a clear and elaborated understanding of the ways in which children differ. Also, the general principles of educational psychology as well as their practical application, can only be meaningful when understood within the context of individual differences, so Part 3 considers the problem of adapting teaching to individual differences. The sequence of chapters in Part 3 is as follows: intellectual factors, emotional factors, physical factors, family influences and social class influences. The chapter on social class influences is placed at the close of Part 3 because it serves to challenge the student to review critically his own value system as it is contrasted with that of others. This is one way of personalizing the learning.

Part 4, consisting of two chapters, is an attempt to reintegrate the major themes of the first three parts of the book. This is done in an analysis of teacher-pupil interaction. This interaction influences the way the child comes to feel about himself and others, how he will learn and how he will develop into a unique human being. The concluding chapter (16) is designed to orient the teacher toward self-understanding and toward using the tasks demanded by his profession in such a way as to become an effective teacher and a significant person.

SUMMARY

The study of educational psychology should assist the teacher in guiding the growth of each student into a responsible citizen, a sensitive human, and a productive and creative person.

The special interests of psychology are closely related to the specific aims of education. Thus an understanding of the psychology of personality should enable the teacher to create the setting for optimal personality functioning. The understanding of learning, problem-solving, thinking, and creativity should enable the teacher to foster the development of rational powers. The psychology of development provides a basis for stating a number of educational aims and for interpreting others. In order to foster individuality, another aim of the educational process, the teacher must have an understanding of individual differences. In implementing the social aims of education, the teacher must operate on the principles of social psychology.

Effective learning, and this applies to the reader of this text also, takes place when the learner first obtains an over-all view of his task, when he understands the basic assumptions of the ideas that he confronts, when he seeks to view these ideas as applied to real situations, and when he seeks to incorporate these ideas in a personally meaningful way.

READING REFERENCES [1]

It is suggested that the reader consult the charts on pages 549–551 in which cross-reference is made between each chapter in the text and thirteen different collections of readings in educational psychology.

Association for Supervision and Curriculum Development 1956 Yearbook, *What Shall the High Schools Teach?* Washington: National Education Association.

Association for Supervision and Curriculum Development 1961 Yearbook, *Balance in the Curriculum.* Washington: National Education Association (particularly chaps. 1 and 5).

Association for Supervision and Curriculum Development 1963 Yearbook, *New Insights and the Curriculum.* Washington: National Education Association.

Dewey, J., *Experience and Education.* New York: Macmillan Company, 1938.

Havighurst, R. J., *Human Development and Education.* New York: Longmans, 1953.

Sayers, E. V. and W. Madden, *Education and the Democratic Faith; an Introduction to Philosophy of Education.* New York: Appleton-Century-Crofts, 1959.

[1] The references given within the chapter will be found alphabetically arranged in the Bibliography beginning on page 521.

CHAPTER 2

DETERMINANTS
OF BEHAVIOR

Because man is a self-conscious creature he has long sought to understand why he and his fellow-man behave as they do. He has developed numerous explanations that have been incorporated into the cultures within which he lives. The teacher, whose task makes him in some ways responsible for the changing behavior of others, is always operating on some kind of motivational theory. In our own society many different and even contradictory assumptions about "what makes people tick" exist side by side. The particular theory that the teacher chooses, even if only implicit, has a most significant effect on the teacher's method of teaching, his system of reward and punishment in the classroom, and in general his perception of his students and his task.

Every description of an activity, every decision in human affairs turns in some measure on our assumptions of motive or need. Teachers even more than others need an orientation to the determinants of behavior that is empirical, practical, and relevant to the classroom. To describe these determinants in a general way so as to explain all human behavior under all circumstances would require a lengthy and controversial discussion, which in the end might not lead to a functional understanding of classroom behavior. This chapter develops a descriptive and explanatory scheme to show how in a school setting behavior gets started, what causes it to persist and to change, and what determines the level of energy being expended in carrying out the behavior. The concept of behavior here refers not only to overt muscular response and internal glandular secretions, but also to thinking and other mental processes. To extend this scheme to explain behavior that occurs in other settings, such as the clinic or the home, and in adults, would require some different emphases, but the essential aspects of the formulation would still be valid.

THE VARIETY OF DETERMINANTS OF BEHAVIOR

The language used by various psychologists to describe the determinants of behavior, appears at first glance to be a veritable hodgepodge. We find such terms as instinct, drive, motive, need, value, incentive, goal, stimulation, reinforcement, and many more, being used in different and sometimes contradictory ways. It would take us too far afield to attempt to trace the history of the controversies in this area. In this chapter and throughout the book a point of view is expressed that is consistent with that of a number of contemporary psychologists (Berlyne, 1960; Butler, 1958; Harlow, 1953a and b; Hebb, 1958; Hunt, 1960; Rethlingshafer, 1963; White, 1959; Woodworth, 1958). To state this view simply: all behavior has its roots in two reciprocal sources, namely, the organism acting on the environment and the environment acting on the organism. When we speak of drive, motive or need, we speak of internal conditions of the organism, either biological or psychological, which compel the organism to act on the environment in more or less specific ways and with greater or lesser expenditure of energy. When we speak of goal, incentive or stimulation we are referring either to environmental factors that have played a part in inducing a condition of drive, motive or need, or we refer to environmental factors toward which these internal conditions are directed. In humans the matter is complicated because of the existence of a psychological environment that in a real sense represents an internal condition. In which case we might have one internal condition, for example a psychological goal, inducing another internal condition, a motive or a need. There is no way of knowing where one leaves off and the other begins. Even the person's behavior itself becomes involved in our description of determinants, inasmuch as behavior is continuous, the end result of one behavior sequence can readily become the antecedent for another.

The following discussion is divided into three parts: (1) The first part deals with those determinants that are universal to man; (2) The second part with those aspects of the classroom environment that determine behavior; (3) The final section takes up the matter of individuality, self, and personality as determinants of behavior. In explaining a particular behavior such as a child's reading in a primer, his throwing spitballs, his attempts to solve an algebra problem or his working a laboratory problem in physics, we must turn to all three classes of determinants to understand why he goes about his task in the manner he does. As the child moves from one situation to another, the relative importance of these classes will change. As the child grows older and has more experiences and as the universal determinants interact with the particular environment, the individual psychological dimension assumes greater and greater significance in the determination of behavior.

THE UNIVERSAL DETERMINANTS OF BEHAVIOR

All living things are motivated to act and to act in certain ways because of the internal physiological and biochemical organization of their bodies. In lower animals, this activity or behavior is more rigidly controlled by their biological makeup than in higher animals. Thus, some animals will go through an elaborate sequence of behavior in nest building, courtship and mating, or the organization of group life as in ants and bees. The entire behavior pattern is unlearned and seems to depend on the animal's inborn, innate reaction tendencies. The environmental factors such as temperature, sounds, and odors, serve simply as trigger mechanisms that set the behavior sequence into motion. When such unlearned behavior is found to be common to a species, it is called *instinctive behavior*. Using this definition of instinct, psychologists generally are in agreement that little if any human behavior is instinctive, that is, so completely determined by internal biological factors. The student will find that some writers (for example, Freud and McDougall) use the term instinct in another sense. In their use of the term the presence of a universal drive is sufficient for the label instinct. They do not require that the entire behavior pattern be unlearned before they use the term instinct. In making a choice of definition the more restrictive definition of the term instinct is more useful and prevents fallacious thinking on the part of the teacher. The teacher who attempts to explain the behavior of a particular child largely in terms of fixed, inherited causes or as being due to the nature of boys or girls at age seven or thirteen, is overlooking the complexity of human behavior and the contribution of environmental and psychological factors in the child's behavior. Although explanations should not rely exclusively on internal forces, an understanding of motivation must take into account the fact that the body is an independent energy system interacting with the energies induced in it by the environment.

Three universal determinants of human behavior are: (1) activity drives, (2) sensory drives, (3) visceral drives, and their interrelationship through homeostasis. These universal drives are shaped from the earliest moments of life by the environment and they change their form of expression from overt physical responses to more covert ideational responses.

Activity Drives

The basic universal force that initiates all behavior is the drive to activity. Many teachers view their motivational task as one of converting students who, from the teacher's point of view, are inattentive, bored, restless, lazy or unmotivated, into students who are attentive, interested, energetic, and motivated. A more fruitful analysis of the motivational problem can be achieved, we believe, by asking a more fundamental type of question, namely: Why do so many children learn so many things? What compels children to change from crawling to walking, from not talking to talking? What compels children in the primary grades to learn to read, to add and subtract, and to take responsibility for so many different activities? What motivates so many students to learn to spell correctly, to develop some scientific notions about the world, to understand the events of history and to relate to others constructively? These events cannot be taken for granted, for in the process of discovering why they occur we touch on the most basic issues in education and psychology.

The point of view that the organism will act only to relieve a state of tension and that it will otherwise be inert has been challenged by a series of animal studies. Thus Butler and Harlow (1954) and Butler (1953) have demonstrated that monkeys will learn to make fine discriminations for no other reason than to explore the environment visually, or to obtain an auditory reward. In earlier studies Harlow (1950) demonstrated that monkeys learned to solve problems for no reward other than that of experiencing the success in making things work. Berlyne (1955) was able to demonstrate similar behavior determinants in the rat.

These and other similar findings on animals have lent considerable support to the theoretical position of Woodworth (1958) and that expressed by Murphy (1947). Woodworth states:

> A large share of human behavior, both playful and serious, is on the face of it directed toward the accomplishment of environmental results without any ulterior intraorganic goal . . . We call attention to behavior that deserves to be taken at its face value in almost all psychological and practical contexts, as being motivated toward results to be accomplished in the environment by the individual or social group . . . Exploratory behavior occurs not when the baby is hungry but when he is free from this primary drive; apparently the behavior has its own drive. It is not motivated by hunger or thirst or fatigue or by a desire for pleasurable bodily sensations. It is directed outward, toward the environment which is being investigated. Its long-range value as the means of making the child acquainted with the world he has to deal with later, and so equipping him through play for the serious business of life, can scarcely lie within the

little child's horizon. His goals are more limited and direct: to see this or that object more closely, to find what is behind an obstacle, to hear the noise an object makes when it strikes the floor, to be told the name of a thing or person. He uses older people as sources of information (pages 76 and 78).

Murphy (1947) in a similar vein states:

> The normal condition is not one of successful escape from activity. Trends toward the reduction of activity and toward the increase of activity are always jointly manifest. The clock is always running down but always being wound up. Even when fatigue, starvation, or illness has forced a violently uncomfortable state of repose upon us, most of the bodily activities go on. The work of the body must be done. Muscular inactivity becomes unbearable; there is a compelling need to do something. At the psychological level something to do, something to occupy one's attention is compellingly experienced. We seek repose, but we also seek activity (page 108).

The presence of this activity drive is both the bane and the boon of the teacher's existence. Out of the activity drive when properly channeled can develop a high level of school achievement and also from it can arise resistance to guidance, negativistic behavior, and strong opposition to the objectives of the school.

Early in life the activity drive manifests itself largely in physical form. The waking moments of the neonate (newborn) are characterized by activity in various parts of the body. The physical activity is gradually molded by internal and external factors into the highly integrated patterns of holding, scribbling, walking, running, making sounds, and a vast array of other patterned responses. With age the physical activity becomes more refined and better integrated, while at the same time the observable aspects of it are reduced in quantity, and the mental activities arising from the sensory drives (see below) such as symbolizing, curiosity, fantasy, and reflection, increase. Contrast the behavior of the preschool child with that of the teen-ager. The young child is constantly on the "go", working off energy in physical activity; at the same time carrying on an endless chain of chatter, playing imaginatively, and asking innumerable questions. Observe the teen-ager over the same time; he may be reading, carrying on a conversation in which he expresses firm opinions, writing a letter, or playing a complex game such as monopoly or one requiring greater energy such as football. In the older child the balance is generally in favor of more passive environmental manipulation.

Because the child's experience with his environment is somewhat limited, he responds to his environment in an undifferentiated manner. His responses to different stimulus patterns in the environment are likely to be erratic and often indiscriminate. By the time the child enters school there is still a great deal of this undifferentiated action upon the environment, but there is also a readiness for the child to have this activity channeled and differentiated. Differentiation as a perceptual and learning phenomenon is dealt with more fully in the next chapter.

The teacher, of course, has some responsibility in directing the activity drive. When the teacher attempts too vigorously to redirect the flow of the child's energy, a phenomenon analogous to Newton's third law of motion may result. This law states that for every action there is an equal and opposite reaction. Forceful redirection may result in the child's use of his energies to resist this force from the teacher. The teacher must also recognize that the energy that lies behind the child's muscle and mental activity is not proportional, nor even directly related, to the amount of stimulation from the external world. The individual relies on his own psychological environment as an object of his drive to manipulate and to explore.

There are striking individual differences in the level and direction of the activity drive. In some part these differences come about as a result of training and experience. In Chapter 14 we shall see how the child's membership in a particular social class will influence his preference for a *motoric* (use of voluntary, large muscles) style of expression or a *conceptual* (manipulation of ideas) style. In part, individual differences can also be attributed to inherited characteristics. Children from birth seem to show marked and consistent differences in their energy expenditure. These differences are more than those related to basal metabolism or the conversion of food intake into caloric energy. Considering that the energy output is partially independent of outer stimulation and basal metabolism, it is small wonder that a group of students will show great variability in their "responsiveness." Observing a class from any grade engaged in an activity will show some who move quickly from one phase of an activity to another, some who are sluggish, some whose movements are smoothly articulated, and others who seem awkward and uncoordinated. These individual differences are basic to all of motivation, indeed, to all instruction. The teacher must understand that although some changes can be introduced by external factors, there are real and definite limits to how much slowing down or speeding up can be induced in the activity drive.

Sensory Drives

The sensory and activity drives are separated for purposes of discussion but the reader should not infer that these are two distinct and different kinds of drives. Sensing and perceiving are very clearly activities, but because they are more subtle and the activity is for the most part nonobservable, they are discussed separately.

As in the case of the activity drive, the natural state of the human is not only one of seeking a state of absence of sensory stimulation. In fact, such a state, if prolonged, is found to be most discomfiting. In one study (Bexton et al., 1954), students were subjected to an environment in which sensory stimulation was reduced, unvaried, and unpatterned. The students were each paid $20 a day to serve as subjects in this experiment. One might speculate that the students would welcome such an opportunity for complete relaxation and "getting away from it all." The results of the investigation were quite to the contrary. During the beginning of the experimental session the subjects spent most of their time in sleep, but as time went on, they became bored and slept less. They tended to stimulate themselves by singing, whistling, or talking to themselves. The subjects could not think productively or systematically and even experienced "feelings of confusion, headaches, a mild nausea, and fatigue." The human body seems to seek sensory stimulation and when the outer world presents too few stimuli it may even resort to creating hallucinatory stimulation. The drive for sensory stimulation is not constantly active; like the activity drive it operates in a cyclical fashion. We seek sensory activity and then seek a period of reduced stimulation.

As in the case of the activity drive, children show individual differences in level and patterning of the sensory drive. Some children seek and enjoy, from the earliest days of life, stimulation of all the sense modalities. They respond readily to music, colors, and the presence of others. Some children, on the other hand, seem less alert to sensory stimulation. We also find that children may specialize in their preferences, preferring musical notes to arrangements of colors, or the kinesthetic senses to the visual or auditory.

As the organism develops it becomes capable of integrating more and more complex patterns of sensory stimulation. When, for a particular level of development, the sensory stimulation is either too constant, insufficiently varied, or else it is of an order that cannot be assimilated because it is of too great or too little intensity, we find that *boredom* or *fatigue* occurs. When this motivational state of boredom occurs one of two things will result. The organism seems to require a change in level of stimulation. This can be achieved either by actively seeking to raise or to lower the level of stimulation. Thus an overstimulated individual will seek an opportunity to rest, to be inactive, and to avoid stimulation by shutting out the world in sleep or in being impervious to his surroundings. In the case of the younger child, however, when overstimulated or when bored, he will seek an even higher level of stimulation. He may show uncontrollable activity, irritability, shouting, running, giggling, and the like. Berlyne (1960) contends that boredom works through an increase in arousal. Commonplace observations of the bored child would support his contention.

Recognizing that the kind of boredom and fatigue discussed here[1] play a significant role in determining behavior, the teacher must constantly be alert to the needs of a particular child or a total classroom group. Children in the first six or seven grades, when returning from an exciting gym situation, may be truly overstimulated but they are likely to respond by becoming hyperactive, easily stimulated to boisterousness and silliness and difficult to control. It is best to introduce quiet, non-competitive activities and to be patient while the excitement subsides. By patience is meant firmness but not punitiveness. In the older student, the motivational condition of boredom or fatigue results in a temporary withdrawal from the situation. The teacher's responsibility is then one of introducing some variation in the sensory stimulation by a change of pace or other appropriate device. In Chapter 11 this question is returned to when emotions as states of arousal are considered. In many respects emotion and motivation are overlapping processes.

The Visceral Drives

The two universal determinants discussed thus far, activity and sensory drives, are "outgoing" motivations—as "directed toward an environmental goal, not toward the satisfaction or reduction of an organic need" (Woodworth, 1958). The visceral drives, on the other hand, serve to reduce a tension or deficiency that, if not satisfied, would lead to "(1) the impairment of the general health and well-being of the organism or (2) the elimination of the species" (Hall, 1961). Because these organic needs are satisfied initially in the home rather than in the school, the discussion of them will be directed to those aspects of these motives or drives that are relevant for the classroom.

Those who trace personality development within the framework of psychoanalytic thought have been very much aware of the relationship of the visceral drives, their modes of satisfaction and later adjustment. Thus Pearson (1954) in a book entitled *Psychoanalysis and the Education of the Child* states:

> I have pointed out that disturbances during the oral period [the period when all energies are directed toward satisfying the hunger and thirst drives] may result in learning difficulties. When a child enters school, his teacher should find out whether he has had such disturbances and what their nature and extent was . . .
>
> It is a general rule in classrooms, both progressive and traditional, that children must not eat while they work because eating interferes with learning and paying attention. On the surface this idea seems at variance with ordinary human experience. It is true that a person does not think

---

[1] In addition to being caused by insufficiently intense or unvaried stimulation, boredom of another kind may have its roots in hostility, anxiety, conflict, and other emotional conditions.

as well as usual after eating a large meal, but it also is true that group discussions on any subject proceed better and with more real interest and profit when accompanied by smoking or nibbling (page 248).

Two points are worth considering briefly with respect to oral need satisfaction. Most of us have experienced the school taboo against gum chewing. If one raises the question with teachers why gum chewing should not be allowed, they usually answer that it looks ugly, it creates a mess, it is distracting, or visitors will misinterpret evidence of gum chewing. All of these reasons are basically unrelated to the issue. Chewing is not inherently a repulsive activity; some children can probably engage in concentrated work better while chewing gum; if proper receptacles are provided, the mess of gum chewing can be avoided. If the teacher views this oral activity as one way of satisfying a visceral need, it is less likely to become a battleground such as develops when the teacher views it as evidence of rebellion and hostility. The truth of the matter is that oral activity, spitting, cursing, and even gum chewing, can be hostile acts, but the latter is likely to become such only when the teacher or others have defined it for the child as taboo behavior.

The other point about oral need satisfaction derives from the ancient understanding that eating together is a basic way of sharing experiences. Under present conditions, the eating period in a school where dining facilities are available is the most hectic and poorly organized period of the day. During this period teachers are assigned supervisory duties or else they seek a few moments of solitude or adult companionship. Teachers should have a few moments for themselves, but perhaps these periods should be at other times of the day so that teachers might be able to spend some time in the "breaking of bread" with their students. This kind of shared experience can be more valuable in strengthening teacher-pupil ties than other periods when instruction is going on. It is likely, too, that through the experience of eating together the teacher will learn to view some kinds of oral activity as a basis for establishing mutuality rather than its opposite.

The one visceral drive that creates many school problems, particularly during the adolescent years, is the sexual drive. It is different from the other visceral drives in that it can be denied direct expression and is much more completely modified by the person's social environment. Many taboos and learned restrictions on behavior are related to the control of this drive. So strong is society's need to control the sex drive that we are even unwilling to consider its educational implications. The existence of the sex drive and its many manifestations in the school setting are real and must be recognized. High school male students will often banter with a young female teacher. They may produce pornographic drawings. Adolescent female students will develop a "crush" on a male teacher. These are often merely the inept expressions of the reawakening sexual drive. It would be difficult to prescribe a particular course of action in dealing with such problems but one objective should be kept in mind. A feeling of fondness of a pupil for a teacher can be useful in encouraging educational achievement. This should not be destroyed as the teacher attempts to cope with the immature expressions of the sex drive. The school's responsibility in the area of sex education has been a controversial issue. Yet the school curriculum could offer many opportunities to set the young person thinking about these issues. The course of history has been determined by man-woman relationships. Literature abounds in sublimated expressions of the sexual impulse and a knowledge of reproduction is certainly a key area in the biological sciences. No program or part of a program will be suitable for all children alike and choices must be made with the awareness that boys and girls differ significantly in the strength of this drive and society produces quite different environments in which they learn the proper forms of expression. The result is that boys are generally more active sexually than girls and significant individual differences exist. Kinsey et al. (1948) have investigated these differences and state:

> Persons interested in sex education look for a program which will satisfy children—meaning all children—at some educational level, overlooking the fact that one individual may be adapted to a particular, perhaps relatively inactive, sort of sexual adjustment, while the next would find it practically impossible to confine himself to such a low level of activity. . . . Meetings of educators who are discussing sex instruction and policies to be followed in the administration of educational institutions, may bring out extreme differences of opinion which range from recommendations for the teaching of complete abstinence to recommendations for frank acceptance of almost any type of sexual activity (pages 197-199).

Homeostasis

The activity and the sensory drives, as we have described them, served the purposes of exploration and acting on the environment for its own sake. These drives also fulfil a maintenance or survival function. In order to survive, a living organism must engage in a constant transaction with the environment, incorporating certain substances, processing them, and producing elimination wastes. Certain of the visceral activities carry on this function. When visceral needs arise and become sufficiently strong, the activity drives are called into the service of satisfying these needs. When the visceral needs are in a reasonable state of satisfaction, the energy of the activity and the sensory drives is used to interact with the environment, to manipulate it, to incorporate it and to be effective in it.

The visceral drives and that portion of the activity drive that serve to maintain the organism, operate in such a way as to keep a relatively constant physiological condition in the body. Cannon (1932) named the regulation of this constant condition and called it *homeostasis*. Cannon described how the body maintains a relatively constant temperature and how the constituents of the blood stream such as water, sugar, protein, salt, acid level, and so on, are kept in constant proportions. When the child's environment permits the maintenance of homeostasis to take place by the expenditure of ordinary energies, then the activity drive can be released for growth or for self-assertion. When, however, the internal or external conditions are such as to place a stress on any one of the organ systems, as in the case of hunger, illness or deprivation, the child's energies are mobilized and directed toward the recovery of homeostasis.

The condition of physiological imbalance is likely to reduce the directed and coordinated character of activity. Harlow (1953b) describes this phenomenon in these terms:

> The condition of strong drive is inimical to all but very limited aspects of learning (directed change of behavior) . . . The hungry child screams, closes his eyes and is apparently oblivious to most of his environment. During this state, he eliminates response to those aspects of his environment around which all his important learned behaviors will be based. The hungry child is a most incurious child, but after he has eaten and become thoroughly sated, his curiosity and all learned responses associated with his curiosity take place (page 25).

A serious state of physiological imbalance will thus inhibit the directed aspects of the other drives that may otherwise be operating. The drives that function for the survival of the individual take precedence over all others and a threat to normal body functioning will reduce the level of activity in other drive areas. Teachers should thus understand that children who are hungry will become restless, that children who have experienced serious deprivation will lose, at least temporarily, the capacity to undertake and maintain directed activity and to seek to satisfy curiosity. Richards, in his *Principles of Literary Criticism* (1926), puts it this way, "The most valuable states of mind then are those that involve the widest and most comprehensive coordination of activities and the least curtailment, conflict, starvation and restriction."

In Maslow's (1954) formulation, the notion that the release of the organism's capacities when the physiological needs are satisfied, is extended through a hierarchy of needs. He suggests that once the physiological needs are relatively well gratified a new set of needs emerges. These needs, he states, are first the safety needs; when these are satisfied the love needs emerge. When the love needs are gratified the esteem needs become primary and when these prior needs are all satisfied the organism develops the need for self-actualization. This last set of needs Maslow describes as a desire "to become more and more what one is, to become everything that one is capable of becoming." This concept is dealt with more fully in a later section of this chapter.

Homeostasis was first proposed as a description of a complex physiological equilibrium that the organism seeks to maintain. The maintenance of equilibrium is not a crucial determinant of behavior. In fact, the human organism seeks states of disequilibrium in order to have the satisfaction of producing his own new point of equilibrium, at a higher level of behavior integration.

ENVIRONMENTAL DETERMINANTS

The universal determinants described thus far are continuously being shaped by the environment. Each of the drives is unique in its expression because of inborn predispositions as well as environmental influences.

The environment of every human is made up of certain omnipresent realities, a particular climate and geography, a political, economic, legal and religious milieu, a stratum within a society, the values, mores and taboos of the social group, and the psychological and material qualities of the immediate family. Each of these is effective to a certain extent in producing certain kinds of behavior forms. Some of these environmental factors are discussed in Part 3, particularly Chapters 13 and 14, which deal with family and social class influences respectively. On a more immediate level, the classroom situation provides some important behavior determinants. For purposes of discussion these are divided into three categories, demand, expectation, and opportunity.

Demand

One aspect of the child's socializing environment to which he is continuously responding is that of demand. Demands are most certainly potent devices in shaping and directing behavior. Children will turn to a particular page in a book, because the teacher has directed the class to do so; most children will proceed to the blackboard and perform the required task if they are told to do so; the school schedule, in a sense, demands that children be at certain places at certain times. The demands of our environment, laws, taboos, and the like, elicit certain behavior forms and inhibit others. In general, the psychological literature has offered the teacher very little guidance in the application of demands as determinants of behavior. Because we have been so concerned with the possibilities of distorting the child's personality by coercion, we have tended to overlook this very important tool in the shaping of behavior and ultimately, personality. It is important to remember that the growing child has no natural sense of determining in which way it is appropriate to express the universal drives. It is only as adults provide direction that the child discovers the paths or channels of expression that are desirable and approved and that can also prove satisfying to him. Demands thus form one important facet of the environmental context in which behavior takes on meaning and expression. While noting the importance of demands in inducing behavior, their limitations must be recognized. We know, for example, that demands frequently are met with resistance, indifference, and hostility. Also, we often have reason to be troubled by outward conformity to demand but an absence of the acceptance of the spirit of the demand. In many cases, children who behave as we require them to behave, do not develop the proper rationale for that behavior and hence are unable to perform in the desired fashion when the demand is no longer operative. This question also arises in Chapter 6 when the development of autonomous morality is considered, and again in Chapter 15 when discussing control.

Teachers, then, face these questions in establishing the demand aspects of the classroom environment: How can I present demands so as to reduce the possibility of arousing negative, resistant behavior? How shall I present the demands so that I do not hinder the child's growth in self-responsibility? The following principles provide a basis for the implementation of demands in the classroom, so that harmful effects are minimized and beneficial ones are maximized.

1. Demands are generally more effective and constructive when they are applied in an atmosphere of positive teacher-pupil relationships. These relationships are described more explicitly in Chapter 15. Teachers who exercise authority without regard to the child's feelings are more likely to engender feelings in the child that will lead to undesirable behavior. However, the demands of the dominative, impersonal teacher appear to be fulfilled at least as often as those of the teacher who is more reluctant to impose his will on his students. In fact, the dominative teacher may create in his students an attitude of unquestioning obedience. This attitude in a child can be a hindrance rather than an asset in his total development. The child's acceptance of the order and the rules necessary for any social function might be slower when he is treated with friendliness, warmth, and respect, but he is more likely to acquire a sense of self-direction and will not require supervision for as long a period of time.

2. The teacher should reserve the use of explicit demands for those situations in which the induced behavior is important for the child or for the group and where the behavior is not likely to occur spontaneously. It is much preferable to allow the behavior to occur because the child recognizes its appropriateness. A corollary of this principle is that the behavior elicited by the demand should at some point enhance the child's adjustment to the world in a larger sense than merely satisfying the teacher's whim. Many teachers' demands for uniformity are not rea-

sonable. The writer has known a sixth-grade teacher who insisted that the students' names on papers submitted should appear exactly one inch from the top and right side edges of the paper, that the name be printed in block capitals and that the date be placed one-half inch below the name in lower-case printing. Most children would resent such nonreasoned prescriptions on behavior and will often manifest their resentment in not fulfilling the teacher's demand or quickly abandoning the form when the occasion seems to permit it. To state the corollary briefly, demands should not be used to assert the teacher's power position in relation to the students.

3. Demands should be consistent and possible of fulfillment. In the high school setting, one often finds that teachers present homework assignments that would require neglect of other teachers' assignments. When a student faces equally forceful pressures and any decision he makes will necessarily lead to nonfulfillment of some demands, he is likely to find himself unable to undertake to do whatever he should be able to do, and will simply ignore all assignments. The teacher does have a responsibility of knowing how his demand is to be met. Teachers who demand the impossible are not providing the student with high standards, but instituting generally impotent instigations to action. The story of the old lady who had so many things to do she went to sleep, may best illustrate this point. The total institution of the school does have the responsibility of setting a tone with regard to such activities as homework, athletic events, after-school remunerative work, and so on. If demands are reasonable and set within the larger framework of expectations consistent with those demands, they will usually be met and this conformity will serve an important role in the development of wholesome personal motives.

4. Demands generally carry with them implications of punishment if not followed. Studies have shown that punishment is more effective in inducing effort than being indifferent to or ignoring the child. These results can be explained by the fact that punishment or the anticipation of punishment is an environmental determinant of greater strength than being treated indifferently. A teacher who punishes may very well be one who cares more than one who does not. A word of caution, however, with regard to punishment is called for. The teacher must recognize that punishment may succeed in deterring wrong or undesirable behavior but this in itself does not direct the child to the correct or proper behavior. Punishments, implied or administered, must be of such a nature as not seriously to disorganize the child's behavior. The denial of opportunity or privilege is an effective means of backing up demands, but the teacher needs to be sure that it is within his power to deny the privilege. Furthermore, the teacher should be careful to assess what is being denied in terms of whether carrying out the threat may not truly

be impossible. Implications of "ever" or "never" are usually indications to the child that the adult is upset and unreasonable but that he would not be able to carry out the threat anyway. Teachers must be careful in their strong desire to back up a demand that they do not bring out the heavy ammunition for minor demands. In short, it may be said that a demand presented as an ultimatum should be used only rarely and cautiously.

5. Demands must be presented in such a way as to be within the range of a child's understanding. Many of the directions presented to young children are not followed simply because the child is unable to understand what the teacher means. Directions stated as general consequences to be avoided such as, "Don't get yourself dirty," or "Don't disturb the other classes," are very difficult for children to fulfill. The adult understands these to mean, take the proper precautions to avoid getting dirty, or keep your voices low enough so that no one will be disturbed by the noise. The child, however, simply does not understand the steps to be taken in not getting dirty or not disturbing others. The teacher would do well at the beginning to spell out the necessary steps in the demand and then to help the child see that he has fulfilled the demand in terms of its general positive consequences. Thus, the teacher should suggest the wearing of a smock or changing to appropriate clothes, keeping voices to a whisper, and then to point out that regular clothes are clean or that the other children have not been disturbed.

In considering the range of a child's understanding, we must also take into account the limitations in his ability to foresee the sequence of events that may follow from his action. Demands that relate to consequences that are too remote in time, too abstract in nature, cannot be fulfilled intelligently by the younger child.

6. Preparation for situations in which new demands will be made is of utmost importance. This preparation should not consist of the teacher presenting a list of "thou shalts" and "thou shalt nots." Rather the preparation should consist of helping the children see what the situation will demand of them.

Mrs. Inham, a seventh-grade teacher of social studies in a school system about seventy miles from the state capitol, had arranged with the school authorities and with officials at the capitol for a tour of the legislative facilities. This tour had usually been reserved for the more advanced grades in the school, but Mrs. Inham was convinced, because of the turn of the discussion in her class, that her seventh graders were ready. She then devoted one class period asking the children to consider the conduct requirements on their trip to the capitol buildings. Many good suggestions were offered with regard to keeping the group together, how they should address legislators and other officials, matters of proper dress were discussed and a list of these and several other topics were placed on the board. Among these topics was also mentioned the need for proper conduct on the bus.

When the day of the trip arrived, three children, who had been absent during the discussion period, appeared in dress not considered appropriate for the occasion. The teacher asked them to join another class, but she first apologized to these students and pointed out that the notification of absentees was one important item that had been overlooked in the planning. On the bus, a few of the boys, who apparently had been fighting during their morning bus ride to school, began to quarrel over a seat. The teacher settled this as amicably as possible by sending both of them to other seats. Along the road, a few of the boys opened the windows and began to throw orange peels from their lunch box at some of the people on the outside and soon began to do this in the bus. The teacher sensed that if she did not help the children to gain control over themselves, the situation would deteriorate. She then asked the bus driver to halt the bus at the nearest convenient spot and she reminded the class that they themselves had set up the rules for conduct for the whole trip, that if they were incapable of meeting the demands of the bus ride, she could not allow them to continue. Some of the boys continued to snicker and act up even while the teacher was talking. Mrs. Inham then added that if she were required to discuss the matter of their behavior again, they would need to return to school. Because the children knew that their teacher was not given to idle threats they began to exert pressure on each other to maintain a reasonable decorum. The teacher's demands did not become unreasonable because of the lapse of discipline and soon the group relaxed into an enjoyable and pleasant trip. This illustration serves to point out that teachers cannot abdicate their assigned authority but must use it cautiously and maturely. Out of the experience of anticipating the demands of new situations children can gradually learn to accept more and more self-responsibility and will eventually be able to direct their own behavior.

7. Demands should not constitute a large portion of the classroom motivating environment. At all levels of education, a teacher may appear to engender a good deal of frenetic activity by means of deadlines, rules, regulations, assignments, and term papers. Students who engage in these activities primarily to avoid the punishments, implicit or explicit, for not meeting the demands, will generally not develop an inspired attitude toward their studies. The environment must consist also of expectation and opportunity if the motivation for learning is to be deep and lasting.

Expectation

Expectation differs from demand as a behavior determinant in two ways. First, expectation is general in that it concerns itself with broad categories of behavior such as levels of maturity, whereas demand is specific to a situation. Second, expectation carries with it the implication of reward and approval if the expectation is met, disapproval if it is not, whereas demand is generally one-sided in its consequences, only implying punishment. Like demand, expectation is a very strong instigator and inhibitor of behavior.

The following statements made by teachers to their students illustrate the more explicit aspects of expectation.

"Boys who are six years old don't cry when they fall."

"I would expect that you would be able to do as well as your sister. She was a very fine student."

"I am disappointed with the work of this class. I had expected that you would all be able to do sixth-grade arithmetic."

"What can you expect from someone who comes from an (Italian, Irish, Polish, Catholic, Jewish) home?"

In addition to the expectations emanating from teachers, reputations that children acquire in a classroom, serve as part of the total expectation environment. "In the naturalistic setting the subjects *receive* stimuli varying partly on the basis of their reputation; they are aware that actions on their part will not be judged completely afresh each time, but will be judged partly in terms of their previously acquired reputation; they know there are fairly stable expectations of the class group with reference to this person" (P. S. Sears, 1957, page 286).

Tryon (1939) has pointed out that adolescents do set for each other certain expectations that must be met if approval is to be gained. Thus, twelve-year-old boys emphasize for their age group the desirability of activity of any sort; they prefer aggressiveness, unkemptness, and boisterousness to their opposites, submissiveness, tidiness, and reserve, and above all, they respect competence in group games. In the case of fifteen-year-old boys, the preferred pattern changes somewhat. Although skill in games, fearlessness and self-assertion are still admired traits, they give equal emphasis to personableness and social ease and poise in heterosexual situations. In the fifteen-year-old boys, boisterousness and hyperactivity are not condoned because they are considered childish behavior patterns, while cheerfulness and a sense of humor become admired traits. Among twelve-year-old girls the characteristics that are related to prestige status are neatness, attractive appearance, quiet good humor, controlled behavior conforming to adult standards and docile social manner. In this age-sex group a certain amount of tomboyishness is acceptable, but contrary to twelve-year-old males, raucous, noisy activity is frowned upon. The importance of being able to attract boys through sophisticated and glamorous qualities becomes apparent in the fifteen-year-old girls, as well as buoyant, rather aggressive, good-fellowship with both boys and girls. While these specific expectations may not apply to every particular group of young people, we must recognize that the expectations of the peer group become increasingly important with age as determinants of behavior (see Chapter 8).

In a study by Tannenbaum (1959) more than 600 eleventh graders were asked to rate the social acceptability of eight hypothetical students. The ranking in acceptability was as follows:

1. Brilliant—nonstudious—athletic
2. Average—nonstudious—athletic
3. Average—studious—athletic
4. Brilliant—studious—athletic
5. Brilliant—nonstudious—nonathletic
6. Average—nonstudious—nonathletic
7. Average—studious—nonathletic
8. Brilliant—studious—nonathletic

These rankings show that the brilliant student is considered much more acceptable if he is nonstudious than if he is studious, and if he is athletic rather than nonathletic. These stereotypes and the resulting acceptance ratings will most assuredly shape the behavior of many high school students. Jersild (1960), from whom the Tannenbaum study is cited, states that preliminary findings by Tannenbaum and his associates "indicate that the studious pupil is likely to be viewed with more favor by his classmates at the elementary-school level than at the high-school level." These latter findings would indicate that in the earlier years the teacher's expectations are adopted more or less uncritically by the students; in adolescence the expectations may be rejected or at least ignored. In a recent study Coleman (1961a) points out that the value systems that are fostered by the powerful adolescent subculture in American schools, will vary in certain details from school to school. Yet in *all* the schools studied academic achievement did not count as much as other activities in school. Coleman states (1961b):

> In every school the boys named as best athletes and those named as most popular with girls were far more often mentioned as members of the leading crowd, and as someone to be like than were the boys named as best students. Similarly, in every school, the girls who were named as best dressed and those considered most popular with boys were far more often mentioned as being in the leading crowd and as someone to be like, than were the girls named as best students.
>
> The relative unimportance of academic achievement together with the effects that have been shown, suggest that the adolescent subcultures in these schools exert a rather strong deterrent to academic achievement (pages 58-59).

Haggard (1957) has shown, however, that the general school atmosphere can be one in which "all the children are concerned about doing well academically, many of them come to idealize intellectual prowess and consider it an essential ingredient to justify self-esteem and acceptance."

One of the ways in which a person expresses his expectation of others is through incentive. Some writers have used the term incentive as applying to all conditions in the external environment that serve as goals for the individual's behavior. Here the term is used in a more restricted sense, to refer to a condition in the external environment (usually some form of reward) defined and controlled by an outside agent, in order to intensify effort. Employers use incentives in the form of bonus pay for extra performance and production; teachers set incentives such as stars, prizes, and good grades for certain kinds of behavior or performance. It is important to recognize that when a person, such as an employer or a teacher, who assumes some responsibility for the effort of others, sets an incentive in order to obtain increased output, he is tacitly assuming that the amount of motive energy that would be expended, should no incentive be present, would be less. Under many conditions incentives do effect a desirable increase of activity. When they are applied uncritically, however, they may produce detrimental results.

The excessive and inappropriate use of incentives can lead to the student being distracted from the intrinsic value of the activity itself, centering his attention on achieving the prize but not perceiving the value and purpose of what he needs to do in order to get the prize. Often the child is led to assume that the teacher offers the incentive with the implication that it is some sort of compensation for doing something intrinsically unsatisfying. That is, the activity itself acquires negative significance as a result of the manner in which the incentive is presented and the development of real interest in the activity is thus endangered. In one school regular attendance was rewarded with prizes and prestige and often children came to school with contagious respiratory infections rather than miss the award. It is desirable, in some respects, for the child to attach value to regular attendance but he should also be taught that he must weigh values. This he cannot learn from indiscriminate application of extrinsic reward.

Each child brings a level of interest and curiosity to his school learning that will in some measure determine the amount of effort that he will expend in gaining mastery and understanding. Incentives can be useful if they support that interest and curiosity. They can be harmful if they are intended to initiate and sustain activity unrelated to the intrinsic interest and the natural curiosity of the child. Relating incentives to intrinsic motives means taking into account the child's current needs and level of maturity. If the rewards for learning and mastery are presented as being only potentially satisfying, they are not likely to be effective, particularly is this true with almost all preadolescents and with a large number of adolescents. A child of the intermediate grades will not exert more effort in his mastery of arithmetic because the principal

*"Have you any comprehension, young man, of your country's
desperate need for scientists?"*

FIGURE 2.1 *A child of the intermediate grades will not exert more effort in
his mastery of arithmetic because the principal points out the country's desperate need for scientists. Drawing by Whitney Darrow, Jr.; copyright © 1957,
The New Yorker Magazine, Inc.*

points out the country's desperate need for scientists. He will, however,
learn the principle of a fulcrum if such understanding will enable him to
apply it to increasing his own mastery of the physical world. The test of
the effectiveness of an incentive system in the classroom is the extent to

which the child's learning is guided by his need to be competent. If the incentive remains the primary goal of the activity, the incentive system has failed. The application of the marking system, discussed in Chapter 9, must be judged in these terms.

In applying incentives it is important to note that easy availability of incentives may eliminate the challenge of the activity. It should also be noted that the incentive system must provide a reasonable expectation of reward for all. A student will not maintain a high level of energy expenditure in a particular direction if he receives his reward for little effort. Likewise, he will give up trying if he fails to be rewarded in spite of much continuous effort. The latter condition occurs when teachers reward the product rather than the effort. Some would argue that the race in life is to the swift, or to the winner, but one can reasonably contend that if we value conscientiousness and responsibility we must express this by rewarding these characteristics as well as high quality performance.

The general effect of expectations was shown in a study by Johnson (1935) who demonstrated that positive expectations led to more effective behavior than negative ones. The adult comment, "You can do it," produced 95 percent completions of a puzzle, as compared to 5 percent when the comment was, "Is it too hard for you?" The study further indicated that positive, unhurried, and specific comments were more productive than those that were negative, hurried, and general. Goethe, the poet, has stated this principle in grander terms. "When we treat man as he is, we make him worse than he is. When we treat him as if he already were what he potentially could be, we make him what he should be."

Opportunity

Although demands and expectations are constantly at work in shaping motivation and determining behavior, an even stronger and more constant environmental determinant is that of opportunity. Baldwin (1955) states that the noticeability or obtrusiveness of the object and its separation from the individual serve to create desire, "we tend to want anything we notice that is not in our possession." Children have great difficulty in refraining from handling the knobs on a television set, the turntable of a phonograph, books, toys, or any object that can be manipulated. Baldwin describes how even adults are sometimes motivated by opportunity. He tells about the dilemma of postal authorities in deciding how to prosecute the person who placed the following advertisement in the newspaper: "LAST CHANCE TO SEND YOUR DOLLAR TO P.O. Box 221." It seems that this person received several hundred dollars by offering people an opportunity without the slightest indication of what the opportunity was.

Teachers do not need to resort to the techniques of the confidence man in order to instigate behavior, but they must be aware that they do create the atmosphere in which the child acts. If the child is surrounded by books, opportunities for nature study, and a positive social environment, he is likely to seize the opportunity to read, to discover the processes in nature, and to relate himself constructively to others.

As the teacher plans the development of educational opportunities, he must keep in mind that opportunities can also play a negative role and detract from learning by serving as distractors. In other words it may be important at times to restrict the range of opportunities in order to focus the student's attention on particular aspects of the learning task. Boguslavsky (1957), in reporting on psychological research in Soviet education, describes one experiment that bears on this issue. In one botany class the students were supplied with real flowers and after some preliminary instruction they were told to practice identification of various parts of the flower, such as the calyx, the stamens, and the pistil. Within the stamens the students were to differentiate the ovary, the style, and the stigma. In a comparable class the teaching procedure was similar except that the students did not receive the flower itself until after the teacher had provided the preliminary instruction from an enlarged drawing of another flower.

A comparison of the mastery of the subject in these two classes showed that the second group was markedly superior to the first, not only in acquiring knowledge but also in applying it to other types of flowers. Boguslavsky quotes from the original Russian report to explain the difference in performance. "A natural object has immediate significance for the child; it elicits interest which has no direct relation to the organs of the flower. During immediate perception of the flower a teacher's words do not produce sufficient effect." By delaying the child's direct experience to the flower and by using charts, the child's attention is not distracted from the essential features that are the object of instruction.

In avoiding distracting features the teacher need not reduce the effectiveness of the educational experience by making it dull or drab. The best way of making an opportunity vivid without introducing distracting elements is to prepare the student by having him focus attention on pertinent aspects of the material in a nondistracting setting and then to give him an opportunity to examine it in a more natural and real setting. Pictures, costumes, field trips, live animals, machines in operation, all can serve to stimulate interest but their use needs careful planning and preparation so that the systematic features for study and understanding are not lost by the irrelevant, albeit immediately interesting, aspects of a situation.

FIGURE 2.2 *A stimulating environment may provide too many distractions. Before planning a field trip the teacher needs to prepare his students so that the features of a situation to which the students are to pay attention stand out in their perception of the situation.* School Management, *Jan. 1960, p. 73, with permission of* School Management *and the Memorial Drive Elementary School, Houston, Texas.*

THE UNIVERSAL DRIVES AND THE ENVIRONMENTAL DETERMINANTS

Implicit in our discussion of the universal drives and the environmental determinants was that the former express themselves with their own power upon a changing and influential environment and that the latter shape and pattern the drives. The interaction of these two produces the unique personality that each of us possesses and provides for the development of a self that operates as another important determinant of behavior.

When the level of *directed* activity in the student is lower than that which the teacher considers appropriate, the teacher is likely to introduce heightened stimulation into the environment. This tendency is based on a widespread assumption that there is a straight-line relation-

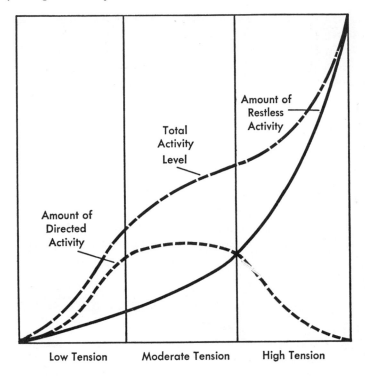

FIGURE 2.3   *The relationship of tension level to amount and type of activity. These relationships can be schematically represented by the graph. The main points to note are that: first, activity increases with tension; secondly, sensitivity to stimulation increases with tension; and thirdly, focused activity is characteristic of the middle ranges of tension. Below the middle range, there is too little responsiveness to be focused; above it the responsiveness is high but generalized. From A. L. Baldwin,* Behavior and Development in Childhood, *copyright © New York: Holt, Rinehart and Winston, 1955.*

ship between stimulation and directed activity, that is, the higher the stimulation the greater the activity. There is good reason to question this assumption. The relationship between environmental input and behavior output is a complex one. Our best information leads us to believe that *directed* activity, the kind so necessary for school learning, first rises then falls as tension increases. This relationship is shown in Figure 2.3. The commonplace assumption is more or less correct only in regard to the total level of activity and in some respects in regard to restless activity, but it does not apply to directed activity.

The implications of Figure 2.3 are such as to demand a careful evaluation of each situation in which the teacher encounters an insufficient amount of directed activity. Many children who exhibit a great deal of restless activity, including daydreaming, may be actually operating under high tension. In such cases the increase of demands, the threat of punishment, the proffer of reward or stimulation through opportunity may result in further increase in tension and consequent decrease in directed activity. For children who appear to be operating at tension levels above the moderate a plan of action to reduce the tension would be recommended; for example, leniency in setting demands, opportunities that stimulate minimally, and expectations that can be met easily. For children who appear to be operating at low-tension levels a plan of action to increase tension would be advised. Such a plan would include firm demands, reasonably high expectations and challenging opportunities. General observation of classrooms and teachers, and even more of parents, would lead us to believe that more problems arise as a result of too much pressure rather than from too little. The teacher should make a differential diagnosis of the situation in cases where directed energy is at a level less than desirable for effective learning. There is no single remedy for all children who present problems of insufficient directed activity.

PERSONALITY AND SELF
AS DETERMINANTS OF BEHAVIOR

The initially amorphous universal drives interact with the various forces in the environment and there gradually evolves from this interaction a differentiated, self-aware person. We note this differentiation when we recognize a given person as the same person even after a lapse of time. Even more marked is the self-awareness that each of us maintains as we stand as separate and unique beings in our own consciousness. Individuality consists of a person's tastes, interests, ambitions, attitudes, values, convictions, and the structure of his self-awareness; it consists also of his style of behaving; it is in short his *Weltanschauung*, his philosophy and his conception of his universe and his place in it.

In the first chapter personality was defined as "the dynamic organization within the individual of those psychophysical systems that determine his characteristic behavior and thought" (Allport, 1961). It was also stated there that the central purpose of the school is to have some significant effect upon the developing personality and the self. It is important to delineate and elaborate this definition of personality and to suggest how the teacher might play a role in influencing this overriding determinant of behavior.

The Search for Meaning

The sensory and the activity drives discussed earlier in this chapter form the raw material from which arises the basic psychological need to understand and to manipulate reality. In human beings the sensory and activity drives culminate in part in an internalization of the outside world in symbolic forms. As this internalization occurs these drives express themselves on this new ideational and symbolic world. Exploratory and manipulative behavior are manifest in the search for the solution of symbolic problems in understanding the forces of nature and creative activity. The tendency to collect various and sundry things and to classify and order them is another expression of the need to explore, understand, control, and act upon one's environment.

The need to give meaning and organization to the concrete and the symbolic world is basic. The prevalence of this need, variously called curiosity, adventure or exploration, has been noted by many writers. Prescott (1938) lists this need as one of the basic ego and integrative needs. He divides it into three categories: the need for contact with reality, harmony with reality, and progressive symbolization. He describes the latter as follows: "the human mind is endowed with considerable power to organize experience, to establish logical arrangements of ideas, and to arrive at general concepts. The development of language, both verbal and postural, affords a basis for mentally manipulating and for expressing these generalizations" (page 121).

Leighton (1959) states as fundamental propositions in his discussion of the foundations for a theory of man in relation to culture that all human beings exist in a state of psychological striving and that striving plays a part in the maintenance of an essential psychical condition. This latter condition is conceived of as a developmental psychobiological equilibrium. Smith, Bruner, and White (1956) also note that personality as a construct is characterized by striving. They suggest that activities such as perceiving, thinking, and remembering not only serve other needs such as obtaining food and approval but seem to be intrinsically motivated: "an 'effort after meaning' or, as Tolman has called it, a 'placing need' which can be activated by a lack of structure in the individual's life space." Allport (1955) refers to this characteristic as "propriate striving." Maslow (1954) describes it as the self-actualizing potentials of personality. According to Maslow these potentials do not become realized unless the prior needs of safety, love, and esteem are satisfied. Within the psychoanalytic framework, the need to know and to understand stem from the child's curiosity about sex. Shortly after the age of school entry the child enters what is called the "latency" period. During this period the sexual curiosity is sublimated or converted into other forms of curiosity such as would support school learning. According to this interpretation children differ as to the age and the ease with which they enter the latency period and also the extent to which they are able to sublimate their early sexual curiosity.

The significant adults in the child's environment provide the circumstances of the outer reality in which the child's curiosity is satisfied. Depending in large measure on these circumstances, the child will acquire a persistent or a weak curiosity, an effective or ineffective set of symbols for acting upon an expanding and changing world, a willingness to tolerate ambiguity or impatience with uncertainty while seeking understanding and meaning. In any event, every human develops his own ways of seeking meaning from his environment. He is seldom if ever "lazy" in the sense that he ceases to strive altogether. Kelly (1958) suggests the following technique for dealing with a student whom the teacher perceives as lazy.

> One technique we came to use was to ask the teacher what the child would do if she did not try to motivate him. Often the teacher would insist that the child would no nothing—absolutely nothing—just sit! Then we would suggest that she try a nonmotivational approach and let him "just sit." We would ask her to observe how he went about "just sitting." Invariably the teacher would be able to report some interesting goings on. An analysis of what the "lazy" child did while he was being lazy often furnished her with her first glimpse into the child's world and provided her with her first solid grounds for communication with him. Some teachers found that their laziest pupils were those who could produce the most novel ideas; others, that the term "laziness" had been applied to activities that they had simply been unable to understand and appreciate (pages 46-47).

Success and Failure as Determinants of Behavior

The consequences of one's action on the environment influence the way in which one approaches a similar action when the opportunity arises. Thorndike's (1921) law of effect is a statement of this relationship. The law of effect states that when a response to a situation is accompanied or followed by a satisfying state of affairs, that response is more likely to be repeated. When the response is accompanied or followed by an annoying state of affairs, its strength or likelihood of being repeated is diminished. The principle of reinforcement, which is an extremely important aspect of programmed instruction to be discussed in Chapter 7, is in essence the positive aspect of the law of effect. Thorndike later suggested that failure or punishment did not produce as predictable results as did success or reward.

In a study by Otto and Melby (1935) a number of second-grade and fifth-grade classrooms were divided into experimental and control groups on the basis of whether the teachers were instructed to avoid or to employ the threats of failure. In the control classes the children were reminded at intervals that if they did not work hard and do well, they would have to repeat the grade. In the experimental classes the teachers told the children several times during the semester that they would all be in the next higher grade. Measures of educational growth in each of these groups of classrooms showed no significant differences. In other words the school performance of children is not beneficially affected by the threat of failure. The teachers in the experimental group noticed no slackening of effort and they could use the positive reminder that the work in the next grade would be easier if the students mastered the assigned work.

Even if the teacher does not apply failure or the threat of failure, the child will inevitably face tasks in which he will make errors and experience a sense of failure. Most children in these instances will continue to work at the task by trying new ways and persevering. Some children lose all interest and become unmotivated at the first signs of failure. Sometimes they become negatively or avoidance motivated and show a reluctance to approach the task. What can the teacher do to help the child whose response to failure is immature? Keister (1943) studied the effectiveness of various procedures for modifying the undesirable responses of preschool children to failure. A group of twelve children, whose responses to an experimental failure situation were judged to be immature, were trained on a set of tasks for a period of six weeks. These tasks required perseverance in order to complete them successfully. While the investigator worked with these subjects she responded to requests for help with comments such as: "I won't need to help you. You can do it all by yourself if you keep on trying." Or she suggested, "Try that piece some other ways. You'll soon find out, by yourself, how it goes." Or, "Keep trying it in different places. You'll get it in the right place in a minute if you keep on trying." When a child had succeeded on a series of easier tasks, he was introduced to more difficult ones. Requests for help were then responded to by the investigator with comments such as, "You did those puzzles in the train story all by yourself yesterday. You will know how to do these by yourself, too, because they are made the same way." The child was encouraged to work alone without requesting help and when he did so, he was praised with such comments as, "Good for you! You kept right on trying until you found the way to do it, didn't you?" Or, "That was fine! You are learning to try hard and not have anyone help you. You did that one all by yourself." At various occasions the children were encouraged by remarks such as: "You need to try some more before you can say, 'I can't,' because you *can* do it if you try a while longer." When the child left the training session he was often told, "You did a good job of making the puzzles in the book today. You were able to do them nicely because you worked hard on them. You kept on trying until you had them finished, and that's a good way to work." It was noted that the child's responses were changed positively during the training session, but more significantly these children showed permanent signs of responding to difficulty with more maturity and perseverance than did a control group. The particular mode of the teacher's response will of course depend on the age of the child, his personality, and the teacher's own preferred way of responding. In one study, Thompson and Hunnicutt (1944), it was shown that fifth-grade pupils who were self-confident and assured, worked better after meeting moderate failure than after success. On the other hand, the less confident, worried student responded better to encouragement and success. Both types of students worked better when their responses were scored success or failure than if their responses were not scored at all. Children prefer some reaction from the environment, even if negative, rather than to receive no reaction.

The essential aspect of the teacher's response to the child's performance is whether it expresses a faith in the unfolding of his potentialities. False praise and destructive criticism can both be harmful because they express a lack of faith. Fromm (1947) maintains that the child's potentialities to love, to use his reason, and to develop his artistic gifts depend on the presence of proper conditions.

> One of the most important of these conditions is that the significant persons in a child's life have faith in these potentialities. The presence of this faith makes the difference between education and manipulation. Education is identical with helping the child realize his potentialities. The opposite of education is manipulation, which is based on the absence of faith in the growth of potentialities and on the conviction that a child will be right only if the adults put into him what is desirable and cut off what seems to be undesirable. There is no need of faith in the robot since there is no life in it either (page 207).

The mature expression of the psychological striving discussed here is to be seen in the urge to be creative and productive and in the appreciation of creative works. The conditions that encourage creative expression are dealt with more fully in Chapter 4. The human personality is an active, seeking system, it strives to function, to exercise its capabilities, to find expression and to unfold its many potentialities.

The Self

Each of us is aware that it is "I" who experiences each experience, that it is "I" who acts upon the environment. We each carry some sense of control and freedom to produce certain conditions in our environment. When we speak of this awareness we are speaking of the *self*. The scientific study of immediate experience, as interpreted by the one who is having the experience, is called *phenomenology*. That which the person experiences as his reality is called the *phenomenal field* and the portion of the phenomenal field to which we refer when we say "I" is called the *phenomenal self* (Combs and Snygg, 1959). Allport (1955) refers to all those regions of our lives that appear to be peculiarly ours, as the *proprium*. "The proprium includes all aspects of personality that make for inward unity."

However this selfness is named, if an attempt is made to understand it, we come closer to understanding why the person behaves as he does. This suggests that understanding the behavior of others involves understanding the other's frame of reference and how he anticipates events (Kelly, 1955). It involves, further, the appreciation that the other person has one basic goal and that is to be effective and adequate in his environment.

The need for adequacy expresses itself very largely in terms of the perceived relationship of the individual's behavior on his environment and the anticipated reaction of the environment. To state this more simply, the individual faces his future in terms of what has happened to him in the past. For most healthy individuals the future promises a little more than the past has offered (Eson and Greenfeld, 1962). The studies of the level of aspiration have shown this relationship to hold true. The level of aspiration is the subjective criterion set by the individual before undertaking an activity that will determine whether the performance will be viewed as successful or not. The grade of B in a course may be seen as highly successful by one student whose level of aspiration had been merely to pass the course and a disappointment to another student whose aspiration level was the grade of A. Sears (1940) has shown that children who have experienced consistent success in school tasks set their aspiration levels slightly higher than their past achievement. They expect that they will become more adequate with time. She found, on the other hand, that those students who had experienced considerable school failure set their levels of aspiration either unrealistically low or, in relation to their ability, exceedingly high. The goal setting of children who have experienced failure is such as to protect the *self* from further failure or to provide a feeling of adequacy. Those who set a low level of aspiration are attempting to assure themselves some success no matter how poorly they perform. They expect their performance to deteriorate with time but they support the self by setting low achievement goals. Those who set exceedingly high levels of aspiration appear to be divorcing goal setting from performance. One can derive some small satisfaction from anticipating a great success even if it is clear that the performance will not measure up to the goal.

Strang (1957) describes the self as having four dimensions. (1) The basic self-concept that she defines "as the individual's perception of his abilities and his status and roles in the outer world." Physical characteristics, various physical and mental abilities possessed by the person, and the reaction of others to these, determine the kind of basic self-concept that the person will have. (2) The transitory perception of self is the self-perception that the person holds as a result of the immediate current situation. This aspect of self is more limited than the basic self-concept. (3) The social self is the self as the person thinks others see it. "This concept may not correspond with other people's perceptions of him; nevertheless it has an important effect on his behavior. If an adolescent has the impression that others think he is 'dumb,' retarded in read-ing, socially unacceptable, he tends to see himself in these negative ways" (page 71). (4) The ideal self is the kind of person the individual aspires to be. It is usually modeled after some real adult within the child's experience, or it may be modeled after a much publicized public hero or fictitious character.

The self-concept changes through the course of development. The manner in which it changes will be determined by kinds of interpersonal relations that the individual has from birth onward, the kinds and levels of anxiety with which he has to cope (Sullivan, 1953), the kinds of "cog-nitive dissonance" (Festinger, 1957) that he has to resolve, and, of course, the culture to which the person is exposed. The teacher influ-ences the course of the development of the self-concept in a number of ways. To the extent that the teacher is a significant person in the child's life he will shape the self-concept. As the teacher seeks the translation of the curriculum into experiences that the student can readily recognize as opportunities for increasing his adequacy, the self-concept will change in desirable directions. By providing tasks at which the student can ex-perience success and reacting appropriately to the student's performance, the teacher can be instrumental in shaping the child's attitudes so that he anticipates the future with reasonable hopefulness and so that he ex-pands his influence on his environment constructively and with con-fidence.

SUMMARY

The human organism is to be viewed as in a constant interaction with the environment. In order to understand behavior it is necessary to examine the universal drives, how they are shaped by environmental de-terminants, and the resulting personality as a determinant of behavior.

The universal determinants of behavior consist of the activity drives, the sensory drives, and the visceral drives. These are interrelated through homeostasis. The visceral drives become operative when there appears a deficiency in the physiological functioning. Homeostasis serves to maintain a biological equilibrium. As the person becomes able to sat-isfy the visceral drives with only a moderate amount of energy expendi-ture and as homeostasis is achieved with relative ease, the individual exercises his activity and sensory drives to expand his environment and to be effective in it. As the individual grows older the activity and the sensory drives express themselves more upon the symbolic and ideational world and less upon the concrete world. There are wide individual dif-ferences in the universal drives. These differences are due in part to in-born tendencies and the uniqueness of each person's environment.

Of the many environmental determinants of behavior, the following three: demand, expectation, and opportunity are discussed. In applying demands in the classroom in order to elicit behavior there are a number of considerations to keep in mind. Demands are generally more effective when human relationships are positive. Demands should not be used to elicit behavior that would occur spontaneously. They should be consistent and possible of fulfillment. Because demands are supported with at least the implicit threat of punishment, the teacher should be sure that he has it in his power to carry out the punishment and he should also be sure that the punishment will not produce disorganized behavior. The teacher should be sure that the child understands the demand before assuming that the child has willfully chosen not to comply. Children often need to be prepared for situations that will require relatively mature forms of behavior. Demands should not constitute the larger portion of the classroom motivating environment.

The teacher's positive expectations of the child, when within the capabilities of the child, will lead to growth. The teacher's expectations become less potent influences as the peer group's expectations become more influential. The teacher must be aware also that he expresses his expectation through setting incentives; if these are unreasonably high or low the child will cease trying to achieve if his only reason for exerting effort is to meet the teacher's expectations.

The third environmental determinant is that of opportunity. The teacher must be careful lest a too stimulating environment becomes a distracting form of opportunity. The introduction of experiences that can be distracting should be carefully planned so that the features of the situation to which the student is to pay attention do not become lost in the irrelevant aspects.

As the teacher applies the environmental determinants in shaping the behavior of his students he needs to recognize that directed activity will rise when greater pressure is applied but after reaching an optimal level further increases in tension will result in a reduction of directed activity and an increase of restless activity.

The personality and the self may be viewed as a third dimension of the determinants of behavior. The self expresses itself in much the same way as do the activity and the sensory drives. The self seeks meaning in the concrete and symbolic reality and it continuously responds to its environment in such ways as to maintain and enhance its adequacy. The teacher plays an important role in shaping the self-concept through the human interaction, by providing the learning opportunities, and by reacting to the child's exploratory and responsive behavior.

READING REFERENCES

Allport, G. W., *Becoming: Basic Considerations for a Psychology of Personality.* New Haven: Yale University Press, 1955.

Association for Supervision and Curriculum Development 1962 Yearbook, *Perceiving, Behaving, Becoming: A New Focus for Education.* Washington: National Education Association (particularly first nine chapters).

Berlyne, D. E., *Conflict, Arousal and Curiosity.* New York: McGraw-Hill Book Company, 1960.

Combs, A. W. and D. Snygg, *Individual Behavior: A Perceptual Approach to Behavior,* rev. ed. New York: Harper & Row, 1959.

Fuller, J. L., *Motivation: A Biological Perspective.* New York: Random House, 1962.

Maslow, A. H., *Motivation and Personality.* New York: Harper & Row, 1954.

Rethlingshafer, Dorothy, *Motivation as Related to Personality.* New York: McGraw-Hill Book Company, 1963.

Woodworth, R. S., *Dynamics of Behavior.* New York: Harper & Row, 1958.

CHAPTER 3

HOW CHILDREN LEARN:
THE ACQUISITION
OF FIXED MEANING

Everyone knows why we have schools. We have them because we want our children to learn. On this we have agreement. When we raise the questions of what they should learn, how they should be taught, or even what learning is, we find ourselves much less certain. Consider the word learning. We use it in describing the child's acquisition of the upright posture and locomotion, we say he learns to walk; we use it also in describing the acquisition of reading skill, he learns to read; he also *learns* to ride a bicycle and he *learns* to appreciate Shakespeare, to solve problems in geometry, to cast a line for fishing, to play the piano and to paint. All of these acquisitions we call learning, yet it is easy to see that each is very different from the other. Almost any change in function and performance we assume is a result of learning. The psychologist differentiates among these acquisitions in terms of the underlying factors that produce the change. He would use the term *maturation* to account for changes in behavior that come about largely as a result of internal biological change. Thus because walking depends more largely on fixed changes in musculature and neurological factors than on interaction with the environment, it is somewhat incorrect to speak of walking as learned. It is extremely difficult to formulate a definition of learning that will include all those aspects of behavior change that we wish to include and exclude those that would not be covered by the concept. Recognizing these difficulties, Hilgard (1956) offers the following provisional defini-

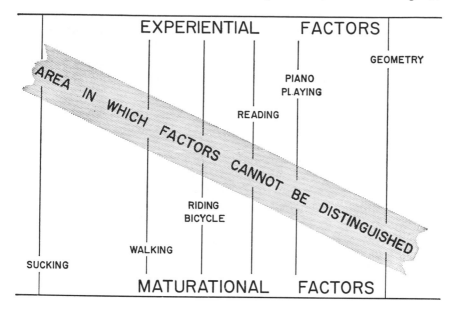

FIGURE 3.1   *This figure shows the relationship of maturational and experiential factors in producing various behavior changes. Each vertical line represents the appearance of a behavior pattern that did not exist before. The portion of the vertical line above the shaded area represents the estimated extent to which the behavior depends on experiential factors. The portion of the line below the shaded area represents the extent to which it depends on maturational or biological factors. Each behavior form requires some contribution from both before it appears.*

tion: "Learning is a process by which an activity originates or is changed through reacting to an encountered situation, provided that the characteristics of the change in activity cannot be explained on the basis of native response tendencies, maturation, or temporary states of the organism (for example, fatigue, and drugs)" (page 3). Changes in behavior are never clearly based on only maturational or only environmental factors; it is primarily a question of which of these sets of factors contributes more significantly to the appearance of a particular behavior form. Figure 3.1 represents schematically the relationship of maturational and experiential factors as they both contribute to various kinds of behavior change.

All change in structure and function, whether resulting from learning or from maturation, is called *development*. Werner (1957) proposes that one regulative principle governs development. This principle "states that wherever development occurs it proceeds from a state of relative globality and lack of differentiation to a state of increasing differentiation, articulation, and hierarchic integration." If we look back upon the course of development of any behavior form, we will find that at first there are no clear signs of that behavior, being incorporated in a global, undifferentiated mass of behavior. Gradually signs of separation of certain aspects of the behavior appear, these become organized or integrated, producing a change in the way the total organism responds.

THE DIFFERENT KINDS OF LEARNING

Learning refers to those changes in behavior that are determined primarily by the individual's interaction with his environment. The changes that can occur as a result of this interaction, even within the school environment alone, are of many different kinds. A student learns to spell a number of words, he learns to solve problems in geometry or he learns to recite a few stanzas of a poem. These learnings are not quite the same as learning to value certain kinds of behavior that we call honest, or learning to be afraid of speaking before an audience. At several different points in later chapters the process of learning in the categories of value change, emotions, social relationships, and motor skills is considered. All of these are most certainly important from the standpoint of making the school an effective institution, yet the school shares with many social agencies the responsibility of fostering these changes. The one large area in which the school has always assumed a prime responsibility is in teaching knowledge, information, and understanding. The various subject matter categories that make up the bulk of the curriculum with which the school is so much concerned are reflections of how seriously this responsibility is taken.

The learnings involved in the acquisition of information and understanding are of several kinds and for purposes of clarification it is necessary to set up an arbitrary classification. The first category within this classification is the acquisition of knowledge of the world as it is or as described by man. This will be the major topic of this chapter. In the following two chapters other kinds of learning are considered, namely, the development of understanding of why events and phenomena occur as they do, and also the acquisition of the ability to apply and to generalize that which has been learned. It must be noted that this distinction among the different kinds of learning is an artificial one. The acquisition of fixed meanings, the development of understanding, and the application of previous learning, generally go hand-in-hand and are inseparable. Thus, for example, when a student learns that water freezes at 32°F, he is learning something about the world as it is described by man; when he learns that upon freezing, water expands, he is likewise learning something about the world as it is; when he can describe why ice forms at the top of a container, he demonstrates the development of understanding; when he proceeds to empty a container or his auto radiator at the onset of cold weather, he is showing that he is able to apply previous learning. A person may remove the water from a container, however, simply because he is told to do so or because he imitates someone else and he may also understand why water expands when it freezes because of a knowledge of molecular action. As we observe a particular behavior we cannot be sure whether it is the result of the acquisition of a fixed meaning, the appearance of understanding, or application resulting from a generalization.

Learning Theory and Educational Practice

The larger portion of psychological research and theorizing on the topic of learning has been concerned with what we have called the acquisition of fixed meanings. On the other hand, the larger portion of educational literature has dealt with the development of understanding and attitudes. Most of the educational literature until relatively recently has failed to note the importance of the school's role in helping the child acquire a knowledge of the world as it is or as described by man. The point of view expressed here is that although the teaching of fixed meanings may not be the only aim, or even the most important aim, of education, it does comprise a significant portion of the school's task. In order for an individual to get along adequately in any society, he must acquire a substantial amount of this type of knowledge. Our society expects the school to teach children to read, to spell, to know certain dates and the events they celebrate, the sequence of the months, the days of the week, the names of the numbers, and much other similar information. Much of this information consists of somewhat isolated segments of verbal learning.

Because of the differences in the work settings of the experimental psychologist and the educational theorist, the application of psychological learning theory to educational practice has not always been apparent. The psychologist is interested in the learning phenomenon itself and he examines it in all its detail wherever he finds it, in the salivation of a dog to a tone, fish swimming toward a light, rats running a maze, or cats escaping from a puzzle box. The findings from the psychological laboratory do not appear to be directly applicable to the classroom situation. Teachers have sometimes commented after studying some of the psychological research on learning that this would be most useful if their students were white rats and if the curriculum consisted of running mazes. Unfortunately, these teachers say, the white rat cannot be taught to read in the human sense, to compose music or to play baseball. Psychologists have examined in great detail how a cat proceeds to free himself from a puzzle box and how he learns to do this with speed and dispatch. But cats cannot learn to knit or to acquire Russian as a second language, nor can they learn about democracy or the scientific method. Even those investigations of learning that have been carried on with human subjects have been done in the controlled conditions of the laboratory rather than in the complex real-life situation of the classroom. In spite of all these limitations of psychological research, the findings do have some bearing on teaching. Two types of learning studies will be described. These basic studies provide us with a framework for looking at the process of acquisition of fixed meanings.

Classical and Instrumental Conditioning

The classical conditioning experiment based upon the work of Pavlov is widely known and often cited. In this experiment meat powder, an *unconditioned stimulus,* was placed in a dog's mouth and it elicited an automatic, natural response—salivation, which is called an *unconditioned response.* It is then established that another stimulus, such as a bell sound, is neutral to the response of salivation. Then if the bell is sounded each time just before the meat powder is placed in the animal's mouth, the tone of the bell will come to elicit salivation. This modification of behavior, salivating to the tone, is called *conditioning* and the new response to the bell is called a *conditioned response* and the tone is called a *conditioned stimulus.* A wide variety of responses have been conditioned to a wide variety of stimuli in a wide range of different organisms. This simple experiment provided a basis for a wealth of laboratory investigations; it enabled scientists to establish empirically the philosophical assumptions about learning that had been asserted as far back as Aristotle; and it became a focus of social-philosophical discussion as, for example, in Huxley's *Brave New World.*

As an example of instrumental conditioning we may take Thorndike's experiment with cats. He placed the animal subject in an enclosed cage. In order to be released from the cage and obtain the food placed outside, the animal was required to manipulate a lever within the box. The manipulation of the lever is a response that is *instrumental* in producing the reward condition, escape and food, and for this reason this type of learning is called *instrumental conditioning.* The acquisition and retention of the instrumental response follow the same principles as that found in classical conditioning. However, because the responses that may be conditioned are not restricted to natural or innate responses to particular stimuli but may be any response in the animal's behavior repertory, instrumental conditioning is much more flexible. Skinner (1948a and 1953) has extended the knowledge about instrumental conditioning and has even attempted in a novel entitled *Walden Two* (1948b) to describe a Utopian society based on this principle of learning. A few characteristics exhibited in common in both forms of conditioning are considered here. For a more detailed discussion the reader is referred to Hilgard and Marquis (1961).

In order for a conditioned response to be acquired and in order for it to be maintained, it must be reinforced. *Reinforcement* is any stimulus condition, such as meat powder or escape, which strengthens the conditioned response. If reinforcement does not accompany the acquired response, it will be weakened and will eventually disappear. This kind of elimination of the conditioned response is called *extinction*. Referring back to our examples above, the dog will eventually cease salivating to the bell tone, if the tone is presented repeatedly without the accompanying meat powder, from time to time. Likewise, the cat will cease manipulating the escape lever if it does not lead to escape and food more frequently than some other escape response. After a conditioned response has been extinguished, it will show *spontaneous recovery* following a period of rest.

If a response is acquired to a particular conditioned stimulus, it will be given to other stimuli that are similar to the original one. Thus the dog who had been conditioned to salivate to a particular bell tone, would also salivate to other similar tones. This phenomenon is called *stimulus generalization*. In the same way if an animal has learned to respond by pressing a lever with the right paw and that paw is tied down, it will respond with the left paw. This is called *response generalization*.

This brief discussion of conditioning will serve as a general background for the discussion in the rest of this chapter on the nature of the fixed meanings and how they are acquired.

FIXED MEANINGS AND CONCEPTS

From the very beginning of a person's acquisition of fixed meanings, he immediately proceeds to sort and classify his learnings into categories. Each child repeats what man has done historically, that is to be able to discern the qualities of things apart from the things themselves. The use of verbal symbols aids immeasurably in this process. The child comes in contact with a number of objects in connection with which he hears the word red, another group of objects are associated with heavy, still another with soft. Out of these experiences a new awareness appears, a concept, having an existence of its own and more manageable than the accidents of the world of concrete objects. The child finds that these concepts are easy to manipulate in thought and that they can be related to each other without the restrictions imposed by the awkwardness of manipulating individual objects. Concepts are ways of organizing experience, giving experiences meaning in terms of some abstract quality of the object or event experienced. The particular kind of grouping and the label attached to it is largely a matter of common usage, agreement, or commonly accepted logic. This is why the acquisition of fixed meaning is learning about the world as it is or as described by man.

Although the verbal symbol is more manageable than the concrete reality, language does set some definite limitations on our transactions with that reality. In his book *Beyond the Mexique Bay* Aldous Huxley (1960) offers some lively comments about the consumer's unreasoned rejection of the off-color oranges of Trinidad. His comments illustrate the way in which language may distort reality.

> Man looks out on reality through an intervening and only partially transparent medium—his language. He sees real things overlaid by their verbal symbols. Thus, when he looks at oranges, it is as though he looked at them through a stained-glass window representing oranges. If the real oranges correspond with the *beau idéal* of oranges painted on the window, he feels that everything is all right. But if they don't correspond, then he becomes suspicious; something must be wrong.
>
> A vocabulary is a system of platonic ideas to which we feel (illogically, no doubt, but strongly) that reality *ought* to correspond. Thanks to language, all our relations with the outside world are tinged with a certain ethical quality; before even we start our observations, we think we know what it is the duty of reality to be like. For example, it is obviously the duty of all oranges to be orange; and if, in fact, they aren't orange, but, like the fruits of Trinidad, bright green, then we shall refuse even to taste these abnormal and immoral caricatures of oranges. Every language contains, by implications, a set of categorical imperatives (page 15).

The growth of fixed meaning depends upon the reciprocal processes of generalization and discrimination. In school learning the process of generalization is at work when the child recognizes that *FUN* in large block capitals is the same as *fun* in smaller lower-case letters, or when the student notes that in algebra $x + y$ can be represented as $a + b$ or $p + q$. When he learns to discern the difference between *fun* and *fire* or between $x + y$ and $x - y$, we say he is discriminating. Generalization enables the learner to incorporate two or more separate experiences into a more comprehensive, new meaning. Through the process of discrimination the learner becomes able to distinguish between classes of events and experiences. Actually we cannot develop accurate generalizations without discriminations, nor can we go far in forming discriminations without establishing some generalizations.

In earlier discussion of the total process of development the terms differentiation and integration were used. The terms discrimination and generalization are these same processes at work in the acquisition of meaning. Just as in the development of manual dexterity there is at first the poorly organized functioning of the hand, with time and some experience the child becomes able to move one finger independently of the others, then to coordinate his index finger and thumb in picking up small objects, then to the skilful use of his fingers in cutting, writing or playing the piano. At each step in the process, differentiation and integration go together. So, too, in the acquisition of meaning discrimination, one concept differentiated from another, and generalization, the integration of separate experiences, go hand in hand.

It should be noted that when the process of deriving meaning from our environment becomes well established, some precision may be lost. Our perceptions tend to be organized in terms of what we expect or what we are accustomed to perceive. This phenomenon can readily be illustrated by the following technique. Look at each of the triangles shown and write on a separate sheet of paper the text printed in each triangle. You may examine each carefully but be sure to write the phrases before reading the explanation of this perceptual exercise.

It is very likely that in each case you failed to note that the first word in the last line was repeated in the preceding line. The vast majority of adults have learned to organize their perceptions so as to overlook certain details. Many more children who are learning to read, in the early school grades, would detect the repetition since their perceptual processes have not become highly integrated and mechanical.

The novelist Richard Hughes describes this phenomenon in the following passage from *The Fox in the Attic:*

> The main house itself now towered in front of them. There were four storeys of stuccoed stone and then four more of steep pantiled roof with rows of dormers in it all boarded up. On the topmost roofridge was fixed a wagon-wheel, supporting a tattered old stork's nest. Augustine took this all in at a glance, for today he was still absorbing everything with the unnaturally observant eye of first arrival somewhere totally strange: not till tomorrow would he even begin to notice less (pages 138-139).

One of the very important aims of education is to enlarge the student's awareness of himself and his world. To accomplish this aim the school must teach for the development of meaning. Each stage in the growth of a concept may be viewed as the expansion of meaning (see diagram in Figure 3.2). The dimensions along which meaning develops are (1) personal, (2) language, (3) analytic, (4) source and process, and (5) sociocultural. The meaning of each experience can be placed along one of these five dimensions, but more significant is the relationship of each step in the growth of meaning with other existing maps of meaning. Thus similar maps can be drawn for the enlargement

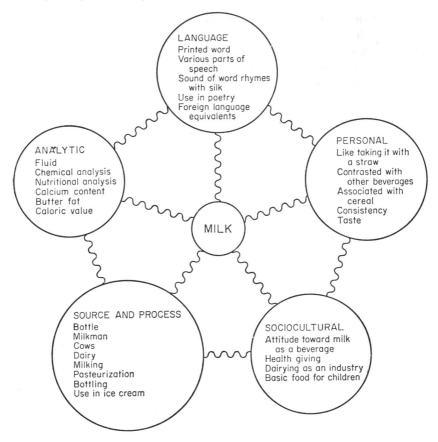

FIGURE 3.2   *Diagram to show the expansion of meaning.*

of meaning for each of the items; fluid, cow, rhyme, and so on that appear on the map for milk. The task of the school is to help enlarge the meaning and to continuously tie in one developing map with another. The history of scholarship is in large measure the development of such meaning. The scholar's task, as well as the student's, is to build out each map in one or several dimensions and relate parts hitherto unrelated. The specialist is the one about whom it has been facetiously said, "He knows more and more about less and less, until eventually he knows everything about nothing." At least he has developed meaning in areas of the territory where very few others have ventured.

It should be noted that experiences lend themselves to particularized patterns of elaboration of meaning. Experiences with certain words in the language may have primarily a language dimension and very little if any of the other dimensions. This would be so, for example, in the case of words like *and, or, then.* Many abstract terms will have a very full dimension of sociocultural meaning as for example, force, honesty, democracy, liberty, and love. In these cases the academic disciplines of psychology, political science, physics, or philosophy provide systems that enable the learner to enlarge the dimension of analytic meaning.

READINESS

One of the problems that the schools face is to determine when children are ready to acquire a designated body of fixed meanings or when they should be exposed to particular learning experiences. It is well known that attempts to teach children certain skills before they are ready, result in frustration and failure. It has also been established as a general principle, that if one delays instruction too long beyond the period of readiness, learning becomes exceedingly difficult and sometimes impossible. For these reasons it is extremely important to establish the developmental periods of readiness.

An examination of educational practice reveals many different assumptions in regard to readiness. Some schools start cursive handwriting from the start, others wait until the third grade. Some schools begin foreign language instruction in grade four or even earlier, others wait until grade six, and still others until grade nine. Some argue that music instruction should begin at kindergarten age, others advise waiting until age nine or ten. These differences exist for a number of reasons. The developmental periods of readiness have not been clearly established by careful investigations. It appears that readiness periods are the result of earlier experience and cultural pressures. In one instance children in an isolated community learned to read before they were five. This was accomplished without any noticeable ill effect and with very few failures. In this community, learning was considered supremely important and children were indoctrinated into the cultural pattern from the very beginning of their awareness. Brownell (1951) has similarly noted that readiness is "amenable to stimulation, direction and control to an extent far greater than is assumed by those who rely upon anatomical maturation." There are divergent assumptions about readiness because the concomitant effects of the timing of instruction are not always easily observed. Does the child have greater difficulty in other areas of adjustment if he is pressured into too early achievement? Does the child lack in self-confidence if instruction is delayed? These questions are very difficult to answer. Yet, although the application of the readiness concept is not directly apparent, certain practical generalizations about its development can be established.

As in all ripening or maturing processes, readiness or ripeness does not appear suddenly as if from out of nowhere, *de novo*. It is rather a slow, gradual development depending on all that has preceded the moment at which we are considering the introduction of the new learning activity. Let us take reading readiness as an example. The child begins to prepare himself for reading from the moment he begins to incorporate and give meaning to his environment and this in a sense starts sometime near birth. The child's ability to derive meaning from printed symbols is part of the total pattern of language development and, language itself is an integral part of the development of meaning. The child's experiences prior to entering school and the process of maturation have served to prepare him more or less for the formal reading instruction. The school's role is to complete the job of preparation and to do it systematically.

Physical Maturation as a Factor in Readiness

A great deal of school readiness depends upon the development of the sensory processes, particularly vision and hearing. The development of these senses depends on maturational factors in the sense organs themselves and in the associated neurological structures. Sometimes this maturation is delayed because of illness, injury, or genetic factors. For this reason a careful medical examination at periodic intervals, with special attention to vision and hearing, to determine which children need special attention and corrective devices, is so essential. The question of physical deficit is examined in some detail in Chapter 12.

Auditory and visual function, however, depend upon more than maturation. They depend also on experience. The school can do much to develop auditory and visual discrimination abilities. A number of activities for this purpose have been suggested by VandeBerg (1953). She points out that the piano provides an excellent tool for teaching differences in sounds, such as loud and soft and high and low. A number of games can be organized such as "Hide the Thimble" playing loudly for "warm" and softly for "cold"; higher notes associated with movement upward, walking or raising hands, for the progression of notes upward and the reverse for the notes downward; the translation of piano rhythms into the rhythm of hand clapping, and distinguishing between notes that are sustained longer and shorter.

The use of the child's voice is another technique for fostering auditory acuity and discrimination, for example, rhyming games, telling stories with appropriate voice parts like The Three Bears, or giving words that begin with the same consonant.

Visual discrimination may be fostered by such activities as having the child sort forms made of colored paper into categories of size, shape, and color; putting together simple jigsaw puzzles and identifying from a group of objects one object that has been hidden from sight.

The Development of Associated Skills and Attitudes

Almost every dimension of development is interlocked with other aspects of development. Thus, the child's readiness to read depends upon his speech and listening skills. The child who does not speak accurately or who uses infantile speech patterns will experience difficulties in learning to read. Garrett (1949) points out that children's speech patterns, pronunciation, sentence structure, and vocabulary range, must correspond sufficiently to the requirements of the reading task, if it is to be successfully undertaken. If children mispronounce words, they will have difficulty learning the regularities of the printed words. Children with inadequate vocabularies may be able to manage the pared down vocabularies of the first year's work in reading, but the limited vocabulary may be a handicap as he moves on to the work of the second and third grade. Readiness must be continuously assessed; readiness for earlier learning does not always indicate readiness for the more advanced forms of the same learning.

In addition to the requisite skills, the learner must have developed the appropriate attitudes in order to undertake a particular learning task. In order to engage in most school learning activities, the child must be capable of refraining from other activities. The activity drive, as described in the preceding chapter, is quite diffuse during the first five years of life and by the time the child enters school it is still expressed primarily in gross muscle movements and in concrete manipulation of objects rather than in symbolic behavior. It is extremely difficult for many children to concentrate the active energy into the sedentary school tasks. These children can be helped by means of activities that can serve as a transition from motoric to ideational activity, for example, the use of crayons, listening to stories, watching a short movie, and so on. These kinds of activities are useful in focusing the activity drive so that the energy can more readily be applied to school learning.

Other readiness factors deal with the maturity of thought processes and the development of intellectual abilities. These will be considered in Chapter 4 and Chapter 10.

The School's Responsibility in Fostering Readiness

If after assessing the child's development, we find that he is not ready for a specific task, what is our responsibility then? Those who view readiness as purely a biological, maturational phenomenon are inclined to advise waiting for the signs of readiness. Thus, for example, the age of school entry is legally fixed at a certain chronological age. However, each child has reached a different point of development at that specified age. Some enter kindergarten at age four years nine months completely ready for the work of the first grade; others reach the age of

FIGURE 3.3 *Some consider school readiness to be a biological, maturational phenomenon rather than one that can be fostered and encouraged by experience. Copyright (1957) by United Feature Syndicate, Inc.*

6½, the age at which formal reading instruction is usually started, lacking many of the requisites for such an experience. Some educators argue that the child who is not ready for school should be kept at home until he demonstrates readiness. This position reflects a common misunderstanding of the readiness concept and, in our opinion, a misunderstanding of the school's role in regard to readiness.

In some instances the school can do a more effective job than the home in systematically preparing the child for school tasks; the school can usually provide better readiness experiences in a more suitable environment. The school program must also take into account those children whose development is advanced over that of their age mates and who are consequently ready for more complex learning tasks. The general problem of school policy such as retardation and acceleration will be discussed in Chapter 7. Olson and Hughes (1944) have pointed out that teachers always must face the problem of adjusting the work of the classroom to suit the various needs of children with different developmental rates.

We need to be concerned about the learner's readiness not only at the beginning of each new learning task but at all levels of education and throughout the course of development of meaning. When we consider readiness within the ongoing stream of the educational process we are dealing with the problem of sequence.

SEQUENCE

From day to day the teacher not only faces the problem of determining when a child is ready for a particular experience, but also the order or sequence of experiences. The teacher must plan each activity so that it accomplishes some particular educational objective. One such objective is the enlargement of meaning, the development of discrimination and generalizations between various parts of the meaning diagram (see Figure 3.2) and between one meaning unit and another. Goodlad (1959) has referred to the starting point of such an experience as an "organizing center" for learning. The enlargement of meaning through such organizing centers will come about if the experience is planned in terms of what the learners have experienced before and if it prepares them for what is to come. "The teacher must ask in planning: To what does this particular catch-hold point contribute? Does it emerge logically from what has gone before? Does it prepare for deeper learning? Positive answers to such questions suggest that the proposed learning is timed well in the sequence of things" (page 56). One scholar has suggested that the child should learn first, what he needs most, to learn more.

The following situation shows how a learning experience is viewed as a starting point for educational development. Miss Mandville planned a trip for her second-grade class to a local dairy. When the children returned they asked many questions and they reviewed their experiences. Some of the statements indicated growth in various dimensions of meaning and also curiosity in the dimension of source and process, which was the teacher's focal reason for planning the trip. Thus, some children asked what kind of work was done in the laboratory? This provided the teacher with an opportunity to make the children aware of the dimension of analytic meaning, explaining simply the work of the laboratory. This same question allowed for the development also of meaning in the sociocultural dimension, the government's concern for the health of its citizens through inspection and standards. One child asked where the cows were, because he had a vague notion that cows were involved in the source. This indicated to the teacher that another experience designed to develop further the source and process dimension should be planned. From a visit to a dairy farm many new dimensions could be developed. For example, the beginning of the development of the language dimension with an analysis of the difference in the way the word "milk" is used in the following sentences: The farmer pours the milk into the can. I milk the cow. The milk bottle is sterilized.

The sequence of experiences can be seen to be determined by the timely development and expansion of meaning. An experience can be evaluated in terms of the following criteria: the extent to which it enables the expansion of understanding in many dimensions, the extent to which it leads to planning other experiences which will further develop meaning, the extent to which it enables the student to see relationships with other concepts and the extent to which it enables students with various levels of understanding and interests to profit from it.

The sequence of teaching may be determined also by whether we want the student to integrate meaning first and then to be supplied with the experiences or illustrations that support the meaning, the deductive method; or whether we wish to supply the separate experiences first and have the generalizations take place afterward, the inductive method. There is a certain glamor for the student in the latter method, it provides him with a sense of adventure and discovery. It is impossible however, for teaching to be done only inductively for it is uneconomical, being generally more time consuming. Also we must recognize that meaning can be derived both deductively and inductively and the student must be made aware of this. Brownell and Hendrickson (1950) state that "In the end, the important thing is that the generalizations taught (at least those that are essential in life) be full of meaning and susceptible to functional use. If this condition is met, it probably makes little difference whether they have been acquired deductively or inductively" (page 123).

THE ROLE OF THE LEARNER
IN THE ACQUISITION OF MEANING

The teacher aims to provide experiences for the learner that he will transform into meaning. How the learner does this and how the teacher facilitates its occurrence are questions to be answered here. The problem is complex and might be clarified by a description of some extreme positions on the issues involved.

One extreme view holds that the learner is passive and analogous to a receptacle into which the teacher pours meaning. The subject matter should be carefully structured and preplanned. Dewey (1902) criticizes this point of view and characterizes it as follows: "The subject matter furnishes the end, and it determines the method; he (the learner) is the superficial being who is to be deepened; his is narrow experience which is to be widened. It is his to receive, to accept. His part is fulfilled when he is ductile and docile" (page 8). This position has

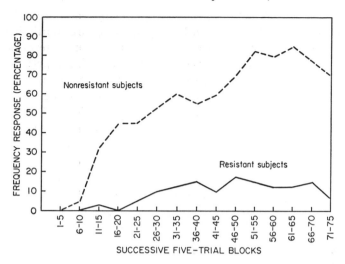

FIGURE 3.4   *The effect of the subject's intent to inhibit response upon the level of conditioning. Subjects who intended to inhibit response (solid line) were instructed as follows: "Be sure you do not wink before you feel the puff." Subjects who did not inhibit response (dotted line) were instructed as follows: "Do not attempt to control voluntarily your reactions to these stimuli. Simply behave naturally and let your reactions take care of themselves." From Eugenia Norris and D. A. Grant, "Eyelid Conditioning as Affected by Verbally Induced Inhibitory Set and Counter-reinforcement," American Journal of Psychology. 1948, 61, 37–49.*

emphasized one aspect of the conditioned response experiments. In classical conditioning the learner's role is completely under the control of the experimenter. The experimenter determines which unconditioned or natural response, such as salivation to food, he wishes to condition. He determines which neutral stimulus he wishes the learner to accept as a conditioned stimulus. By presenting the unconditioned stimulus, food, simultaneously or in close temporal contiguity with the conditioned stimulus, the learner will respond to the latter with salivation. Because the experimenter, who serves as a teacher, can have the learner change the meaning of his environmental stimuli, it is reasoned that we need only to create a controlled environment in order to facilitate the acquisition of meaning.

Although the conditioning experiment does offer some suggestions for the guidance of the learner, the intent of the learner must be taken into consideration and the proper reinforcement schedule must be employed. Certain kinds of fixed meaning can be taught to a willing learner by conditioning procedures. The unwilling learner cannot be successfully taught by conditioning procedures. This has been demonstrated in one conditioning experiment where subjects were given different kinds of instructions. In Figure 3.4 it can be noted that the conditioned response hardly gets established when the subject is instructed to inhibit the response. The same results could be expected when the learner resists the learning for reasons of his own.

Another extreme position on the role of the learner proposes that we discard any preconceived notions with regard to subject matter, that we wait for the appearance of felt needs and these determine the subject of the lesson. It is a teacher with this orientation that provoked the cartoon in which the child asks, "Teacher, do we have to do what we want to today?" The absence of guidance can lead to unsystematic and often arrested development of meaning. The child cannot on his own arrive at any high level organization of his experiences. The long historical process of sifting and sorting in which man has engaged should not be overlooked. The person who does not draw on this investment cannot achieve full self-realization. In this way the lack of guidance defeats the very purposes for which this kind of education is instituted.

Given the tools, the maps, and instructions for finding his way, the learner will constantly enlarge his meaning, or his understanding of the world as it is or described by man. The curriculum serves the teacher in that it enables him to plan the environment of the learner. Dewey (1902) summarized this middle point of view by stating that the primary value of the curriculum or the course of study

> . . . is for the teacher, not for the child. It says to the teacher: Such and such are the capacities, the fulfilments, in truth and beauty and behavior, open to these children. Now see to it that day by day the conditions are such that *their own activities* move inevitably in this direction, toward such culmination of themselves. Let the child's nature fulfil its own destiny, revealed to you in whatever of science and art and industry the world now holds as its own (page 31).

This suggests that the curriculum is viewed as the accumulated wisdom of mankind that the child can incorporate a large segment of this wisdom and make it part of his personality, if he is guided in his own terms to doing so. Guidance does not mean imposition from without. It is rather the freeing of the child's energies for their own most adequate fulfillment. This suggests further that in order for learning to take place the learner must be actively involved in learning, he must sense that the enlargement of meaning will make him more adequate, will enhance his phenomenal self, as he engages in the complex business of living. Activity does not necessarily mean bodily overt activity, it means also thought, meditation, and covert experiencing. The realization of purpose in the acquisition of meaning must be in large measure immediate, within the classroom itself.

The realization of purpose and the clarification of meaning can be accomplished at the same time. By offering children an opportunity to explain to others, purpose is provided, and we involve the learner actively in his attempt to achieve clarity. This point of view is supported by many studies on the benefits of recitation. For example, in one study children in the fifth and sixth grades learned to spell most effectively when they spent 60-80 percent of their study time in recitation, least effectively when all the time was spent in reading the words (Forlano, 1936). In another study by Weir and Stevenson (1959) it was shown that children learn visual discrimination tasks more efficiently if they verbalize or talk about what they are doing. Ray (1957) reports similar findings on adults, namely, that they learn the task more quickly if they were required to tell their plans beforehand. In general the more the learner is involved in acquiring meaning, the more effective is the learning. He becomes involved largely on the basis of being motivated and interested but involvement comes about also when the experiences are multiple and varied. The use of vision, hearing, manipulation, speech, and other sense modalities and response avenues will enhance the acquisition of meaning. Carefully planned field trips, laboratories and other experiences should form a basis for teaching meaning. As the student grows older and moves into college, the need for these kinds of first-hand experiences may be less than in the earlier grades, but at all levels of learning they have some place.

THE COURSE OF MEANING ACQUISITION: LEARNING CURVES

One way of understanding the acquisition of meaning is to examine the course of its growth. Learning curves provide us with the means for such an examination. Although learning curves do not tell the whole story, since the acquisition must be translated into performance before it can be traced on a curve, they provide us with some basis for understanding the many kinds of meaning development. The measure of mastery or success is plotted on the vertical axis and the amount of practice, time spent or number of trials, is plotted on the horizontal axis. The measure of success may be as in typing, the number of words per minute, in which case we would expect the curve to start low, few words in the early trials, and rise; the measure may be the amount of time to type 100 words and in this case we would expect the curve to drop. More typically the measure of success is plotted so that the curve rises. Three different kinds of learning curves and their implications for guiding the learner are considered here.

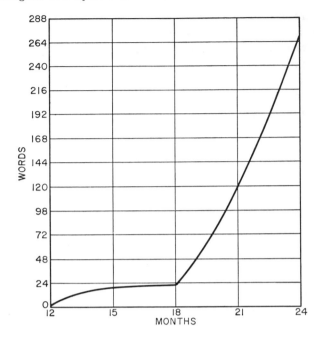

FIGURE 3.5   *The increase in the average number of words in children's vocabulary during the second year, a positively accelerated curve. From H. L. Kingsley and R. Garry,* The Nature and Conditions of Learning, *2d ed. © Englewood Cliffs, N. J.: Prentice-Hall, 1957.*

Positively Accelerated Learning Curves

The shape of the curve as shown in Figure 3.5 indicates that later gains are larger than earlier gains. Thus, in plotting the increase in the average number of words in children's vocabulary during the second year each succeeding three month period (with the exception of the period fifteen to eighteen months) shows a greater increase than the preceding three-month period. The increment in the number of words during the first six month period is approximately twenty, whereas in the second six month period the increment is about two hundred and forty words.

> Curves of learning informational or logical material such as content in history, psychology, or mathematics are often positively accelerated; the more one learns, the more he can learn the new material. Learning the basic vocabulary in the vernacular or in a foreign language makes progressive improvement in reading possible (Gates et al., 1949, page 355).

The slow improvement in the early phases of learning may also be due to the fact that the learning or development that is taking place is of such a nature as not to be manifest and thus does not appear on the curve. Thus a measure of the *spoken* vocabulary shows the curve is positively accelerated (slow acquisition in the early stages). At the same time, however, the *aural* or *listening* vocabulary may be increasing rapidly.

The positively accelerated form of learning may create some problems of motivation in the early phases of learning. The learner is strongly stimulated by success and where this is lacking he may give up before he can realize more measurable amounts of success. Fortunately much of this kind of learning takes place in the case of the younger person who is more readily satisfied with his performance or level of meaning acquired and does not clearly realize the difference between his level and the more integrated or perfected level.

It is most important for the teacher to understand that, even though the gain insofar as it can be plotted on the learning curve may be rather slight, this phase of the learning activity is inevitable and forms a necessary foundation for the later greater progress. Once the slow progress of the early part of learning is overcome, the learner can be encouraged by having his attention called to his continuing increase in progress. Theoretically, it should be noted that as long as we are compelled to consider learning in terms of what the learner is able to do or to demonstrate, we will quite frequently encounter periods of little or no apparent learning as at the beginning of a positively accelerated curve or in the case of the plateau (Figure 3.7). However, we must not overlook that learning may consist of changes within the learner that cannot become manifest until by accumulated practice and experience the learning acquires a certain degree of structure or precision. The period during which this takes place is the period of little or no apparent progress. It is analogous in some ways to observing the erection of a building, much of the essential work underground on which the rest of the structure depends cannot be assessed by the casual observer. The teacher must be aware that a certain amount of teaching is ground work and must be viewed as an investment with long range returns. Children often absorb a great deal of meaning and information before they can demonstrate what they have acquired.

Negatively Accelerated Learning Curves

When the improvement in the initial phases of learning is greater than in the terminal phases, the learning curve is negatively accelerated. This type of curve occurs in many kinds of school learning. One such curve is shown in Figure 3.6, where the increase in the ability of translating into telegraph code for sending purposes occurring during the first eight weeks of learning is unequalled in any similar period of time. The amount of gain during the last twenty weeks seems hardly worth the effort. Very similar types of progress occur in various school situations.

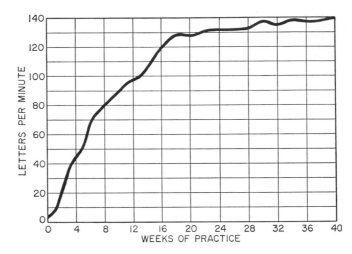

FIGURE 3.6 *Progress in learning to send telegraph code, a negatively acceler-*
ated learning curve. Bryan and Harter (1897), from whom this figure is taken,
were among the first to plot the progress of skill acquisition. Their method of
plotting progress is essentially the one used today.

The enthusiasm in approaching a new learning situation and the use of
previous learnings, related to the present task and overlearned, account
for the rapid gains at the beginning. The wearing off of the novelty of a
new learning with the resultant drop in interest and the difficulty often
encountered in the more precise aspects of the final learning, lead to
slower gains. The teacher has several reasons for doing all he can to
encourage the learner to continue in his learning. (1) Not all the benefits of practice and effort are readily apparent. (2) Overlearning or continued use of a previously acquired meaning or skill is essential for efficient retention. (3) Although the gains during the final phases of learning may be minimal, these gains may be crucial for acceptable performance. For these reasons the teacher must encourage the learner by
rewarding effort and by making note of progress.

The Plateau and Limits in the Learning Curve

In some instances, usually when the rate of learning is negatively
accelerated, the progress in learning levels off and then increases again
if practice continues. In Figure 3.7 we have such a case of flattening out,
called a plateau in the learning curve. The plateau can easily be mistaken for the limit of learning and when both the teacher and learner
take it for such, it is not likely that further progress will be made. In
actuality the plateau can be accounted for in terms of a sublimit; that is
the limit for a particular part of the entire task. In receiving telegraph
code the learner acquires first the skill of hearing certain code combi-

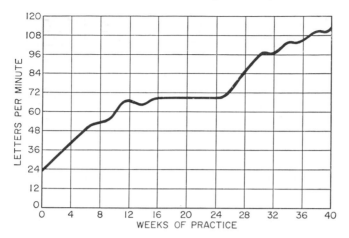

FIGURE 3.7 *Progress in learning to receive connected discourse in telegraph code, a negatively accelerated curve with a plateau. This curve is taken from Bryan and Harter (1897), who offered an explanation for the occurrence of the plateau which is still widely accepted.*

nations and assigning the proper letters to them, a simple kind of meaning acquisition. This takes place rapidly. The learner then proceeds to put these letters together and receives words rather than single letters, a more complicated kind of meaning acquisition. Words can then be put together into phrases and sentences. At any point when the shift from one type of meaning to another type takes place, the learner goes through a period of consolidating the early learning before going on to more complex forms. If the teacher is alert to the existence of various levels of complexity within the acquisition of meaning it is possible to assist the learner over onto the next level. However, real limits do exist; limits that can be accounted for in terms of the physiological makeup of the learner at a particular period in his development or in terms of the task to be mastered. A three-year old cannot readily acquire meaning from the printed page and a mature reader cannot surpass a certain rate of reading with material of given difficulty.

If the process of acquiring meaning is examined as it takes place over a long period of time, the various kinds of progress described are found. This general learning curve shown in Figure 3.8 can be divided into six parts. The discussion of learning curves can be reviewed as follows.

1. A period of negligible progress. This will occur in those cases of exposure to experiences before readiness of various kinds has developed or it may represent the period during which learning is taking place but is not well enough established to manifest itself in measurable performance.

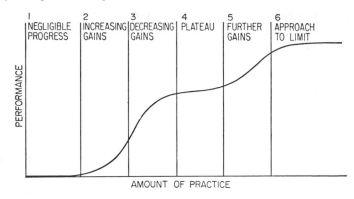

FIGURE 3.8   *A general learning curve. From L. J. Cronbach,* Educational Psychology, *copyright 1953 ©, 1962, 1963, by Harcourt, Brace & World, Inc., and reprinted with their permission.*

2. A period of increasing gains. After the foundations have been acquired new meanings can be built upon these and increasing gains can show themselves.

3. A period of decreasing gains during which the more complex aspects of meaning are being encountered and mastered.

4. The plateau, a period of negligible gain that may result from the loss of motivation or interest, or the consolidation of previous learnings and the slow beginning of new learnings, somewhat like period 1.

5. A period of further gains resembling period 3.

6. An approach to the limit determined by the stage of development of the learner, by the nature of the task, or the procedure used.

MEMORY

The over-all result of our school learning is an expansion of knowledge and an enlargement of meaning. Children know and understand more at the end of the ninth grade than they did at the end of the fifth. Yet many specific items of information that we once learned and knew are now no longer remembered. At one time or another in our school career we knew the names of the capital cities of many countries, we could give the nonmetric values for various metric measures, we could spell and give a satisfactory definition of a great number of words that are now strangers to us, and we could rattle off the declension and conjugation of various nouns and verbs in a foreign language. A host of specific facts were known and are now forgotten. Were it not for the fact that a great deal of useful information is retained, we might well ask if there is any value in learning. Forgetting is an inevitable concomitant of learning. A study of how forgetting takes place should enable us to direct and guide learning so as to maximize retention and to make the acquisition process more efficient.

The Causes of Forgetting

A common misconception about forgetting attributes it completely to a process of fading, analogous to the disappearance of a crease in a pillow with the passage of time. A more adequate explanation would describe forgetting as a process in which the learner is actively and completely involved just as in the learning process itself. Different kinds of forgetting can be explained in different ways. Each of the explanations and descriptions of the process will view the human organism as continually reacting, developing, changing, and adjusting to a large number of situations each day. The quality and quantity of memory will depend on what the learner does while he is having the experience and the kind of experiences that follow. "Those events which produce only a transitory limited reaction are speedily forgotten, while those which evoke extensive reactions and which result in modifications of our subsequent activity are remembered, at least as long as those modifications persist in a form similar to their original" (Cameron, 1947, page 46).

The development of meaning itself paradoxically accounts for certain kinds of forgetting. In the early phases of meaning acquisition certain details are important for understanding. As meaning expands, the understanding no longer relies on these details. As we understand something as a whole and more adequately, we are inclined to forget some of the particulars that were needed for the earlier less complete forms of meaning. Remembering is thus like perception in which we naturally give up a certain amount of detail for the sake of economy, efficiency, and better organization (see triangle demonstration on page 59). As the typist becomes more proficient he may have greater difficulty in recalling the location of a particular letter on the keyboard; many specifics in music are better known to the beginner than to the accomplished musician. The adult beginner in the study of foreign language is more painfully aware of grammatical features of the foreign language that differ from his native tongue than the person who uses the language fluently. For some aspects of the development of meaning, forgetting permits the establishment of more complex and coordinated understanding. The need to forget errors is obvious. On occasion where forgetting fails to occur we witness the perseverative response or the repetition of a response where it no longer is appropriate. This positive aspect of forgetting implies that the teacher needs to recognize that although it may be useful to remember certain things, some learnings can be profitably forgotten since their usefulness may be limited only to a certain phase of meaning development.

Thus far we have looked at forgetting as a positive and beneficial feature of the enlargement of meaning. In many cases, however, forgetting represents a loss or reduction in the quality and amount of meaning when compared to the mastery at the height of the acquisition. We forget the date of an historical event that was known to us a few weeks ago, or the answer to a question of fact; after once being able to make the distinction, a child confuses the letters "b" and "d" or a student of physiology confuses "diastolic" and "systolic." The psychologist explains this kind of forgetting or loss as being due to *interference* or *retroactive inhibition*. By this we mean that all of the learner's experiences interact with each other; what he experiences at one time may affect detrimentally the impact of an experience at another time. McGeoch and Irion (1952) suggest that the extent to which forgetting or retention occurs or appears to occur is related to the following conditions:

1. The procedures used to measure retention.
2. The characteristics of the original learning, such as the kind of material and the degree of mastery.
3. The characteristics of the experiences between the time of acquisition and recall.
4. The psychological state of the learner at the time of learning and at the time of recall.

Measures of Retention

The procedure we use in measuring retention will determine the amount of the original learning that appears to be retained. Thus, we may measure retention by means of *reproduction,* the learner may be required to reproduce, verbally or in writing, a poem or some other material that he has previously learned. A second procedure for measuring retention is that of *reconstruction*. This technique requires the learner to reassemble a scrambled presentation of the original material. In some cases, items that are not contained in the original may be introduced also, and he is required to distinguish between the relevant and irrelevant. This involves the use of another measure of retention—recognition. A third procedure for measuring retention, more adaptable to the psychology laboratory than to the classroom is that of *relearning*. Ebbinghaus (1913) in his classical laboratory studies of memory employed this measure of retention. He would learn a list of nonsense syllables, such as FEJ, BEX, DOQ, or XAB, in series or in pairs, to a given level of mastery; for example, one, two, or three perfect recitations. After a specified interval, he would relearn the same list and would designate the amount retained as the number of trials saved, the savings being the difference between the number of trials to learn and the number of trials to relearn to the same level of mastery. This measure is probably the most accurate measure of retention, but as already noted, it does not lend itself readily to the classroom situation. A fourth procedure for measuring retention is *recognition*. In this procedure, the subject is required to identify the correct responses from a group of possible choices. This is the technique relied upon in many multiple choice examinations and may be used in conjunction with the procedure described above, namely, reconstruction. Recognition allows the learner to use minimal cues and hence will give higher retention scores than any of the other procedures. Each of these measures of retention, by testing retention differently, would indicate different amounts retained (Luh, 1922). Thus, the teacher in estimating the amount of forgetting or retention must keep in mind that the scores obtained on a test designed to measure retention are a function of the procedure used. If the teacher desires to encourage the learner he may use a test of recognition. If, however, the learning must be used in a setting demanding an exact reproduction, such as in spelling, the most appropriate measure of retention should, of course, be reproduction.

The Original Learning—A Factor in Retention

The learner's response to the material at the time of learning will determine how he will remember it. The kind of meaning he is able to assign to it, the kind of organization he can give to it, and the extent to which it can be integrated into previously established learnings, will determine the quality of retention. In essence this means that retention is continuous with the original learning. Effective acquisition of meaning usually brings with it effective retention. A child who is able to learn his spelling list rapidly will be slow to forget it and conversely the child who is slow in learning the same list will tend to forget it rapidly (Underwood, 1948).

Each learning task involves the learner in a search for meaning. If necessary we "recode" the substance of the current learning task, oversimplifying if need be, so that it will fit the categories established by previous experience (Bruner, 1957). The learner may achieve meaning in a variety of ways. One influential basis for assigning meaning is to give the experience a name. If a perceived form is given a name later reproductions of the form from memory will resemble the object bearing that name. In Figure 3.9 we see how subsequent reproductions of a conventionalized figure of an owl come to resemble a cat, and in Figure 3.10 we note that the name given to a figure by the experimenter influences the manner in which the figure is reproduced later from memory. Wulf (1922) has called this process whereby the memory assimilates to some familiar form or object, *normalization*. Other changes were classified by Wulf under the categories of *leveling* and *sharpening*. In the former the retained material becomes more symmetrical, better balanced

Original Drawing   Reproduction 1   Reproduction 2

Reproduction 3   Reproduction 4   Reproduction 5   Reproduction 6

Reproduction 7   Reproduction 8   Reproduction 9   Reproduction 10

FIGURE 3.9   *The original drawing of a rather unusual figure carrying a strong suggestion of some realistic representation becomes, on repeated reproductions, elaborated in the direction of that familiar representation. From F. C. Bartlett,* Remembering, *England: Cambridge University Press, 1950, p. 180.*

and somewhat simpler, than the original. In the latter some outstanding feature or characteristic becomes accentuated or exaggerated as the material is processed in memory.

Organization facilitates the original learning and also enhances retention. Compare how much more difficult it would be to learn and to remember the following code:

A=⌋, B=⌉, C=⌐, D=⌊⌋, E=□, F=⌈⌉, G=⌊, H=⌈, I=⌈,

than if the code were presented as follows:

A	D	G
B	E	H
C	F	I

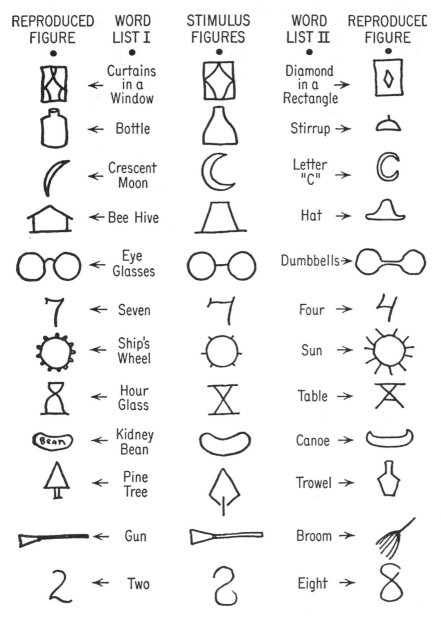

FIGURE 3.10 *The stimulus figures were presented to two groups of subjects. Each presentation was preceded by the words in List 1 for the first group and those in List 2 for the second group. The reproductions tended to conform to the forms suggested by the words in the respective lists. From L. Carmichael et al., "An Experimental Study of the Effect of Language on Visually Perceived Form,"* Journal of Experimental Psychology, *1932, 15: 73–86.*

In the first case the learner is faced with the task of acquiring and re-taining nine separate pieces of information, whereas in the second he need remember only two, namely, the order of presenting the letters and that of the pattern made by the four lines. It is obviously easier to re-member two "chunks" of information than to remember nine. Miller (1956) suggests that the memory span for information depends on the extent to which the learner is able to recode or process the informa-tion into organized units; the larger the unit the more the person re-members. In fact, this is what we do when we employ mnemonic de-vices to aid our retention. The mnemonic device is an organizing aid to enable us to retain more information.

> Thirty days hath September
> April, June and November
> All the rest have thirty-one
> Excepting February with twenty-eight.

This mnemonic verse reduces our problem to four or five units of infor-mation rather than twelve. To remember the name ROY G. BIV repre-sents three units of information, which is easier than the seven in nam-ing the colors of the spectrum in order, red, orange, yellow, green, blue, indigo, and violet. These devices are somewhat artificial in that they are often unrelated to the material being learned. In most class-room situations the teacher's mastery of the subject enables him to or-ganize it so as to make it more efficiently learned and hence more ac-curately remembered. Ausubel (1960) has shown that providing the learner in advance with "appropriate and relevant subsuming concepts (organizers)" greatly facilitates the learning and retention of unfamiliar but meaningful verbal material.

The level of organization achieved in the original learning will determine how well the material is retained. Practice and repetition which lead to overlearning are for this reason often effective means of establishing meaning. Mere repetition of a poorly organized response will not improve retention. Practice and repetition where they lead to observable improvement in organization, serve to improve retention. Where material is mastered to a high level of organization, the loss over equal periods of time will be considerably less than if the original mas-tery is only to a moderate level (see Figure 3.11). In line with this prin-ciple is the common observation that meanings that are used frequently and through repetition develop a high level of integration will generally be retained better than those that have little application.

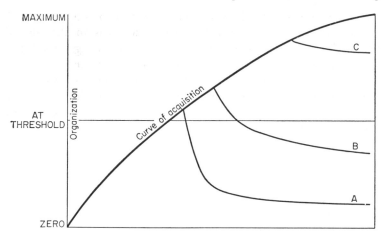

FIGURE 3.11 *Rate for forgetting for different levels of organization in the original learning. Curve A shows the rapid forgetting which occurs when the organization is at the threshold of response. Curve B shows a slower rate of loss when the organization acquired is somewhat above the threshold. Curve C shows little loss when the acquired organization approaches the maximum. The reading skill of many adults would follow Curve C. From A. I. Gates et al.,* Educational Psychology, *New York: Macmillan Company, 1949, p. 394.*

The Experience between the Time of Acquisition and the Time of Recall

In addition to retention being a function of the quality of the original learning, it is also a function of the kind of experience and activity that follows the original learning. Later experiences can support or interfere with the earlier learning. Interference will be minimal if the original learning is well established and if the two learning activities are dissimilar. For example, in beginning reading the letters *b* and *d* are frequently confused. It might be a good idea to introduce one letter and wait for reasonable mastery of it before introducing the other. In learning a foreign language it would be well for the student to master one meaning of a word before learning another meaning of the same word. If two learning tasks are conceived as similar in stimulus value, response, or the context, interference is maximized. The general principle governing the relationship of similarity to interference is that if two learning tasks are short of being identical, interference is greatest (Robinson, 1927). Furthermore, interference will be greater when the new learning occurs shortly after the preceding learning activity. The implications of these generalizations for educational planning are such that the schedule of class periods should be examined so as to keep interference at a minimum and the over-all program should be such as to allow sufficient mastery before introducing a subject matter that may interfere. For instance students should not undertake a second foreign language until the first has been reasonably mastered.

Each autumn the teacher is faced with the task of assessing what the students have retained over the summer vacation. Although the loss may appear considerable, it is soon overcome by means of review. Also forgetting occurs differentially, that is, it affects different subject areas and different students differently. After reviewing a number of studies on this topic Seagoe (1956) concludes that the following characteristics of the material or the learner account for summer loss:

1. *Specificity of subject matter.* Fundamentals of arithmetic and spelling show greater losses than subjects that allow for some broader generalizations such as science and geography.

2. *Degree of mastery.* As shown in Figure 3.11 the degree of organization determines the rate of forgetting. Children who left for vacation with mastery at the point where forgetting Curve A starts will have lost more than those whose original mastery was at the level where Curve C begins. This would suggest that spring review especially in arithmetic and spelling in order to bring the skill to a high level of mastery would be advisable.

3. *Application of school learning to summer activity.* School learnings such as reading are much more likely to show gain over the summer. Whereas, arithmetic will ordinarily show loss. Children whose summer programs are guided such as at camp or in the use of library facilities will show gain in reading and science. The teacher can help children and parents plan some summer activities that will enhance the work of the school.

> It is clear, then, that the teacher must expect a pattern of differential forgetting over long vacations. If the child knows a skill well, can use it independently, and finds it useful in out-of-school activities the vacation will cause little loss. It may result in gain. If the child is just beginning to learn a skill, cannot use it independently, and if his out-of-school activities do not allow it to function, that skill will show a rapid loss during the vacation. Arithmetic fundamentals and spelling are particularly susceptible to loss under such conditions (Seagoe, 1956, page 235).

Review is one of the most important safeguards to retention. It generally serves to raise the organization and stability of meaning above the highest level that existed previously and thus serves to retard forgetting. A proper schedule for review is of course dependent on the time available, and on the kind of material in question. Assuming that scheduling is flexible and that the initial learning took place over a period of four or five days, the best review schedule would allow for the first review four or five days later, the second about a week after the first and the third, fourth and fifth review sessions would follow at intervals of ten days, two weeks and three weeks respectively. Some of the review sessions can take the form of examinations.

Motivation and Retention

Our discussion of memory would be incomplete if it did not include at least a brief discussion of the relationship of such dynamic factors as motivation, emotion, attitudes, and the organization of memories. In Chapters 6 and 11 the effect of value orientation on the learning process is discussed. After learning has taken place the learner's purposes, his attitude-value system and his general frame of reference will continue to shape the organization of what has been learned. After reviewing a number of studies dealing with the differential retention of pleasant and unpleasant experiences, Edwards (1942) concludes:

> (a) That experiences that are consistent and which harmonize with an existing frame of reference will tend to be learned and remembered better than experiences which conflict with the frame;
> (b) That experiences or materials which are in opposition to the frame of reference will tend to be recast so that they may be more readily assimilated (page 52).

As previously pointed out, when the meaning of an experience is not consistent with the categories of meaning established by previous experience, significant changes will take place in remembering the experience. These changes will be in the direction of simplification and more customary meaning. This type of change is *normalization*. The following story, The War of the Ghosts, possesses a quality of strangeness and when reproduced it shows changes that indicate the tendency to give the story meaning consistent with previous experiences. The story and the reproductions are taken from Bartlett (1950).[1]

The War of the Ghosts

One night two young men from Egulac went down to the river to hunt seals, and while they were there it became foggy and calm. Then they heard war-cries, and they thought: "Maybe this is a war-party." They escaped to the shore, and hid behind a log. Now canoes came up, and they heard the noise of paddles, and saw one canoe coming up to them. There were five men in the canoe and they said:

"What do you think? We wish to take you along. We are going up the river to make war on the people."

One of the young men said: "I have no arrows."

"Arrows are in the canoe," they said.

"I will not go along. I might be killed. My relatives do not know where I have gone. But you," he said, turning to the other, "may go with them."

[1] From F. C. Bartlett, *Remembering*, Cambridge University Press, New York, 1950, pp. 65-71.

So one of the young men went, but the other returned home.

And the warriors went on up the river to a town on the other side of Kalama. The people came down to the water, and they began to fight, and many were killed. But presently the young man heard one of the warriors say: "Quick, let us go home: that Indian has been hit." Now he thought: "Oh, they are ghosts." He did not feel sick, but they said he had been shot.

So the canoes went back to Egulac, and the young man went ashore to his house, and made a fire. And he told everybody and said: "Behold I accompanied the ghosts, and we went to fight. Many of our fellows were killed, and many of those who attacked us were killed. They said I was hit, and I did not feel sick."

He told it all, and then he became quiet. When the sun rose he fell down. Something black came out of his mouth. His face became contorted. The people jumped up and cried.

He was dead (page 65).

Eight days later one subject remembered the story as follows:

The War of the Ghosts

Two young men from Edulac went fishing. While thus engaged they heard a noise in the distance. "That sounds like a war-cry," said one, "there is going to be some fighting." Presently there appeared some warriors who invited them to join an expedition up the river.

One of the young men excused himself on the ground of family ties. "I cannot come," he said, "as I might get killed." So he returned home. The other man, however, joined the party, and they proceeded on canoes up the river. While landing on the banks the enemy appeared and were running down to meet them. Soon someone was wounded, and the party discovered they were fighting against ghosts. The young man and his companion returned to the boats, and went back to their homes.

The next morning at dawn he was describing his adventures to his friends, who had gathered round him. Suddenly something black issued from his mouth, and he fell down uttering a cry. His friends closed around him, but found that he was dead (page 67).

Another subject attempted to reproduce the story after an interval of four months and he dictated it as follows:

I have no idea of the title.

There were two men in a boat, sailing towards an island. When they approached the island, some natives came running towards them, and informed them that there was fighting going on on the island, and invited them to join. One said to the other: "You had better go. I cannot very well, because I have relatives expecting me, and they will not know what has become of me. But you have no one to expect you." So one accompanied the natives, but the other returned.

Here there is a part that I can't remember. What I don't know is how the man got to the fight. However, anyhow the man was in the midst of the fighting, and was wounded. The natives endeavoured to persuade the man to return, but he assured them that he had not been wounded.

I have an idea that his fighting won the admiration of the natives.

The wounded man ultimately fell unconscious. He was taken from the fighting by the natives.

Then, I think it is, the natives describe what happened, and they seem to have imagined seeing a ghost coming out of his mouth. Really it was a kind of materialisation of his breath. I know this *phrase* was not in the story, but that is the idea I have. Ultimately the man died at dawn the next day (page 71).

Paul (1959), by using modifications of the stimulus story used by Bartlett, found that by eliminating gaps and ambiguities in the story, by changing the content so that it would be a more familiar story for the learner, and by making the stimulus material more coherent, learning and remembering could be facilitated and forgetting, distortion and fragmentation could be avoided. He found also that there were individual patterns of remembering and forgetting. Some of the subjects in the study seemed to strive after meaning or structure in the whole of the stimulus material while others sought primarily to master the detail. Some subjects tended to elaborate the memory by adding to the original, others tended to contract by leveling and erasing some of the original content.

A number of studies have shown that a person's value orientation will affect his memory. In these studies a dimension of the student's frame of reference is established, such as theistic-atheistic (Watson and Hartmann, 1939), pro-New-Deal-anti-New-Deal (Edwards, 1941), pro-communist-anticommunist (Levine and Murphy, 1943). The student is then exposed to material that favors or opposes his point of view. In each of these studies it is demonstrated that the student remembers better that which is consistent with his beliefs and tends to forget that which conflicts with them. The implications of these findings for classroom instruction are that before instruction begins the proper frame of reference must be established, the student must be helped to recognize the consistency of the new ideas with those which he presently has. One cannot force acceptance, the student will quickly reject or forget those meanings that do not fit his existing meaning maps.

The purposes for which a person learns are most significant in determining not only how effectively he will learn, but also the conditions of his remembering. In one study two groups of subjects learned the same material. One group was told that the learning task was an intelligence test, the other group was simply asked to learn the same material as part of a routine learning experiment. The students who viewed the learning as a test of their intelligence showed better retention than the others (Alper, 1946). A student who studies for purposes of doing well on an examination will remember the material better for the examination day than if he had studied the same material without the exam ination in mind. This is basically the reason for students' objections to surprise quizzes. The kind of examination, objective or essay, for which a student prepares will determine the organization of what he remembers. This does not mean that the teacher orient the student primarily toward passing the examination, for once the learning has served its purpose, forgetting is likely to be rather rapid. The best assurance of maximum retention is to provide learning experiences that are self-enhancing. Examinations can be self-enhancing when they are used diagnostically, do not threaten the ego, and they direct the student's attention to ways of improving his performance. This suggestion is elaborated in our discussion of evaluation in Chapter 9.

The learner does not approach his learning tasks passively nor is his retention a passive affair. Learning and retention are both determined by many dynamic factors such as motives, needs, attitudes, values, and frames of reference. These factors shape what will be remembered and are responsible for what is forgotten. They will facilitate or inhibit recall, they will transform, introduce confusions and distortions and in some cases enhance the organization of memory.

The acquisition of meaning depends upon three general factors: motivation and emotion, orientation to the task, and organization of the material. The following ten general principles should be kept in mind in designing a practical program of teaching (Bureau of Child Development and Parent Education):

1. Meaning develops only as we are ready for the particular learning.

2. We learn most efficiently what is related to our own purposes and interests.

3. We learn best and retain longest when the learning becomes incorporated into our way of living.

4. We do not learn efficiently when resistance is present in a learning situation. Prejudice against, resentment towards or hatred of the subject matter or the teacher, interferes with or entirely obstructs the learning process.

5. We learn best when we are actively involved in the learning.

6. We learn certain things from fear and shock. This is a dangerous form of teaching. Used outside of really hazardous situations, it quickly breeds anxiety or indifference. We may indeed become impervious to further learning in these areas.

7. We learn inefficiently in anticipation for future use, especially if such use is for some vague remote date.

8. We acquire meaning through processes of discrimination and integration. These are complementary processes and take place simul-

taneously. Discrimination cannot take place until earlier meanings are integrated and integration depends upon previous discrimination.

9. Repetition assists in the learning process when used appropriately. If it creates resentment or boredom, or if it is substituted for meaningfulness or is given to a learner before readiness for the material has been reached, it tends to obstruct learning and cause confusion.

10. The emotional state of the learner is of great importance. Anxiety checks learning. An over-all feeling of inferiority, a temporary humiliation, defiance or anger, a sense of being rejected, and other disruptive emotions affect the learning process. The reverse is true, a feeling of well-being and of being respected by others stimulates an alert mind, willingness to participate, and an attitude conducive to learning.

SUMMARY

Learning is defined as the process that accounts for relatively permanent changes in behavior that result from the interaction of the individual with his environment. The process of learning is distinguished, at least theoretically, from a similar process called maturation, which is a process accounting for changes in structure and function resulting primarily from biological forces. All behavior change, in actuality, depends on both learning and maturation and the total course of behavior change is development. Development proceeds by a process of differentiation and integration, from a condition of relatively unorganized and amorphous behavior to one that is organized and articulated.

Learning differs from one situation to the next depending on the way in which the learner approaches the particular learning task. In this chapter the process of learning as it is applied to those tasks in which the learner acquires information about the world as it is or as it has been described by men of a particular culture has been considered. The contributions of Pavlov and Thorndike in describing classical and instrumental conditioning, provide the background for understanding how fixed meanings are acquired. In both these forms of conditioning a new response is acquired, but it is a response that is arbitrarily set by the experimenter and which the learner is either compelled to produce or else he must discover what the experimenter (teacher) demands of him. The various characteristics of the conditioned response, such as its extinction, the range of stimuli to which it is given, and so on, have a bearing on educational practice.

The sorting and classification of the various fixed meanings that the learner acquires, lead to the development of concepts and generalizations. The growth of concepts may be visualized as the development of the meaning map with its five dimensions: personal, language, analytic, source and process, and sociocultural. This, like the whole process of development, depends on learned discriminations and generalizations among various experiences.

In order for the learner to acquire the fixed meanings and to place them in effective relationship to each other, he must be *ready* for the experience. Readiness is not purely a maturational phenomenon for which we must wait passively. It is a developmental process that must be nurtured by means of proper experience. The school must take an active part in providing those experiences that foster readiness.

The sequence of experiences for the acquisition of fixed meanings should be such that each experience should build naturally on what has gone before and should be planned as an "organizing center" for the enlargement of various meaning maps. The sequence should consist of both inductive and deductive processes; that is, they should proceed from the generalization to the detail, deductively, and from the specific instance to the discovery of the generalization, inductively.

The role of the learner in the acquisition of fixed meanings should be such as to allow active and purposeful participation, but in a direction set by the teacher who recognizes that the child may fulfil himself and realize his potentialities in the accumulated wisdom of man.

Learning curves provide us with some basis for understanding the course of meaning development. Some learning starts slowly and then picks up rapidly (positively accelerated), other learning proceeds in the reverse direction, rapidly at first and then more slowly (negatively accelerated). At other times we can note in the learning curve a period of little or no apparent gain, a plateau. A number of different factors account for the different shapes of the learning curve. Motivation is one of these factors. At other times the shape of the curve depends on the fact that a learning task is made up of a number of learning tasks some of which may have been acquired prior to the task being considered, sometimes these associated learnings must be mastered before the skill that we are measuring can manifest itself, and sometimes as the learner moves from one level of task organization to another, the manifest learning will level off.

Another aspect of the acquisition of meaning is memory and retention. Some forgetting is useful in that the amount of detail necessary for effective functioning may be less than was needed in the early stages of acquisition. Often, however, the quality of that which has been learned deteriorates as a result of forgetting. Forgetting is an active rather than a passive process. It depends on the quality of the original learning, what has transpired after the learning, the condition of the learner at the time of the learning and at the time of recall, and on the methods used for measuring retention. The following relationships apply: the better organized the original learning, the more effective the retention, the more active and involved the learner at the original learning, the better the retention, and the more continuously useful the original learning, the longer the period of retention. Purposeful review becomes an essential procedure for the development of stable learned structures that can be maintained against the interference of other learnings.

In order for the teacher to guide the pupil in the acquisition of fixed and arbitary meanings, the pupil's motivational and emotional condition must be carefully considered. It is difficult to teach against resistance and indifference but the teacher can expect that most children will enjoy the sense of competence and mastery involved in school tasks if they are ready for the task, if the learning has been properly sequenced and paced, and if his total environment supports this learning.

READING REFERENCES

Anderson, G. L. and A. I. Gates, The general nature of learning. In N. B. Henry (Ed.), *Learning and Instruction.* Forty-ninth Yearbook (Pt. I) National Society for the Study of Education. Chicago: University of Chicago Press, 1950.

Association for Supervision and Curriculum Development 1959 Yearbook, *Learning and the Teacher.* Washington: National Education Association (particularly first four chapters).

Deese, J., *The Psychology of Learning.* New York: McGraw-Hill Book Company, 1958 (chaps. 8 and 10).

Rivlin, H. N., *Improving Children's Learning Ability.* Chicago: Science Research Associates, 1953.

Trow, W. C., *The Learning Process* (What Research Says to the Teacher No. 6). Washington: National Education Association, 1954.

CHAPTER 4

HOW CHILDREN LEARN: THE DEVELOPMENT OF UNDERSTANDING

In addition to the fixed responses and definite meanings that the child must learn he must also learn to think, to reason, to understand, and to explain. These latter activities characterize the educated person. "The educated person is, among other things the *thoughtful* person, that is, one who is equipped to deal reflectively rather than impulsively with life's problems" (Hartmann, 1941, page 259). The previous chapter dealt with the school's responsibility in transmitting the cultural heritage or at least that part of it dealing with information about reality that the culture has established and accepted. This type of learning has been called reproductive learning. This chapter deals with the school's responsibility in helping the student to understand the principles that explain why these realities are accepted by the culture and to help the student explore ways of testing these principles. This type of learning has been called productive or creative learning. If the teacher acquires an understanding of the thought process, if he becomes able to recognize the various kinds of immaturities in thinking, and if he comes to appreciate the individuality of thinking, the process of teaching itself may become a more productive enterprise.

This chapter describes: (1) the various forms of thinking, (2) the various characteristics of immature thinking and suggests teaching procedures designed to overcome these immaturities and (3) the conditions that foster the outward expression of systematic and objective forms of thought that result in creativity and originality.

WHAT IS THINKING?

Thinking takes many different forms. For this reason it is difficult to offer a single definition that will cover all the different types of thinking and the different kinds of situations in which thought occurs. Thinking occurs when the individual responds to a relationship or a generalization in his experiences. Thinking often involves *symbolic representation*, that is, responding to an aspect of reality by means of some ideational substitute of that reality. Language is one form of symbolic representation and much thought involves the use of language. It should be noted, however, that thinking as a response to relationships without verbal concomitants does occur, as for example the problem-solving behavior of preverbal children and infrahuman organisms. In addition to thinking without language it should be noted that not all language is truly the product of thought as in the young child's imitation of sounds or in the adult's use of language to conduct the social amenities of life. Because thinking is a *covert activity,* taking place in nonobservable ways, analysis of the process is difficult. In fact the analysis of overt responses is used to deduce the form and the structure of the thought. Thinking (the use of symbolic representations) goes on during almost all of our waking hours and to a lesser extent even during sleep.

Thoughts can be classified in terms of two different characteristics (see Figure 4.1). These characteristics are the extent to which the thought is systematic or random and the extent to which the thought is egocentric or objectified.

> Egocentricity . . . is marked by the fact that the self is confused with the external world and with other people; the vision of the world is falsified by the fact that the personal point of view predominates, almost to the exclusion of all others. . . . Then, as the child discovers that others do not think as he does, he makes efforts to adapt himself to them, he bows to the exigencies of control and verification which are implied by discussion and argument, and thus comes to replace egocentric logic by the true logic created by social life (Piaget, 1930, pages 301-302).

Using these two dimensions of thought a fourfold classification can be used as follows: (1) egocentric-unsystematic (dreams, fantasy, childish reasoning), (2) egocentric-systematic (prejudices, attitudes, and many beliefs), (3) objectified-unsystematic (the trial and error behavior found in attempts at solving puzzles), (4) objectified-systematic (scientific problem solving and appreciation, also creation in science and the literary and graphic arts). This distinction of the four types of thinking

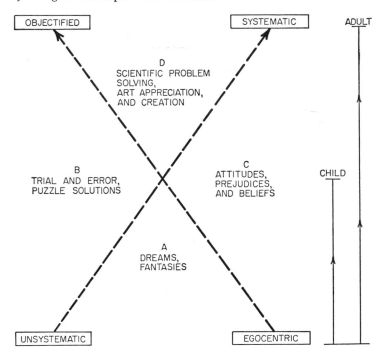

FIGURE 4.1   *The growth of thinking along the dimensions of system and objectivity.*

is an arbitrary one. In actuality, "Thinking is a fluid enterprise. Like raindrops coursing down a windowpane, intellectual operations coalesce and separate and run together again" (Johnson, 1955, page 23). For example, the solution to a scientific problem may have its source in unsystematic, random, trial and error thinking; dream and fantasy often furnish the raw material for creative production; and prejudice can be modified by means of objective analysis of the premises on which the prejudice is based. What distinguishes the thinking of the adult from that of the child is the distribution of the various kinds of thinking. The child's thought processes are more likely to be unsystematic and egocentric. The adult's thinking, although never entirely free of these immature characteristics, is characterized by the more frequent presence of more mature forms of thought. It should be further noted that as the adult acquires systematic and objective modes of thinking his manner of using the egocentric and unsystematic modes changes. The normal adult's use of these latter modes is called autistic thinking. Vygotsky (1962) is of the opinon that autistic thought is "a late development, a result of realistic thought and of its corollary, thinking in concepts, which leads to a degree of autonomy from reality and thus permits satisfaction in fantasy of the needs frustrated in life" (page 22). In Freudian terminology the more impulsive thinking is called the primary process and the more reality oriented thinking is called the secondary process (Rapaport, 1951).

Problem Solving

A problem is defined as a situation in which the learner seeks to discover a route to a goal, where the various elements of the route are knowable to the learner but they have never appeared in this organization or pattern. The goal may be to have a correct answer or a better understanding of a situation. Much of the problem solving in school is designed to develop comprehension. As pointed out in Chapter 2 this can be a potent motive and can serve to keep the student interested in school work involving thinking if he has not been continuously frustrated in his attempts to understand. The definition of problem solving can best be illustrated by having the reader engage in the activity. The following three problems each illustrate a different aspect of the process.

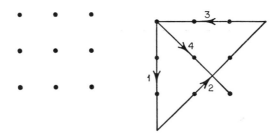

FIGURE 4.2   *The nine-dot problem.*   FIGURE 4.3   *A solution to the nine-dot problem.*

PROBLEM ONE (THE NINE-DOT PROBLEM)   Draw nine dots in the form of a square as shown in Figure 4.2. The problem is to draw through each of the nine dots with four straight lines without taking the pencil off the paper and without retracing a line. Lines can cross each other if necessary. As the reader attempts to solve the problem he is attempting to achieve some understanding of the relationship of the nine-dot square and the four lines. He is likely to try the simple solution of going around the periphery but discards this because he uses up the four lines and still one dot remains. The next step is to try to draw a diagonal line but the same result occurs. At this point an impasse is reached. The problem appears insoluble. The configuration suggests that the solution must be found within the confines of the square. As soon as the reader discovers that the solution should be sought outside the boundaries of the square he will after a short period find a satisfactory solution that will be some variant of the solution presented in Figure 4.3.

PROBLEM TWO (THE X-RAY PROBLEM)   The nine-dot problem demands a minimum of symbolization. The next problem has many similar elements but in addition demands a considerable amount of symbolic representation almost to the point of talking to oneself. The problem is stated as follows: given a human being with an inoperable stomach tumor, and rays that can destroy the tumor tissue. The intensity of the rays required to destroy the tumor will also destroy the healthy tissue that surrounds it. By what procedure can one free the patient of the tumor by these rays and at the same time avoid destroying the healthy tissue? Duncker (1945) presented this problem to a number of college students with the request that they think aloud. He kept a record of their thinking. The attempted solutions to the problem parallel those of the nine-dot problem. Each subject started out by offering an impracticable solution, or one that violated the conditions of the problem. Thus one suggestion was to "send the rays through the esophagus," another was to "desensitize the healthy tissue in some way." One subject suggested that the intensity of the rays on their way through the healthy tissue be lowered. After several ineffective solutions he suggested that one give weak intensity in the periphery and concentrate the intensity in the place of the tumor. He then was able to suggest the use of a lens to accomplish this. This solution approximates the best solution, which states that several weak bundles of rays are emitted from various sources crossing at the tumor.

As in the preceding problem all the elements of the solution are knowable. It remains for the subject to reorganize these knowable elements, which we may call the *cognitive field,* in such a way as to produce a solution.

PROBLEM THREE (CODING)   In the nine-dot problem and in the X-ray problem one solution solves the entire problem. Most problems, however, consist of a series of separate and different types of solutions. Our third problem is one of this type. In the following set of letters substitute a digit from zero to nine for each letter so that the sum is correct. Each different letter must be assigned a different digit.

$$
\begin{array}{r}
S\ E\ N\ D \\
M\ O\ R\ E \\
\hline
M\ O\ N\ E\ Y
\end{array}
$$

In this problem each digit-letter substitution represents a separate problem and calls for its own kind of solution. The first problem is, "Where do I start?" Starting at the right does not lead into an opening, whereas at the left there is one solution. By trying various possible substitutions for S and M we may become aware that M in the sum is always one. This solution is confirmed when we check it against a principle that is usually unstated, namely that the sum of any two different single digits cannot be larger than seventeen (eight plus nine representing the largest such sum). Armed with this solution, M = one, we then proceed to attempt a solution to the letter S in SEND and O in MONEY. The solution process for S is not as definite as for the letter M. It may proceed somewhat as follows: M in MORE is one, S plus M must add to at least ten, therefore S should be nine; but a doubt arises, we are permitted to carry from the previous sum so S may be eight. Considering this possibility we begin to become aware of the fact that O must be equal to zero. We then are inclined to assign the digit nine to S, since E and O (with O = zero) would not add to more than ten to provide one for carrying. We now have solved three substitutions M = one, O = zero, and S = nine, and we have taken care of five of the thirteen places in the problem.

In turning to the next column we use a different solution process, one involving the relationship of the values to be assigned to letters E and N. It can be seen that the value assigned to N will be one greater than that assigned to E, since O is zero and E and N must be assigned different digits it must be that the preceding sum produced one to carry. We then proceed to solve for the values of E and N by a process of elimination. All digits except zero, one and nine are possible. We may start with assigning a value of two to E and work our way up the series or start with E assigned the value of eight and work our way down. If we decide on assigning eight to the letter E we must assign nine to N and since nine has been assigned to S, E cannot be eight. We would then try seven and checking this we would find that we cannot complete the coding since R would have to be nine. Assigning six to E will likewise not not work because either D or Y would require a previously assigned digit. We then assign the value five to E and by means of little further elimination for finding the values for the letters D and Y, our complete solution appears as follows:

$$
\begin{array}{cccc}
\text{S} & \text{E} & \text{N} & \text{D} \\
9 & 5 & 6 & 7 \\
1 & 0 & 8 & 5 \\
& \text{M} & \text{O} & \text{R} & \text{E} \\
\hline
1 & 0 & 6 & 5 & 2 \\
\text{M} & \text{O} & \text{N} & \text{E} & \text{Y}
\end{array}
$$

Problem Solving as Restructuring the Field

In each of the three problems the solution depended upon the recognition of new relationships and a new organization of the knowable parts. This process is the restructuring of the cognitive field. In order to

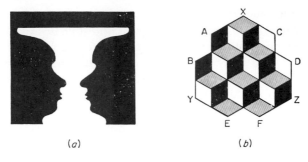

(a)   (b)

FIGURE 4.4   *The ambiguity of the figures results from*
fluidity of the perceptual field.

understand this concept we should examine perceptual experience. Each perception depends on the organization of the perceptual field. Certain segments of the field are assigned by the perceiver to figure or foreground and certain segments are assigned to ground or background. The meaning obtained from the perception depends on which segments are assigned to figure and which are assigned to ground. Thus in Figure 4.4a the black portion is usually assigned to ground and it appears as a white vase. If, however, the black portion is assigned to figure, the white becoming ground, the figure is perceived as two human profiles. Likewise in 4.4b, the number of blocks perceived will depend upon whether the diamond-shaped pieces X, Y, and Z are assigned to ground giving a perception of seven blocks or whether these pieces are assigned to figure and others A, B, C, D, E, and F become ground, producing the perception of six blocks. The six-block perception may be easier to achieve if the page is turned upside down. This same process takes place in problem solving. The cognitive field, like the perceptual field, is made up of figure and ground. A satisfactory solution to a problem depends essentially on the proper relationships of figure and ground within the cognitive field.

Thinking and Logic

Thinking, as we have seen, is a process whereby the cognitive field is continuously reorganized. In order to find the appropriate cognitive field organization many different techniques are used. Bruner et al. (1956) have studied the various strategies employed to arrive at concepts and categories. One of the formal ways of organizing the cognitive field is that of logic. Logic is one technique for checking the validity of the steps in analyzing a problem situation or in testing a conclusion. There are a number of different ways of conducting an abstract logical inquiry. One common way is that of the syllogism consisting of two premises and a conclusion. If all A is contained in B and all B is contained in C, then all A is contained in C. Logic leads us to accept this abstraction as true. This is confirmed when applied to a real situation, for example all of Cleveland (A) is contained in Ohio (B), all of Ohio (B) is contained in the United States (C), therefore all Cleveland (A) is contained in the United States (C). The following abstraction might be more difficult to follow, but the student of logic will recognize it as false: All A's are B's and all C's are B's, therefore all A's are C's. It may be helpful to make the abstraction more concrete: all monkeys (A's) are animals (B's), all men (C's) are animals (B's), therefore all monkeys (A's) are men (C's). Training in formal logic can help improve the thinking process, but the ability to use logic per se is of very limited benefit. A person who knows how to check the validity of conclusions is not necessarily able to sense the existence of a problem and he may not be able to devise the necessary steps to arrive at a checkable solution. A person who is skilled in logic but is not able to engage in creative thinking is almost like someone with a solution in search of a problem.

When the individual faces a real problem, a statement of real events or a situation in which the solution has some particular value to him, he will generally find it difficult to apply the principles of logic. In the case of the monkeys and men, the statement is rejected by most individuals because of the conclusion not because of the false logic. A student facing the possibility of failure in his examinations might accept the following as true:

> Failure leads to demoralization
> Demoralization leads to cheating
> Therefore all students should be passed

Another factor that makes difficult the application of logic is that of "atmosphere" or the general impression created by the premises. Sells (1936) demonstrated that when a single premise is stated in the affirmative, such as all X's are Y's, the subject tends to accept the invalid converse. When two premises are stated in the affirmative such as in the syllogism just given, all A's are B's, and all C's are B's, the affirmative atmosphere of the premises leads to the acceptance of the invalid affirmative conclusion, all A's are C's. Sells demonstrated similar atmosphere effects for "negative" propositions and those containing the word "some."

DEFICIENCIES IN THINKING

The general line of development in thinking as the individual grows from early childhood to adolescence is to establish systematic objective thought patterns and also to modify the egocentric unsystematic forms (see Figure 4.1). This development occurs as a result of the continuous interaction with the social and physical environments. Although as the child grows older he uses more of the systematic objective forms of thinking, he never dispenses with the other forms. As previously noted the normal adult uses autistic forms of thought that are the adult kind of egocentric unsystematic thinking. The task of the school, therefore, is not to eliminate egocentric unsystematic thought patterns but rather to establish the systematic objective forms. Suggestions for the kind of environment that fosters these kinds of thought processes follow after a description of the obstacles that the teacher may encounter in attempting to induce these problem-oriented forms of thinking.

Egocentrism

The major deficiency in the child's thought process stems from the lack of awareness of the self and the fact that the child is not aware that he thinks and reasons. In an attempt to obtain a sample of the content of children's consciousness, this writer interviewed a number of children between the ages of six and eight asking them to tell him what they had been thinking about and talking about during the past two weeks. The responses indicated that children were aware of their actions but gave no evidence that they realized that they thought. Their statements were of this type: I played ball, I raked the leaves, my daddy took me for a ride and so on. The responses indicated an absence of self awareness particularly in regard to the process of thinking. This absence of awareness is noticeable also in the younger child in regard to the physiological processes. Children under five seem incapable of knowing that they are hungry or tired. They give indications of heightened irritability and restlessness but they lack sufficient awareness of self to know the state of affairs within their person. Between the ages of seven and ten the self awareness increases gradually and the child becomes somewhat aware of the thought process as he engages in it. It is difficult for the child consciously to correct a process of which he has so little awareness.

In describing this lack of consciousness of self and the consequent difficulties in analyzing one's response, Piaget (1928) writes as follows:

> He [one of the subjects of his study] appeared in a manner to be unconscious of his own reasoning process, or at any rate incapable of immediate introspection or retrospection. To recall an example: the expression "5 times faster than 50 minutes" was sometimes identified with "45 minutes." As such, this answer has no particular interest for us. But the method and the degree of consciousness in the reasoning process are suggestive. As the number of questions was increased, analysis showed, that the child simply takes away 5 minutes, as though "5 times less" meant "—5." But when he is asked to explain what he has done, he can neither describe his process of reasoning nor even say that he has "taken away 5" from 50. He answers, "I tried" or "I found 45." If we go on to ask "How did you find?" and press him to reveal the steps of his reasoning, the child invents a new cal

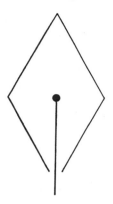

FIGURE 4.5 *An example of the child's lack of need for verification in problem solution. He is instructed to show a plan of search for a purse lost in the field. He has drawn a single line and stated he has found it. From L. M. Terman and Maud A. Merrill,* Stanford-Binet Intelligence Scale, *Boston: Houghton Mifflin, 1960.*

culation which is perfectly arbitrary and presupposes the answer 45. One boy, for example, told us: "I took 10 and 10, and then 10 and 10 and then I added 5" (pages 210-211).

Absence of Need for Verification

Egocentricity may be further described as the absence of the need for verification. There exists no greater obstacle to discovery and persistence in problem solving than the satisfaction with an incomplete or inadequate answer. This deficiency in understanding is illustrated in the response sometimes given to one of the items in the Stanford-Binet Intelligence Scale. The item is Plan of Search in which the child is shown a diamond-shaped figure with a small gap (see Figure 4.5). He is given a pencil and the examiner says to him: "Let's suppose that your purse with a lot of money in it has been lost in this big field. Take this pencil and start here (pointing) at the gate and show me where you would go to hunt for the purse so as to be sure not to miss it" (Terman and Merrill, 1960, page 102). Some children draw a single line and say "Here it is." The feeling of certainty in a response without the need for verification is a serious obstacle to understanding. Goldstein (1943) describes a similar deficiency in the thought processes of brain-injured patients. He calls it "secondary rigidity" and characterizes it as the preference for an incorrect response to no response at all when faced with a too difficult problem.

Set and Mechanization in Problem Solving

The unverified solution procedure for a particular type of problem shows itself also in the more mature, experienced problem solver. If a particular form of response is made several times in succession to a number of similar problem situations and this response leads to a solution of the problem, there is a strong general tendency to repeat this response in succeeding similar situations. Luchins (1939) has demonstrated this phenomenon called *Einstellung,* set, or mechanization in problem solving. Table 4.1 presents the series of water-jar problems that Luchins used in his study. Problem One was used to illustrate the general principle of using the containers in order to obtain the desired amount of water. Problem Two was presented as a practice trial and after the subjects had tried to solve the problem on their own, the experimenter presented the solution by stating "One fills the 127-quart jar and from it fills the 21-quart jar once and the 3-quart jar twice. In the 127-quart jar there then remain the 100 quarts of water." This method of starting with the largest of the three containers and pouring off once into the next smaller container on the left and twice into the smallest container on the right, can be used in Problems Three through Six. This same procedure may also be used in Problems Seven and Eight. However in these latter problems simpler solutions can be employed by subtracting three from twenty-three and adding three to fifteen. Subjects tended to use the method learned in the earlier problems even when a more direct method was available. In Problem Nine, which could not be solved by the more direct method, some subjects persisted in their attempts to apply the inappropriate procedure and insisted that the problem was

TABLE 4.1   WATER-JAR PROBLEMS TO DEMONSTRATE MECHANIZATION
IN PROBLEM SOLVING

Problem	Given the Following Empty Jars as Measures			Obtain the Required Amount of Water
1.	29	3		20
2.	21	127	3	100
3.	14	163	25	99
4.	18	43	10	5
5.	9	42	6	21
6.	20	59	4	31
7.	23	49	3	20
8.	15	39	3	18
9.	28	76	3	25
10.	18	48	4	22
11.	14	36	8	6

Source: A. S. Luchins "Mechanization in Problem Solving—The Effect of *Einstellung*," *Psychological Monographs*, **54**, no. 6, 1942, p. 1.

wrong rather than abandon their solution procedure. This confirms our contention that in some cases having an answer is a hindrance to problem solving.

Luchins (1942) found that some subjects, among bright children between the ages of ten and fourteen, did not show an *Einstellung* effect or set:

They looked at each of the tasks anew, trying to find the proper way to deal with it. So little did they think of merely repeating what they had done before that they had sometimes to be reminded, "Why don't you use the method you used before?" This seemed to them clearly not the way they liked to do things. They were not suspicious. Their attitude basically was one of directly looking at the problem at hand in order to discover the proper way of solving it (page 33).

Inadequate Part-Whole Relationships

As we have seen, thinking and reasoning involve the establishment of relationships between parts of the cognitive field. One of the deficiencies in the thought process is the confusion of parts and wholes and the inability to establish these relationships. For this reason many concepts in geography are difficult for the child. He cannot understand how he can be in Albany and in New York State at the same time. Very often this leads to logical inconsistency. The child will attribute a reason to a phenomenon and will under other circumstances attribute an opposite reason to the same phenomenon; at least insofar as the adult reasoning is concerned the phenomenon is the same. Piaget (1928) calls this deficiency *syncretism*. He cites the case of a $7\frac{1}{2}$ year old as an example. The boy is asked why water rises in a container when a pebble is dropped into the container. He answers that the water rises because the pebble is heavy. When wood is used the boy explains that the water rises because the wood is light. In another study Piaget (1955) analyzed the reasoning behind the child's improper connection of a proverb with a statement that is supposed to give the meaning of the proverb. Piaget refers to the following as a case of almost pure syncretistic reasoning:

> Kauf (8-8) . . . connects the proverb: "When the cat's away the mice can play," with the following phrase: "Some people get very excited but never do anything." Kauf, who would understand the meaning of each of these sentences if they were separate, yet declares that they mean *"The same thing."*—"Why do these sentences mean the same thing?"—*"Because the words are about the same."*—What is meant by 'some people' . . ." etc?— *"It means that some people get very excited, but afterwards they do nothing, they are too tired. There are some people who get excited. It's like when cats run after hens or chicks. They come and rest in the shade and go to sleep. There are lots of people who run about a great deal who get too excited. Then afterwards they are worn out, and go to bed"* (page 149).

The tendency to give an answer without verification, the use of problem solving set, and the presence of syncretism in thinking, all represent a kind of fusion or cohesion in the thought process. These deficiencies can be attributed to the lack of differentiation and integration in the child's thought processes (see discussion of these terms in Chapter 3). The immature thought process is characterized by the absence of proper generalizations and integrated thought patterns. The process of

FIGURE 4.6   *An example of immature thinking. Copyright (1960)
by United Feature Syndicate, Inc.*

differentiation and integration in mature thinking depends upon the
use of induction and deduction. These processes are used in only a limited way by the child. He generalizes from particular cases and is completely unaware of the contradiction of his conclusions (see Figure 4.6).

Lack of Value Development

The child's understanding of relationships is not the same as that
of the adult because of the differences in value orientation or anchoring
points in the analysis. A fire that has wiped out the family possessions
may be viewed as tragic by the child because she has lost her rag doll.
The child in Sunday school who views a picture of Christian martyrs in
an arena with a group of lions may sympathize with "the poor lion behind the pack of animals because he is not going to get anything to eat."
Value orientations serve as focal points for the organization of the cognitive field. Children's organizations will often prove surprising because
they simply have not acquired the value orientation of adults. The differences in value orientation that arise out of different cultural experiences
also account for differences of opinion or the differences in systematic
organization of the cognitive field with strong egocentric bias.

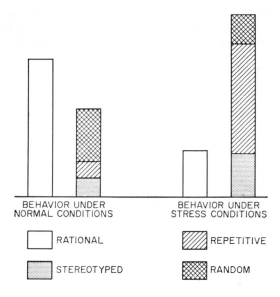

BEHAVIOR UNDER
NORMAL CONDITIONS

BEHAVIOR UNDER
STRESS CONDITIONS

☐ RATIONAL   ▨ REPETITIVE

▦ STEREOTYPED   ▨ RANDOM

FIGURE 4.7   *Under conditions of emotional stress problem solving behavior becomes less rational and more unsystematic. Data from J. R. Patrick,* Journal of Comparative Psychology, *1934, pp. 167 and 178.*

Effects of Stress

Strong motivation and emotional excitement will interfere with systematic thinking. This relationship has been demonstrated in one study (Patrick, 1934) that investigated the differences in problem-solving technique under conditions of minimal tension and under conditions of emotional excitement. Problem solving behavior was classified into five types as follows:

1. Rational inference tendency
2. Unmodified searching tendency—previously acquired information is not applied to the solution
3. Tendency to adopt stereotyped modes of searching
4. Repetition of unsuccessful response
5. Automatism—subject behaves in a relatively unplastic unadaptive manner

It is readily noted that these five types of problem solving behavior range from the most to the least systematic. In Figure 4.7 the shift from the rational inference type responses to stereotyped, fruitless repetitions, and thoughtless automatic type responses is shown.

The implications of the results of this study for classroom practice are stated by the investigator as follows:

This would seem to establish just what one observes in the nature of "random," "useless," "repetitious," responses (both verbal and overt) in the behavior of those about us when they are disturbed and excited due to some mix-up in every day life. A concrete example would be the reactions of men under a "hard boiled" foreman set over them when they are in the beginning stages of learning a job; or the random reactions of pupils made under a teacher who "snaps" at her pupils while they are learning the use of certain formulae in algebra (Patrick, 1934, page 189).

Gaier (1952) similarly found that college students who were described as anxious individuals spent a great deal of time thinking about themselves and about things unrelated to the problems being considered by the class. He suggests that teachers should strive to reduce the feeling of threat that hinders some students in carrying on effective problem-solving activities.

THE TEACHER FOSTERS THE DEVELOPMENT OF UNDERSTANDING

The techniques discussed in Chapter 3 for the teaching of fixed meanings are on the whole inappropriate for fostering the development of understanding. Understanding and problem solving depend upon a deeper grasp of relationships. This grasp may be interfered with if the teacher presents the problem and the solution in such a way that the relationships become fixed. Many textbooks present the figures to represent certain concepts in a fixed manner and thus preclude the students gaining a broad understanding of the concept. Right-angle triangles are shown with the right angle at the base; parallelograms are presented with the longer side at the base; and radii are presented either horizontally or vertically. These rigid presentations make it difficult for the student to make use of his understanding when the concept must be manipulated in a variety of contexts.

Wertheimer (1959)[1] has illustrated how the understanding of relationships is hampered by teaching by formula. He describes his visit to a classroom in which the teacher reviews a previous lesson during which the students had learned to find the area of a rectangle. One pupil announces that the area of a rectangle is equal to the product of the two sides. The teacher checks by presenting a number of rectangles of varying sizes which the students all solve easily.

"Now," says the teacher, "we shall go on." He draws a parallelogram on the blackboard ⟋▱⟍ : "this is called a parallelogram. A parallelogram is a plane quadrilateral the opposite sides of which are equal and parallel."
Here a pupil raises his hand: "Please, teacher, how long are the

[1] From M. Wertheimer, *Productive Thinking*, 1959, pp. 13-16, Harper & Row, Publishers, New York and Tavistock Publication Ltd., London.

sides?" "Oh, the sides may be of very different lengths," says the teacher. "In our case one line measures 11 inches, the other 5 inches." "Then the area is 5 × 11 square inches." [2] "No," answers the teacher, "That's wrong; you will now learn how to find the area of a parallelogram." He labels the corners *a, b, c, d.*

"I drop one perpendicular from the upper left corner and another perpendicular from the upper right corner.

"I extend the base line to the right.

"I label the two new points *e* and *f.*"

With the help of this figure he then proceeds to the usual proof of the theorem that the area of a parallelogram is equal to the product of the base by the altitude, establishing the equality of certain lines and angles and the congruence of the pair of triangles. In each case he states the previously learned theorem, postulate, or axiom upon which the equality or congruence is based. Finally he concludes that it has been proved that the area of a parallelogram is equal to the base times the altitude.

"You will find what I have shown you in the text book on page 62. Do the lesson at home, repeat it carefully so that you will know it well."

The teacher now gives a number of problems all of which require finding the areas of parallelograms of different sizes, sides and angles. This being a "good" class, the problems are all correctly solved. Before the end of the hour the teacher assigns ten more problems of this kind for homework.

At the next meeting of the class, one day later, I am there again.

The lesson begins with the teacher calling on a pupil to demonstrate how the area of a parallelogram is found. The pupil does it exactly. One sees that he has learned the problem. The teacher whispers to me: "And he is not the best of my pupils. Without a doubt the others know it as well." A written quiz brings good results.

Most people would say, "This is an excellent class; the teaching goal has been reached." But observing the class I feel uneasy, I am troubled. "What have they learned?" I ask myself. "Have they done any thinking at all? Have they grasped the issue? Maybe all they have done is little more than blind repetition. To be sure, they have solved promptly the various tasks the teacher has assigned, and so they have learned something of a general character, involving some abstraction. Not only were they able to repeat word for word what the teacher said, there was easy transfer as well. But—have they grasped the issue at all? How can I clarify it? What can I *do?*"

I ask the teacher whether he will allow me to put a question to the class. "With pleasure," he answers, clearly proud of his class.

I go to the board and draw this figure.

---

[2] This is an example of the interference of set that was discussed earlier, also known as negative transfer effect (see Chapter 5).

Some are obviously taken aback.

One pupil raises his hand: "Teacher, we haven't had that yet."

Others are busy. They have copied the figure on paper, they draw auxiliary lines as they were taught, dropping perpendiculars from the two upper corners and extending the base line. They then look bewildered, perplexed.

Some do not look at all unhappy; they write firmly below their drawing: "The area is equal to the base times the altitude"—a correct subsumption, but perhaps an entirely blind one. When asked whether they can show it to be true in this case, they too become perplexed (pages 13-16).

Thus Wertheimer demonstrates the weakness in the kind of teaching that attempts to teach understanding by means of having the student slavishly imitate or copy the teacher. Wertheimer goes on to suggest that the student sense the difference between what he already understands and what he is trying to understand; and by having the student seek the verification of his solution in broad general terms rather than verification limited to one problem. It should be noted, however, that the understanding of relationships depends upon previously acquired knowledge and meaning. A child cannot be expected to work understandingly on a problem involving the area of a parallelogram without the previous knowledge of units of measure, the process of addition, and the like.

Organizing the Field by Means of Visual Models

The organization of the cognitive field demands manipulation of abstractions. This is a difficult process even for the mature thinker. The difficulties can be overcome by reducing the abstractions to some direct perceptual experience. In physics the use of lined arrows to represent vectors serves this purpose. The graph in psychology and the map in geography are examples of the same thing. The clearest example of the use of visual models in order to anchor the cognitive field is found in the teaching of fractions. To teach the abstraction of the fractional unit it is useful to have available a number of models, blocks of wood, plastic figures that can be taken apart and, of course, the blackboard. The sequence in which the experiences are provided should afford many opportunities for manipulation and visualization of many different kinds of fractional units and should make it possible for the pupils to understand clearly the following kinds of relationships, "a. The more equal parts into which a whole is divided, the smaller each equal part will be. b. Denominators tell the size of the fractional unit and numerators tell the number of equal parts in the fraction" (Buswell et al., 1955, page 9).

FIGURE 4.8 *Studying fifteen.*

FIGURE 4.9 *Coins worth a dollar.*

FIGURE 4.10   *The component parts of six are seen in relation to the whole.*

FIGURE 4.11   *Dramatizing four groups of three.*

FIGURE 4.12   *The regular classroom teacher checks up. Ida Mae Heard, "Our Arithmetic Class Was a Talking Thinking Class,"* A Monograph for Elementary Teachers, *New York: Harper & Row, 1959, no. 92.*

Figures 4.8 to 4.12 show some of many ways in which visual models may be used to foster the development of understanding.

Organizing the Field by the Analysis of Riddles and Humor

People of all ages enjoy riddles and jokes. Some writers have suggested that of all the world's creatures, humans are alone in their appreciation of the humorous. This is another way of saying that human beings have the capacity to appreciate the incongruity in some unexpected or inappropriate organizations of the perceptual or symbolic fields. It may start early in life with the enjoyment of seeing someone put a sock on his hand as if it were a glove. The appreciation will appear in a more developed form when the child has mastered various aspects of the language. Thus a first and second grade child will enjoy riddles like these.

Why did the sparrow fly over the wall?
He couldn't fly through it.
What is the first thing a man plants in his garden?
His foot.
What makes more noise under a gate than a pig does?
Two pigs.

As the child grows a little older he can discern the humor in a more complicated story such as the following:

John (reading a newspaper): They have just published statistics which show that there are more steers in Texas than horses.

Henry: That's strange, isn't it? Steers are slaughtered all the time and you would imagine that there are more horses than steers.

John: But you forget that horses are constantly stolen.

When the border between Canada and the United States was being fixed, a controversy arose as to whether a certain farmhouse should be included in Canadian or U.S. territory. After a lengthy argument it was decided that it belonged to the United States. When this information was published, the owner of the farmhouse told his wife that he was a happy man.

"I'd rather have my house in the U.S. than Canada any time," said the farmer.

"Why so?" asked the wife.

"Because," replied the husband, "we shall henceforth be spared the rigors of the Canadian winter."

Diagnosing and Correcting Problem-Solving Deficiencies

An interesting approach to the study of problem-solving processes of college students is reported by Bloom and Broder (1950). They compared the thinking processes of successful and unsuccessful students. They were careful to eliminate from the latter group those who did not possess the basic information necessary to solve the problems. After analyzing the "thinking-aloud" protocols of these two groups of students they were able to develop a diagnostic check list consisting of four major categories that distinguished the successful from the nonsuccessful problem solvers. A similar study was conducted by Buswell and Kersh (1956) in which they concluded that:

> . . . some deficiencies in problem solving reside in certain conditions preliminary to the central logical thinking employed in solving the problems. Better training (a) in reading problems in order to sense relevant, irrelevant, or needed data, (b) in estimating reasonable answers, (c) in following a superior sequence of operations, and (d) in using abstract symbols might be expected to contribute to competence in problem solving (page 135).

These four steps suggested for the improvement of problem solving and thinking are similar to those proposed by Bloom and Broder that are used here for the framework of the discussion.

UNDERSTANDING THE NATURE OF THE PROBLEM   In order to be able to solve a problem the student must have some awareness of the dimensions of the problem. The nonsuccessful problem solver shows a tendency to misinterpret the problem. He seems to start with an answer and then converts the given problem to suit that answer. This is similar to the immaturity in thought pattern described above. How can the teacher help the student overcome this difficulty? With the older student it may be sufficient to help him identify this deficiency and to provide opportunity for working on problems with constant attention to the directions and to restatement of the problem. With the younger student this procedure is not sufficient. It is important for the teacher to foster a questioning attitude; to emphasize the question rather than the answer. The teacher must be cautious not to carry over the more rigid procedures appropriate for the teaching of fixed meaning into the teaching of problem solving. In teaching spelling for example the question is merely a cue for the correct answer. In teaching for understanding the question or the problem is a framework for the answer. Much more attention must be given to the question to determine how to structure the solution. "If, in general, teachers would shift their major concern from the answers obtained to the methods of thinking by which answers are obtained, there is a possibility that more effective thinking would result" (Buswell and Kersh, 1956, page 138).

UNDERSTANDING OF THE IDEAS CONTAINED IN THE PROBLEM Bloom and Broder found that although the successful and nonsuccessful students in their study did not differ in the amount of necessary information possessed, they did differ in the extent to which they could bring this relevant information to bear on the problem. If the problem differed in form from the ones they had encountered in their reading and lectures, the unsuccessful students were unable to translate the novel situation into terms that would enable them to solve the problem. This bears on the question of transfer of training or the ability to apply what one has learned in one situation to a new problem (the next chapter deals with this topic). The teacher can foster the understanding of the applicability of ideas by demonstrating the many settings in which the same idea has relevance.

GENERAL APPROACH TO THE SOLUTION OF PROBLEMS Bloom and Broder found that the successful and nonsuccessful students differed in the extent to which they used systematic and sustained reasoning processes.

> The analysis of the protocols indicates that the successful and the nonsuccessful problem-solvers differ in three general respects in their approach to the solution of the problems. These are: extent of thought about the problem, care and system in thinking about the problem, and ability to follow through on a process of reasoning. . . .
> Contrast the solutions to [this] problem: "Give the reasons which

would have influenced a typical Virginia tobacco farmer to support the ratification of the Constitution in 1788, and the reasons which would have influenced him to oppose the ratification."

George H: "Well, uh, I have to read the statement over, I haven't had any history for three years, and, uh, 'Give the reasons which would have influenced the typical Virginia tobacco farmer to support the ratification of the Constitution in 1778 and reasons which would have influenced him to oppose ratification.' Well, uh, to tell the truth I never had anything on the reasons of a Virginia tobacco farmer and at present I couldn't think of any."

Ralph R: (Reads the statement of the problem.) "Tobacco farmers are quite wealthy, I imagine. He has to pay, ratification of the Constitution, well, what rights did the Constitution give him? Well, starting at the end, well, from the standpoint of money, which one would be more to his advantage? Well, prior to the Revolutionary War, he would have to pay taxes to England, but that isn't applying here. Support ratification of the Constitution. Well, as any other citizen of the colonies, I suppose he would approve of the Constitution, but as a Virginia tobacco planter, well, I think he would approve of it for patriotic reasons, and from the standpoint of money he wouldn't have to ship his tobacco to England or anything. Well, he wouldn't have to pay the taxes" (pages 28-29).

The teacher can encourage systematic reasoning by eliciting hypotheses about the solution and following these through to a conclusion. It is important that the teacher not reject an hypothesis simply because he knows that it will ultimately not solve the problem. The students should be permitted to see this for themselves and they should be commended for offering the hypothesis. Hypothesizing or guessing a framework for the solution is essential. A student who is attempting to find a solution should not be expected to offer only correct hypotheses. The testing of the hypothesis allows for the understanding of the problem even when it does not lead to a solution. The teacher's role is largely that of encouraging the student to offer possible frameworks for the solution, helping the student stay within the framework until he arrives at a conclusion, and allowing him to test or verify his conclusion.

ATTITUDE TOWARD THE SOLUTION OF PROBLEMS   Most school problems require an objective, nonpersonal orientation. The introduction of personal considerations and egocentrism into a problem reduces the effectiveness of the problem solving. This was demonstrated in the discussion of the application of logic. The objective attitude can be developed by having the student approach problems that state, "assume the following to be true," where the assumption clearly contradicts a commonly accepted "truth." Keeping the assumption before the student as he proceeds through the problem can help him keep egocentricity to a minimum. There is little or no danger that the student will become dishonest in his thinking as a result of such experiences. On the contrary, submitting one's opinions to systematic, objective examination can only lead to a set of more valid beliefs. Hartmann (1941) states that: "To every assertion there is conceptually possible some counter-assertion, *i.e.,* every affirmation may be negated and every negation may be affirmed. Awareness of this grammatical or logical 'universal' may often prove helpful in arriving at a true solution to a problem" (page 268).

In some cases the personal attitude is of such an extreme nature that it interferes with even the simplest problem solution. The case of Karl, a brilliant college freshman, will serve as an illustration. In spite of outstanding performance on his college admission tests, Karl was doing poorly in most of his subjects. He was referred to this writer for counseling. It soon became apparent that the boy had had a difficult relationship with his father and had generalized his attitudes toward any authority figure including his instructors. He was very critical of his teachers and in class he made it a point to argue and to show up the instructors. He sometimes succeeded in carrying his point of view. He always succeeded in irritating his teachers. Examinations in his college were prepared and administered by a Board of Examiners so that he could have passed his courses by performing well on examinations. However, he carried his belligerency over into his examination period. One true-false question on a physical science examination read as follows: "1 cc is equal to 1/1000 of a liter." He answered false. His counselor was certain that Karl knew the correct answer and tried to understand why he had accidentally or deliberately answered the question incorrectly. Karl produced his textbook and showed the counselor the statement which read somewhat as follows: "For our purposes we shall consider that 1 cc equals 1/1000 of a liter." A footnote reference was given in which several authorities on quantum theory were cited which called this statement into question. Karl had gone to the library and read these authorities and he was determined to show his instructors that he was right, even though the loss was his. Many counseling sessions were required before Karl could look at academic problems objectively and not as the battleground for working out his personal problems.

CREATIVE THOUGHT

In the discussion thus far thinking and problem-solving processes have been analyzed and suggestions for their improvement have been offered. No attention has been given as yet to the source of the problem. In fact the discussion has implied that the dimensions of the problem, or the substance about which thought centers, is provided by some external agent such as the teacher. Another level of thinking is that in which the problem and the substance of thought are provided by the learner himself. When the individual, on his own, becomes aware of a problem and presents a solution method for it, he is engaging in creative thought.

Minor forms of creative thought occur regularly in the daily lives of most individuals, that is, they become aware of problems and arrive at unique solutions. This ordinary creative thought parallels in many respects the historically significant and recorded forms of creativity. This latter kind of creative thought can be divided into two major categories. The first is that of the generalizations with which we understand the physical, natural, and social world. The person who demonstrates creative thought in this area is able to note certain inadequacies or inconsistencies in these generalizations and he is then able to suggest more satisfactory generalizations. The history of science, philosophy, and politics offers a number of examples of this kind of creative thought. The second area of creative thought is that of literature and art. The substance used in this kind of creativity is the individual's own feelings and even his fantasies. It must be noted that in this kind of creativity an objectification of these feelings and fantasies must occur before creative activity takes place. That is to say the person must be able to be aware of his feelings and he must find a way of expressing them so that he communicates the universal aspects of them to others. Cassirer (1944) states this point of view very well.

> To be a poet, declared Henrik Ibsen, means to preside as judge over oneself. Poetry is one of the forms in which a man may give the verdict on himself and his life. It is self-knowledge and self-criticism. Such criticism is not to be understood in a moral sense. It does not mean appraisal or blame, justification or condemnation, but a new and deeper understanding, a reinterpretation of the poet's personal life. The process is not restricted to poetry; it is possible in every other medium of artistic expression. If we look at the self-portraits of Rembrandt, painted in the different epochs of his life, we find in the features the whole story of Rembrandt's life, of his personality, of his development as an artist (page 75).

Creative thought relies on the skilful use of certain tools. In some cases the understanding of mathematical procedures, and the scientific method or knowing how to work with others would seem to be essential. In other cases, language skills, musical understanding, or the use of tools and colors would seem to be basic. In all instances, creative thinking depends on the mastery of fixed meanings and, more important, the skills through which creative thinking emerges. In fact it may be argued that these meanings and skills form an integral part of the creative process. It is questionable whether the creative act can occur without them. However, the procedures for acquiring fixed meanings and the development of understanding wherein the teacher consistently presents the correct answer or poses the question, are antithetical to the development of creativity. Therein lies the dilemma: How to teach the requisite skills and problem-solving processes without destroying the urge to act creatively.

Various writers have analyzed the stages through which the creative thinker moves in arriving at a creative production. Most investigations have found that the fours stages described by Wallas (1926) seem to describe the creative process. These stages are: (1) preparation (2) incubation (3) illumination (4) verification.

The period of *preparation* is the end result of the working out of the awareness of the problem and it represents also a restatement and definition of the problem. During this period, appropriate material and information are gathered. In many creative enterprises this period of preparation ends in no satisfactory solution and the problem is often set aside, at least insofar as conscious attempts at solution are concerned. The period during which the creator is not aware of the problem, but during which some kind of nonconscious activity is going on, is called the period of *incubation*. Our understanding of this stage in creative effort is deficient because we cannot obtain introspective reports on it. We assume its existence because of the marked difference in the appearance of the problem at the end of the preparation stage and the time when it appears with the sudden realization of its solution at the moment of *illumination* or insight. Seldom does the solution appear in finished form in the period of illumination. The solution must be tested and refined. The period during which this takes place is called the period of *verification*.

These four stages do not appear sequentially. Various creative people have emphasized different aspects of the creative effort. Thomas Edison's remarks about invention being 90 percent perspiration and 10 percent inspiration suggests that he emphasized the preparation and verification aspects of the process. The report of Poincaré, the creative mathematician, as recorded by Ghiselin (1952) points to the significance of incubation and illumination.

> Most striking at first is this appearance of sudden illumination, a manifest sign of long, unconscious prior work. The role of this unconscious work in mathematical invention appears to me incontestable, and traces of it would be found in other cases where it is less evident. Often when one works at a hard question, nothing good is accomplished at the first attack. Then one takes a rest, longer or shorter, and sits down anew to the work. During the first half hour, as before, nothing is found, and then all of a sudden the decisive idea presents itself to the mind (page 27).

Encouraging Creativity

Not all the spontaneous outpourings of children in expressing their imaginings and feelings are to be considered creative. "Creativity implies a fresh response unique to the creator; it is characterized by personal initiative and conscious effort; it involves thinking and doing according to self-applied tests; and is finally judged as an accurate expression by the initiator" (Association for Supervision and Curriculum Development, 1949, page 121). If this definition is accepted the conclusion follows that the person who is more mature in his thinking and better able to apply tests involving self-criticism, would be more capable of creative work. Yet many people have commented on the decrease of spontaneous creative thought as the individual grows older. It is true that awareness of the limits of the real world and the acceptance of the *status quo* serves in part to restrict the range of imagination and in some measure creativity. However, it should be noted that the urge to be creative can be kept alive and nourished and may actually be enhanced by the development of self-criticism, a more complete understanding of reality and the acquisition of skills of expression. As we shall see in reviewing the suggestions for fostering creativity, the need for self-actualization (see Chapter 2) is the key to the whole process.

The Importance of Individuality

Creative individuals cannot be produced on an assembly line. The person whose thoughts and expression are replicas of someone else's is by definition not creative. Yet the effort in school must be directed to producing people who spell alike, count alike and so on. This effort must, however, be cautiously directed so that it does not stifle the individuality so necessary for creative thinking. Various attempts to discover the basic characteristics of creativity have come, more or less, to the same conclusions. The characteristics are as follows:

1. Sensitivity to problems
2. Spontaneous flexibility
3. Ability to think abstractly
4. Originality
5. Ideational fluency
6. Ability to see differences and similarities
7. Ability to rearrange, to organize, and to elaborate
(Guilford et al., 1951, Lowenfeld and Beittel, 1959)

Although some of these characteristics are descriptive also of intelligence, (see Chapter 10), it is interesting to note that there may be some definite distinctions between creative and so called intelligent individuals. For example, Getzels and Jackson (1962) have shown the creative student is not as highly regarded by the teacher as the student who is, by some definitions, labeled intelligent but not creative. The creative student is likely to place greater value on humor and playfulness as desirable personal qualities, whereas the intelligent group places greater value and emphasis on success. Torrance (1959) has found similar results with elementary school children. He writes: "In other words, the highly creative pupils achieve as well as do the highly intelligent pupils, without appearing to strive as hard. My guess is that these highly creative children are learning while they appear to be 'playing around,' possibly through manipulative and/or exploratory activities which the teacher tries to prevent" (page 312). In another report Torrance (1960a) confirmed the findings of Getzels and Jackson, indicating that those children who can be identified as creative are considered by their teachers to be less desirable pupils, less ambitious, less hard-working and studious. If teachers are alerted to the distinction between creative and the more conforming children they may be able to develop the kind of environment that fosters creativity. It is generally true "that the environmental conditions which foster creativity are those which encourage independent thought and which are permissive of new ideas" (Wilson 1958, page 117).

Although we have little or no research evidence on the specific characteristics of the classroom environment that is conducive to creative effort, Rogers (1953) has suggested that two conditions are essential for the emergence of creativity, namely psychological safety and psychological freedom. Our discussion in Chapter 2 on fostering a sense of self-adequacy is relevant here. Rogers sees the inner conditions of constructive creativity to be:

1. Openness to experience, which is the opposite of psychological defensiveness. The person who is open to experience does not prevent or distort experiences as they come into awareness. He is able to be honest about what he experiences, he can tolerate ambiguity. "The more the individual has available to himself a sensitive awareness of all phases of his experience, the more sure we can be that his creativity will be personally and socially constructive" (page 77).

2. An internal source of evaluation that makes possible the evaluation of the creative product by means of criteria established by the creative person himself rather than in terms of the praise or criticism of others. The only questions that matter for the person who is being creative are: Does this creative product express what I want it to express? Does it satisfy me? Does it clarify my own feelings? If these questions are answered more or less in the affirmative, it is likely that it has served to actualize the creating person's potentialities. No further evaluation is really necessary. Generally a satisfactory evaluation by the creator will be favorably received by others and the creative person will thus be able to satisfy the desire that usually accompanies creativity, namely to communicate and share his creation.

3. A willingness to manipulate ideas and various dimensions of reality such as colors and shapes. "It is from this spontaneous toying and exploration that there arises the hunch, the creative seeing of life in a new and significant way" (page 78).

The environmental conditions that foster the growth of these inner characteristics are psychological safety and psychological freedom. Psychological safety is made up of three associated conditions:

1. An unconditional faith in the child's unfolding potentialities and in his basic worth. This faith creates a climate of safety and the child can gradually learn that he can be whatever he is and he can experience fully, without distortion, the full impact of his interaction with his environment.

2. Minimizing external evaluation. Evaluation by others is usually threatening, creating a need for defensive reaction and induces the denial of experience to awareness. This does not mean that the teacher should cease having reactions to what children produce. In fact the teacher should exemplify freedom of response and should be free to say "I don't like your expression." It should be noted that this reaction is subtly different from the kind of evaluation in which the teacher states, "What you are doing is bad, (or good) and this evaluation is assigned to you from some external source." The first reaction still permits the student to maintain an internal source of evaluation, whereas the second form of evaluation subjects the student to outside sources that lead him away from individuality and hence from creativity.

3. The teacher understands empathically. This requires that the teacher attempt to understand what it is that the child is trying to express. If the teacher can in a certain sense take the point of view of the child, it is more likely that he will extend an empathic understanding and in this way provide the psychological safety so important in fostering creativity.

The second feature of the environment that fosters the development of the inner conditions that permit the emergence of creativity is psychological freedom. The basic ingredient in this quality of the classroom atmosphere is the child's awareness that he is free to feel whatever he feels even when the feeling is that of hatred or antipathy. As long as he chooses a nondestructive avenue of expression, as long as he finds ways of sublimating this feeling, he need have no fear of expressing his real feelings. This subject will be expanded in Chapter 11.

Creativity Takes Time

Creativity cannot be forced. Since by definition the creative effort requires that the student become aware of his own feelings and the inadequacies in accepted generalizations, it should be clear that this awareness must be the student's own, it cannot be imposed from the outside. Several procedures may encourage the development of this awareness. The following example from Mursell et al. (1946) illustrates how children may be made conscious of how an artistic production can express feelings.

Examining the Effect of a Painting

Larry's painting, fastened to a board where all could see, was the topic.

"I like the way his picture makes me feel that it is a cold day," remarked Mary. (Larry's picture dealt with two boys making a snowman.)

"I like that too," said the teacher. "How did he give us that feeling?"

"The snowman makes you feel cold," was Jim's answer to the teacher's question. Then in succession came the following remarks:

"Just seeing a snowman wouldn't give you that feeling. I think it's the color he's used. There's a lot of blue and gray which makes me feel cold."

"I believe it's the mittens and sweater. The boys look all bundled up."

"There is much more cool color than warm color so that the little bit of red in the scarf makes the blues and gray seem all the colder" (pages 207-208).

Similar kinds of analysis of poetry and music can be used to help children recognize the many different ways for objectifying and expressing feeling and personal experience. A number of such illustrations are given in Chapter 6, *Fostering Creativity,* in the 1949 Yearbook of the Association for Supervision and Curriculum Development. Torrance (1960b) has developed many ideas for developing creative thinking abilities through the language arts in the fourth, fifth, and sixth grades. He starts with the characteristics of creative thinking described by Guilford and proceeds to outline suggested procedures for the development of these characteristics. It should be noted that these procedures and those to be described here take more time than if the teacher were to point out the various salient features of the creative product. This investment of time is well worth while if creative understanding is the result.

Originality

To foster originality children should be encouraged, on occasion, to be whimsical and fanciful and to share these ideas with others. The appreciation of literary works that represent the very skilfull expression of whimsy and fancy should be nurtured. Children seem to enjoy the writings of Dr. Seuss, Jules Verne, Lewis Carroll, and Jonathan Swift. The work of these authors and others can serve to stimulate the child's fancies.

The Development of Technique

The creative urge must find an outlet in some medium of expression such as language, art, music, movement, and so on. These are techniques and they form an integral part of creativity. The danger insofar as teaching is concerned lies in the emphasis on mature technique when the thought processes and the emotional experience lying behind the creative urge are not yet mature. Lowenfeld (1959) states that three things are important in developing technique.

1. The teacher must recognize *"that the child must develop his own technique."* The teacher must not consider that merely showing a "correct" technique will suffice. The child cannot incorporate a strange technique and make it his own before he is ready. It is the teacher's task to note when the child is ready to use more difficult material and to introduce it at the appropriate time.

2. The child should be given an opportunity to see how particular materials and techniques contribute most relevantly to his needs. If the creative expression is accomplished more effectively, the child should be able to recognize this and choose this approach.

3. Different stages of development and different needs call for different techniques. When the child is in the so-called scribbling stage in artistic expression, the crayon serves best. When the need is to depict atmosphere, the transparency of water color is best. If the mood is exhiliration, it may best be expressed by a young child in dance rather than poetry.

Under proper conditions nearly all of us can learn to express ourselves creatively but we cannot be creative in every medium. Teachers should help the student develop expressive skill in at least one major technique to the point where it can become functional in the creative effort. In the other media of expression we shall need to be satisfied with an appreciation of the creative product of others. Although appreciation is a more passive process than the creation itself, it still represents a measure of creativity and it serves to expand sensitivity, which may be translated into the favored creative medium.

SUMMARY

Thinking is defined as the covert process of symbolic representation. This process produces what might be called a cognitive field. Problem solving is the process of restructuring of the cognitive field in order to reduce an incongruity or a dissonant quality in it. Creativity is another level of thought activity in which the individual becomes independently aware of a problem and seeks a solution method for it.

Thinking develops from egocentric forms to objective forms and from unsystematic to systematic procedures. Combining these two gradients of development there are four different kinds of thinking, namely, (1) egocentric-unsystematic, (2) egocentric-systematic, (3) unsystematic-objective, and (4) systematic-objective. The last occurs only in the more mature individual and serves to change the quality of the other three kinds of thinking.

Immature forms of thinking are characterized by the following: egocentricity or an incomplete separation of the self from others and from the objective world; absence of the need to verify the outcome of the thought process; susceptibility to set or an inability to approach each problem afresh; inadequate part-whole relationships shown in generalization from particular cases and lack of awareness of the contradiction in inadequate generalization; lack of a socialized value system that serves as anchoring point for the organization of the cognitive field; susceptibility to anxiety and stress.

The teacher can foster the development of mature forms of thinking by providing opportunity for the student to acquire a deeper grasp of relationships. This is interfered with if the teacher emphasizes the answer rather than an analysis of the problem. The teacher fosters a problem-solving attitude by reducing abstract problems to visual models, by the analysis of riddles, humor and language-structured cognitive fields. The teacher should learn to diagnose various kinds of problem-solving deficiencies such as the lack of understanding of the nature of the problem or its contents, the general approach to the problem and improper attitudes.

Creative thought seems to have four phases: preparation, incubation, illumination, and verification. These do not follow in a fixed sequence in the creative enterprise. The teacher fosters creativity when he teaches in such a manner as to allow for individuality and openness to experience. The teacher should place the burden of evaluation on the learner by minimizing external evaluation. The acquisition of technique is a *sine qua non* of all creative activities. Above all, adults need to recognize that creativity takes time, it can neither be rushed nor mass produced.

READING REFERENCES

Association for Supervision and Curriculum Development 1963 Yearbook, *New Insights and the Curriculum*. Washington: National Education Association (particularly chaps. 13 and 14).

Bartlett, F. C., *Thinking*. London: George Allen & Unwin, 1958.

Bruner, J. S., *The Process of Education*. Cambridge: Harvard University Press. 1960.

Flavell, J. H., *The Developmental Psychology of Jean Piaget*. Princeton, N.J.: D. Van Nostrand Company, 1963 (particularly chaps. 8-10).

Thomson, R., *The Psychology of Thinking*. Baltimore: Penguin Books, 1959.

Wallach, M. A., Research on children's thinking. In H. W. Stevenson (Ed.), *Child Psychology*. Sixty-second Yearbook (Pt. 1) National Society for the Study of Education. Chicago: University of Chicago Press, 1963.

Wertheimer, M., *Productive Thinking,* rev. ed. New York: Harper & Row, 1959.

Wilson, R. C., Creativity. In N. B. Henry (Ed.), *Education for the Gifted.* Fifty-seventh Yearbook (Pt. 2) National Society for the Study of Education. Chicago: University of Chicago Press, 1958.

CHAPTER 5

TRANSFER
OF TRAINING

It is important to consider the question for what purposes the subject matter of the curriculum is taught. We teach for the mastery of the particular areas of the school curriculum, geography, history, spelling, science, music, and so on, but we also hope that this mastery will lead to more effective behavior in other settings in and out of school. We expect that after a student has assimilated what has been taught in the classroom that he will be able to utilize it in other learning activities as well as in the application to the practical matters of human affairs. Teachers expect that children will derive benefits from school learning, benefits that are greater than mere knowledge of facts, whether rules of grammar, dates of historical importance or scientific laws.

A teacher of mathematics might suggest that in addition to being able to solve problems in algebra and geometry, his students will also learn to think logically and to reason well. A social studies teacher may argue that the study of history will induce patriotism and loyalty in the students. Writers of textbooks in science often state that the study of science would increase the students' objectivity toward life. The teacher of speech is generally convinced that the student's experiences in speech class will make him better able to communicate in other out-of-class situations. In fact teachers of every subject field at all levels of education claim values that transcend the subject matter itself. It would be a sorry educational program indeed that did not claim such values, for it would require such specific and minute detail that the student would be immobilized. He would need to learn every word in his vocabulary in every possible setting and every combination in arithmetic for every possible application. This would be truly an impossible educational undertaking. This chapter will examine the process of transfer of training, the application and utilization of learning, and determine the validity of the claims made upon this process. From this discussion the teacher will be guided to a clearer determination of why he teaches. This expectation itself is based on the assumption that transfer of training takes place.

DEFINITION

Imagine a student having two educational experiences separated in time. The first (A) is the study of a foreign language vocabulary list and the second (B) the study of the periodic table of chemical elements. These two educational experiences will interact with each other and will have both beneficial and detrimental effects on each other. There are four possible end results from such an interaction. The learning of B may interfere with the retention of A; this is called retroactive inhibition (see Chapter 3). The learning of B may facilitate and improve the retention of A; this is called reminiscence, a phenomenon in which the learner is able to recall more of what he has previously learned than he was able to immediately after learning. Reminiscence and retroactive inhibition are phenomena of memory or retention. Transfer effects are observed when the effect of A upon B is measured. If the learning of A facilitates the learning of B we speak of proactive facilitation or positive transfer effect. When the learning of A inhibits the learning of B we have proactive inhibition or negative transfer effect. It is a well known fact that both positive and negative transfer do take place. Disagreement arises when we attempt to explain how transfer takes place, how best to teach so that transfer benefits will be greatest and which subject areas and teaching procedures produce the most direct transfer values.

This then is the subject of transfer of training; the carrying over, the utilization of a previous learning experience into a new situation. There is, perhaps, no topic in educational psychology that has greater significance for the educational process and no topic about which there has been so much controversy. Every teacher is concerned with transfer. How will the student use his learning of arithmetic in his later study of algebra and in situations involving quantities and space? To what extent will the student apply his knowledge of grammar in analyzing poetry and in communicating effectively?

HISTORICAL ORIENTATION: THEORIES OF TRANSFER

Various theories that have been offered to explain the transfer phenomenon are examined here. Some aspects of these theories are not valid in the light of research evidence, and in the light of our present understanding of the learning process. These theories are presented in spite of their deficiencies for two reasons. First, many respected educators seem to hold to them despite contradictory evidence—careful examination can protect the student from being misled by the statements of prominent men invoking invalid transfer theories. Second, the student can come to an understanding of the strongest position on transfer only after a careful review of all the opposing arguments.

Formal Discipline

The theory of formal discipline is the oldest of all transfer theories. In its original form it was based on what is known as faculty psychology. Faculty psychology conceives of the human mind as being made up of separate and independent faculties. These faculties were sometimes grouped into three categories: the intellect, consisting of reasoning, memory, judgment, and the like; the emotional faculties, consisting of affections, appetites, and the like; and the faculties of will and volition (Butts and Cremin, 1953). According to the formal discipline theory, transfer takes place when these faculties are exercised. As physical exercise develops body muscles, mental exercise improves the faculties of the mind. Through tradition certain subjects appear as best qualified to improve the mental powers of man. Mathematics strengthens the ability to reason, history improves memory and develops loyalty, and literature enhances the imaginative powers. Mental growth thus takes place through formal exercise or discipline. The task of education is to provide the exercises (subject matter) that will develop the mind most effectively.

What are the implications of such a position? How would an advocate of the formal discipline theory of transfer approach educational issues such as decisions on curriculum content and teaching method? Historically the theory of formal discipline became the basis for resisting the inclusion in the curriculum of such subject matter areas as modern languages, chemistry, biology, and physics. It was argued that although these latter subjects might be more apparently useful or practical they simply lacked the values for *training the mind* possessed by mathematics and the classical languages and literatures. The value of any subject matter depended on its service as a mental exercise. It is also to be noted that mental exercise value was, by some magical formula, the exclusive possession of those subjects already in the curriculum, and most newly included subject matter areas, such as the sciences and modern languages, invoked the same mental discipline value as soon as they became respectable.

An educator who believes that transfer takes place on the basis of formal discipline would tend to make certain assumptions about the content of the curriculum and teaching method. He would not be interested in changing the content of what is taught. Suppose you were a teacher of mathematics with a formal discipline orientation and the unit is that of ratio and proportion. You would have no concern for any observable application of the learning. The value of the lesson resides in the mind training to be derived from the mastery of the concept of ratio and proportion. You would present what you considered the best solution system and insist that students follow this system. Further, the doctrine of formal discipline implies that the amount of learning is unimportant, but that how hard the student works is important. Any attempt to make the subject matter interesting by extending its applications, or by using lively and interesting materials, would be opposed because such innovations would tend to make the subject less difficult to master and would thus decrease its discipline value.

A Critique of the Formal Discipline Theory

Thorndike (1921, Volume 2) has criticized this aspect of the formal discipline position as follows:

> The notion that doing what is irksome and distasteful in school gives one power and willingness to work for truth and justice in the world is a sample of the naïve verbal thinking that still too often pervades education. In the first place, the habit formed is often that of *not* doing it. . . . In the second place, the habit formed is sometimes that of doing the disagreeable with blind confidence—a superstitious puritanism which expects that out of aimless subjection of oneself to the disagreeable, good will come by magic. It will not. . . . To suffer simply so as to stand suffering would be as foolish as to learn falsehoods so as to be able to unlearn them (pages 422-423).

In this modern world of ours the theory of formal discipline becomes obsolete. The worth of any idea or theory is measured in terms of its actual consequence. The scientific method itself, which has impressed itself on many aspects of our thinking, demands that ideas are tested in experience. Before a conclusion about the effects of a particular kind of educational experience is accepted, there must be an empirical demonstration that these effects actually do take place. When the theory of formal discipline is subjected to this test, it is found not to have validity. For the truth of the matter is that transfer does not take place through unrelated formal mental exercises. For more than half a century, psychologists have shown time and again that the theory of formal discipline is inconsistent with the results of controlled studies on the transfer of training.

The simplest experimental design in transfer studies is to have subjects practice on task A and to have before-and-after-tests on task B. An early study by William James (1890, Volume 1) employed this design. He tried to discover whether a certain amount of daily training in memorizing poetry would reduce the time it would take to learn an entirely different kind of poetry. The results with other individuals as subjects confirmed what James found when he acted as subject himself. His task B was the memorization of lines from Victor Hugo's *Satyr*. On the foretest he found that it took almost 132 minutes to learn 158 lines (task B). He then worked on task A, memorizing all of the first book of *Paradise Lost*. This task took twenty minutes daily for thirty-eight days. He was interested in discovering how this extended practice in memorizing *Paradise Lost* would affect his ability to learn more lines of Victor Hugo's poem. His aftertest on 158 new lines of *Satyr* took about twenty minutes longer than the foretest. That is, before training in memorizing, he memorized at the rate of fifty seconds per line; after training his rate was fifty-seven seconds per line. The then popular view of formal discipline would have predicted that the ability to memorize poetry would improve after a period of training. The results contradicted this prediction.

The type of experimental design used by James can be criticized for the lack of control groups. Even if he had found positive transfer effects, one could have attributed the gain to the practice effect during the foretest rather than to the benefits of the training itself. Sleight (1911) repeated James' study but included a control group. His experimental design can be described as follows:

Control group:	Foretest in B	No practice in A	Aftertest in B
		Groups equated on foretest scores	
Experimental group:	Foretest in B	Practice in A	Aftertest in B

His results confirmed those found by James, namely, that there appeared to be no general faculty of memory that could be improved by training.

If the faculty of memory could not be substantiated, it was possible that gains in other faculties as a result of studying certain academic subjects might not take place. Thorndike (1924) addressed himself to this problem. He modified the experimental design just described as follows:

Group 1:	Test of intelligence	Curriculum including subject A but not B	Test of intelligence
		Groups equated	
Group 2:	Test of intelligence	Curriculum including subject B but not A	Test of intelligence

After comparing various groups of students whose programs of study were the same except in one course, Thorndike was able to make two significant conclusions. (1) "Those who have the most to begin with gain the most during the year. Whatever studies they take will seem to produce large gains in intellect." (2) "After positive correlation of gain with initial ability is allowed for, the balance in favor of any study is certainly not large." These findings were confirmed by Brolyer et al. (1927) and more recently by Wesman (1945). These studies demonstrated conclusively that the mind is not like a muscle that can be trained by exercise in particular subjects.

For those who wonder how it is that so many men of prominence seem to have been trained in what we might call a formal discipline approved curriculum, Thorndike (1924) had the following to say:

> The expectation of any large differences in general improvement of the mind from one study rather than another seems doomed to disappointment. The chief reason why good thinkers seem superficially to have been made such by having taken certain school studies, is that good thinkers have taken such studies, becoming better by the inherent tendency of the good to gain more than the poor from any study. When the good thinkers studied Greek and Latin, these studies seemed to make good thinking. Now that the good thinkers study Physics and Trigonometry, these seem to make good thinkers. If the abler pupils should all study Physical Education and Dramatic Art, these subjects would seem to make good thinkers. These were, indeed, a large fraction of the program of studies for the best thinkers the world has produced, the Athenian Greeks (page 98).

After reviewing the experimental studies on transfer of training, an intelligent teacher would not tacitly assume that the subject he teaches has the magical benefits that may be ascribed to it by the formal discipline theory. On the other hand teaching and learning do produce positive transfer effects; therefore, it is necessary to consider the ways in which transfer values accrue and then institute a teaching program and procedure that would offer the greatest transfer value. Thorndike offered such a theory. As initially stated, it contained many philosophical and logical weaknesses; however, much constructive teaching was done in its name and as the theory has been elaborated and explained, it has become indistinguishable from later transfer theories. An examination of Thorndike's transfer theory, called *identical elements,* follows.

The Theory of Transfer Based on Identical Elements

The writer was once invited to observe a fifth grade in a large, new school in a midwestern city. The occasion was the culmination of several weeks' work on money and arithmetic. Before the class met, the teacher outlined to the writer all that had previously taken place.

During a period devoted to discussion of personal experiences, one of the students told the class of the new savings account that he and his father had just opened. This prompted one of the students to ask the question, "Where does money come from?" Other members in the group could give only very hazy answers, and often as not, their answers gave rise to further questions. The teacher suggested that perhaps the students would like to work together to find the answers to these questions and any others that might occur to them. The response from the students was enthusiastic and with the teacher's help, they compiled a list of the things they wished to find out about money. Inasmuch as the list was rather lengthy, the teacher suggested that the class might best decide on the order in which they were to accomplish them. A period of discussion, ending in a class vote, decided the order in which the problems were to be answered. The following day the class discussed means by which they might answer their questions and find out about money. They planned a visit to the local bank, a visit to a department store, setting up their own bank, store, and mint in order to make their own money—for classroom use only, the teacher pointed out.

The class selected committees to investigate the possibility of accomplishing each of these projects and to determine, if possible, whether it would be worthwhile for the whole class to participate in them. The committee on visiting the bank and the department store had written letters to the head of the bank and store respectively asking if it would be possible to come over for several hours during the day. The committee on setting up the mint had arranged within itself to discover how the federal mints operate and then to make money out of scraps of colored paper and cardboard. The committee on the store had the responsibility of assembling enough stock—either borrowed from mothers or simulated—to meet the demands of their purchasers. The committee on the bank set up a bank in class that was to make change and maintain a very simple system of accounts.

By the time the writer observed the class, the students had already made several trips in their community and had had one guest speaker. Now they were ready to operate their own businesses.

During the period of observation, the students alternated jobs so that all had a chance to make money, to make change, to operate accounts, to sell groceries, to purchase groceries, and to carry on all the simple but essentially lifelike operations involved. One other task not mentioned above was included and that was that one group of students was working arithmetic problems presented by the teacher. This group, however, changed jobs with the rest.

The teacher afterward explained to the writer her reason for encouraging the students to carry on this activity. It was that she wished to present to them situations and skills *in the manner in which they would later find them in everyday life,* so that they would be able to carry over from their schoolwork to life the skills, understanding, and knowledge that would be useful.

In this illustration, the teacher attempted to achieve a transfer of training through the theory of identical elements. According to this theory, the effect of the learning in one situation upon the learning in another situation depends largely upon the similarity in the skill or concept to be mastered in the two learning situations. In the class just described, the teacher hoped to present to the students problems that would be almost identical to those that they would meet in actual handling of money in everyday life. Although the money was not real, the denominations were equivalent and making change was identical whether the change was made with scraps of colored paper or with actual coinage.

Critique of the Theory of Transfer
Based on Identical Elements

Teaching based on the assumption that transfer takes place insofar as there are elements in situation A that are identical to those found in B, is subject to two kinds of criticism.

First, the theory, as originally interpreted, assumes that life problems remain static and that the solutions to these problems are predetermined and fixed. In a dynamic, changing society such as ours, this assumption is a difficult one to justify. The conditions under which each succeeding generation lives are so vastly different that it would seem impossible to prepare children in one generation for a fruitful life in the next, if transfer took place according to the theory of identical elements. The education would literally be preparing children for yesterday. A person holding to this theory of transfer is in danger of assuming that knowledge and the application of knowledge would remain static. The English writer, Herbert Spencer, took such a position in the middle of the last century. The following statement from his essay *What Knowledge is of Most Worth?* shows how the theory of identical elements can direct one's thinking into false prediction, "Numerous attempts have been made to construct electromagnetic engines, in the hope of superseding steam; but had those who supplied the money understood the general law of the correlation and equivalence of forces, they might have had better balances at their bankers." Further, the theory seems to assume that all school learning should lead to demonstrably useful results in the mundane activities of everyday life. Many would argue that the learner's experiences may be justified in terms of his becoming ready for more complex learning experiences and also for the sheer pleasure of learning and understanding. Man is a symbolizing and searching creature and not all learning activities are to be justified in their practical, social utility value.

The second criticism stems from psychological theory itself. Allport (1937, page 285) has criticized the theory of identical elements on the following grounds: (1) While it may be possible to identify elements in objective reality, the human personality as it responds and interacts with that reality does not respond in any elementary way. (2) Even if one were to allow for a generous interpretation of element, it would be impossible to find any element of experience identical in two situations. (3) Finally,

> . . . on the experimental side there is no evidence for proportionality of transfer, that is to say, for the contention that transfer occurs in proportion to the number of approximate identities between two fields of stimulation. The falseness of this contention is especially apparent in all cases where trauma or emotional learning is involved. In these instances, transfer passes all bounds of expectation. In such cases identities cannot be involved, for the whole personal life is saturated with the effects. All in all, experimental data, the discoveries of modern neurophysiology, the canons of theoretical psychology, and simple common sense, unite in rejecting this view of mental organization.

In spite of these criticisms, many psychologists feel that the research data do not fundamentally invalidate the theory of transfer based on identical elements. They would emphasize the learner's perception or cognition of similarity rather than the objective existence of an identity (Loree, 1959). When the theory is stated this way it comes close to the theory that transfer takes place as the learner is able to generalize from learning situation A and to apply this generalization to situation B.

The Theory of Transfer by Generalization

According to the theory that transfer takes place by generalization, we are supposed to look to the intellectual and mental changes within the learner, rather than to the subject matter itself. Although this may appear to be what the formal discipline theory propounded, there are some subtle and yet significant differences between the concept of transfer by generalization and transfer based on formal discipline. These differences should become apparent in the discussion that follows.

The experimental support for the theory that transfer takes place on the basis of the learner's awareness of generalizations, came originally from a study reported by Judd (1908). A later study by Hendrickson and Schroeder (1941) investigated the same phenomenon, namely the effect of the knowledge of a principle on the later behavior in a situation where the principle applies. This latter study reports findings that differ in some respects from those reported by Judd; however, the two studies lead to the same general conclusion, namely, that the understanding of the theoretical principle or generalization that underlies an experience contributes greatly to transfer effects.

In both studies the task involved was that of striking an underwater target. This task is complicated by the refraction of light by water, which creates the illusion that the target is where it actually is not. Hendrickson and Schroeder used three groups in their experiment, one control group and two experimental groups. The control group was permitted to practice hitting the target when it was placed at a depth of six inches and when successful at this task, the control subjects undertook the second task, which consisted of hitting the target at a depth of two inches. The first experimental group was given a simple explanation of refraction of light before practicing. The second experimental group received a more complete explanation of refraction that explained that the error of refraction was greater when the object was deeper. The results showed that the theoretical explanation was of value in facilitating transfer and that the more complete the explanation the greater the transfer. Table 5.1 shows the results of this study.

TABLE 5.1   SUMMARY TABLE SHOWING DIFFERENTIAL TRANSFER EFFECTS

Groups	Mean of Trials Required At 6 Inches	At 2 Inches	Gain in trials	Percentage of improvement
Control (no theory)	9.10	6.03	3.07	34.1
Experimental group 1 Partial explanation	8.50	5.37	3.13	36.5
Experimental group 2 Complete explanation	7.73	4.63	3.10	40.3

As seen in Table 5.1 practice without theory increases the difficulty of the task and the more complete the explanation the easier the initial task. In adapting to a new task all groups show the benefits of transfer with the experimental group receiving the more complete explanation benefitting the most.

Judd's control group, made up of younger subjects than those used in the Hendrickson and Schroeder study, did not transfer the learning from the initial task to the changed conditions of the second task. A study by Kendler and Kendler (1961) suggests that older control subjects would tend to develop their own generalization.

In a study investigating the effect of external direction on transfer, Kittell (1957) found evidence suggesting that:

1. In addition to organizing the materials used in learning, teachers should aid pupil discovery by suggesting meaningful relationships on which learners may base discovery and by providing practice with those relationships.
2. Providing statements of underlying relationships without specifying answers fosters learning, retention, and transfer to different situations (page 403).

An Application of the Theory of Transfer
by Generalization

The following incident was brought to the writer's attention in a conversation between a mathematics instructor and a science instructor who had been working together rather closely in preparing their units of work. The science instructor had decided to wait in introducing the laws relating the volume of a gas to the pressure and temperature until the mathematics instructor had covered the concept of ratio and proportion. After the mathematics instructor had completed the unit on ratio and proportion, the science instructor felt that the students did not understand sufficiently well the concept of ratio and proportion and their preparation in mathematics did not contribute significantly to his science class. The science teacher was suggesting that there seemed to be no value in the cooperative planning of units. Had the science teacher not felt some personal admiration for his colleague, he might have suggested that there was no value in teaching mathematics. The mathematics instructor, on the other hand, produced evidence that this concept had been thoroughly covered in class and examinations indicated that thirty of the thirty-five students had answered correctly 90 percent of the problems on the examination covering the unit of ratio and proportion.

Why were the students in this high school situation unable to use in the science class the learnings acquired in the mathematics class? It might be explained in terms of forgetting. The students may have forgotten what they learned in mathematics. This possibility was discarded when it was shown, on a final examination in mathematics given several months later, that the students still remembered how to solve this type of problem. In fact, some of the students did somewhat better on the final examination in this particular section testing ratio and proportion than they had done previously. A careful study of the situation led both instructors to the conclusion that they had each been teaching very specific skills, which the students were mastering, but the application of skills to a variety of situations was not being developed.

Why had this happened? Had the mathematics instructor taught ratio and proportion by a method that made his students unable to apply it to situations and problems outside the math class?

Essentially, the mathematics instructor had done something that occurs at all levels of teaching and in all areas; that is, he taught a concept as an abstraction with the assumption that the learner would then make applications in other appropriate situations. In this case of proportions, the abstraction becomes the relationship between certain quantities as expressed in numbers. In order to simplify instruction, the mathematics teacher expressed the relationship as follows:

$$5 : 15 : : 6 : X$$

The units of measure were not specified. The teacher then proceeded to indicate the process for finding X. The students were instructed to multiply the center terms (means) and then the outer terms (extremes) and then solve for X by the process of division. The students were cautioned against using alternate methods for fear that they might become confused.

Teaching the problem in this way, the abstract concept of the general relationship between quantities was lost as the specific manipulation of a fixed arrangement of numbers was emphasized. The understanding that proportions may occur in many ways in life was lost because of the expectation that a person will be asked to solve an expression that is always presented in the same form even though the specific numbers may be changed. As is frequently the case, the test of the effectiveness of this teaching was in the form on an examination that presented the problem in the same form as it was taught. It can be seen that such a series of steps in teaching restricted rather than increased the possible variety of situations in which the qualities might have been related.

The following year, the mathematics instructor used a variety of concrete illustrations taken from the students' own experiences and developed the concept of ratio and proportion. For example, the teacher used a series of situations such as increasing or decreasing the size or amount of food recipes, numbers of yards of materials needed to make table cloths or drapes for larger or smaller tables and windows, increasing or decreasing distances in laying out a little-league baseball diamond, and so on. After each of these situations, the teacher allowed time for a group discussion of the problem and for a discussion of its relationship with other problems met in class.

He found that some of the students did not do as well on the type of examination that he had been accustomed to giving. This might be accounted for by the fact that the students now needed to arrange their thoughts and select a method of solution from several possible methods available to them. The science instructor, however, found that the application of learnings in the mathematics class to the problems of science was much greater. He was able to cover the unit on relationship of volume to pressure and temperature more efficiently and the students' grades, and more important, their understandings in science were much improved.

In attempting to teach the abstract concept of the relationship of numbers involved in ratio and proportion, as he did the second year, the mathematics instructor through helping the students form generalizations or relationships from their own experiences was attempting to accomplish transfer according to the theory of transfer through generalization.

This theory states that transfer from one learning situation to another takes place to the extent that the individual sees the relationships and generalizations in one situation and applies them to another.

As the mathematics instructor first taught ratio, he did not permit the students to generalize. Instead he presented them with only one type of problem and allowed the students to solve it in only one way, thereby denying any attempts on the students' parts to reason out a relationship between the numbers. Instead they were provided with a mechanical rule, multiply the means, then multiply the extremes and solve for X by division, which the students soon realized would solve those problems which they might face in this class. It should be noted that the bright student often is able to generalize his learning without assistance from the teacher.

Without generalizations the students were unable to transfer what they had learned in mathematics to the work with volume, temperature, and pressure of gas. Only when the mathematics instructor changed his method or presentation of the concept of ratio and proportion, when the students were led to form their own generalizations from a number of learning situations that involved ratios in several forms, were the students able to transfer learnings to the science classroom.

To bring the problem of generalization a little closer to home, consider your position as a reader of this material and as a student in an educational psychology course. As you read this material and any additional supplementary readings that might be required by your instructor, you cannot be expected to remember every situation described, every interpretation of the various theories presented, every research investigation, case study and the like. If you did, you would find yourself hopelessly bogged down. Your aim should be instead to consider how the generalizations that are developed here might be applied to the teaching of the age level and the subject matter areas with which you expect to be working as a teacher. Your observations of teaching should be directed toward making these textbook generalizations meaningful and more widely applicable.

Teaching for generalization does not always produce positive transfer effects. Certain kinds of generalizations can be hindrances to application or transfer. For example the rounding out of decimals is a process that may be considered a generalization. One teacher had presented this concept in the usual way, explaining the rule of rounding out to the nearest whole number. One of the practice problems was stated as follows: One gallon of paint will cover 200 square feet of surface; how many gallons will be required to cover a surface 34 feet by 20 feet? Students worked the problem by finding the area of the surface obtaining the correct answer of 680 square feet. They then divided by 200 to determine the number of gallons required and they came up with the an-

swer, 3.4 gallons. Rounding out to the nearest whole number they submitted the answer of 3 gallons, which the teacher accepted as correct. One
boy insisted that the surface would not be covered with 3 gallons of paint
and that anyone wanting to cover the whole surface would have to purchase 4 gallons or at least $3\frac{1}{2}$ gallons. If the teacher mismanages a situation like this the student is likely to learn that school is a place in which
reality is ignored and that school learning operates in terms of its own
rules. Bode (1927) has attacked this condition in the following statement.

> The moral of all this is that if we devote ourselves to the proper de-
> velopment of concepts, transfer of training will cease troubling. We have
> had a problem of transfer because we have failed to develop concepts so
> as to give them proper usefulness outside of the classroom. The fact that
> the problem of transfer is, in the first instance, a "school problem" raises
> the suspicion that we have this problem on our hands because of the
> cleavage between the school and the life outside of the school. In the
> world of everyday affairs we do not seem to be troubled so much by the
> problem of transfer. But a school subject which, in Judd's language, is "so
> organized that it rotates around its own center" does not carry over, and
> this calls for explanation. The remedy lies obviously in the reorganization
> of the curriculum and teaching method so as to remove the cleavage. The
> problem of transfer is symptomatic of a defect in our educational aims and
> ideals. If we can bring the school into right relations with the life outside
> of the school, the problem of transfer will take care of itself (pages 202-
> 203).

TRANSFER AS "LEARNING HOW TO LEARN"

Another question arises about transfer of training. Is the person
who acquires a number of generalizations in a better position to make
new generalizations than the person without previous experience in
generalizing? The answer to this is a qualified yes. Harlow (1949) has
demonstrated the existence of a learning how to learn factor. He was
able to show that monkeys and children who had been trained in discrimination tasks were able to approach new tasks much more effectively
than those who had not been trained. Harlow calls the learning how to
learn factor *learning set*. He states that the learning set converts a problem that would be difficult for the subject "into a problem that is so
simple as to be immediately solvable. The learning set is the mechanism
that changes the problem from an intellectual tribulation into an intellectual triviality and leaves the organism free to attack problems of another
hierarchy of difficulty" (page 56). Harlow goes on to speculate that his
subjects may also have developed social-emotional learning sets.

Ward (1937) showed that learning sets are acquired also in the
rote learning of nonsense syllables. Using university students as his subjects, he presented them with a different list of twelve nonsense syllables

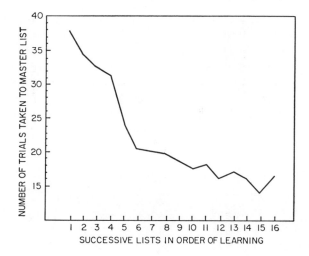

FIGURE 5.1 *Subjects learn how to learn nonsense syllable lists. Adapted from L. B. Ward, "Reminiscence and Rote Learning,"* Psychological Monograph, **49,** *no. 4, American Psychological Association, 1937.*

on each of sixteen trial days. He found that whereas it took almost forty trials to learn the first list to one correct recitation, it required only twenty trials on the sixth day and an average of only fifteen trials for the last two days. His subjects had learned how to learn nonsense syllables (see Figure 5.1).

The following statement by a man who was training to be a teacher after a career in engineering demonstrates the operation of learning sets.

Over fifteen years have elapsed since I attended high school. In view of this, it is particularly interesting to think back and ask myself the question: What did I learn? The first thought that comes to mind is that I have forgotten almost everything I was expected to learn. I'm sure I couldn't pass a final exam in Latin or history; I suspect I would do very poorly in advanced algebra and trigonometry. I would in all probability fail an exam in grammar if I had to explain the various rules of usage. I doubt whether I would do much better if I were tested in most of the engineering subjects that I studied at the university, even though after graduation I worked successfully for nearly ten years as an engineer and metallurgist. On the other hand, this forgetting has never particularly hampered my work; I imagine that I could go out tomorrow and get a job with any number of engineering firms if I so desired. If I had not gone to high school or college this would be impossible. Why is this so? In part the reasons are rather complex dealing with such things as standards, the selective function of the school and the like, but more important is the fact that I am a different person having attended high school and college. Any value that school still holds for me must now be due either to the direct

"It's probably my early training in mathematics
that gives me my edge over you in all our arguments."

FIGURE 5.2 *An illustration of learning set. Drawing by*
Mirachi, copyright © 1958, The New Yorker Magazine, Inc.

transfer effects or to changes in personality and self-concept. In other words, school has provided me with a readiness for particular learning situations over and above that which I would have had had I not gone to school.

The cartoon in Figure 5.2, although exaggerating the point, also directs our attention to the value of learning sets.

A study by Dorsey and Hopkins (1930) showed that the learning set can be more readily brought into play when the teacher orients the student to the applicability of the learning set. Using college students as subjects they found that by giving instructions such as, "Use the method of study that you have learned, or your knowledge of Latin or geometry as you approach this new material," the student is better able to transfer his previous learning to a new situation.

Within the school situation the teacher faces the problem of how much guidance to give the student as he is involved in deriving the proper generalization. This issue was discussed in Chapter 3 when inductive versus deductive approaches to teaching were considered. The research evidence is somewhat contradictory. On the one hand the opinion of Herbert Spencer is quoted by Spitzer (1951) as being consistent with research findings. "Children should be led to make their own investigations and to draw their own inferences. They should be told as little as possible and permitted to discover as much as possible." On the other hand Craig (1953) concludes "that subjects of all ages use and benefit from all the help given in their search for bases determining correct responses." He concludes from his data that the teacher should freely offer suggestions that will aid the learner in discovering the principles of organization.

One thing is clear from the various studies of transfer based upon generalization and that is — the learner benefits little and will not transfer widely a general principle that he has mastered as a mere verbalization without understanding.

DERIVING MAXIMUM TRANSFER VALUES

Thus far the transfer phenomenon has been considered in a limited way in terms of the specific benefits to be derived from a well-defined learning situation. When the teaching task is designed to attain maximum transfer effects of this order the following generalizations can be made (Stephens, 1960):

1. The feature or the idea that can be transferred should be clearly identified and highlighted. Mathematics should be taught so that the logic inherent in it stands out clearly. Latin should be taught so that the realtionship to English and general linguistic structure is clearly identified.

2. Learning experiences should be integrated so that meaningful generalizations can be derived. The teacher should be reasonably certain that the generalization is not a mere verbalization. Where the student behaves in such a way as to indicate that a sound general principle underlies his behavior, he should be assisted to formulate a conscious awareness of the principle.

3. Experiences with the generalization should be varied. As pointed out in Chapter 4, the generalization and concepts that are useful in thinking are those that can be stated in a variety of ways. Right-angled triangles should be approached with the right-angle in a variety of positions; algebra problems should be worked with the unknown as a, m, p, as well as x, and so on.

4. Generalizations should be applied as extensively as possible. The soundness of this principle is demonstrated in the findings of two early studies on transfer of training. In the first study by Bagley (1911) a group of third-grade students were subjected to persistent drill in the preparation of neat and accurate papers in arithmetic. Nothing was said of either neatness or accuracy in other school work during the period of

investigation. The papers in arithmetic were compared with those in language and spelling. It was discovered that while three weeks' persistent drill resulted in neater papers in arithmetic, the papers in language and spelling showed a general decrease in both accuracy and neatness. In the second study by Ruediger (1908) habits of neatness were emphasized as having general application in dress, business and home. The seventh graders who were the subjects in this study did show that transfer of training takes place when the initial learning is broad in its application.

5. The student should be helped to acquire and transfer as many generalizations as possible. As we pointed out in citing the work of Harlow, it appears that the ability to transfer is itself in large measure acquired through successful transfer experiences. Jensen (1956) has called this an "attitude of transferability" and suggests that teachers should foster this attitude.

In addition to the transfer effects of the type considered here, transfer effects of a more general nature also occur. The learner's intellect does not function independently of his total personality. The effects of a learning experience on the learner's motivational system, his values, and his self-concept must also be taken into account. Dewey (1938) has commented on the weakness of certain kinds of education from the standpoint of the limited transfer values that they offer:

> One trouble is that the subject matter in question was learned in isolation; it was put, as it were, in a water-tight compartment. . . . If exactly the same conditions recurred as those under which it was acquired, it would also recur and be available. But it was segregated when it was acquired and hence is so disconnected from the rest of experience that it is not available under the actual conditions of life. . . .
>
> Perhaps the greatest of all pedagogical fallacies is the notion that a person learns only the particular thing he is studying at the time. Collateral learning in the way of formation of enduring attitudes, of likes and dislikes, may be and often is much more important than the spelling lesson or lesson in geography or history that is learned. For these attitudes are fundamentally what count in the future. The most important attitude that can be formed is that of desire to go on learning (pages 48-49).

It is reasonable to assume that every experience, that is every meaningful interaction or transaction with the world, will have some impact on the learner's personality. It is quite probable that we will never be able to predict with accuracy in what ways a particular experience will affect a particular child at a particular time. However, teachers can become increasingly sensitive to the fact that certain kinds of classroom procedures and teacher-pupil relationships can encourage the students' growth in powers of self-analysis and evaluation, toward a positive orientation to intellectual activities, in the appreciation of esthetic experiences and in constructive attitudes toward other people. The seeming paradox and at the same time the great challenge of transfer is that it can be derived mainly in and through current experiences and not by using the current experiences as investments for enhancing the future activities of the learner. As Dewey (1938) states it:

> We always live at the time we live and not at some other time, and only by extracting at each present time the full meaning of each present experience are we prepared for doing the same thing in the future. This is the only preparation which in the long run amounts to anything (page 51).

SUMMARY

The study of transfer of training is the study of the effects of earlier learnings upon the acquisition and retention of later learning tasks. It has long been recognized that transfer does occur. Controversial opinions exist in regard to the explanation of how it occurs and how best to insure maximum transfer benefits.

The most ancient and still widely-held position on transfer is that of formal discipline. This position maintains that the mind is like a muscle and that the subject matter is material on which the mind exercises itself. It further maintains that certain subject matters have inherently superior powers for inducing transfer. Careful experimental investigation has shown that transfer does not take place on the basis of faculty psychology or formal discipline theory.

Another extreme position is that of identical elements first proposed by Thorndike. It suggests that transfer takes place insofar as the later learnings have elements in common with the earlier ones. This transfer position tends to narrow the curriculum so as to prepare the student for those activities that he will use at some later time. This position also is subject to criticism because it does not conform to experimental data and to accepted principles of theoretical psychology.

As the theory of identical elements was later interpreted, it came close to the position of transfer by generalization. This position holds that if the student masters the general principle underlying his earlier learning task, his learning of a later task in which this principle is involved, will be more efficient. The experimental data not only supports this position, but also tends to support the idea that one learns how to learn or that one acquires learning sets.

An understanding of the transfer process should make the teacher aware that the transferable feature should be clearly identified, the student should grasp the underlying relationship, he should see how it functions and applies to a wide variety of settings, and he should be helped to develop an attitude of "transferability." The most important challenge in transfer is the recognition that the acquisition of under-standing changes the personality of the learner and it is the personality change that carries forward to the new learnings.

READING REFERENCES

Bugelski, B. R., *The Psychology of Learning.* New York: Holt, Rinehart and Winston, 1956 (chaps. 7 and 14).

Buswell, G. T., Helping children learn how to learn. In Association for Super-vision and Curriculum Development 1959 Yearbook, *Learning and the Teacher.* Washington: National Education Association.

Cronbach, L. J., *Educational Psychology,* 2d ed. New York: Harcourt, Brace and World, 1963 (chap. 10).

Deese, J., *The Psychology of Learning.* New York: McGraw-Hill Book Company, 1958 (chap. 9).

Grose, R. F. and R. C. Birney (Eds.), *Transfer of Learning.* Princeton, N.J.: D. Van Nostrand Company, 1963 (particularly selections 1, 4, 5, 6, 8, and 10).

CHAPTER 6

TEACHING
FOR VALUES

The problem of discussing morality and ethics as applied to teaching in our modern democratic society is particularly difficult. The philosophy underlying the American democratic society reflects the conviction that it is possible and desirable to develop unified action out of diverse and sometimes conflicting points of view. This unified action can only occur if these diverse points of view are based on some common value assumptions. These basic value assumptions have been explicitly avowed or implicitly affirmed by most of the major religious faiths. Psychological thought and research has contributed to our understanding of the validity of these values (Feuer 1955 and Montagu 1955) and in suggesting the most effective means of aiding the growing individual incorporate these values.

Because a great deal of our concern about moral conduct stems from the existence of serious deviations from acceptable norms (dishonesty, crime, and delinquency), we are prone to ignore the importance of the positive aspects of morality. Positive morality assumes more than the mere absence of immorality. Consider for a moment how uninspiring it would be to teach a robot-like individual who does nothing wrong but does everything that he is told; a person who gives back exactly what the teacher puts in. The teacher who rejects this view of moral training must develop a clear conception of character in psychological terms, that is, as a dynamic interacting process. The result of such understanding will be to view the objectives of education in terms of helping children develop integrated personalities. The person with an integrated personality is committed to the aim of enhancing his own personality, that is, to be productive and creative in such ways as not to interfere with the attempts of others to enhance themselves. The person with an integrated personality is furthermore committed to the recognition that a most significant avenue for self-enhancement is in the enhancement of others.

The first part of this chapter will outline the common basic value assumptions of our society. The next step will be to describe how the child comes to incorporate these values into his own value system. The chapter concludes with a consideration of the teacher's role in fostering moral and ethical behavior and his role in instances where the behavior demands corrective attention.

COMMON BASIC VALUES

The basic value of our society from which all others are derived is that of human life. Human life is not only the biological entity but also the incorporated acquired individuality, the personality, the psychological component of human existence. This then implies that the basic aim of our society is to develop healthy personalities in a healthy society. Jersild (1960) puts it this way:

> The child's development may take a healthy or an unhealthy turn and the society in which he lives may also be healthy or unhealthy. A state of health prevails when the influence in society combined with the impetus of a child's own growth help him to realize his potentialities. An unhealthy condition prevails when a child's development is distorted by forces in a society which imposes stifling stereotypes. "Social adjustment" is not synonymous with healthy development. For example, in a given community, adjusting to a society may mean that a child must suppress his capacity for being friendly by yielding to the prejudices that prevail or by bending all his energies toward being competitive. This form of adjustment reflects an unhealthy state both in him and in the society to which he belongs (page 15).

This great value that we place on the human personality leads to a number of other moral concepts. For example, the human personality is valued in those settings where the individual acquires a sense of *moral responsibility;* where he recognizes that *common consent* and voluntary cooperation are more desirable social arrangements than rule by power and violence; where he recognizes that the human intellect functions most effectively where there is *free access to information;* where the *same moral standards* are applied in judging all persons; and where each individual is free to choose his own enrichment and pleasure alone or in groups of his own choosing as long as this pursuit does not in any way restrict others (Educational Policies Commission, 1951).

The positive expression of these moral concepts grows out of those situations in which the individual establishes satisfying meaningful relations with others. The human need to interact and to associate with other people is so pervasive and universal that many early psychologists were inclined to list gregariousness as a human instinct. Modern psychologists, who have considered the basic needs of man, regularly include the personal-social needs. Havighurst (1953) uses the concept of the developmental task to describe the process of human development and he considers that getting along with others is a recurrent and significant developmental task. (See page 11 for the definition of developmental task.)

The two dimensions of social interaction that are relevant to the development of mature morality are affection and control. Genuine affection is important in the child's life to enable him to develop ethical relationships with others. The child who has received a measure of love and control will have received the proper foundation for an ethical value system.

Love and affection have many different qualities but these four of the many given by Montagu (1955) are especially important for the teacher.

1. A most important quality of love is that it must be communicated and appropriately expressed. "While love begins as a subjective state, it must be activated and made objective, that is, it must be demonstrative if it is to be fully realized" (page 294).

2. Genuine affection must be given freely and not as a reward for good conduct. Love is like oxygen; we would not consider providing a high altitude aviator with oxygen as a reward for a successful flight, it must be provided in order to make the flight.

3. Love is expressed in firmness and this firmness "conveys to the loved one that both one's 'Yea' and one's 'Nay' are equally firm evidence of one's love" (page 294).

4. "Love is reciprocal in its effects, and is as beneficial to the giver as it is to the recipient. To love another means to love oneself as well as the other; in this sense love is the highest form of selfishness as well as the highest form of unselfishness, the best of all forms of conduct for the development of the self, one's ownself and the selves of others" (page 295).

The issues of control and obedience in human relations are also central to the theme of morality and ethical conduct. Some view these issues, when it comes to children, as that of breaking the unwilling bronco to the saddle. In this view the process of socialization represents a forceful imposition of control from the outside. This view further emphasizes that the acceptance of social limits and the norms of civilization represent a demanding sacrifice for the individual (Freud, 1957). It is our contention that there is no major inconsistency between the proper kind of socialization or adult control that stems from a love for children, and the integrated personality. The acceptance of limits and controls does not result in a greatly conflicted personality. It is only when children are subjected to excessive control or to too little and where this inadequate control is accompanied by a lack of affection that we witness personality difficulties. A child who experiences such deficient control will react with extreme passivity and cease to strive toward self-directed accomplishment. Some children subjected to excessive control become negative and resistant and will become discipline problems or, even worse, will show extreme forms of antisocial behavior.

THE GROWTH OF MORAL JUDGMENT

Piaget (1932), whose work was reviewed in the discussion of the development of understanding (Chapter 4), has also examined the development of moral judgment in the child. By means of careful observations of children's responses to the rules of marble playing and by means of careful interrogation, Piaget has been able to formulate the general trends in the development of moral judgment. As the child grows older, and as he participates in group activities, changes occur in his approach to rules and his evaluation of situations involving moral issues.

The infant is essentially amoral, for his behavior is not guided by moral considerations. As he begins to participate in structured play activity, he will observe a few of the rules. His aim in doing so is largely to imitate and to feel himself a part of the society of older children. However, he is unable to participate truly in the game because he lacks the understanding of the place of the rule in the management of the social interaction involved.

As the child acquires the requisite skills for engaging in the game, he gradually acquires an understanding of the function of the rule and more important he learns that the rules are the same for everyone. However, his conduct with regard to the rules is provisional and specific to the situation. His behavior is not yet guided by a general code or underlying ethic. The classical studies of Hartshorne and May (1930) have pointed to the greater consistency of character traits as children grow older. Thus they state, "There is a tendency . . . for children to become more integrated or consistent with advance in age" (page 326).

Alongside these two developments certain changes in attitudes toward rules take place. One important change is from the attitude that rules are sacred and in a sense external, to an attitude from which rules are viewed as adaptable and arising from within the person. This shift represents growth from a heteronomous state (one in which moral and ethical judgment must be imposed by others, the child shows no initiative in this regard) to an autonomous state (one in which the child can act independently and make his own decisions in situations demanding moral judgment). While the child is in the heteronomous state he will act as if he believed that to obey the will of the adult is right and to have a will of his own is wrong.

In studying the development of moral judgment, Piaget presented his subjects with a pair of stories. The stories differed in one regard, namely, in one of them a child causes much damage but does this unintentionally; in the other he causes minor damage while engaging in an act of disobedience or wrongdoing. The following is an example of one pair of stories used in Piaget's studies:

> A. There was a little boy called Julian. His father had gone out and Julian thought it would be fun to play with his father's ink-pot. First he played with the pen, and then he made a little blot on the table cloth.
> B. A little boy who was called Augustus once noticed that his father's ink-pot was empty. One day that his father was away he thought of filling the ink-pot so as to help his father, and so that he should find it full when he came home. But while he was opening the ink-bottle he made a big blot on the table cloth (page 118).

By presenting stories such as these and asking his subjects a number of questions Piaget was able to demonstrate that children show a strong tendency to judge the child in the second story as having committed a greater wrong. They seem incapable of taking into account motive or intent in their moral judgment. Piaget calls this "moral realism" as opposed to "moral relativism." When the child's morality is dominated by the former he is inclined to consider the result as having much more significance than the purpose or the intent of the act. When moral realism is mixed with heteronomy the child's evaluation of a wrongdoing will be determined in part by the severity of punishment that follows a misdeed. During this period of moral realism the child tends to view moral rules in the same way that he views physical laws. "Just as we trip, independently of any carelessness, we fall on to the ground in virtue of the law of gravity, so tampering with the truth, even unwittingly, will be called a lie and incur punishment" (page 187). Piaget points out that the child's growth from moral realism to the more mature stage of moral relativism is hampered by the kind of constraint that many adults impose upon children. The imposition of too many rules, the too frequent attempts to break the child's will can be seen as the reinforcement of moral realism. "It is perhaps in this domain that one realizes most keenly how immoral it can be to believe too much in morality, and how much more precious is a little humanity than all the rules in the world" (page 189).

THE DEVELOPMENT OF AUTONOMOUS MORALITY

The morality of childhood, as we have seen, is inclined to rest upon external moral constraints. Yet the adult's behavior is often guided by an internal sense of obligation and by a self-referred judgment of appropriateness or right. Whereas the child's moral decision is guided by fear of punishment and a feeling of external enforcement, the adult's morality is more likely to be based on a maintenance of his self-respect and the attainment of his ideal self image (Allport, 1955). How does this shift take place? It can be accounted for in two general processes. The first of these is called identification and the second directed conscious guidance.

The Process of Identification

The concept of identification, first described by Freud, has been adopted by many non-Freudian psychologists and other social scientists to explain the general similarities between one generation and another. At a descriptive individual level, identification is the process of "modeling oneself in thought, feeling or action after another person" (Symonds, 1949). R. Sears (1957) uses the concept to account for two major developments in a child's personality, the growth of autonomous control over impulse through the development of conscience, and the acquisition of appropriate sex-typed role behavior. After a careful review and analysis of the literature on the topic, Bronfenbrenner (1960) concludes that the term is applied to three broad classes of phenomena. Identification is used to describe *behavior* that is modeled after the behavior of another; usually the actual behavior of another, though sometimes the ideal standard set by another. Identification is used also to refer to a *motive* to imitate or the disposition to act like another. A third class of phenomena to which the term is applied is that of "the psychological forces that impel the child to emulate a model." It is this last meaning of identification as a *process* that is considered primarily here. Out of an understanding of the dynamics of the process of identification we can become more deeply aware of why the child behaves as he does and of the effects we may have on his developing personality.

Pearson (1954) writing from the psychoanalytic point of view describes the importance and the operation of identification as follows:

> The need of the child to identify with the adult is a most important mechanism in the ability to learn, to acquire ego skills, particularly the ego skills of an academic nature. The child envies the power, self-sufficiency and apparent freedom from fear of the adult and desires to be like him so as not to be tormented with feelings of fear, inadequacy, and incapability. The adult is also the source of pleasure because he gratifies the instinctual desires of the child. When the source of pleasure is absent the child be-

comes apprehensive lest he suffer pain and discomfort, for then he may feel his instinctual desires but will be unable to gratify them. The child believes that if he could himself become the source of pleasure, the adult, then he would no longer be apprehensive when the adult was not present, for he would never be exposed to feelings of pain and discomfort. In short, the child wishes to be the adult in order to avoid his feelings of anxiety and dread. Consciously and unconsciously from the time he becomes aware that his ego is separate from his environment he attempts to identify with the adult (page 142).

Anna Freud (1946) describes another facet of identification when she suggests that identification with the aggressor is one of the ego's weapons in dealing with certain anxiety arousing interpersonal relations. By using identification when subjected to punitive treatment and by impersonating the aggressor and assuming his characteristics, the child is able to feel that he is no longer the threatened person but the person who administers the punishment.

She tells of the experience of August Aichhorn in advising in the case of an elementary school boy. The boy had been referred because of a habit of making faces.

> The master complained that the boy's behavior, if he were blamed or reproved, was quite abnormal. On such occasions he made faces which caused the whole class to burst out laughing. The master's view was that either the boy was consciously making fun of him or else the twitching of his face must be due to some kind of tic. His report was at once corroborated, for the boy began to make faces during the consultation, but, when master, pupil and psychologist were together, the situation was explained. Observing the two attentively, Aichhorn saw that the boy's grimaces were simply a caricature of the angry expression of the teacher and that, when he had to face a scolding by the latter, he tried to master his anxiety by involuntarily imitating him. The boy identified himself with the teacher's anger and copied his expression as he spoke, though the imitation was not recognized. Through his grimaces he was assimilating himself to or identifying himself with the dreaded external object (page 118).

One of the consequences of the process of identification is the development of the super-ego. The super-ego is the aspect of the personality that develops when the child internalizes those external restrictions upon impulse that were originally set by adult authority. Freud (1933) describes the development of the super-ego, which serves as a kind of autonomous morality, in the following terms:

> The role which the super-ego undertakes later in life, is at first played by an external power by parental authority. The influence of the parents dominates the child by granting proofs of affection and by threats of punishment, which to the child, mean loss of love, and which must also be feared on their own account. This objective anxiety is the forerunner of the later moral anxiety; so long as the former is dominant one need not speak of super-ego or of conscience. It is only later that the secondary

situation arises, which we are far too ready to regard as the normal state of affairs; the external restrictions are introjected, so that the super-ego takes the place of the parental function, and thenceforward observes, guides and threatens the ego in just the same way as the parents acted to the child before. . . . The basis of the process is what we call identification, that is to say, that one ego becomes like another, one which results in the first ego behaving itself in certain respects in the same way as the second; it imitates it, and as it were, takes it into itself (pages 89-90).

Although the literature on the subject of identification suggests that the early identification of the child with his parents, dating back to the time when he is completely dependent on them, is the most profound and influential, there is also the suggestion that the child learns to identify per se or to model his behavior after other significant people. Whether or not the teacher will be such a significant person will depend on a number of factors. In a study on the development of the ideal self in childhood and adolescence, Havighurst and his co-workers (1946) found that when youngsters were asked to describe the person they would most like to be like, one fifth-grade group that happened to have a very attractive teacher, mentioned this teacher frequently in their essays, although teachers generally were not mentioned very often. Even if children do not mention their teachers, they may nevertheless identify with them in many ways.

Stoke (1950) postulates a number of factors that influence identification. Among the factors he lists are the following:

1. The extent to which the person with whom the child is identifying accords him affection. Pearson (1954) suggests that the strongest reinforcement for identification is for the child to be loved by the adult with whom he is identifying. Of course, the way in which a teacher demonstrates his love for a child would differ from the way of the parent.

2. Identification depends on the extent to which the child's needs are satisfied by the person with whom the child is attempting to identify. In the case of the parents, the needs that are satisfied are basic and the child's dependence is greater. The teacher must satisfy the psychological needs involving adequacy and esteem. This does not mean that the teacher makes no demands upon the child. R. R. Sears (1957) hypothesizes to the contrary, that the strength of identification would vary positively with the severity of the demands placed on the child. He qualifies this hypothesis with the following: "As with affectionate nurture, there is probably an upper limit of severity beyond which severity is negatively related to identification; if the mother sets standards entirely beyond the child's capacity for accomplishment, he will either never get loved (if affection is contingent on success) or the demands will not be true demands (if affection is given anyway)" (page 160).

3. Identification depends on the degree of clarity of the behavior pattern or role and the child's acquaintance with that role with which identification is to take place. In a simpler economy and in a more clearly sex-role differentiated society, growing boys and girls have ready access to the unequivocal role of the parent of the same sex with whom they can identify. In our industrial society, which is characterized as becoming less differentiated in regard to sex roles, the child's task of identifying becomes difficult. Children tend to see only segments of the sex-role appropriate behavior and these are often ambiguous. Parsons and Bales (1955) maintain that the urban middle-class boy experiences difficulty in adopting the male role because of the difficulty of understanding many middle-class adult male occupations because they are remote and as they do not involve physical prowess or skills, they do not patently symbolize masculinity. The absence of the adult male role also weakens the adult female role, since sex-typed role behavior is reciprocal, and consequently girls also experience difficulty in this aspect of identification.

4. Identification depends on the extent to which the child's ability, his temperament, his aspirations, and his self-concept permit him to adopt the behavior patterns of the model. Thus Bronfenbrenner (1960) arrives "at the notion that exposure to a model who exhibits effective mastery of the environment might, through capitalizing on an already existent activity or exploratory drive, stimulate the child to adopt the father's 'adventurous' pattern of activity." The child will face some choices in his post parental identification and the choices he will make will depend upon the previous identifications that have led to his present self-concept and his current aspirations. In the selection of the ideal self, Havighurst et al. (1946) have shown that there is a developmental trend, such that in childhood the identification tends to be with a parental figure, in middle childhood and early adolescence the identification is characterized by romanticism and glamour, and in late adolescence identification tends to be with an attractive, visible young adult or an imaginary figure who symbolizes the desirable characteristics.

The result of the various identifications that the child makes is to provide him with a sense of self as a distinctive yet typical being, as both a part of the group and apart from the group. Erikson (1959) calls this sense of self "ego identity," which he describes as follows:

> The sense of ego identity, then, is the accrued confidence that one's ability to maintain inner sameness and continuity (one's ego in the psychological sense) is matched by the sameness and continuity of one's meaning for others. . . . The growing child must, at every step, derive a vitalizing sense of reality from the awareness that his individual way of mastering experience is a successful variant of the way other people around him master experience and recognize such mastery (page 89).

Erikson is correct to point out that the individual's identity as it emerges in a more or less final form at the end of adolescence is more than the sum of all the identifications that the child has made. It represents all the significant identifications, each of them somewhat altered so as to form a "unique and a reasonably coherent whole of them." The formation of a person's identity in addition to being the Gestalt, or unique configuration of previous identifications, is dependent also on the way in which the group *identifies* the person, assigns roles to him and expresses its expectations of him. The reader will note the relationship of this to the discussion of the self at the end of Chapter 2.

What are the implications of this discussion for the school and for the teacher? Understanding the process of identification is theoretical and general rather than empirical and practical. At the present we cannot predict with any certainty what would be the specific results of exposure to a particular person. We do know that the process generally takes time and that there are many subtle, conscious, and unconscious influences that operate. With some caution, therefore, the following suggestions for educational practice are offered. Teachers should be capable of expressing affection appropriately toward their students. Pearson (1954) points out that prizes, merit badges, and even marks are taken by the child as signs of the teacher's love. He criticizes the discarding of these signs in the name of progressive education. In any case, the teacher must be aware that the student often depends upon some observable sign, at least of the teacher's concern for him as a person. Children should be exposed to a wide variety of desirable models. Because children differ, no one model would be appropriate for all. Some will find congenial the more extroverted, energetic, effervescent teacher and identify with him; some will be able more readily to identify with the more stolid, methodical, deliberative kind of teacher. In view of the problem of sex-role identification the presence of the male teacher in the primary grades, would ease the difficulty in this area. Finally, if the aim of the school is to foster cognitive development, learning, and a desire for learning, it is important that children be exposed not only to teachers who are competent but who themselves are learners. If the student sees the teacher as one who is interested in learning, he too will perforce become interested in learning in order to be like him and so be loved by him.

THE CLASSROOM FOSTERS AUTONOMOUS MORALITY

The preceding discussion of identification and its general implications for school organization fails to indicate some of the procedures that the teacher can use in the classroom. Although the content of the curriculum may support or obstruct the development of mature morality, the method is of utmost importance. In a study of moral values in public education carried on in Kentucky, one of the guiding principles in setting up the program emphasizes this very point.

> In a democratic society which seeks to educate growing persons as free and responsible participants in a free and dynamic society, method should seek to develop the abilities and habits of discrimination, constructive criticism, self-reliance and cooperation. The center of education shifts from teaching to learning. The role of the teacher as an understanding guide and counselor in assisting the young to achieve competence in dealing intelligently and effectively with moral issues assumes unprecedented importance (Hartford, 1958, page 6).

Dewey's (1909) statement reflects a similar point of view and offers further suggestion for curriculum and method. "Ultimate moral motives and forces are nothing more or less than social intelligence—the power of observing and comprehending social situations—and social power—trained capacities of control—at work in the service of social interest and aims" (page 43).

Classroom Method

The classroom method that is most effective in producing sound character is that which applies the principles of positive transfer discussed in the previous chapter. That is the method that develops the principle (in this case the moral principle), sharpens its meaning and then provides opportunities for application of the principle. This generalization about character training is well supported by the findings of Jones (1936) who studied the relative effectiveness of various classroom procedures in character and citizenship training. Using seventh- and eighth-grade pupils he studied the gains made under each of the following conditions applied for one school year:

1. No conscious or directed instruction in citizenship and character —control groups
2. Providing activities designed to induce moral conduct such as respect for property and the rights of others but with no attempt to generalize the learning
3. Verbal instruction but with no provision for the application of the principles
4. Combination of (2) and (3)

The results of this study indicated that the largest gains in tests of honesty, cooperation, and the like were made under conditions in which the moral principle was developed in classroom discussion and the students were then provided with active opportunities to apply the principle. Although methods (2) and (3)—discussion alone or experiences alone—proved superior to the control group in which no guidance or instruction was given, they either failed to produce the full awareness of the principle or its application to specific situations. Quillen (1947) in describing the task of the teacher in developing the meaning of basic social and moral concepts suggests that there are essentially three steps to the process: (1) to identify the concept to be taught; (2) to select experiences in which these concepts will be applied in a way that is appropriate for the developmental level of the student; and (3) to guide the students to a fuller comprehension of the meaning of these concepts as they would be applied to various situations of their environment.

Another finding of the Jones' study that is of interest points to the importance of good group morale in fostering character growth. He found that the class with the best group morale made the greatest gain during the course of the year. The gains made under conditions of good group morale, *group-linked gains,* tended to be less permanent than those made as a result of classroom procedures. In reviewing his own study Jones (1946) states the following:

> This concept implies that, if a child rather suddenly shows improved character responses in a social setting where the group morale favors superior conduct, it does not necessarily follow that such conduct has become firmly interiorized at this level. . . .
>
> It seems that group linked gains and losses become interiorized gradually. On the side of remedial treatment this would seem to mean that a child who rather suddenly deteriorates under bad influences may be saved from much of his loss by speedy removal from these surroundings. In the case of a child whose conduct has improved under the impetus of superior surroundings, it means that provision should be made for rather protracted exposure to such conditions to allow the gains to become integrated into individual standards and habits (page 728).

These recommendations will be referred to again later in this chapter when the teacher's role in correcting values is considered.

Textbooks and Values

Teachers are inclined to overlook the extent to which the content of the curriculum guides in the development of values. When this dimension of the reading material, for example, is overlooked, children are likely to acquire some undesirable and unrealistic value orientations. The reading material made available to children should be reviewed by the teacher for its possible effects on children's values. It may be assumed that the events of a story are reacted to by a child as if he were actually experiencing it in real life. Child and others (1946) examined a series of thirty third-grade readers in order to assess the possible effects of the various incidents or themes in these stories on values and personality development. Some of the values that were reinforced by the reading material would be judged desirable; others, however, were found to be questionable and unrealistic. Thus, for example, effort as a way of reaching goals is consistently rewarded in these stories. On the other hand, intellectual activity is not encouraged and in fostering constructive behavior only one story concerns itself with a nonmaterial product, a poem. The central character seldom receives encouragement for original thinking and self-initiated activity. The need to explore and to satisfy curiosity tends to be punished when the child seeks to satisfy this need independently, whereas it is almost consistently rewarded if it is satisfied by means of dependence upon authority. These investigators also point out that this reading material fails to identify the variety of possible solutions when the child's needs for affiliation and nurturance (the need to help others) are frustrated. Their findings indicate also that the stories offer few suggestions to children who experience failure in competition and those who find their desires interfered with by other and more powerful persons. They suggest that reading material should include incidents in which children who express these kinds of needs at first experience failure but discover that only after a new approach, more suited to the situation, is hit upon can these needs be satisfied. These investigators temper their criticism of the reading material by noting that "the development towards autonomy must be a gradual process and a considerable amount of dependence on superiors is necessary, not only at this age but even on into adult life" (page 48).

This review of Child's study should serve to alert the teacher to the possible inadequacies of the reading material to which children are exposed. This implies that in selecting reading material the teacher needs to be sensitive to the value implications that it may contain. Where a story or an incident serves other worthwhile purposes but is somewhat deficient insofar as some positive value is concerned, the teacher can engage the class in a discussion in which other possible outcomes in the story are presented by the class. In this way the teacher can arrange to introduce rewards for independence, autonomy, intellectual activity, and the like, to compensate for whatever deficiencies are recognized in the reading material.

Religion in the Classroom

Many well-intentioned people have suggested that the teaching of religion would solve many of our problems in the development of character and moral behavior. These people ignore the pluralistic nature of our society and when they seek the common religious denominator they are likely to resort to a bland meaningless religious practice such as a nondenominational prayer or other ritualized behavior. They would be surprised to discover that the game of bowling was used some five centuries ago for such religious ceremonial purposes. The naves of the great cathedrals served as bowling alleys. The bowling pin was a symbol of evil. If a bowler was able to knock down his pin, it was taken as an indication that he was devout and could overcome evil. However, poor aim indicated that the religious fervor of the bowler was not strong enough to conquer evil and more faithful church attendance was required. It is of interest to note that Martin Luther was an enthusiastic bowler (McDonough, undated).

Our intention is not to deny the worth of organized and formal religion, but as already indicated the American community is founded on the conception that the particular religious or nonreligious sanction for moral behavior is not a public concern. The following two illustrations of the use of religion in public education are adapted from a paper by Benne (1955).[1] They offer an interesting contrast. In the first it will be noted the teacher fails to recognize the legitimate privacy of certain religious beliefs and practices; in the second the teacher uses these differences to educational advantage.

A TEACHER MISUSES RELIGION IN INSTRUCTION   Miss A is a fifth-grade teacher in an urban school. Recently, at a teachers' meeting the superintendent intimated that the teaching about religion might be a desirable thing. He hinted also that a majority of the school board favored the idea. He gave no directive but Miss A thought that she ought to contribute directly to the character development of her students and she decided to proceed accordingly.

One morning that week, during their planning period, Miss A questioned her students to find out where they went to Sunday school and church. Some students named Methodist, Baptist, and Holiness churches among others. Some students hesitated a moment and then seemed to choose one of the churches already mentioned, as if they felt compelled to offer just any name. Finally, Jack's turn came. He is an able student and is respected by his classmates as well as by the teacher. Jack responded, "We don't go anywhere regularly, Miss A." Miss A seemed somewhat surprised, "But surely you must go somewhere to church and Sunday school, Jack. All the others have told us their churches. Now, Jack, tell us, where do you go to church?" Everybody in the group was looking at Jack now. Jack squared his shoulders and said, "But I told you, Miss A, we don't go to any church regularly." Miss A was completely unaware of the feelings, thoughts, and actions which she had aroused in this brief interplay as she moved on to other matters.

That noon as the children were coming home for lunchtime Jack's mother, Helen, noticed that something was wrong in the group that regularly came by the house. The group was chanting, "Jack doesn't believe in God," and Jack was protesting ineffectually, "We *do too* be-

[1] Adapted from K. D. Benne, "What Teachers Should Know About Religion," *The Educational Year*, the American Association of Colleges for Teacher Education, 1955, **8**, pp. 213-221.

lieve in God." The taunting children became silent when they saw Helen on the porch. Helen calmed Jack who began to sob after the children left and through his sobs and his complaint, "They wouldn't even listen to me, Mama," she learned of the problem. Helen and Mike, Jack's father, decided to let things ride and to talk to Miss A about the incident the next time they saw her.

The next day Miss A had planned to implement her aim to teach religion during the art period. She suggested that each student draw his or her picture of God. Soon most students were busy drawing some version of a large old man with a long beard. Jack didn't draw. When Miss A asked why he wasn't drawing, Jack said, "I don't think you can draw God." "But, Jack, all the other children are drawing. Why do you think you can't draw God?" "Because," and here Jack raised his voice, "when we talk about God at home, He means everything that is very good. He is everywhere anything good is. You can't draw that." Jack refused to draw despite the obvious displeasure of Miss A and the furtive glances of the class.

That evening Jack reported his experience to his father and mother and expressed concern over the resentment he seemed to be inducing in the teacher and the class. Mike and Helen reassured him and tried to point out that doing what one thought was right was not always easy or popular. Further discussion about Jack's conception of God as everything anywhere that is good led to Mike's asking if there was something good that he could draw even though it wasn't God to him. Jack thought awhile and said he thought he could honestly draw the sun as something very good for man.

The next day during art period the children continued their previous day's activity. When Jack started to draw Miss A was obviously relieved. Later in the period she noticed that Jack had colored a heavy black shadow over most of the bright sun he had drawn first. "Why did you put a shadow over most of the sun, Jack?" "Because, Miss A, there are people who think you can draw God."

This statement from an otherwise cooperative boy should have alerted Miss A that something was wrong but she did not understand that her efforts to teach about religion had misfired until she spoke to Jack's parents later that week. Her discussion with them led her to wonder what ideas about religion she had actually communicated to her students.

A TEACHER MAKES USE OF RELIGIOUS DIFFERENCES   Miss B is also a fifth-grade teacher in a similar community. Miss B takes pride in being able to work out human relations problems in her class but now she sensed that she was facing a difficult problem. About three weeks earlier a new student, Ruth, had been placed in her class. Ruth's mother, Mrs. Levy, had come with the girl on the first day and had chatted a while with

Miss B. Mrs. Levy explained that they had previously lived in a larger city in a neighborhood that had a number of Jewish families. She was concerned now about how her daughter would make out in a school where so few children were Jewish. Miss B admitted that Ruth would be the only Jewish child in the class, but she assured Mrs. Levy that the class would make Ruth feel at home. At this point she was wondering if Ruth was being made to feel at home.

The hospitality committee in Miss B's room had at first welcomed Ruth and treated her like company, but as Ruth was there to stay the special hospitality efforts dropped off after a few days. Miss B noticed that Ruth had no secure place in the group. She sought out Miss B before school and during play periods, and she seemed not to have found a congenial group of girl friends. Miss B speculated as to the cause of this exclusion. She could find nothing in the child's behavior that could account for it until Miss B overheard some of her children on the playground whispering to children from another fifth grade that Ruth was a Jew. Then Miss B began to give some thought to the problem of how she could help the other students achieve a better understanding and appreciation, not only of Ruth's religion, but also of their own. Miss B knew her problem was most difficult. She herself didn't know much about religion, but she knew enough to sense how touchy the whole subject was to many people.

Miss B sought advice from a number of people. Her principal encouraged her to work something out and hoped she would be able to report success at an early faculty meeting. Her own minister, a Congregationalist, asked her frankly what *she* thought about Judaism as a religion. She confessed that she knew very little about it but she thought that it was one among many religions and that she wasn't sure, from an objective point of view, whether it was more or less valid than her own faith. She felt that her minister agreed with her and he suggested that Miss B talk to the rabbi in the community. After discussing the matter the rabbi gave her two bits of advice: (1) to use informed laymen rather than members of the clergy if she brought adults in to talk about their religions and (2) not to overlook the legitimate needs of those children who were not affiliated with any religious group.

Miss B's next step was to invite a parents' group to discuss the situation. In addition to Ruth's mother who was present, there were several Protestant parents; a few Roman Catholic mothers; and the wife of a faculty member in a local college, a secularist, whose son Jim was in the class. She said frankly that Ruth's coming into the group had reminded her how little each child knew about the religious faith of the others, but that she thought the problem was not one of an individual child. She suggested that she was thinking about a social-studies unit on various religious outlooks and she asked if the parents would cooperate with her. The parents agreed to help. Miss B went over her plan and some of the parents objected to her idea that the children might visit different worship services, so she deleted that from her plans. The parents also agreed to report any reaction to the program, good or bad, and to evaluate the unit with her at the end.

Miss B introduced the unit in social studies to her class as an opportunity to learn more about the interesting differences among religious points of view and practices. She related the unit to others, in which they had studied about different ways of life across the world and even in their own town, and suggested that they might start by talking about the different ways in which families celebrated the winter holidays that were coming soon. The children were surprised to learn of the differences in Catholic and Protestant Christmases and the "national" and "denominational" aspects of the celebration. The children listened attentively to Ruth's talk about Chanuka, the feast of lights, the story of the Maccabees and their fight for religious freedom. They were almost envious of the several days of gift giving that she described. Jim talked about his father's reading the *Christmas Carol* every year just after the family had decorated and lighted the tree. Everyone talked to an interested audience.

Miss B organized committees to prepare a presentation on some type of religious belief and observance. Each committee was expected to invite and to brief the outside layman who came to talk to the class about that religion and to prepare the class for the ensuing discussion. The secularists were also represented on one day when Jim's father spoke. Miss B and the parents rated the unit highly. She felt that she as well as the students had learned a good deal about the variety in the community's religious life. She noticed that Ruth had found a more secure place in the classroom group and Jim had not lost his.

Against the background of these illustrations Benne suggests that the teacher must know the following if he is to teach about religion successfully.

1. The teacher should appreciate the variety of religious positions in America and in the world.
2. "The teacher must have objectified his own religious outlook . . . to see that it is one among many approaches to ultimate values and their interpretation and that these approaches have some degree of intelligibility and possible validity in their own right."
3. The meaning of religious freedom and the pluralistic character of our society should be clear to every teacher who attempts to teach about religion.

4. The teacher should understand that religion can have a strong emotional implication in the lives of many people and that resentments, oppression, and antipathies can be easily aroused.

These four statements can also serve the teacher as guides in the teaching of science or other subject matter that may conflict with a student's religious views.

CORRECTING VALUES

Every teacher will observe some behavior that is indicative of an undesirable value orientation. The teacher must be prepared to cope with this behavior. Each time an incident or situation of this type occurs, the behavior must be analyzed for its meaning before corrective steps are taken. The behavior itself is symptomatic of something psychodynamically deeper. Procedures designed to eliminate the specific behavior, without regard to its fuller meaning, may well result in a reinforcement of the negative value. A few of the kinds of situations that can arise in the school will be analyzed and the importance of viewing the student as an integrated psychologically active being will be demonstrated. Four kinds of situations are discussed: a situation wherein an elementary-grade youngster innocently commits a dishonest act, the problem of cheating in the high school grades, the more serious form of antisocial behavior commonly known as delinquency, and finally the problem of value distortion shown in intergroup prejudice.

Innocent Dishonesty

Johnny happily informs the teacher that the clerk at the candy store had mistakenly given him a dime instead of a penny when he purchased some candy at noon. He is perplexed and disappointed when the teacher suggests that he ought to return the dime and receive a penny in exchange. This type of innocent dishonesty occurs quite frequently and can provide some of the substance for character education. Many paths are open to the teacher. Some of these are described in the following discussion adapted from the Educational Policies Commission[2] (1951) statement on moral and spiritual values in the public schools.

The teacher can emphasize fair play and justice by saying something like this: "It isn't only the dime. It isn't fair for you to profit from the clerk's error. We must always try to live by the principle of fair play. Do to others what you expect them to do to you."

The teacher may attempt to show that law is law regardless of the amount. In general this approach reinforces the moral realism of the child and adopts an overly simple view of transfer. In this case the teacher

2 Adapted from Educational Policies Commission, *Moral and Spiritual Values in the Public Schools.* Washington, D. C.: National Education Association, 1951, pp. 39-45.

would say something like this: "As you grow up you will be tempted to have things that do not belong to you. You must learn to resist the easy temptations now so that it will be easier for you to resist the stronger temptations later on. We have laws against stealing and if you do not obey the law, you will be punished."

The teacher can exercise his authority. This approach would, of course, reinforce the heteronomy. A teacher applying this approach would say something along this line: "I insist that you return that dime. If you do not, I shall be forced to punish you by keeping you after school to-morrow. Do you understand?"

Another approach would be to invoke group disapproval. The teacher using this approach would say: "The other children in the class will find out that you kept a dime that the clerk gave you by mistake. They will feel that you are a person who cannot be trusted. They won't want to play with you any more. You don't want that to happen, do you?"

Along the same line the teacher may invoke the child's inner conscience. He would say, "You know that it is wrong to take something that belongs to someone else. Whenever you will be reminded of this you will be unhappy with yourself. The two candy bars that you could buy with the dime are hardly worth the guilty feelings that you will have. Don't you agree?"

Another approach would be to lead the child to an awareness of the various facets of the situation. The conversation between the teacher and the child might proceed along these lines.

Teacher: How will the clerk feel when he discovers his mistake?

Student: He's dumb, not to be able to tell the difference between a dime and a penny.

Teacher: Were you able to tell the difference when you picked it up?

Student: No, I thought I had a penny until I came to school.

Teacher: Then you couldn't tell the difference either.

Student: Well, I get the idea. We can all make mistakes.

Teacher: How would you feel about it if you were the one to be the loser because of your mistake?

Student: I guess I'd feel sorry.

Teacher: What will happen this evening when the clerk checks the cash register?

Student: It will show ten cents missing, wouldn't it?

Teacher: Not really, it will show nine cents missing. The difference between a dime and a penny. How will the clerk explain the missing nine cents?

Student: He can just say that he made a mistake.

Teacher: If you were the owner of the store what would you do if money was missing and the clerk said that he made a mistake?

Student: I don't know, but I suppose I'd make the clerk pay for it.

Teacher: Now put yourself in the clerk's place. Would you like to pay it?

Student: I wouldn't like to pay it but if I made the mistake I would deserve it.

Teacher: Would you feel the same way if you were the clerk and you were short nine dollars instead of nine cents?

Student: I guess it would be a lot harder to have to pay nine dollars.

Teacher: If you had gone to the store for your mother and the clerk had given you a ten-dollar bill instead of a one what would you have done?

Student: I'd take it back because I wouldn't want him to have to pay nine dollars.

Teacher: How do you feel about the nine cents?

Student: It's not really very much money.

Teacher: How much money would it have to be before you thought you should return it?

Student: I don't know. I hadn't thought about it that way. Do you really think I ought to take it back?

Teacher: What I think doesn't matter. What do *you* think?

It is important to note that bringing the child to the point of correct behavior is by itself not sufficient. The teaching procedure must be evaluated in terms of the basis or the reasons for the child's action. Jahoda (1956) suggests that conforming behavior may have its roots in four different processes.

1. Compliance represents a response brought about by some pressure of authority or power. The teacher who succeeds in obtaining the desired behavior by means of the threat of punishment that is unrelated to the issue is obtaining conformity based in compliance. This type of pressure, even if seemingly successful, will, if used consistently, prolong the child's heteronomous morality. (See Figure 6.1.)

2 Conformance is a form of conforming behavior that arises from a desire to remain a member in good standing with a valued group. The finding by Jones (1936), referred to earlier in this chapter, that group-linked gains or losses in character take place where group morale is high, can be explained as changes in moral behavior brought about as a result of conformance. The teacher who suggests that the group will disapprove of the child is developing morality based on conformance. This sanction for moral conduct is moderately effective but the interiorization of the gains made under these conditions takes considerable time.

3. Convergence "represents a process brought about by an argument on an issue related to but not identical with the main issue; no change in beliefs on the main issue occurs." Children will conform to the rules made by a school administration or faculty not because they have accepted the principles underlying these decisions and not because they have abandoned their own beliefs, but because it seems reasonable to conform at this time. Convergence represents a compromise on the part of the student.

4. Consent represents the firmest basis for moral action. The individual changes his belief and accepts the principle underlying the desired conduct because he personally wishes to do so. It has been said that the ultimate basis for morality in an individual is his desire to act morally. When the individual changes his point of view and is convinced that the moral decision is the right decision for him, he is acting out of consent.

The teacher cannot be satisfied with correcting the undesirable action alone; he must come to discriminate between the various sources from which conformity stems. Jahoda emphasizes the importance of this distinction when she states:

Consider the perplexing situation in which our school teachers find themselves occasionally when they learn that a boy who apparently showed no noticeable deviation in his behavior in class is suddenly caught up in an act of juvenile delinquency. If we could help our teachers to refine their diagnosis of such a child's earlier conformity to the school's standards and values in terms of the four processes—if they distinguished between genuine consent to the school's standards and values, compliance with them out of fear, conformance with the social pressures in the immediate environment of the classroom, or convergence with classroom regulations with the calculated anticipation that inconspicuous behavior at school might one day serve as an alibi, an earlier diagnosis of pre-delinquents might become possible (page 238).

Cheating

A somewhat more serious manifestation of inappropriate values is found in those school situations in which students cheat. The teacher needs to be concerned about this. He needs to understand the meaning of this kind of behavior so that he can constructively prevent it and rationally cope with it when it does occur. The following brief description of a cheating incident and the analysis of the dynamics involved will provide a framework for deriving some useful principles of instruction for character development.

In one large high school the senior class had participated in widespread cheating on the final examination. The teachers suspected that something of this sort had occurred when they discovered that students who had performed poorly all year long did unusually well on this final examination. After a little investigation it was revealed that some enterprising students had removed examination copies from a locked room. Copies of the examination were sold at quoted prices. Students whose honesty and integrity made them reluctant to participate in this kind of activity were convinced by the others that they risked failure if they maintained these virtues. They were led to believe that since many other students had availed themselves of the advance copies, the virtuous few might find themselves with the poorest grades.

Various members of the faculty and administration voiced differing opinions as to what needed to be done. Some suggested that all those who could be incriminated should be failed and the ringleaders dismissed from school without a diploma. Some suggested that the students be re-examined and no other particular notice given to the incident. Some argued that the results on the final examination be ignored since each teacher had accumulated sufficient evidence of student performance during the course of the year to assign a final grade. One small group insisted that the concern with immediate procedures for handling the situation, while important, should not lead to overlooking the basic causes of the difficulty. In the opinion of this group treating the symptom alone was not satisfactory since they felt that the fact that such an incident occurred indicated that there was something basically unsound in the atmosphere of the school. The principal suggested that two committees of faculty be formed; one with the immediate goal of recommending procedures for handling the assignment of final grades and for dealing with the students involved, and the other a continuing committee to look more critically at the school policy as a possible contributory cause to the cheating incident.

The first committee made a number of recommendations that met with the approval of the faculty. Among these recommendations were the following: (1) to rely on grades achieved during the year for the final grade, (2) to meet with the students in small groups to explain the faculty's concern over this form of behavior, (3) to meet individually with the ringleaders and their parents to point out the seriousness of the violation with the hope that they would come to understand the meaning of their action.

The second committee presented its report to the faculty several months later. The report pointed out a number of deficiencies in the school's policies that the committee felt had contributed greatly to the cheating incident. The report was emphatic in stating that the students' behavior was not to be condoned, but the school should not contribute to the normlessness that seemed to be prevalent in the school community. The committee report made the following observations:

1. Instruction throughout the high school was largely impersonal and although much of this could not be avoided because of the departmentalization, some improvement of teacher-pupil relationship could be sought. One suggestion was that teachers be assigned to a class group for as long a period of time as possible.

2. Grades were to a too large extent determined by the final examination.

3. Final grades were used to make a number of irrelevant decisions about the student. For example, participation in varsity athletics and other extracurricular activities were contingent on the final grades in the academic courses. The committee was divided on the modification of this ruling. Several members of the committee felt it was neither psychologically nor educationally sound to prohibit a student from excelling and satisfying important status needs in an area in which he might be capable, such as athletics or band, simply because he showed deficiencies or inadequacies in some other area. The faculty finally agreed that each case of extracurricular participation in which low academic performance was involved would be reviewed by a faculty committee that would receive recommendations from the various teachers of the student in question.

4. The committee emphasized the need for a faculty reappraisal

of its orientation to examinations. Both students and faculty had come, to a certain extent, to view examinations as punitive devices rather than as essential educational procedures. (The discussion in Chapter 9 is relevant to this point.)

5. Finally the committee noted the serious lack of opportunities for students to engage in self-evaluation. In order for students to accept some responsibility for their own continuing education they must be helped to become capable of appraising their own efforts and to be realistically self-critical.

In the case of the younger child the analysis would proceed along different lines. A child in the first grade who copies from the child sitting next to him is not engaging in cheating in the sense just described. We do the child an injustice in judging his behavior in terms of our adult standards. He has not yet become aware of the subtle requirement of working alone under certain conditions. Making an issue merely serves to confuse the child and to reinforce his tendency to believe that having a will of his own is wrong.

When cheating occurs the teacher must recognize his responsibilities in two directions. First, he must respond to the immediate situation and deal with it in such a way as not to preclude implementing long-range action. Second, he must view the incident as possibly symptomatic of negative pressures that have operated to produce it. Some of these negative forces can be eliminated to prevent the recurrence of such behavior. At the level of prevention, teachers must seek ways of reinforcing the positive aims and behavior rather than to act as policemen who would punish any deviation.

Delinquent Behavior

Juvenile delinquency has become one of the major concerns of our society since the dramatic increase in incidence after World War II. Although the vast majority of our children between the ages of seven and seventeen years grow up as essentially law abiding young citizens, an increasing number become involved in violations of the legal code and are brought before juvenile court authorities. One writer has estimated that if the present trends continue, it is likely that one boy in five will have a record of delinquency before reaching draft age (Kvaraceus, 1958).

The schools can play an important part in the control of juvenile delinquency. In order for teachers to participate with other agencies in coping with this problem they ought to be informed about its dimensions. They should be able to detect the early signs of predelinquency and they need to have some understanding of their role in dealing with children whose value orientation is such as to classify them as delinquent or predelinquent.

Much of the discussion in the newspapers and popular literature makes the error of lumping all forms of delinquent behavior together. Medical science would have made little progress in disease control if it had considered all fevers or other symptoms indiscriminately as belonging in single categories of illness. It is important that we differentiate one delinquent act from another in terms of what is going on within the child's personality. Redl (1956) has suggested a number of such categories or areas in which personality disturbance may lead to delinquent behavior. He proposes that the delinquency will have quite different meaning if it develops as a result of the child's being subjected to a series of traumatic experiences, as opposed to his becoming involved in the excitement or intoxication of group vandalism. Delinquency may arise from uneven development in the various aspects of the child's physiological and psychological development. Certain forms of anxieties and neuroses when occurring in certain environments may lead to delinquent patterns. For example an anxiety-ridden youngster may act tough or do daring things because he believes that if he does not do these things others will consider him "chicken" and will beat him up.

One writer has considered delinquency as a solution to a sociological conflict to which many youngsters are subjected. Cohen (1955) suggests that the American social class system (see Chapter 14) appears to define achievement and status in such a way as to make it seem that status is equally available to all, while at the same time a number of children from lower-class homes find it impossible to achieve any mark of success or a sense of worth. Some of these youngsters find that their peer subculture provides "criteria of status which these children *can* meet." This subculture is not specifically delinquent, it rather expresses the rejection of the middle-class criteria of success and the adoption of a contrary set of criteria. The status achieved in this manner is dependent upon participation within a group that holds these values. Each person who joins the group becomes committed to its criteria of status and finds it difficult to leave because he will be further rejected by the society for having participated in the delinquent subculture.

One extensive study (Glueck and Glueck, 1950) that compared 500 delinquents with a similar number of nondelinquents on a number of criteria, although it failed to differentiate between the various bases for delinquent action, does offer some information on the general characteristics of delinquent youth. This study showed that the signs that distinguish the delinquent from the nondelinquent youth appeared quite early. About half of the cases of delinquents were under eight years of age when the first clear signs of maladaptive behavior were shown and all but 12.4 percent were under eleven. Some of these signs to which the teacher should be alerted are impulsiveness, lack of self-control, defiance, and destructiveness. The delinquents as a group showed less fear of failure, less concern about meeting conventional expectations, and were less sub-missive to authority. "To a greater extent than the control group, they express feelings of not being recognized or appreciated." The delinquent group tends to perform well on those tasks of the intelligence tests that require direct, immediate, and concrete responses, but not as well on those that require the use of symbols or abstractions. School misbehavior was five times more prevalent in the delinquent group and appeared three years earlier than in the nondelinquent group. The delinquent shows his resentment toward the restraints of the school by persistent truancy. Other kinds of school misconduct in which delinquents greatly exceeded the nondelinquents were disobedience, disorderliness, stub-bornness, sullenness, and impertinence. The homes of the delinquent youth were more likely to be characterized by lack of understanding, affection, and stability and parents were more likely to provide inade-quate identification figures.

How can the school, as an institution, or the teacher, as an in-dividual, help? Kvaraceus (1958) states:

> Three factors that tend to immobilize the potential force of the school agency and which tend to dissipate its energy must be mentioned at this time. They include the delinquency trilogy of anonymity, boredom, and failure-frustration. These, in turn, frequently can be viewed as natural consequences of bigness, both in size of school and in size of class, fostering a mass system of instruction which vitiates the basic principle of individual differences (page 15).

If the classroom situation is favorable, the teacher can help by identifying the early signs of predelinquent behavior. Kvaraceus has de-veloped a delinquency proneness check list consisting of eighteen factors

TABLE 6.1   DELINQUENCY PRONENESS CHECK LIST

1. Shows marked dislike for school	11. Is a child who seriously or persist-ently misbehaves
2. Resents school routine and restric-tion	
3. Disinterested in school program	12. Destroys school materials or prop-erty
4. Is failing a number of subjects	
5. Has repeated one or more grades	13. Is cruel and bullying on the play-ground
6. Attends special class for retarded pupils	
7. Has attended many schools	14. Has temper tantrums in the class-room
8. Intends to leave school as soon as the law allows	15. Wants to stop schooling at once
9. Has only vague academic or vo-cational plans	16. Truants from school
	17. Does not participate in organized extracurricular programs
10. Has limited academic ability	18. Feels he does not "belong" in the classroom

Source: W. C. Kvaraceus, "Juvenile Delinquency," *What Research Says to the Teacher Series,* no. 15, Washington, D. C.: National Education Association, 1958, p. 17.

all of which can be evaluated within the school setting. "Since these 18 factors have been shown to be significantly characteristic of delinquents when contrasted with nondelinquents, it is suggested that classroom teachers keep a weather-eye open for those pupils in their classes who show a *saturation of these characteristics*" (page 16).

If the teacher arrives at the estimate that a particular child shows significant signs of predelinquent tendencies, he must then attempt to interpret the behavior. Attempts to punish children of this sort, without considering the consequences of such punishment, will in all probability aggravate the situation. The teacher should rather embark on a program of raising the child's self-esteem, finding activities that will prove interesting and worthwhile, and eliminating the sources of failure and frustration within the classroom. If the child's problem is of a more serious nature, these attempts on the part of the teacher may prove to be in vain. In this case the school must become involved with other community agencies such as child guidance services, juvenile court authorities, and social service agencies in helping the child achieve a satisfying and satisfactory relationship with his environment.

Prejudice

Different writers on the topic of prejudice emphasize one or another aspect of the concept in their definitions. Simpson and Yinger (1953) define prejudice as "an emotional, rigid attitude (a predisposition to respond to a certain stimulus in a certain way) toward a group of people." This definition does not distinguish between positive or negative attitudes. Allport (1954) makes this distinction when he defines negative ethnic prejudice as follows: "Ethnic prejudice is an antipathy based upon a faulty and inflexible generalization. It may be felt or expressed. It may be directed toward a group as a whole, or toward an individual because he is a member of that group." The definition given here is not intended to improve on those already available but rather to place the concept more clearly within the framework of the discussion of values. A prejudice is a negative attitude toward an identifiable group and the individual members thereof, which serves to enhance the status of the bearer of the prejudice by means of disenhancing the victims of the prejudice. Prejudice represents a distortion of the basic value presented at the beginning of this chapter.

The existence of prejudice within an individual can express itself in various forms of negative action. Allport (1954) lists the types of activities that may arise from prejudiced attitudes and beliefs.

1. *Antilocution.* Many people show their prejudice only through verbal expression.
2. *Avoidance.* Some individuals with more intense prejudice will

avoid members of the disliked group, even perhaps at the cost of considerable inconvenience.

3. *Discrimination.* When the prejudice reaches a higher, more organized level, the prejudiced person will attempt to exclude all members of the group from opportunities of finding their legitimate fulfillment, such as employment, education, housing or political rights. "Segregation is an institutionalized form of discrimination, enforced legally or by common custom."

4. *Physical attack.* Under particular conditions when prejudice is at a high level, resort to violence can occur. Gang wars between different ethnic groups, desecration of places of worship, and the bombing of homes of a member of the disliked group are some examples of actions that issue from prejudicial attitudes.

5. *Extermination.* "Lynching, pogroms, massacres, and the Hitler program of genocide mark the ultimate degree of violent expression of prejudice."

In order for the school to prevent and correct the distortion of values and the destructive behavior represented in prejudice, it is important to gain some understanding of how prejudices are acquired and how they are sustained. Prejudice has its roots, like all other values, in three sources, namely, the general culture or subculture, the family, and the individual personality. These sources or determinants may operate separately or in concert. Figure 6.2 presents schematically the various bases of prejudice.

The Culture and Its Prevailing Norms

The differential geographic distribution of prejudice toward the Negro in this country is basically due to the effect of prevailing norms. Although this difference can also be accounted for on the basis of historical and economic factors, it does not negate the fact that the institutional patterns in southern communities are more supportive of prejudice toward the Negro than those of northern communities. After conducting an extensive study of the development of prejudicial attitudes toward Negroes, Horowitz (1936) concludes: "It seems that attitudes toward Negroes are now chiefly determined not by contacts with Negroes, but by contact with the prevalent attitudes toward Negroes." A later study by Radke et al. (1949) concluded similarly that prejudice is largely based on "conformity to environmental standards and expectations."

Teachers no less than other members of the community are subjected to the influences of the prevailing norms and standards. They might, however, gain some self-understanding and objectivity if they understood the effects of these norms. Merton (1957) has described how prejudice produces what he calls a self-fulfilling prophecy, defining this phe-

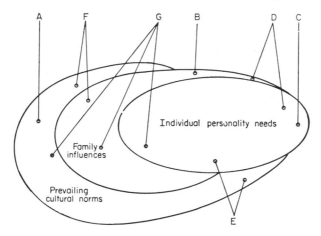

FIGURE 6.2 *The varied bases of prejudice. A represents prejudice based upon prevailing cultural norms not mediated by family and not integrated into personality needs. B represents prejudice based upon family influences, not supported by cultural norms and not integrated into personality needs. An example might be a college student's compromising reaction to the particular prejudice of his parents. C represents the individual prejudice arising from basic personality needs, not mediated by the family and not supported by the cultural norm. D, E, F, and G represent other forms of prejudice based upon various combinations of A, B, and C factors, for example G is the most virulent form of prejudice. It gains support from the family and the culture and is integrated into the personality. This form of prejudice can readily lead to discriminatory and violent action.*

nomenon as follows: "The self-fulfilling prophecy is, in the beginning, a *false* definition of the situation evoking a new behavior which makes the originally false conception come *true*." This suggests that attributing characteristics of inferiority to a group, where originally these characteristics were not evident, can evoke those characteristics. Reacting to a child, because he is a member of a particular group, with suspicion or as if he were dull, will induce sneakiness and dullness. Even an unprejudiced teacher will sometimes begin to wonder about a particular group, because the children of that group show many of the stereotyped characteristics as a result of previous encounters with prejudiced adults. Merton states that the failure to comprehend the operation of the self-fulfilling prophecy has led many Americans of goodwill to retain (often in opposition to personality trends) enduring ethnic and racial prejudices. Merton does not hold out too much hope for educational campaigns that bring the "truth" before the prejudiced group. He asserts that "enacted institutional change," motivated by positive moral sentiments, is the most effective procedure to counteract the circular effects of the self-fulfilling prophecy. A number of studies have demonstrated that under controlled conditions, members of various racial and ethnic groups can overcome their prejudices toward each other (Star et al., 1949; Deutsch and Collins, 1958; Festinger and Kelley, 1951; and Yarrow et al., 1958). The United States Supreme Court, in making its decision of May 17, 1954, seemed fully aware of the social-psychological implications of institutional support for prejudice. Mr. Chief Justice Warren in delivering the opinion of the court stated:

> To separate them from others of similar age and qualifications solely because of their race generates a feeling of inferiority as to their status in the community that may affect their hearts and their minds in a way unlikely ever to be undone. . . . We conclude that in the field of public education the doctrine of "separate but equal" has no place. Separate educational facilities are inherently unequal.

The Supreme Court documented its position by citing a number of psychological studies that have clearly demonstrated the detrimental effects of prejudice, both on those who hold the prejudice and those against whom it is directed. The court also quoted from an earlier court decision.

> Segregation of white and colored children in public schools has a detrimental effect upon colored children. The impact is greater when it has the sanction of the law; for the policy of separating the races is usually interpreted as denoting the inferiority of the Negro group. A sense of inferiority affects the motivation of a child to learn. Segregation with the sanction of law, therefore, has a tendency to retard the educational and mental development of Negro children and to deprive them of some of the benefits they would receive in a racially integrated school system.

In one study (Yarrow et al., 1958), previously cited, the dynamics in children's adaptations to a new social situation, namely a desegregated summer camp, were analyzed. Among other factors these writers point to the importance of leadership in facilitating the adaptation to new norms. The teacher, as the camp counselor in the research study, is a key figure in the success of the desegregation process once it is instituted. He can facilitate the development of new norms by clarifying immediately what is appropriate and what is expected. He occupies a "strategic position in giving definition to an ambiguous situation, and in communicating the norms to the children. The manner in which he deals with the racial issue *for himself* (i.e., how he copes with his feelings of anxiety, anger, or tension) plays a decisive role."

In general, the teacher's responsibility in fostering and supporting enacted institutional change is that of a responsible and informed citizen. It is important for the teacher to express a long-range view when critically evaluating the effects of such institutional change.

Personality and Prejudice

While it is true that a person whose prejudice is derived primarily from the cultural environment, will in time give up his prejudice if the institutional patterns of his social environment change or if he moves into a society that does not hold that prejudice; this is not true in the case of prejudice that serves deep-seated personality needs. A series of studies in which the personality structure of highly prejudiced individuals was contrasted with that of those showing little prejudice have produced some interesting findings. These studies have shown that the expression of prejudicial attitudes is a natural outgrowth of certain kinds of personality structure. One study (Gough et al., 1950) showed that those children who were highly prejudiced were more likely to agree with each of the following personality inventory items than those who showed little prejudice.

1. The best rule is to play fair with your gang, and let the other children look out for themselves.
2. There are only two kinds of people: the weak and the strong.
3. Teachers should tell the children what to do and not worry about what the children want.
4. I have often been punished unfairly.
5. If a person doesn't like the way our country does things he should just keep his mouth shut.
6. I refuse to play some games because I am not good at them.
7. I often feel as if I had done something wrong or bad.
8. Most people are honest because they are afraid of being caught.
9. Most people will cheat if they can gain something by it.
10. Most of the other countries of the world are really against us, but are just afraid to show it.
11. Most people hate it when they have to help someone else.
12. It is really true that you will have bad luck if a black cat crosses your path.
13. I have more than my share of things to worry about.

Other studies have shown that items like these that at first glance seem to be irrelevant to prejudicial attitudes, are integrally related to the total value-attitude system. This general finding supports the contention that "prejudice is frequently woven firmly into a style of life" (Allport, 1954). The style of life or the personality dynamics that characterize the highly prejudiced individual have been shown to be composed of the following (Frenkel-Brunswik, 1948; Adorno et al., 1950):

1. A tendency toward self-glorification, ascribing to oneself predominantly positive traits and the denial or rationalization of negative traits.

2. A tendency to view the masculine and feminine roles in dichotomous terms, the male as energetic, assertive, and decisive, the female as passive and soft. The prejudiced individual will not admit to possessing any of the traits of the opposite sex.

3. A tendency to view justice in nonabstract terms and to be guided largely by conventionalism and moralism.

4. A tendency to express aggression explosively and diffusely without clear awareness of the cause.

5. A tendency toward rigidity, to conceive values and religion in their most dogmatic form and the inability to tolerate ambiguity.

6. A tendency to repress (to deny from consciousness) fear, weakness, sex impulses, and aggressive feelings against authority figures.

7. A tendency to seek power, to manipulate others, and the inability to establish "affectionate and individualized interpersonal relations."

8. A tendency to view the outside world as threatening, dangerous, and untrustworthy.

The following case description, adapted from Frenkel-Brunswik (1951), demonstrates how prejudice is woven into the fabric of the personality of an eleven-year-old boy. Karl is somewhat unusual in that he exhibits so many of the characteristics found statistically in the prejudiced group but seldom converging in one individual. He may be considered an archetype.

Karl's statements about minority groups reflect a deep-seated prejudice. Karl says about Negroes: "They make trouble, start wars. I wouldn't mind if they moved all the Negroes out of my city. I would like to have a couple of them for good fighters. They are good fighters when they fight with a knife." About Jews he says: "They think they are smart and go anywhere they please. They think they are hot. They dress up in all kinds of jewelry. Some just kidnap girls and boys and use them for slaves." Karl gives his reaction to Hitler as follows: "He was a little bit O.K. Sometimes he got a little bit too mean and did dirty stuff like putting lighted matches in the toenails of Americans." Speaking of the Germans and Japanese he says, "We should put all the Germans and Japs on an island and put an atom bomb to it."

Karl is described as being an unusually fat and passive boy with a history of many illnesses. Throughout the interviews he shows a strong underlying anxiety of being lost and of being deprived of food. He is much more concerned about the well-being of animals than that of people. His emphasis on order, regularity, and cleanliness in the external physical environment is in sharp contrast to the turmoil and chaos that he recommends in his human environment.

Karl's attitudes toward his teachers reflect an ambivalence to authority. He first states, "I like everything about teachers." Later on he complains about unjust treatment by teachers: "A lot of them make you go to the principal's office or out of the room for something you didn't do. I had that happen a lot of times." Karl begins his description of the perfect boy with the quality of perfect obedience to teachers. Like other prejudiced children, Karl tends to view the adult-child relationship as one in which the weak child is expected to exhibit a self-negating surrender to the stronger adult. Karl seems unaware that he hardly fulfills his own requirement of submissive obedience to authority. He exhibits an identification with the aggressor as described earlier in this chapter. He is possessed by destructive inclinations that he can direct only in part toward the authority figures to whom he feels an allegiance, but that he feels free to express toward those individuals and groups considered by him to be underdogs. Karl tells of corporal punishment at home and indicates that he is in favor of very severe punishment of children for relatively minor misconduct. His own reactions to anger are explosive and violent. He says, "When I am angry I do anything I can—bite, pull hair, kick, tear into them."

He has a rigid conception of sex roles, stressing politeness in girls and assertiveness in boys. In most of the stories he tells to the pictures of the Thematic Apperception Test, a murder is commited and it is the man who is the victim. He tends to see the woman as safe and provided for. In more overt expression of hostility Karl shows more of this feeling toward his mother than toward the father. On a rating of attitudes toward parents, Karl earns the extreme rating of 6 toward both parents, indicating the feeling of being threatened and victimized by their hostility.

There is evidence that much of the boy's personality structure can be traced to the home situation. The interviewer describes the home as crowded, with overstuffed and dreary oak furniture and with lace doilies on the tables. All this seems to represent a determined effort on the part of the parents to stress their middle-class identification and to avoid the possibility of being grouped with the underprivileged. This anxiety stems at least in part from the fact that the socioeconomic history of the family is highly unstable.

Both parents come from broken homes. The father does not like to talk about his own father, whom he describes as a drunkard and psychopath who deserted his family. He is much more ready to discuss his grandfather, by whom he was raised: "My grandfather was really strict. He had thirteen children, and even when they were grown up there wasn't one of them that would talk back to him and he could handle any of them." Karl's mother experienced her parents' divorce and then a series of stepfathers. Both Karl's parents continue to fantasy about achieving fame some day.

In discussing their children, Karl's parents emphasize that they made rules for them that had to be strictly obeyed. For instance, the children had to be in bed "sharp at six without fail." Asked whether the children ever had tantrums, the mother said: "I should say not. They had better not. If they got mad I just sat them in a chair and said to stay there until they could behave. I guess they never really had tantrums." This is at variance with boy's description of his temper outbursts whose report is probably much closer to the truth.

Both parents report that they use spanking as a method of discipline. The father openly favors a rigid dichotomization of the sex roles: "Boys shouldn't do work in the home." In explaining her children's personalities the mother relies heavily on astrology. About Karl she says: "He is a dreamer of far places. He will go far and wide. The stars show that."

Both parents are ethnically extremely prejudiced. They consider Negroes America's biggest problem. The mother tells how, when she was a waitress, she personally took it on herself to put Negroes in their place. She would give them a glass of water and then ignore them. "When they went out we smashed the glass behind the counter good and hard so they were sure to hear it. The Chinese and Japanese should be separate too." About the Jews the mother says: "The Bible says they will always be persecuted. You know it wasn't a small thing they did—crucifying Christ— God said they would be punished till the end of time."

This description of the personality that exhibits a tendency toward prejudice should make the teacher aware that the approach to prevention and remediation of prejudice cannot be direct. Such procedures as providing information, punishment, or enforced contact are not very likely to touch on the basic personality structure. On the contrary these procedures often lead to reinforcement of the prejudice. There is a story told of such a person who held a prejudice toward women drivers. One day he noticed a car proceeding erratically down a street and he commented, "There goes a woman driver." When he drew alongside the car and caught a glimpse of a man behind the wheel he modified his statement, "He drives just like a woman driver." When the prejudice serves deep-seated personality needs it distorts perception and understanding so that information, enforced contact, and other direct procedures are generally misinterpreted by the prejudiced person.

A person showing a number of the characteristics listed above is not a likeable kind of individual. He is likely to induce behavior in others that will confirm his negative view of the world and his restricted value scheme. The teacher must not be drawn into this net. To overcome the tendency toward self-glorification, the teacher must provide experiences to establish an adequate basis of self-esteem from which objective self-evaluation can grow. To overcome the tendency to view justice in non-abstract terms, the teacher must provide consistency in the application of justice; consistency in terms of abstract principles not in terms of superficial criteria of uniformity or a rigid code of rules. To overcome the tendency to express aggression without a clear awareness of the cause, the teacher must accept the legitimacy of hostile feelings and provide opportunities for discussion of situations that would ordinarily induce hostility. The discussion of role playing in Chapter 8 and the discussion of aggression in Chapter 11, elaborate on this point. The tendency to seek power and to manipulate others without establishing individualized relationships can be counteracted by the teacher's example of warm, nonexploitative relationships with pupils. The tendency to view the world as threatening and untrustworthy can only be countered by security-giving and dependable forms of social interaction. These statements are not intended as prescriptions for the treatment of personality distortions that lead to prejudice. They are rather an attempt to summarize what has been stated earlier in this chapter when the importance of love and consistency in the fostering of a mature autonomous morality were discussed. It is the teacher's painstaking task to lead children to a realization that they can achieve true self-enhancement when they accept themselves and consequently permit the enhancement of others.

SUMMARY

The teaching of values in our pluralistic society contains in it the seeds of controversy. However, if we view the task as that of helping children develop integrated personalities, so that they seek to enhance themselves by being productive and creative, the school's role in teaching values is clarified.

The kind of environment that fosters the basic value assumptions of our society is one characterized by moral responsibility, where social conflict is resolved by common consent, where there is free access to information, and where moral standards are equitably applied.

The two dimensions of social interaction that are crucial in the development of sound moral judgment are affection and control. Genuine love must be made objective, it must be given without contingency, one shows love by denying as well as by consenting, and love is beneficial to the giver as well as the recipient. Control of children's behavior is essential if the behavior is to have design and meaning. Too much or too little control leads to conflict with the moral values that support integrated personalities. Both love and control are the essential ingredients in the process of identification, through which the child incorporates the values of the meaningful adults in his environment.

In the early stages of development children's behavior is amoral, that is, it is not guided by moral considerations. As they interact with their social environment they imitate the rules and accept them as provisional and specific to the situation. The next stage in moral development

is one in which the attitude toward rules is that they are sacred and external to the individual, moral heteronomy. The mature stage of moral development, moral autonomy, is one in which the individual can make
independent moral decisions that have the consistency derived from being
referred and guided by an internal sense of appropriateness.

The acquisition of a value system hinges on the process of identification as well as on directed conscious guidance. The process of
identification is defined as the modeling of oneself, usually unconscious,
in all behavior, after another person. It is through identification that one
acquires a superego and a conscience, as well as appropriate sex-typed role
behavior. The process is most influential when the one making the identification is dependent on and feels an allegiance toward the one with
whom he is identifying. Identification is facilitated when the role with
which the child is trying to identify is clear and when it is consistent
with his abilities and his self-concept. One of the most important characteristics of the teacher in terms of harnessing the energies of identification
for achieving educational aims, is that the teacher be a learner.

Classroom activities can be designed to foster a mature value system.
In the actual instruction the teacher needs to identify the concept to be
taught, he needs to select activities in which moral principles are applied,
and the students need to be made fully aware of the principle and its
applications. Textbooks also are instruments for value inculcation. Often
they are deficient in this regard, and the teacher must carry the instruction to a point where the appropriate values are experienced.

Because sectarian religious practice in public institutions is not
sanctioned by law, formal religious instruction in the public schools cannot be employed to foster the growth of moral judgment. Nevertheless,
religious diversity is a fact of our social community and this can be used
to foster a respect and acceptance of differences. In order to do this teachers themselves need to have objectified their own religious position, and
they need to appreciate the true meaning of religious freedom and the
pluralistic nature of our society.

Children can behave in accordance with a moral principle on a
number of different bases. The behavior may be described as *compliant,*
resulting from the pressure of authority or power. Behavior that is consistent with the rule may be described as *conformance,* or arising from the
desire to maintain the regard of the members of a valued group. Another
basis for the behavior is *convergence,* representing a practical compromise
or opportunistic submission to the rule. The soundest basis for moral
behavior is *consent* in which the behavior is the outgrowth of the incorporated value system.

When the teacher encounters a violation of moral principle, such
as cheating, he must analyze the motivation of the behavior. Without
sanctioning the behavior, the teacher should determine to what extent

external, teacher controlled, conditions have contributed to the violation. Correction measures aimed at the immediate situation should not preclude constructive long-range action.

A more serious manifestation of value distortion is found in delinquent behavior. Delinquent behavior has many sources. It may arise from neurotic tendencies, psychotic reactions, or it may be an adjustive reaction to the inequities of our social order. The first signs of maladaptive behavior in school that are indicative of later delinquency, usually appear before the age of eleven. In general these signs include a resentment toward the constraints of the school and a rejection of the school's aims. When it is determined that the behavior of a particular child is symptomatic of delinquency, the school must mobilize its own resources and be prepared to coordinate its efforts with other social agencies to help the child.

Prejudice is another form of value distortion. It is defined as a negative attitude toward an identifiable group and the individual members thereof, which serves to enhance the status of the bearer of the prejudice by means of disenhancing the victims of the prejudice. Prejudice may show itself in speaking about the group in a hostile way, *antilocution.* It may show itself in avoidance, discriminatory action, physical attack, and in extreme form, extermination. Prejudice has its roots in three sources, in the prevailing cultural norm, in family influences, and in individual personality needs. Institutional change, such as integrated schooling and housing, can change the prevailing cultural norm and can counteract the effects of the self-fulfilling prophecy. In dealing with the child whose personality needs are such as to require a group against which he can express his hostility, the teacher must be careful not to be induced to respond in kind toward the hostile child. The teacher's behavior needs to be such that: the child will come to have some esteem of himself; he will come to see the abstract principle covering a code of conduct; he will feel free to recognize and accept his feelings, even his hostile ones; he will identify with the teacher's warm and accepting attitudes toward others; and he will find in the classroom security-giving and dependable forms of social interaction.

READING REFERENCES

Allport, G. W., *The Nature of Prejudice.* Garden City, N.Y.: Doubleday Anchor Books, 1958. (Originally published by Addison-Wesley, 1954) (particularly chaps. 1, 9, 10, 18, 19, 25, 27, 30).

Association for Supervision and Curriculum Development 1963 Yearbook, *New Insights and the Curriculum.* Washington, D. C.: National Education Association (particularly chaps. 9-12).

Bandura, A. and R. H. Walters, *Social Learning and Personality Development.* New York: Holt, Rinehart and Winston, 1963 (particularly chaps. 2-5).

Clark, K. B., *Prejudice and Your Child,* 2d ed. Boston: Beacon, 1963.

Fromm, E., *Escape from Freedom.* New York: Holt, Rinehart and Winston, 1941.

————, *Man for Himself.* New York: Holt, Rinehart and Winston, 1947.

Kvaraceus, W. C., *Juvenile Delinquency* (What Research Says to the Teacher No. 15). Washington, D. C.: National Education Association, 1958.

Peck, R. F. and R. J. Havighurst, *The Psychology of Character Development.* New York: John Wiley & Sons, 1960.

Piaget, J., *The Moral Judgment of the Child.* New York: Free Press of Glencoe, 1948 (first published in French, 1932).

EDUCATIONAL PRACTICE

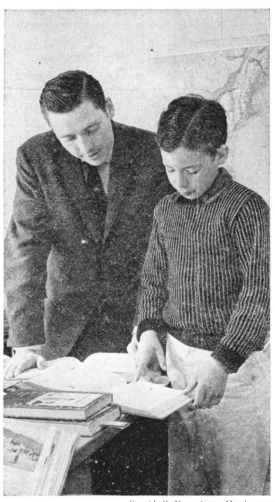

Campbell Hays from Monkmeyer

PART 2
EDUCATIONAL PRACTICE

CHAPTER 7

THE MANAGEMENT
OF LEARNING

In the six chapters of Part 1 the various psychological principles that should guide the teacher in planning the most effective instruction have been considered, starting with the theory and showing its application to practice. In Part 2, the practical problems in education are considered first, and analyzed in psychological terms.

Educational practice has changed markedly over the past five decades and it is reasonable to expect that it will continue to change. In part the change can be attributed to more comprehensive statements of educational theory, in part to the changes in our society in technology and social outlook, and in part to the insights derived from psychological research. It is this latter basis for educational change that is elaborated here. The matter of educational practice or the management of learning is not one of finding a specific solution to a specific problem but rather one of change in the educational instrumentality, the method, based on an understanding of the outcomes and on a desire to bring the method into harmony with a changing conception of educational aims.

THE SIZE OF THE LEARNING TASK
AND THE DISTRIBUTION OF TIME

A fundamental decision that the teacher must make in the management of learning is to determine the size of the unit of instruction and the distribution of time. In each area of instruction, be it beginning reading, elementary arithmetic, high school chemistry or college history, these decisions must be made. Some parts of the decision are made for us by tradition and by administrative necessity but a large measure of freedom still remains to the teacher. To illustrate the issue: shall we start in reading with the phonemes (the units of speech sound), the whole word or the entire statement? Should we teach five or six spaces on the typewriter keyboard until these have been mastered or shall we teach the entire keyboard? Similar questions have been considered in Chapter 3, in the discussion of the sequence of instruction. Related to the issue of the size of the instructional unit is that of the most effective distribution of the time to be devoted to the learning task. Should we keep the learner at the task in blocks of time as large as possible or shall we distribute the time? These issues have been studied under the heading of "Whole versus part learning" and "Massed versus distributed practice."

Whole Versus Part Learning

The terms whole and part are somewhat ambiguous when applied to learning tasks. A definition of whole will depend upon the learner's capacity to see relationships. In general we learn by wholes when the activity that results from the learning is unified, functional, and independently integrated. We learn by parts when the activity resulting from learning needs to be incorporated into a larger context of activity before it becomes functional. Considering the learner's capacity and the ways in which he would use the learning, a sentence such as "This is a dog," would be a whole for the beginning reader with each of the words and letters being parts of that whole. In senior high school the plot of the Shakespearean play would be the whole and the various acts, scenes, and segments of dialogue would be considered parts of that whole. In the examples used it is obvious that the wholes would, from another point of view, be considered parts; the sentence in primary reading could contribute meaning to a series of sentences and the entire play could be viewed as contributing to an appreciation of all of Shakespeare's works or Elizabethan literature generally. Nevertheless, these examples of wholes do have the quality of unity in the context they are used, whereas what we have called parts would at best have only tenuous meaning and function if removed from within the context of the more unified whole.

The early laboratory evidence dealing with this problem demonstrated that whole learning was superior to learning by parts. This evidence accumulated in spite of the fact that the learning tasks were lists of nonsense syllables and the pair of syllables could be considered as much a whole as the entire list of syllables. Nevertheless, it was shown that going through a list of nonsense syllables from beginning to end over and over again was more economical and efficient than memorizing the first pair, then the second and so on. It was shown that the amount of time spent in putting together the separate parts was of such an order as to make the part procedure uneconomical.

Symonds (1958) has reviewed the literature on this topic and he points out that one investigator demonstrated the superiority of the whole method in the learning of typewriting; in another study the sentence unit was shown to be superior to the word-unit method in learning shorthand, and a third study likewise concluded that in learning piano music the whole method was more efficient.

The reader may well wonder at this point how this principle is to be applied to a course in history or a play by George Bernard Shaw? How can the student attempt to learn a long piano piece by going over the whole piece over and over again? The finding that the whole approach is superior does not suggest that the learner never become aware of the details. It suggests rather that the learner have a bird's eye view of his task before proceeding to obtain a more detailed view. Thus, he might read a précis of the play, a few paragraphs outlining the period in history, or he might listen to the piano selection on a recording. After gaining a general overview of the learning task, the learner is prepared to work out the separate details and their contribution to the whole pattern. It is important to note that for many learning tasks, effective performance will require a mastery of the separate parts of the task and an understanding of the individual components. As Bugelski (1956) points out, "one does not seek the services of automobile mechanics who know the nature of the internal combustion engine in general." One may however seek the services of a mechanic who started his career by understanding the principles of chemistry and physics underlying the operation of the automobile.

Gray (1948), who has contributed much to the development of reading instruction, in discussing the importance of the child's word attack skills in reading, makes note of this point:

> Skill in phonetic analysis is essential for independence in identifying new printed words, but this skill should be based on fundamental understandings of how sounds and their letter symbols *function* in our language; and these understandings should develop as generalizations based on the child's experience with words—*words which he learns visually as meaningful wholes, rather than mechanically as a series of letter sounds* (page 32, italics added).

Hovland (1951), who has studied this problem carefully, makes note of the necessity of taking into account the learner's capacity in determining the appropriate size of the task. He states: "The best advice seems to be to learn by using the largest units that are meaningful and within the individual's capacity. The older the individual, the higher his intelligence, the more practice he has had, the greater is the size of the unit he is able to handle."

It has been reported that the learner's motivation is better sustained when he achieves success through mastery of the simpler segments of a learning task. It should be noted, however, that the procedure recommended should lead to a high level of interest and motivation. Becoming familiar with the overall organization will serve to make the learning of contributing parts more efficient and this success will maintain motivation. Nevertheless the teacher should not wait too long to give the learner an opportunity to break up the learning task into smaller units. The size of the unit for the absorptive phases of learning can be larger than that appropriate for the more active, performing aspect of the learning, where the reinforcements for successful performance need to come more quickly.

Distribution of Time

The distribution of time is related to the division of the material to be presented. In many instances the school schedule determines how often and how long a period of time will be allotted to a given subject area. Within the restrictions of the school schedule, however, the teacher does have a certain degree of freedom in determining, for example, whether to spend all of a class period on one task or to divide the period among several tasks. This might be illustrated by stating the question as follows: If we have seventy-five minutes to devote to spelling each week, how should this time be distributed? Should we allow two periods of thirty-five to forty minutes each or five periods of fifteen minutes each? The problem of distribution of practice time has been studied intensively in the psychological laboratory. These studies have shown consistently that spaced or distributed practice periods produce better results than massed practice. These studies have also demonstrated that for each type of learning activity, a different amount of rest between practice sessions is indicated. The findings of Lorge (1930) are typical. In his study subjects practiced mirror drawing and code substitution under three different practice conditions. The first group practiced without rest intervals, a second group was allowed to rest for one minute between trials, and a third group had one day intervals between trials. As can be seeen in Figure 7.1 the time per trial for the groups with distributed practice dropped rapidly after the first trial as compared with the group working under conditions of massed practice.

Although it is generally true that short practice sessions with long rest periods are more efficient than massed practice sessions without rest intervals, there are some exceptions to this rule. If the task is of such a nature as to require a great deal of preparation, warm-up and clean-up, as for example in art instruction, then a larger number of short periods would use more time not directly focused on the task. If the total time required to master a skill is short, massed practice seems preferable. Cer-

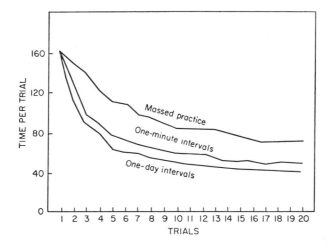

FIGURE 7.1 *Although the three groups start out equally, the group with rest intervals between trials (distributed practice) improve their performance more rapidly, taking less time per trial, than the group woking continuously through all twenty trials. From I. D. Lorge,* Influence of Regularly Interpolated Time Intervals Upon Subsequent Learning, *Contribution to Education no. 438, New York: Teachers College, Columbia University, 1930.*

tain kinds of tasks, such as problem solving and creative thinking, must be worked on in a continuous block of time in order for the student to arrive at a satisfactory solution. In this kind of learning interruption would be detrimental. Where interruption is inevitable, as in a high school class period, time should be set aside to summarize at the end of the first period and to review at the beginning of the next session.

With these qualifications in mind, the teacher will find that both for purposes of improving a skill such as in shorthand or for the sake of long-term retention, schedules that permit distribution of time are superior. This is particularly true in the case of beginning learning and where the learning task is complex and difficult. Fatigue, boredom, and a number of other inhibitory factors cause the massed effort to be less productive. In spite of the fact that distributed practice permits forgetting to take place between trials, there seems to be sufficient consolidation of the response during the rest interval, to result in better performance when practice is distributed.

In some instances the situation demands mastery of a skill in a short time, for example, if one is planning a trip to a foreign country and desires to learn something of the language in two months or so, or in the case of cramming for an examination when circumstances would not permit the distribution of learning over a longer period of time. (In the case of cramming, research evidence points to much greater long-term loss than when learning is distributed.) In these special cases there is little alternative to massing of practice but periodic rest periods, ten minutes out of each hour or so, have been shown to result in greater learning than if the rest period is eliminated and the time used for continuation of study. The spacing of practice can also be accomplished by changing to different aspects of the same task. In fact it has been argued (McGuigan, 1960) "that much of the superiority of the whole method is due to the fact that it entails distributed practice."

The following description of the sequence of work during one week of spelling activity based on the fifth-grade speller of a popular spelling series (Patton and Johnson, 1956), will demonstrate the principles of whole, spaced, and varied learning activities.

On the first day the students are introduced to the new words that appear in a story. The new words (sixteen to twenty in number) are underlined in the story and appear separately in a list printed to the left of the story. The student is encouraged to look at each word and to say it, to note what letter stands for each sound and whether any letters are silent, to spell the word to himself without looking at it, and to write the word from memory. During the second day the student works on a series of exercises that develop the primary and secondary meanings of the new words. On the third day the student takes a trial test in which the teacher dictates the words, using them in sentences. The student makes note of any misspelled words and enters these correctly in a separate section of his notebok. The exercises for the fourth day are designed to "concentrate attention on recognition of phonetic elements, on development of word-recognition and word-building skills, and on special spelling difficulties in words." On the fifth and last day the student takes a final test on these words. This program is followed for five weeks, each week with a new list of words. On the sixth week the previous work is reviewed and special skills such as the use of the dictionary are developed. This type of systematic program serves to arrange the learning activity so that the learning is whole rather than part; provides for distribution of practice and variation of activity.

GUIDING THE STUDENT'S LEARNING ACTIVITIES

In addition to blocking out the learning task and arranging for the proper distribution of time, the teacher faces a number of other difficult decisions in guiding the student's learning activities. These decisions center around the timing, the amount and the kind of guidance to be provided. Although the research literature does not provide sufficient evidence to support a series of definitive suggestions, it does lead to a number of useful principles for guiding the student's learning.

The aim of instruction is to help the student become an independent, systematic learner, capable of defining his own problem and inde-

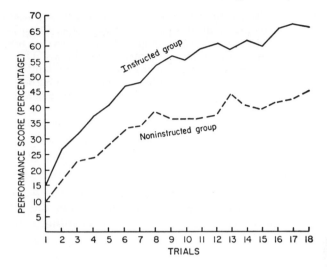

FIGURE 7.2 *Differences in acquisition of skill under conditions of instruction and noninstruction. From D. R. Davies,* "*The Effects of Tuition Upon the Process of Learning a Complex Motor Skill,*" Journal of Educational Psychology, *1945, 36, pp. 352–365.*

pendently applying the appropriate problem solving techniques to it. To achieve this aim the teacher is required to assist and guide the learner.

That guidance and formal instruction are beneficial has been demonstrated in a number of different studies and is commonly recognized as a consequence of the usual educational experience. In a study by Davies (1945), for example, two groups of students were given different kinds of experience in acquiring skill in archery. One group was given preliminary verbal instruction before using the bow and arrow as well as systematic guidance while practicing. The other group practiced without instruction. As might be expected the group receiving instruction surpassed the group that practiced without instruction from the first trial to the end of the experiment (Figure 7.2). It should be noted, however, that the learner in the instructed group received more than verbal instruction; he was given as much opportunity to practice as the noninstructed learner. These results are as would be predicted from the studies in transfer of training reported in Chapter 5.

Davies states that instruction increases the flexibility of the learner's behavior and prevents him from adopting a procedure that will cause his performance to level off below his potentialities. She states that in providing instruction the teacher aids the student in these ways:

(a) He directs the learner's attention to more adequate techniques than those the learner has been employing. He thus stimulates the learner to break up faulty techniques, even at the temporary loss of achievement. In teaching a complex skill, this process is repeated again and again.

(b) The teacher promotes the growth of intellectual insight on the part of the learner into the factors related to his success. The instructions given by the teacher make a major contribution to the improvement of the learner's conception of the skill that he is attempting to master.

(c) Finally, the teacher's attitudes and encouragement serve to give the learner a feeling of security and confidence in giving up a familiar mode of behavior and seeking one that is better (Davies 1945, page 364).

The teacher can use different techniques in guiding the learner. He must select the one that seems appropriate for the particular learning task. The teacher may provide verbal instruction, a model for imitation or mechanical guidance. In the case of verbal instruction the teacher must guard against assuming that what is clear and meaningful to him, will also be clear and meaningful to the learner. The teacher's background experience is generally such as to invest a verbal statement with meaning that may not necessarily be conveyed to the learner. Most observers of educational practice have been critical of the heavy reliance that teachers place on verbal instruction. Nevertheless, it should be recognized that combined with actual experience, verbal instruction is most effective. The second mode of guidance, a model for imitation, is useful in guiding the student in the acquisition of an observable skill. The model should be of such a nature as to demonstrate clearly the relationships of the various aspects of the skill without distorting the total performance. The slow-motion film is useful in this regard for demonstrating motor skills. Here again it must be recognized that the learner cannot learn merely by observing someone else's performance, he must become actively engaged in the learning. Mechanical guidance, such as directing the child's hand while he writes or plays the piano or providing model letters for tracing, can be useful if it provides the learner with a feel for the act as a whole; it can be detrimental if it deprives him of the sense of confidence and initiative that he will need in performing on his own.

McGeoch and Irion (1952) have summed up the research findings on the usefulness of guidance as follows:

> The effectiveness of guidance is a function of its amount and of the point in practice at which it is introduced. Small numbers . . . of guided trials early in practice . . . are the most effective in facilitating learning. The influence of guidance diminishes as its amount increases and as the point of its introduction is moved away from the early stages of practice. Large amounts of guidance, or amounts given at unfavorable points during practice, may hinder learning (pages 288-289).

SELF-INSTRUCTION MATERIAL AND DEVICES

In addition to the practical concern about the size of the instructional unit, the distribution of practice time, and instituting appropriate forms of guidance, the teacher must concern himself with the internal arrangement of the content of the learning task. This again is a problem of sequence first introduced in Chapter 3. The arrangement of the material so that the learner can use it without the aid of the teacher is considered here. Such devices have been used as long as there have been books, workbooks, and assignment note books. The recent developments in programmed instruction, self-instructional materials, or teaching machines, based on the work of Skinner in instrumental conditioning (discussed in Chapter 3), represent an attempt to design the material of instruction so that large segments of the curriculum can be adapted to self-instruction. Programmed instruction has been described by a number of writers, for example, Skinner (1958), Galanter (1959), Lumsdaine and Glaser (1960), Green (1962), and Deterline (1962). It should not be presumed from the recent dates of these publications that the idea is an entirely new discovery. Pressey (1926) had developed a device primarily for evaluation that is recognized as a forerunner to the teaching machine and Richards (1943) recommended the sequencing of instruction very similar to that found in most modern programs. Yet it remained for the more recent workers to bring these instructional procedures into the framework of psychological theorizing and laboratory research.

Although there are many different kinds of programmed material, they all have these characteristics in common: (1) the material is presented in small sequenced units, (2) the learner makes frequent responses as he proceeds through the material and, (3) the learner receives immediate information (feedback) about the adequacy of his response. Before elaborating on these features, here are some examples and the external features of one form of programmed instruction.

The preparation of the material for a program of instruction requires a careful, step by step, analysis of the stages through which the learner must proceed in acquiring a fully developed skill or grasp of the concept. Table 7.1 shows the 6 steps that would be needed to teach the spelling of the word "manufacture" and Table 7.2 shows a larger unit in physics on light and heat. The programmed material is installed in a machine such as is shown in Figure 7.3. The word to be learned with a definition and an example of the word in context appear in the slot of the machine as frame 1. The student copies the word. He checks to see if it is correct and when it is he brings up frame 2 by pushing a lever. In this frame discrimination and generalization are established. The learner must discriminate a part of the word manufacture from the whole word and he must generalize the relationship of manufacture to factory. Frame

TABLE 7.1   A SET OF FRAMES DESIGNED TO TEACH A THIRD- OR
FOURTH-GRADE PUPIL TO SPELL THE WORD MANUFACTURE

1. Manufacture means to make or build. *Chair factories manufacture chairs.* Copy the word here:
   □ □ □ □ □ □ □ □ □ □ □

2. Part of the word is like part of the word factory. Both parts come from an old word meaning *make* or *build*.
   m a n u □ □ □ □ u r e

3. Part of the word is like part of the word manual. Both parts come from an old word for *hand*. Many things used to be made by hand.
   □ □ □ □ f a c t u r e

4. The same letter goes in both spaces:
   m □ n u f □ c t u r e

5. The same letter goes in both spaces:
   m a n □ f a c t □ r e

6. Chair factories □ □ □ □ □ □ □ □ □ □ □ chairs.

Source: B. F. Skinner, "Teaching Machines," *Science*, 1958, **128**, p. 972.

3 does the same thing with another part of the word. In the next frame the student begins to spell the word without copying and because he must insert the same letter in two places, the chances of giving the correct response are greatly increased. The same procedure is followed in frame 5. In the last frame the student is required to spell the word completely. The same careful kind of programming can be done for teaching some aspects of arithmetic, the factual aspects of science (see Table 7.2), geography, and the like.

Glaser (1960) has indicated that the number of frames required to teach school subjects can be high indeed. Four grades of spelling may require 25,000 frames. A high school physics program used 3,000 frames to teach six weeks of a course.

Skinner points out that it is not the machine that teaches but rather the presentation of programmed material. He calls it a labor-saving device in that it can bring one teacher into contact with many students. This is the effect of a textbook, except for the fact that with the machine the student remains active and involved. Because the machine paces the material according to the individual needs of the learner, it allows for individual differences to a greater extent than either lectures or textbooks. Crowder (1960) has introduced a variation in programming, called branching, so that the learner proceeds by larger or smaller steps through the content of the learning task, depending on the extent of his understanding

FIGURE 7.3   *Student at work on a teaching machine. One frame of material is partly visible in the left-hand window. The student writes his response on a strip of paper exposed at the right. He then lifts a lever with his left hand, advancing his written response under a transparent cover and uncovering the correct response in the upper corner of the frame. If he is right, he moves the lever to the right, punching a hole alongside the response he has called right and altering the machine so that that frame will not appear again when he goes through the series a second time. A new frame appears when the lever is returned to its starting position. From B. F. Skinner, "Teaching Machines,"* Science, *1958, 128, p. 971.*

of the previous material. The questions in the program are so constructed as to diagnose the student's needs, and the program provides alternate materials suited to the different needs. The student's answer to a particular question determines which items he will work on next. If the

TABLE 7.2   PART OF A PROGRAM IN HIGH-SCHOOL PHYSICS.[a]

Sentence to be completed	*Word to be supplied*
1. The important parts of a flashlight are the battery and the bulb. When we "turn on" a flashlight, we close a switch which connects the battery with the _____.	bulb
2. When we turn on a flashlight, an electric current flows through the fine wire in the _____ and causes it to grow hot.	bulb
3. When the hot wire glows brightly, we say that it gives off or sends out heat and _____.	light
4. The fine wire in the bulb is called a filament. The bulb "lights up" when the filament is heated by the passage of a(n) _____ current.	electric
5. When a weak battery produces little current, the fine wire, or _____, does not get very hot.	filament
6. A filament which is *less* hot sends out or gives off _____ light.	less
7. "Emit" means "send out." The amount of light sent out, or "emitted," by a filament depends on how _____ the filament is.	hot
8. The higher the temperature of the filament the _____ the light emitted by it.	brighter, stronger
9. If a flashlight battery is weak, the _____ in the bulb may still glow, but with only a dull red color.	filament
10. The light from a very hot filament is colored yellow or white. The light from a filament which is not very hot is colored _____.	red
11. A blacksmith or other metal worker sometimes makes sure that a bar of iron is heated to a "cherry red" before hammering it into shape. He uses the _____ of the light emitted by the bar to tell how hot it is.	color
12. Both the color and the amount of light depend on the _____ of the emitting filament or bar.	temperature
13. An object which emits light because it is hot is called "incandescent." A flashlight bulb is an incandescent source of _____.	light
14. A neon tube emits light but remains cool. It is, therefore, not an incandescent _____ of light.	source
15. A candle flame is hot. It is a(n) _____ source of light.	incandescent
16. The hot wick of a candle gives off small pieces or particles of carbon which burn in the flame. Before or while burning, the hot particles send out, or _____, light.	emit
17. A long candlewick produces a flame in which oxygen does not reach all the carbon particles. Without oxygen the particles cannot burn. Particles which do not burn rise about the flame as _____.	smoke

[a] The machine presents one item at a time. The student completes the item and then uncovers the corresponding word or phrase shown at the right.

TABLE 7.2 (*continued*) PART OF A PROGRAM IN HIGH-SCHOOL PHYSICS.

Sentence to be completed	Word to be supplied
18. We can show that there are particles of carbon in a candle flame, even when it is not smoking, by holding a piece of metal in the flame. The metal cools some of the particles before they burn, and the unburned carbon _____ collect on the metal as soot.	particles
19. The particles of carbon in soot or smoke no longer emit light because they are _____ than when they were in the flame.	cooler, colder
20. The reddish part of a candle flame has the same color as the filament in a flashlight with a weak battery. We might guess that the yellow or white parts of a candle flame are _____ than the reddish part.	hotter
21. "Putting out" an incandescent electric light means turning off the current so that the filament grows too _____ to emit light.	cold, cool
22. Setting fire to the wick of an oil lamp is called _____ the lamp.	lighting
23. The sun is our principal _____ of light, as well as of heat.	source
24. The sun is not only very bright but very hot. It is a powerful _____ source of light.	incandescent
25. Light is a form of energy. In "emitting light" an object changes, or "converts," one form of _____ into another.	energy
26. The electrical energy supplied by the battery in a flashlight is converted to _____ and _____.	heat, light; light, heat
27. If we leave a flashlight on, all the energy stored in the battery will finally be changed or _____ into heat and light.	converted
28. The light from a candle flame comes from the _____ released by chemical changes as the candle burns.	energy
29. A nearly "dead" battery may make a flashlight bulb warm to the touch, but the filament may still not be hot enough to emit light—in other words, the filament will not be _____ at that temperature.	incandescent
30. Objects, such as a filament, carbon particles, or iron bars, become incandescent when heated to about 800 degrees Celsius. At that temperature they begin to _____ _____.	emit light
31. When raised to any temperature about 800 degrees Celsius, an object such as an iron bar will emit light. Although the bar may melt or vaporize, its particles will be _____ no matter how hot they get.	incandescent
32. About 800 degrees Celsius is the lower limit of the temperature at which particles emit light. There is no upper limit of the _____ at which emission of light occurs.	temperature
33. Sunlight is _____ by very hot gases near the surface of the sun.	emitted

TABLE 7.2 (*continued*)   PART OF A PROGRAM IN HIGH-SCHOOL PHYSICS.

Sentence to be completed	*Word to be supplied*
34. Complex changes similar to an atomic explosion generate the great heat which explains the _____ of light by the sun.	emission
35. Below about _____ degrees Celsius an object is not an incandescent source of light.	800

Source: B. F. Skinner, "Teaching Machines," *Science*, 1958, **128**, p. 973.

student answers incorrectly he is given an item containing information designed to correct the error before he continues through the sequence. If he answers correctly he moves on to more advanced material. If the material is carefully programmed it can help the student give the correct answer almost every time. This sense of achievement is a strong motivator. The greatest advantage of the machine over the usual classroom situation is that it corrects and reinforces the student each time he makes the response. This form of immediate feedback cannot be achieved easily in any other teaching setting.

Another virtue of the automated teaching device is that it takes into account individual differences in learning and allows for the learner to determine his own rate of progress. At one time the ideal of a program was the attainment of errorless learning. Even though this ideal is now considered not feasible, when the student fails in acquiring the right response, it is assumed first that something is wrong with the material rather than with the learner's motivation. Although the willingness of the student to learn determines the effectiveness of the teaching machine, where the learner grows in his capacity to adjust to his environment, his cooperation can readily be enlisted. If this growth in adjustive capacity takes place in a setting wherein the student is optimally involved, his readiness taken into account, and his responses are corrected and reinforced immediately, the learning will be efficient and motivated. The usefulness of the teaching machine rests on the premise that effective teaching will induce successful learning and successful learning is a potent motivator for further learning. In regard to the question of maintaining the learner's motivation in programmed instruction, Richards (1963) makes an important point. He urges that those who make up programs should use as much as possible analogy, proportion, similarity, opposition, in short relationship, rather than contiguity. He gives as an example of the latter *a b c ? e f* and as an example of the former *a:c::d:?*. Richards states, "Unluckily, contiguity is much easier for program writers to use. It needs less imagination and invention and can get along on mere mechanical assiduity instead. Correspondingly, it is likely to generate *in the learner* mere mechanical procedure, which is boring and dehumanizing, in place of constructiveness and exploratory enterprise which are enjoyable and restorative."

The use of programmed learning and automated teaching devices described here is limited to those areas of learning where the response is more or less fixed, where the expansion of meaning takes place along predetermined lines. Where we wish to develop the student's questioning attitude, exploratory behavior, creative imagination, self-awareness, or critical thinking, it is doubtful whether much use can be made of the teaching machine. In fact it would seem that the fixing of definite responses by whatever means, although essential in knowing about the world as it is or described by man, is in some respects inimical to the development of many desirable student qualities. However, insofar as the school has the responsibility of teaching predetermined bodies of subject matter, the teaching machine offers promising avenues of exploration. It may free the teacher for those kinds of teaching activities that take time and demand more involved teacher-student interaction.

Not all materials that go under some label such as programmed instruction, are worthy of adoption. The user of such material must evaluate these proposed materials. To aid the educator in this process of evaluation, the governing boards of the American Psychological Association, the American Educational Research Association, and the Department of Audio-Visual Instruction of the National Education Association, have approved a statement reflecting their position on the evaluation of self-instructional materials and devices. The following is adapted from that statement.[1]

Any evaluation of a teaching machine requires an assessment of the availability and quality of programs for each type of machine, as well as its mechanical dependability. Only those programs compatible with a particular machine can be considered as available for use with it. (A list of commercially available programs and devices may be obtained for fifty cents from the Department of Audio-Visual Instruction of the National Education Association in Washington, D. C.)

In evaluating the specific content that a self-instructional program purports to teach, the program can be examined to determine what the student is required to do and whether it reflects the kind of competence the educator wishes to achieve. Just any set of question and answer material does not constitute a self-instructional program. The steps in a program can be examined to see if they embody a careful, logical progression of the subject matter, if they require the student to respond to the critical aspects of each item or to perform the important operation that that item was meant to teach.

---

[1] The statement in its entirety may be found in the *American Psychologist*, 1961, **16,** p. 512.

An important feature of almost all self-instructional materials is the record of the student's responses, which provides a basis for revising the program. The prospective purchaser should ask about the extent to which revision has been based on student response and how the preliminary tryout was conducted. The effectiveness of a program can be assessed by evaluating students' learning and retention. The prospective purchaser should determine if such evaluation data are available.

Active experimentation with self-instructional materials and devices in school systems is to be encouraged prior to large-scale adoption.

INDEPENDENT LEARNING

It is obvious that the teacher cannot constantly be at the side of every student guiding him in his learning activities, nor can programmed material take care of all the student's learning activities. Even if this could be so it would not be desirable, as our aim is to allow the student to become an independent learner and our means for accomplishing this aim cannot contradict the aim itself. Students cannot become independent if the educational procedures foster and encourage dependence. In some traditional classrooms the independent learning activities were considered necessary evils. These learning activities were assigned as "busy" work to a part of the class so as to enable the teacher to give direct instruction to another group. The group not receiving this direct instruction had to be kept from interfering with the current work of the teacher and the students often sensed this. One child referred to these assignments as "seed" work having misheard the teacher's name for it, "seat" work. Rather than have periods during the day in which the child goes to "seed," it is preferable to establish a classroom organization in which these independent activities are planned for and designed to accomplish the worthwhile objectives of the class. Smith et al. (1958) have described this kind of classroom organization in which children are able to work in such ways as to develop characteristics of cooperativeness, independence, and social responsibility. This type of classroom organization will allow each child to be involved in meaningful and purposeful activity during every part of the school day. It serves to meet the individual needs of all children by using flexible groupings that are determined by abilities and interests. The following description of a school day, as presented by Smith,[2] will serve to point up the importance of classroom organization in developing independent learning abilities.

2 From J. A. Smith et al. (Eds.), *Independent Learning Activities*. Albany, N.Y.: Capital Area School Development Association, State University of New York at Albany, 1958, pp. 16-17.

A School Day (Grade 5)

9:00 A.M. The children have come. They have brought many things. As they enter, the teacher greets each one and examines him critically but in a friendly manner for any signs of sickness or uncleanliness. She notes that Mary's eyes are heavy, and asks Mary if she feels well. Mary tells of a restless night.

The teacher suggests she go down to see the nurse in the office and perhaps rest on a cot in the nurse's room. To John she says, "I bet you played ball on the way to school, Johnnie. How do I know? You guess!" And Johnnie, grinning, runs off to wash his hands.

The teacher goes to the front of the room and sits waiting. As the children see her there, one by one they stop their work and join the circle. They look over the list of plans left on the board from yesterday. Together they plan today and check their plans to be sure they alternate between sitting and activity.

Then the teacher says, "Do we have any contributions today?" Each child who has something, shows it to the group and tells what he knows about it. No "contribution" is brushed over or ignored. Helen brings in a painted pig, which a friend has brought her from Mexico. The class is studying Mexico and they are very interested. Bobby stands up and shows a rock he has picked up on the way to school. The teacher is inwardly overjoyed—for Bobby has never contributed before. This is a great moment for which she has been striving, but she meets it calmly and gives vent to her emotions on the 3x5 card she carries which she will later drop in his folder. "Bobby brought a rock to school today and presented it to the group! His first time before the group!" To insure further participation by Bobby, she calmly asks questions about the rock and the children also ask questions. Bobby cannot answer them so teacher says, "Let's put these questions on the board! Then some of us may find the answers in other places like our science books. Perhaps Bobby would like to look up some of the answers in work period?"

Bobby says, "I can't read the science books." So teacher reassures him at once with, "It is hard, but perhaps you and I can read them together."

9:20 A.M. The class moves into the planned work period which they had set up the last part of the previous afternoon. A group that is slow mentally is making a mural of Mexican industries. A group with a high average I.Q. is doing research on the Government Agencies and Education in Mexico. They plan to make graphs and present a report. Three children are writing letters to the Pan American Union to ask for resource materials. One girl who is not yet socially adjusted to all the children works on a scrap book cover for the reports on Mexico. One group of boys makes paper maché Aztec masks for a play they will present. One very bright girl writes the script for the play. Others prepare reports to be made in the conference period. Teacher gets a book on science and reads to Bobby.

He tells her the answers to the questions on the board from what she has read, and she prints the story simply on a sheet of paper in his words. This he is able to learn to read quickly. He then joins the group making the mural to do his part on it. Teacher circulates, taking notes, helping where she can, and jotting down ideas for future work, for individual help, and for group help.

10:30 A.M. The group comes together for a conference. One group is reporting on "Shelter in Mexico." They use activities to make their report. Bobby, who cannot read well, gives a demonstration on how to make adobe. Harry, another poor reader, has collected pictures or drawn pictures of different homes in Mexico. Sarah and Michael who read very well, read the written report which answers the questions asked by the class—questions which have resulted from their research. The report is evaluated by the class—checking with a chart they have made, "What Makes a Good Report?" The work period is also evaluated in this manner.

Bobby gives his report. Each child briefly tells what he has done during the work period and what he must do tomorrow. This is listed on the board. Also a list is made of "materials we will need tomorrow."

11:00 A.M. Time out for lunch and the teacher teaches a new Mexican Hat Game she has found in her reading.

11:15 A.M. Words are taken from the Vocabulary Chart which will need to be learned. This is Monday, so a pre-test of the words will be given to determine which ones each child will have to study. Each child makes out his own list of words to study for the week. For the slow learners, the teacher underlines the most important ones so they can begin there.

11:30 A.M. The remainder of the morning is used in studying scripts and learning how to write them so those writing scenes from the plays will know the right techniques. The teacher noted the previous day that no one was doing this correctly, so some scripts are read and examined and a chart is made bringing out the main points in writing a script. Then the teacher and the pupils write a short act together on the board, putting to use what they have learned.

1:00 P.M. Children come to front of room, check off jobs done in the morning, and review plans for the afternoon.

1:10 P.M. Reading groups

Group 1: (Good Achievement) continue research on difficult questions relating to their unit.

Group 2: With the teacher reading on a second grade level, make charts to read together and read some stories from a low difficulty level reader.

Group 3: Weak in selecting main points in a story, are doing mimeographed exercise prepared by the teacher.

Group 4: Three or four individuals, capable but not up to grade level, getting help from Mary who is a good reader. Mary has been coached by the teacher and is telling words to the children who do not know them. They are reading a story silently, later will read the stories aloud to each other striving for speed. Teacher finishes with her group and checks all the others, giving needy individuals help.

2:00 P.M. The group has made arrangements to have the gym teacher in to help them with a Mexican dance they are learning for presentation to the parents.

3:00 P.M. The class is working on a Mexican meal they are to have. Joe has brought in a recipe for chili con carne; they must increase it four times to feed a class of 32. The recipe has been printed by teacher on a large chart, so now she puts it before the group and utilizes it to teach concepts about fractions. Increasing $1\frac{1}{4}$ cups kidney beans four times presents a stimulating real-life problem which each child works out in his own way until answers agree. Teacher shows an economical way to add $1\frac{1}{4}$ four times and the children have fun trying some of those examples. Those who "catch on" help those who don't. Teacher helps those who need her.

3:30 P.M. Quick evaluation of the afternoon. "We did a lot today." "We learned much." "We had fun." "What is there to do tomorrow?" (pages 16-17)

The reader can visualize how a particular child would spend each part of a day in a class such as this. Whether the child is working alone or with a group, under the direct guidance of the teacher, or without such guidance, he is engaged in purposeful and meaningful activity of the kind that forms the primary basis of productive learning.

This classroom description is somewhat extreme in being so project-centered and having the appearance of being unstructured. Although in this class the teacher and the children know what they are about, in most classes the teacher would prefer to rely on a schedule that would, for example, call for reading or arithmetic groups to meet all at the same time. In the high school where different teachers teach different subjects, such wide-ranging projects would of course be impossible. The illustration is offered not as a model but rather to show how one teacher handled the problem of independent learning in the classroom. There are many other ways of fostering independent study in the classroom.

INDEPENDENT LEARNING AS HOMEWORK

Another educational practice that depends on the student's ability to learn independently is that of homework. The research evidence on the topic is inconclusive and at some points contradictory. For example, Strang (1937) in a survey of high-school students found no relation between amount of time spent on homework and school achievement. On the other hand Anderson (1946), who investigated the problem experimentally, using experimental and control groups, found that in the eighth grade, students who were assigned homework in English, social studies, and mathematics showed greater achievement gains than a comparable no-homework group. It is likely that the differences in experimental design, the use of students of different ages, and different kinds of homework assignments, account for the different findings in these and in other studies.

The studies with positive findings do indicate that when the curriculum is a challenging one and where homework grows naturally from such a curriculum, achievement can be expected to benefit. We should also note that homework, at least in the upper elementary grades and throughout the high-school years, is expected by the great majority of pupils and even more by parents and teachers. Although many parents, pupils, and even teachers, may favor the practice for the wrong reasons, their expectation cannot be ignored. The absence of independent study outside of school hours in a particular school may be taken by parents to be indicative of a basic weakness in the curriculum.

Bard (1958) offers a ten-point home assignment program for the secondary-school teacher. He elaborates by giving a number of practical suggestions in the various subject matter areas of the high school. His program consists of such items as: acquiring specific information through reading, listening, and observing; drilling in skills to develop accuracy and facility; classifying data; applying general principles learned in class to out-of-school situations; stimulating esthetic and emotional responses. Whatever the particular assignment, the teacher must take into account the students' home situations and other needs in making the assignment.

Strang (1960) offers four objectives to be achieved by home study. The homework assignments should be varied so that they serve generally to accomplish all of these objectives.

1. Homework should aid in the development of a sense of independence and responsibility through self-directed activity. In order to accomplish this objective the student should participate in setting the assignment, he should understand its educational purpose, and he should have an opportunity to budget his time over a period of two or three days or even longer.

2. Homework should encourage those leisure interests and activities that grow naturally from school learning. To accomplish this objective the teacher should encourage the use of the library, critical reading of various sections of the newspaper, listening to music, selective and critical TV viewing (see Chapter 13) and a number of such activities.

3. Homework should make productive use of out-of-school facilities for the enrichment of the school experience. The school environment has definite limitations and these can be overcome by the use of home and community facilities. High school students can make meaningful surveys of community conditions, they can carry on biological field surveys, prepare scrapbooks, and the like. In making assignments of this sort the teacher should be careful not to overburden the home or the community. If the student has to work alone the assignment should be within the range of his capacity to complete it independently. Most parents willingly accept the responsibility of helping out but they justifiably resent being overburdened with complex assignments. The following example given by Langdon and Stout (1957) will illustrate this point. One mother told this story.

> Jimmy had to reconstruct the skeleton of an animal for his biology class last year. I bought a hen and cooked it all day to get the meat off the bones. We couldn't use the pressure cooker for fear of softening the bones too much. We finally did get all the meat off, but it was so messed up we just threw it away.

That night Jimmy took the bones out to the workshop in the garage and started polishing them a little. Then he tried to glue them together, but in a couple of hours he came in and said it was hopeless.

We looked it over, and it looked hopeless to us, too. However, his father promised to help him the next day.

In the morning they got a diagram of a chicken skeleton and went to work. It took all of Sunday morning and most of the afternoon. We thought it was all done except for letting the glue set and dry. Then Jimmy called me from school on Monday and said that the skeleton had to be painted.

I put the spray attachment on the vacuum cleaner and sprayed the bones with some quick-drying paint.

Tuesday morning Jimmy took the skeleton to school. It made a hit and he got an A on it. He worked hard, but I wonder if we were right in helping him. He said he would fail if he didn't get it done, so his dad and I both pitched in.

This year he had to make a motor and a transformer. This wasn't so bad, because his father knows more about electricity. But do assignments like these mean much when they have to be turned into family projects? (page 372)

4. The homework assignment should reinforce school learning through practice and application. The amount of homework assigned to accomplish this objective should be carefully limited. If drill and repetition are assigned in excess the child will come to resent any kind of homework assignment and the other worthwhile aims will be defeated. However the teacher can expect that the child will review his spelling list at home, prepare sentences using his new spelling words, become more skilful in the use of arithmetic computations, and read correlated subject matter. This kind of assignment when appropriately assigned will result in improved achievement.

It should be noted that homework that is assigned in an improper spirit, perfunctorily, as busy work, or as punishment will frequently result in copying, parent resentment, or student indifference.

GUIDING THE STUDENT TO MORE EFFECTIVE STUDY

Although we recognize that when the student is interested in his study he will generally work out his own effective study procedures, there are many instances where the teacher will be required to give attention to the study procedures. Students often need help in budgeting time, in becoming aware of the requirements of proper study facilities, in checking vision or other health conditions. More important, however, is helping the student achieve a proper orientation to the learning task. A number of studies have shown that instruction in study techniques can be useful to college students. In an early study Pressey (1928) showed that college students who were having difficulty and were given instruction in study techniques were much more likely to do passing work than similar students who received no help. In a later study Ranson (1955) showed that a group of students who spent between ten and fifteen hours in a study skills clinic had a significantly higher grade-point average than an equated group of students who had not made use of the clinic. Howell (1950), working with children in grades four to eight, was able to demonstrate that a year of intensive emphasis on work-study skills produced considerable improvement in achievement. The program of instruction made the school library and the librarian the focal point around which the procedures rotated. The particular skills that were taught were: map reading, use of references, use of an index, use of the dictionary, reading graphs, charts, and tables. It is interesting to note that the greatest improvement appeared in grades four and five, indicating that instruction in work-study skills can profitably begin in these intermediate grades.

Robinson (1961), who has organized highly successful how-to-study courses, has drawn a caricature of an all too typical high school or college student.

> Once started, how does our typical student go about studying? Having found the first page of the assignment, what does he do next? He probably looks for the last page, holds the assignment up to see how thick it is, and then leaves a finger at the end of the lesson as a goal indicator. Have you ever noticed how students, after reading a while, will hold up the part read and the part to be read in order to compare their relative thickness? Also indicative is the student who, when asked what the lesson was about, looked at the length of the lesson and said "about thirty pages."
>
> Note how many students follow the lines with their fingers as they read. One almost gets an impression of dutiful line following so that the next day they can truthfully say "I don't remember, but, honest, I read every word." Some so carefully mark the cadence of their eyes that their fingernails seem to be plowing each line under. Not all are "line plowers" but certainly few reach the stage of using headings and context clues.
>
> Most readers feel that they understand the material as they read; the trouble comes later in trying to remember it. Thus as they read along they can continually murmur "mmhm," "uhhmm" as they see each idea, much as a mirror passing over the book might clearly reflect what was printed. On finishing, they push the book aside with a sigh. To an impolite inquiry as to what ideas were discussed, the typical reader has a nebulous feeling that there was much he had understood but it now is jumbled. Rather than dwell on this discomfiting fact, he prefers to say, "Well that's done! Now for the next lesson." . . .
>
> Some conscientious students try rereading their lessons in order to raise the level of their comprehension accuracy and to retard forgetting. But simply rereading a lesson several times in one sitting does not help comprehension accuracy very much; thus in one experiment the average reader got 69 percent right on an easy test after one reading of the text and only 74, 75, and 74 percent right with two, three, and four successive readings, respectively (pages 13-14).

Robinson suggests a method, called Survey Q3R. The method derives its name from the five steps recommended, namely, survey, question, read, recite, and review. The method represents an attempt to incorporate the principles of learning and retention into a program of effective study. A brief description of each step and its relationship to the appropriate principles of learning discussed previously follows.

SURVEY The student should learn how to skim over his reading assignment so as to obtain the major core ideas around which the study assignment is organized. This first step is consistent with the findings on whole-part learning discussed earlier in this chapter. There it was found that the learner is well advised to get the over-all sense of his learning task before proceeding to the details. Starting by surveying the assignment will accomplish this.

QUESTION Textbook material generally appears with section or topic headings. These headings should be converted into questions. This step will serve to orient the student to finding the answer and will thus provide a purpose to his reading. As indicated in Chapter 4, an essential characteristic of the successful problem-solving attitude is the formulation of a question for which an answer is sought. This is a difficult step to teach but students obtaining practice under supervision can acquire the skill of converting a topic heading into a question that will support the reading.

READ The first reading of the assignment becomes a search for an answer to the question. During this phase, the student needs to avoid distraction, he should seek to grasp the organization of the answer and to note how the separate details fit into this organization. In the discussion of retention in Chapter 3 it was pointed out how important the sense of organization was both for effective acquisition and for optimal retention.

RECITE Recitation is a crucial step. The student must present to himself an answer to the question that he originally formulated without referring to the book. He may find at this point that his question was not related to the reading and he will need to formulate a different question and re-read the material. The student must exercise self-criticism and evaluate his own response. He should pretend that he is explaining the idea to someone who knows nothing of the topic. Will such a person understand the explanation? Writing down a few cue ideas will provide the necessary notes for future review. This step is consistent with the point made in Chapter 3 that for learning to be effective the learner must be involved in the learning task, and that recitation is one way of accomplishing this. Learning needs to proceed to the point where it becomes demonstrable; otherwise, it is not measurable and will be easily interfered with and forgotten.

Each topic or headed section is approached this way; a survey of the assignment, the formulation of a question, reading for the answer, and recitation.

REVIEW   When the entire assignment is completed as just described, the student should go over his notes to obtain a better understanding of the organization of his assignment. Review should consist of attempting to reconstruct the outline of the entire assignment, the major headings, and the subtopics. Before starting a new assignment the student should review the preceding ones. A few minutes spent this way will keep the old learning intact and will enhance the new assignments. The retention curves (Figure 3.11) demonstrate how continual review supports retention.

SCHOOL POLICY AND LEARNING

The management of school learning is mediated not only through the procedures employed by the teacher but also by over-all school policy. By setting such policy the administrator participates indirectly in guiding the students' learning. In determining promotion policy or establishing the criteria for class groupings he is involved in the educational development of his students.

Promotion Policy

A number of alternatives are open to the school administrator in determining the promotion policy for his school. He can set up grade standards of achievement and require that each student meet those standards before moving on to the next grade. This was general school policy up to the end of the first decade of the present century and many find it attractive even today. At the other extreme the administrator can set a policy in which every student remains with his age group throughout his school career regardless of achievement level. A third alternative might be found in some compromise between these two as, for example, in setting up minimum-grade standards for achievement but not applying them when the student is two years older than the average age for the particular grade. Whatever the policy, it should be determined by what is best for the individual student rather than in terms of a vague concept of justice or retribution. When the child's educational growth shows signs of being retarded he should not be punished. Even when it is assumed that the reason for the retardation is due to lack of effort, a punitive school policy will not increase effort. Those who favor a measure of achievement as a criterion for promotion do not necessarily intend to be punitive. They may argue reasonably that the child should be held back in order to help him overcome his educational deficiencies and to avoid the frustration of failure in the next grade. The policy should not be set purely by logical argument. Let us see what guidance is offered by the research literature on this topic.

Coffield and Blommers (1956) carried out a careful study on the effects of nonpromotion on educational achievement in the elementary school. By selecting a group of students who failed once in grades three to six and matching them carefully with promoted students whose achievement, intelligence, socioeconomic status, and so on were similar, they were able to obtain a measure of the effects of the failure. They found that the promoted group made from four to six months more progress than the nonpromoted group, as measured on school achievement tests, during the ensuing year. In fact the promoted group showed almost as much growth in one year as did the nonpromoted group in two and when they reached the seventh grade both groups were typically on a par, even though the promoted group had spent one year less in school. The level of achievement of the seventh-grade pupils who have experienced failure once is about eight months less than their counterparts who were promoted and were now in the eighth after spending the same number of years in school. These investigators found that the conclusions seem to apply no matter in which grade the failure was experienced and that the general achievement level in a school was not significantly related to the rigidity or leniency of its promotion policy. The findings of Hall and Demarest (1958) generally confirm these conclusions. Thus we cannot justify, at least as a general policy, the practice of nonpromotion that is intended to enable the student to make up a deficiency in subject matter achievement.

A careful study of the effects of promotion policy on the social and personal adjustment of children was carried out by Goodlad (1954). Using a personality inventory, peer rating data, and a teacher rating scale, Goodlad was able to show that in general nonpromotion is to a greater extent associated with consequent undesirable social and personal adjustment characteristics than promotion. In view of his evidence and the evidence from other studies he seriously questions the usefulness of nonpromotion as a general educational policy.

One must not conclude from this research evidence that a policy that automatically keeps each child with his age group is in itself a solution. A child who is not performing as well as his classmates can easily acquire a sense of inadequacy. This danger is more continuously present in the case of the promoted than in the case of the nonpromoted child. In fact, Goodlad found that promoted children were rated by their teachers for cheating more frequently than their nonpromoted counterparts. The promoted children were unhappier over low marks and reported more frequent feelings of being unwanted at home.

It seems that the child with inadequate achievement is subjected to a number of forces whether promoted or not. One is a sense of adequacy or inadequacy as he compares himself with his classmates, another is the expression of confidence or lack of it shown by his teacher when he recommends that the student be promoted or not, and still another force acting on a child is the achievement expectation present in the classroom. It seems that promotion mobilizes more of these forces positively than does nonpromotion. However, the particular context in which a child is advanced or retarded in his school progress is more important than the policy itself. The teacher must do whatever is possible to eliminate the stress and anxiety in a promoted child whose performance is below the majority of his grade. On occasion the teacher may decide that nonpromotion is indicated, in which case this must be done so that it does not convey the impression that the teacher has lost faith in the child and so that the lower achievement expectation will not have detrimental effects.

Many of the same considerations apply in the case of the child whose educational development is accelerated. Accelerated promotion is discussed in more detail in Chapter 10.

Classification and Grouping

One of the challenges facing the teacher and the school administrator is that of dealing with the vast array of individual differences found in every age-grade group. Many have attempted to cope with this challenge by programs designed to reduce the range of pupil differences. A presumed secondary gain of the grade standard of achievement policy of promotion was that it would tend to create more homogeneous groups; that is groups that performed more or less alike. Studies have shown, however, that the range of abilities within a grade is about the same in schools having high rates of nonpromotion as in those with low rates. In most schools, regardless of promotion policy, the range of academic achievement is about five years in the third grade and nine years in the eighth grade. That is, in a typical third grade the range of achievement will be from about the middle of grade one to the middle of grade six, and in a typical eighth grade the range will be from about fourth-grade level to college-freshman level.

Another proposed solution to the challenge of individual differences is the grouping of children by scores obtained on standardized tests of intelligence and achievement, or teacher grades. This practice is called ability grouping. Various experts have reacted differently to this practice. For example, Sorenson (1948) in a widely used textbook in educational psychology, states the following:

> Ability grouping should be a means for bringing about effective instruction for children of all abilities. Obviously, in a heterogeneous group, instruction directed to the dull is not suitable for the average and the bright, and instruction suitable for the bright is not adapted to the aver-

age and dull. Consequently, when children are classified into ability groups, the content of the courses and the method of instruction should be adapted to their learning capacities (page 234).

Admitting that the research evidence is far from adequate, Sorenson feels the results of studies indicate that ability grouping leads to slightly superior achievement and better personal adjustment.

On the other hand, Lane and Beauchamp (1955) are strongly critical of the practice of ability grouping. They state:

> Standardized group tests continue to be used as the principal basis for homogeneous grouping. Tests are alleged to be superior to opinion in their freedom from the bias and halo-effect that favor the more pleasant, quiet, and "well-bred" children liked by teachers. We have yet to find a group test that purports, even in its advertising, to be a precise measure of the achievement of an individual. They are, by title and definition, made to test groups, to test outcomes of experimental methods, and to secure data for use in research, NOT to measure the ability and achievement of individuals in groups. Yet we all know instances of a person other than the child's teacher ordering the child's removal to another group on the basis of his few quantitative scores and in sheer ignorance of the child's personal needs and attitudes or of the probable influence of the change upon his parents and their attitude toward him (page 307).

Lane and Beauchamp go on to point out that in society at large there are few instances, indeed, in which effective social groups are homogeneous. Bettelheim (1958) also takes a critical view of the proposition that the gifted should be separated from other children of average or lower than average ability. His criticism stems from his speculation that behind the conscious concern for the gifted expressed by some parents and educators is the less desirable motive of social-class segregation. Our discussion in Chapter 14 is relevant to this point. Bettelheim also points out that children who are intellectually able might benefit more from the security gained from feeling competent in a regular classroom than from the pressure of a very demanding curriculum.

Cronbach (1954) presents a view that is most in accord with that of this writer. Those who criticize the practice of ability grouping on the basis of its contribution to a caste system and to the loss of self-esteem in those assigned to the low-ability groups, fail to recognize that pupils "who do poorly in academic work have a feeling of inferiority under any plan." Cronbach goes on to say:

> Ability grouping does not solve our problem. Because different aspects of readiness are only slightly correlated, *pupils who are homogeneous in one respect differ in other dimensions almost as much as unselected pupils.* Even within a group where pupils are selected so that their mental ability is above average, there are still differences in reading and arithmetic ability that require adaptation in teaching (page 230).

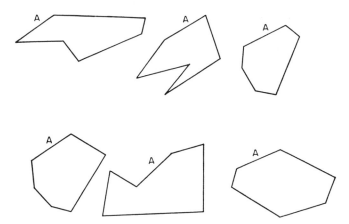

FIGURE 7.4   *Side A in each of the geometric designs is of equal length, so do these figures form a homogeneous group? Similarly, grouping children on the basis of one characteristic, such as intelligence, will not significantly reduce the range of differences in other important characteristics.*

In Figure 7.4 is a graphic representation of this concept. Children cannot be homogenized. The recognition of individual differences and of pupil individuality is of great importance in fostering human development.

Although the procedure of ability or homogeneous class groups does not meet the challenge of individual differences, there are many things that the teacher can do within the classroom. The use of flexible subgroups is a useful procedure for meeting the many needs of individual pupils. Thus the teacher would organize a group of several pupils who need help on word analysis, or long division, or on how to prepare a bibliography. At another time groups could be organized along special interest lines or for social purposes. The size and composition of the group would be determined by the particular demands of the occasion. In order to facilitate such grouping and to encourage the teacher to engage in flexible grouping patterns, the administrator or supervisor should not insist on uniform achievement levels and should provide a variety of instructional materials.

If one were to predict the character of the school of the future it is likely that the arrangement of pupils within groups would differ markedly from what is common today. Anderson (1962) notes that there has already been some movement away from the allocation of pupils to relatively permanent classes or sections to a pattern in which there is a considerable amount of flexible subgrouping and reallocation. Thelen (1960) indicates that there is some evidence, by no means conclusive, to favor the practice of students selecting their teachers. Where these choices are based on sufficient, direct interactive evidence, it is reasonable to assume that groups resulting from such a procedure would be more congenial than those arising from ability or random grouping. It is hoped that the grouping policy that will emerge will be based on sound research findings to answer such questions as those raised by Wrightstone (1957). What technics can be used to adapt instruction to individual differences? How may groupings within the class be used for more effective instruction? What types of class organization are needed to adapt secondary-school instruction to various student needs and abilities? What are the dynamic characteristics of groups that affect the pattern of learning? This last question is considered in the next chapter and the other questions in Part 3 where the topic of individual differences and their implications will be discussed in five chapters.

SUMMARY

The teacher has the responsibility for organizing the material of instruction and determining the most effective distribution of time. Psychological research indicates that the learner should approach the learning task first in terms of the largest units that are meaningful and within the learner's capacity. He should then proceed to analyze for details and finally to discern the larger interrelationships of ideas. A similar problem is involved in the distribution of class time for various aspects of the learning task. The research would support a program of distributed practice rather than one of massed practice. Although there are some common-sense qualifications to this recommendation, rest intervals between trials allow for beneficial consolidation of the learning.

The teacher's inclination to offer the student guidance needs to be tempered by an awareness that at certain times, certain kinds and amounts of guidance can be detrimental to learning. In general, guidance should be given near the beginning of learning, it should be of the kind that does not deprive the learner of his independence and a sense of adequacy, and should be limited in amount.

Self-instructional material or programmed instruction is an educational procedure based on the laboratory work in instrumental conditioning. Programmed material is prepared by setting up a series of logically related, sequenced, small units that require frequent responses from the learner and then provide him with immediate information about the adequacy of his response. The general attitude toward the learner and toward the learning task is a constructive one. However, the limitations must also be noted. Programmed instruction is limited to those kinds of learnings in which the responses are more or less fixed and the development of meaning is predetermined. Where this is not the case, as in exploratory behavior and in the growth of creative imagination, this kind of teaching approach is not useful. Before adopting a self-instructional program and the associated mechanical device the educator must evaluate carefully. He should know whether the device is mechanically reliable and suited to other programs, whether the contemplated programs have been carefully prepared, and whether they have been adequately tested on appropriate subjects.

The work in the classroom requires that students be engaged in independent learning. The classroom organization that is most productive is one in which the student is engaged in some activity that has meaning and purpose to him. The teacher should not overlook the use of group activities that foster attitudes of cooperation and social responsibility for parts of the school day when the student is working independently of direct teacher guidance.

Although the research literature on homework is somewhat ambiguous, there is ample evidence to support certain kinds of homework assignments. The objectives of homework should be to foster a sense of independence and self direction, to encourage certain kinds of leisure interests and activities, to enrich the school learning by applying it to out-of-school situations, and to provide practice for certain kinds of skills. The general program of homework assignments needs to be examined to see if it meets these objectives.

All students need to be guided to more effective study procedures. Students in the intermediate grades of the elementary school can be helped to acquire the requisite study skills and students at the college level also benefit from systematic help in study techniques. One program that grows out of our understanding of learning suggests that the student first survey his learning task, then formulate the questions that his study is designed to answer, then read to answer these questions, then recite or actively present his understanding, and finally review.

Various aspects of school policy have effects on achievement. One of these is the promotion policy. The decision whether or not to promote a particular student whose achievement level is deemed inadequate, needs to be made on an individual basis. The research data on the question would indicate that, in general, promoted students achieve more in an equivalent period of time than do matched nonpromoted students. It appears that more positive educational influences are mobilized when the policy favors promotion, with occasional purposeful nonpromotion.

Another school policy affecting achievement is that of ability grouping. The suggestion that children be grouped in terms of ability is based on a conception of the organization of student abilities that is not in accord with actuality. Homogeneous grouping does not effectively reduce the variability in most classes. In large school systems and in specialized programs a certain amount of grouping might be justified. In the more typical school situation the teacher is better advised to make constructive use of pupil differences rather than vainly wish that they didn't exist.

READING REFERENCES

Association for Supervision and Curriculum Development 1954 Yearbook, *Creating a Good Environment for Learning*. Washington, D. C.: National Education Association (Pt. 1, first six chaps.).

Bard, H., *Homework: A Guide for Secondary School Teachers*. New York: Holt, Rinehart and Winston, 1958.

Galanter, E. (Ed.), *Automatic Teaching: The State of the Art*. New York: John Wiley & Son, 1959.

Goodlad, J. I. and R. H. Anderson, *The Nongraded Elementary School*. New York: Harcourt, Brace and World, 1959.

Henry, N. B. (Ed.), *Individualizing Instruction*. Sixty-first Yearbook (Pt. 1) National Society for the Study of Education. Chicago: University of Chicago Press, 1962 (particularly the four chaps. of Section 3).

Lumsdaine, A. A. and R. Glaser (Eds.), *Teaching Machines and Programmed Instruction: A Source Book*. Washington, D. C.: National Education Association, 1960.

Robinson, F. P., *Effective Study*, rev. ed., New York: Harper & Row, 1961.

Strang, Ruth, *Guided Study and Homework* (What Research Says to the Teacher No. 8). Washington, D. C.: National Education Association, 1955.

CHAPTER 8

USING THE
CLASSROOM GROUP

Teachers do not teach a collection of individuals; they teach groups. The distinction is important, for a group has a uniqueness that goes far beyond the mere sum of the characteristics of the several individuals. The same is true of all other organizations. We cannot describe completely or understand the nature of a building by examining the various parts that went to build it. A human being, as well, is more than a collection of living cells; these cells are functionally related to each other and interact with each other to produce a unique person. The individual cells have one meaning when considered in isolation; they acquire broader and more complex meaning when they are viewed in an interrelated context. The very nature of the cell changes as it interacts with those surrounding it. So it is with groups. A group has a meaning all its own and the individuals that compose this union are changed and acquire new significance as they interact with others in the group.

The following discussion of the classroom group has three objectives:

1. In understanding the dynamics of groups, the teacher can extend his understanding of how personality develops and functions. Children learn from others about themselves and the world. In their interaction with others, children check, correct, and extend their concepts of reality, they learn about feelings and how to cope with them, and as pointed out in Chapter 6, their values are in part determined by the group.

2. Many dynamic aspects of the group that used to be considered irrelevant to the main objectives of teaching are now recognized as important determinants of whether or not the cognitive goals of the classroom will be accomplished. Jensen (1960) points out that "the social-acceptance dimension of the instructional group can either facilitate or impede the development of effective problem-solving and work-relationship requirements for the achievement of a given set of learning objectives." Gibb (1960) also points out that group maintenance goals may obstruct or support the achievement of the stated goal of the instructional group. Similarly, Morse (1960), in applying the generalizations from group dynamics research to the school learning situation, states that "the power of the group can support or oppose the learning goals of the teacher . . . it is clear that group attitudes can influence individual learning performance."

3. Teachers can acquire the necessary skills for recognizing and dealing with the various psychological forces operating in the group. The teacher who is able to teach children to work with each other, to cooperate, to compromise, to lead, to follow, to communicate, to contribute to the accomplishment of group goals, and so forth, is teaching skills that are in themselves in some ways as important as those of reading, writing, and arithmetic and that are essential developmental correlates of cognitive development.

The classroom group differs from other groups in many ways. It functions along two poles of interaction. The first is the teacher-pupil interaction, the second is the pupil-pupil interaction. Although the former influences the latter, the pupil-pupil interaction can be studied more or less independently. In this chapter the focus will be on this aspect of the classroom group, namely, the interaction of the pupils among themselves. The teacher's leadership role in this chapter is viewed from a relatively limited perspective. In Chapter 15 the teacher-pupil interaction is considered from a more analytic and broader perspective.

THE NATURE AND THE EFFECTS OF THE CLASSROOM GROUP

A group is more than a mere aggregate of individuals. In a technical sense the individuals in a classroom form a group only when two or more persons accept a common goal and develop a pattern of interaction that is determined both by the nature of the goal and by the individual personalities of the individual members. In some classrooms the interaction may, at least on the surface, be limited to that initiated by the teacher in his relationship to the class as an audience or to individual pupils. Some teachers may allow a greater variety of interaction patterns. But in any case the control and leadership of the classroom group are vested in the teacher and this authority is sanctioned by law and custom. This feature of the classroom group, plus the facts that the stated objectives of the group are mandated in the form of the curriculum and that the attendance of the classroom group members is compulsory, make the classroom group somewhat different from the groups that have been studied for the determination of the principles of group dynamics (Getzels and Thelen, 1960).

Yet, in spite of the uniqueness of the classroom group, there are a number of features that can be profitably examined, such as, the question of cooperative vs. competitive interaction patterns, and the related group phenomena of norm formation and need satisfaction.

Cooperation and Competition

Of the various kinds of interaction patterns that may emerge in the classroom and in the school, cooperation and competition among group members and between groups are the most noteworthy. It has often been noted that the social interaction pattern most encouraged in American schools is that of individual competition. The process of evaluating the student's individual performance and the resulting comparison with other group members leads generally to a competitive atmosphere. It is quite apparent that schooling and other cultural factors in our society encourage competition. Greenberg (1932) found that as children advance through the elementary grades the strength of competition as an incentive increases. In other cultural contexts children do not show the same type or amount of competitive striving (Erikson, 1950, and Faigin, 1958).

Because of the kind of training received by children in our culture, it is not surprising that Maller (1929) found that student effort was greater when their achievement was credited to them as individuals than when the effort contributed to the achievement of the group. On the other hand, Deutsch (1949) found when he compared the performance in cooperative and competitive student groups, there were more positive features to be noted in the cooperative groups. For example, in the cooperative groups the productivity rate was higher and quality of production was better; the pressure for achievement was greater; the relations between members were friendlier; the efforts of the group members were better coordinated through a greater division of efforts; the process of communication was more effective; and the group members derived greater satisfaction from their activities. Blair et al. (1954) noted that the effects of competition or cooperation depend upon such factors as the nature of the task, the structure of the group, as well as the age, previous experience, and the needs of the group members involved. Although under certain conditions competition may appear to produce better results, several inherent dangers in this kind of interaction need to be guarded against, such as, the discouragement for those who are unable to compete successfully, the excessive stress that may result in deterioration of performance, and the depersonalizing effects that develop when competing students cease to care for the feelings of fellow students (Association for Supervision and Curriculum Development, 1949).

Another facet of this issue is that of the interaction between groups. Insofar as school groups are permitted to relate to each other, they may relate by cooperation within each group in order to compete with other groups or cooperation among groups for accomplishment of over-all group aims. This aspect of human group interaction has been empirically studied and reported by Sherif and Sherif (1953 and 1956). They arranged for two groups of boys, twenty-two boys of about eleven years of age, to be studied in a summer camp setting. The groups were studied under three conditions, namely, a period of in-group formation during which each group acquired a structure and norms of its own, a stage of intergroup friction and conflict during which intergroup rivalry and competition produced intergroup hostility, and finally a stage of reduction of intergroup friction. During the first stage a definite group structure with differentiated status positions and related roles emerged in each group. The boys interacted with each other in such ways that provided goals with common appeal to all members of the group and which required interdependent effort for their attainment. During the second stage, the one in which competitive activities brought about a condition of intergroup friction and conflict, the observers noted a considerable amount of unfavorable attitudes and stereotypes in relation to the out-group. The groups displayed a greater amount of in-group solidarity yet there were some changes in the structure of the group. In one of the groups, for example, a boy, who had achieved a leadership position in the first stage, lost this position in the second stage because he was unable to serve in a leadership role during periods of intense intergroup competition. During the third stage the experimenters studied various methods for the reduction of intergroup conflict. They found that by itself the method of introducing social contacts under pleasant conditions did not reduce tension. The second approach did reduce intergroup tension to a degree but it led to other larger conflict situations. This approach consisted of providing a common enemy against which the conflicting groups had to contend. The technique that proved most effective was the introduction of a series of superordinate goals that required intergroup interaction and the combined effort and resources of both groups. This technique led to a marked reduction of friction between the groups.

The use of competition as a school incentive to increase motivational energy has many inherent dangers. Some elements of competition are probably inevitable in the school. The teacher should control and direct competitive activities so that the harmful effects of competition are minimized and controlled. The teacher's efforts to define group goals so that every individual in the group can come to feel the need for co-operation and to find his satisfaction in group accomplishment, will lead to healthier personalities and a stronger society.

Groups Satisfy Individual Needs and Shape Norms

Many of the person's needs are satisfied or frustrated in the group interaction. Within the classroom various needs will arise and the student will attempt to use the group as an instrument for his need satisfaction. For example, a group member who has a need to share some anxiety or other feeling will turn to the friendship aspect of group interaction to satisfy this need. If this type of relationship is not possible in the class, the need will go unfulfilled. Group members also bring to the class various kinds of socially oriented needs that they hope to satisfy. These needs will center on such matters as adequacy, control, influence, esteem, and relationships with the opposite sex. Some of these needs are reciprocal between group members, that is, the individual member can become the means of satisfying the need of another by making the other feel adequate, providing him with an object for control or influence, or the individual relies on group members to make himself adequate or to control others and so on. The kind of group structure that emerges in the classroom will determine which of these needs will be gratified, which will be deprived, and which interaction patterns will be employed. The consequences of group structure in the classroom play a prominent role in class morale, individual and group achievement, and the discipline situation (Jensen, 1960).

In the discussion of the identification process in Chapter 6, it was pointed out that when the child is dependent on his parents for his basic need satisfaction, he identifies strongly with his parents and through this process acquires his early value orientation. In a similar fashion, the individual, being dependent on the group for the satisfaction of many of his social needs, identifies with the group and adopts many of the group's values. When this occurs the group is called a *reference group*. In Chapter 6 group-linked gains and losses in value development in the classroom were discussed.

A number of studies have documented the fact that the group is capable of exerting significant influence on the judgment and the value orientation of the individual. Asch (1956) reported on a series of experiments related to this topic. The basic experiment consisted of placing an individual in a group-pressure situation. A group of seven to nine college students was assembled and instructed to make discriminatory judgments about the length of lines. Each subject was asked to announce out loud which of the lines on a comparison card matched the line on the standard card (see Figure 8.1). All but one of the subjects

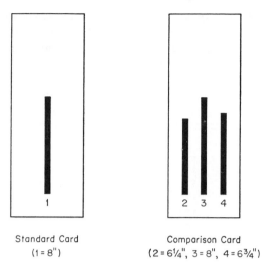

Standard Card
(1 = 8")

Comparison Card
(2 = 6¼", 3 = 8", 4 = 6¾")

FIGURE 8.1 *An example of the type of stimulus cards used in the Asch and Berenda experiments. In one of the pressure trials the majority of rehearsed subjects chose line 2, for example, as being the one of the three lines in the comparison card that matches the line on the standard card.*

were planted by the experimenter who had instructed these subjects beforehand to respond incorrectly on certain of the line-judgment trials. The naïve subject, whose responses were the dependent variable in the experiment, found himself giving his answer on certain critical trials after the other members of the group had given their responses. If he chose the correct line, his answer would disagree with a unanimous majority of the group. In one set of experiments Asch found that 37 percent of the responses of 123 naïve subjects were incorrect, that is, they conformed to the incorrect unanimous majority. Virtually no incorrect responses were given in the absence of group pressure. There were marked individual differences, some subjects yielded all the time, others were consistently independent, and others went along on some judgments and resisted on others. Most of the subjects who resisted expressed a "longing" to agree with the majority.

The subjects in Asch's studies were adults. The effects of group pressure on school-age children are even more interesting. Berenda (1950) conducted a series of such studies using essentially the same procedure as that followed by Asch. The results of one of Berenda's experiments are shown in Table 8.1. Under control conditions 93 percent of the younger subjects gave the correct response to the critical lines, yet when faced with eight bright classmates who gave the wrong response, only 43 percent of these same children responded correctly. In the older population the figures were 94 percent correct under control conditions, 54 per-

TABLE 8.1 CHILDREN'S "FOLLOWING" RESPONSES ON LINE-JUDGMENTS WHEN FACED WITH A UNANIMOUS MAJORITY OF EIGHT RESPONDENTS GIVING INCORRECT RESPONSES IN SEVEN CRITICAL TRIALS

Number of times "following"	Younger children (Ages 7-10)		Older children (Ages 10-13)		Total population (Ages 7-13)	
	Number	Percent	Number	Percent	Number	Percent
0	3	7	11	20	14	15.5
1	7	18	7	13	14	15.5
2	4	11	8	15	12	13
3	4	11	4	8	8	9
4	4	11	6	12	10	11
5	4	11	4	8	8	9
6	2	2	6	12	8	9
7	10	26	6	12	16	18
Total	38	100	52	100	90	100
Average	3.5		2.5		2.7	

Source: Ruth W. Berenda, *The Influence of the Group on the Judgments of Children,* New York: Columbia University Press, 1950.

cent under group pressure. It will be noted from Table 8.1 that the younger subjects are more prone to yield and less prone to remain independent when compared with the older subjects. Berenda could find no observable relationship between the yielding scores and IQ, or teachers' ratings of the subjects on submissiveness.

Observing the behavior of the children during the group-pressure situation, the investigator concluded that it was not easy for children to follow. The children who were the test subjects manifested much distress when faced with the incorrect majority response. "Many a child would stand up in his seat, rub his eyes, look at all the others and then at the lines with a puzzled, embarrassed, and frightened expression on his face."

After being told the truth about the experimental situation, the subjects were interviewed to obtain further information on the qualitative aspects of the yielding or conforming response. One child stated: "Maybe I don't see so good; maybe I need glasses." Another responded as follows to the question "How did you feel during the test?" "I felt funny. I know it will be silly, but when they said an answer and I didn't think it was right, I felt like my heartbeat went down." Another child said: "I know they were wrong, but it was like a jury—we were nine and I was the only one against eight. The majority wins. Besides, how could I prove I was right?" One girl of eleven said: "I had a funny feeling inside. You know you are right and they are wrong and you agree with them. And you still feel you are right and you say nothing about it. Once I gave the answer they didn't give. I thought they would think I was wrong. I just gave their answers. If I had the test alone, I wouldn't give the answers I gave."

It is interesting to note that when the children faced the teacher who gave the incorrect line judgment they yielded much less frequently than they did to their peers. In seven critical judgments in opposition to the teacher, 40 percent of the younger subjects and 83 percent of the older subjects gave no yielding responses. This compares with 7 and 20 percent respectively of no-yielding responses in the case of peer group pressure as shown in Table 8.1. No children in either group yielded more than three out of seven times to the teacher's incorrect judgment. It is interesting to note that children were able to justify their opposition to the teacher by such statements as: "She just don't see correctly—bad eyesight." "She knows most in class. Maybe she made a mistake in her vision. Might have been blurry." These comparisons indicate that the prestige position of the teacher is not as influential in inducing "following" behavior as is the majority opinion of peers.

In the typical real-life situation, different individuals with different judgments come together in one group setting. Attempting to approximate this type of situation, yet maintaining the controls of a laboratory situation, Sherif (1936) studied the effects of the group by using the autokinetic effect. This effect is the apparent movement of a stationary point of light when viewed in a darkened room. Sherif found that each of his subjects in a series of estimates established his own standard or norm and his own range of distance judgments for the apparent movement of the light. When various persons who had established their own norms in their own individual sessions were assembled for a group session, their differing estimates tended to converge.

These various laboratory findings are consistent with those of Newcomb (1943) who studied the change of attitudes within an actual institutional setting. He studied the effects of a small, liberal-arts college (Bennington College) on the political attitudes of students who came to college generally with the conservative attitudes of their parents. The prevailing faculty attitudes were termed politically liberal. The great majority of the students adopted the college community as its reference group in regard to political attitudes. In other words, the college community became the group to which the individual related himself in such a way as to adopt its frame of reference for making political judgments. Liberal attitudes in this setting served the purpose of gaining emancipation from parents and their attitudes, as well as gaining prestige and acceptance in the college community. The following statement of one of the students illustrates this. "Every influence I felt tended to push me in the liberal direction: My underdog complex, my need to be independent of my parents, and my anxiousness to be a leader here." Those students whose attitudes did not change in the direction of the prevailing college attitude were found to maintain their affiliation with out-of-college groups, generally with parents.

In certain respects these findings are disconcerting. What hope is there for our democratic way of life if individuals submit so uncritically to the will of the majority? Teachers should consider ways of fostering an attitude of loyal opposition on the part of the individual and tolerance of dissenting opinions on the part of the group. Morse (1960), in discussing this issue, suggests that the teacher can help the individual student deal with the group pressure by fostering a sense of personal adequacy and independence based on self-confidence. The teacher can help pupils maintain independence by making the task less ambiguous. "The more support and the more information supplied, the less conformity."

This brief review of the nature and the effects of the group should make the teacher aware that many attitudes of the individual, including aspects of those attitudes having to do with the pupil's orientation to learning, have their source in the groups of which he is a member. The studies just referred to, and others (such as Lewin, 1947; Miles, 1959) would suggest that changing certain properties of the classroom group might be a more effective means of changing individual attitudes than attempts to influence the individual more directly as an individual.

STUDYING THE INTERACTION OF CHILDREN

We might conceive the classroom of children as a society and our procedures for studying this society might in some ways parallel those of the social anthropologist. One of the first steps in studying a society is to determine its network or web of interaction.

The Sociogram

For classrooms or groups of about thirty individuals where the members have had the opportunity to become acquainted with each other and also have the social maturity to be sufficiently aware of other people (usually not before age eight) the sociogram may prove a useful tool. A sociogram is a chart that shows the group structure at one point in its development. It presents subgroup organization, friendship and rejection patterns, and the relation of any one pupil to the class group as a whole. To obtain the information necessary to construct a sociogram, a variety of questions may be presented to the students. It is recommended that questions involving working with other pupils on subject matter should be avoided because the student making a choice may place more stress on academic skill than sociability. It is best when the information is gathered in a natural manner. The situation described here is one example of how a teacher might proceed.

The teacher had taught the group for one year in the third grade and was now teaching the same group in the fourth grade. One day during the first month of the second year, the teacher provided each child with a pencil and a sheet of paper and said to them:

> We have been reading together a book about three little friends. These three were very close friends. I would like to know whom you would choose as your best friends. It might help me to plan things for you. Will you write on a piece of paper the names of those you choose as your best friends? Do not write more than three names, even though you have more than three friends. After the children had done this the teacher continued:
> Now if there are some whom you would not choose for friends, write their names also. You may not know any, you may wish to name one or you may have several in mind. Please do not write more than three names (American Council on Education, 1945, page 295).

The children were not surprised or bothered by this request. They responded readily because they trusted the teacher and accepted the explanation that their answers might aid in planning for them.

The actual sociogram may be constructed in several different ways. The procedure described here is one that has proven most satisfactory for those who are inexperienced. A card is made out for each child that appears as shown in Figure 8.2.

Child's name:

Children selected as friends	Those who chose this child
1.	1.
2.	2.
3.	3.
	4.
	5.
Children rejected	Those who rejected this child
1.	1.
2.	2.
3.	3.

FIGURE 8.2 *Card form for constructing sociogram.*

After the teacher has transferred the information to these cards, they can be arranged and rearranged on a large surface until a suitable pattern for a sociogram is formed. It is best to start by placing the card of the student most frequently chosen (counting all choices, first, second, or third) in the center.

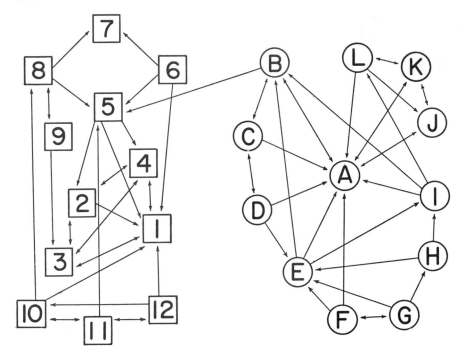

FIGURE 8.3 *Friendship choices in an eighth-grade group. Circles and letters represent girls, squares and numbers represent boys. Note that all choices are within sex group except for girl B's choice of boy 5.*

The sociograms shown in Figures 8.3, 8.4, and 8.5 are of an eighth-grade class. It is possible to show by means of colored lines which choices were first, second, or third. Several significant points can be made as a result of examination of these sociograms.

Although boys and girls in the junior-high-school grades are attempting to establish heterosexual relations, sociograms reveal that they generally choose members of the same sex. Girl B, a very mature girl often seen in the halls talking with boys, is the only girl choosing a boy. Her choice of boy 5 is odd, because on the substitute rejection sociogram in Figure 8.5 we find that this boy thinks that girl B would want to have as little as possible to do with him. The individual frequently misinterprets social overtures made to him by others. Individuals vary markedly in the degree to which they are accepted by their age mates. Boy 1 and girl A (see Figure 8.3) are called "stars" in sociometric terminology because a large number of choices converge on them. Individuals such as these, who are chosen by many others, can be used by the teacher to help a child who is rejected or isolated in the group. It is interesting to note that girl A and boy 1 do not reject any one as shown in both rejec-

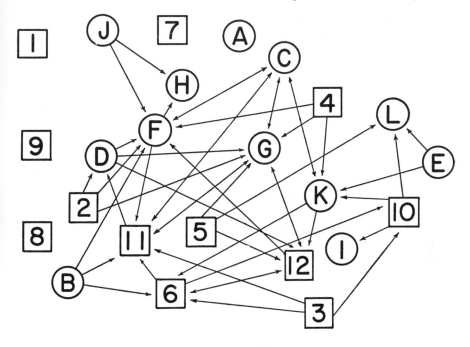

FIGURE 8.4 *Rejection choices in same eighth-grade group. Note that rejection choices frequently cross sex lines.*

tion sociograms (Figures 8.4 and 8.5). Most children who feel generally comfortable and accepted in the group tend not to express rejection toward others in the group, except in cases where the group itself has strong need to reject and the leader shows the way in the expression of this need.

The use of questions such as the one just suggested "Now if there are any whom you would not choose for friends . . ." which require the student to identify those classmates whom he rejects is a debatable procedure. The authority just quoted seems to find the procedure acceptable. On the other hand Cunningham (1951) states:

> Some investigators recommend the use of negative questions, such as "Who are the three people you like least?" in gathering basic material for sociograms. We tried this approach in several groups but found it very difficult to use. Whereas answering the positive questions was seen by group members as being an enjoyable experience, when the negative question was asked, there was considerable feeling of discomfort. In our culture children are taught that to love thy neighbour is a virtue, and not to like people is naughty. Thus identifying people who were disliked gave rise to guilt feelings. Moreover children who suspected they might be named as persons disliked showed increased insecurity. We decided that the harm done to personal trust and group climate through the use of the negative

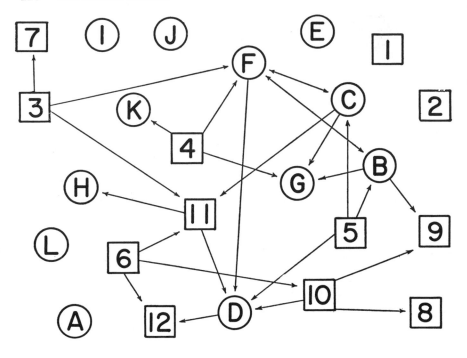

FIGURE 8.5   *Substitute rejection choices on basis of following direction: name those students in the class who you think would like to have as little as possible to do with you.*

question was not compensated by the added knowledge the result gave the teacher (page 160).

In those instances where the teacher has not yet completely won the confidence of the group or where the group members do not know each other very well, this argument would be a valid one. Helen Hall Jennings, who has done noteworthy work in the field of sociometry, has suggested that in order to overcome the objections to rejection items, the following instruction might be used: *Name those students in the class who you think would like to have as little as possible to do with you.*

This type of question might be a compromise but it does provide much of the same information provided by the rejection question. Figure 8.5 is a sociogram based on the results obtained from the question just stated when put to the same eighth-grade group. Note that girls F and G are reacted to in much the same way on both rejection sociograms. The high number of rejections received by these two girls might be a partial explanation for the mutual choice in the friendship sociogram, Figure 8.3. Children who are rejected by the group may seek each other out in order to give each other some kind of acceptance—"Misery likes company." It might also be suggested that one of these girls may be the ini-

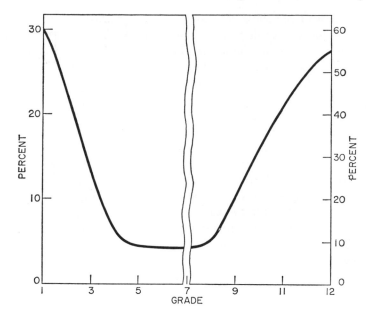

FIGURE 8.6 *Percentage of heterosexual friendship choices at various grade levels. Data from J. L. Moreno, "Who Shall Survive?"* Nervous and Mental Disease Monographs, *1934, and R. G. Kuhlen and Beatrice J. Lee, "Personality Characteristics and Social Acceptability in Adolescence,"* Journal of Educational Psychology, *1943, 34, pp. 321–340.*

tiator of rejection by the group and the association with this child may cause the group to extend its expression rejection, a kind of "guilt by association."

In comparing the first sociogram, showing friendship choices, with the other two showing rejection, the interaction of boys and girls across sex lines takes place almost exclusively at the level of rejection. This will be found to be true of the social organization of children's groups between the ages of about nine and thirteen. It is a phenomenon that is probably related to normal processes of psychosexual development and the problems associated with acquiring appropriate sex-role identity. During this period, called the latency period, the child is struggling to establish for himself an appropriate sex role and he rejects anyone of his age who represents the role of the opposite sex. The teacher who attempts to establish positive relations between boys and girls must be aware that this will be viewed by the children as a threat and will often result in extreme forms of reaction. Boys will see the teacher's attempt as suggesting sissy-like behavior, and girls will interpret it as suggesting unladylike behavior. It might also be noted that before and after the latency period friendship choices across sex lines are quite common (see Figure 8.6). The cross sex choices in the early grades are based on quite different reasons from those that apply in the twelfth grade. In the case of the first graders it is due to a lack of awareness and the absence of differentiation of sex roles; whereas in the case of the twelfth graders, boys and girls will choose each other precisely because of established sex roles that permit and foster this kind of relationship.

The Classroom Social-Distance Scale

The questions that the teacher asks to construct a sociogram impose some artificial considerations on children with regard to their friendship choices. The first choices made by two different children may be made with varying degrees of intensity, yet in our examination of the sociogram we are not able to differentiate the intensity involved in each choice. In order to be able to examine in a more exact manner the kinds of feelings involved in the interpersonal relations in the class, the classroom social-distance scale is suggested. It is patterned after the scale devised by Bogardus (1933) to measure attitudes toward various national and ethnic groups. The following description of the classroom scale is adapted from Cunningham (1951).

Each child is given a sheet containing the instructions, the names of all the children in the class, and the attitudes by which each child is to be rated (see Figure 8.7).

It is possible by means of the classroom social distance scale to arrive at an acceptability score for each student. Let us assume that a particular child in a classroom of thirty students receives the following combination of check marks from his associates: 4 checks in column 1 (best friend), 9 checks in column 2, 10 checks in column 3, 6 checks in column 4, 0 checks in column 5 (wish he weren't in our room).

$$
\begin{aligned}
4 \times 1 &= 4 \\
9 \times 2 &= 18 \\
10 \times 3 &= 30 \\
6 \times 4 &= 24 \\
0 \times 5 &= 0 \\
\hline
&76
\end{aligned}
$$

This boy's social-distance score is 76. The lower the score the greater the acceptance by the group—the less social distance. The maximum social distance in this class would be 30×5 or 150; the minimum would be 30×1 or 30.

We can also determine how this boy feels about the group by examining his paper. We find, for example, that he checked his paper as follows: 2 names checked in column 1; 5 names in 2; 8 in 3; 13 in 4; and 1 in 5. Multiplying as above we find his self social-distance score to be 91. Interpreting the difference in these two scores one can conclude that

CLASSROOM SOCIAL-DISTANCE SCALE

Instructions:

We don't like all of our friends in the same way. Some we like more than others. There may be some people we don't like at all.

The check list on the next page will give you a way of telling how close an acquaintance you would like to have with other boys and girls in your room. Next to each name listed on the page, put a check in the space below the statement which most nearly describes your feeling about the person. Of course you are to substitute "her" for "him" in your thinking when checking a girl's name.

When you come to your own name, check the space which describes how you think most of the boys and girls feel about you.

No one in your room will see this paper but your teacher.

Name	1. Would like to have him as one of my best friends	2. Would like to have him in my group but not as a close friend	3. Would like to be with him once in a while but not often or for a long time	4. Don't mind his being in our room but I don't want to have anything to do with him	5. Wish he weren't in our room
1.					
2.					
3.					
4.					
5.					
6.					
7.					
etc.					

FIGURE 8.7 *Suggested form for obtaining social-distance data. Adapted from Ruth Cunningham et al.,* Group Behavior of Boys and Girls, *New York: Bureau of Publications, Teachers College, Columbia University, 1951.*

the acceptance of this boy by the group is greater than his acceptance of the group.

The scores or results obtained on the classroom social-distance scale or the sociogram are not to be considered ends in themselves. The results are actually a beginning point. They may be viewed as analogous to a temperature or blood pressure reading in a medical diagnosis. As Cunningham has stated, "Perhaps the greatest value in an examination of results is that it directs attention to certain aspects of interpersonal relations which lead to further observation of individual and group behavior." As the teacher gains understanding of the group structure, of interpersonal relations, possible reasons for certain aspects of structure, he might then be able to cope with those problems which may be obstructing the most effective functioning of the group.

GROUPS RESPOND DIFFERENTLY

The illustrations that follow show how principles of group dynamics can help the teacher achieve more effective classroom leadership.

Two eighth-grade social-studies classes were studying the problem of bicycle safety in the community. The selection of the topic was made on the basis of expressed interest in each of the classes. One question which came up repeatedly in the exploratory discussions was concerned with the desirability of initiating a driving test and village license for bicycle riders. The teacher, Mr. Lane, used the early periods to help the children understand the responsibility of the community to its citizens, the purposes of licensure and other points of this sort. The interest in the original problem was maintained until the teacher proposed that both classes hold debates on the topic. The pupils accepted this suggestion with enthusiasm. The debate topic was: "Resolved that a driving test and licensing procedure be instituted for bicycle riders in this community."

The whole procedure in these classes was sound in that it built upon the experiences of children and enabled them to generalize from these to larger problems. The teacher acted as a guide but not without regard to the interests and experiences of the students. This topic was not fixed upon by Mr. Lane and pulled out each year for the eighth-grade class. One can always pay lip service to children's interests and then find ways of ignoring them. This is illustrated in a charming story told about a well-intentioned teacher who had taught third grade for many years. When a new principal, with a progressive point of view arrived on the scene, she resolved to try to meet his expectations. After a lengthy teachers' meeting, she came to her class determined to be guided by the interests of her students and she proceeded to elicit from the children the topics they would like to discuss. One youngster suggested turtles, another suggested animal pets, a third something else and so on until finally much to the teacher's satisfaction one little boy suggested they study about Indians; whereupon the teacher pulled out the old Indian unit that she had used these many years.

The eighth-grade social-studies classes chose teams and prepared for the debate. The teacher participated in the small group discussions and helped the teams gather information and prepare their presentations but, of course, took no part in the debates. A student chairman took charge during the debates and during the general class discussion which followed. No attempt was made in either class to determine which team won nor was a final answer to the debated question agreed upon. This may be seen by some as a failure to bring a topic to a close, but it also serves the valuable purpose of allowing greater use of self-evaluative powers.

A significant difference developed between the two class situations during these activities and became strikingly apparent in the actual debate sessions. One class maintained a high level of interest throughout. The teams worked diligently to find information. Almost all class members eagerly awaited the debate. The debate itself drew almost complete attention in the class. The team members were enthusiastic and made forceful presentations. The argument was heated, but it proceeded in an orderly manner. The general class discussion which followed was carried on at a high level.

In the other class, the team members made superficial and uncoordinated preparations. The debate was poorly organized, and the presentations were weak. Arguments tended to be heated but based more on feelings than on facts. The class discussion which followed lacked organization.

The teacher searched for explanations for these differences. He considered several possible factors. Homogeneous grouping was not practiced in the school, and random scheduling placed a cross-section of the pupil population in each class. Therefore, he could not explain the difference in response on the basis of class composition. The debates were held on the same day. Unusual disrupting activities, such as the distribution of grade cards, or pep meetings for athletics, were not present. The same teacher worked with both classes, and both classes initially entered eagerly into the activity. It appeared that the classes were clearly similar in most respects.

Mr. Lane decided to construct a sociogram for each class and also to apply the classroom social-distance scale. After examining the results, striking differences in the groups became evident. In the class which carried on the highly successful debate, the debate teams were composed of the most sought after members of the class. Team members were mutually receptive to each other. The speakers enjoyed a high degree of prestige in the class. In the less successful class, some of the team members were sought after persons, but most of those who had volunteered to participate in the debate were not chosen as close associates by the other members of the class.

It is difficult to control or even to discern the factors that resulted in the differing situations. It may have been that the first pupil to volunteer in the more successful class was in the well-accepted group and that his friends followed. Perhaps a less accepted pupil volunteered initially in the other class and his more favored classmates hesitated to join him. Mr. Lane could not recall whether or not this was actually so. The above analysis is not intended to suggest that only the favored or popular students should be given the opportunity to make a presentation, rather it only serves to point out that the social structure of a class group materially influences the success of activities in which pupil participation is a factor.

The quality of the group's reaction is an important factor in determining the effectiveness of teaching and learning and the satisfactions gained by the teacher, as is illustrated in the following:

> When I taught high-school physics, I had two beginning classes which, as far as I could tell, were composed of children who were equally bright, had equal social standing in the community, and, on individual interview, expressed the same range of interest in physics. Yet teaching one class was like pulling teeth and teaching the other like singing around the piano. In one class, I had the immediate response of apathy to everything I did; in the other class, the feedback was of challenging questions and meaningful ideas for the group to pursue (Thelen, 1954, pages 43-44).

PROBLEMS ARISING FROM INADEQUACIES IN GROUP-INDIVIDUAL INTERACTION

Jensen (1960) identifies a number of different kinds of disruptive behavior that are possible manifestations of the structure of instructional groups. She indicates that when decision-making power is too heavily concentrated in the role of the teacher, the dependency problems of individual students are likely to be aggravated. In other students the need to be self-assertive or rebellious may be brought to the surface. Another problem of group structure that leads to disruptive behavior is the incompatibility of the learning goals established by the teacher and the learning needs of some of the students. This situation leads to lack of interest and to boredom. Those students who cannot obtain satisfaction from working with the group, may seek to gain satisfaction from working against the group, belittling the group, engaging in attention-seeking behavior, and so on.

Jensen also speaks of collusive relationships between students as a form of disruptive behavior arising from the conditions of group structure. She states: "Probably nothing is so disturbing to teachers as collusion on the part of students to 'defeat' the teacher's testing, assignment, and grading endeavours or to resist and weaken the teacher's authority for direction-setting and decision making." Collusive behavior leads to the "gentleman's C," cheating, copying, and an atmosphere of hostility and suspicion.

Collusive behavior sometimes occurs also in the student-student relationship. Such conflict between members of the class group can be disruptive of educational progress. It can also erupt into scapegoating and other forms of hostile action of the group directed against one or two individuals. The following illustration is one of such collusive behavior resulting in a social problem that solved itself.

A Social Problem That Solved Itself

Children tend to assume exaggerated patterns of behavior as their social awareness develops. Gradually, the child learns to moderate these extremes in behavior (for example, extreme acceptance, dependence, rejection, and rebellion). Interference by an adult, however well-intentioned, may sometimes retard the appearance of more moderate interaction patterns.

The situation here may be considered the problem of Judy's classmates or it may be Judy's problem; it is probably best to consider it a common problem of the early adolescent girl who seems to depend, more than the boy, on intimate relationships with members of the same sex (Thompson and Horrocks, 1947).

Judy's mother was frantic with worry when she called the junior high school principal in the late fall. When school had opened in September, Judy had been one of the more popular members of a group of eighth-grade girls. The group often met at her home. They walked or rode their bicycles together to and from school. Judy was included in all of their banter and was thoroughly happy.

Now only seven weeks later, everything had changed. Judy had been given to understand that she was not welcome in the group. The other girls ignored her completely at school. They became silent and moved away when Judy approached.

The same things were true of her life out of school. All of the girls stayed away from Judy's home. No one telephoned her. On the way to school the girls avoided Judy's home so it was necessary for her to go back and forth alone.

This group of girls had depended on each other for companionship and although they were rather popular with others among their classmates, they had no close friendships with other girls. As a result, Judy was almost completely deprived of association with her peers.

Why should early adolescent girls do this kind of thing? Two basic feelings of humans furnish some clues. As people learn to be conscious of themselves they need status with their peers. Also, they need to feel a sense of belonging. As awareness of human relationships continues to grow the feeling of status and belongingness take on comparative aspects. Degrees of status become important. For some persons to enjoy prestige means that some others cannot. The discussion of prejudice in Chapter 6 and competition earlier in this chapter are relevant here. There are degrees of belongingness. The infant probably does not discriminate so much. He either belongs or he does not because he does not comprehend how much his brother or sister is wanted. This partially explains why sibling rivalry, when it exists, is usually initiated by the older sibling.

At the junior high school level children are capable of fine discriminations in status. Neugarten (1946) and Stendler (1949) have pointed out that a sharp awareness of social class and a tendency to place peers on a status scale has developed by the age of thirteen (see Chapter 14).

The girls in Judy's peer group were about equal in status and security in the group. They enjoyed considerable prestige among their other classmates but this was probably not enough. Perhaps they felt the need to have a person with whom to compare themselves. When the most sought after member of the group suggested that Judy be snubbed for a while, there was ready agreement.

After this analysis of the situation, the teacher decided to seek an opportunity through role playing, using the sociodrama Ins and Outs,[1] or some other literature from which she might get into the problem of exclusion. However, this proved unnecessary for not long after Judy's mother called the principal to report that the relationships had changed again and Judy was taken back into the group. It is difficult to say how this experience of exclusion would affect the girl. No one was ever able to note any factor that caused the girls to welcome Judy back into the peer group. Neither the principal nor the teachers could discover any personal influence that made a difference. Judy's parents had done nothing that they could identify. Judy was simply in the group again.

Insecurity in Group Relations

Another problem that may arise in group relations in the classroom is that of the individual's insecurity in the group. Any child who moves into a well-established class group is likely to encounter a modicum of difficulty in finding his place within that group. Insecurity does not refer to a well-defined entity, but to the reaction of a person when he is uncertain of the world in which he lives. Insecurity may have many causes that are rooted in the parent-child relationship. Also an increasing number of school-age children face the insecurity that arises from frequent family moves. The geographical mobility of families has increased markedly since World War II. The teacher can use certain aspects of the group situation in ways that will help the insecure child with his problem. The case of Ruth presented in Chapter 6 illustrates certain

---

[1] *The Ins and Outs* by Nora Stirling, 1948. A dramatic sketch for and about teen agers with Discussion Guide by Lawrence K. Frank—reveals the relationships of the "Ins"—those who belong to a group, with an "Out" who tries to belong but is excluded.

aspects of the problem of insecurity and ways of coping with it. The case of Peter, which follows, considers other aspects of the problem.

Peter's family had moved many times while he was in elementary and junior high schools, and by the time he was in tenth grade he had attended six different schools. This last school year Peter started in the tenth grade in an upstate New York school where he made a satisfactory adjustment but then he moved to the Middle West in November of that same year.

In this present school, Peter showed himself to be unusually timid. He was deferent to a painful degree in the presence of teachers. He associated little with his classmates and usually entered and left classes alone.

His work in class showed considerable ability. His written work was much better than his oral presentation. He rarely volunteered to participate in class, but when he did so his statements were usually correct. The homeroom teacher consulted the guidance office. It appeared that the information about the boy transmitted by his previous schools dealt primarily with academic achievement, which was reported adequate in all subject matter areas.

The boy's problem centered primarily in his withdrawal from the group. A reluctance to participate is in and of itself not symptomatic of poor adjustment. Many children are quite satisfied with only a few intimate human contacts and these may be outside of school. However, in Peter's case it was quite obvious that his lonesomeness was acute and that he was unhappy in his withdrawal. In discussing the problem with other teachers, the homeroom teacher realized that she was not alone in her evaluation of the situation. Several teachers agreed to seek ways of helping the boy by means of using the group's capacity for satisfying individual needs. Some little progress was made during the months of November and December, but apparently not enough. After Christmas vacation, Peter's father telephoned one of the high school teachers at home and asked to have a conference concerning Peter's adjustment to school. He requested an evening conference when he would not be seen talking with one of his son's teachers.

At this conference a number of facts were brought out. Peter's development was normal. He had liked elementary school but as the family had moved about he had shown an increasing tendency to dislike school and to make fewer friends. In the last school he had attended in New York State, Peter made one close friend and practically all of his out-of-school activity was carried on with that one friend, a boy about his age. Peter had been upset and had cried when notified of the impending family move and was most reluctant to leave this friend.

It was apparent that the boy was reacting to the separation from this close friend and there was not much that could be done about his unhappiness until he could relate to someone else in this fashion. The teachers and the parents could only leave the door open for Peter's adjustment to the new school and the new community. The rest would have to take its own time.

The Development of Social Skills Depends on Experience

In times of increased mobility in the population Peter's situation is a common one. Children in these circumstances do not have enough time to establish relationships with new friends before they must begin again in another school.

Children do not learn the social skills involved in carrying friendships out to a mature point if they do not remain in one community long enough to reach this stage. Neither do they have an opportunity to experience the results of deep friendships. The feeling of security in anticipating others' reactions to ideas and situations does not develop. The transient child is usually acting without knowledge of what to expect from those around and inevitably makes social mistakes. Sometimes, there is no chance for the child to evaluate his own social overtures to see his degree of success in the long term.

The child who is rebuffed because of his social ineptness is likely to withdraw and cease his attempts at relating to his schoolmates. Such withdrawal aggravates the problem as less and less social experience ensues. Serious damage to the personality may result.

Dimock (1941) found that a substantial number of adolescent boys, in his study population 15 to 25 percent, possessed an acceptability status that was judged to be below the minimum needs for wholesome and satisfying personality development. Lippitt and Gold (1959) found that the position of a student in a class group with respect to whether he is liked or disliked is rapidly established and is maintained with a high degree of stability throughout the school year. Laughlin (1954) in a study of the peer status of children in the sixth and seventh grade, found that the level of acceptance during the sixth grade was positively related to the same students' acceptance in the seventh grade, even though between the sixth and seventh grade these students had transferred from the elementary school to the junior high school and had joined other class groups. She concludes that "by the time these children reached junior high they had established a fairly consistent personality pattern, which in turn influenced their acceptance by others." In view of these findings, she suggests that opportunities for establishing constructive peer relationships must be provided from the early grades.

Lippitt and Gold (1959) in studying the low status, rejected child in the classroom concluded that the difficulties are created and maintained by a circular social process to which the child himself, his classmates, and his teacher contribute. The child himself contributes by reacting with hostility, withdrawal, or ineptness to his own negative self-evaluation, and by "his insensitive and defensive reception of feedback from others which might potentially give him more guidance for his own behavior." The class group contributes to the problem situation by rapidly attaching an evaluative label to a child and then tends to act in certain ways so as to perpetuate the negative social reputation. The group generally responds to the social difficulty of an individual child by ignoring or rejecting him rather than by sympathetic guidance. The teacher contributes to the situation by the following:

> (1) a lack of teaching effort focused on developing personal attitude and group standards about good human relations; (2) a lack of interpersonal grouping practices and other procedures guided by mental health goals; (3) a lack of clear presentation of constructive behavior patterns toward low status children which could be imitated by her other pupils (Lippitt and Gold, page 49).

In instituting a procedure that would correct the problem of an individual child, the teacher must be careful not to disrupt the positive features of the group structure. In attempting to solve a problem of group structure, the teacher must be careful not to sacrifice the well-being of the individual. In an excellent pamphlet on discipline in the classroom group, Sheviakov and Redl (1956) refer to this principle as *the law of marginal antisepsis* by which they mean that a technique that is right for resolving the child's problem must at least be harmless to the group and a technique chosen for its effect on the group must at least be harmless to the individuals involved.

The establishment of relationships among humans and especially among children and youths is a complex process. Part of this process goes on through first-hand experiencing, part goes on vicariously. First-hand experiencing is probably the more important of the two.

Commonly, our most successful human relationships are those with our parents or with brothers and sisters. To refer to the case of Peter, the only persons who were with him through all of his moves were the members of his family. All others among his relatives, friends, and acquaintances were left behind at each move. However, even the family relationships were being shaken by Peter's unhappy experiences with his peers.

The human infant begins to establish relationships very early with those who come near him. He stops crying when someone picks him up. He may learn to resume crying when put back in bed. Reactions will depend on the consistency in the sequence of events. If comfort and satisfaction regularly follow the appearance of his mother, the child will react with signs of approval when she comes near.

As the child grows older and encounters new situations and new people, he will react to familiar elements in each new experience in ways learned previously. Unfamiliar elements in situations are likely to cause doubts concerning the proper response. Some responses may be unfortunate. For example, a newcomer may attempt to joke about a matter being taken very seriously by others present. In general newcomers are likely to be greeted by an unfriendly response when they attempt to join in the activities of an established, cohesive group. Later, the person who has established himself with the group will probably join in putting another newcomer "in his place."

Other responses to new situations may prove more successful. Responses that bring satisfactions tend to be repeated. In interpersonal relationships, responses are successful if the reactions elicited from others bring about mutually satisfying consequences. People vary in their needs and in their perceptions in such ways that identical responses, if such are possible, will cause different reactions in different people. If a person can learn to predict reactions he can select more successfully among possible approaches to others. Members of certain interest groups tend to be predictable in certain respects. The athletic lettermen's club is likely to respond favorably to talk about sports. Members of the chorus may be interested in the coming operetta, and so on.

With respect to other matters members of groups may be less predictable. The discovery of acceptable methods for establishing a common ground of interest and agreement with other people is a complex process. Except for those persons who lose contact with reality, most humans work at this process throughout their lives. If there is insufficient continuity of contacts to enable a person to form generalizations about a given group, the resulting inappropriate responses will lead to social failure. In Peter's case the frequent moves from one community to another and the final separation from a close friend were the cause of the problem. In the case of Ruth in Chapter 6 it was the child's anxiety about being accepted and the group's inexperience with someone who was different. Another cause of this kind of difficulty lies in the fact that schools have become large, classes are often crowded, and teachers overburdened. All of these form barriers to constructive interpersonal relations between teachers and also among pupils. Many children resist the tendency toward "anomie," namelessness or a lack of identity, but in doing so they are likely to adopt exaggerated forms of response, such as excessive conformity to group standards, the extreme reliance on a best friend, and the seeking of a steady boy- or girl-friend at early ages. If the teacher would foster healthy social development, he must do what he can to recognize each child as an individual and to foster in him a healthy identity.

SOCIODRAMA AND ROLE PLAYING IN THE CLASSROOM

Throughout this chapter it has been suggested that there is much that the teacher can do to establish the kind of group structure that will satisfy the needs of children, support the learning process, and contribute to healthy personality development. The procedures that the teacher may employ to accomplish this cannot be specified in detail and they grow out of the teacher's general orientation to the teaching task. This is discussed in Chapter 15. There is, however, one specific technique that can be used from time to time and under particular conditions for the development of individual and group social attitudes, and that is sociodrama or role playing.

This technique is based on the assumption that the person can come to understand another person when he is in his position. No one can, of course, be exactly in another person's position but by role playing he can begin to understand the feelings and the condition of another. Children do this quite naturally in their play activities. The little girl who tries on her mother's high heels is trying to get the feel for this adult role which she vaguely anticipates she will play. Preschool children spend a good deal of time at role playing—taking the part of father, mother, doctor, nurse, police, robber, cowboy, fireman, and almost any role that comes vaguely within the realm of their experience. These activities, which are manifestations of the process of identification described in Chapter 6, produce understandings, the value of which is frequently underestimated. This desire and ability to put one's self in another's position is one of the most important avenues for achieving personal and social maturity. The person who cannot feel for another person is likely to be cruel and destructive, or erratic and eccentric.

One study (Hartley et al., 1952) of children's play was able to distinguish eight different functions served by dramatic play in typical group situations within the preschool and kindergarten period.

> Through this activity the child is given an opportunity (1) to imitate adults; (2) to play out real life roles in an intense way; (3) to reflect relationships and experiences; (4) to express pressing needs; (5) to release unacceptable impulses; (6) to reverse roles usually taken; (7) to mirror growth; and (8) to work out problems and experiment with solutions (pages 27-28).

The self-initiated dramatic play of the four- to six-year-old gradually gives way to more organized and structured forms of play. The purposes fulfilled by dramatic play are only partially satisfied in these other play activities. Some form of dramatic activity, such as role playing and sociodrama, can also enable the individual to explore and practice various approaches to a social situation which may be threatening if tried without some tentative trials. The adult may do this by means of discussion with someone he trusts or simply by the process of reflection and imagination. The younger person may find it easier to carry on this exploration by means of trying various courses of action in a pseudo-realistic setting.

In an educational psychology class a student who was planning to substitute in a high school class asked if she could try her lesson plan in brief form before her fellow students. In order to make the situation easier the instructor suggested that the students recreate several different kinds of class situations. The students assumed different roles: the obstructionist student, the dull one, the indifferent, the capable, and the interested. The student making the original request was surprised at the difficulty in conducting the class. The instructor and class members analyzed the causes of the difficulty. The student reported the following week that her substitute teaching assignment might have proven very discouraging had she not had the role-playing experience. Students going out on job interviews can be helped considerably by role-playing activities.

The role-playing situation can be useless or even harmful if certain cautions are not exercised. Excessive use of the sociodrama technique can become boring. Any single sociodrama should be brief and the enactment should be cut at the height of interest rather than to wait until the players or actors have run out of ideas. This may be after three minutes but should not be longer than ten. The sociodrama, if initiated in a classroom, should not be carried on if no time is left for discussion and analysis of why people did certain things and how certain incidents made the participants feel. If it is appropriate, the teacher should lead the class to a general formulation of social behavior. Under no circumstances should rehearsal of script or dialogue take place, but a brief description of the situation should be given, with an assignment to the actors that they are to characterize certain individuals with certain kinds of opinions on the issue at question. The teacher must exercise extreme caution in setting up the characterizations to be portrayed. The following brief descriptions of sociodrama in the classroom, taken from the Educator's Washington Dispatch,[2] will serve as illustrations.

> *Stella's Manners:* An elementary-school teacher, by means of sociodrama, aided her boys and girls in learning how to make social introductions. Success of the project encouraged her to tackle table manners— a need revealed by observation in the cafeteria. But she underestimated the knack of the young to see through devices which an adult thinks have been cleverly camouflaged.
> Instead of leading into the second role-playing as a natural sequence

2 From "Educator's Washington Dispatch," *Portfolio of Teaching Techniques,* New London, Conn.: Croft Educational Services, 1951, p. 26.

to the first, she abruptly asked a group one day after lunch to pretend they were eating in the cafeteria, using the worst table manners they could think of. This was to be followed by a dramatization of good manners.

Johnny, both mischievous and malicious, started imitating Stella. Everyone, including Stella, herself, immediately recognized the girl in the caricature. The youngsters laughed. Stella cried.

Susan Makes Friends: Another elementary teacher, more adroit in dealing with children, had better luck with a somewhat similar effort.

Noticing the thoughtless way in which Susan, a newcomer, was excluded from activities during recess, the teacher waited for an opening so that she could introduce the idea she had in mind. Not long afterward, Marilyn mentioned how much she liked school. Asked why, she gave "being with my friends" as one answer. Would she enjoy being in a new school? Yes! It wouldn't take two minutes to make friends. Kay agreed. Penny thought it would be awful to be in a strange school.

The sociodrama developed so naturally that no one knew exactly when it started. Kay was to pretend she was the new pupil; Marilyn to be well-meaning but inconsiderate. Two girls, Penny and Susan, were to "do what came naturally." For Penny to have played the part of the unaccepted newcomer would have been too near her real-life role of always-on-the-fringe-of-things. The teacher doubted if Penny could be aggressively friendly or unfriendly. It would be interesting to study her action—which turned out to be an amazingly positive one that carried over into the playground the next day.

The teacher purposely wanted Susan, the actual new pupil, to be one of the role players, lest as an onlooker she self-consciously felt as though she were the object of everyone's thoughts. Also Susan's gestures of friendship toward the "new pupil" might give the others hints as to the overtures for which she had been longing.

The teacher attributed to this role-playing incident Susan's easy and quick integration into the group very soon thereafter (page 26).

GROUP INTERACTION FOSTERS INDIVIDUALITY

In any discussion of the relationship of the individual to the group, there is bound to arise the implied criticism of the group's tendency to stifle individuality. The previous discussion in Chapters 2, 4, and 6 is consistent with the point of view that a critical aspect of the healthy personality is identity and individuality. Riesman (1950) refers to autonomy and self-directedness as characteristics of the mature personality. Maslow's (1954) use of the term self-actualization (discussed in Chapter 2) also implies that a differentiated personality is essential for effective living. These descriptions, as well as others, assert that although it is important for the individual to work out a constructive and unique mode of coexistence with others, he must learn to live creatively with and within himself.

This quality of independence becomes particularly urgent today in a world where conformity to ideas and fashions has become the order of the day. The mass media, the recent emphasis by some thinkers upon the group, and the tensions of a world in crisis, all encourage men to huddle closer and closer together. There is a two-fold threat in this growing cult of conformity and group dependence. First there is the threat to the individual today. A person can become so immersed in the crowd that he can completely lose himself; creative activity, independent thought, and reflection can now be exchanged for ready-made answers. But if we believe that the individual should be allowed and indeed encouraged to develop to his fullest capacities and abilities, then we cannot allow that person to lose himself—to escape.

Another consequence of the loss of individuality has more far-reaching consequences. When a society begins to discourage differences it invites disaster. Advances are made by persons who are willing to step outside the customary circle and try something new. A society without eccentrics is a society without the sources of new ideas. To the extent that we insist that our children conform to the mode—and only the mode, we discourage creativeness and individuality.

Education for individuality is directly related to our study of groups. Those who wish to help develop the uniqueness of each individual student, within broad culturally accepted norms, must not lose sight of two important facts. First, that before the individual can become autonomous and self-directive, he must first be dependent and guided by others and before the child can give up the need to be directed by others he must be allowed to participate with others in shaping his own values. Second, the roles (see Chapter 15 for definition of "role") that a person plays in expressing his personality have meaning only as others play coordinated roles. Playing the role of a first baseman depends upon others taking the role of other positions; playing the role of the child depends obviously on others who act the role of parent. The meaning of a person's existence depends upon the social context of his life.

As Drucker (1959) points out, the strength of the group lies in the individuality and independence of its separate members and the strength of the members depends upon the strength of the group. He states that the group depends "on the individual acting as an individual and committing himself as an individual. His act must be voluntary; the more a 'man' and the less of a 'cog' the individual member, the stronger the organization." On the other hand, the individual depends on the group even for his individuality. Thus, ". . . the individual, in order to be effective as such, not only has to find access to the organization; he has to accept its reality, has to affirm its objectives and values, has to form his values, knowledge and efforts on its needs and opportunities." In this view the individual and the group are not antithetical elements, but reciprocal and complimentary. Our aim should be to develop the kinds of groups that encourage individuality in their members.

SUMMARY

One of the most important dimensions of the person's reality is that of other human beings. His attitudes, his values, and other essential aspects of his motivational system are shaped through group interaction. Also the group serves as an instrument for the gratification of the person's social-psychological needs. It is in the group that a person becomes aware of himself as an individual. In the group context he learns the approved ways of behaving and the accepted ways of looking at things.

Among the various interaction patterns that the teacher can foster are cooperation and competition. In our society competition is relied on excessively as an incentive for effort in learning. There are many inherent dangers in this form of social interaction in that it can discourage the less able and it can foster considerable hostility. Conflict and friction between groups, leading to out-group hostility and stereotypes, are often the result of excessive competition. By establishing over-all group goals that can be achieved only through the combined efforts of individuals or groups, cooperative effort is fostered. In general this kind of group interaction produces better results and a greater amount of personal satisfaction. It is the teacher's task to devise the kinds of group goals that call for cooperative effort and that are consistent with the instructional aims of the school.

Because the group satisfies individual needs, the individual comes to identify with the group. The group then becomes a reference group and the individual accepts the norms of the group and conforms to them. This phenomenon has been studied in the laboratory where it has been demonstrated that the group is a more potent influence in gaining conformity than is the teacher. Studies in a college community indicate that college students accept the prevailing attitude as a means of gaining emancipation from parents and as a means of gaining prestige and acceptance in the group. These studies would suggest that the teacher, by accepting differences, can foster an attitude of loyalty to the group even in opposition, and a willingness on the part of the group to be tolerant of dissent.

The techniques that are presently available for the study of group structure and member interaction, are the sociogram and the classroom social-distance scale. In the former, the teacher asks each student to indicate the names of those with whom he would choose to interact and, in a rejection sociogram, the names of those with whom he would prefer not to interact. The classroom social-distance scale introduces the factor of intensity into the measurement. That is, it establishes the degree of acceptance or rejection. By constructing and studying the sociogram the teacher can find out a great deal about an individual student's status in the class. This can serve to help those whose acceptability status is inadequate. An examination of the sociogram can sometimes reveal why group efforts seem to work well at one time and then fail at other times.

Many problems of conducting the class have their basis in inadequate group-individual interaction patterns. Excessive teacher domination can produce dependency or rebelliousness problems. Excessive reliance on competition can lead to a situation in which certain students have difficulty in gaining satisfaction from group participation. Collusive relationships among students can obstruct the achievement of educational aims and can lead to exclusion of certain individuals from various group activities. Another difficulty is that of the feelings of insecurity that one individual may have in relating to others. This is common in the case of the new child entering the group and occurs more frequently as our population becomes more mobile geographically.

The development of social skills depends upon social experience. Exclusion, rejection, or low status within the group can deprive the individual of the necessary experience. This can lead to a circular pattern in which lack of acceptance in the group tends to induce unacceptable behavior, which leads to further rejection by the group and so on. The teacher needs to help break this chain by establishing constructive group standards of human relations and by presenting model behavior patterns toward low status children for other pupils to emulate.

Sociodrama and role-playing activities build upon the natural tendency for children to try out in their play the roles of various individuals. In sociodrama the aim is to provide a means for the child to become more keenly aware of another person's feelings. When this is achieved, the child can play his own role more effectively and can relate more satisfactorily to others. Role playing is useful also in more specific situations such as the preparation for the employment interview, the teaching of a class, or a court trial.

The either-or conception of the individual's relationship to the group is not a useful one. It must be realized that only through the group, through organized social experience and action, can the separate person achieve individuality and personal significance, and only through the voluntary commitment of single individuals can the group achieve any integrity, cohesion, and meaningful action.

READING REFERENCES

Association for Supervision and Curriculum Development 1963 Yearbook, *New Insights and the Curriculum*. Washington, D. C.: National Education Association (particularly chaps. 7 and 8).

Coleman, J. S., *The Adolescent Society*. New York: Free Press of Glencoe, 1961.

Cunningham, Ruth et al., *Understanding Group Behavior of Boys and Girls.* New York: Bureau of Publications, Columbia University, Teachers College, 1951.

Gronlund, N. E., *Sociometry in the Classroom.* New York: Harper & Row, 1959.

Henry, N. B. (Ed.), *The Dynamics of Instructional Groups: Sociopsychological Aspects of Teaching and Learning.* Fifty-ninth Yearbook (Pt. 2) National Society for the Study of Education. Chicago: University of Chicago Press, 1960 (particularly chaps. 3-6, 9, 11, and 13).

Shaftel, G. and Fannie R. Shaftel, *Role Playing the Problem Story.* New York: National Conference of Christians and Jews, 1952.

Smith, L. M., *Group Processes in Elementary and Secondary Schools.* (What Research Says to the Teacher No. 19). Washington, D. C.: National Education Association, 1959.

CHAPTER 9

PURPOSES AND
PROCEDURES
IN EVALUATION

Each of us has been subjected to and has participated in such a vast array of measurement and evaluation activities, that we have come to take the whole process for granted. From the time of our arrival on this earth, witness the notice of our weight accompanying the birth announcement, we are continually measured, tested, weighed, judged, and compared. We in turn make similar evaluative judgments of people, things, and events. The result of all this is that we tend to lose sight of the purposes and the consequences of our many evaluative acts. Such a casual attitude may be only moderately harmful in the conduct of everyday human affairs, but it can be seriously detrimental if it invades the realm of educational practice. Whenever a teacher evaluates the learning of his students without being aware of the proper role of evaluation in teaching, it is likely that the instruction has become rigid and aimless. On the other hand, when the teacher understands how to weave the evaluation into the whole of the instructional process, the teaching and the learning become increasingly more purposeful and more effective. The intention in this chapter is to examine the various purposes and procedures of evaluation, so that this essential aspect of teaching becomes clearly understood.

If we wish to think scientifically about educational problems and to discuss educational issues in systematic and realistic terms, we must rely on concepts and techniques developed in measurement psychology.

Thus, if we desire to determine to what extent the curriculum and the methods of instruction are achieving the established educational aims, then we must use evaluation and measurement procedures. Also, if our purpose is to teach so that each student's educational needs are taken into account, the appropriate instruments should be used to assess those needs. Furthermore, to guide the student into some specialized program of training or to select from a group of candidates those most likely to benefit from such an experience, we must have the kind of information derived from test scores. Although the field of psychological measurement has other purposes as well, insofar as its application to education is concerned it serves these purposes: to tell us how well we are meeting our educational aims and to suggest changes in curriculum and methods so that these aims are more closely achieved; to identify the special needs of students so that special arrangements can be made to satisfy those needs; to guide and to select students. Before considering these purposes in detail the characteristics of educational and psychological measuring instruments will be discussed.

THE CHARACTERISTICS OF PSYCHOLOGICAL MEASUREMENT

Because the measurement of various phenomena is so closely related to our philosophical assumptions about reality, it is important that we understand some of the characteristics of psychological measuring instruments. Thus Thorndike's (1918) assertion that whatever exists at all, exists in some amount; and anything that exists in amount can be measured, reflects an attitude toward reality that is not wholly acceptable. The poet Burns is much more realistic when he states: "What's done we partly may compute, But know not what's resisted." It has been noted, for example, in Chapter 3, in the discussion of learning curves, that much of what goes on in learning is not directly measurable, in Chapter 4, that much of what we experience in achieving insight and understanding is beyond measurement, and Chapter 2 and Chapter 6, that the more significant aspects of values and personality structure are not subject to direct measurement. An examination of the characteristics of instruments used to measure such qualities as educational achievement will reveal some of their limitations. Yet in spite of these limitations, the contributions of measurement psychology to the advance of educational practice have been considerable. In order to understand the nature of these contributions the reader should become familiar with a few fundamental notions in statistics and with the procedures for interpreting test scores. For a more extended introduction the reader is referred to a beginning text such as Smith (1962) or Garrett (1953).

Some Concepts in Descriptive Statistics

The following scores in arithmetic and spelling tests were obtained by students in a hypothetical fifth-grade class:

Spelling scores: 80, 78, 52, 92, 98, 77, 69, 75, 90, 91, 65, 89, 78, 86, 98, 92, 75, 74, 86, 73, 78, 75, 94, 86, 88, 76, 48, 64, 70, 82.

Arithmetic scores: 71, 85, 64, 78, 90, 81, 82, 64, 85, 97, 60, 75, 78, 80, 92, 89, 81, 78, 88, 84, 73, 68, 99, 96, 80, 89, 67, 88, 83, 88.

It would be difficult to say very much about these scores when they are in this form. One way of bringing order to these figures is to arrange them in a frequency table as in Table 9.1.

TABLE 9.1   TALLY AND FREQUENCY TABLES FOR 30 SCORES IN SPELLING AND 30 SCORES IN ARITHMETIC

	Spelling[a]			Arithmetic[b]	
Step	*Tally*	*Frequency*	*Step*	*Tally*	*Frequency*
95-99	11	2	97-99	11	2
90-94	11111	5	94-96	1	1
85-89	11111	5	91-93	1	1
80-84	11	2	88-90	11111/1	6
75-79	11111/111	8	85-87	11	2
70-74	111	3	82-84	111	3
65-69	11	2	79-81	1111	4
60-64	1	1	76-78	111	3
55-59		0	73-75	11	2
50-54	1	1	70-72	1	1
45-49	1	1	67-69	11	2
			64-66	11	2
			61-63		0
			58-60	1	1

a The mean of the spelling scores is 79.3, the standard deviation is 12.
b The mean of the arithmetic scores is 81.1, the standard deviation is 9.9.

The frequency distribution enables us to see some order in the disorganized series of scores. It would be more convenient if we characterize the performance on each of the tests by a single number. The most usual way of doing this is to use one of the measures of central tendency, the mean (the arithmetic average) or the median (the score at the middle of the distribution of scores). The mean is obtained by adding all the scores and dividing by the number of cases. When this is done the mean in spelling is 79.3 and in arithmetic the mean is 81.1. The median is that point in the distribution of scores above which and below which

50 percent of the scores fall. Turning again to our spelling and arithmetic scores we find the median in the former to be 78.8 and in the latter 82.9. (The frequency table was used to compute the median. It would be accurate enough to use the figures 78 and 83 respectively for the medians of the two distributions.)

In describing the performance of the group, the measures of central tendency do not tell us about how the scores are distributed, how they are dispersed or spread through the distribution. In comparing the performance of two groups it would be useful to know not only the means of the scores, but also how the scores are dispersed. Does one group have the scores cluster closely to the mean and the other have them spread far away from the mean? A measure of dispersion is useful in describing the group performance. It tells us, among other things, about the homogeneity or heterogeneity of the performance of the group. One measure of dispersion is the range of scores or simply the highest score less the lowest score. In the example above the range in spelling is $98 - 48 = 50$ and in arithmetic it is $99 - 60 = 39$. The range as a measure of dispersion is, however, too greatly affected by extreme, atypical scores, furthermore, it does not sufficiently take into account other scores. The most common and most useful measure of dispersion that overcomes these deficiencies of the range is the standard deviation (SD, also written as sigma, σ). The following are the steps necessary for obtaining the standard deviation:

1. Determine how much each score deviates or differs from the mean. For example, the first score for the ungrouped spelling scores, 80, deviates from the mean, 79.3, by 0.7. The other deviations are similarly determined.
2. Square each deviation. The 0.7 obtained in step 1 would be squared to give us 0.49.
3. Sum all the squares obtained in step 2.
4. Divide this sum by the number of scores. In the case given it is necessary to divide by 30.
5. Obtain the SD by taking the square root of the quotient in step 4. In the examples the SD for the spelling scores turns out to be 12 and for the arithmetic scores it is 9.9.

When there is a large number of unselected cases the scores generally fall into a bell-shaped frequency distribution approximating the one shown in Figure 9.1 This bell-shaped curve, commonly called the *normal curve,* has certain mathematical properties that provide the basis for many different kinds of statistical analyses and inferences. A few of its features are noted here. The number of scores is greatest in the middle and gradually drops off as we move out to the high and low scores. The curve is symmetrical. The larger the population, the more the fre-

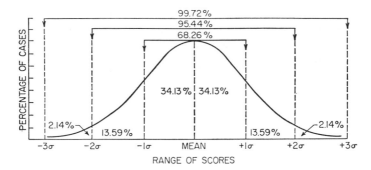

FIGURE 9.1   *A normal curve. This form of distribution, with a large percentage of cases at or near the mean and with decreasing percentages as the scores become larger or smaller, is what we expect when the characteristic being measured occurs as a result of chance factors in a large population.*

quency distribution will resemble the idealized normal curve shown in Figure 9.1.

The Nature of the Scale

In most of our experiences with measurement, for example measures of weight or distance, two obvious and basic assumptions can be made. We can assume that the units on the scale are always equal wherever they are found, an inch is an inch and a gram is a gram, throughout the whole scale. We can also assume the zero position is a true or absolute zero representing no amount. Using such instruments we can conclude that 50 grams is twice as heavy as 25 grams and that a child who has grown 4 inches in a year has grown twice as much as one who has grown 2 inches.

Wood (1960) points out that most educational and psychological tests meet neither the condition of equal units nor that of absolute zero. A child who makes an error in every word in a spelling test and who receives a score of zero, cannot be assumed to have no knowledge of spelling. Usually he will even demonstrate that he understands some principles of correct spelling even within those words spelled incorrectly. Moreover, in that same spelling test, the student will usually receive one additional point for answering correctly one additional item. As the items on the test are not likely to be completely equivalent, the score units or the intervals on the scale are not equal. Measures of school achievement generally have neither equal units nor an absolute zero point. As we shall see in the ensuing discussion, there are ways of dealing with these facts that make test scores usable for the purposes just outlined.

The raw score or the number of items answered correctly on a test must be interpreted. The most common basis for interpretation is to compare the score with the scores obtained by others on the same test. The simplest way of comparing scores is to rank them. However, as the size of the group may be large or small, ranking does not permit us to interpret the score clearly. For example, should you receive a score of 78 on a test, you would know very little about your level of accomplishment. Should your score place you at rank 27, you would still be unable to interpret your accomplishment unless you knew the size of the group. The simplest way of making ranks comparable is to convert the rank to a percentage value thus obtaining percentile or centile ranks. In using a standardized test the manual will often provide a table allowing the conversion of the raw scores into percentiles. The percentile score is not a measure of the percentage of correct responses. A score at the 75th percentile bears no direct relationship to the number of correct responses, it merely indicates that the student has performed better than 75 percent of the population with which he is being compared, the standardization population.

In many test manuals tables are provided that convert the raw scores into *age* or *grade* scores. Age scores are measures of performance for those abilities that show improvement with age. For example, if the raw score on a reading test is converted to an age norm it might be reported as 9-2, meaning that this reading performance is equal to that of the average of a population of children who are nine years and two months old. A ratio measure or quotient can be derived by computing the ratio of age score to chronological age. Age scores and quotients will be described further in the next chapter in connection with concepts of mental age and intelligence quotient (IQ). Grade scores are analogous to age scores. A raw score converted to a grade score may read 6.3 meaning that this performance is like that of the average of pupils who have spent three months in the sixth grade. Cronbach (1960a) points out that the uncritical use of grade norms can be misleading.

> Grade norms are based on samples of pupils throughout the nation. Some sections of the country are far superior to others, because of differences in pupil ability, differences in the quality of teachers, and differences in expenditures for education. No teacher or superintendent from a superior school can take pride if his group merely reaches the national norms; no one from a handicapped school district should be condemned if his group cannot attain the national average. The only fair basis for comparing schools is to judge each school against schools with similar organization, similar curricula, and similar promotion policies. Rarely are published norms based on such meaningful segments as "New England public elementary schools, in cities with population 2,000 to 10,000" or "Southern rural elementary schools."
>
> Norms are not "standards." It is a common mistake to assume that all pupils in the ninth grade should reach the ninth-grade norm. This is of course a fallacy; 50 percent of the pupils in the standardizing sample fall

below the norm. Furthermore, the test shows only what schools are doing at present. It is highly unlikely that the schools are doing so well that the national average represents what pupils could attain with the best teaching methods. The teacher whose class reaches the average has no cause for complacency. There is much room for the development of better educational methods (page 385).

A grade score may be useful in the placement of a pupil who transfers from one school system to another where there are several classes for the same grade, each with a somewhat different distribution of achievement scores. Let us imagine that a youngster is being entered into a school in January. He is eleven years and seven months of age (CA 11-7) and has been in the sixth grade in a different school system. The school that he is entering has four classes of the sixth grade with the following mean scores on an achievement test administered in September: 5.7, 6.3, 6.8, and 7.1. The same test is administered in January to the entering student and he achieves a grade score of 6.6. It would appear that he should be placed in the class that scored 6.3 in September as the average performance in that class is most similar to his. (Assuming that the mean performance of this class would be 6.7 by January.) The range of ability in each class would need to be considered beforehand, as well as the student's interests and any special abilities or deficiencies that might be revealed in his test scores.

It can be demonstrated that although different parts of the percentile scale or the grade-norm scale are presented as equal, in actuality they are not. A student who improves his score from the 80th to the 90th percentile shows greater change than one who improves from the 40th to the 50th percentile although both have gained 10 percentile points. In order to overcome this deficiency in percentile ranking and grade norms a more stable measure has been devised, that of the *standard score* and its derivative the *T-score*. These scores, like percentile scores, tell us where a given raw score would fall in comparison with the standardization population.

In converting raw scores to standard scores, the average or mean score is assigned a value of zero and each standard deviation is given a value of one. Returning to the spelling and arithmetic scores given above, a raw score of 79.3 in spelling would be designated as "0" standard score and 91.3 (79.3 + 12) as 1; in arithmetic 81.1 would be designated "0" standard score and 81.1 + 9.9 or 91.0 as a standard score of 1. A standard score of 2 would be that raw score corresponding to the mean score plus two standard deviations. In spelling this would be 79.3 + (2 × 12) = 103.3 (a score that does not occur in actuality here but might occur theoretically); in arithmetic a standard score of 2 would correspond to a raw score of 81.1 + (2 × 9.9) = 100.9. Minus standard scores can be obtained by proceeding in similar fashion but subtracting the value for the standard deviation from the mean instead of adding. Standard scores can also be obtained that represent fractional values of the standard deviation, for example, $\frac{1}{2}$ standard deviation above the mean and so on. In order to facilitate reporting, the minus sign and decimals are eliminated by using a modification of the standard score, the T-score. When using the T-score the mean of the distribution is arbitrarily assigned a value of 50 and each standard deviation has a value of 10. Thus 79.3 in spelling and 81.1 in arithmetic would be assigned T-scores of 50, and a score of 91.3 in spelling (the score equivalent to one standard deviation above the mean) would have a T-score of 60, and so on.

One of the purposes of converting raw scores to percentiles, or to standard or T-scores, is to enable us to compare the performance of an individual on two different tests. For example, if Susan has raw scores of 91 in spelling and 73 in arithmetic in the example above, she would have T-scores of 60 and 45 respectively. We can say that her performance in spelling is better than the average and in arithmetic somewhat below average. These converted scores are directly comparable with each other where raw scores are not.

Theoretically the range of scores may extend from infinitely small scores to infinitely large ones. Practically, however, in most sets of scores, as for example the ones shown in Figure 9.1, the range of scores is usually encompassed by three standard deviations above the mean and three below. Each standard deviation is an equal distance in score from the mean. The percentage of cases obtaining scores between the mean and one standard deviation above or below the mean is 34.1 The percentage of cases between various points using the mean and standard deviation values can be computed from Figure 9.1.

Thus we see that scores in educational measurement are based largely on comparisons of one pupil with appropriate groups of pupils. The fact that certain achievement qualities exist does not mean that they can be measured in the sense that we usually take the term measurement. Our procedures in educational measurement must fit the task and the purposes of measurement.

Reliability

Another important characteristic of educational and psychological measuring instruments is their reliability. The consistency, accuracy, and stability with which a test measures is said to be its reliability. The reliability of a test score is its dependability. The factors that influence the reliability of a test score arise from three general sources, the scoring, the content of the test, and the instability of the test response of the person being examined.

If the test score requires the subjective estimate of a judge, the re-

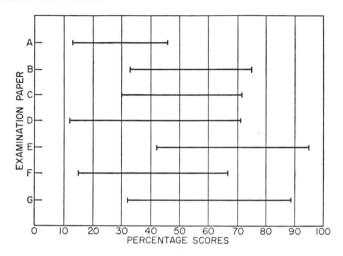

FIGURE 9.2 *Seven examination papers in home economics are scored by twelve different teachers. The horizontal lines indicate the range of scores assigned by these teachers to each of the seven papers. Adapted from Clara B. Arny,* Evaluation in Home Economics, *New York: Appleton-Century-Crofts, 1953.*

liability will tend to be low. The same response, let us say an essay written in a test, will receive a different score if the scoring is done by the same judge at different times or by different judges. This problem arises particularly in the evaluation of creative productions, compositions and essays, form in athletic performance, and so on. Figure 9.2 shows the wide range of judgments given by twelve raters to seven essay papers in a home economics examination. Paper D, for example, is judged to be worth 10 points by one judge and 70 points by another and paper G's scores range from less than 40 to 90.

The assignment of a letter grade to the student's performance in a course is similarly subject to the unreliability of the teacher's subjective judgment. When different instructors teaching different sections of the same course use different bases for assigning letter grades, much dissatisfaction can result. In Table 9.2 we have such a situation. The data were obtained from six different instructors teaching a total of twelve sections (more than 350 students) of a college freshman history course. As far as could be determined the students were assigned to these sections on a random basis.

The meaning of each letter grade to each of these instructors is quite obviously based on different considerations. One would suspect that instructors H and I have some sort of absolute standard in mind, albeit different ones, whereas instructor J seems to be using some sort of fixed percentage distribution judging from the symmetrical distribution with the C grade as the mode. It is reasonable to assume that similar

TABLE 9.2   PERCENTAGE OF STUDENTS GIVEN EACH LETTER GRADE BY
SIX INSTRUCTORS IN A FRESHMAN HISTORY CLASS

	Grades				
Instructor	A	B	C	D	F
H	5	8	40	30	17
I	20	38	40	2	0
J	3	20	55	20	2
K	25	30	40	3	2
L	8	15	65	10	2
M	22	15	28	19	16

performances have been assigned different grades by the different instructors. If a student were primarily interested in the letter grade he
would be well advised to try to enter a section taught by instructor K
who assigns A and B grades to 55 percent of his students and to stay out of
those taught by H who assigns D and F grades to 47 percent of his
students.

This problem of the lack of reliability introduced by the subjective element of teacher judgment can be somewhat controlled. This can
be achieved by improving the form of the test item and also the instructions to the person grading the test paper. We discuss these questions
below.

The content of a test introduces another source of unreliability.
If the directions are vague, if the questions are not clearly stated and invite guessing, and if the test is too short for the breadth of subject matter
being examined, the test is likely to be unreliable. The score obtained
on one such test by a student would not be the same as the score he
would obtain on another form of the test intended to examine the same
subject matter. Thus in a spelling test sampling 150 words, a list of fifteen words is selected. The teacher reads these words one at a time and
uses them in sentences. If the directions are not clear and the sentences
used are misleading, the scores obtained by the different students would
in all likelihood be different should another list of fifteen words be
used.

This source of unreliability stemming from the content of the test
can be avoided by careful analysis of the test so that the breadth of the
content of the test reflects adequately the scope of the subject matter being tested. This issue is also of concern in establishing the validity of the
test. To reduce this source of unreliability the test must be long enough
and attention should be given to clarity of the directions and the test
questions.

It is commonly recognized that the performance on a test is influenced by conditions not directly related to the ability being measured.

That is, there are a number of temporary factors such as fluctuation of motivation, the presence of distraction, physical discomfort or illness, emotional upset and the like that could depress a test score. If the person were to be examined again under more auspicious circumstances his score would be higher. We must recognize that such factors can influence the test score even though some students use them as an alibi to explain away their poor performance. All testing should be done under the most favorable conditions possible so that this source of unreliability is minimized.

The reliability of the test score also refers to its precision or accuracy. There are many occasions when a test result is treated as if it were much more precise than is actually warranted. Walker (1948) emphasizes the approximate nature of educational measurement in the following statement.

> The approximate nature of all measurement is an important idea for educated people in general, but especially important to teachers who may do great harm to their pupils if they place too literal trust in unreliable measures of those pupils. The inescapable unreliability of measurement can be made vivid even to relatively immature pupils if appropriate experiments are arranged. Over and above the needs of the average person, the teacher needs to have some idea of the meaning of the conventional measures of test reliability and the qualities to be sought in selecting standardized tests as well as methods of determining the reliability of teacher-made instruments.
>
> There is an inexhaustible supply of amusing illustrations of the ordinary person's misplaced faith in the precision of his measurements. The particular episode which has grown gray in my service at this point comes from the days when I taught a high school class in trigonometry. The students had been brought up in the tradition which makes a fetish of complete accuracy and I had spent most of one period trying to blast out their belief that it was a mark of merit to carry computations to a large number of decimal places. Finally, with a yardstick scaled only to the quarter inch I measured the length of a desk with well worn edges and stated the result as 43.4672 inches. What was their appraisal? It took them no time at all to say I was either bluffing, joking, or hopelessly stupid. The very next morning in a school assembly the high school principal read the average grade of each member of the graduating class to four decimal places. As a device for reinforcing my teaching the experience was admirable but I fear it did not enhance the prestige of the principal in the eyes of this class (page 209).

Correlation

The reliability of a test is usually reported in the form of a correlation coefficient. In addition to providing a method for determining reliability, the correlation procedure has many other applications in psychological measurement and in the analysis of psychological data.

Correlation is used, for example, to determine the validity of a test instrument as we shall see below, to obtain a measure of the degree of relationship between various abilities as in factor analysis, to determine to what extent certain factors such as level of parent's education are related to intelligence or other abilities, and so on.

There are a number of different ways of computing a correlation coefficient. Whatever method is used for computing the correlation coefficient, the end result is a measure of the degree of correspondence or relationship between two or more variables or sets of scores. In the case of establishing the reliability of a test we would need to obtain two scores for each subject from one of the following sources: (1) the scores assigned by each of two judges rating the same performance of each of the subjects, or one judge rating each performance, let us say an essay, twice, (2) the scores obtained by each of the subjects taking the same test twice or taking alternate, equivalent forms of the test, (3) by assigning a separate score to each of two halves of the test (odd numbered items and even numbered items). The decision whether to use one or another procedure for establishing the reliability of a test instrument will depend on the nature of the measurement. In some instances two procedures are equally applicable and may give somewhat different reliability coefficients. The reliability coefficient or the relationship between any of these two sets of scores may take different forms.

One type of relationship that may exist between two variables is "strong positive." This means that individuals obtaining high scores in one variable tend to obtain high scores in the other variable, middle scores tend to go with middle scores, and low scores with low. Such a strong positive relationship can be illustrated in the scores of sixteen students on two equivalent forms of a spelling test. The data are presented in Table 9.3 and have been transferred to a scattergram in Fig-

TABLE 9.3   SCORES OF SIXTEEN STUDENTS ON TWO EQUIVALENT FORMS OF A SPELLING TEST

Student	Score on Form 1	Score on Form 2	Student	Score on Form 1	Score on Form 2
1. Anne G.	40	39	9. Sue B.	33	30
2. Henry F.	38	38	10. Larry F.	32	28
3. Alan M.	39	36	11. Linda P.	30	27
4. Sue G.	36	35	12. Elizabeth S.	29	26
5. Judith L.	34	34	13. Edward N.	25	27
6. Barbara A.	34	33	14. John T.	28	23
7. Charles M.	33	33	15. Don P.	25	21
8. Gerald L.	32	33	16. Carol G.	20	21

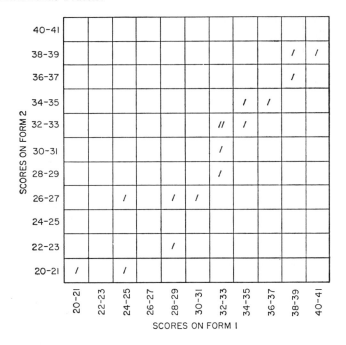

FIGURE 9.3 *A strong positive correlation. Data is taken from Table 9.3. Each student's pair of scores is represented by a tally in the box representing the point at which the score on Form 1 meets the score on Form 2. The correlation is + 0.93.*

ure 9.3 so as to represent the correlation graphically. Another illustration of a strong positive correlation is to be found on page 310 (Figure 10.2), where the relationship of the scores obtained by a group of subjects on two forms of the Stanford-Binet intelligence test is represented in a scattergram. In both these scattergrams it will be noted that the tally marks are arranged on or near the diagonal going from the lower left corner to the upper right. This diagonal is the line that represents a perfect positive correlation (+1.00). If all the tallies fell along this diagonal, the individuals obtaining the highest scores on variable one would obtain the highest scores on variable two, those obtaining the lowest scores on variable one would obtain the lowest scores on variable two and so on, and we would be able to predict perfectly, at least in standard score terms, from one test score to the other.

A less pronounced and somewhat more typical reliability relationship is shown in the scattergram in Figure 9.4. The scores of 104 subjects on two equivalent forms of a Word Fluency test, a subtest of a group intelligence test, are represented on the scattergram. It will be noted that the tendency is for the tallies to be distributed along the same diagonal

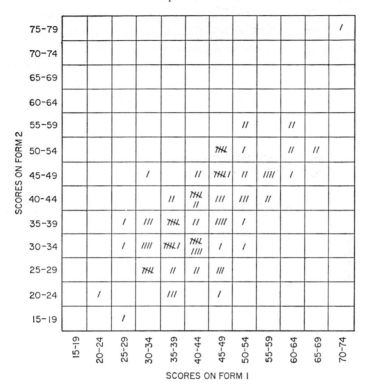

FIGURE 9.4 *A reliability coefficient of 0.72. Forms 1 and 2 are two versions of a word fluency test. From Anne Anastasi,* Psychological Testing *2d ed., New York: The Macmillan Company, 1961, p. 117. Based on data from Anastasi and Drake (1954).*

as in the two previously mentioned scattergrams. The tendency however is not as pronounced. This reliability coefficient is reported as 0.72.

Another possible form of the relationship between two variables is a "negative" correlation. This would be the case if the tally marks fell on or near the diagonal running from the upper left corner to the bottom right. When this happens it can readily be seen that low scores on variable one are associated with high scores on variable two, high scores on variable one are associated with low scores on variable two, and middle scores with middle scores. It is important to note that negative correlations provide us with as much ability to predict from one set of scores to another as do positive correlations, when they are both of the same magnitude.

In addition to the positive and negative forms that a correlation may take, we may find that two variables do not vary in any consistent way with each other. This is the absence of relationship or a zero correlation. In this case the tallies would be so arranged on the scattergram so that high scores in each variable would be more or less evenly distributed through low, medium, and high scores on the other variables, and medium and low scores of one variable would be likewise randomly associated with high, medium, and low scores of the other. When this occurs we obviously cannot predict except by chance from scores in one variable to scores in the other. When coefficients of reliability are at or near zero, we could not depend on the scores to be the same if the test were taken again, if it were scored by another judge, or if we correlated the scores on one half with the scores on the other.

There is a strong tendency for the uninitiated to interpret correlation coefficients as percentage values. They are not. The magnitude of the correlation tells us how much better than chance our predictions would be but not in terms of percentages. In Table 9.4 are presented

TABLE 9.4   SOME CORRELATION VALUES AND THEIR INTERPRETATION

Correlation	*Interpretation*
0.80-0.97 +	These are generally considered very high correlations. We would find correlations of this order on some test-retest reliabilities; in judge reliabilities involving ratings on a simple aspect of performance such as word counts.
0.65-0.80	These are considered high correlations. We would find correlations of this order in correlating such scores as "one intelligence test with another; reading test with vocabulary test; height with weight," Commins and Fagin (1954); also achievement test scores with scores on group intelligence tests.
0.40-0.60	Correlations of this order are usually not acceptable as reliability coefficients. They are useful however in some cases of predictive validity (see discussion below). This magnitude of correlation might be expected, for example, in predicting school grades from intelligence test scores.
0.20-0.40	These are low correlation values and we would expect to find correlations of this order when correlating mechanical ability with vocabulary scores; group intelligence test scores with grades in performing arts, and the like.
0.00-0.20	These are very low correlations. They occur in correlating height, strength, coordination, handwriting, and so on, with intelligence test scores. Correlations of this magnitude occur also as a result of chance factors.

some ranges of correlation coefficients and their interpretations.

It should also be noted that correlations do not establish cause and effect relationships. If two variables are correlated there is no reason to assume that one produces or causes fluctuations in the other. The relationship may be due to a common third factor or may result from attributing certain unjustified characteristics to our scores. The correlation of intelligence and achievement scores is usually high but not because intelligence produces achievement but because the tests are made up of very similar tasks.

The Use of Essay and Objective Test Items

As already intimated in the discussion of reliability the form of the test item is an important consideration. Test items are usually classified into essay type and objective type. A list of the advantages and disadvantages of essay and objective forms of examination might be mistakenly used as a basis for concluding that one form is better than another. In truth, each form has a contribution to make in the evaluation of pupil performance. If each form is used in its proper place and if the deficiencies to which each of these forms is prone are avoided, it is not necessary to decide which of these is better.

Tinkelman (1958) describes the contribution of the essay question as follows:

> The fundamental contribution of the essay question is that it requires the pupil to develop an answer from his own background and fund of experience, without benefit of suggested possibilities or alternatives, and to express that answer in his own words. Where this is a crucial element in the measurement picture, the use of essay rather than objective questions is indicated. By requiring pupils to present evidence, to evaluate, to analyze and to solve new problems or approach problems in a new way, essay questions can serve to measure some higher level abilities and thus contribute to knowledge about the pupil (page 9).

The rating of an essay question introduces a factor of unreliability. In order to increase the reliability of the essay question the following procedure is suggested. In framing the question the scope of the answer should be clearly delimited. The answers should be scored with a model answer in mind. The student's answers should be compared with this model answer and the shortcomings of the student's answer should be noted; the grade can be assigned accordingly. It is further suggested that all the answers to one question be scored at one time.

In order to assure adequate coverage of the material several short essay questions are preferable to one long one. If it seems desirable to offer the student some choice in selecting the questions, the teacher should be careful that the choices available are of similar difficulty, that they do not change the range of coverage of the subject matter, and that reasonable comparability of pupils' scores is maintained.

The major advantages of the objective-type questions are that they permit broader sampling of the content thus increasing the reliability and the ease of scoring. Objective-type items may be grouped into four categories: (1) Completion items. These represent the only form of the objective item that relies on recall rather than recognition. (2) True-false items. These should be limited to statements that are unequivocally true or false. It should be noted also that true-false items invite guessing. (3) Multiple-choice items. (4) Matching items.

The objective part of an examination should be checked carefully to see that it meets a number of criteria. The following questions, adapted from Tinkelman (1958), may serve as a checklist for the classroom test.

1. Are the items presented in clear and simple language, with vocabulary kept as simple as possible?
2. Does each item have one and only one correct answer?
3. Are negative statements avoided?
4. Are trick questions avoided?
5. Is excessive "window dressing" avoided?
6. Is the item free from specific determiners such as "always" and "never," and extraneous clues due to grammatical inconsistencies, rote verbal associations, length of response, and the like?
7. Are items of the same type requiring the same directions grouped together in the test?
8. Are items arranged from easy to more difficult within the test as a whole and within each major subdivision of the test?

In order to improve the quality of the test item, a record of the performance of the class on each item should be kept. The teacher should maintain a card-file library of test items, both essay and objective. Each time the item is used a notation should be entered on the card and appropriate changes in the item should be made. For the objective items the teacher can record the number of correct answers to each item made by those who scored high on the total test (the top 25 percent) and those who scored low (the bottom 25 percent). By analyzing each item the teacher can determine the difficulty of each item, how well it discriminates between good and poor performers, and whether the item needs to be revised.

The concern for good test items should not divert our attention from one important fact. Our purpose in administering a test is to provide the teacher and the student with information that should be used to improve teaching procedures and the learning process.

Validity

The most important quality of a measurement procedure is its validity, that is, the extent to which it measures what it purports or claims to measure. Another way of stating this is that the validity of a test is the extent to which it truly satisfies the purpose for which the test is administered. As we might have different purposes even in administering the same test, the test would have a different validity for each purpose. Anastasi (1961) states: "No test can be said to have 'high' or 'low' validity in the abstract. Its validity must be determined with reference to the particular use for which it is being considered."

We tend to look to the title of a test to tell us the purpose for which it has been designed. However it must be noted that titles of standardized published tests can be misleading and may have been chosen to attract sales. As in selecting a book or a novel the title is generally a poor indicator of the content. This writer recalls an incident in which the title of a test misled a group of students in a class in educational psychology. These students, who were being trained in youth work and who were serving as youth-group leaders, were requested to participate in trying out a paper and pencil test called "A Test of Leadership." The form was administered to several hundred young people and after being scored was returned to the youth-group leaders. In going over the results, several of the college students commented that the test results were most revealing. Some of the children who had been withdrawn from the group and who had not actively participated, had scored high on the test. The students had failed, however, to investigate the validity of the test instrument. The observational measures were in this case a better measure of leadership than this particular paper and pencil test. Educators need not give up faith in their own observational measures as a basis for assessing certain qualities. These are often more valid than paper and pencil devices purporting to measure such qualities.

The validity of a test is determined, in general, by measuring the extent to which the scores on a test are related to other independently derived information about the characteristic being measured. The American Psychological Association (1954) has issued a bulletin entitled *Technical Recommendations for Psychological Tests and Diagnostic Techniques*. In this publication the various procedures for determining validity are classified under four categories, namely, predictive, concurrent, content, and construct validity. A consideration of each of these types of validity follows.

Predictive Validity

Very often a test is given with the purpose of predicting the possible future performance of those examined. The validity of such a test is its predictive validity or the measure of the extent to which this test enables us to make such predictions. To establish the predictive validity of such a test we need to obtain a measure of the future performance on a population of individuals that we would call our validating population. The extent to which the test scores correspond to the future performance scores would be the predictive validity of the test. If this is sufficiently high we could use the test on other individuals as a predictor of their future performance. The measure of future performance obtained on the validating population is called a *criterion measure*.

The most common situation in which the predictive validity is useful, is in a test administered for selection purposes. The primary purpose of using tests in selection is to differentiate between the potentially more able and the potentially less able candidates. Selection tests are designed to provide information that would enable the selecting agency to choose individuals who have those characteristics that are essential for quality performance on a task. The selection problem is complicated by the multiple and variable requirements of the tasks or the training programs for which we select people. Thus a teacher, army officer, or stenographer may be called on to deal with so many different kinds of activities that it is well nigh impossible to state with clarity what a particular job demands in the way of human qualities. This means that it is difficult to obtain a good measure of the criterion. In spite of this problem, selection programs can accomplish two things. They can eliminate those who have critical deficiencies such as a lack of intelligence, or basic aptitude, and they can reduce the error that would occur if less systematic approaches were applied. The following illustration should clarify the values and limitations of selection test batteries in the educational setting.

The British Education Act of 1944 requires local school authorities to provide a variety of educational opportunities suitable for children of differing abilities and aptitudes. The education act does not specify the procedures for selecting children, but a pattern has developed country-wide called the eleven-plus examinations. Children who have reached the age of eleven take standardized objective tests of intelligence, English, and arithmetic. After teachers administer and score the tests, the Education Office of the local authority establishes order-of-merit lists, based on the three scores. Depending on the number of places available in the grammar schools, the selective academic secondary schools, a number of those at the top of the list are offered an opportunity to attend these schools. Those who score low on the tests are considered poor risks for the secondary grammar schools and are assigned to either the secondary modern or secondary technical schools. An estimate of the effectiveness of this selection procedure is presented in Table 9.5. The data in the table are hypothetical and based on two assumptions; first that the selection test scores correlated 0.90 with the measure of success in the grammar school (the criterion measure), and second that the admission rate to the grammar school was 20 percent. When these two conditions apply we note that one fourth of the small number of those selected for the grammar school, are destined to be unsuccessful. If, however, the same standards were maintained in the grammar school and all children

TABLE 9.5   THE PREDICTIVE EFFICIENCY OF THE ELEVEN-PLUS
EXAMINATIONS

	Number successful in work of grammar school	*Number unsuccessful in work of grammar school*
Passed by selection Procedures (total N = 20)	15	5
Failed by selection Procedures (total N = 80)	5	75

Source: **P. E. Vernon** (Ed.), *Secondary School Selection*. London: Methuen, 1957, p. 76.

were admitted without selection, we would find that four fifths (80 out of 100) would fail. That is to say that a test that has reasonable predictive validity can only reduce the error in selection, it does not eliminate it. A consideration of some of the possible undesirable effects of selection testing follows.

Some Dangers of Selection Examinations

A selection procedure generally carries with it prestige implications, such as, admission to the college of one's choice, scholarship or status, and recognition. Even the selection of a child to carry a note from one classroom to another will bring forth a number of "choose me" responses. Those who take a selection examination usually hope that they can perform well enough to be selected for the job, scholarship, or admission. This hope and striving is strong enough in most cases so that the student will prepare himself for the examination. He will cram if this is possible, he will seek tutoring help, and in general will try to obtain an advantage over his competitors. In the case of the eleven-plus examination it is common practice for parents to engage private tutors to prepare the child for this examination. The school staff, desiring to reduce the possible advantage of the home tutored, may introduce coaching classes at school for a considerable period before the examination. The effects of coaching may or may not be detrimental. They will be harmful if the preparation for the tests leads to a narrowing of efforts on the part of the teacher or the student with performance on the examination becoming the major purpose of schooling. If the examinations are very broad in scope and rely but little on specifics, it is not likely that they will have any negative results.

In one important respect selection examinations are based on a point of view that is inconsistent with sound educational practice. It is true that they are used to meet the practical exigencies of a situation. For example, we have only limited funds for scholarships, a limited num-

FIGURE 9.5 *With an inflexible target there will always be some failures. Copyright (1957) United Feature Syndicate, Inc.*

ber of places in an entering class, or the task for which we are selecting requires a certain minimum preparation or level of performance. In general this runs counter to what schools have accepted as their motto; to give to each what will benefit him the most. Selection examinations do not ordinarily concern themselves with the needs, personal or educational, of those who do not make it (see Figure 9.5). Although we must recognize the usefulness of selection procedures, we must guard against the encroachment of the impersonality that must accompany them.

Concurrent Validity

Concurrent validity is essentially another form of predictive validity. The difference between these two forms of validity is the time during which the criterion measures are obtained on the validating population. In predictive validity the measure on the criterion can only be made at a future date, as when in validating a selection test for medical school students we would have to wait until such time as the program of study was completed. In concurrent validity the measure on the criterion is immediately or even previously available.

Cronbach (1960a) describes concurrent validity as follows:

In many situations for which tests are developed, some more cumbersome method of collecting information is already in use. If the existing method is considered useful for decision making, the first question in validation is whether the new test agrees with the present source of information. If they disagree, the test may have value of its own, but it is certainly not a substitute for the original method. Validation again requires an empirical comparison. Both the test and the original procedure are applied to the same subjects, and the results are compared. For example, tests intended for clinical diagnosis are compared with the judgments made by a psychiatrist who interviews each patient. A test of proficiency in radar maintenance may be compared with ratings given by an instructor who watches each man in the shop. This type of empirical check on agreement is called *concurrent validation,* because the two sources of information are obtained at very nearly the same time (pages 103-104).

Content Validity

Of the four types of validity under consideration, content validity is of most direct application to the educational test. We determine the content validity of a test by examining whether the content of the test corresponds to the content of the subject matter under consideration. Anastasi (1961) points out that mere inspection of the test is usually not sufficient to establish its content validity. We need to know whether the test measures all of the objectives set for the particular course of study.

There is a tendency to overgeneralize test results. A test of foreign-language ability may emphasize reading or grammatical construction; a high or low score on such a test does not reveal anything about the individual's ability to speak the language. Also, an objective multiple-choice test that measures ability to recognize correctly and incorrectly spelled words may or may not be a good measure of ability to spell in dictation, spontaneous writing, or other kinds of activities requiring spelling ability.

A critical review of an examination with the following questions in mind will improve its content validity: Does the test evaluate all the objectives of the course? Is there a reasonable balance of test items covering such objectives as mastery of technical terminology, application and extrapolation of information? Too many tests emphasize specific knowledge to the exclusion of other teaching objectives. Does the test adequately sample the various parts of the subject matter? For example in a course in history covering a particular period does the test concentrate too much on one segment of the period? Content validity may thus be seen to be a matter of adequate coverage of material and of objectives. A later discussion of evaluation of the cognitive aspects of the curriculum will further clarify the concept of content validity.

Construct Validity

Tests are sometimes used to measure a theoretical construct, a hypothesized psychological trait, or to test an aspect of a more general psychological theory. The extent to which the test succeeds in doing this is its construct validity. Cronbach and Meehl (1955) in elaborating on the statement of construct validity found in *Technical Recommendations* of the APA, state the following: *"Construct Validation* is involved whenever a test is to be interpreted as a measure of some attribute or quality which is not 'operationally defined.' "* They go on to say that construct validity would be involved in seeking answers to such queries as: To what extent is this test culture-free? To what extent is reading ability a factor in a particular test score? Anastasi (1961), although she agrees that there is a useful place for the concept of construct validity, takes issue with the statement just quoted and is of the opinion that such a definition can lead to fuzzy thinking about test scores and the traits they measure. Bechtoldt (1959) goes still further and states that the concept of construct validity contributes nothing to the process of building a theory of behavior, that it leads to unnecessary confusion, and a nonempirical, nonscientific approach to the study of behavior. On the other hand, Campbell (1960) reviews the various criticisms of the concept and finds them generally unjustified. He points out that under certain conditions construct validation is a useful procedure for determining whether a test truly measures the psychological construct in question.

Cronbach (1960b) points out that in education construct validation is important when we attempt to measure the degree to which we are meeting some of the less traditional objectives of instruction such as "freedom from prejudice." A measure of prejudiced thinking could not be validated against a body of content and we would have difficulty checking it against some kind of behavioral criteria. It would need to be validated indirectly. In order to determine to what extent the test measures what it purports to measure, such as prejudiced thinking, we would first need to determine to what extent the scores are correlated with such measures as reading ability, knowledge of specific subject matter, and other presumably irrelevant factors. If these correlations were high we would presume that our test had low construct validity. It is necessary to determine to what extent the scores are influenced by specific instructions. If such influences are substantial the test also would have low construct validity. Eson (1956), for example, has shown that scores on the Minnesota Teacher Attitude Inventory are substantially influenced by the ability to recognize the "right" responses. It is easier to demonstrate that a test has low construct validity than it is to show that its construct validity is high. A person trying out a test on which he must claim construct rather than other forms of validity, needs to gather as much evidence as he can that the test instrument is not measuring factors other than the one being claimed "before the test can be confidently used to evaluate instruction. Similar questions arise in connection with tests of artistic judgment, reasoning abilities, character, and personal-social adjustment" (Cronbach, 1960b). It should be recognized that the measurement of such qualities as outcomes of education with instruments that have demonstrated high construct validity is still more a wish than a reality.

EVALUATION AND CURRICULUM DEVELOPMENT

Evaluation procedures, educational objectives, and learning experiences form together an organic whole. Examinations cannot be considered outside the context of their objectives and the necessary learning experiences to be provided in order to achieve those objectives. The kind of objectives stated will determine the kinds of learning experiences for which provision is needed and the construction of the examination should follow from these. In this context the test or the evaluation device is not intended so much to check on the students but rather to assess in some systematic way to what extent a particular content or teaching procedure leads to the accomplishment of objectives; whether a particular sequence has a more desirable cumulative effect than another. Achievement testing thus becomes a device for examining curriculum and teaching procedures for the sake of developing a sounder more effective curriculum.

The statement of objectives of a curriculum can be arrived at in a number of ways. The formulation of these objectives is largely a matter of value decision and for this reason a subject of controversy. The literature on curriculum development has pointed more and more in the direction of teacher involvement. In order for teachers to understand fully what they are trying to accomplish, they need to know and appreciate not only the particular content but why the content has been selected. In Chapter 5, it was pointed out that there is no magical value inherent in any particular content. The teaching procedure or the learning experiences are in many instances of equal, if not greater, importance in achieving the aims of education. For this reason it is imperative that the teacher participate in the formulation of objectives and the consequent selection of content so that everything he does will eventually be focused on the appropriate goals.

The present knowledge in the area of evaluation measures is unevenly developed. This fact has created some distortion in the relationship of testing to curriculum. Our greatest skill is in measuring verbal behavior and consequently the emphasis has been on this one objective of the curriculum. Other legitimate objectives such as attitudes, emotions, self-direction, group cooperation, receive little attention even though they often appear in the statement of course objectives. A famous English schoolmaster stated some three centuries ago, "I can tell you about the student's state of grammar but not his state of grace." We have continued to be concerned with verbalization but are beginning to be uncomfortable at the neglect of the development of the student's personality. Schools more and more will be concerned with the development of appreciations, sensitivities, and other characteristics that might be termed emotional development. Teachers will attempt to develop in children a sense of self-worth and concern for others through the understanding of the nature of the group and its effect upon individuals. However, the evaluation of success in these areas will remain in some measure subjective and clinical. McKim (1957) has summarized the comparative status of our knowledge of evaluation as follows:

> 1. We know more about norms for separate aspects of development than we do about the interrelationships among these aspects of development in the growing organism.
> 2. We have more techniques for studying the learner in the light of norms and averages than we have techniques for studying him in the light of his goals and his concept of himself.
> 3. We know more about how to develop skills such as reading and handwriting and about how to teach facts, than we do about how to develop concepts or attitudes.
> 4. We know more about how to study the outcomes of a child's work than we do about how to study the processes by which he works—the steps he takes in solving an arithmetic problem, the way he reasons in drawing conclusions.
> 5. We have more techniques for evaluating growth in skills and knowledge than we have techniques for evaluating growth in such areas as attitudes and feelings (page 34).

Although the techniques available to the teacher for assessing progress in certain areas of school objectives are not as adequate as we would like them to be, a great deal can be done to improve the curriculum by evaluating achievement in what has been called the "cognitive domain" (Bloom, 1956). The evaluation of progress in the acquisition of meaning, understanding, and transferability, as discussed in Chapters 2, 3, and 4, can be carried out in such a fashion as to clarify objectives and to balance the program of teaching.

Clarification of Objectives

When the process of constructing examinations is closely related to one's teaching objectives, the latter tend to become clearer. Tyler (1949) describes how this close relationship induces clarification of objectives and modification of curriculum.

Our achievements tests were constructed on the basis of specifications drawn up in each case by the staff of the particular course or field. The staff was asked to state these specifications precisely enough to describe just what kinds of behavior the course was expected to develop in students. Thus in one of the biology courses, the staff worked a good many hours in clarifying its own conception of what the objectives were and what these objectives meant; finally being able to define each of them concretely in terms of behavior.

Clear and concrete description was especially difficult for such an objective as developing skill in the scientific method, although this goal was commonly accepted by all the staff as an important objective. It was not clearly defined until a good deal of exploration, reading, introspective examination of their own behavior and discussion produced an increasingly clear concept of what scientific method is, especially as carried on by the student in biology. The staff saw the importance of defining objectives clearly because as soon as they were clearly defined, it became easier to find testing devices which would give evidence of their attainment. It became quite clear to me and to the instructional staffs in Ohio that the task of working on achievement tests served to clarify objectives, and not only was such a clarification essential for testing; it also provided a more adequate basis for outlining the course and deciding on teaching materials and methods (page 397).

The following classification of course objectives adapted from Bloom (1956) can be applied to most areas of the curriculum and should serve as a guideline in balancing each examination. Every subject matter area might be viewed in terms of knowledge; understanding, analysis, and synthesis; and application and value judgments.

KNOWLEDGE The category of knowledge includes those objectives that might be called the acquisition of meaning as described in Chapter 2. In the elementary school curriculum this would include such items as the names of the days of the week, months of the year, measurement terms, some aspects of spelling, and so on. In secondary school and college this would cover the mastery of a technical terminology, formulae, rules of punctuation, classification schemes in science, history, and literature.

The following are three examples of test items that would test achievement in this category.

The antonym of a word is one which:
1. Has the same meaning
2. Sounds like the word but has a different spelling
3. Has the opposite meaning
4. Has the same spelling but means something different

The English conquered Canada from the French
1. Ten years before the American Revolutionary War
2. During the time of the War of 1812

3. During the time of the French Revolution
4. In the early part of the 16th century

In a normal distribution the percentage of cases included between one standard deviation below the mean and one standard deviation above the mean is:

1. 34
2. 50
3. 68
4. Depends on the shape of the curve.

Although the knowledge aspect of the curriculum is important and essential for other aspects of cognitive development, undue emphasis in teaching and testing in this area should be avoided. Many examiners and teachers are too readily satisfied with the thought that memory of these specifics implies ability to comprehend and analyze or to apply this knowledge. These latter categories demand separate consideration in curriculum development and in evaluation.

UNDERSTANDING, ANALYSIS, AND SYNTHESIS   As shown in Chapter 4, this area represents a very important segment of the school curriculum. Achievement in this area would be represented in the ability to break down material into its various parts, to note the relationships among the parts, and to discern the organizing principles if such exist. Test items in this category would include translation from a foreign language, working word problems in arithmetic, the translation of verbal symbols into mathematical formulas, predicting the outcome of the interaction of given physical forces, the reading of charts and maps and extrapolating from data, distinguishing the relevant from the irrelevant, distinguishing cause and effect relationships from coincidental variation, and understanding the techniques of persuasive materials as in advertising and political propaganda. Although objective test questions can be used successfully for measuring ability in comprehension and analysis, essay-type questions serve to check how well the student has learned to express himself in regard to his comprehension and analytic skill. In the use of the essay test such factors as spelling, handwriting, and general neatness should not influence the teacher's judgment of achievement in this category. Test items used to measure achievement of comprehension and analytic skill should rely on data and material unfamiliar to the student, otherwise we are likely to be measuring recall of specific interpretations that would represent mastery of knowledge rather than comprehension.

The development of the ability to synthesize is an important objective in modern education. We wish to see in our students the ability to think and act creatively and to integrate their experiences into their unique "apperceptive mass." The ability to synthesize is essential in all artistic, literary, and scientific undertakings. As pointed out previously (Chapter 4) the development of this skill depends on a proper balance of direction from the teacher and the student's self-direction. It should be noted that the strict application of normative standards in evaluating the student's work in this area can result in nullifying our efforts to encourage the student to express himself in his own unique way. On the problem of evaluation of the creative effort, Lowenfeld takes an extreme position when he states: *"Creative works must be evaluated on their own individual merits.* This is highly significant and is true for all levels of teaching. *The meaningfulness of the work to its creator must never be disturbed by 'objective evaluations'"* (1957, page 44). Yet in many situations the final product of the learner needs to be evaluated in order to determine the effectiveness of the curriculum in fostering creative growth. In obtaining the product for evaluation we must be careful to leave the student sufficient opportunity to demonstrate his creative skill. Objective questions are therefore not very useful. However, this does not mean that essay questions automatically measure the development of this skill. In too many instances the student in writing an answer, in hopes of being rewarded with a high grade, will not be creative but will more likely produce that which he thinks the evaluator would like to see. Poems, essays, paintings, and the like that are produced in a nonevaluative setting are likely to be better for evaluation purposes than those produced for evaluation itself. On the actual evaluation we must consider the developmental level of the student, his background of experience, and what he is trying to express. With these factors in mind we may then estimate the quality of the organization of the work and its coherency. Although synthesis and creative effort would be listed as legitimate objectives for a number of parts of the curriculum, the evaluation itself should not be of such a nature as to hinder its growth.

The following questions (Tinkelman, 1958) are illustrative of the types of items that may be used to evaluate achievement in the areas of understanding and analysis:

A person will feel more uncomfortable on a hot, humid day than on a hot, dry day. What is the biological explanation?

Show how each of the following has been a factor in the development of democracy in the United States:
1. The characteristics of life on the western frontier
2. The public schools
3. Newspapers and periodicals (page 17)

In an experiment, two mice are fed the same food except that one is given milk and the other is given coffee. The mouse that is given coffee dies. What does this experiment prove?
1. Coffee is poison to mice
2. Everyone should drink milk

3. Milk is a better food than coffee
4. None of these is proven (page 39)

The social-studies test item shown in Figure 9.6 is another illustration of a test item designed to measure understanding of principles. The students are asked questions about the map that would require that they demonstrate various kinds of understanding such as:

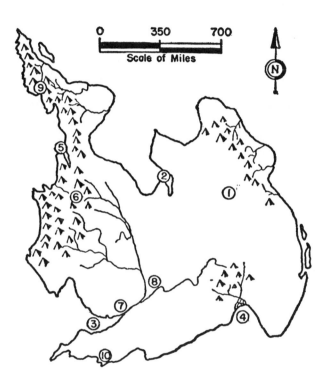

FIGURE 9.6 *Map of an imaginary island suggested for use as a social studies test item in grades four to six. From E. G. Wandt and W. Brown,* Essentials of Educational Evaluation, *copyright* © *New York: Holt, Rinehart and Winston, Inc., 1957.*

1. If explorers came to this island by ship, where would they find the safest harbor? (Circle the correct answer)

    a 2   b 4   c 9   d 10

2. Which of these places is on a peninsula? (Circle the correct answer)

    e 4   f 6   g 7   h 9

APPLICATION AND VALUE JUDGMENTS   In almost every field of teaching we are most interested in helping the student draw value-oriented conclusions and to apply these to situations involving practical matters of everyday living or to problems of scholarship. There are many instances where the student gains knowledge about the important elements in wholesome nutrition and where he comprehends the basis for their effects, yet he does not act on this knowledge and comprehension in matters affecting his health.

In attempting to measure the extent to which the student is able to evaluate a course of action and to act on this evaluation, we are faced with the problem of measuring the transfer effects of learning. This cannot be done easily by means of the usual paper and pencil tests; the observation of students under real-life situations is a preferable procedure for assessment of transfer. These real-life problems are ordinarily difficult if not impossible to set up and there are many serious difficulties in evaluating the student's solutions to these problems. The externship in medicine and practice teaching in teacher training are the most difficult aspects of the curriculum to evaluate.

Questions such as "What would you do if . . . ?" do not really get at this skill since the student may know and understand the answer but he may not be able to act on this knowledge and understanding. In the laboratory courses, particularly in such areas as home economics, shop and technical training, one can develop model situations that simulate the real and that can serve to evaluate the transfer effects of learning.

One interesting example of such a model situation designed to evaluate how the student would apply his knowledge and understanding is the Tab Item (Glaser et al., 1954). This testing procedure was originally developed as one of a series of measures of a mechanic's proficiency in maintaining a radar-computer system. It can, however, be adapted to many situations. It consists essentially of a series of diagrams stating the problem. For example, a description of a TV set that is not functioning properly, a series of check procedures that the mechanic might employ to determine the cause of the malfunctioning, and a list of units or components in the set that could be defective and cause the described malfunctioning might be used. The person being examined is directed to select the check procedures that he thinks might yield him the information needed to solve the problem. By removing a tab he obtains this information. After he has gathered enough information by pulling information tabs he then selects the solution by pulling another tab. By examining the tab sheet we can determine whether the student has demanded more information than necessary (pulled too many tabs) and the number of incorrect solutions before solving the problem correctly. This examination technique can be applied in such courses as qualitative analysis in chemistry, in physics, in certain phases of agriculture, and in other fields where the evaluation of a course of action and the application of knowledge and comprehension follow fairly clear sequential steps. In other fields the teacher might see if the student can determine the dependability of data, the extent to which he will generalize before he has adequate data, or the extent to which he appears overly cautious in arriving at generalizations.

Evaluation for Supervision

Closely related to evaluation for curriculum development is the use of standardized achievement tests for supervision. In the minds of many lay people responsible for the educational program, school-board members and the like, the most efficient way of measuring the effectiveness of teaching is to administer a battery of achievement tests. The results of these tests are then to be compared with national norms and the staff should accordingly be fired, retained, or promoted on the basis of what they produce. This sounds disarmingly simple. In many states the concept is further reinforced by the statewide testing program. Although tests can contribute to the quality of educational supervision, when educational measurement is used as a primary supervisory tool the effects are more likely to be harmful than beneficial.

When the student's performance on a test is used as a basis for judging the competence of the teacher, the teacher will try to prevent the poorer student from taking the examination. An absolute measure of poor student performance is not sufficient basis for concluding that the teaching has been poor. The student's improvement during the course of instruction is a somewhat better measure of teaching effectiveness, but before and after measures of achievement are seldom used in the ordinary course of supervision. A further defect of supervisory tests is that they tend to dictate to teachers specifically what they should teach down to particular interpretations. This stultifies the entire teacher-learning process. When supervision relies primarily on test results, the teaching is bound to become regimented and mechanized with cramming and memorization as the major tools for passing the test. Vernon (1957) suggests that the English eleven-plus examinations take on a supervisory aspect. He states:

> The reputation of a primary school is largely affected by the success of its pupils at 11+. Thus it is only natural that many teachers should still further increase the strain by devoting all their efforts in the last year or two cramming those pupils who have a chance of passing, and neglecting school subjects or activities which do not directly contribute to this end. Working for examinations or tests is very liable to have a stultifying effect on progressive educational practices, to discourage experimentation with activity methods, group work and self-expression or creative subjects (page 62).

A further harmful effect of supervisory examinations is that some students are forced to attempt learning activities for which they are not ready or that in general are inappropriate for them because of lack of background experience and particular aspirations, while they are compelled to ignore those learnings for which they are ready and that would prove beneficial. Other students are encouraged to overlearn what is expected on the exam and not to attempt challenging projects and reading outside the strict scope of the course outline, as profits are measured by examination results.

To the extent that these defects result from an improperly applied supervisory test, the standards of a school will be lowered and distorted. In one instance where a large statewide school system was subjected to a common final examination, it was found that over a period of years large numbers of students were being failed in a particular subject. The writer, after surveying the problem, suggested that curriculum, teaching methods, and subsequently, the examination be modified. The state supervisor responded that any changes that might lead to greater numbers of students passing would represent to him the lowering of standards. The argument that standards are being maintained while one witnesses constant inadequate performance represents a contradiction in terms, viewed as noncontradictory only by means of semantic blindness.

The proper use of tests for supervision depends first on a proper relationship between teacher and supervisor. The elements of this relationship will be discussed in Chapter 16. When tests are used to provide the teacher with feed-back and with knowledge of teaching results, they can lead to proper redirection of effort. Test results can help evaluate the results of teaching in the light of the kind of student taught. The supervisor can assist the teacher to define the circumstances in which he is teaching. The class group should be carefully described in terms of the previous achievement of the students, the range of ability in the class, the socioeconomic background, health factors, educational history, and so on. After this has been determined, the teacher and the supervisor can determine the realistic educational objectives for the particular group. The supervisor in consultation with the teacher, or with a group of teachers working in similar teaching situations, can set final examinations to determine how well these objectives have been met. Standardized tests can be used for this purpose but as previously pointed out they must always be interpreted in the light of the particular circumstances and should generally be supplemented by special evaluation instruments. The report of test results should be complete, containing information about the groups used for comparison, the areas in which success was achieved, objectives not fully accomplished, and some statement about the students who have made exceptional progress and those who seem to have progressed less than one might have expected. The supervisor must consider the differences in circumstances among those being supervised; this consideration involves adopting appropriate standards for each situation and assisting the teacher to do what almost all teachers want to do: the most they can do for each student. The use of tests in supervision thus can be seen in a total context of the relationship of the supervisor to the teacher and his responsibilities to him. Tests of academic achievement are tools that can help the supervisor and the teacher answer the question, "How well are we doing in fostering pupil growth in desirable and realistic directions?"

Every test can serve the needs of the individual student. After examining the results of an achievement test a teacher can determine in which ways his teaching method and subject matter content need to be modified in order to better achieve the stated objectives. Also, he can tell which students need particular kinds of help. One student may need the aid of a teaching machine, such as described in Chapter 6, in order to review factual material; another may need to think aloud through several problems to check his problem-solving procedures and so on. This implies that the teacher should make a diagnosis of the student's learning needs.

EVALUATION FOR DIAGNOSIS

The primary justification for the usual evaluation carried on in the classroom is that of diagnosis. This means that the teacher employs evaluation techniques to discover what aspects of the learning process can be improved. The evaluation techniques to carry on such an analysis will range from standardized testing procedures and teacher constructed tests to careful observation of the individual at work.

The effectiveness of evaluation procedures for diagnostic purposes depends primarily on the attitude of the pupil and the teacher toward the discovery of deficiencies in the learning process. A pupil who suspects that the findings of an evaluation will in some way be used against him will seek some means of obscuring the deficiency and will consequently be unable to accept help in overcoming it. Diagnosis depends upon the awareness of the individual that any identified defect is not a reflection on him but a stage in his achieving greater adequacy. The teacher must be careful not to make the student defensive. The student's sense of growing adequacy should be safeguarded.

In diagnosing and correcting the pupil's learning the teacher must be able to describe the current performance in some meaningful way. Brueckner and Bond (1955) suggest six dimensions of performance along which the learning can be described. These are: (1) rate of response, (2) accuracy, (3) quality, (4) the level of development or depth of ability, (5) the breadth of experience or the range of ability and (6) methods of thinking or process. The following discussion demonstrates how the teacher can approach the student's learning and performance by analyzing it for these characteristics as they appear singly and in combination.

Rate and Accuracy

Rate and accuracy are related variables. They may occur in various combinations as shown in Table 9.6.

TABLE 9.6 A CLASSIFICATION SCHEME FOR ANALYZING STUDENT PERFORMANCE WITH REGARD TO RATE AND ACCURACY

Rate	Accuracy		
	High	Average	Low
High	1 High in both rate and accuracy	2 High in rate—average in accuracy	3 High in rate—low in accuracy
Average	4 Average in rate—high in accuracy	5 Average in both rate and accuracy	6 Average in rate—low in accuracy
Low	7 Low in rate—high in accuracy	8 Low in rate—average in accuracy	9 Low in both rate and accuracy

Source: L. J. Brueckner and G. L. Bond, *The Diagnosis and Treatment of Learning Difficulties,* Appleton-Century-Crofts, New York, 1958, p. 18.

Students in category 1 are able to work rapidly and accurately. If there are no observable difficulties in the other four characteristics, these students would benefit from opportunities to use their time in further enlarging the breadth of their experiences or developing special talents.

Pupils whose performance is average or high in both accuracy and rate (categories 2, 4, and 5) do not usually present any problem. On those tasks where they show this combination of characteristics, they can be encouraged to improve either rate or accuracy or both.

The student in category 7 is one whose performance is unusually slow but his product is near perfect or without error. This combination, low rate and high accuracy, is often a sign of exaggerated strivings for security. Teachers may aggravate this situation by hurrying the child and by criticizing his slow rate, because in doing this they make the child more insecure. The teacher needs to view this child as one who requires long-range security producing experiences. His inadequacies need to be minimized and the teacher should not give praise to the pupil's accuracy; too much praise will tend to reinforce it. The striving for perfection at the expense of rate can best be overcome by providing a noncritical, reasonably structured environment.

Children who work rapidly but seem careless and make a large number of errors, category 3, need to be helped to be more self-critical. One of the ways in which this can be done is to provide the child with techniques for checking the results of his work. He may be helped first by having him evaluate his answers for reasonableness, in spelling the sounding out of the word as written may help, in arithmetic the estimate of the answer before determining it exactly may be beneficial, also the reworking of the problem in subtraction and division by addition and multiplication will provide the student with ways of improving his accuracy. Just as in the case of the slow, highly accurate child, the child who works rapidly but carelessly will not be helped by being told to slow down. He must be provided with suggestions for improving the accuracy of his work; also, a more complete understanding of the meaning of the task will lead to a reduction of errors.

The cases of the children in groups 6 and 8 may be considered as modifications of the problem described in the previous paragraph. However, the absence of a fast rate of working when the child is low in accuracy, or the absence of a high rate of accuracy when he is exceedingly slow, makes the diagnosis more difficult. These children might be considered for special remedial help.

Students who are low in both rate and accuracy, category 9, present the most serious problem. This combination of characteristics is frequently accompanied by poor quality, absence of depth or special talent, narrowness of range, and inadequate methods of work. In most instances referral is indicated. Referral would include careful medical examination and consultation with the staff of a child guidance clinic if such services are available. Where special facilities within the school or the community are not provided the teacher has no alternative but to do what he can to bring some order out of chaos.

Altitude and Range of Abilities

The analysis of the various combinations of altitude and range of abilities and their implications, parallels that of the possible combinations of rate and accuracy. The nine-type classification presented in Table 9.7 may serve as a guide to the teacher in instituting diagnostic and remedial procedures. Note that altitude and range are two characteristics used in describing intelligent behavior (discussed in the next chapter).

Students in category 1 who are able to undertake almost any kind of school learning task in any area and acquire a high degree of com-

TABLE 9.7 A CLASSIFICATION SCHEME FOR ANALYZING STUDENT
PERFORMANCE WITH REGARD TO RANGE AND DEPTH

	Depth		
Range	Deep	Average	Shallow
Broad	1 Mastery of difficult skills in broad range	2 Average difficulty or depth over broad range of skills	3 Superficial mastery of many skills
Average	4 Mastery of difficult skills in average range	5 Average depth— average range	6 Superficial mastery over average range of skills
Narrow	7 Deep and narrow	8 Average depth— narrow range	9 Superficial mastery of few different skills

petence are generally those who bring great joy to a teaching faculty. One need not dwell too long in considering the teaching of these children except for the occasional problem of indecision among many alternatives when the individual must choose a career or a field of specialization. It is to be hoped that future research might help us understand how this type of person develops, that is, what are the factors in his constitution and his developmental experience that produce the intensive and extensive competence.

Students who fall into categories 2 and 4 should not present a problem in the usual school setting. The student who has been able to perform in an average manner over a wide range of skills, category 2, might be encouraged to find one or two specific skills that he might develop to a higher degree. This is not always indicated, as many individuals can derive the greatest sense of self-fulfillment from a wide range of activities without excessive concentration in any particular one. Even more, the individual whose interests are not excessively broad but prefers to master well whatever he chooses to perform should not be strongly urged to give up his concentrations. It is out of his sense of mastery that a sense of well-being and security will develop. Out of this can grow an assuredness that will transfer to other areas.

Very much the same kind of recommendation can be made with regard to students in category 7, those who have a narrow range of skill mastery but who master a few skills to a high level of perfection. If the particular skills that are mastered are relatively complete in themselves, for example the various graphic arts, athletic competence, mathematics, then the teacher has little reason to be concerned. If, however, the mastery is restricted to parts of these then it might be well to expand the student's awareness of the inter-relationships of these parts and to support the student as he ventures into areas where he has already given evidence that he can succeed.

Students who demonstrate that they can achieve an average level of competence over an average range of skills are generally not problems and comprise the majority of the school population. The particular selection of skills to make up this range differs, however, in each case so that we can only consider them alike in principle. Actually, these average students are very much different from each other.

Students in categories 3 and 6, those who seem to lack the ability to master any skill in depth, may present problems. The first of these, group 3, suggests a butterfly constantly moving from one attraction to another. Inconstancy of activity or experience precludes development of any real mastery. A student in this group, like those in group 6, may need some help in concentrating his interests. He may exhibit a fear of failure so that he seeks to protect himself by moving to another activity before he is forced to admit or recognize his failure. The teacher should be aware of the real benefits to be derived from at least average success in the performance of any activity. He needs to assure the student that initial contacts with a skill will generally be awkward but improvement itself can bring satisfactions.

For students in group 8 who are able to function to average levels of depth, but in a very limited range, the question arises as to whether to attempt to extend their range of ability first or to deepen the level. The answer would, of course, depend upon the combination of factors in the particular case. Generally, extending the range would be preferable and more readily accomplished, particularly if the areas chosen depend upon similar types of skills as those being used in the present limited range of activities.

Students in group 9, those who show little ability insofar as level is concerned and who choose few activities in which they can demonstrate even these meager abilities, can present a real problem to the teacher. The teacher should try first to provide the child with as much security as possible so that he may venture into one area where he is likely to achieve some modest level of mastery. The benefits in self-assurance from modest achievement where there has been little before might be considerable. In most instances, these children require intensive diagnosis, medical and psychological, beyond the competence of the classroom teacher and they also require special educational procedures not usually possible in the ordinary classroom.

Assessing and Improving the Quality of Performance

The assessment of the quality of a student's performance implies some standards or criteria against which to judge the product. For example, in the case of handwriting the degree of legibility would be a practical criterion. If it is determined that the quality of the writing is such as to make it difficult to read, a careful analysis should be made to determine the specific deficiencies that need to be corrected. Brueckner and Bond (1955) point out that the letters that contribute most to illegibility are *a, d, e, u, r,* and *t.* In other areas of performance, such as composition or speech, a similar determination of specific difficulties should be made rather than over-all ratings of quality such as poor, fair, good, and excellent. If the evaluation is diagnostic it will point out as clearly as possible the nature of the weakness in the performance with statements such as these: "The underlined words are not used in the right context," "Watch the rules of punctuation, see page 94 of text for use of semi-colon," "You need some help in expanding your speaking vocabulary, see me during homeroom for some suggestions." Statements such as these can direct the student's attention to his particular deficiencies in quality and indicate how he might overcome them. The teacher's concern for quality performance demonstrated by pointing out particulars is probably the one most effective diagnostic and remedial procedure.

Evaluation of Method, Procedure, and Form

In most areas of school learning and performance there are many different kinds of acceptable procedures, forms or styles. The particular style or procedure adopted by the student can be considered an expression of his individuality, unless the teacher knows from previous experience that such a style would be a hindrance to the development of a more mature form or style. The teacher should be aware of the various ways in which skills can be organized to produce an adequate form. For example, if the rate of performance in primary arithmetic is low, the teacher might suspect that the student is counting on his fingers. It then becomes important to help the student overcome this inadequate procedure so that he can advance to more complex arithmetic. In writing and reading we may find as we analyze the inadequate performance, for example, the pupil is using an impossible form in holding the pencil or that he is vocalizing in silent reading. In such instances the teacher, by avoiding a condemnatory attitude, needs to help the child overcome these handicapping tendencies.

Identifying Faulty Methods in Arithmetic and Reading

Children may devise roundabout and inefficient methods that are uneconomical and wasteful. Many of these faulty methods prevent the development of mature skills. The following illustrations of handicapping procedures in arithmetic from Brueckner and Bond (1955)[1] are commonly found in the middle elementary grades.

> A fourth-grade boy reported failing in arithmetic found the answer to the subtraction example below by counting back from 81 to 37 by ones. He had devised a way of keeping a mental record as he counted. He had used this method in all cases when regrouping was required. When asked to subtract two larger three-place numbers, he balked and refused to attempt to find the answer.

$$\begin{array}{r} 81 \\ -37 \\ \hline \end{array}$$

> A fourth-grade girl persistently worked subtraction examples in which regrouping in the minuend was necessary by subtracting the smaller number in ones' place in the minuend from the larger number in ones' place in the subtraend. This seemed to her to be a procedure logically correct.

$$\begin{array}{r} 72 \\ -26 \\ \hline \end{array}$$

> This pupil does not understand the role of 0 as a place holder, as is shown in the incorrect work in the division example.

$$\begin{array}{r} 6\ 7\ \text{r}5 \\ 6\overline{)\ 3647} \\ 36 \\ \hline 47 \\ 42 \\ \hline 5 \end{array}$$

> This boy, grade four, IQ 118, 1.4 years below grade in arithmetic, had devised many ingenious but awkward methods of finding answers to problems, as illustrated by the following:
>
> He was asked to read the problem below and to give the answer:
>
> If 2 loaves of bread cost 42¢, how much does 1 loaf cost? Quick as a flash he said, "21¢." When asked, "How did you find the answer?" he replied, "Well, 20 and 20 are 40, and 1 and 1 are 2, so 21."
>
> The example 2$\overline{)42¢}$ was written on the blackboard, but he was unable to work it (page 228).

Another illustration of faulty methods in arithmetic is the case of the girl who knew her multiplication tables exceedingly well but never

[1] From L. J. Brueckner and G. L. Bond, *The Diagnosis and Treatment of Learning Difficulties.* New York: Appleton-Century-Crofts, 1955.

seemed to obtain the correct answer in multiplication problems such as these:

38	42	64	72	83
$\times 7$	$\times 6$	$\times 5$	$\times 8$	$\times 4$
566	302	400	646	362

A careful analysis of her answers will reveal that she was not carrying properly. She appeared anxious to get rid of the number that had to be carried and she added it to the tens digit in the multiplicand before multiplying. Thus she added the 5 from her product of 7×8 to the 3 digit in 38, rather than to the product of 7×3. This is a case of negative transfer from carrying in addition.

Many similar illustrations of faulty procedures can be detected in a careful analysis of motor performance, music, laboratory science, and almost any area of the curriculum. Much has been written on the diagnosis and correction of reading difficulties. Bond and Tinker (1957) suggest that there are forty-five particular kinds of deficiencies in eight major categories of reading difficulty. This list can be condensed to the following items:

1. Sight vocabulary limited
2. Word attack skills inadequate (for example, inability to make use of context, inability to analyze words into syllables or phonic elements, guessing)
3. Omissions and reversals
4. Silent reading with unnecessary vocalization and lip movement
5. Faulty eye movement pattern (for example, frequent pauses, reversals) and inappropriate return from end of line to beginning of next line
6. Inflexibility of reading pattern and inability to adjust to the particular or different types of reading material; not able to scan or to read carefully as the case may demand

In many cases the detection of the specific reading difficulty will itself suggest appropriate corrective procedures. These procedures will consist of modifications of those used in ordinary reading instruction for the development of sight vocabulary, word attack skills, and the like. In some instances, however, the problem is complex and deep seated. Schools are turning more and more to the services of a remedial reading specialist to handle those problems that lie beyond the usual skills of teachers. In general, however, the task of diagnosis and remediation in reading and in other subject areas remains that of the classroom teacher.

EVALUATION FOR GUIDANCE

In a general sense the discussion of evaluation for diagnosis might be considered evaluation for guidance in so far as a teacher's purposes are to stimulate and guide the individual to make the most of his potentialities. There is another sense in which the term guidance is used. That is to make the person aware about his unique characteristics, his abilities, his temperament, and his interests, and to make him aware about certain features of the environment such as a course of study or a vocation so that he may be guided in making the proper decisions in academic programming and vocational planning.

Guidance has often been likened to the fitting of square pegs in square holes and round pegs in round holes. There is a danger of oversimplification in viewing the problem this way. The characteristics of the holes cannot be definitely determined in advance, that is, a course of study or a particular vocation cannot be described in such a way so that we would be permitted to say that it has these and these dimensions or qualities of roundness or squareness. The holes are in many respects amorphous or at least multipatterned—no vocation, no curriculum has form aside from that given to it by the individual. The pegs (in this case the students) are even more difficult to describe. Students are not constant entities, they change with time and experience. Our ability to describe an individual with respect to significant characteristics is seriously limited. The extent to which the student will find his fulfillment as a result of a decision involving so many dynamic factors is not easy to assess in advance.

The process of guidance and counseling has become increasingly complex and has increasingly demanded special training. It is not expected that teachers should carry on in this area without appropriate training. Teachers do, however, need to appreciate what it is that the guidance counselor does, what kinds of information he uses, and how he uses this information, so that the classroom teacher can contribute to the guidance effort, participate in it, and support it.

When the student stands at a point of making an academic or a vocational decision, which course of study to choose and which subjects within the course of study, for which occupation to prepare, there are many factors that must be taken into account. The basic personality needs of the student and the extent to which a specified occupation or program of study can satisfy his needs, is a primary consideration. In addition, the student's assets and handicaps in physique, intellect, cultural background, and financial status must be carefully weighed. The counselor must be able to interpret the broad range of possibilities, substitutions and changes that exist in the environment into which the student is moving. Ultimately it is the purpose of appraisal in the guidance program to enable the student to better understand his choice and above all to understand himself. The student cannot be viewed as a passive, static entity that can be measured and described and then placed in a fixed environmental space. The information gained from testing must in some way be interpreted to him and the demands and possibilities of his environment described or preferably experienced by him so that he can make a wise decision; a decision for which only he can be responsible and hence only he can make. In a democratic society no one can force important life decisions on another. Counselors and teachers can provide information and proper experiences so that the student comes to understand himself and his environment and thus can act autonomously in making his choices.

Both the teacher and the counselor can help the student gain some understanding of himself by systematically gathering and recording information derived from various sources. This task should not result in an attempt to reduce the student to a set or a pattern of statistics and figures but rather in providing a basis for understanding of oneself as a unique person with a unique role to play in a diversified and free society.

The record maintained in the guidance office should contain information in the following categories:

1. The social context in which the student lives
2. The student's emotional, motivational, and personality characteristics
3. Teacher's observational and anecdotal records
4. Self-assessment statements by the student
5. Measures of vocational and academic interest
6. School achievement, intelligence, special abilities, and disabilities

In describing the social context of the student's life the teacher might have some useful information about the socioeconomic level of the student's family; parental attitudes toward education and toward the student; sibling relationships and sibling's attitude and performance in school. In many instances the teacher will have some information about the student's adjustment to peers, based on sociometric information; relationship to the opposite sex; and attitudes toward authority. In preparing statements in this area the teacher should be as much descriptive and as little evaluative as possible. Some of the aspects of social development were considered in Chapter 8, and social context will be considered in Chapters 13 and 14.

It is extremely difficult for the teacher or the guidance counselor to obtain an objective record or measure of the student's emotional and motivational characteristics. Many of the techniques, such as the projective tests, require considerable training and experience for administration and interpretation. These specialized techniques are not likely to find a place in the routine phases of the school guidance program and their validity would be questionable should they be administered routinely. The paper and pencil tests are of very little value in the guidance of students. As Buros (1949) says of personality assessment:

> On the whole, the faults of the *California Test of Personality* are those of personality questionnaires in general. Such devices vainly seek the pot of gold at the end of the rainbow: a simple, cheap, foolproof method for studying human personality. Teachers, administrators, and school counselors who are tempted to consider the use of such devices would be benefited by a psychological insight into the fact that their own great need to do something about personality problems leads them to the delusion of accepting instruments of very low objective value (page 26).

The insights that teachers gain in their everyday relationships with students, provide a better source of information about the students' emotional needs and motivational patterns. In addition to the need for objectivity in recording such information, it is important that the teacher refrain from appearing "snoopy" but rather be alert to events as they occur naturally. Another problem in gathering observation data is that of time. In the elementary grades the teacher might set aside cards with the names of four or five students for a particular week and seek to enter a meaningful anecdotal comment about each of these students. This procedure would provide some five statements for each student during the course of a school year. In the high school, with departmentalization, this becomes much more difficult but by no means impossible.

Another source of information about personal needs and motives is the student himself. A problem check list, such as the one developed by Mooney and Gordon (1950), may serve as a jumping-off place for personal counseling and also for curriculum development. This particular check list is available in various forms for different student groups. It consists of several hundred problems covering such general areas of concern as health and physical development, vocational, financial, social-recreational, and so on.

The specially designed written assignment can reveal a great deal about the student's feelings toward himself, others, and his environment. One such assignment could be to write a future autobiography. The student would be asked to pretend that he is now fifty years of age and writing the biography of his life. If such an assignment is given in an English class it can be used for improvement of writing style and composition. In addition, the composition can be evaluated for over-all mood, self-concept, ambition and aspiration, and orientation to others. Another type of assignment that is similarly useful would be "Describe the Person You Would Most Like to be Like." Still another assignment would be, "If you had three wishes what would they be?" The following four papers were submitted in response to assignments of this type. The analysis of the responses would indicate clearly that these youngsters, all approximately thirteen years of age, exhibited different levels of maturity, and different states of harmony with their environment as well as different levels of skill in writing.

If I could wish, I would wish that for once there would be peace in this world. In peace time everyone can be satisfied, or rather, everyone should be satisfied. Peace would mean happiness for many, many people; it would mean united nations; it would mean prosperity.

A second wish would be that there would be a solution to my mother's greatest desire. Her desire being to see her parents once again. We live in America; my grandparents in Germany. As I said before peace would help greatly.

My last wish would be to make the people around me happy. There is nothing better than pleasing people and being well-liked. I wish people to be happy.

If I had three wishes I think my first one would be that I was sixteen so I can drive a car.

My second one would be that I passed all my school years.

My third one would be that I make all the sports in school.

Portrait of the Person Whom I Would Most Hope to be Like

She was one of my elementary school teachers, but her work isn't why I admire her.

Physically, she was very attractive. Young, slender, of average height, her pleasant face was framed with shining dark hair.

The big thing about her was her smile. No matter what she was doing, it appeared frequently. This wasn't just a surface smile, but one that seemed to come from deep down.

All the members of our class adored her. She was patient with us, but never tried to slow us down. She talked to us on our own level, although she didn't appear to be condescending.

Her attitude—about everything from predicate nouns to long division—was that it was great fun and we should learn it like a new and exciting game.

The way in which I would most be like her was the way she was supremely happy about her work, and evidently about things in general—and, more important, she showed it.

The Person I Want Most to be Like

The person I am about to describe is the person I want most to be like. This person is not selfish by any means. When it come to the needs of other people she immediately puts off all the plans she may have had in order to help those people. She is always doing favors for other people no matter how much or how little other people may have done for her. If you ask a favor of her she doesn't keep putting it off for an indefinite length of time, instead she does it at her earliest possible convenience. She is generous in every way that she can possibly be. Of course this person is not perfect but she is one of the few people that I have seen so far that has filled so many requirements necessary to become so.

The teacher can obtain considerable understanding of his students by occasional writing assignments of this sort and can without too much additional effort transmit this understanding to his colleagues via the guidance folder.

Vocational and academic interest inventories serve the purpose of clarifying for the student his own interests and attitudes in relation to various aspects of a vocation or an academic program. Academic interest inventories have not been commonly used because students generally do not need assistance in systematically investigating their attitudes toward bodies of subject matter. Vocational interest inventories, on the other hand, have been widely used. In making a decision with respect to his vocational future the student must answer two questions. What are my skills and abilities presently and potentially? What would I like to do or what are my interests? We too often assume that each person has a clear idea of his interests and desires and if he is provided with information of his abilities plus those demanded of the various occupations, the decision about vocational choice can be readily made. Actually, the student requires assistance in analyzing his interests and needs to know more completely how his pattern of interests fits the various vocations. It is easy for the student to fake his answers on a standardized interest blank and to produce results that would make it appear that he has a particular kind of interest. For this reason it is unwise to use the vocational interest forms as a part of a selection program or in evaluating the effectiveness of instruction. In the guidance setting the student should be impressed with the importance of honest reactions to the statements in order for the information derived from the inventory to be of any use. The analysis of a student's interests helps to define his disposition to behave in certain ways and the satisfactions that he will derive from achieving certain goals.

Perhaps the most important information about the student in school guidance is the record of his achievement, and the estimate of his abilities. For this purpose standardized achievement, aptitude, and intelligence tests can be most useful in supplementing the record of grades assigned by the teacher.

The great number of achievement and aptitude tests available on the market creates a problem of choice for the school administrator. Once an achievement test battery is selected for a school, it is wise to continue the same battery for a number of years. Also, because it is important to obtain some picture of the development of an individual, the battery should be administered at least every three years. For these reasons care should be taken at the outset in selecting a test so that its reliability, validity, and standardization population are all such as to satisfy the requirements of the school. The test should be constructed so that different forms can be administered to the same group of students at various stages of their schooling. The achievement-test battery has the advantage over the individual-subject test in that it permits comparisons of pupil achievement in various subject areas. Rather than describe the particular tests, the reader is referred to Buros' *Mental Measurements* Yearbooks. The yearbook is issued every few years and contains descriptions and critical reviews of many different kinds of tests.

Some standardized tests of achievement and aptitude report the results in the form of a profile. Examination of the profile can be of considerable assistance in counseling with the student. A good example of such an instrument is the Differential Aptitude Tests (published by the Psychological Corporation). This aptitude-test battery is appropriate for grades eight to twelve and provides separate measures for the following: verbal reasoning, numerical ability, abstract reasoning, space relations, mechanical reasoning, clerical speed and accuracy, language usage: 1 spelling, 2 sentences.

The following case[2] taken from a casebook prepared by the authors of the Differential Aptitude Tests (Bennett et al., 1951) may serve as an illustration of the counseling procedures that can develop from the use of the test.

Constance T.

Problem: Constance, with no real problem, sought advice about her educational plans. Differential Aptitude Tests, Grade 9. [See Figure 9.7 for profile]

Report of Counseling in Grade 9

Constance has a distinctive speaking voice. She expresses herself clearly and in good English. Her health record is good; she has no outstanding defects. Her varied interests include playing the piano, reading, and playing softball. Constance began to take piano lessons when she was in the sixth grade; she has become steadily more interested in music. Last year she decided to specialize in classical rather than popular music. Her grades last year were excellent in every subject.

Constance has no vocational preference. She says she wants to go to college but doesn't know which one.

In this case the *Differential Aptitude Tests* are consistent with other information. As the *Manual* states, superior students often score low on the Clerical Speed and Accuracy test. This proved true in the case of Constance. After the counselor had stressed to Constance the importance of speed, she was retested. Her second score for this test placed her in the 76th percentile for girls on local norms. (Some of this gain, of course, may have been due to practice).

Comments

In a school which tests all its students in the eighth or ninth grade, the early discovery (or, as in this case, verification) of talent becomes administratively simple. Constance really has no problem requiring intensive counseling now. The counselor, however, is distinctly aware of her as a high-level achiever from whom society can expect much, and therefore a pupil who needs the very best training commensurate with her abilities. Care should be taken to prevent her coasting through high school with deteriorating work habits or finding herself frustrated by lack of direction.

We shall assume that the counselor has, or can develop, a plan for effective communication to the teachers about girls like Constance. Constance needs exposure to the information about—or better yet, bits of experience in—the more challenging occupations open to able women (pages 72-73).

An important principle to be kept in mind in examing guidance data is to consider the child as a growing and developing individual. If

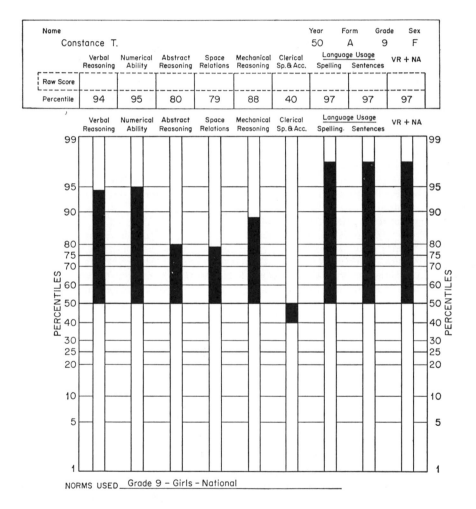

FIGURE 9.7 *Profile obtained by ninth-grade student on the Differential Aptitude tests. From G. K. Bennett et al.,* Counseling From Profiles, *copyright 1951, New York: The Psychological Corporation. Reproduced by permission. All rights reserved.*

we wish to guide growth we must cease giving all our attention to how a child compares with others at any one point in his development, but we must consider the pattern of the child's growth. Understanding of a pattern depends upon the examination of test results obtained over a period of time. Various patterns may appear. The student's growth in achievement may have been consistently at a high rate. For example, he may have gained the equivalent of three grades in achievement every two calendar years so that by the time he is in eighth grade he shows achievement equivalent to the twelfth grade. This information may be used to help the student choose activities that will enrich his experience outside the classroom, to help him achieve further breadth and depth in those areas where his achievement indicates an already high level of development, and by building up skills and understanding that are comparatively under-developed. For vocational guidance purposes these students should be helped to develop and maintain a high level of motivation toward an academic curriculum and to encourage the student to select a vocation that would require academic preparation.

The student's growth in achievement may have been consistently at a low rate. For example, he may have gained the equivalent of two grades in achievement in every three years of schooling, so that by the time he is in the ninth grade he shows achievement of the sixth-grade level. This information should lead the teacher to seek out areas that will enable the student to experience success outside the academic area; the manual arts, music, athletic activities, or social relationships. This does not mean that this student is likely to show great development in these nonacademic areas, but if he has not been defeated by his lack of success it is highly probable that he can acquire satisfactions from craftmanship, appreciation of certain forms of arts, from the expert use of his body, and from understanding of abstractions and theoretical concepts at his level of comprehension. In vocational choice the student of this type can be helped to recognize the many avenues available to him that would enable him to make a contribution to society and at the same time find self-fulfillment in areas other than outstanding academic achievement.

The test data obtained over the years may indicate an average rate of development, that is, a gain of approximately one grade in achievement for each year of schooling. In that rather common type of case, the teacher and the guidance counselor should attempt to discover and develop any special talents. The decision about a vocation will likely hinge on sociocultural and motivational factors. The choice of a curriculum should be as broad as possible, to permit maximum development of appreciations, citizenship understanding and responsibility, as well as a variety of practical skills required in modern day living. The child who shows sporadic and irregular growth may present a difficult guidance problem. Two types of patterns appear here. One pattern shows regular or accelerated development and then a slump; another pattern is one in which development is retarded for a number of years and then appears to pick up. In the case of the first pattern we should be alerted to some significant change in the experiences of the child. Has he experienced some emotional trauma? Is there a physical illness? Is there something in the teacher-pupil relationship that accounts for the child's problem? Identification of these possible causes of the "slump" in growth may be the first step in their correction. In contrast to the child who "fizzles" in his growth we have also the "late bloomer." Olson (1957) cites a case of this type.

> We can only illustrate the problem by the records of one child (Sam M.) who graduated with honors from a leading university. A very thick file containing much case material is available for him. The growth curves . . . show delay in reading (RA) to almost age ten, an unusual "splitting" or divergence of the various curves and a steady rise in intelligence (MA) and achievement (RA) toward the close of the period . . . (five to sixteen years). The associated data indicate delayed secondary sex characteristics, late maturation as a family trend, and an academic record which placed him near the bottom of his high school graduating class. Under the usual criteria for a selective philosophy of education he would have been considered unpromising material for secondary school or college. His "second chance" came through a delay of several years while serving in the armed forces and under the combined influences of added maturation and experience, he attained later distinction (page 28).

In all guidance decisions, the growth pattern in achievement is more important than a description of status based on one set of test data.

In offering the student guidance the teacher can contribute a great deal by simply taking an interest in the personal welfare of the student. The following transcript of a five-minute interview with a fifteen-year-old boy leaves one with a feeling that this boy's needs have been sadly overlooked.

> *Teacher:* Will you tell me something of your high school experience, mentioning especially how the school can help you?
> *Albert:* There's nothing I care about. All I want is to get out and get a job. But I'm only fifteen. I have to wait another year.
> *Teacher:* You want to leave school now?
> *Albert:* Yes, I don't like school, especially business training. It's mostly spelling, and I'm poor in writing and spelling. The teacher doesn't help, and I haven't asked.
> *Teacher:* Why not?
> *Albert:* She thinks I can't do it, and I guess I can't.
> *Teacher:* What do you do outside of school?
> *Albert:* My mother works, so I have to go home after school and take care of the house.
> *Teacher:* Do you belong to any clubs?
> *Albert:* I belong to the patrol boys. I like it. I can't belong to the others because of the housework.

Teacher: How do you get along with the reading?
Albert: I can read, but it's the words I can't pronounce. I read books out-side sometimes—Boy Scout books. I take books from the library sometimes.
Teacher: Have you gone to any parties in the school?
Albert: Went to two dances.
Teacher: Do you know what you would like to do when you leave school?
Albert: I want to be an electrician. I don't see the use of the subjects I'm taking (Strang, 1953, pages 204-205).

SUMMARY

The field of measurement has contributed much toward making teaching and learning more effective. In order to understand the applications and the limitations of measuring instruments, the teacher must be able to evaluate the measuring instrument in terms of its essential characteristics. These characteristics include the nature of the scale, the reliability of the instrument, and its validity.

It is important to understand the differences between the usual measurement in education and that ordinarily applied to our physical reality. In the latter we usually start with an absolute zero point and the intervals on the scale are equal throughout the scale. In educational and psychological measurement these conditions do not obtain. We can compare among different performances by various forms of ranking such as percentile scores, standard scores, and age and grade norms. When using a standardized test, one in which the scale has been established on a standardization population, one must be sure that it is appropriate to compare the specific person or group with the standardization population.

The reliability of a test is a measure of its accuracy, consistency, and stability. The reliability of test scores is affected by the subjectivity of the judges, the ambiguity of test items and directions, and temporary fluctuations of performance in the persons being examined. We can improve the reliability of a test by providing judges with models of various quality levels and directions for scoring; by the use of objective test items that are clear in intent; by improving the form of the essay question and its scoring procedure; and by making test conditions as favorable as possible.

Validity is a measure of the extent to which the test measures what it claims to measure or the extent to which it satisfies the purpose for which it is administered. Since we have various purposes in administering tests, we have different kinds of test validity. Predictive validity is the extent to which a test has been able to predict future performance on a criterion task. Selection examinations have predictive validity. Concurrent validity is another form of predictive validity, the difference being that the concurrent validity relies on an immediately available criterion. Content validity depends on the extent to which the test assesses the achievement of educational objectives and the extent to which it adequately covers the range of the subject matter. Construct validity is the extent to which the test measures a psychological construct. This last type of validity cannot be determined directly and various scholars are in disagreement over the usefulness of the concept.

Evaluation can be used to measure the degree to which the objectives of instruction are being met and to indicate what changes in curriculum need to be made. The different objectives of instruction require different kinds of test procedures. A test of factual knowledge is the easiest to construct but should not be emphasized over other objectives such as the development of understanding, analytic skills, application of knowledge, and the growth of value judgments. The use of achievement tests for supervision of teaching must take into account student growth and the characteristics of students and should not turn to absolute measures of student performance to evaluate teaching effectiveness. This latter practice can be detrimental to creative and effective teaching.

Evaluation for purposes of diagnosis and correction of learning should assess the rate of work and its accuracy. When the relationship of these is inverse the student will need to be helped to become more secure so that he can give up his need to be perfect or he may need help in gaining accuracy by using checking procedures where possible. The same type of analysis can be done on the depth of ability and the range over various abilities. Corrective procedures for problems in depth and breadth should take into account the positive feelings associated with mastery of a skill. The quality of performance should be assessed in terms of specifics, if the student is to be helped to improve his quality. A careful analysis of the student's approach to problems, his style or method of performing, can be helpful in indicating how he might overcome any crucial deficiencies.

Teachers participate in the specialized guidance function of the school by gathering and interpreting data in the following areas: The social context of the student's life, including sociometric data, family and socioeconomic background; the student's emotional and motivational characteristics, which are better assessed by self-descriptions written by the student rather than by specialized personality measures; measures of achievement that describe, in the form of a profile, the student's stronger and weaker areas of performance. For all guidance the student should be provided with the necessary information about himself and about the world in which he lives, and he should be encouraged to make his own decisions.

READING REFERENCES

Bloom, B. S. (Ed.), *Taxonomy of Educational Objectives, Handbook I: Cognitive Domain*. New York: Longmans, 1956.

Brueckner, L. J. and G. L. Bond, *The Diagnosis and Treatment of Learning Difficulties*. New York: Appleton-Century-Crofts, 1955.

Cronbach, L. J., *Essentials of Psychological Testing*, 2nd ed. New York: Harper & Row, 1960 (particularly chaps. 2, 5, and 6).

Findley, W. G. (Ed.), *The Impact and Improvement of School Testing Programs*. Sixty-second Yearbook (Pt. 2) National Society for the Study of Education. Chicago: University of Chicago Press, 1963 (particularly chaps. 1-3 and 12).

Rothney, J. W. M., *Evaluating and Reporting Pupil Progress* (What Research Says to the Teacher No. 7). Washington, D. C.: National Education Association, 1955.

Wandt, E. and G. W. Brown, *Essentials of Educational Evaluation*. New York: Holt, Rinehart and Winston, 1957.

Wood, Dorothy A., *Test Construction: Development and Interpretation of Achievement Tests*. Columbus, Ohio: Charles E. Merrill Books, 1960.

PART 3

ADAPTING TEACHING TO INDIVIDUAL DIFFERENCES

From Devaney

CHAPTER 10

INTELLECTUAL
FACTORS

The vast majority of teachers would agree that the one kind of human difference that truly makes a difference insofar as schooling is concerned is the quality of intelligence that the student possesses. What they generally mean by this is that teaching and learning are greatly influenced by the student's ability to master the content of the curriculum and it is assumed that this ability is synonymous with intelligence. Many teachers proceed from this more or less tenable position to a number of unwarranted assumptions about the characteristics of intelligence, the sources from which it is derived, and the course of its growth and development. The technical and research literature on the subject is vast and at many points contradictory. A study of some of this literature makes it clear that the last word is yet to be said if indeed it ever will be. The purpose of this chapter is to reveal some of the issues involving the concept of intelligence and to develop in the reader a judicious caution in the application of intelligence test results.

THE NATURE OF INTELLIGENCE: A DEFINITION

Many students are surprised to learn that the popular notions about intelligence are vague and ambiguous, but this is bound to result when a term receives such widespread use. They are even surprised to learn that psychologists are in basic disagreement on the meaning of the term. One point of disagreement is whether intelligence is to be conceived as capacity or ability. Most of those who use the term capacity or potentiality in defining intelligence convey their belief that intelligence is innate, inborn, or untaught. Those who use the term ability, on the other hand, do not commit themselves on the question of the source of intelligence, and they would argue that what we observe is ability and that we cannot observe and record potentiality unless it has developed into some kind of performance. The writer recalls being questioned by a group of parents of children afflicted with cerebral palsy. They wanted to know the *real* intelligence of their children. They seemed to assume that the psychologist measured some hidden quality, perhaps even that he was able to examine the genes and chromosomes that contribute to intelligence. No one can even guess how these afflicted children would have performed were they not so handicapped. Such a guess would serve little purpose except to alleviate some of the guilt with which these parents were surely burdened. The view held here is that intelligence is a quality of behavior and performance.

The next question to be raised is: What kind of ability? Binet, the father of modern intelligence testing, described intellectual ability as "the tendency to take and maintain a definite direction; the capacity to make adaptations for the purpose of attaining a desired end; and the power of auto-criticism" (Terman, 1916, page 45). Terman, who was responsible for the popular American adaptation of the Binet test—the Stanford-Binet—defined intelligence as the ability to do abstract thinking.

Stoddard (1943, page 4) presents a comprehensive description of intelligence when he defines it as: "The ability to undertake activities that are characterized by (1) difficulty, (2) complexity, (3) abstractness, (4) economy, (5) adaptiveness to a goal, (6) social value, and (7) the emergence of originals, and to maintain such activities under conditions that demand a concentration of energy and a resistance to emotional forces."

Difficulty as an attribute of intelligent behavior is determined by the age of the typical child that can carry on such behavior. It is assumed that older children can accomplish more difficult tasks than younger ones. The level of difficulty of an intelligence test item is established statistically by computing the percentage of various age groups that can pass the item. It should be noted that difficulty cannot be considered as an independent attribute of intelligence; it has meaning in the description only insofar as it fits the over-all definition. Complexity, the second attribute, refers to breadth of intelligence. If two individuals show behavior that is equivalent in all the other attributes, except that one is able to undertake successfully a larger number of different tasks, it is assumed that he is more intelligent. Complexity and difficulty are closely intertwined in a functioning intelligence.

Abstractness may be described as thinking, symbolic representation that is objective and systematic (see Figure 4.1, p. 92). Stoddard correctly points out that this attribute lies at the heart of his definition and that it appears in every formulation of intelligence. The greater the difficulty and complexity of an individual's ability to use symbolic and abstract thinking, the higher is his intelligence. Economy as an attribute of intelligent performance, refers to the efficiency with which the person carries out the task. Economy and efficiency are functions of time and accuracy.

The attributes adaptiveness to a goal and social value may be considered together. They are difficult to describe directly but may be understood from a description of their opposites. Behavior that is aimless and that shows lack of awareness of social appropriateness is unintelligent. In order for behavior to be considered intelligent it cannot be aimless, unsystematic, or rigid. The schizophrenic generally shows little loss in the other characteristics of intelligence, but he does lack an awareness of social appropriateness and is likely to exhibit behavior that is bizarre. The same is true to a certain extent of the criminal whose behavior may be described as intelligent even in regard to adaptiveness to a goal but it lacks social value or appropriateness.

The emergence of originals is an attribute that distinguishes different types of intelligence at the higher end of the continuum. The discussion of creativity in Chapter 4 deals with this attribute of intelligence.

THE ORGANIZATION OF INTELLIGENCE

Whether intelligence is a global characteristic or made up of different amounts of various abilities has been the concern of measurement psychologists for many decades. It is important that the teacher develop a point of view on this question in order to deal appropriately with individual differences.

Binet and those who followed the philosophy inherent in his approach considered intelligence to be a general and a unified ability. Spearman, a British psychologist, applied statistical analysis to intelligence test results and concluded that performance on intelligence tests was due first to the presence of a general, g, factor and then to specific abilities, s, factors. Using a different statistical approach, factor analysis, Thurstone developed a test that measured what he considered to be primary mental abilities. The number of these primary abilities or factors varies with the age level but generally included are the following: verbal meaning, word fluency, memory, number, reasoning, and spatial relations.

Guilford (1959) approaches the study of intelligence from yet another factor analytic view. He first considers the many different ways in which intelligent behavior may manifest itself. He then suggests that intelligent behavior consists always of some operation or mental activity, dealing with some content or material and resulting in some outcome or product. After this analysis he attempts to devise tests that will measure the interaction of these three, namely, operations, content, and product.

Guilford specifies five different kinds of operations. These are:

1. Cognition, which means discovery or recognition. The discussion of the cognitive field in Chapter 4 describes this operation.
2. Memory, which refers to the retention of what is cognized.
3. Divergent thinking is described as the ability to produce a large variety of responses.
4. Convergent thinking "leads to one right answer or to a recognized best or conventional answer."
5. Evaluation is the ability to determine how good, correct, or adequate is our knowledge or thinking at a particular time.

Each of these five operations can be applied to each of four kinds of material or content:

1. Figural content is concrete material involving the senses.
2. Symbolic content is made up of the conventional symbols such as letters and numbers and their systematic organization.
3. Semantic content appears in the form of verbal meaning and interpretation.
4. Behavioral content is added purely on a theoretical basis inasmuch as no particular tests to measure this content have yet been developed. Guilford suggests that this content area is sometimes called "social intelligence."

Each of the five kinds of operations can be involved in each of the four areas of content so as to produce six different kinds of products. These are: (1) units, (2) classes, (3) relations, (4) systems, (5) transformations, and (6) implications.

To aid in visualizing the interaction of three facets of intelligence, operations, contents, and products, Guilford presents a three-dimensional model of intelligence (see Figure 10.1). This conceptualization provides 120 cells, each corresponding to a specific factor of intelligence. Only about half of these factors have been operationally identified. Thus, for example, a person is asked to produce as many words as possible from a series of scrambled letters. This type of task would represent the factor that falls at the intersection of divergent thinking (operation No. 3), symbolic content (content category No. 2) and units, (product No. 1). The student might find it interesting to find the factor for each of the sample items from the Stanford-Binet scale on page 308 below.

It is interesting to note that Guilford is of the opinion that appropriate educational experience can improve the development of each

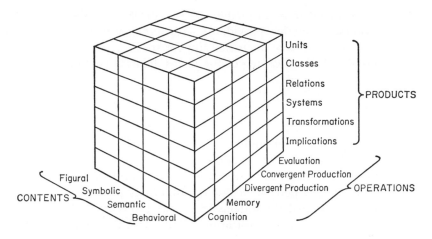

FIGURE 10.1 *A cubical model representing the structure of intellect. Each of the 120 small cubes in the model can be described in terms of operation, content, and product, for each cube lies at the intersection of a unique combination of these three facets of intelligence. From J. P. Guilford, "The Three Faces of Intellect,"* American Psychologist, *14, no. 8, 1959, p. 470.*

intellectual factor. The school would, of course, have greater interest in some factors than in others.

Garrett (1946), who defines intelligence as the comprehension and use of symbols in the solution of problems, proposes a developmental theory of intelligence. He concludes, after examining a great deal of research evidence, that intellectual ability tends to be unified and general during the early school years, but as age increases this generalized ability becomes reorganized and differentiates itself into a number of fairly distinct and independent abilities.

Hunt (1961), in an excellent book on intelligence and experience, marshals evidence to show that the findings of the factor analytic studies would not contradict the notion that a general global intellectual ability is the developmental forerunner of the various factors that have been identified. He attributes the presence of independent factors to the fact that the data used in the factor analytic studies of intelligence were obtained on adult subjects.

THE MEASUREMENT OF INTELLIGENCE

Although the person who constructs an intelligence test must begin with a reasonably clear definition, the test user is better advised to rely on the more operational definition of intelligence, which states that intelligence is whatever intelligence tests measure. In other words, the characteristics of intelligence such as the ability to use abstractions, or the ability to remember, must ultimately be converted into intelligence test items. It is these items that provide us with our measure of intelligence. Before the various kinds of items that appear in the most commonly used tests are presented, the meaning of the terms mental age and intelligence quotient will be clarified.

Mental Age

Alfred Binet, who first used the term mental age, assumed that during the childhood and adolescent years intellectual ability improved with age. On this assumption he administered a number of test items to a large number of subjects of different ages. He retained only those items that showed a larger percent of older individuals passing than younger ones. Later he grouped these items into year levels in terms of the age for which these items were most appropriate. The mental-age score that a person obtains is simply a conversion of his success score on the items. The Stanford-Binet Intelligence Scale, the most widely known American adaptation of the Binet test, is arranged so that each year level from two through four has twelve items in it, from five through fourteen there are six items at each year level, and beyond the age fourteen level there are twenty-six test items divided into four separate levels. The value assigned to each test item is such as to give the subject a total score of twelve if he passes all the items in a particular year level. (The four levels beyond age fourteen level provide a maximum possible credit of 106.) The score of twelve for each year level corresponds to twelve months of the year and credit points are called months of mental age.

Let us consider a hypothetical child whose calendar or chronological age (CA) is five years and six months and let us assume that he performs as follows: He passes all the items at the year four level, five of the six items at year five, two at year six and none at year seven. As the items are arranged in order of difficulty it can be assumed that he would fail all the items beyond year seven and that he would pass all those below year four. Credit is given him for the tests that he is expected to pass, thirty-six months in this case, twelve months for passing all the items at year four, ten months credit for the five successful items at year five, and four months credit for the two items at year six. This gives him a total of sixty-two months or five years and two months credit. Hence his mental age is 5-2. It should be noted that although the mental age is simply a score (Wechsler, 1944), a particular mental-age score obtained by a child tells us that his performance compares with children whose chronological age is the same as his obtained mental age. In the case of the hypothetical child, his mental age score of five years two months indicates that he performed like children whose chronological age is approximately five years and two months.

The Intelligence Quotient (IQ)

The intelligence quotient is an index that enables us to indicate the relationship between the ability that a child has and what is expected of him on the basis of his chronological age. Referring again to the hypothetical child, as he is five years and six months of age, a score of 5-6 on the test might be expected; his obtained score was 5-2. His measured ability is somewhat less than his expected ability. This relationship is expressed in the form of a ratio as follows:

$$\frac{\text{Obtained mental age score in months}}{\text{Expected mental age score in months (CA)}} = \frac{62}{66} = 0.94$$

In order to remove the decimal multiply by 100 and this child's IQ would be reported as 94.[1]

Thus if a child's test performance gives him a score that equals that of his age group his IQ is 100; if the score stated in months of mental age is greater than the expected score (his chronological age) the IQ would be more than 100. The IQ is essentially an index of the child's brightness.

One feature of mental age and intelligence quotient should be noted. As we move up the age ladder our expected scores increase. It is assumed that seven-year-old children as a group will do better than six-year-old children, ten-year-olds better than nine and so on. However, we know that the twenty-year-old group does not perform better than the nineteen-year-old group, and the nineteen-year-old does not obtain higher scores than does the eighteen-year-old. Each intelligence test has a maximum age beyond which we would not expect the age groups to differ in their performance. This maximum age for the Stanford-Binet is sixteen. The expected score for an individual over sixteen years of age is 192 months of credit (sixteen by twelve) and a person of chronological age of sixteen or over who receives a mental age score of 192 months (sixteen years) would receive an IQ of 100. With individuals sixteen or over the denominator in the ratio remains fixed at 192 months.

Description of Intelligence Tests

The development of a useful intelligence test is a long arduous task. We have a number of tests available for our use. In most schools the general testing program will include a group test of intelligence. When a child is being considered for special purposes (possible mental defi-

---

[1] The 1960 Revision of the Stanford-Binet does not use the ratio procedure in determining the IQ. The IQ tables presented with the test manual (Terman and Merrill, 1960) use deviation or standard score IQ's. The standard score IQ has a mean of 100 and a standard deviation of 16 (see discussion of standard score on p. 252). The IQ of the hypothetical case turns out to be 93 if it is derived from the tables provided in the manual.

ciency, behavior problem, or special-class placement) an individual test should be administered by a competent psychologist.

Individual Tests

The most widely used individual test of intelligence is the Stanford-Binet Scale. As just described, it is an age scale or a test in which the items are grouped according to difficulty appropriate for various chronological ages. A trained examiner (only trained individuals should administer the test if the results are to be meaningful) knows where to start with a particular subject and how to proceed. The usual examination takes almost an hour. A few of the items from the current revision of the Stanford-Binet Scale (1960) are shown here.

> Year Six
> *Vocabulary:*   At least six words known in a graded vocabulary list. At this level words are: tap, gown, roar.
> *Differences:*   Example: What is the difference between wood and glass?
> *Number concepts:*   Demonstrates understanding of numbers up to ten by counting blocks.
> Year Nine
> *Verbal absurdities:*   Finds absurdity in an incongruous statement.
> *Memory for designs:*   Is able to reproduce a design after looking at it for ten seconds.
> *Rhymes:*   Example: Tell me a number that rhymes with tree.
> Year Twelve
> *Vocabulary:*   At least fifteen words from graded vocabulary list. At this level words are: brunette, muzzle, haste.
> *Digit span:*   Repeating five digits reversed.
> *Abstract words:*   Knows the meaning of such words as: pity, curiosity.

The Wechsler Intelligence Scale for Children (WISC) is another widely used individual test. It is constructed as a point scale rather than an age scale. Instead of providing a mental-age score, it provides scaled scores for each of the ten subtests usually administered. The scaled scores can be converted into a full scale IQ as well as verbal IQ and performance IQ. There are some clinical values in a test in which the performance of various kinds of subtests can be compared with each other. The verbal IQ is derived from the scores on the following subtests: information, comprehension, arithmetic, similarities, vocabulary, and digit span as an alternate test item. The performance items are: picture completion, picture arrangement, block design, object assembly, coding, and mazes as an alternate item.

As just indicated, the administration of an individual intelligence test takes about an hour and requires a well trained examiner. It is not likely that a school would arrange for an individual test for each student, nor would the amount of interpretive information obtained be useful. For these reasons, most school systems use group tests of intelligence.

Group Tests

The Differential Aptitude Test briefly described in the previous chapter on page 291 combines tests of intelligence such as verbal reasoning and abstract reasoning with tests of special ability like clerical speed and accuracy along with achievement tests of language usage.

The Cooperative School and College Ability Tests, known as SCAT, published by the Cooperative Test Division of the Educational Testing Service (1957), is another example of a group intelligence test. This test assumes that scholastic ability is more or less synonymous with intelligence. The test has five levels extending from grade four to college level. The test measures four skills and is divided into four parts: (1) sentence meaning, (2) arithmetic computation, (3) word meaning, and (4) arithmetic problems. Scores on parts 1 and 3 give a verbal score; scores on parts 2 and 4 give a quantitative score.

The California Test of Mental Maturity published by the California Test Bureau (Sullivan et al., 1957) is a widely used group test of intelligence. Like the SCAT, it provides a language and nonlanguage score. The separate parts of the test are: memory, spatial relationships, logical reasoning, numerical reasoning, and verbal concepts. The test has seven forms appropriate for kindergarten through adult levels.

It should be noted that group tests generally demand reading and children whose reading skill is deficient are penalized. It should also be noted that the tasks on a group test are similar to school tasks and children who are poorly motivated in school work are likely to receive poor scores. If the test is being used as a predictor of future school performance, poor reading and poor motivation will often predict poor future performance as much as low intellectual ability. However, it is important for the teacher to understand that there is a complex of causes which produces a score on a test and it is dangerous to assume that scores on a group test are the result of only intellectual ability.

THE STABILITY OF INTELLIGENCE TEST SCORES

Many important decisions about children are made on the basis of one or two intelligence test scores. Schools that practice homogeneous grouping rely heavily on intelligence test scores. Much of the guidance that a student receives particularly in junior and senior high school is based on such test scores. Students' scholastic achievement is often evaluated and termed over- or under-achievement with expected achievement

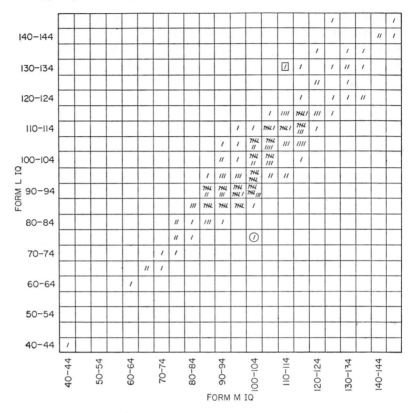

FIGURE 10.2 *A scattergram showing the IQ scores obtained by a group of seven-year-olds on two forms of the 1937 Revision of the Stanford-Binet. From L. M. Terman and Maud A. Merrill,* Measuring Intelligence, *Boston: Houghton Mifflin, 1937, p. 45.*

based on intelligence test performance. Because of such great reliance on the intelligence test it is important to consider two characteristics of these scores, namely, reliability and constancy.

Reliability on Intelligence Test Scores

The concept of reliability or error in measurement was discussed in the previous chapter. It is considered here with particular reference to the measurement of intellectual abilities. If we were to give another form of the same test to the same individuals within a short time after the first test, how much change would we expect to find? There is a partial answer to this question in Figure 10.2. In this figure are presented the scores obtained by some 200 seven-year-old children on two forms of the Stanford-Binet Test. The test reliability for ages six to thirteen is reported to be 0.91. This is a highly reliable test indeed. The reliability figures for group tests are not usually higher. Let us examine the scatter-gram in Figure 10.2 for the kinds of errors that might result if we had only one measure. The tally mark which is circled represents a child with a Form L IQ of 75-79. On the basis of this score we would have reasonable doubts of his ability to complete the usual elementary school curriculum. We note that his Form M IQ is 100-104, which would lead us to believe that he has a 50-50 chance of completing an academic high school curriculum. The tally marked with a square represents a child whose Form M IQ is 110-114. If we were making some judgments about this child based on this score we would believe that he would not merit being placed in an accelerated or enriched program group. Yet his Form L IQ of 130-134 would place him in the definitely superior group. While it is true that we have selected the extreme cases and that the majority of children obtain very similar scores on both tests, we must not lose sight of the fact that these are real children, not simply tally marks. Classifying a child on the basis of a single test score may do him a serious injustice. Also a scattergram on group tests would show many more individuals whose scores would differ significantly. The test constructor is of necessity an actuarial psychologist. That is, he is interested in scores of populations, not individuals. The teacher on the other hand must always retain an orientation to the individual and interpret the sample performance on a test with the utmost caution.

The Error of Measurement and Over- or Underachievement

It is common practice for teachers to compare the score obtained on an intelligence test and that obtained on an achievement test. If the score on the former is higher, the student is labeled an underachiever; if the latter is higher, he is labeled an overachiever. This practice cannot be justified (Dyer, 1960). Cronbach (1960a) has pointed out that a typical intelligence test and an achievement test overlap in what they measure to about 71 percent. The error of measurement would account for an additional 14 percent of each test score. He concludes that "among children with the same achievement *about half of the individual differences in IQ are due only to random errors. . . .* For most children, a group mental test leads to the same prediction that a comprehensive achievement test would."

It is true that some children with high level intellectual ability are poorly motivated in the classroom and do not make full use of their ability and there are others who by dint of hard work perform well on school tasks even while they have only modest intellectual ability. However, we cannot make a decision about whether one or the other is the case by comparing the scores on two tests that measure essentially the same thing, general scholastic ability.

So far only the reliability of a test measure has been considered.

The question has been, how certain can we be that the measure we have is a true reflection of the child's performance? The next questions are: Assuming the reliability of a test measure, how stable is the process of mental growth? Do children who show signs of rapid, average, or slow growth during the early years fulfill the prediction of these signs later on? These questions can only be answered by means of longitudinal studies. In a longitudinal study the same individuals are studied over an extended period of time. This type of study is costly and difficult, but it is only from data obtained in this fashion that we are able to understand how children grow.

In one study (Honzik et al., 1948) more than 150 children were tested at specified intervals over a sixteen-year period from ages two to eighteen. As we are interested primarily in the school-age period, only the conclusions on the age period six to eighteen will be examined. This study showed that only 15 percent of the group showed change of less than 10 points of IQ. More than half of the population changed from 10-20 IQ points. About one third of the group, showed changes of 20 points or more in IQ and about one in ten children changed 30 or more IQ points.

In another longitudinal study reported by Bayley (1949, 1955), it was conclusively shown that test performance on infant scales does not indicate later intelligence. She concludes from her data that intellectual growth through the first eighteen years of life is a "resultant of varied and complex factors." As in the previous study, Bayley concluded that the total life experience of a particular child can provide disturbing or stabilizing influences and these, together with the inherited predispositions for growth, determine a child's mental growth pattern. On the basis of a careful longitudinal case study of a single child, Richards (1951) likewise concluded that fluctuations in IQ measures were related to important characteristics of the child's current life situation.

Similar results of fluctuation in IQ are reported in another well-designed longitudinal study by Sontag et al. (1958). Samples of the mental growth patterns obtained in this study are shown in Figure 10.3. At the extremes there is Case 1 showing an almost constant, marked rise in IQ from ages three through twelve, and Case 139 showing a constant decrease in IQ. In between these extremes there is every kind of fluctuation. It should be noted that, although the IQ's reported in this study were obtained in such a way as to rule out most sources of error in measurement, almost two out of three children studied changed more than 15 IQ points in either direction.

Another significant contribution of this study is the finding that a number of personality factors are associated with different patterns of mental growth. Using a number of carefully applied rating scales, Sontag and his colleagues demonstrated that personality dimensions related to

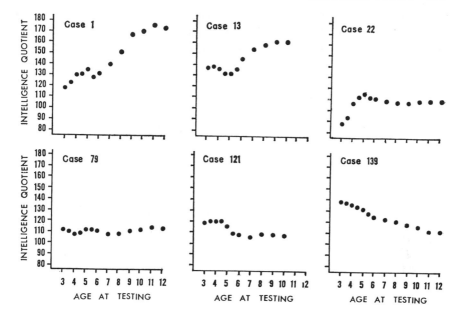

FIGURE 10.3   *Samples of mental growth patterns. From L. W. Sontag et al., "Mental Growth and Personality Development: A Longitudinal Study,"* Monographs of the Society for Research in Child Development, *23, no. 2, 1958.*

the need for achievement were associated with the direction and degree of change in the mental growth pattern.

These studies show that intelligence is not a static function, predetermined at birth and fixed thereafter, but is rather organically related as a quality of any behavior to emotions, attitudes, and motivation (Fromm and Hartman, 1955). Bayley (1955) has stated it as follows:

> It becomes evident that the intellectual growth of any given child is a resultant of varied and complex factors. These will include his inherent capacities for growth, both in amount and rate of progress. They will include the emotional climate in which he grows: whether he is encouraged or discouraged, whether his drive (or ego-involvement) is strong in intellectual thought processes, or is directed toward other aspects of his life-field. And they will include the material environment in which he grows: the opportunities for experience and for learning, and the extent to which these opportunities are continuously geared to his capacity to respond and make use of them (page 813-814).

HEREDITY AND ENVIRONMENT IN INTELLIGENCE

Ever since intelligence tests have come into widespread use, a controversy has raged among measurement experts as to whether intellectual ability is an inherited or an acquired characteristic. Those who argue that genetic or inherited factors are the primary determinants of intelligence would state their case more or less in this fashion. At the time of conception the individual receives from his parents his gene structure. This gene organization will determine the course of his growth. A poor environment may inhibit growth but a stimulating environment could not counteract the limits set by genetic constitution.

The evidence for this point of view is derived from a number of different sources. A number of studies, dating back to the beginning of the century, have demonstrated that the correlation of intelligence test scores of children and each of their parents is about 0.50. In order to control the influence of a common environment the intelligence of children placed in foster homes has been correlated with that of their true parents as well as that of their foster parents. As these children reached adolescence the correlation of their intelligence with that of their foster parents tends to be near zero, whereas the correlation with their true parents' intelligence approaches 0.50. If we compare the correlations of the intelligence scores of siblings, fraternal twins, and identical twins, it can be shown that the greater the degree of genetic similarity the greater the degree of correlation. Identical twins reared apart were more similar than nonidentical siblings. There is then a substantial body of evidence to support the contention that genetic factors play an important role in determining the level of intelligence.

On the other hand, a significant body of evidence has accumulated to support the point of view that environmental influences make a great difference in intelligence test scores. In one study (Sherman and Key, 1932), using four different tests of intelligence, it was clearly demonstrated that children who lived in more isolated mountain communities with poorer educational facilities scored significantly lower than those who lived in more favorable conditions. There was good reason to believe that the genetic constitution of the various populations was similar. This study further showed that the older the children the greater the impact of the environment on the score differences.

A study by Lee (1951) confirmed an hypothesis presented by Klineberg (1935). Klineberg had explained the fact that Northern Negroes obtain higher scores on intelligence tests than do Southern Negroes on the basis of improved environmental conditions. However he was not able to control for the possibility of selective migration factors. Lee's study obtained longitudinal data that demonstrated that whereas during the first grade the Negro children who had recently moved to Philadelphia scored lower than those who had been born in the city; by the time the migrant group reached the ninth grade their IQ's were almost equal to the native group.

It has been established that when economic and educational improvements take place in a community the IQ scores of children from the same community and largely from the same families tend to rise significantly (Smith, 1942 and Wheeler, 1942).

In analyzing the results of the National Merit Scholarship selections for 1956, Bond (1960) shows that children of professional and technical workers account for 45 percent of the talented high school graduates, whereas children of laborers account for only 0.2 percent. Both groups of parents represent similar sized segments (8.5 percent) of the total population, yet of a total of 28,000 talented youth, the former produced 12,649 talented youth while the latter produced only 54. It is difficult to argue that the pools of genes that may be operative in the development of academic talent are so highly differentiated along occupational lines in a society as young as ours.

The awareness that children from different socioeconomic groups perform differently on intelligence tests has led to serious attempts to develop tests that do not discriminate against children of lower socioeconomic levels. Using data provided by Eells (1948), Davis and Havighurst (1948b) report that 90 percent of the items in a group of four tests of intelligence discriminated significantly between children of high and low socioeconomic levels. They state their conviction that: "There is no evidence, and no theory shared by the leading human geneticists, to the effect that the underprivileged socioeconomic or racial groups are genetically inferior to the more prosperous socioeconomic groups" (page 312). This kind of thinking and research has led to the development of the Davis-Eells Test of General Intelligence or Problem Solving Ability. This test is discussed in Chapter 14.

Related to the topic under consideration are the questions whether or not there are racial and ethnic differences in intelligence, and if such differences do exist should they be attributed to hereditary or environmental factors. The kinds of answers given to these questions are of very great social significance. There exists a widespread, long-standing, and harmful misconception, probably arising out of prejudicial needs as described in Chapter 6, that personality and mental differences among racial groups parallel physical differences and that the so-called white race is unquestionably superior. Tyler (1956) points out that even some eminent scientists of the recent past such as G. Stanley Hall and Francis Galton, supported such a point of view. The danger of such a view is that if inferiority is attributed to a group this may induce that characteristic in the group. (See discussion in Chapter 6 of self-fulfilling prophecy and also reasoning surrounding the U. S. Supreme Court decision of 1954.)

There are many problems connected with conducting research in the area of race differences. For a detailed discussion of these problems the reader is referred to Anastasi (1958) and Tyler (1956). Some of the more obvious problems are mentioned here. Races, ethnic groups even more, are not fixed and differentiated populations, hence it is extremely difficult to select samples that represent separate racial or ethnic groups. Imagine someone planning to study the differences in some psychological characteristic in American Negroes and whites. The definition of the racial group is a difficult problem, for most individuals who are ordinarily classified as Negro can trace to some white ancestors in their lineage. Which subjects should he select for his white sample, Italians, Irish, or Scandinavians? If one extends the range of research to study individuals in different parts of the world one encounters the problem of selecting appropriate testing instruments when testing individuals with different language backgrounds and different socializing experiences. Even if one overcomes these difficulties, he still faces the problem of selecting from each group samples that would be comparable in socioeconomic status and comparably stratified throughout the range of the characteristic in question.

Yet in spite of these difficulties a great amount of research on this question has been done. The single most important educational implication of this research is that knowledge of an individual's group membership cannot be a basis for predicting his test performance or for attributing specific characteristics to him. Anastasi (1960) states: "Even when statistically significant differences are found between groups, they are of little practical value for dealing with specific persons. Mean differences *between* groups are always far smaller than differences *within* groups." It has been repeatedly noted that even in those cases where group differences can be demonstrated, there is extensive overlapping of the scores of the distributions. Overlapping is a measure of the extent to which the scores in one distribution reach or exceed the median of the other. Complete overlapping occurs when 50 percent of the scores of one population reach or exceed the median score of the other population. Even with the effects of past and present cultural and educational inequities, in comparing Negro and white populations, at least 25 percent of the intelligence test scores of Negroes reach or surpass the median of intelligence test scores obtained by comparable white subjects. That is, the overlapping is at least half the maximum possible. Moreover it is worth noting that the ranges within the distributions are almost identical, meaning that extremely gifted individuals (as well as extremely deficient ones) will be found in both groups. Because of this extensive overlapping and identity of ranges, it is essential that we judge each individual on his own merits and not on the basis of his race or ethnic group.

No definitive statement in regard to race equality can be made. However, the dogmatic position in regard to racial superiority can be rejected. When more is learned about the forces that shape the development of that quality called intelligence, and when some of this understanding in the form of appropriate developmental experiences is implemented, it should be possible to increase the overlapping of scores between groups to approach the maximum 50 percent, and to realize greater intellectual ability in all populations. This prediction is based on such findings as those just referred to (Lee, 1951) and those of Strodtbeck (1958) that showed that the value orientations of families from different ethnic groups produced different attitudes toward achievement and independence. In essence the position is that we haven't done nearly as much as we can in improving intellectual growth of all children by arranging the environmental conditions, so that it is not necessary at this point to concern ourselves with the hypothetical limitations and differences in genetic qualities.

The controversy as to the relative influence of genetic and environmental factors in producing the characteristics of behavior that are called intelligence cannot truly be resolved. For as in the case of any behavior the two factors, heredity and particular past experience, must interact before the behavior appears. Hebb (1953) writes that to ask what proportions of a behavior are due to heredity and what proportions are due to environment is like asking how much of the area of a field is due to its length and how much to its width. Liverant (1960) in examining intelligence as a concept is critical of the genetic point of view and also suggests that *interaction* of a *specific genetic structure* operating within a *specific environment* produces any characteristic. He states that "genes set the limits within any given environment but these limits may vary as the environment varies" (page 103).

The practical implications of viewing intelligence as a resultant of the interaction of heredity and environment should be clear. The teacher who explains the difference in problem-solving skill between two children as being due to differences in intelligence is making a tautological or circular statement. He might as well say that differences in problem-solving ability are due to differences in problem-solving ability. In viewing the present level of school performance and problem-solving ability as the result of the interaction of a very complex pattern of genetic processes and a vast array of past experiences, the task for the teacher becomes one of careful environmental manipulation. The teacher must believe that even within the limited framework of the school environment every child's intelligence can be improved. Bond (1960), whose analysis of the National Merit Scholarship results was reported above, argues that if we could provide for every child in the land appropriate "opportunities for intellectual stimulation now enjoyed by the children of professional, technical, and kindred workers, we would increase our 'talent pool' five fold" (page 133). If we provided the right kind of educational experiences for children who already evidence high ability, their ultimate destiny would be to provide the creative leadership that our world so sorely needs.

STUDENTS WITH HIGH ACADEMIC ABILITY

Most school programs are designed for children of average and slightly above average academic ability. In order to educate properly the child with high ability the school must be able to identify the academically talented and to make appropriate curriculum adaptations.

Identification of the Gifted

The primary bases for identifying the gifted child are teachers' judgment and observation and the standardized tests of intelligence and achievement. The usefulness of the teachers' observation is limited by the tendency of many teachers to overrate nonintellective factors and to overlook some characteristics that are important in high order intelligent behavior. The Educational Policies Commission (1950) has noted this difficulty in the following statement:

> Some teachers overrate the intelligence of children who are neat, pretty, obedient, friendly, or talkative. A child who does what is expected of him wins his teachers' approval, whereas the child who is independent in his thought or behavior or asks embarrassing questions may antagonize his teachers; yet, originality and curiosity are characteristics of superior intelligence (page 36).

The teacher should also be aware that the picture of the intellectually superior child as one who is inferior in other respects is a false one. Terman and Oden (1947), who studied the childhood and adult characteristics of a group of about 1500 gifted children, have demonstrated quite clearly that "the popular stereotype of the child prodigy so commonly depicted as a pathetic creature, overserious and undersized, sickly, hollow-chested, stoop-shouldered, clumsy, nervously tense and bespectacled," is not supported by the facts. On the contrary there is a tendency for positive characteristics such as good health, mature interests, academic ability, and so on to be positively correlated. That is, the data shows that children who rate high on one characteristic show a slight tendency to rate high on another characteristic; the reverse is true for those rating low.

Although no list of characteristics of the gifted child will describe any particular child, the teacher should be alerted to the various ways in which intellectual superiority may manifest itself. The following list is made up from the descriptions of children with high mental ability presented by Dunlap (1958), Kough and De Haan (1957), Warren and Heist (1960), and Witty (1958). According to these writers, gifted children will show a number of the following characteristics:

In the language area:
1. A large vocabulary used with precision
2. Enjoyment of reading and interest in ideas expressed in words
3. Ability to read rapidly and with good comprehension
4. Ability to express themselves with originality and to give a novel twist even to old ideas
5. Enjoyment of writing stories and poems

In other areas of intellectual activity:
1. Curiosity manifested by frequent questions
2. Discovery of cause and effect relationships and ability to generalize
3. Ability to concentrate for long periods of time
4. Interest in science, clocks, calendars and history, and varied intellectual activities
5. Enjoyment of research, classification, and collecting hobbies
6. Proficiency in drawing, music, and other artistic activities

In personal social area:
1. Strong desire to excel, sometimes outspokenly critical of themselves and others
2. Tendency to show initiative and independence, sometimes rebellious and unwilling to accept instruction
3. Good sense of humor
4. Tendency to seek older companions and to enjoy being with adults

Along with teacher participation in the selection of the intellectually superior student, the school should use standardized tests of achievement and intelligence. The particular level of performance on these tests that will be set for the selection of children with high ability, will of course, depend upon the kind of program contemplated and the facilities available in the school. If the school plans to work in some particular way with the upper 10 percent of the general population, an IQ cutoff point of about 120 would be indicated. Because of the great amount of fluctuation found in IQ scores, a policy that is as open and as flexible as possible is advisable. Any indication of the possibility of ability should be a basis for taking a chance in providing special educational opportunities for a child.

De Haan and Havighurst (1957) cite the case of a sixth-grade boy whose IQ measured between 129 and 139 on different group intelligence tests. His performance on achievement tests and his marks in class work were only average. His teacher thought that he should not be included in her classroom enrichment program. However, the boy was not lazy as the teacher had supposed. He was handicapped by a disturbed family situation in which his mother worked to support the family because of the father's irresponsibility and alcoholism. The teacher's understanding of this situation led to her acceptance of the boy as a special challenge.

PROGRAMS FOR THE GIFTED

It is far simpler to identify the gifted student than it is to plan appropriate educational experiences for him. To a certain extent the kind of program will determine the type of screening and selection. The program in turn will depend upon the size of the school, the attitudes in the community, and the readiness of the staff to undertake such an activity. Havighurst and others (1955) surveyed the programs available to gifted children in various communities and found that the three basic types of programs are: acceleration, grouping for specialized instruction, and enrichment within the regular classroom. These may be implemented in various combinations such as grouping for specialized instruction so that three or four grades may be completed in one year less than the usual (that is, grouping combined with acceleration).

Acceleration

Children who show signs of maturing intellectually very rapidly can complete the usual curriculum in a shorter period of time than the typical child. One way of permitting the precocious child to accomplish what he is able to accomplish is to advance him more rapidly through his schooling. Usually children with superior intellectual ability are also advanced in their physical and social development so that they are not likely to be seriously handicapped by such rapid promotion. Terman and Oden (1947) in their follow-up study of gifted children have pointed out "that more than half of the children with IQ's of 135 or above had already mastered the school curriculum to a point two full grades beyond the one in which they were enrolled." They also point out (1954) that gifted children who are accelerated are usually more successful in later life than equally bright children who have not had the opportunity to be accelerated. In considering the rapid advancement of a particular child, several cautions must be observed. Is the child ready for this experience socially and emotionally? Is the curriculum in the advanced grade appropriate for him and has he mastered the requisite skills? Is the teacher in the advanced grade able to provide the individual attention that this child may require? If these questions can be answered in the affirmative the child can appropriately be advanced. This kind of adjustment in program can be instituted also by permitting early entrance to kindergarten (Birch, 1954), the junior or senior high school or college (Pressey, 1949).

Grouping for Specialized Instruction

This kind of program adjustment for the gifted may range from special groups meeting one or two hours a week to special schools with selective admission standards. The most common procedure is to set up special classes for the intellectually superior students. Dunlap (1958) states that:

> Gifted children respond well to grouping. In the company of other bright, zealous youngsters, incentive to grow in knowledge, understanding, and skill is enhanced. Certainly in the intellectual areas of the school program these children need the mental stimulus which they can give each other. Since much of formal learning is intellectual, grouping of children with unusual aptitudes for learning should be as logical as grouping for remedial reading, speech correction, music, art, or varsity athletics (pages 164-165).

Another advantage of the special-class group lies in its facilitation of proper attitudes toward study and intellectual activity. The usual climate of opinion within a class will often discourage the gifted child from developing his special talents. A study by Tannenbaum (1959), referred to in Chapter 2, reveals that the climate in a school toward studiousness and other characteristics may easily be such as to direct the able student away from any clear demonstration of his ability. He found that among eleventh graders athletic skill was rated by peers consistently higher than studiousness or brilliance. The highest ratings were received by the hypothetical students described as athletic and nonstudious whereas the lowest ratings were given to the nonathletic and studious.

Some of the disadvantages of grouping have been discussed in Chapter 7. These are briefly reviewed here. Segregation of the gifted child deprives the average child of the stimulation that the more able child can provide. It does not permit the able child to use his abilities to help others. Intellectual ability is many-faceted and special-class groups generally operate on the assumption that it is unidimensional. Intellectual growth is variable. In the process of keeping a child in a nonspecialized class we may inhibit a growth spurt because of the lower expectancy that generally prevails in a class from which most of the able students have been removed. Some have argued also that separating children, particularly placing them in specialized schools, is contrary to our democratic tradition and introduces an elitism that is unacceptable. For these reasons it would seem that grouping should be kept flexible and should be limited rather than general.

Enrichment Within the Regular Classroom

Enrichment is administratively the simplest procedure for taking care of the able student but at the same time it is the most difficult and least specified procedure for the classroom teacher. Passow (1958) describes the concept as follows: "Basically, enrichment consists of the selection and organization of learning experiences appropriate to youths' development. It is not, therefore, 'special education' in the meaning in which the term is generally used—giving attention to students with unusual problems—but rather the essence of good education" (page 193).

Most of the schools in our nation do not have special provisions for the gifted child. Therefore it becomes the responsibility of the regular classroom teacher to provide for their enrichment. In Chapter 4 the fostering of problem-solving skill and creative thought were discussed. These procedures, while appropriate for all children, are essential for the gifted child for it is in these areas that he excels and needs encouragement.

In providing educational experiences for the able student the teacher must keep several objectives in mind.

1. All children in the class must come to realize that instruction is individualized and that it is not unfair for children to have a variety of assignments, each according to his need.

2. Enriching the curriculum for the gifted youngster does not mean doing more of the routine practice exercises. The gifted student needs less practice rather than more.

3. The teacher must do all in his power to foster an atmosphere where the students come to respect intellectual brilliance, studiousness, and scholarship. This cannot be accomplished by being disdainful of nonintellectual activities.

THE SLOW LEARNER

Between the group of children who would be classified as mental defectives (IQ below 70) and those who would be classified as normal or above (IQ above 90), we have a group of children, about 15 percent of the total population, called the slow learners. "The slow learners, although less seriously handicapped than the mentally retarded, usually find the traditional type of school program too difficult to handle without some modifications of the program to adjust requirements to their normal capacity for achievement" (Kelly and Stevens, 1950, page 238).

Identifying the Slow Learner

As in the case of the gifted child, identification of the slow learner depends upon teacher observation and standardized tests. In using group tests of intelligence or achievement tests, the teacher must be aware that these tests depend upon reading skill and although reading skill and intelligence are related abilities they are not the same. Reading disability may have its roots in a number of causes unrelated to intelligence. Therefore the score on a group test should be cautiously interpreted. It is advisable to arrange for a competent administration of an individual intelligence test in those cases where slow learning or inadequate school progress is evident.

Although the more seriously mentally handicapped child often shows sensory or motor defects, the slow learner is less often afflicted with such defects. His disability is more likely to be found in the more subtle area of thinking. In some instances because of adult attitudes toward the slowness of intellectual development, the child shows signs of immaturity in the areas of social and emotional adjustment. The slow learner finds it difficult to think in abstract terms and in symbolic forms. He is less able to see relationships and to form generalizations. Because many teachers are impatient with slow educational progress, the slow-learning child may become a motivational problem. He quits trying to do even what he can do. He often senses that his age mates do not have respect for him as a person and he may find himself degraded by their name-calling such as "dummy," "stupid," or "stew-pot" and the like. Little wonder then that many of these children become school problems, showing their hostility in truancy, bullying, and disrespect for adults. Their view of the school is that of a place where their sense of adequacy is threatened and they resist becoming involved in those areas that are most threatening to them.

THE EDUCATIONAL PROGRAM FOR THE SLOW LEARNER

The primary objective of the educational program for the slow learner is to establish optimal patterns of personal and social adjustment. Johnson (1958) states that:

> All children have certain basic needs that will promote the development of healthy attitudes and aid them in becoming emotionally healthy individuals. These basic needs consist of opportunities to participate in worthwhile activities, to feel that they are valuable, contributing members of a group, to be accepted for what they are, and to have success in the performance of these worthwhile activities. It is extremely difficult and in many instances impossible for a mentally handicapped child to satisfy these needs within a regular classroom situation (page 193).

Johnson further suggests that the special class for the slow learner be formed early without waiting for the development of behavioral problems that are likely to occur after two or three years of educational failure. The decision on placement in a special group would depend upon the teacher's estimate of the child's ability to function effectively in a regular class.

The curriculum for the slow learner should be designed to provide him with the basic essentials that will enable him eventually to live as an economically self-sufficient and responsible citizen. He should learn how to read and to communicate effectively, to handle numbers, to get along with other people, and to care for his own health. The selection of curriculum materials should be such as to meet the interests of the student and at the same time not be beyond his readiness level. For example, there are available a wide variety of reading materials that can meet the interests of the older student, yet the vocabulary and complexity of writing are suited for the usual slow learner. The slow learner requires more drill and exercise in acquiring reading skill (Hegge et al., 1936) and the arithmetic fundamentals. At the same time, the slow learner requires more concrete and direct experience.

SUMMARY

One of the most important qualities of behavior insofar as the school is concerned, is intelligence. It is defined as an ability to do abstract thinking that is directed to a goal and that has social value. In order to be able to carry on such abstract thinking efficiently, the motivational and emotional aspects of the personality must be coordinated so as to support intelligent behavior. Intelligence is a developmental characteristic and thus as the individual grows older, at least into adolescence, he becomes more able to undertake activities that are difficult and complex. Creativity is another attribute of intelligence but it is generally *not* measured by our present-day intelligence tests.

Psychologists are not in agreement as to the organization of intelligence. Some suggest that it is a global and unified characteristic of behavior, others view it as made up of more or less independent factors. The latter position grows out of the findings derived from the statistical procedure known as factor analysis. It is reasonable to suppose that when behavior is undifferentiated, as in the early years, intelligence will be undifferentiated also; but with the increase in behavior differentiation with age, intelligence will also become differentiated.

The best way to understand the operational meaning of intelligence is to examine the items contained in intelligence tests. We find items that test for immediate memory, the detection of incongruities, and the noting of differences. The particular format of the test and the procedures are determined in part by whether the test is an individual or a group test, and whether it is an age scale or a point scale. The scores on many tests are given in years and months and called mental age (MA). The score that we would expect the person to obtain is likewise given in years and months and is derived from his actual chronological age (CA). The intelligence quotient (IQ) is the ratio of mental age to chronological age multiplied by 100.

The stability of a measure obtained on an intelligence test is a function of the test's reliability and also of the individual's growth pattern. Both of these factors make a single measure of intelligence a rather unstable quantity and would suggest extreme caution in making predictions. These factors would also suggest that assumptions of over- or under-achievement are not well founded as the achievement tests measure similar abilities and are also subject to errors of measurement.

The controversy as to whether intelligence is largely an inherited characteristic or one largely determined by the environment, is a difficult one to resolve. There appears to be sufficient evidence in correlational studies of intelligence within families, in foster-home studies and other types of studies, to support the contention that intelligence is inherited. On the other hand, there is convincing evidence that environmental conditions produce predictable changes in the growth patterns of intelligence test scores, both in individuals and in groups. The evidence suggests that intelligence, as the teacher sees it in the level of school performance and in problem-solving ability, is the resultant of the interaction of complex genetic and environmental factors. For every particular effect of this interaction at a particular time of development there is an optimal environment that the teacher can help create.

The schools need to provide appropriate adaptations of the curriculum to accommodate to the wide range of differences in intellectual ability. In identifying the gifted child, teachers need to guard against paying too much attention to irrelevant factors such as neatness and conforming behavior and also against penalizing independence and curiosity. In addition to the problem of selection, the school must decide on the kind of program adjustment. A number of alternatives are available: acceleration, grouping for specialized instruction, or enrichment within the regular classroom. Each of these presents advantages and disadvantages. In the application of any procedure, as well as in the selection of the students for special educational treatment, the most important consideration is flexibility to allow for errors in measurement and changes in growth patterns. The program itself should be critically viewed to determine both its positive and negative effects and appropriate changes introduced. The program should be designed so as to produce in all students a wholesome respect for intellectual ability.

Problems in teaching the so-called slow learner require similar adaptations. The adjustments required for the slow-learning child should be introduced before he comes to feel so inadequate as not to be able to reach a level of function that will be satisfying for him and useful for the society.

READING REFERENCES

Cruickshank, W. M. and G. O. Johnson (Eds.), *Education of Exceptional Children and Youth*. Englewood Cliffs, N.J.: Prentice-Hall, 1958.

De Haan, R. F. and R. J. Havighurst, *Educating Gifted Children*. Chicago: University of Chicago Press, 1961.

Getzels, J. W. and P. W. Jackson, *Creativity and Intelligence: Explorations with Gifted Children*. New York: John Wiley & Sons, 1962.

Henry, N. B. (Ed.), *The Education of Exceptional Children*. Forty-ninth Yearbook (Pt. 2) National Society for Study of Education. Chicago: University of Chicago Press, 1950 (chaps. 13 and 14).

————, *Education for the Gifted*. Fifty-seventh Yearbook (Pt. 2) National Society for the Study of Education. Chicago: University of Chicago Press, 1958 (particularly chaps. 8-12).

Hunt, J. McV., *Intelligence and Experience*. New York: Ronald Company, 1961.

Kephart, N. C., *The Slow Learner in the Classroom*. Columbus, Ohio: Charles E. Merrill Books, 1960.

Jenkins, J. J. and D. G. Paterson (Eds.), *Studies in Individual Differences: The Search for Intelligence*. New York: Appleton-Century-Crofts, 1961 (particularly selections 6, 8, 28, 36, 37, 44, 53, 58, 63, 66).

Piaget, J., *Psychology of Intelligence*. Paterson, N.J.: Littlefield, Adams, 1960 (first published in French, 1947).

CHAPTER 11

EMOTIONAL FACTORS

Any teacher describing the children in his classroom would, in one form or another, use terms indicating differences in emotional response. The roster of descriptive terms might include: Susan is shy and withdrawn; George is aggressive and always fights; Henry is well adjusted and resists distraction; Mary is a happy child; Betty is sad and worries a good deal; and so on. As teachers we tend to take notice of those emotions that disrupt routine or in some way interfere with the students' learning activities. We sometimes lose sight of the positive contribution of emotions to classroom learning, for without the enjoyment of learning and growing, very little of worth could take place in the school. This chapter attempts to show that emotions are, figuratively speaking, a double-edged sword and that they are involved in the constructive aspects of life as well as the disruptive.

In training children to a wholesome expression of emotion the school's objective should be to help the student experience his feelings and to help him find appropriate ways for expressing them. Too much of present-day training has emphasized a negative, unwholesome type of emotional control. In a study by Jersild (1952) it was shown that a large percentage of pupils included in their self evaluation frequent mention of inability to conceal emotion as a characteristic that they disliked about themselves.

The idea of "control," in the form it often takes, is not healthy, but false, insidious, and morbid. It frequently stems from a philosophy concerning emotion which is unwholesome, but which many psychologists and many educators seem to accept. . . . Emotion repeatedly is defined only in negative terms. It results from blocking or thwarting. It is "disorganized behavior." It is what strikes a person when he's struggling with a problem that's too much for him. He is stirred up. But given time and good luck and a chance to simmer down, his emotion will pass and he can then return, like an oyster, to his previous well-organized, unstirred, unemotional state (pages 39-40).

The teacher's task is not to reinforce the denial of the existence of emotions, but rather to recognize their importance in learning, indeed in all human activity. The existence and the arousal of emotion are prerequisite to a positive orientation to any task. Our aim in education should be neither to eliminate emotion nor to induce controls that produce stylized, expressionless human beings, but rather to use the energy engendered by this aspect of life to the advantage of growth and maturity.

In modern psychological literature there is a threefold classification scheme of the various mental processes: cognition or knowing, affect or feeling, conation or striving. As in any attempt to analyze a living activity that occurs in such a way as to combine all three processes, we introduce an element of distortion when we separate one for particular consideration. The reader thus will see that often there is a fine line between this chapter on emotion and Chapter 2 on motivation. The derivation of the word "emotion" and the behavior in which it expresses itself make quite clear the notion that emotion and motivation are overlapping categories. These two processes, that of affect and conation, are in turn intimately related to the third, cognition. Perception, intellect, and the process of learning are very much dependent on how we feel and what we strive for. Recognizing these interrelationships it is profitable to examine emotion as a separate phenomenon.

The four major topics of this chapter will be: (1) the nature of emotions, (2) emotional development through the school years, (3) the disruptive aspects of emotion, and (4) the teacher's role in fostering growth toward emotional maturity.

THE NATURE OF EMOTIONS

Because of its complexity and its pervasiveness in all psychological phenomena, emotion as a separate process is very difficult to define. The one definition that requires the least modification to fit our general conceptualization of emotions is that of Young (1943), who offers the following criteria for defining an emotion: "(1) An emotion is a disturbed [aroused] state of the organism. (2) An emotion includes vis-

FIGURE 11.1 *Models used in satiation study. From J. S. Kounin, "Intellectual Development and Rigidity," in R. G. Barker et al. (Eds.),* Child Behavior and Development, *copyright 1943, p. 185. New York: McGraw-Hill Book Company, Inc. Used by permission.*

ceral changes due to increased activity of the autonomic nervous system. (3) An emotion originates within the psychological situation" (page 44).

Emotions as an Aroused State

In order to engage in an activity the organism must be aroused or alerted. The major problem in education is to achieve the proper condition of arousal for the particular task. "It seems likely that there is an optimal level of activation for each type of task, and perhaps for each subject. For example a moderate level of activation would seem optimal for playing chess, whereas a relatively high one would be best for sprinting" (Schlosberg, 1954, page 82). Thus, the teacher's task is to help children become adequately aroused before engaging in a particular kind of activity. Sometimes this calls for stimulation by means of competition or some hilarious humor. Other times the teacher may need to insist on a few minutes of rest. In either case, stimulation or sedation, the teacher must be aware that once the level of arousal is established it continues of its own momentum, so that it should be stopped somewhat short of the desired point. It should also be recognized that arousal is a generalized process, that is to say, if a child is aroused or quieted in one activity, he will start another activity with approximately the same level of arousal.

This carry-over of feeling from one activity to another was very ingeniously demonstrated in a study by Kounin (1943). He presented a group of youngsters ranging in age from six years to seven years and nine months, with normal IQ's, an opportunity to participate in drawing activities (see Figure 11.1).

> Each subject was shown how to draw cats, bugs, turtles and rabbits until he felt confident and secure in these activities. He was then allowed to draw cats, until he became satiated and wanted to draw no more. After having become satiated with the drawing of cats, he was asked if he wanted to draw bugs. After having become satiated with drawing bugs, he was asked if he desired to draw turtles. Finally, after having become satiated with drawing turtles, he was asked whether or not he felt like drawing rabbits (page 184).

The normal subjects showed a great amount (in general, more than 90 percent) of cosatiation. That is, the degree of satisfaction or satiation reached in one activity carried over into the next activity.

> Other marked cosatiation effects in addition to the quantitative time measures were revealed in the case of the young normal subjects. They paused more frequently and for longer time intervals, engaged in non-drawing activities more often, and generally exhibited relatively more satiation symptoms (such as variations and mistakes) in the later drawing tasks than in the first drawing task (page 186).

The fact that feeling tone is transferred from one activity to another like activity has some important implications for teaching. It is wise to avoid satiation in one activity by moving on to another while interest is still high. If boredom does develop it is wise to change to an activity that is very dissimilar. It also is wise to maintain a flexible schedule in order to capitalize on appropriate states of aroused emotions.

Emotional States Have Physiological Correlates

Emotional arousal and physiological condition are reciprocal factors. In fact, the mental experience of emotion and the physiological change that accompanies it are so closely intertwined that William James concluded that the existence of the latter underlies the actual emotion. These physiological changes that all of us have experienced in and out of school, such as the pounding heart and the shaking knees, have been very carefully studied in the psycho-physiological laboratory. Most of these changes can be measured and recorded. Every organ system of the body seems to be affected. For example, when a person is emotionally aroused the circulatory system responds by showing an increase in blood pressure and pulse rate; the digestive system decreases its activity and this is subjectively felt as a dryness of the mouth and "butterflies" in the stomach; a modification of the condition of the skin in the form of temperature change and increased level of perspiration; respiration increases in depth and rate; the amount of energy available to the muscle system increases because of the release of blood sugar (this may show itself in knee shaking or hand tremors). These and many other physiological changes are generally associated with the emotions of fear and anger. It should be noted that the arousal of the organism to a condition of fright or rage serves to prepare it for the momentary critical demands of physical "flight or fight."

The next chapter examines the further consequences of these physiological changes if they are maintained for long periods and produce psychosomatic disturbances and the lowering of physical resistance. The physiological conditions accompanying the pleasant emotions have not been as carefully investigated in the laboratory; but there is good reason to believe that the pleasant feeling accompanying an enjoyable experience in art, music, literature, also the successful solution of a problem in mathematics or science—any school activity—produces optimal physiological conditions. It is very likely that when the person is meeting the demands of his environment effectively and enjoyably, the circulatory, digestive, and skeletal-muscle system are functioning in such a way as to make the activity possible and to produce the sense of well-being. Emotional responses are natural and serve to enhance our capacity to adjust.

> Emotional responses, as we have seen, are physiological functions, derived from our mammalian ancestry, which have enabled humans to survive in a precarious and often dangerous world. This way of viewing emotions may help us to see that they are not, initially at least, moral questions. Emotional reactions like hunger, elimination, and sleep are basic organic functions essential to living; but they must be regulated, patterned, often transformed, for us to live in a social order as personalities in a symbolic cultural world. We can therefore regard emotions as normal legitimate functions, like all other functions, which fluctuate continually as the organism-personality strives to maintain a dynamic equilibrium in its unceasing intercourse with the continually changing environment of events and other persons and their approaches and responses (Frank, 1954, pages 26-27).

Emotions Originate Within the Psychological Situation

As the conditions of the external environment are perceived and interpreted, the appropriate emotional response is organized. This response will possess qualities of individuality as well as those of human generality. To the extent that people share a common perception of a situation as a result of similar socializing experiences and similar physiological characteristics, they will respond to that situation with the same emotion. But more significant for the teacher is the uniqueness of our perception. The individuality of perception and emotional organization has been fully demonstrated by the projective techniques of personality assessment (such as the Rorschach Inkblot Test and the Thematic Apperception Test) where the subject is given an unstructured stimulus and responds to it in his own unique way revealing the individual aspects of his personality. The level of development of the person and the background experience determine to a great extent the quality and impact of the external environment.

The organism reacts to the field as it is experienced and perceived. This perceptual field is, for the individual "reality".

> This is a simple proposition, one of which we are all aware in our own experience, yet it is a point which is often overlooked. I do not react to some absolute reality, but to my perception of this reality. Snygg and Combs give the example of two men driving at night on a Western road.

An object looms up in the middle of the road ahead. One of the men sees a large boulder, and reacts with fright. The other, a native of the country, sees a tumbleweed and reacts with nonchalance. Each reacts to the reality as perceived. . . .

To understand this concept that reality is for the individual, his perceptions, we may find it helpful to borrow a phrase from the semanticists. They have pointed out that words and symbols bear to the world of reality the same relationships as a map to the territory which it represents. This relationship also applies to perception and reality. We live by a perceptual "map" which is never reality itself. This is a useful concept to keep in mind, for it may help to convey the nature of the world in which the individual lives (Rogers, 1951, pages 484-485).

This concept should make the teacher aware that the level and kind of emotional response to a particular experience will differ quite naturally from child to child. Every parent has experienced the disappointment of the young child's enthusiastic involvement with the colored paper used to wrap an expensive gift, while ignoring the gift itself. Children's likes and dislikes are highly individualistic. The teacher should therefore not be disappointed if after some elaborate preparations, several students in the class behave in a disinterested fashion. It is simply that these students' perceptions, being unique, do not produce the expected emotional arousal. The external situations that ordinarily arouse the emotions of fear and anger are also highly individualized in their perception and hence produce different kinds of responses.

The relationship of perception and emotional bias has been established experimentally. In one study (Postman et al., 1948), the impact of personal values as selective factors was demonstrated as follows. A series of thirty-six words were selected so that groups of six words would represent each of six different value orientations.

Value Orientation	*Words Selected*
Theoretical	theory, verify, science, logical, research, analysis
Economic	income, useful, wealthy, finance, economic, commerce
Esthetic	beauty, artist, poetry, elegant, library, graceful
Social	loving, kindly, devoted, helpful, friendly, sociable
Political	govern, famous, compete, citizen, politics, dominate
Religious	prayer, sacred, worship, blessed, religion, reverent

The following data were obtained on each of twenty-five college students: (1) time required to recognize each of the thirty-six words by means of brief exposure technique (tachistoscopic presentation), (2) attempted solutions preceding recogntion of the actual words, (3) score profiles on the Allport-Vernon Study of Values Test. The results of the study seem to indicate that various kinds of "selective mechanisms" seem to be operating.

Value orientation acts as a sensitizer, lowering thresholds for acceptable stimulus objects . . . *selective sensitization.* Value orientation may, on the other hand, raise thresholds for unacceptable stimulus objects . . . *perceptual defense.* Finally the perceiver, whatever the nature of the stimulus, favors the presolution hypotheses which reflect his value orientation. He will, therefore, perceive more readily stimulus objects which lie within the same value area as his preferred presolution hypotheses. This third mechanism we shall term *value resonance* (pages 151-152).

The implications of this study and others that support these general conclusions, for understanding what transpires in the classroom, have not as yet been established. But in a general way we can begin to understand why certain words in spelling may be continuously misspelled by a particular youngster; why certain types of word problems in arithmetic such as those involving giving or dividing may arouse perceptual defenses, why certain concepts in history involving revolution or war may produce certain behaviors consistent with value resonance. The greater our understanding of the relationship of emotion and perception the more accurate our diagnosis of a child's behavior and the greater our capacity to assist his growth.

THE DEVELOPMENT OF EMOTIONS

One of the outstanding characteristics of growth is the change in the emotional make-up of the person. The suggestion that a child or an adolescent "act his age" usually stems from witnessing behavior that conflicts with an unstated table of norms of appropriate stages of emotional development. The changes that take place may be analyzed in two categories: the range and change of stimuli that are capable of arousing response and the change of response pattern when aroused.

The Change of Stimuli

The younger the child the more his emotions tend to be aroused by tangible events that impinge directly upon him. As he grows older he becomes increasingly responsive to signs and symbols that betoken furtherance or hindrance of his welfare and his wishes, and more and more of his emotional reactions concern anticipated events. Also, of course, as a child grows older, emotions become associated with an enlarging repertoire of activities, plans and interests, and he becomes increasingly able to entertain lingering or recurrent fears, joys, and resentments (Jersild, 1946, page 759).

Because the child grows in his understanding he encompasses larger aspects of his external environment into his experiences and his interpretations of his reality. Also because of the changes in needs, changes due to social and psychosexual development, different stimuli take on different meanings as the child grows older. The dog may not be seen as a threat at first in the preschool years, the same stimulus may then become a source of fear and then later on a friendly companion on which to lavish affection. Often children change markedly in either acquiring or discarding emotional response patterns in relatively brief periods of time. In early adolescence the symbolic value of members of the opposite sex becomes a significant force in emotional arousal. The appreciation of humor grows increasingly subtle as the child grows older. We find also that ideals acquire effectiveness in arousing a sense of loyalty, defense, or violent opposition.

Change in Response Pattern

When emotionally aroused the avenues of response are different for different age levels. The problem of coping with a kindergarten child who is thwarted is much different from that of a high school senior. This difference in emotional response pattern is based essentially on the following: (1) intellectual growth that allows for intricate ways of coping with feeling such as the use of writing, painting, and music; (2) language-symbolic development that not only changes the interpretation of emotion arousing stimuli but also permits one to express one's feeling in words; (3) growth in physical skill that allows for the elimination of obstacles or the sources of frustration and that also provides an avenue for emotional expression through sports and other constructive activities.

PATTERNS OF EMOTIONAL DEVELOPMENT

Just as a child grows and changes systematically in his physical action pattern, intellectual ability, and social interests, so too does he grow and change in the area of emotions. It is true that many of the characteristics of emotional development are fixed by the interaction of a unique physiology and a unique socializing experience, we can, nevertheless, detect some general patterns of change. To state that the "typical" five-year-old can be described by particular types of emotional attributes and the seven-year-old by another set, is carrying the generalization about patterns too far. The statements that follow about the emotional characteristics of various age groups are intended to make the teacher aware of gross differences to be found in classes of different ages, but this does not deny the existence of differences between two classes of the same age group. (The following discussion is based on Gesell and Ilg, 1949 and Gesell, et al., 1956.)

The Early School Years—First Three Grades

Upon entering school the child is likely to be noisy, boisterous, and easily excitable, enjoying slapstick humor and resorting to name calling, using such terms as "skunk," "rat," "I'll kill you." He is likely to appreciate praise and approval and is easily aroused to aggression both physical and verbal. Toward the end of this period the child exhibits a decrease in spontaneous aggressive acts (this is particularly true of the girl), he will show some concern about his place in the group, and is likely to burst out into tears and to have laughing jags. The girls more frequently than boys will have fits of giggling. Frequent arguments and name calling based on physical characteristics, "fatty," "teeny," and open fantasy expression of aggression can be observed.

The Middle School Years—Grades Four to Six

In these grades there is enjoyment in competitive activities and children enjoy picking teams. There is enjoyment of subtle humor. We observe a great amount of *empathy* or actually experiencing the feeling that another person is undergoing. At this age level the child responds well to compliments and signs of approval. He will show some fears and most children of this age seldom cry. At about age eleven frequent anger outbursts are reported. It should be noted that during these years of late childhood there are marked differences between boys and girls in the stimuli that arouse emotion and the manner in which emotion is expressed. It is during this age that the boy is likely to overact the so-called malelike characteristics such as stoicism, toughness, and rowdiness and the girl is likely to express, in exaggerated form, the femalelike characteristics such as tenderness, sympathy, and sedateness.

Pre- and Early Adolescence—Grades Seven to Nine

This period is one in which the child changes from being expansive, outgoing, and enthusiastic to being thoughtful, inwardized, and self-contained. During this period the previously described difference between the sexes is continued. As in the preceding period, many children exhibit worries around homework and lessons, but at this age there is also great concern over grades. This junior high school period is marked by great group variability in emotional aspects of growth, as well as in other aspects, due to the rapid psychosexual development of some and the retarded development of others. In general, we find that during this period there is present at first a robust type of emotional expression, then a sensitive more delicate pattern, followed again by an expansive outgoing pattern.

Middle and Late Adolescence—High School Years

The popular view that the adolescent years are characterized by emotional stress and strain has not been substantiated by the research literature.

The inconsistency of these data, as well as certain inadequacies in the studies calls into question the conception of adolescence as a period of *generalized* storm and stress. Increase in anxiety and stress in adolescence seems instead to be relatively specific to certain areas of adjustment typical of the teens—family relations, ideological developments, heterosexual relations, vocational orientations. The existing data do suggest the possibility that girls may experience more generalized stress and anxiety at adolescence than do boys, a finding which would seem reasonable in view of the greater control that is maintained over their development and their resulting lag in self-reliance (Pressey and Kuhlen, 1957, page 352).

Analysis of age in relation to fingernail biting, total number of worries, admissions to mental hospitals, and rates of suicide per age in the general population (all of these may be taken as symptoms of emotional tension) show the age period under question to be either one of decrease in signs of emotional tension or simply at a point in line with a general increase with age (Kuhlen, 1952). During this age period we find also some evidence of the detrimental effects of the environment on the suppression of emotional expression. Youngsters report conscious attempts not to show feeling, to "suffer in silence," "grin and bear it." Anger responses are less frequent and are less frequently overt, except for some youngsters whose emotional development is characterized by disturbance. All sorts of evaluations, at work or at school, produce definite signs of worry and anxiety.

FEAR AND ANXIETY

The point has been made that emotional arousal is equivalent to tension arousal and some tension is required and beneficial for the maintenance of the directed effort necessary for the solution of many of life's problems. In Chapter 2 the relationship of level of tension to the amount of directed activity was described and it was demonstrated that though responsiveness is high when tension is high, much of the responsiveness is directed into restless activity. Extreme forms of emotion are equivalent to high states of tension. It is necessary for the teacher to understand the effects of fear and anxiety, anger and hostility and methods of dealing with these disturbing levels of emotional arousal.

The studies of the emotions of school-age children show that they express many fears and anxieties. For example if the school maintains a policy of nonpromotion and when this policy is well publicized though only seldom practiced, children will express great concern about being "left back" or "flunked." In one study (Jersild et al., 1941) more than half of about one thousand pupils responded on a check list that they sometimes or often worried about being "left back," whereas objective examination of the results of the promotion policy indicated that only about one percent would be retarded in grade. The reader may comment "If they don't worry about being promoted they won't try." This assumes a single straight-line effect of tension on directed activity. But the effects of anxiety on the child's performance are variable, sometimes increasing efficiency and often reducing it. Threat of failure as a motivational device has been shown to be of only limited use.

Under the general category of fear and anxiety two types can be differentiated: fear that arises out of objective situations of danger; neurotic anxiety that may manifest itself in general apprehension and worry or in the form of phobias that are irrational fears and withdrawal reactions to particular situations.

Objective Fears

Freud (1935) has described fear arising out of objective situations of danger as follows:

> Now real anxiety or dread appears to us a very natural and rational thing; we should call it a reaction to the perception of external danger, of an injury which is expected and foreseen; it is bound up with the reflex of flight and may be regarded as an expression of the instinct of self-preservation. The occasions of it, i.e., the objects and situations about which anxiety is felt, will obviously depend to a great extent upon the state of a person's knowledge and feeling of power regarding the outer world. It seems to us quite natural that a savage should be afraid of a cannon or of an eclipse of the sun, while a man who can handle the weapon and foretell the phenomenon remains unafraid in the same situation. At other times, it is knowledge itself which inspires fear, because it reveals the danger sooner; thus a savage will recoil with terror at the sight of a track in the jungle which conveys nothing to an ignorant man, but means that some wild beast is near at hand; and an experienced sailor will perceive with dread a little cloud on the horizon because it means an approaching hurricane, while to a passenger it looks quite insignificant (page 342).

Objective fear may show itself in various school activities, such as in science laboratories, physical education, and some extracurricular activities. When fear of this type leads to caution it serves a constructive purpose. When, however, it leads to withdrawal and refusal to participate, corrective measures are indicated.

The Treatment of Objective Fears

The following discussion presents a brief statement of each of seven possible procedures for coping with fear. Some of these procedures are definitely harmful, some have limited effectiveness and some are more generally recommended. In one study (Holmes, 1936) it was found that a group of well-educated parents resorted at one time or another to all of them in responding to their children's fears.

ENFORCED CONTACT WITH THE FEARED SITUATION When adults become impatient with the child's fear or if they underestimate its importance, they may resort to this technique. The swimming instructor who does not know better will throw the child who fears water into the deep end of the pool. The parent who locks the child into the darkened room and threatens corporal punishment if he expresses his fear by crying may find that the child will eventually become subdued. In contemplating this approach two negative consequences should be considered; first, that the child's reaction to the adult involved in later situations may be one of resentment and distrust, and second, that enforced contact may confirm the fear because the discomfort is likely to reinforce the anxiety.

RATIONAL EXPLANATION   Many teachers who have little knowledge of the nature of emotions will try to reason with the child who demonstrates a fear reaction. The adult will explain that the human body is lighter than water and hence cannot sink or that the dead frog cannot do any harm. It is important to understand that being in the presence of the fear-producing stimulus produces fear and all its physiological concomitants. These cannot be reasoned away any more than can the heart beat or the salivary response. Verbal explanation will be effective to the extent that it conveys a feeling of support and understanding—it will fail if it represents verbal pressure, ridicule, and invidious comparison.

AVOIDING THE FEAR STIMULUS   One basic principle to be kept in mind is that one cannot acquire mastery of an emotional response that may be presenting a problem, outside of the context in which it arises. The only basis for considering avoiding contact with the fear stimulus would be that as the person grows older the stimulus may take on other meaning and may be more easily mastered by the more mature person. This would suggest that a temporary avoidance might have a beneficial effect. More generally, however, the teacher's or parent's attempts at side-stepping the feared situation convey a sense of justification of the fear to the child and thereby compounds the difficulty in overcoming it.

GRADUAL EXPOSURE   In some instances the situation that arouses the fear is effective primarily because of the degree of its strength; were it of a weaker order, it might be more acceptable. A child may show no fear to a small, quiet dog, but a large barking one may readily arouse fear, or a child may show no fear in a room where there is a dim light, but will be frightened if the room is completely darkened. Fear stimuli often are characterized by having different levels of potency and we can help the child respond more favorably by slowly increasing the strength and time of exposure. For example, if we are trying to help a child overcome his fear of insects or live animals, it would be wise to discover the contexts in which fear of these objects does not appear and gradually build up from there. This procedure requires a considerable amount of patience because often the fearful child will recognize that the stimulus is at or beyond the threshold and respond fearfully; if however we proceed with caution, we can usually help the child overcome fear by gradually and slowly increasing the potency of the fear stimulus.

ACQUISITION OF SKILL Helping a child acquire skill in meeting the threat of a situation is the most constructive approach to elimination of fear. In the process of safety education we often establish reasonable fears. In the chemistry laboratory we establish cautions about breathing toxic substances, explosions, acid burns, and the like. Whenever a child uses sharp-pointed scissors we try to convey a sense of caution; in general we try to induce some fear of dangerous situations. Parents and teachers who emphasize the danger but offer little in the way of suggestions of coping with it will constrict the child's development. A principle that the teacher might well keep in mind is that of *positive prophylaxis,* that is, the child should be taught to handle situations that have implications for danger rather than to avoid these situations. The child should be taught to handle fire rather than to avoid it, he should be helped to use dangerous substances in the laboratory and elsewhere rather than to be made afraid so that he will consistently avoid these situations.

The following illustrations from a class studying the "Preparation and properties of chlorine" may serve to illustrate our point.

> Miss G., a chemistry teacher, . . . always dreaded "dangerous" experiments, . . . because someone in the class usually, apparently through carelessness, would get too large a dose and have to be taken, choking and coughing, to the nurse's office. Mr. K., another chemistry teacher, almost never had any trouble with "dangerous" experiments. Miss G. and Mr. K. seemed for the most part well matched with respect to strictness, knowledge of chemistry, . . . and the like.
>
> Miss G. always introduced the chlorine laboratory activity by saying that it was dangerous and frequently resulted in someone being overcome; that under no circumstances must anyone use larger quantities than the directions called for; that if the flame was turned too high, they would be unable to handle the volume of gas produced. Mr. K. introduced the laboratory work with the question, "What are some points of special precaution today?" and then calmly joined in the discussion from time to time (Thelen and Tyler, 1950, page 312).

It is through growth of skill and knowledge that our patterns of fear reactions are modified; in general, however, the more skilful the person becomes in dealing with various aspects of his environment, the less fearful he will be. The teacher can contribute much to a child's growth in skill in meeting threat situations and avoid the tension that appears when the threat is given the appearance of being more or less insurmountable.

IMITATION   One of the sources of fear is imitation of others. Children rely heavily on cues from adults and in the preadolescent and adolescent years they will rely also on the peer-group leaders for cues that indicate the proper mode of response. They will generally follow the lead of a trusted adult or friend when the stimulus situation is unfamiliar. If the teacher is afraid to approach the snake that a child brings to school, or as in the case just cited, the teacher is concerned about the preparation of chlorine, many children will recognize the fear and if any doubts existed in their mind about the nature of snakes or chlorine, they now become certain of the danger and are naturally afraid. Likewise if the fear response is diffused and it is counterbalanced by the sense of curiosity to know what snakes are like or what chlorine is like, the child will approach if indications of danger are not overemphasized. Even where the fear is already established, the child's need to find favor with the teacher or the peer group may be so strong as to submerge the fear.

RECONDITIONING   Many fears develop through the process of conditioning, that is, when a stimulus that is neutral, insofar as the fear response is concerned, is associated with a feared stimulus, the neutral stimulus acquires the potency of the feared one. A study by Watson and Rayner (1920) is often quoted in the discussion of the development of emotional response. Using an eleven-month-old boy, Albert, as subject, the investigators paired a previously neutral stimulus, a white rat, with a startle-producing stimulus, a sudden loud sound. Albert was made clearly afraid of the rat. Moreover the fear response was given in a *generalized* fashion to many furry objects. Jones (1924) showed in a later laboratory study that by associating a feared stimulus with a pleasant one, such as food that is liked, the fear response and its generalized pattern could be eliminated. These laboratory studies make us aware of the manner in which emotional responses arise; however, the process of reconditioning assumes that there exists a control over the learner that is not generally characteristic of the classroom situation. It should also be noted that unless the factors that might be operative in the situation are carefully watched, we might find that the positive stimulus may be responded to as to the feared stimulus; in other words, in reconditioning, we must be alert to possible "backfiring" results. There is however one important point for all teachers to learn from the studies of conditioned emotional reactions, a child who is uncomfortable about one of many things while studying arithmetic, reading, science, and so on, may acquire a dislike of the subject matter as a result of this unrelated discomfort. This is particularly significant in the introducing of new subject matter. Conditioning works positively, too. One college professor suggested that children attending summer symphonic concerts be served ice cream. They would then be conditioned to the enjoyment of music. A pleasant atmosphere, freedom from discomfort, can contribute greatly to a child's general positive orientation to his studies.

Anticipatory Fear Reactions

We have already seen that as a person develops in intellect and skill, his emotional response to various situations will change. One of the most significant changes in human development is the expansion of the life space in the time dimension. As the child grows he incorporates into his awareness an ever expanding time boundary. Our entire motivational process as well as our emotional response pattern depends on this time coordination development. Although this expansion of the life-time-space contributes to the maturity of the individual in significant ways, it also creates some problems in emotional adjustment. The young child responds to discomforts more readily but he achieves equilibrium more quickly as well. As the child enters school he has begun to anticipate and to organize his responses around an enlarged future orientation. His behavior becomes in some respects controlled by the anticipation of rewards if not too distantly placed, or by the contemplation of consequences of some course of action. This influences markedly the individual's emotional reactions. We anticipate events, respond to them as if they were immediately present, and we carry with us the effects of past experiences as if they were currently acting upon us (Lewin, 1946).

Let us consider an example of how growth in anticipation may be helpful in school adjustment. Marc is almost five years old and his mother takes him to school in the spring in order to register him in kindergarten for the fall term. She dresses him in his best clothes, associated in the little boy's mind with pleasant adventure (this might have been otherwise), and proceeds to the school building. At the school he is offered an opportunity to explore the play equipment and also to play with some of the children he knows well from his home neighborhood. The entire experience seems pleasant to him. Whenever school is mentioned his eyes light up, he smiles, and comments on his anticipated attendance in September. Though his awareness of September as a specific future date is vague, he is anticipating with enthusiasm this forthcoming experience. This positive anticipation can be capitalized on in introducing him to school procedures and the necessary restrictions of school life.

On the other hand, it is possible that anticipatory reactions may be so strongly negative that the individual may be unable to move into the future. When this occurs we speak of neurotic anxiety. The school itself is seldom the basic cause of neurotic anxiety but it may readily become the object of anxiety expression. This may happen when the child is unable to start school or it may express itself later in the kind of anxiety that we call school phobia.

Reluctance to Attend School

Each year a number of children present a problem of resistance in starting school for the first time. Several previous painful separations from mother may be the cause of this emotional state; or unwillingness to have a younger sibling at home to the exclusive attention of mother; or a home in which there is a great deal of friction between parents may cause the child to anticipate tragedy should he leave home. Obviously the school cannot deal with this type of underlying basis of the anxiety. However, there is one suggestion that can be offered to the teacher and the principal and that is a firm insistence that the child attend school and that he not be permitted to absent himself. One clinician, Klein (1945), who describes several cases of this type points to "the great importance of bringing about a return to school at the earliest moment, on any level of school participation that the child can tolerate" (page 278).

> Before the teacher can do anything to help, the child must of course, be in school. It is far better for him to be in school than at home, and if the school and the father state firmly to the child that he must come to school, this firmness will often be enough to keep him coming. . . . Once he is in school, the teacher can try to help in a number of ways. . . .
>
> If the teacher and the mother are working together to keep the child coming to school, the mother can assure the child that she wants him to go to school, that she knows he will be all right when he is away from her, and that she will be all right, while he is away from her. This is very important, for he is afraid that his bad wishes toward her might come true in his absence. The mother will need to do this repeatedly over a long period of time. If she can do this and if the father can take a strong positive stand toward the child's going to school, he will gradually gain the feeling that it is good for him to be there (D'Evelyn, 1957, pages 84-85).

School Phobia

After a child has been in attendance for sometime he may exhibit strong symptoms of anxiety about his continued attendance. These anxiety symptoms might be called *school phobia*. It should be noted that a child with school phobia differs in significant respects from a child who is truant. In the latter case there is usually found a surreptitious element, in that the pupil is likely to attempt to deceive his parents and members of the school staff and to conceal his whereabouts and activities during the period when he absents himself from the classroom. Essentially the truant is acting out feelings of aggression and defiance. The phobic child, on the other hand, may have shown what appeared to be a genuine liking for school until shortly before his phobia began. In the latter instance, the child has usually attended school regularly and his school performance was usually adequate and sometimes superior. The child does not attempt to conceal his absence and may offer such reasons as "the teacher yells too much" or "the other children pick on me," which on closer examination are found to be based on the child's own feelings of self-rejection rather than objective descriptions of fact.

When a teacher encounters a child with school phobia, it is important to keep several principles in mind and for the teacher to avoid self-incrimination or defensiveness. First, the child's anxiety about school and the occasional expression of criticism of the teacher or classmates, represent a *displacement* of feeling from the proper object to a safe impersonal one. The child is really "talking about something else" in his negative statements about the school. Second, there are precipitating events, recent but not deeply significant causes that have brought the situation to a climax. Third, there are deep underlying causes or dynamics that reach far back into the child's life history and the entire complex of the relationships within his family. In many instances where the expression of neurotic anxiety takes the form of school phobia, the teacher is likely to require help from a school psychologist or from a child-guidance clinic. The following case is taken from the files of such a clinic and is intended not only to illustrate the dynamics of school phobia but also to show how the school receives and offers help in working with another community agency.

Six weeks after the opening of the fall term, Mr. Parks, an elementary school principal was informed by the fourth-grade teacher that one of the students, a girl named Ruth, had been consistently absent, attending only nine days intermittently in school. Mr. Parks checked the child's record and found that she had moved last spring from a somewhat better neighborhood of the city to that of the present school, a more crowded section of the city. The transcript from her previous school indicated that Ruth had done average third-grade work, that Ruth had appeared unhappy at times but in general she seemed to respond well to the encouraging overtures of the teacher. The record contained no clue to explain the absences. The principal telephoned the mother to request a visit to the school. In his first interview, Mr. Parks discovered from the mother, who was pregnant, that the family had been experiencing serious financial difficulties. The husband had failed in business and because of strained finances, the family had been forced to give up their attractive home, which was heavily mortgaged. The family moved to this less expensive section of the city and was renting a second-floor flat over the landlady's flat. Ruth's father worked overtime, and when he was home with the children, there were two younger girls besides Ruth, he was cross and impatient. About the time school had started, Ruth fell from her bicycle, jabbing the handlebar into her abdomen. Medical examination had revealed no physical injury, but Ruth developed imaginary stomach pains and recurrent nausea. To Mr. Parks' inquiry if each absence was due to these periods of illness, the mother reported that in addition Ruth had complained tearfully about school. She had reported that her teacher was "mean and sneaky" and that her classmates hated her. Mr. Parks knew that this was quite likely not true, since the teacher had been a successful teacher having helped him solve many difficult classroom problems over the years. Plainly, Ruth was inappropriately attaching her anxiety feelings, which arose elsewhere, to her classmates, teachers, and school. The principal suggested that the local child-guidance clinic might be of service and the mother accepted the suggestion.

The clinic undertook to study Ruth's case and substantiated what the mother had reported to the principal. The situation had even grown worse. Each school morning, Ruth hid beneath the bedclothes and cried or vomited. The mother tried to drag her bodily out of bed. Once, when she got as far as the staircase, they struggled and both fell downstairs; this experience naturally frightened both of them very much.

The clinic discovered that childhood experiences of the mother had been such as to make her unable to cope with her environment and made it impossible for her to provide consistent love and opportunity for Ruth's growth. Ruth's emotions were *ambivalent;* she felt both love and hate for her mother. Her hatred made her guilty. At times she wished so strongly that some evil would befall her mother, that she felt it actually would. The focus of Ruth's anxiety was not so much at school but rather, she feared absenting herself from home.

How could all this affect Ruth's relationship with her teacher? The teacher as a surrogate mother can easily become a target for the hate element in the ambivalence. She may be seen as a "good mother" who gives love and knowledge, but she also may be seen as the "bad mother" who prohibits and deprives. These ambivalent feelings, which Ruth had long had toward her mother, were pointed up and strengthened by the precipitating events just mentioned. Because Ruth was unable to express her feelings openly at home they were displaced upon Ruth's new teacher, and then upon the entire school experience.

As a result of the treatment received at the clinic, mother and daughter were assigned to separate therapists with whom positive relationships were established, Ruth made slow but definite progress. The reaction against coming to school gradually faded away as both the mother and the child gained some understanding of their relationships and of the causes behind the phobia.

General diffuse anxiety should be taken by the teacher as a danger sign. The child who turns in overly meticulous work and whose overconscientious behavior requires him to use excessive time in preparing his lessons, may be using these behaviors to control an overwhelming anxiety. Sometimes neurotic anxiety may manifest itself in thumb sucking, masturbation, and other habit manipulations. Very often at the onset of the anxiety state the child will complain of somatic ailments for which no physical basis can be found, or the onset of the anxiety may coincide with the arrival of puberty.

In dealing with school phobia and other symptoms of neurotic anxiety there are three points to keep in mind.

1. The teacher should not take personal offense at the child's stated dislike of him or expression of fear. These usually represent displaced expression of feeling.

2. The teacher, principal, and other school personnel who may become involved in the case, should not become judgmental about the parent's relationship to the child. The parents themselves are the products of forces that produced an inability to conduct their lives more constructively.

3. Referral to professional psychological and psychiatric care, either directly or through some other community agency, should be considered. The school can help the clinician by providing information about the problem and also in carrying out the clinician's recommendations in the day-to-day contacts with the child.

ANGER AND AGGRESSION

Several surveys (Schrupp and Gjerde, 1953; Stouffer, 1952; Wickman, 1928) of teachers' concerns about children's behavior indicate that problems of control of the expression of hostility and aggression rank very high. The following list is a composite of the findings of several surveys and includes the ten most serious problems as viewed by teachers.

Most Serious Problems of Classroom Behavior as Seen by Teachers

1. Cruelty and bullying
2. Stealing
3. Impertinence, defiance
4. Heterosexual activity
5. Disobedience
6. Untruthfulness
7. Destruction of school materials
8. Unreliableness
9. Unhappiness, depression
10. Cheating

With the exception of items 4, 8, and 9, these items represent ways in which children overtly express their anger and hostility. The various studies show that different groups of teachers will rank these problems differently, but all show that the expression of aggression causes more concern to teachers than any other single emotion. A moment's thought will confirm the generalization that in all areas of living the greatest problem we face is in the control and direction of the aggressive impulse. The great problem of modern civilization is the threat of war, which is essentially a massive organized expression of hostility. The teacher must come to understand the emotion that underlies aggression, for by understanding the causes one can institute preventative measures and one can direct the expression of anger and hostility into constructive channels.

As pointed out in the general discussion of the emotions earlier in this chapter, anger is a natural emotion and is essential for survival. Out of this emotion grows the drive for controlling and directing one's environment and more important the development and the assertion of selfhood. There are two general meanings given to the term aggression. When we characterize a child as aggressive, we may be applauding his leadership qualities, his ability in influencing and persuading others, or his use of energy to achieve his ends. On the other hand, we may be decrying the child's destructiveness, his general inclination to injure others, and his defiance of authority. It is this latter type of aggression that will be our concern here and we shall consider how this type of emotional energy can be directed into more positive channels of expression.

The Underlying Basis of Aggression

We may select from two theoretical approaches the explanation of how aggression arises. A psychoanalytic interpretation is presented by Flugel (1955). He suggests that:

> Aggression springs from a perennial source of energy deeply rooted in our very nature and ultimately independent of any external thwarting or frustration. This [position] may seem to provide a more adequate explanation of many apparently unprovoked acts of violence and destruction and of the joyous participation in, or contemplation of, destruction generally (page ix).

Although it may be difficult to disprove this explanation, it offers, however, little in the way of suggesting a remedial approach to problems of aggression. Another widely accepted position is simply that an aggressive act arises out of the frustration of an "instigated goal response." If an individual is about to perform certain acts, or if he is in the process of attempting to satisfy certain needs and some external agent, a person or an inanimate object, or a deficiency on the part of the person himself, interferes with this activity, we say that the person is frustrated. According to the frustration-aggression hypothesis, all acts of aggression arise from frustration. It is important to note that not all aggression is immediately recognizable as such, for often the aggressive act is disguised.

> Many of the common forms of aggression can be instantly recognized by an observer who belongs to Western society. Acts of physical violence are perhaps the most obvious. Phantasies of "getting even" with galling superiors or rivals, calculated forays against frustrating persons (whether the weapon is a business deal, a gun, a malicious rumor, or a verbal castigation, is of little moment) and generalized destructive or remonstrative outburst like lynchings, strikes and certain reformist campaigns are clearly forms of aggression as well. It hardly needs special emphasis that tremendously complex learned skills such as the boomerang and machine gun, may occur in these aggressive behavior sequences (Dollard et al., 1939, page 9).

The sequence of frustrating experience leading to the aggressive act is not always direct. The aggressive act may be expressed in different ways and under some circumstances may be so completely modified as to be socially approved and even socially useful.

The selection of one of the four possible responses to frustration shown in Figure 11.2 will depend on (1) the strength of the instigated goal response, (2) the kind of frustration, this being measured subjectively, (3) the maturity of the person and the degree of insight he has into his own behavior. Bandura and Walters (1963) have demonstrated that children's frustration-reactions are shaped through modeling, that is, the form of response chosen by the frustrated child will conform to the type of adult frustration-reaction that the child has observed. If children observe physical aggression, yelling, withdrawal, or other behaviors as adult reactions to frustration, they will adopt these themselves when they are thwarted. The understanding of the effects of frustration is a lesson in psychology that children as young as age eight can begin to learn; a lesson that is most useful in leading to the understanding of others and one's self.

Direct Aggression

Parents and teachers find the expression of anger in the form of direct aggression very difficult to tolerate. This difficulty can be accounted for on the following grounds. Most adults, even teachers and intelligent parents, have not completely resolved the conflicts and anxiety arising from the instigation to aggressive action. The child's aggressive outburst often serves to frustrate the adult and the unresolved control of aggression manifests itself in the adult's reaction of hostility toward the child. We often witness that a parent or a teacher knowingly or unknowingly frustrates a child, the child becomes aggressive and this in turn produces further aggression on the part of the adult. The situation is resolved only when, because of physical power, the adult succeeds in subduing the child. When the controlling factor in resolving such a con-

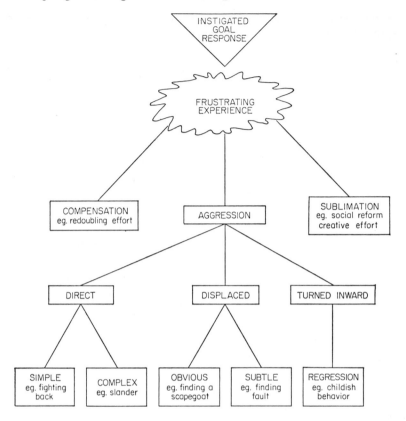

FIGURE 11.2   *The various forms of response to frustration of instigated goal response.*

flict is physical power, two dangers result; first, the child learns that might is right, a concept that, if widely accepted, can do much damage to our social structure, and second, this position of power is not to be permanently held by the adult and when the child grows bigger and stronger the process of working through a frustrating experience cannot be learned anew. It must be noted that in a conflict between two children or when one child becomes directly aggressive toward a group of children, the teacher has an obvious responsibility for the physical welfare of all the children. This responsibility must be expressed in such a way as to safeguard not only the physical welfare but also the psychological relationships involved. It would profit a teacher little to isolate a child permanently on the pretext of the possible damage he might do to others, if by this isolation the teacher and the child have no basis for future cooperation. The prevention of physical outbursts is indeed complicated, but the skilled teacher is fair, objective, and concerned both

with resolving the immediate problem and also the possible future outcomes of this resolution.

Displaced Aggression

Very often the child or the adult cannot deal with the source of
frustration directly. For example, the child may not be able to attack
directly the older child who is blocking his goal response or who may be
restricting his freedom of movement. He must in a sense swallow his
aggression momentarily but he will need to find some outlet for it. He
may express it against inanimate objects and thus destroy some of his
own toys or he may choose another person, such as a smaller or weaker
child against whom he can more safely express this feeling. In some instances the pent-up hostility of deprived youth in a community will express itself in acts of vandalism against school buildings and other public
institutions. When our diagnosis leads to the conclusion that the vandalism is due to such displaced aggression, it might be well for the authorities not to add fuel to the smoldering fire by administering punishment or frustration to the already frustrated individual. It is well to
note that not all vandalism is displaced aggression and not all punishment is ill-advised; a diagnostic approach is needed when symptoms of
difficulty arise.

Displaced aggression is not always displayed in violence. The
teacher who is frustrated by a principal who belittles him, or who
thwarts a favored plan, may feel unable to express this frustration toward his superior and may turn his aggression then toward the children
and become excessively punitive or harsh with his students. The teacher
needs always to be alert to the sometimes hidden causes behind any exaggerated tendency in his response. It is remarkable how just this awareness of the working of displaced aggression can reduce the need to be
aggressive in a specific situation.

A caricature of displaced aggression as a kind of chain reaction
will illustrate our point. Dad cuts himself while shaving in the morning,
has a flat tire on the way to work, and is bawled out by the boss for an
error in his accounts. When he comes home he finds fault with the pota-
toes, which appear excessively lumpy and the steak, which is too well
done and he picks an argument with Mom. Mom knows too well that
fighting back may lead to much unpleasantness. However, she notices
that Junior did a rather poor job of washing before supper, his clothes
have not been hung up, and his bike has not been put away. All the
things that a ten-year-old boy would ordinarily do, irritate her to the
point of slapping him. Junior doesn't understand why this happens but
he has learned that Mom won't listen to reason when in this mood. So
he decides to go to the basement and work with his tools, but Rex, his dog,
is blocking his path and receives a kick for his inconsideration.

Social scientists have attributed a great deal of racial prejudice and the behavior of bigoted persons to the presence of displaced aggression. In the classroom we find similar phenomena occurring and it might be well for the teacher to look into the possible frustrations behind a particular youngster's displaced aggression. The bully who picks on younger children, the sly, aggressive child who destroys secretly what belongs to others, and so on; these children are often acting out of a sense of generalized frustration by choosing safer outlets for their aggression, that is displacing their hostility.

Aggression Turned Inward, Regression

Regression is defined as reverting to a less mature pattern or level of behavior after having achieved a higher form. Thus the child who for some time has been toilet-trained, starts to wet his bed at night (becomes eneuretic), or the child who has developed a more mature pattern of speech acquires some infantile characteristics in his speech, we speak of regression. This phenomenon is to be distinguished from fixation, which refers to a child's retention of immature habits because of excessive anxiety about growing up or undue satisfaction derived from immaturity. We must also distinguish between true regression and the natural process of maturation, which involves movement forward and backward. The natural maturation phenomenon can best be seen in the acquiring of upright locomotion. As a child begins to walk he may take a few steps but then revert to crawling. On succeeding days he gradually walks more and crawls less but there will be periods during which he will crawl only. Maturing resembles an irregular progress line in which the periods of apparent lack of progress are really pauses to gather strength for the next lunge forward.

What causes a child to regress? Again we may turn to the frustration-aggression hypothesis for an explanation. When the frustration is of such a nature as to produce feelings of guilt or feelings of unworthiness, it is then likely that the aggression will be expressed toward the self and will show itself in some form of regression.

Regression arising from frustration has been studied experimentally in one ingeniously designed investigation (Barker et al., 1943). Each of thirty children, ranging in age from two years to five years who were used as subjects, was given an opportunity to play without restriction with a set of standardized play materials. These materials consisted of a little chair on which a teddy bear and a doll were seated, a cup, a small truck and trailer, a saucer, a teapot, an ironing board and an iron, a telephone receiver, crayons and writing paper, a small motorboat, a sailboat, a celluloid duck and frog, and a fishing pole with a line and a magnet for a hook. The manner in which each child played with these toys was carefully studied and each child was scored on his level of constructiveness of play. The scoring was done on a continuum ranging from rather primitive, simple, little structured activities to elaborate, imaginative, highly developed play.

Following this rating of the children, most of the standardized toys were incorporated into a more elaborate and attractive set of toys that had been put behind a partition in the room. The elaborate play set up consisted of a large doll's house, large enough to admit the child, with complete furnishings, and a toy lake filled with water, also elaborately equipped. The child was given enough time in this attractive play arrangement to become thoroughly involved in it. The experimenter then collected the standardized toys and took the child to the other part of the room and lowered a wire partition and fastened it by means of a large padlock. The part of the room containing the attractive toys was visible through the wire but inaccessible. In this frustrated condition each subject was observed as he played with the standard toys and a second constructiveness-of-play-score was obtained. The results indicated that twenty of the subjects regressed as a result of frustration. Three did not change and five increased in their constructiveness score. The over-all change when expressed in mental-age equivalents was an average regression of 17.3 months. That is to say that on the average a child who had played with the standardized materials at the constructive level of a usual 4½-year-old, after frustration, played with these same materials at the level of a three-year-old. The investigators' interpretation can be extended by speculating on the meaning to the child of being removed from the elaborate play-room atmosphere. Being deprived in this way may well be interpreted by the child as an indication that the adult is punishing him because he has done something wrong, so that not only is he frustrated by having his desires thwarted but there may also exist a feeling of guilt. For this reason the frustration leads to regression rather than direct or displaced aggression. This type of response to frustration has been called intropunitive to differentiate it from the extropunitive response (Rosenzweig, 1934).

Several illustrations of the regressive effects of frustration can be cited. The college student who sleeps most of the day, being unable to stay awake during lectures or while studying, is regressing. The frustration is the inability to meet the demands of college study accompanied by feelings of self-deprecation and guilt.

Sears (1961) has shown that the different kinds of early socialization experienced by boys and girls in our culture, result in different patterns of aggressive behavior in middle childhood. He found that "girls are significantly higher on prosocial aggression and aggression anxiety, while boys are substantially higher on antisocial aggression." That is, girls show a tendency to express their aggression in ways that support the norms and standards of the group. They will be punitive and aggressive toward those who are inclined to break the rules. Prosocial aggression is that kind of aggression that might be shown in a policeman's maltreatment of a suspected criminal. At the same time girls show more aggression anxiety, which means that the aggressive impulse would be converted into avoidance behavior, somatic symptoms, feelings of guilt, and expectations of injury and attack. The aggressive impulse in boys, on the other hand, is more likely to be acted out in overt destructive behavior.

One can readily see that these differences in expression of anger would elicit different responses in teachers. To the extent that the teacher is inclined to resort to prosocial aggression, the girl is more likely to be accepted as a teacher's ally in counter-aggression toward the overt aggression of the boy. Because the girl tends to repress the feeling of anger, its presence is more likely to be unnoticed by teachers than in the case of the boy.

Compensation and Sublimation

Not all responses to thwarting and frustration are expressed in terms of destructive hostility and aggression. In cases where the frustration arises from a generalized threat to the strivings for a sense of adequacy, the reaction may take the form of *compensation*. The compensatory reaction may result in attempts to overcome the deficiency or it may produce behavior designed to build up the sense of adequacy in some activity unrelated to the deficiency. Demosthenes, the orator of ancient Greece, is often cited as an example of compensation resulting in overcoming a deficiency. It is said, that in his youth, Demosthenes suffered from a speech defect so that he could not be easily understood. He practiced assiduously by placing pebbles in his mouth and speaking against the roar of the sea, thus overcoming his speech defect. Many such cases of people of fame have been used to illustrate the phenomenon of compensation. It is more common for the compensation to take place in such a way as to develop skill in an area where one's deficiency is not a handicap. The blind person who develops a great sensitivity to sounds and in the sense of touch; the deaf person who sees more keenly, or in a more general way the child who because of physical disability cannot participate in sports and turns to books for his satisfaction. Thus we see that certain kinds of frustration lead to constructive attempts to meet a threat to the feelings of adequacy. In other instances the threat to adequacy cannot be coped with constructively and the compensation may appear in the form of bullying, belittling, and attempts to reduce the adequacy of others so that self does not appear as inadequate in comparison.

Many occupations that serve the useful purposes of society depend in some measure on controlled and constructive channeling of aggression.

The editor or drama critic who corrects and challenges his author, the skilled baseball player whose aim it is to "knock the pitcher out of the box," the comedian who entertains and reduces tension by poking fun at himself and at society in general, the playwright who organizes thoughts of violence and rebellion; these are examples of the constructive conversion of aggressive impulses. This transformation of aggression into socially approved behavior is one form of *sublimation.* All human beings face frustrations as a result of the failure of their surroundings to bring immediate satisfaction to their desires. This generalized frustration can lead to aggression that is antisocial or socialized. It is the responsibility of the school to channel the aggressive impulses by showing children that one can use written expression, art, drama, the development of critical ability, competitive sports, and so on, as methods of expressing emotion in desirable and useful forms.

DEVELOPING EMOTIONAL MATURITY

The mature or integrated personality has been described at various points in the book. The description can be extended to include emotional maturity or stability. The integrated person is one whose emotional life is organized to a point where he can withstand a reasonable amount of stress, where he maintains an awareness of the emotion, and he derives a degree of satisfaction from his emotion. The expression of emotion in the maturing individual is satisfying to himself and at the same time brings satisfaction to others. When the individual is frightened, restless, unhappy, or irritated, and when this condition interferes with his approach to the world of things or people, we can say that his development toward maturity is being hampered. When others feel uncomfortable and threatened in his presence, we can say also that all is not well in the realm of emotional maturing.

One might reword Rogers' description of the therapist or the counselor to make it more directly applicable to teaching aimed at fostering emotional maturity. The teacher's role is best described by the terms *warmth, permissiveness, acceptance,* and *understanding* (Rogers, 1948). The teacher bases his work upon a warm interest in others. He shows a willingness for the student to be what he is, to feel what he feels. The teacher must be committed to the principle that the student has the capacity of responsible choice. He creates an atmosphere in which the student can gradually come to be himself. Axline's (1947) description of the therapist in a play-therapy setting can be similarly reworded to apply directly to the teaching situation. The teacher must develop a warm, friendly relationship with the child, in which good rapport is established as soon as possible. The teacher accepts the child exactly as he is. The teacher maintains a deep respect for the child's ability to solve his own problems if given an opportunity to do so. The responsibility to make choices and to institute change is the child's. The teacher does not attempt to hurry the growth process along. It is a gradual process and is recognized as such by the teacher.

Although these ideas of acceptance and permissiveness in redirecting the behavior of children are not new, many teachers are unwilling to consider their use in the classroom situation. The idea prevails that growth takes place in a restricting, pushing atmosphere rather than in a warm, accepting atmosphere.

The following description of a classroom situation illustrates that permissiveness, encouragement, and patience can be effective in fostering growth toward emotional maturity. The boy in this case showed evidence of rather serious disturbance and the teacher might better have been advised to have referred the child to a children's psychiatric facility. She chose, instead, to "treat" the child herself. Her "treatment" worked, but one wonders whether the risk was not excessive and whether the unnoticed effects on other children in the class were altogether beneficial. This case is selected not to encourage teachers to imitate Mrs. Hillis but rather to show how acceptance works and, with a limited focus, how effective it can be.

The school opened with a short registration period on Friday. Charles was the only child of the thirty-four who was not present to meet Mrs. Hillis, the first-grade teacher. His mother, however, did appear and explained very nervously that her son was seriously ill. As the mother and teacher talked, it was apparent that the mother needed someone to visit with and she relaxed as the conversation progressed. This mother, with her anxious manner, remained in the teacher's thoughts. However, Charles remained only a name and a birth date.

On the following Monday the teacher prepared an individual name card for each child. These cards were placed around the room and each child was helped to find his own card and was asked to tell about himself. An interesting activity for the children, it proved also to be a source of information about each child. The kindergarten teacher who had had him last year, while visiting in the room, noticed Charles' card and said, "I couldn't do a thing with this child. He was my first failure."

Mrs. Hillis questioned his former behavior and found that he was hyperactive, aggressive, and destructive. He ruined every story and project. He kicked the teacher one day after he deliberately hit a child with a hammer for no apparent reason. He had been taken to the office and his mother called for a conference with his teacher and the principal. This conference was on record for Mrs. Hillis to use. In addition, she knew there was much information available to her if only she extended herself.

She was not surprised to see him hale and hearty so soon after his "serious" illness. The first impression of the boy as a whole was pitiful. His little-boy face was drawn and tense; his eyes fearful. One good quality was noticeable, he was spotlessly clean and very appropriately dressed. The teacher commented on her reaction to the child. "Someone is very concerned about this little fellow. He is my first problem."

Charles talked constantly. Occasionally his talking was replaced by gun noises, loud singing, or whistling. He would not sit at his desk, he refused to listen to stories or to play games. The only positive action that first morning was that he went to the cupboard, selected a piece of paper, and drew a bright picture with his crayons. The teacher tried to get near him in order to praise him about his splendid picture, but he ran away every time she came near.

Many anxious moments occurred during that first week of school. Charles ran to the pencil sharpener and was successful in making a sharp point which he immediately used as a sword on his fellow class-mates. The teacher restrained her horror as well as her voice and went quickly to the supply of crayons that were to be part of the first-grade equipment. She smiled as she gave the first box to the child who was crying about his injury. Charles came up to grab his box. Mrs. Hillis was firm about the fact that he must not have both the crayons and the pen-cil. She knew, from the picture he had drawn using a box of old crayon pieces, that he loved color. Mrs. Hillis had used this first opportunity to be firm with Charles concerning his relations with other people. He responded to this quiet suggestion and watched the teacher tape his name to the pencil before it was stored in the box. All the time that he watched Mrs. Hillis, he shifted from foot to foot nervously, breathing hard. The teacher commented about her feelings saying, "I wanted to take him in my arms and love him until he was relaxed and happy, but I knew many bridges must be crossed before he would be ready to re-spond to love." This pencil-crayon trade was the first bridge; it had been crossed safely. The injured children responded to a hug and the incident was past history.

While the teacher was setting a limit to Charles' behavior, she was careful not to reject him. The name on the pencil served as evidence for him that he was being respected and his individuality was regarded. Of course, this train of thought is not verbalized by a first grader but inter-pretations are still made at the feeling or affective level. The teacher can-not expect that the successful management of one critical situation will lead to a personality transformation. Other problems are likely to de-velop as can be seen in the description that follows.

The attention span of this child was so short that he soon tired of his new crayons. This time he took thumbtacks out of the name cards and proceeded to stick children with them. The teacher called Charles over to help her get the cards back in place. He seemed to enjoy the task of punching thumbtacks into the rubberized composition and seemed to forget about his former activities. After a series of experiences like that of the pencil jabbing and the thumbtacking, the teacher found herself walking unconsciously between Charles and the class because he was as quick as lightning and just as unpredictable. Mrs. Hillis continued to teach the class giving them interesting things to do. She felt that Charles must come of his own accord to realize that a positive response would ultimately bring greater satisfactions. She attempted to rely upon his need for contact and harmony with reality, which can be satisfied by a variety of rich and meaningful experiences.

The children often asked why Charles wasn't doing what the rest did and the teacher timed her answer in a low, steady, pleasant voice so it would be heard by Charles when he hesitated to get a fresh start. "Charles isn't ready for first-grade fun." As days and weeks passed, Charles started to come closer to examine the class projects. She was aware of the fact that the surface behavior of this child could possibly be changed by becoming tough, suppressive, and threatening, but she realized that this would have led to more serious and complicated consequences.

One day in October, Mrs. Hillis duplicated a fire engine for each child and explained briefly how they would be put together and showed them a complete sample. She then built upon this experience by telling them that she had a nice story about *The Little Fireman* (by Lois Lenski) that she would read first and then after it was read, each could make a fire engine toy. Charles rushed forward and grabbed at the stack of materials that were to be used for making the toys. "Let's hear the story first," said Mrs. Hillis as she succeeded in putting her arm around his shoulders and asked him if he cared to sit next to her. He sat quietly for a few moments and then got up and moved slowly away. All of a sudden he grabbed the long pointer and thrashed it through the air narrowly missing several children. The teacher grabbed the stick and again placed her arm around his shoulders. This time she said, "Charles, we all love you and we just can't understand it when you hurt us. We want you to make a fire engine too, but if you waste our story time, you can't make a toy to take home." Mrs. Hillis was firm yet she did not raise her voice. She was sensitive to the fact that Charles was ambivalent; that is, he seemed to be pulled in opposing directions, he wanted to be the tough, rough nonconformist and yet he desired to do as the others were doing. The teacher was attempting to encourage the positive rather than the negative tendency in his behavior.

Mrs. Hillis suspected that some of the tensions and frustrations causing Charles' behavior were caused by something in the home. This was confirmed one morning when his sister, a fourth grader, appeared at the door holding Charles by the collar. She exhibited an injury below her eye and explained that it had been caused by a pair of scissors that Charles had thrown at her the night before. Mrs. Hillis expressed her sorrow to the sister and cordially dismissed her, sensing the tension that her presence created. She said nothing to Charles hoping that her confidence in him might help him settle himself. Her hope was unfounded, for Charles grabbed a pair of scissors from her desk and stood poised ready to throw them at the first intruder. The teacher was in a dilemma. She could not risk the welfare of the class and she was uncertain how sound was her own relationship with this angry boy. She stood between the boy and the few children who were in the room and quietly told the children to leave for a few minutes and to wait outside with the others who were arriving. She then told Charles to give her the scissors so that she could show him how they should be held. He followed her instructions and she was able to explain to him that the scissors must always be carried with the points together in the closed hand. This procedure illustrates the principle of positive prophylaxis previously described. In a few minutes the teacher was able to invite the class into the room and asked Charles to demonstrate the proper way of carrying scissors.

Mrs. Hillis noticed that Charles' mother often wheeled the baby to school to walk home with Charles and his sister. The teacher used this opportunity to meet her on a casual, friendly basis. She learned that the sister was in fourth grade and an excellent student. The mother conveyed the impression that her daughter was bossy with Charles. One day, the mother frankly said, in front of Charles, that she hoped that the teacher could handle him at school; she couldn't do a thing with him at home. Mrs. Hillis turned to Charles and looked right into his eyes, realizing that this last remark could easily be interpreted as a lack of faith and confidence and said, "Charles knows I can handle him at school and he knows there are many ways he can help us." This seemed to be a turning point for Charles. From this time on, he began to show a moderate degree of respect for his classmates, and he began to react with pleasure when he was praised. He seemed to enjoy knowing that he was "being handled" like one of the group. The teacher's reliance on the boy's capacity for positive change had finally borne fruit.

As the boy learned to respond more positively at school he became more accepted at home, which further encouraged his growth toward emotional maturity. In the teacher's estimate of the situation it was worth treating this child within the regular classroom but other teachers could, with justification, have decided otherwise initially and called upon more expert attention or a special class setting.

Our central point is that the teacher needs to rely as much as possible on what Rogers (1948) has referred to as the basic motivation for change being a socially and biologically based preference for harmonious rather than antagonistic relations, for mutuality rather than complete selfishness, for a high degree of individual independence rather than submissiveness. The force that operates to bring about change, as described in Chapter 2, is the growth capacity of the individual, the tendency toward maturity and self-actualization that is the mainspring of human life, group or individual.

The teacher and the school can encourage the development of affective maturity by:

Providing:	*Avoiding:*
1. Skills that will enable the child to meet the threats of his environment	1. Threatening the child who expresses fear or anger
2. A permissive atmosphere in which the child can express what he feels	2. The error of identifying oral expression of feeling with the acting out of feeling
3. The awareness of the causes of certain feeling states	3. Excessive repression and attempts to develop excessive control
4. The identification of proper and constructive ways of expressing feeling	4. Condemnation and guilt feelings about emotion

SUMMARY

Emotions as psychological processes are in reality not distinguished from conation, motivational processes, or cognition, knowing or awareness processes. All three function together in an integrated fashion. The distinctions are made for ease of discussion.

Emotions have three components. They represent (1) a state of arousal, (2) visceral changes, and (3) are individualized responses dependent upon psychological interpretation. The level of arousal appropriate for different kinds of activities will differ. The visceral changes serve to mobilize the organism for "fight or flight." If this mobilization occurs continuously as a result of psychological threat, psychosomatic disorders can occur. The fact that emotions represent an individualized response means that different children will react to the same stimulus situation in different ways.

As the individual grows his emotional experiences change from amorphous reactions of excitement to more highly differentiated sensitivity to the environment and a wider range of responses. Emotions are modified through the process of socialization and physical maturation.

One of the emotional conditions that disturb is that of fear. Fear inhibits action, sometimes serving to protect the individual from harm and at other times limiting growth toward maturity. When the latter occurs the teacher has several avenues open to him. He may use enforced contact, rational explanation, avoidance of feared situations, gradual exposure, teaching of skills, imitation, and reconditioning. All of these procedures have their limitations. Some of them when properly applied can release the child's growth potential.

School phobia is another manifestation of fear. The points to keep in mind are as follows: the child should be brought back to school as soon as possible; the child's expression of negative feeling toward the school and the teacher are displaced feelings usually originating in the home; and psychiatric treatment is usually indicated.

Another emotional condition that disturbs is that of anger. Here also the resulting action can either be useful in providing energy for overcoming obstacles or it can be harmful in a number of ways. The feelings engendered by frustration, anger, can be displaced and directed against innocent persons or it can be turned inward leading to regression. Other usually more constructive ways of handling the feeling of anger are by compensation and sublimation.

The school can contribute significantly to the development of emotional maturity. This can be done where there is an awareness that feelings and emotions are a natural and integral part of a healthy existence and where control of emotional expression is not the primary aim of teaching. The child will become more mature emotionally when he is accepted and treated warmly, when he acquires the skills for sublimating and constructively dealing with his feelings, and when he can be free to recognize the existence of his own feelings.

READING REFERENCES

Berkowitz, L., *Aggression: A Social Psychological Analysis*. New York: McGraw-Hill Book Company, 1962.

D'Evelyn, Katherine E., *Meeting Children's Emotional Needs: A Guide for Teachers*. Englewood Cliffs, N.J.: Prentice-Hall, 1957.

Henry, N. B. (Ed.), *Mental Health in Modern Education*. Fifty-fourth Yearbook (Pt. 2) National Society for the Study of Education. Chicago: University of Chicago Press, 1955 (particularly chaps. 7-10).

Jersild, A. T., *In Search of Self*. New York: Bureau of Publications, Columbia University, Teachers College, 1952.

May, R., *The Meaning of Anxiety*. New York: Ronald Press Company, 1950.

Redl, F. and D. Wineman, *The Aggressive Child*. New York: Free Press of Glencoe, 1955.

Sarason, S. B. et al., *Anxiety in Elementary School Children*. New York: John Wiley & Sons, 1960.

CHAPTER 12

PHYSICAL FACTORS

The most readily noticed and apparent differences among pupils are those of health, physical appearance, and motor skill. Some children are robust, handsome, and graceful, others are sickly, plain, and awkward, while most are somewhere between these extremes. The physical body gives rise to the child's first awareness of a self separate and apart from others and it is the physical body that to a certain extent determines the reaction of others; this in turn has a significant influence on the child's concept of self. We no longer think of the body as an outer shell housing the more significant entity called the mind. Mind and body are intimately related and each experience is an interaction of a total organism with its environment. For example, we may refer to anger as an emotion, implying that it is exclusively psychological or mental, but as indicated in the preceding chapter, anger and all the so-called emotions have very significant physiological components. On the other hand a so-called physical problem, such as a prolonged illness, endocrine or neurological imbalance, or a deficiency in the sensory or motor apparatus cannot be without profound effect upon the feeling, striving, and reasoning processes.

Much of the change in behavior that results from school learning manifests itself in a physical response. Although reading is largely a function of the process of acquiring meaning and the application of understanding, it depends in some measure on the use of the eyes. Simi-

lar considerations apply to handwriting, speech, playing a musical instrument, and many other perceptual-motor skills.

The major topics of this chapter will be: (1) the nature of the relationship between what we normally conceive of as the body and personality, (2) the problems that arise in the normal process of physical
development, (3) the effects of deviation in bodily growth and function
on personality development, (4) the effects of psychological stress on
physiological functioning (psychosomatic disturbances), and (5) the
necessary considerations in helping different children in the acquisition
of the perceptual-motor skills.

BODY-FORM AND PERSONALITY

The first and often the most important impressions are created
by outward appearance. Our folk literature is replete with references
indicating a relationship between body build or facial characteristics and
qualities of temperament or personality. The square jaw is taken as a
sign of determination and a receding chin is a sign of a weak will. The
high forehead (the egg head) is considered a sign of intellectual interest
and ability and sometimes of impracticality. The person with red hair is
assumed to have a volatile temper. The roly-poly person is said to have a
jolly nature, the thin individual is considered likely to be moody and distant, and tallness is associated with qualities of leadership.

In addition to these folkloristic characterizations there is an extensive literature, dating back to the ancient Greeks, dealing with this topic
directly. Sheldon (1944) has reviewed the history of the many attempts
to establish the relationship of body-form and personality. The weakness
in many of these formulations lies in the absence of validating studies or
controlled tests to determine whether the assumed relationship between
various body characteristics and temperamental traits exists in reality.

The work of Sheldon and others (1940, 1942) is the most systematic
and attempts empirical validation. After examining several thousand
photographs of male college students, Sheldon concluded that the
body types could be described as varying along three dimensions, *endomorphy, mesomorphy* and *ectomorphy*. He set up a seven-point scale
for each of these dimensions. When endomorphy is most pronounced and
the other two dimensions are not, the individual is classed as 7-1-1 and
he would have the characteristics in which the digestive viscera are prom-
inently developed. The person who is predominantly mesomorphic would
be classed 1-7-1 and his body structure would emphasize bone and muscle.
His build would be athletic and muscular. When ectomorphy predomi-
nates the classification is 1-1-7, and the body build is one which is fragile
and linear. "The ectomorph has long slender, poorly muscled extremities
with delicate, pipestem bones, and he has, relative to his mass, the great-

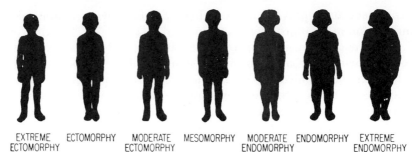

EXTREME   ECTOMORPHY   MODERATE   MESOMORPHY   MODERATE   ENDOMORPHY   EXTREME
ECTOMORPHY   ECTOMORPHY   ENDOMORPHY   ENDOMORPHY

FIGURE 12.1   *Silhouettes of seven body types in children. From M. Massler and T. Suher, "Calculation of 'Normal' Weight in Children,"* Child Development, **22**, *1951, p. 80.*

est surface area" (Sheldon, 1944, page 540). Figure 12.1 shows the silhouette outlines of some body types as they might appear in school-age children.

After developing this classificatory scheme for somatotypes (physique) Sheldon attempted to establish the relationships of personality traits to these body types. Using a Scale of Temperament that he developed out of his interviews with a population of young adult males. Sheldon was able to demonstrate a number of correlations of body build to temperament. He found correlations of endomorphy with viscerotonia, mesomorphy with somatotonia and ectomorphy with cerebrotonia. These qualities of temperament are listed in Table 12.1.

TABLE 12.1   BODY TYPE AND TEMPERAMENTAL QUALITIES

Physique	Temperament	Personality characteristics
Endomorphy	Viscerotonia	Relaxed in posture and movement. Love of physical comfort. Slow reaction. Tolerant. Amiable. Complacent. Dependent on social approval.
Mesomorphy	Somatotonia	Assertive of posture and movement. Adventurous. Energetic. Love of risk and exercise. Competitive. Appears more mature.
Ectomorphy	Cerebrotonia	Restrained in posture and movement. Quick reaction. Love of privacy. Inhibited in social situations, apprehensive.

Sheldon's work has been criticized on several counts. One of the criticisms of his procedure stems from the fact that in his studies, the person making the personality evaluation is aware of the hypothesis regarding the relationship of body type and personality. This knowledge could introduce a bias in the results. Hanley (1951) tried to control for this bias by having junior high school pupils rate each other on personality ratings obtained by means of the guess-who technique. He correlated these ratings with somatotype at age eighteen. He was able to show that boys who were mesomorphic at age eighteen were more likely to have been rated in junior high as "Takes chances," "Good at games," "Real-Boy," and "Leader." Boys who at age eighteen were ectomorphic had been rated in junior high as "Bashful" and "Not Quarrelsome." Hanley's results in general show associations between somatotype and peer ratings that are congruent with Sheldon's hypotheses but the correlations obtained by Hanley were of such a low order that the teacher would not be justified in assuming any personality traits in a particular student from observing his body type.

Another point at issue in the Sheldon conclusions is that of the basis for the relationship between body type and personality. Sheldon suggests that whatever determines the former (presumably genetic factors) also determines the latter. Others who have concerned themselves with this problem have considered that social-psychological processes may be operative to a more significant degree. Hanley states: "There exists, of course, the possibility that a stereotype, equivalent to a vulgar version of Sheldon's hypotheses, affected the ratings of the reputation judges" (page 256). Anastasi (1958) also considers the possibility that social stereotype may operate to produce some fairly consistent relationships between physique and temperament. She states:

> Whether a person is conspicuously tall or short, fat or thin, muscular or puny, blond or brunet—these and many other characteristics may serve as stimuli for the responses of other people toward him. They may influence the attitude he encounters, the opportunities he is given, and even his own self percept. Through these channels, his behavior may gradually tend to approximate that demanded by the stereotype (page 128).

This point of view is consistent with that developed in Chapter 2 when the effects of social expectations on behavior were described, also with the discussion of the self-fulfilling prophecy in Chapter 6. The teacher should be on guard against his own stereotyped assumptions about fixed relationships between outward appearance and personality. Although some of these stereotypes can be definitely harmful, the teacher should be aware that physical development has significant implications for the child.

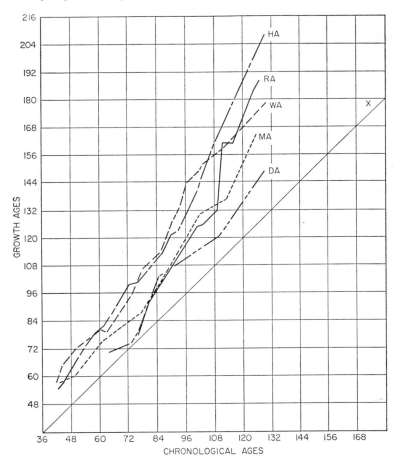

FIGURE 12.2 *This figure and the one which follows contrast the organismic development of two girls. Note how HA (height age), RA (reading age), WA (weight age), MA (mental age), and DA (dental age) develop more rapidly than would be expected (solid diagonal) in the first case and more slowly than expected in the second. X is the expected rate of growth. W. C. Olson and B. O. Hughes, "Growth of the Child as a Whole," in R. G. Barker et al. (Eds.),* Child Behavior and Development, *copyright 1943, pp. 200-201. New York: McGraw-Hill Book Company, Inc. Used by permission.*

THE PROCESS OF PHYSICAL DEVELOPMENT

From previous chapters it should be clear that the child grows in many different dimensions. He grows and changes in scholastic ability, in emotional response, and in physical size, strength, and skill. Although growth in these dimensions is not always parallel, research has shown that "there seems to be an underlying growth rhythm in the organism as a whole" (Simon, 1959). Olson and Hughes (1943) have shown that for

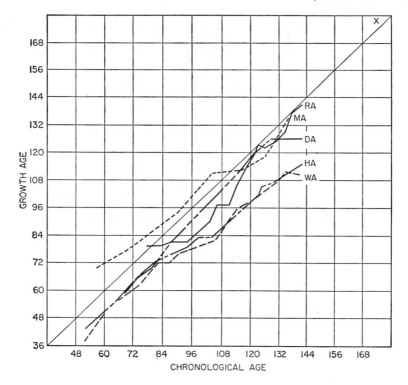

FIGURE 12.3 *See legend for Figure 12.2.*

most children the development of reading ability (reading age) and mental ability (mental age) parallel the development of such physical characteristics as height, weight, strength of grip, dentition, and skeletal development. The over-all growth pattern is called the organismic development and at any particular point, organismic age. In Figures 12.2 and 12.3 are shown the contrasting growth patterns of two girls, one a rapid grower and the other a slow developer.

Simon (1959) has shown that the body configuration undergoes discernible and measurable changes between the ages of five and seven, and that these changes are associated with school readiness. She states:

> From the present study and other evidence cited it would appear that it takes an over-all developmental age of body and mind of about 6-6 to attain school readiness in our culture. Obviously, physical maturity is more than skin-deep: it is reflected not only in superficial body features but in the maturational status of the central nervous system which in turn underlies such behavior as readiness to submit to restraints and the application to tasks (page 508).

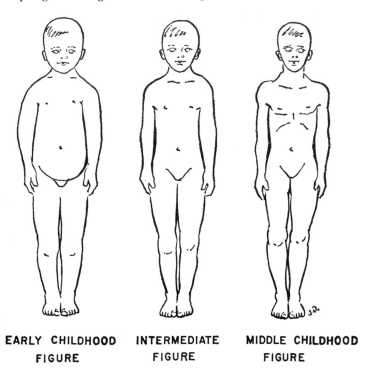

EARLY CHILDHOOD   **INTERMEDIATE**   **MIDDLE CHILDHOOD**
FIGURE   **FIGURE**   **FIGURE**

FIGURE 12.4   *Between the ages of four years six months and seven years five months, most children grow from the early childhood body configuration toward the one of middle childhood. There are marked changes in body proportions, facial structure and expression, the neck and shoulder line, the trunk and abdomen, body surface texture, and the lateral body outline being formed by adipose tissue in earliest stages and by muscles and joints in the later stages. Simon (1959) found that in a population of first-grade students "failing students tended to be more immature on a battery of anthropometric indices than successful students." Adapted from Maria D. Simon, "Body Configuration and School Readiness,"* Child Development, *30, 1959, pp. 493-512.*

Simon was able to show that children who showed less mature body configurations tended to do less well during the first grade than those whose body configurations were more mature. This was true even when the children were matched for age, IQ, and socioeconomic status.

This discussion does not imply that the school has no responsibility in fostering the child's readiness for learning, or that there is nothing to be done but wait if physical maturation and other aspects of readiness are retarded. On the contrary, it suggests, as pointed out in Chapter 3, that the school must always take into account the child's developmental status and pattern in planning his educational experiences.

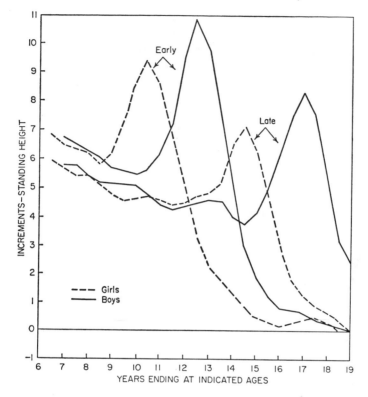

FIGURE 12.5 *Increments in height tend to slow down before the growth spurt. The spurt may take place early—about age ten for girls and age twelve for boys; or it may take place late and in a lesser degree—at age fourteen plus for girls and age seventeen minus for boys. From Nancy Bayley and R. D. Tuddenham, "Adolescent Changes in Body Build," in N. B. Henry (Ed.), Adolescence, Yearbook of the National Society for the Study of Education, 43, Pt. 1, Chicago: University of Chicago Press, 1944. (After Shuttleworth, 1939.)*

Physical Changes and Their Correlates

The period of adolescence is one in which marked physical changes having significant behavioral implications take place. The most pronounced of these changes are the growth spurt in which there is a rapid increase in height and weight and the appearance of secondary sex characteristics, voice change, beard, and pubic hair in the boy; and breast development, change in body configuration and pubic hair in the girl. These changes are associated with the ripening of the reproductive organs and the arrival of the biological aspects of sexual maturity.

The pubertal growth phase takes from five to seven years and may start as early as eight or as late as sixteen. Boys as a group enter this phase of growth about one and a half years later than girls. There are marked variations in the time of entry. In Figure 12.5 we see how early and the late maturing boys and girls change in height during this period. The changes in weight follow a similar pattern. At ages twelve to fourteen many more girls than boys have experienced the pubescent growth spurt. This may present some problems in those school activities in which boys and girls participate together. The writer recalls an elementary school graduation exercise in which boys and girls were paired as they marched down the auditorium aisle. The girls appeared so much taller and more mature. One could sense the discomfiture of both the boys and girls as they came down the aisle under the scrutiny of their beaming parents.

What are the correlates of the pubescent growth spurt and the appearance of the secondary sex characteristics? The maturing body is closely associated with the achievement of personal independence. Starting with the acquisition of walking and the attainment of bowel and bladder control, the maturing physiology plays an important role in personality. Erikson (1950), in delineating the various stages through which the human personality grows, points out that the development of autonomy and initiative or their inhibitory counterparts shame, doubt, and guilt, resides in these physical maturation processes of early childhood. During adolescence this matter of physical maturing becomes more focused and conscious. It has been shown that the interests and behavior patterns of children are closely allied with the pattern of physical and physiological development. Stone and Barker (1939) studied the attitudes and interests of premenarcheal and postmenarcheal [1] girls of the same chronological ages and the same socioeconomic background. They found that the girls who were more advanced in their physical maturation differed from their less advanced agemates in the following interest categories: they showed a stronger interest in heterosexual activities, in adornment and display of person; they were more inclined to engage in imaginative daydreaming activities; they were less interested in strenuous activities; and they showed a slight tendency to have fewer fears.

Jones and Bayley (1950) have studied the behavior characteristics of early- and late-maturing boys. They used skeletal development as indicated by X-rays as their criterion of physical maturity. The boys who matured late were rather small between the ages of thirteen and fifteen (see Figure 12.5); they were also relatively weak and showed lower scores on tests of athletic ability. They found significant differences favoring the early-maturing boys on the following characteristics: attractiveness of physique, grooming, matter-of-factness or absence of attention-seeking behavior, unaffectedness, and relaxation. The late-maturing boy is likely to encounter a sociopsychological environment that is less

---

[1] Menarche refers to the first menstruation period and is usually taken as a sign of the onset of pubescence.

favorable than that encountered by early-maturing individuals. Mussen and Jones (1957) studied the self-concepts, motivations, and attitudes of early- and late-maturing boys and found that those who were retarded in physical development (late-maturers) were "more likely to have negative self-conceptions, feelings of inadequacy, strong feelings of being rejected and dominated, prolonged dependency needs, and rebellious attitudes toward parents." On the other hand early-maturers were more likely to be capable of playing an adult role in interpersonal relationships; more of them showed attitudes of self-confidence and independence. An analysis of the case-histories of these adolescent boys showed that the "rate of physical maturing may affect personality in crucially important ways." The authors caution, however, "that in any particular case the effects of early- or late-maturing may be significantly modified by the individual's psychological history and present circumstances."

Adolescents show a wide variety of concerns about their physical development and appearance. One study (Frazier and Lisonbee, 1950) showed that two thirds of a large group of middle-class tenth graders expressed a desire for some change in themselves physically. In another survey (Elias, 1947) of about six thousand high school seniors it was shown that about half worried about some aspect of appearance, size, or complexion. In the California Study (Jones, 1939) as reported by Stolz and Stolz (1944) a group of boys and girls was studied over an eight-year period. About one third of this group showed definite signs of disturbance over some aspect of their physical characteristics at some time during this period. These studies show that there are similarities and differences in the concerns shown by boys and girls. Boys are likely to be concerned with shortness, thinness, lack of muscular strength, and facial blemishes; girls are likely to be concerned with tallness, thinness, fatness, facial features and blemishes, and small breasts.

Stolz and Stolz (1944) suggest several reasons for the acuteness of concern over physical features during adolescence as compared with earlier or later periods.

One obvious reason for this is the enhanced awareness of their bodies which adolescents acquire partly from the consciousness of their own physical development and partly from their increasing identification with culturally determined ideals concerning appropriate physical characteristics for men and for women. Another probable reason is related to the time dimension of life. In childhood, years of growth stretch indefinitely ahead and growing-up, adequate in every respect, is taken for granted. But during puberty, boys and girls begin to realize that the years of growth are numbered and they are faced with the reality of permanent differences of size in relation to other people. Perhaps a third reason why differences in height become more significant to individuals as they approach their mature stature is because these differences as measured in feet and inches are actually greater even though relative heights may remain the same (page 87).

The case that follows will serve to demonstrate that physical factors can initiate a series of school adjustment problems.

A Late-Maturing Boy

"Midge" Brown had another name of course. His parents called him Paul. But a boy who weighs barely 100 pounds when he is graduated from high school is likely to acquire a name like "Midge."

"Midge" had been rather small for his age all through the early years of elementary school, but no one considered this unusual. He played at the same games his larger friends enjoyed, and they responded to him with no particular consideration to his size.

"Midge's" teachers thought of him as the smallest one in the class and as a cute little boy who looked young for his grade. Paul (as his teachers called him) did average work in school, so there never seemed to be any particular reason for concern. Each year he was advanced to the next grade and his cumulative record folder was filled with such comments as "an average pupil—a bit small for his grade."

When most of the girls and later the boys began to show signs of more rapid growth before and during the onset of pubescence, Paul remained small. The difference in his size became more and more apparent and began to be somewhat of a disadvantage. Soon Paul was "Midge" to all but his teachers and family. Although the nick-name was usually used without aggressive intent it did serve to set Paul apart and to make him more acutely aware of his small stature with its implications of inferiority.

As the class interests changed, Paul tried to keep up with his age mates but his adjustment was not always easy. He went to dances after basketball games but usually stood around with the boys all evening. Most girls were a head taller than he was and he would feel ridiculous dancing with them. He was appointed manager of the football team in his senior year, but the gesture had the flavor of being mascot. He seldom engaged in team activities and the only success he experienced was in swimming and ice skating.

His high school teachers considered him a "low-average" student. They often reported to the guidance counselors that Paul seemed to lack initiative and maturity of judgment. Paul looked forward to his course in chemistry at the beginning of his junior year because he had always enjoyed his chemistry set at home and he expected this to be his favorite subject. However, the chemistry teacher reported that Paul did not tend to business during laboratory periods and his class-work was only fair. His record for chemistry during each of the marking periods was average or lower. Paul decided not to enroll in physics.

Paul finished high school with a rank of thirty-seven in a class of eighty-two. He entered a large liberal arts college where his father had been graduated. He decided to try again in chemistry with the tentative plan of taking a premedical course if he were successful. He failed college chemistry, was marked D in college algebra, and withdrew after one year because of poor work and lack of objective. He went to work for a small magazine published in his home city.

The name of "Midge" went with Paul to the magazine job and stayed with him in spite of the fact that in three years at the new job he grew four inches taller and gained thirty-two pounds. He found that he wanted to know much more as he worked with the staff at the publishing house, and he spent most of his time reading widely. He asked to read manuscripts submitted to the magazine. His comments concerning the writing proved helpful to the editors, and they recommended him for a better position when there was an opening. Paul decided to return to college instead where he majored in English, graduating as an honor student in that department. His work in other courses was satisfactory. Upon graduation he was recommended for a good position on the staff of another magazine where he is enjoying exceptional success.

Paul's good vocational adjustment is not typical of the late maturing boy. Jones (1957) found that at age thirty-three, even though physical differences between early and late maturers have disappeared, the late maturers were as a group more impulsive, rebellious, dependent, and fewer members of this group had made good vocational adjustments. Another case study demonstrating the interaction of physical factors with other aspects of development is to be found in Stolz's (1940) report entitled *Shorty Comes to Terms with Himself.*

PHYSICAL ILLNESS, PHYSIOLOGICAL, AND SENSORY DEFECTS

In spite of the remarkable advances in medicine during the past several decades, illness and physical disability are still widely prevalent and present a problem to the teacher. One health survey (Collins et al., 1955) found that in a population of 1000 children ages five to fourteen, the incidence of illness averaged more than one illness per child in a year and almost three fourths of these illnesses were of a severity such as to keep the child out of school for a period of ten days or more. Added to this number are the many children with permanent physical disabilities and the many with visual and auditory impairment. One can readily see that the dimensions of the problem are of great magnitude. Although it is not the teacher's role to make a medical diagnosis, the information that the teacher is able to gather about a particular child may be vital to the physician who views his patient as more than a physio-chemical system. Most long-term therapy recommendations will involve some adjustments in the school program. It is therefore important for the teacher to have some understanding of the child who suffers from illness, physical handicap, and sensory impairment.

It should be noted that a child with a physical problem does not lose his individuality. The adjustments to physical deficiencies are as varied as those made by children of good health. A child who might under ordinary circumstances tend to be shy, or attention seeking, will exaggerate this tendency when coping with chronic ill-health or a physical handicap. Also, the presence of a health problem may introduce feelings that would ordinarily not occur. For example, a child who must undergo surgery or experience prolonged bed rest, as in the case of rheumatic fever, will show fear and anxiety as well as guilt. Many children assume that the illness is the consequence of disobedience or naughtiness (Connor, 1958). A teacher who is sensitive to these possibilities and who is accepting of the child's feelings, will help alleviate some of the problems associated with these emotions.

The discussion here is limited to some of the problems associated with neurological dysfunction, orthopedic or crippling disorders, and sensory defects. For more extensive discussion of this general topic the reader is referred to Barker et al. (1953), Cruickshank and Johnson (1958) and Wright (1960).

Neurological Dysfunction

Extensive damage to the central nervous system leads to extreme effects resulting in mental deficiency, paralysis, or uncontrolled muscle activity. Recent research has shown that damage to the central nervous system may be of a less dramatic nature also. Pasamanick and his associates (1956a, 1956b), and Kawi and Pasamanick (1959) have postulated that brain damage incurred in the prenatal period and during the birth process may lead to a "gradient of injury." In the last cited study the authors conclude:

> Such findings have led to the formulation of a hypothesis that there is a continuum of reproductive casualty with a lethal component consisting of abortions, stillbirths and neonatal deaths and a sublethal component consisting of cerebral palsy, epilepsy, mental deficiency, and behavior disorders in children. This investigation suggests that some of the reading disorders of childhood constitute a component of this continuum (page 61).

The findings in these and other studies suggest strongly that some of the difficulties manifested by some children such as distractability, clumsiness, and inability to master school learning tasks, may not be due to simple motivational causes as is so often assumed. They may have their roots in neurological damage. The central nervous system serves as an integrating mechanism and it is possible that when minimal damage occurs, the child's handicap may not become manifest until demands for high level integration within the nervous system arise. This would be the case when the child begins formal school learning.

A word of caution is necessary here. The diagnosis of minimal brain damage requires a very careful medical and psychological study of the child. The notification of parents should be left to those who are able to interpret the findings of the various tests. The teacher's role would consist of suggesting to parents that restlessness, hyperactivity, and distractability might be the basis for a thorough physical examination. A teacher who approaches a school learning or behavior problem with more than the assumption that the child is improperly motivated, will be more accepting and considerate of the child's needs. On the other hand, the teacher should not assume that all classroom problems arise directly from neurological dysfunction. It should be noted, however, that awareness of this problem, both medically and educationally, is very recent and the suggestions offered here are tentative.

One teacher (Freidus, 1959) described a child with brain damage. His learning and behavior patterns are peculiar. He doesn't respond the way other children do and he causes the teacher to "go home exhausted and confused and puzzled every afternoon." The medical report on the child may have contained a statement such as "post-encephalitic" or "diffused brain damage." She goes on to say that there are great differences among these children. Some are hyperactive, others are phlegmatic. Some are highly verbal but cannot seem to perform even a simple task; others can carry out complex routines but cannot verbalize. Some enter into activities with enthusiasm but stay with them for about a minute and give up, while others can't seem to get started until the teacher warms them up, "gets them rolling—and this may take ten or fifteen minutes—and then they're in business." In general, children with this kind of brain damage present problems of distractability, poor memory, short attention span, and perceptual distortions, all of which lead to learning difficulties. These problems can easily be mistaken for impertinence, wilfulness, or indifference.

The treatment for a child of this sort will usually consist of medication, special remedial education, psychotherapy for the child, and guidance for the parents. The area in which the teacher can help is in providing a highly structured, nonpunitive environment. School administrators must recognize that if a teacher is willing and able to work with a child who demands constant attention, then he will not be able to work with a large number of children in the class. Freidus states that the teacher of the child with neurological dysfunction must maintain objectivity and must have an inordinate amount of patience. She goes on to say the following:

We must learn what to look for specifically in the way of perceptual problems. . . . We must be willing—and this is important—to search for and recognize the child's mechanisms for avoiding failure, mechanisms for covering up an anticipated inadequacy, mechanisms for avoiding anxiety—compensating mechanisms of all kinds. For example, the very verbal young man who can talk such an impressive line one day heard me start to cough. He said, "Uh, why don't you—uh—you know, down the hatch—uh, you know, those poison pellets you've got?" Well, this may sound like humor, but it wasn't exactly humor—it was that he couldn't think of the words to say, "Why don't you take a cough drop?" He couldn't think of the words, so he took a fast detour—he is always doing that. It's sad. It's doing things the roundabout way because he can't do them the simple, direct way. . . .

We have to break things down and structure them step by step and get the child into the habit of structuring step by step as he goes along. It's not easy, and it must be done individually (pages 20-21).

Orthopedic Handicaps

Although orthopedic handicaps do not represent a very common disability, they do serve as a clear illustration of the effects of physical deviation on the psychological functioning of the individual. With some exceptions, our understanding of the crippled child will apply to any child who deviates physically in any noticeable way as for example extreme obesity, malformation of teeth, the wearing of a hearing aid, and the like.

A physical disability does not in and of itself lead to personality distortion, but it does introduce an obstacle to adjustment. Some children can encounter such an obstacle and overcome it without serious emotional disturbance. Others do not adjust well to their handicap; however the reactions to it will vary. A government pamphlet prepared by Lesser (1952) describes the various kinds of reactions of children who are not well adjusted to their handicaps. Some children interpret their disability as being due to lack of devotion or care from significant persons in their lives. They feel that they are victims of injustice. They may express these feelings in withdrawal or in open hostility. This places a burden on parents and teachers. They must accept these feelings and at the same time demonstrate by patience and unobtrusive indications of friendliness and understanding that true devotion does exist and that the world is just and trustworthy.

Other children respond to their handicap by being proud and sometimes rebellious. They will reject any offers of assistance and will interpret these as signs of pity. They feel that their disability is degrading and their behavior can be viewed as an attempt to generate respect from others. Parents and teachers can help the child by never being patronizing and by showing signs of appreciation for the child's courage and strength.

Another reaction to physical handicap is that of excessive depend-ence and demand. These children find it difficult to act independently even in areas where their disability is not relevant. Adopting a role of helplessness seems to assure them of the amount of attention they desire. This kind of behavior may provoke some rejection from those caring for the child and this in turn induces the child to act more dependently. In helping the child with this kind of reaction the adult must combine a great amount of attention with a friendly but insistent demand that the child contribute to the effort being made on his behalf. The child must learn through experience that the nonfulfillment of his demands is not due to lack of love but because the reality of the world is such that not all of one's demands can be fulfilled. In addition parents and teach-ers must direct the child into a new awareness. Such children may have come to feel that only by being helpless can they generate kindliness. Parents and teachers must help them discover that striving and achieve-ment can be more greatly rewarding in terms of admiration and affec-tion from others as well as in self-respect. There is also the danger that the afflicted child will become narcissistically attached to his disability. The teacher can prevent this by avoiding undue attention to the child's impairment and by treating the child as an ordinary individual.

Not all teachers can work constructively with children who have a physical disability. Wright (1960) surveys the various attitudes held toward persons with atypical physique and shows that many of the non-disabled unconsciously believe that crippling is associated with evil and sin. It is very likely that many teachers would be repelled by marked physical deviation and this feeling would obviously be harmful for the afflicted child. Teachers who can perceive the child as one with a disa-bility that requires accommodation to that disability alone, rather than as a generally disabled child, will help develop a personality that is re-ality-oriented and with a sense of adequacy.

Drawing on a publication of the National Foundation for Infan-tile Paralysis and the Citizenship Education Project (1956), Wright (1960) summarizes a list of suggestions for the teachers of the intermedi-ate elementary grades in guiding their students toward more realistic and favorable attitudes toward persons with disabilities. Wright lists the fol-lowing:

> 1. Use of a social-distance-scale technique [see Chapter 8] to indicate the feelings of the children about boys and girls with various kinds of dis-abilities as portrayed in pictures.
> 2. Discussion of the children's ratings on the social-distance scale.
> 3. Discussion with the children of stereotyped statements about people with disabilities, such as "I feel I should be especially friendly to people like that" or "A person like that can't do the things other people do."

4. Seeking further information by arranging discussion with local physicians and nurses, and if possible with an employer who welcomes employees with handicaps, contacting national and local disability organizations and reviewing the lives of individuals who coped successfully with their disabilities.

5. Completion of a picture story involving a boy with a disability in order that the children may apply the knowledge and constructive attitudes which it is hoped have been accrued in some measure through the preceding activities. The stories are then acted out.

6. Discussion of an incident involving a girl with a disability in order to give the class an opportunity to evaluate the attitudes of someone else toward a person with a disability (pages 268-269).

It can be readily seen that this kind of teaching procedure is another illustration of the teaching for values that was discussed in Chapter 6.

Sensory Defects

Perception and thinking, the processes whereby particular meaning and significance are derived from our environment, depend upon sensation. Sensation in turn is dependent upon the proper functioning of a complex sensory apparatus. Such proper functioning in the case of each sense modality, such as vision or hearing, may be viewed as consisting of a number of levels. First a specific form of energy must be received, focused, and concentrated. In the case of the eye we rely on cornea, pupil, and lens; in the case of the ear we have the outer ear with the external auditory canal, the middle ear with the eardrum, and the chain of small bones known as ossicles. These serve to focus the energy of light or the sound. The second level depends upon the sensory nerve endings, which when stimulated by the concentrated energy, convert it to neural energy. This is accomplished in the case of the eye by the rods and the cones distributed in the retina and in the case of the ear by the nerve cells located in the cochlea. The next stage is the process of transmitting this neural energy by means of nerves; in vision the optic nerve and in hearing the acoustic nerve. Finally the appropriate area of the central nervous system is activated and the integration of the various neural impulses takes place. A defect or loss of sensation may result from the malfunction of the sensory apparatus at any of the stages. The discussion here is limited to certain defects of vision and hearing that are commonly encountered in school.

VISION   Almost every adjustment in and out of school depends in some measure on the sense of sight. The development of concepts and generalizations very often begins with the visual experience. Defective vision is therefore a problem of great concern to school. Furthermore, a large number of children (nearly 40 percent) suffer from some form of

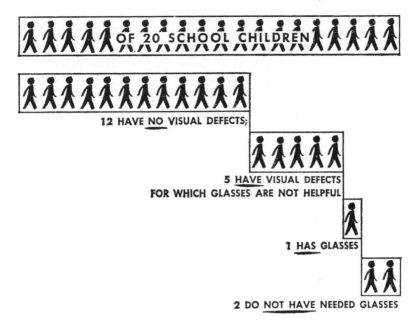

OF 20 SCHOOL CHILDREN

12 HAVE NO VISUAL DEFECTS;

5 HAVE VISUAL DEFECTS
FOR WHICH GLASSES ARE NOT HELPFUL

1 HAS GLASSES

2 DO NOT HAVE NEEDED GLASSES

FIGURE 12.6 *Distribution of visual defects among school children. From H. B. English,* Dynamics of Child Development, *copyright © New York: Holt, Rinehart and Winston, Inc., 1961, p. 272.*

visual deficiency. Figure 12.6 shows the incidence of visual defects in school children.

Defective vision can result from abnormality at any of the stages in the visual process. The condition of the cornea, the shape and flexibility of the lens, the function of the rods or cones in the retina, the shape of the eyeball, the condition of the optic nerve, the coordination of the two eyes, these and many other factors determine the effectiveness of the visual process. Many visual deficiencies have not been fully studied so that we do not know what, if any, adjustments are necessary. Color blindness is one such deficiency. At the present time we have no educational literature that considers in what ways, if any, the color-blind student is handicapped in his learning experiences. On the other hand many visual defects are easily detected and corrected. It is these that we shall consider here.

The teacher is often the first person to note the symptoms of visual difficulty. Since so much of school work demands the use of the eyes, visual adjustment that may have been adequate for out-of-school activities may break down in school. The symptoms of visual difficulty are as follows: generalized tension when doing visual work; poor sitting posture involving tilting of head or head thrust forward; body tense when looking at blackboard or charts at front of room; noticeable movements of head while reading; frequent rubbing of eyes; avoidance of close visual activities; frequent loss of place in reading (Knox, 1953). These symptoms of visual difficulty may arise from a number of causes that can be determined by a careful examination. It should be noted that the *Snellen Chart* or its modification the *E Chart,* which is most commonly used as a screening device, can only detect nearsightedness and is of little use in the detection of other visual deficiencies. Nearsightedness or myopia is seldom associated with school-learning difficulties. The child who is myopic has difficulty in seeing clearly those objects that are at a distance. He tends to bring his reading matter close to his eyes. He may have difficulty in reading the blackboard and he may suffer from fatigue of the eye muscles after prolonged reading. However, the nearsighted child experiences even greater difficulty when playing games that require distance vision and if he suffers from no other visual deficiencies will tend to spend much of his time in reading and study.

The other refractive errors (deficiency in the focusing of the light energy) are astigmatism, blurring of vision due to the uneven curvature of the cornea; and hyeropia or farsightedness. Astigmatism when corrected by eyeglasses may result in better than average reading. Bond and Tinker (1957), after reviewing various studies in which good and poor readers are compared, conclude that reading disability cases show a high incidence of hyperopia or farsightedness. English (1961) points out that the discomfort arising from close discrimination in the case of hyperopia may lead to irritability and avoidance of school work. The child is likely to associate this discomfort with the place and the activity in which it occurs, namely school and reading. He may find that while engaging in sports and play that he achieves more success and he feels more comfortable. This complex of influences leads then to lack of interest and poor performance in school work.

Other visual difficulties arise from the lack of coordination in the use of the two eyes. These include muscular imbalance, technically known as strabismus and commonly referred to as cross-eyes or wall-eyes, and slowness of fusion of the images in both the eyes. The child who suffers from one or both of these deficiencies may be seriously handicapped in adjusting to school learning activities and unlike the child with hyperopia will also be uncomfortable in tasks requiring vision of distant objects.

The teacher should not be disappointed if the correction of a visual defect does not lead directly to improvement in school performance. "Once the correction has occurred, other aspects of the disability which have arisen through handicapped learning must be identified also and appropriate remedial training instituted to achieve the total improvement in reading that now has become possible" (Bond and Tinker, 1957, page 90).

The teacher needs to be alert to signs of visual discomfort, to re-fer children whose vision appears to be deficient, to arrange lighting so that glare, shadow, or insufficient light are avoided, to arrange seating so that no child's vision is strained, to provide reading materials with type of appropriate size, and to vary activities so that children's eyes do not become fatigued from prolonged close work. In some instances the teacher will need to give some attention to adjustment problems of the child who must wear glasses and feels sensitive about this.

HEARING   Although hearing deficiences are less common than visual defects, occurring in about 5 to 10 percent of children, they are more likely to be overlooked and the symptoms are likely to be mistaken as being due to other causes. For example the child may be considered inattentive or disobedient when the difficulty may be due to defective hearing. The hard-of-hearing child may also be judged to be dull be-cause of the language retardation that frequently accompanies hearing deficiency. Much school work requires the coordination of visual and auditory processes. The teacher presents a visual stimulus such as a word and says it orally. The child who cannot hear the word clearly will have difficulty in learning the necessary relationship. It is no wonder then that Fiedler (1949) found that children with impaired hearing were named by teachers more frequently as presenting classroom problems than were normal children.

Here again we have a situation in which the reaction of others to the handicap takes on as much or more significance as the handicap itself. The teacher should suspect hearing impairment if the child mis-understands directions, frequently requires repetition of statements, or seems inattentive. If the child complains of ringing or buzzing in the head or earache, the teacher should refer the child for medical atten-tion. Other signs of hearing strain can be noticed by the child's tilting of the head, turning one ear toward a speaker or answering to a name other than his own.

If the presence of hearing loss is established the child may require special attention in speech-reading instruction, auditory training, extra tutoring in school subjects and in the use of a hearing aid. O'Connor and Streng (1950) suggest that favorable seating in the classroom should be arranged for the slightly hard-of-hearing child. If the loss is greater in one ear, the more efficient ear should face the side of the room from which speech emanates. In general the teacher would do well to exercise patience and to reduce the unfavorable psychological impact of inappropriate expectations usually imposed on the acoustically handi-capped.

PSYCHOSOMATIC DISORDERS

Up to this point the possible impact of physical form or deficit upon the psychological functioning of the individual has been considered. This relationship has been called *somatopsychological* or *somatopsychic*. The reverse of the process is the *psychosomatic* problem—the physiological correlates of emotional life. In the preceding chapter it was briefly pointed out that when a person is emotionally aroused, the various physiological systems, such as the circulatory, digestive, and respiratory, are affected. These changes are ordinarily transitory and they can be useful in the total adjustive process. When the individual is subjected to prolonged emotional stress, the reaction of the autonomic nervous system, which is useful in mobilizing the body for short-term emergencies, is overextended and this ultimately leads to tissue damage and disruption of the physiological processes. Although the underlying basis for the disorder is psychological, the symptom and the discomfort are caused by immediate and actual organic factors.

In a comprehensive survey of psychosomatic medicine, Weiss and English (1949) estimate that about one third of the patients who consult a physician "do not have any bodily disease to account for their illness" and another one third "have symptoms that are in part dependent upon emotional factors." It is becoming increasingly clear that when the individual experiences long-term emotional tension significant changes in body chemistry occur that may be the basis for organic symptoms.

Selye (1956) in describing the *general-adaptation-syndrome* has provided an experimentally based theoretical framework for the understanding of the psychosomatic reaction. Briefly stated, Selye's theory postulates that when the organism is subjected to prolonged stress either psychological or physical, the pattern of physiological response changes and three levels of reaction appear. The body's first response to stress is the alarm reaction. When the individual first meets a stressful situation such as loss of love, threat of rejection, or accident, a change in body chemistry occurs that leads to a feeling of generalized malaise, chills, headaches, nausea, and a loss of energy. If the stress situation continues, further physiological changes occur and the alarm reaction is then followed by the stage of resistance. During this stage the bodily resources seem to be mobilized so as to resist the particular stress involved and the physical symptoms seem to subside. However, during the stage of resistance the tolerance for other stresses is lowered. If the stress provoking situation continues the stage of resistance is followed by a stage of exhaustion. The symptoms of physiological dysfunction that occurred in the stage of alarm reappear and other organic symptoms develop.

The teacher must not be deceived by the apparent toughness of some children who have been subjected to severe environmental stresses. The appearance of toughness may be viewed as the stage of resistance in the general-adaptation-syndrome. If the stress provoking situations are not removed very serious harm can come to the child. Furthermore, the person who has suffered severe deprivation and stress is much more susceptible to other minor strains in adjustment. There are many, including parents and teachers, who believe that the child should be trained to meet the inevitable frustrations and disappointments of life by being subjected to failure during childhood. Although challenge and the overcoming of challenge by application are certainly useful experiences, the severe constant strain of failure can have harmful consequences. The development of a healthy personality should not be viewed as resulting from a toughening up process but rather analogous to the effects of diet on a healthy physiology. The body does not learn to do without essential nutrients; on the contrary, if these are lacking for a long period of time the result will be physical breakdown and illness. So, too, in personality development, affection, recognition, acceptance, and success serve as the essential ingredients for a well-integrated personality. The person cannot function effectively if deprived of these for extended periods.

Prolonged emotional tension can result in a variety of physical symptoms. Why the tension should lead to one symptom in one person and to another symptom in another is not clear. It probably depends on a number of factors such as the developmental period during which the stress was imposed, constitutional factors, and the kind of emotion (anger or fear) that is aroused. It should be pointed out further that the somatic symptoms listed below can occur as a result of infection or other purely organic causes as well as from psychological stress.

Many psychosomatic disorders are associated with the functioning of the gastro-intestinal system. Being fed and being loved are closely related in infancy and we never completely outgrow the equation of food with love (Grinker and Robbins, 1954). As previously noted, the achievement of bowel control is associated with the development of autonomy and independence as well as with assertiveness and aggression. In the psychoanalytic description of personality development, the first two phases through which we grow are called the *oral* and the *anal* periods. According to this view the experiences associated with the gastro-intestinal functions are assumed to be of great importance in determining the kind of adult personality. Certain kinds of psychological disturbances can lead to gastro-intestinal disturbances. As for example:

1. *Inordinate appetite.*   Excessive eating can lead to obesity. Bruch (1947), who studied a large number of obese children clinically, concluded that in the vast majority of cases the parent-child relationship was a dis-

turbed one. Once obesity develops it can become a somatopsychological problem as well, leading to teasing and rejection by other children.

2. *Loss of appetite.* This may be associated with vomiting. This symptom may be based on strong wishes for attention and love, resentment and jealousy, as well as guilt feelings.

3. *Chronic constipation or diarrhea.* These symptoms are usually based on problems of dependence, resentment, depression, and difficulty in accepting responsibility. Of chronic psychogenic constipation Saul (1944) says the following: "It results from a typical constellation, in which there are usually feelings of being rejected and unloved, distrust, especially regarding dependence upon others, and a pessimistic outlook" (page 279).

4. *Peptic ulcer.* Although this disorder is not common in children, there is good evidence for the belief that its occurrence in the adult is based upon childhood experiences. It seems to occur in adults whose childhood was characterized by overindulgence or by over-bearing and demanding parents.

Psychosomatic disturbances can also affect the respiratory system. Although most respiratory difficulties are caused by virus organisms or allergic hypersensitivity to specific substances, there is good reason to believe that psychological tension produces tissue changes that provide a favorable medium for the virus or the allergen (Grinker and Robbins, 1954). Two respiratory disturbances that may have a psychosomatic component are common colds and asthma:

1. *Common colds.* One study has shown that the incidence of colds is in part related to emotional tension. In comparing eight preschool children from broken homes with a matched group of eight children from well-adjusted homes, it was found that the incidence of colds in the former group was twice as great as in the latter. The investigator feels "that in some cases internal tensions due to psychologically traumatic situations may be operating among other factors contributing to individual cold susceptibility" (Despert, 1944 cited in Stone and Onqué, 1959).

2. *Asthma.* Various studies have shown that most asthmatic children are insecure and overanxious. This personality condition is the reflection of extreme parental overprotection. It should be pointed out that an asthmatic attack is a terrifying experience for both the child and the parent and the overprotection on the part of the parent may be due to realistic concern. However, in many cases the overprotective attitude precedes the onset of the asthmatic condition. As pointed out in the next chapter, parental overprotection is frequently a reaction formation resulting from the unconscious repression of strong feelings of rejection. Miller and Baruch (1948) have shown that maternal rejection is a sig-

nificant factor in allergic conditions of childhood. There is danger in the too glib assumption about the psychosomatic relationship. Parents who must care for an asthmatic or allergic child need least of all to be further burdened by the aspersion that they have rejected their children.

Emotional tension can be a factor in making the skin sensitive to allergens and can also lead to self inflicted sores resulting from scratching and picking. The condition known as essential hypertension of the circulatory system may likewise have a psychosomatic aspect. As in the case of peptic ulcer, the symptom of essential hypertension is not a common condition in childhood. However, the pattern of maladjustment leading to this condition is developed in childhood. The emotional condition that lies behind essential hypertension is in the improper management of feelings of anger and aggression (White, 1956).

Other symptoms affecting the endocrine system, the genitourinary system, and musculature can develop as a result of prolonged emotional tension. These are not all the possible symptoms that are assumed to have a psychosomatic component, but a few to make the teacher aware of the complexity of the human organism and to underscore the fact that physical and physiological functioning are part and parcel of the total person including how he feels about himself and others. The symptom in a psychosomatic ailment is real and should not be equated with malingering or feigning of illness in order to avoid an unpleasant situation. The teacher's understanding of the psychosomatic relationship should lead to a classroom atmosphere in which states of extreme anxiety and excessive tension are not prolonged.

PERCEPTUAL-MOTOR SKILLS

By perceptual-motor skills is meant the coordination of perceptual processes with motor responses. All observable responses, whether habitual or cognitively directed, are essentially perceptual motor in character, in that the motor component is in some way tied in with the perceptual component. Thus in walking, dancing, reading, writing, speaking, and so on, the ongoing activity is dependent in part on cognitive direction, in part on stimuli from the moving muscles themselves, and on stimuli from the external environment. Cronbach (1954) refers to the stimulus component as a *cue* and defines it "as any stimulus from outside or from within the body that helps a person recognize a situation or recognize the correct moment for action." Cronbach points out that every perceptual-motor act consists of tries and corrections and as the performance becomes more skillful, the tries are not carried out as far and the corrections are introduced sooner and the response is not carried back as far in the opposite direction. He refers to this total process of sensing and correcting as *feedback*. Even when the response is developed to a high level of skill and is highly habituated, as in the adult walking, the feedback process is essential. When the customary feedback mechanisms are interfered with the behavior becomes distorted and awkward. The reader may experience this result of interference with feedback by tracing a pattern in a mirror using an arrangement where the tracing hand is covered from direct view and can be seen only in the mirror. Smith (1962), working with various types of delayed sensory feedback procedures, proposes a "neurogeometric" theory based on innate neural mechanisms to account for perceptual-motor integration. This theory posits that certain neurons (single nerve cells) of the central nervous system are sensitive to differences in neural activity at different points of the neuron endings. "Each such neuron is related to two specific points, either within the same or different receptor systems, and is activated when some inequality of stimulation exists between two points." This theory raises a number of questions many of which can only be answered by further developmental research on direct, distorted, and delayed sensory feedback.

For purposes of this discussion the perceptual-motor skills are divided into three categories. The first group consists of those skills that are acquired early, apparently with little systematic guidance or teaching. The child acquires skill in locomotion and becomes able to speak largely as a result of maturational processes within the usual adult environment. The child comes to school with a vast array of these skills developed at least in their fundamentals. The task of the school is to build on this foundation and sometimes to remedy faulty habits.

The second category of perceptual-motor skills are those in which the school has a primary interest because they support the achievement of the central objective of the educational program. Handwriting and eye movements in reading are good examples of this kind of supporting skill. The child's ability to read and to write is of course dependent on many other developments but these perceptual-motor aspects are most certainly important. A later section of this chapter is devoted to the matter of handwriting.

The third category of perceptual-motor skills consists of those skills that are systematically taught more or less for their own sake. This applies to certain aspects of the curriculum in industrial arts, home economics, and physical education. In these courses the student learns how to use tools, to perform specific motor acts and skilled movements. This is not to say that the person becomes a physical or motor being during these parts of the school day and a thinking, ideational being during others. It is only that the starting point is primarily motor in one case and primarily verbal in the other. In our society as more and more time becomes available for leisure and as less and less work activity demands the use of motor function, the person is likely to need recreational outlets that depend on motor skills. It is important that the school provide opportunities for the acquisition of motor skills. No special section is devoted to this topic because evidence from studies on the learning of perceptual-motor skills has been used to support the various points made about learning and development. The work of the teacher in industrial arts, home economics, or physical education must be guided by the same principles as apply to the teaching of other subject matter.

The general pattern of development in the perceptual-motor area is very similar to that presented in Chapter 3 in the discussion of how children learn. Many of the same considerations apply. In Chapter 3 the terms discrimination and generalization were used to describe how the child gradually comes to deal in an organized and consistent fashion with the world of ideas and concepts. In the acquisition of motor skill similar processes are even more obviously at work. The infant's motor response is undifferentiated. For example the sounds he makes with his vocal mechanism are varied but unpatterned. With time and experience, through a process of imitation and reinforcement, certain sounds disappear while certain sequences and patterns become established. This is largely a process of *differentiation* and *integration* of motor response. These two processes describe the development of motor response as it progresses from a disorganized whole to differentiated part responses and to the integration of these parts into patterned and organized wholes. The same processes are at work in the development of all motor responses. Of course this development depends also on development in the perceptual area.

The principle of readiness (discussed in Chapter 3) derives much of its evidence from studies on motor development. A number of studies have shown that the acquisition of certain motor skills is little influenced by the opportunities for practice. Other studies have shown that training and practice do have a beneficial effect on the development of motor skills. All the evidence seems to point to two basic principles. The first principle is that there is a "critical phase" for providing training opportunities. Jersild (1960) describes it as follows:

> A phase of growth may be "critical" because what happens during this phase may have a marked effect on the later course of development. It appears that certain types of behavior may especially be influenced by what happens at a particular time in the sequence of development and that there are times when the organism is especially vulnerable to harm (page 23).

The second principle relating training to readiness is stated in the form of an hypothesis called *stimulus-induced maturation*. This hypothesis suggests that once the maturational process is induced, training becomes a less significant factor in the development of the skill. Baldwin (1955) considers the implications of this hypothesis in the following statement:

If such a hypothesis is adopted, it would be reasonable to suggest further that the sensitivity and responsiveness of the organism to stimulation and challenge depend in large part on the level of maturation that the organism has already attained. A further implication of the point of view is that some of the normally expected abilities of the adult in any culture depend upon the occurrence of such stimulus-induced maturation. The culture normally induces the maturation of special abilities that are required in that culture. Because of this dependence upon stimulus-induced maturation, an impoverishment of the environment that strips it of its challenging characteristics deprives the organism of an opportunity to mature. The result is a retarded child or an adult with unrealized potentialities (page 392).

Most studies of training in motor skills conclude that training in motor activity before the neural mechanisms have attained a state of readiness, is useless. This principle is not altogether applicable to the school learning situation where the activity itself is so complex that training in related skills leading up to the larger skill is possible, and the period of readiness can be induced. This is not to suggest that all individual differences can be eliminated but only that the whole range of performance can be improved.

We see in motor development what appear to be natural sequences for the appearance of certain behavior forms (the importance of sequence was discussed in Chapter 3). These sequences have been called the laws of developmental direction. Development proceeds from the head region to the tail region, from the top downward. This is called the *cephalo-caudal* direction of development. It also proceeds from the central axis of the body out toward the extremities. This is called the *proximo-distal* direction of development. That is to say, the motor skills that depend upon coordination of the larger muscles in the shoulders (nearer the central axis) will appear before the coordination skills of the fingers. The child will come to use his hands (nearer the head region) before he can use his legs. If we examine our direction for handwriting we note that we proceed from the top of the page downward and for right-handed individuals from the central axis to the extremity (proximo-distally). This is discussed further in the next section.

The Teaching of Handwriting

As previously noted, handwriting is a fundamental skill for which the school has primary responsibility. It is obvious that the child must learn to write if he is to be literate and if he is to be able to communicate his thoughts beyond the restrictions of oral communication. Although attention in this brief discussion of handwriting is directed toward the form, we must not lose sight of the fact that the content and the meaning of what is written is far more significant than the form.

After we have learned to write we are likely to forget how complex is the handwriting act. Freeman (1954) points out that when we write across the page, the pressure of the fingers on the writing instrument and the pressure of the pen or pencil point on the paper, are continually changing. These changes in pressure are quite complicated and delicate. The speed of movement is likewise continually changing as we write. The rate at which we form each letter varies as we make the various turns and as we change direction. If pressure and speed changes are wrong for the particular letter, the movement is awkward and the form of the letter is distorted. If one observes a child who is just beginning to write, one will note a great deal of irrelevant movement, for example tongue and legs become involved as energy irradiates through all response outlets. In order for the child to use the feedback mechanism so that the writing becomes smoothly articulated, he must have the appropriate level of biological maturation and he must have opportunity for practice. Eventually when handwriting becomes habituated the writer is able to make the necessary changes in his muscles and joints without being aware that he is doing so.

The teacher's responsibility in helping the child acquire handwriting skill is a continuing one, at least through most of the elementary grades. The purpose of attending to the details of the writing act is that the child will be able to produce legible writing at a reasonable speed and with some facility. The approximate average rates of letter production are given in Table 12.2. In Figure 12.7 are shown samples of good quality handwriting for grades two, four, and six.

TABLE 12.2   APPROXIMATE AVERAGES OF SPEED OF WRITING IN LETTERS PER MINUTE FOR EACH GRADE

Grade	2	3	4	5	6	7	8
Speed	30	40	50	60	67	74	80

Source: F. N. Freeman, "Teaching Handwriting," *What Research Says to the Teacher Series,* no. 4. Washington D. C.: National Education Association, 1954, p. 4. (By permission of the Department of Classroom Teachers and the American Educational Research Association.)

There are three aspects of handwriting that the teacher must keep in mind in order to help the child achieve the rates indicated in Table 12.2, or higher ones, and to write legibly and comfortably. These aspects are, the placement of the paper, the grip on the writing instrument, and the writing movement. The recommendations made here apply to the right-handed child. The left-handed child is considered in a separate discussion. The paper should be placed on the desk so that the top tilts downward to the left and the bottom of the paper forms an angle of approximately 30° with the front edge of the desk. This paper placement is appropriate for cursive writing. For manuscript writing

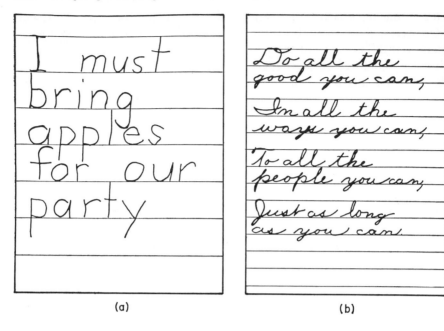

I must
bring
apples
for our
party

(a)

Do all the
good you can,
In all the
ways you can,
To all the
people you can,
Just as long
as you can.

(b)

When you go out
riding
On your horse
or bike;
When you go out
walking
Or when you
take a hike;
Morning, noon or
night;
Keep to the left
of traffic
Not to the right!

(c)

FIGURE 12.7 *Samples of good quality handwriting at grades two (a), four (b), and six (c); 50 percent of the original size. Bureau of Elementary Curriculum Development,* Handwriting, *Albany, N. Y.: New York State Education Department, 1955.*

the bottom edge of the paper should be almost parallel with the front of the body. The grip and writing posture are related. Freeman (1954) describes the recommended posture and grip as follows:

The forearm should rest on the muscle pad at its largest part and should be able to move freely from left to right to carry the hand across the page, and to a lesser degree in any direction to contribute to forming the letters. The hand should rest on the last joint of the last two fingers and should slide easily upon them. It should be turned somewhat to the right, but not more than half way, so that the wrist is at an angle of not more than 45°.

The penholder should be grasped lightly by the thumb and the first two fingers, with the first finger on top, the second finger at the side and the same distance from the point, and the thumb above the first finger. The fingers should grasp the penholder not less than an inch from the penpoint (pages 18-19).

The manner in which the index finger grips the writing instrument is indicative of the pressure being applied. Some children achieve satisfactory handwriting with the index finger lying more or less flat against the pen or pencil, most, however, prefer to have the instrument rest almost in the crotch between the thumb and the index finger with the index finger slightly hunched up on the pencil. There is no reason to interfere with individual preference in regard to this aspect of the grip.

On the matter of handwriting movement there has been much controversy in the past. Some contended that movement should be exclusively in the arm. Beginning writers seem to resist this movement and generally resort to finger movement. If the writer is not helped to achieve a combination of arm and finger movement, the letters will be difficult to read and the person will not be able to write for lengthy periods without fatigue. The movement that combines both arm and finger in the formation of letters and words is the one generally recommended.

In the earlier literature on handwriting there is a disagreement as to whether the handwriting should be vertical or slanted. It is now generally agreed that a moderately slanted style is preferable.

The teacher needs to decide whether to use manuscript (separated letters similar to print) or cursive (connected letters) style of handwriting. The vast majority of schools introduce the child to handwriting by way of manuscript. This choice would appear to be a wise one for the following reasons. (1) Manuscript writing requires simpler movements and children can generally write legibly at an earlier age. (2) Manuscript writing is perceptually simpler inasmuch as the child does not need to learn how the letter appears in different kinds of settings or when joined to different letters. (3) Because the letters in manuscript writing are similar to those which the child will encounter in reading, the writing activity supports the development of discrimination in reading. (4) The child will be better able to note whether or not he has spelled a word correctly when using manuscript writing, that is, the feedback is clearer.

Once the reading skill has been well established and manuscript writing has been mastered, the child can be readily trained to the cursive style. The time at which the change from manuscript to cursive is to take place depends on the level of the child's motor and over-all educational development. The research literature would suggest that an educational achievement level of about the middle of grade two, is the appropriate level for the change-over. If the teacher prefers to have all the pupils in the class change at once rather than to provide individualized cursive handwriting instruction, then he ought to wait until the first half of the third grade in order to be sure that nearly all the children will make the change easily.

In working toward a legible style, the teacher must recognize that the quality of the handwriting will continue to improve and that it will continue to develop its individual characteristics well into the adolescent years. Also, some aspects of handwriting, as is true of all manner of perceptual-motor expression, are the outward manifestation of personality. The teacher should understand, for example, that some distortions of letter formation are caused by excessive tension that may be more general than merely the grip or the pressure on the paper and the child's handwriting might not be improved by direct suggestions but rather by attending to the causes of the generalized tension. Handwriting is an instrument for the expression of meaning and also the expression of self. While it is essential in the earlier grades to devote periods of practice to the improvement of the form of the letters, and to the development of good posture, position, and movement, the child should not come to consider the writing task as one in which he shapes meaningless forms on the paper (Freeman, 1954).

Teaching the Left-Handed Child

One of the basic characteristics of much of human perceptual-motor activity is that it is initiated from one side of the body. In spite of man's bilateral or two-sided and seeming symmetrical body structure, he tends to face and act upon the world from one side, his dominant side, while the other side serves a coordinated supporting function. Hildreth (1949) indicates that with regard to handedness "individuals vary in the degree of consistency they show in dominant handedness. Invariability in handedness is the exception, not the rule." Nevertheless, by school age a large proportion of children show a sufficiently consistent preference for one or the other hand to be labeled either right- or left-handed.

The reasons for one person becoming right-handed and another left-handed are not clearly understood. One theory ascribes the preference to the dominance of one of the hemispheres of the brain. Because the motor nerve pathways cross over from their cells of origin in the cortex to the opposite side of the body, the dominant hemisphere is on the opposite side from the dominant side of the body. Among those who hold to the cerebral dominance theory of laterality, there are some who believe that hereditary factors produce cerebral dominance and consequently the particular sidedness. This hereditary explanation has been criticized by various writers. For example, after reviewing the evidence on the relation of sidedness to hemisphere dominance, Hildreth (1949) concludes that "the theory of cerebral dominance as a *cause* of handedness rests on weak foundations." A more reasonable view of the relationship of laterality and cerebral dominance is that both develop concomitantly as a result of experience and training. Hildreth marshals considerable support for the social-developmental theory of the origin of handedness. This theory suggests that nearly all individuals can become either dominantly right- or left-handed if training is begun sufficiently early and continued over a period of time.

The practical question about laterality that teachers of the primary grades are likely to ask is the following: Should the child who shows a preference for the left hand be trained to use the right? Although the left-handed person is no longer looked on with suspicion or with disdain as was the case in times gone by (witness the Latin word for left, *sinister,* or the French word, *gauche*) there is implicit in the question a realistic awareness that the left-handed child may face some inconveniences in and out of school. For example, athletic equipment, such as baseball gloves and golf clubs, as well as certain tools, such as scissors, are designed for the right-handed person and the left-handed individual may have difficulty locating items designed for his needs. Even school equipment such as tablet arm-chairs and also lighting arrangements in the classroom serve the right-handed person rather than the left-handed. The acquisition of hand-writing skill, as we shall see, may present some special difficulties for the left-handed child. In spite of these problems, if one holds to a genetic or hereditary explanation of handedness, one would recommend the adjustment of the environment to the left-handed child. That is, the teacher would recognize the special needs of the left-handed child and would provide for those needs wherever possible. This hereditary explanation has been widespread since early in this century and under its influence teachers and parents were inclined to avoid changing the left-handed child's preference. As a result of this attitude the incidence of left-handedness rose from about 3 percent in 1913 to about 11 percent in 1957 (Enstrom, 1957).

A social-developmental explanation for the origins of handedness, even though it recognizes the learning component, could also agree that in those instances where the child shows a clear preference for the left hand that he be permitted to continue in its use. The social-developmental explanation recognizes that motor patterns that are acquired early and that are overlearned, as is often the case with the use of the left hand, are difficult to unlearn. However, the child who comes to school lacking a clear tendency to use one or another hand, indicating that the training has not been consistent, should be encouraged to use the right hand. Those children who show a clear preference for the left hand should be helped to become skillful in the use of this hand and will need special attention for this purpose. Yet the teacher must exercise some caution in giving this special attention lest children whose preference is not fully determined and even some who are moderately right-handed, sense that left-handedness is a desirable mark of distinction. At the same time by accommodating to the left-handed child, the teacher can demonstrate that individual needs and unique characteristics are important and should not be overlooked. The situations in which the instruction needs to be varied are frequent. For example, Hildreth (1949) cites the case of a left-handed teenage pupil who had difficulties in learning to play the drums. The teacher had demonstrated the drumming technique that was appropriate for right-handed pupils and because the class was large, had not noticed that this left-handed pupil was having difficulty with the technique.

The left-handed child faces some special difficulties in acquiring handwriting skill. It has been noted above that the natural tendency is for arm movements to proceed from the central axis of the body outward, in a proximo-distal direction. This means that for the right-handed person the natural direction of movement is from left to right and for the left-handed person from right to left. This natural tendency to move in a proximo-distal direction can be confirmed by observing preschool children who have been asked to draw a horizontal line first with one hand then with the other. After a year or two of schooling the left-handed child, under pressure of the school environment, draws the horizontal line from left to right or against his natural proximo-distal tendency.

The direction of our script and print is consistent with that of the right-handed individual.[2] In learning to form individual letters and digits most children show some reversal confusion in the early stages of writing. This problem may be more acute for the left-handed child. The digit 7 may be used as an example. It is likely that the child's initial perception is that of a horizontal line with a vertical line dropped from the end. As he proceeds to form the digit the child makes the horizontal line; if he is right-handed the line is more likely to go from left to right,

[2] It is interesting to note that some older scripts, such as Hebrew and Arabic, are written from right to left. Some have speculated that this may have resulted from the greater incidence of left-handedness in ancient times. A more likely explanation is that ancient scripts were first chiseled in stone and this required a hammer and a chisel, the hammer being held in the right hand and the chisel in the left by the right-handed individual. The natural direction for this kind of operation is from right to left. It is interesting to note that individual letters in modern Hebrew script are designed generally for left to right motion as they are in our Roman script.

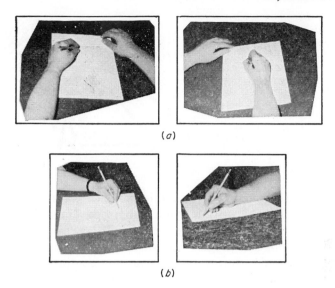

(a)

(b)

FIGURE 12.8 (a) *One view of the most commonly recommended handwriting position.* (b) *Another view showing more specifically the grip on the pencil.*

if, however, he is left-handed he is more likely to go from right to left and then drop the vertical line, producing a reversed digit. Each child's tendency to produce reversals needs to be overcome, with the left-handed child this may require even greater patience and understanding.

In addition to the formation of the particular letters and digits, the over-all act of handwriting needs to be carefully considered when adjusted to the left-handed child. The position of the paper, the placement of the hand, wrist, and arm and the grip on the writing instrument as described above, need to be modified for the left-handed child. The most widely recommended position is shown in Figure 12.8. The arrangement differs from that of the right-handed in these particulars: (1) The position of the paper is reversed so that the tilt of the top edge of the paper is downward to the right rather than to the left. (2) The index finger is about 1½ to 2 inches from the point of the writing instrument to allow for a better view of writing. (3) Some authorities also recommend that the desk surface be lower for the left-handed child than for the right-handed. This also permits a better view of the writing. Enstrom (1962) has studied carefully fifteen different handwriting arrangements of arm, wrist, paper, and so on, commonly adopted by left-handed individuals. He concludes that in addition to the arrangement described in Figure 12.8, there are three others that result in comfortable, legible handwriting and that allow for developmental improvement. Two of these represent more extreme turning of the paper. The third of

FIGURE 12.9 *An acceptable hooked wrist handwriting adjustment for habit-bound advanced-grade left-handed pupils. From E. A. Enstrom, "The Extent of the Use of the Left Hand in Handwriting and the Determination of the Relative Efficiency of the Various Hand-Wrist-Arm-Paper Adjustments," unpublished doctoral dissertation, University of Pittsburgh, 1957.*

these positions, shown in Figure 12.9, is marked by a pronounced hooking at the wrist and the writing hand is above the line. The position of the paper is the same as for the right-handed person. This position along with all hooked wrist adjustments is generally condemned. However, Enstrom considers this to be an appropriate adjustment for "habit-bound advanced-grade pupils" who are committed to more extreme hooked wrist adjustments.

SUMMARY

The body, its physical attributes, its physiological functioning, and the pattern of its growth, are significant factors in determining the individual's concept of self and his adjustment to his environment. They are, moreover, factors producing individual differences that are important for schooling.

The body-form or somatotype is related to personality characteristics. There is a slight tendency for the endomorphic person, one with a rounded physical build, to be slow reacting, amiable, and dependent on social approval. The mesomorphic person, one whose body-type is characterized by a predominance of bone and muscle, tends to be more assertive, adventurous, and competitive. The ectomorphic person with a body build that is slender and delicate, shows a tendency to be inhibited in action, apprehensive, and to avoid social contact. The position taken here is that the correlations between body build and personality are of a very low order and that whatever relationship does exist is induced by social norms and consistent social expectations, rather than by genetic factors.

The over-all growth pattern is called organismic development. There appears to be an underlying growth rhythm so that different aspects of development, both physical and psychological, tend to follow parallel patterns of acceleration or retardation.

The period of pubescence is associated with a number of significant physical and physiological changes that may produce psychological

repercussions. Youth who enter pubescence early are more likely to behave in more mature ways and to have more mature interests than those
of the same age who have not yet experienced the pubescent change.
Boys who, because of late pubescence, are shorter than their peers may
experience difficulties in making various adjustments. In general, a
large number of adolescents are seriously concerned over some aspect of
their physical development.

Physical illness is so prevalent that the teacher may expect that
during the course of each year nearly every child will be absent for a period of ten days or more because of such illness. These problems are
not as difficult to manage as those which arise from permanent physical
damage. Children with minimal brain damage with symptoms of distractability, clumsiness, and hyperactivity need to have learning experiences designed so that they proceed slowly to a mastery of the various
essential skills. Children with orthopedic handicaps may present reactions that require sensitive management by the teacher. Some of these
children manifest attitudes of resentment and hostility. Some are exceedingly resistant to help of any kind, and others are over-dependent
and immature. The teacher can institute procedures that can help clarify the feelings of nonhandicapped children toward individuals with
physical handicaps.

Sensory defects in vision and hearing can obviously interfere with
the child's learning. The incidence of defective vision rises markedly
when school learning activities make such direct and consistent demands
on the visual function. The teacher is often the first person to note the
signs of visual discomfort and of vision difficulty. The type of visual disorder will determine the kind of adjustment problem. Thus, children
with hyperopia or farsightedness, because they are uncomfortable when
doing close work like reading, will show a preference for sports and will
avoid desk activities. The reverse is true of children with myopia or
nearsightedness. The child with a hearing difficulty likewise faces a number of obstacles in school learning. Hearing impairment is easily overlooked and the child's lack of responsiveness is often attributed to poor
motivation and inattentiveness. Certain adjustments within the classroom can contribute to the learning effectiveness of the child with a
hearing deficiency.

An understanding of the concept of *psychosomatic* disorders,
where the underlying basis of the symptom is psychological and emotional while immediate and real organic changes have occurred, should
make the teacher aware of the unity as well as the complexity of the
human organism. Deprivation, stress, and prolonged states of anxiety
and anger can lead to a disturbance of function of one of the physiological or organ systems. Some individuals who are subjected to prolonged
psychological stress will suffer from gastro-intestinal disorders, others will

show respiratory symptoms, and still others will show heightened sensitivity to skin irritants and other allergens.

The proper development of perceptual-motor skills is important in many areas of school learning. Reading, speaking, and writing, for example, depend on eye movements, voice muscles, and hand-eye coordination. Beginning with early infancy and extending through the life span, the use of body muscles in acting on the environment plays an important role in all of the person's development. The acquisition of perceptual-motor skills illustrates many of the principles of development and their implications for teaching practice. One observes in the acquisition of motor skills the reciprocal processes of *differentiation* and *integration*. The need to consider the principles related to readiness for training can be clearly demonstrated in the development of motor function. The importance of knowledge of results or *feedback* is even more apparent in the development of motor skill than in other areas of development. The *sequence* of motor development is a natural one in that the direction of development and action is from the head region downward, *cephalo-caudal,* and also from the central axis of the body outward, *proximo-distal.*

One of the perceptual-motor skills for which the school has primary responsibility and in which many of the above principles of development are of practical significance, is that of handwriting. For a number of reasons, the child should be taught manuscript writing first and switched to cursive handwriting at the end of second or the beginning of third grade. The teacher needs to learn to recognize that certain features of the handwriting style are expressions of personality and unless these interfere with legibility or they produce fatigue, the teacher should not attempt to change them. The teacher should also remember that handwriting is an instrument or a means primarily for the expression of thought, not an end in itself.

Because the left-handed individual faces a number of practical difficulties in developing and using his perceptual-motor skills in a world that is designed for a predominantly right-handed population, the teacher needs to give special consideration to the instructional needs of the left-handed child. The position taken here is that handedness is not primarily determined by genetic factors but that it is an outgrowth of social-developmental factors. In most instances these factors become operative in the early years and by the time the child comes to school his preference for the left hand is likely to be overlearned and rather than attempt to change hand preference the child should be helped to become skillful in the use of the left hand. Where the preference is not firmly established, it is recommended that the child be trained to use the right hand. One area where the left-handed child needs special attention is that of handwriting. The direction of the script from left to right is opposed to natural, proximo-distal, direction of movement for the left-handed. This produces greater possibilities for letter and digit reversals. In addition, the left-handed child needs to learn to avoid the smearing of his writing since his hand follows rather than precedes the writing; and he needs to overcome the difficulty caused by his hand blocking his view of his writing. Adjustments in hand, arm, wrist, and paper position need to be made so that the child can write comfortably, legibly, and make the expected developmental improvements.

READING REFERENCES

Cruickshank, W. M. and G. O. Johnson (Eds.), *Education of Exceptional Children and Youth.* Englewood Cliffs, N.J.: Prentice-Hall, 1958 (particularly chaps. 7 and 9-12).

Dunbar, Helen F., *Emotions and Bodily Changes,* 4th ed. New York: Columbia University Press, 1954.

Freeman, F. N., "Teaching Handwriting," *What Research Says to the Teacher Series,* Washington: National Education Association, 1954.

Henry, N. B. (Ed.), *The Education of Exceptional Children.* Forty-ninth Yearbook (Pt. 2) National Society for the Study of Education. Chicago: University of Chicago Press, 1950) (particularly chaps. 8-11).

Selye, H., *The Stress of Life.* New York: McGraw-Hill Book Company, 1956.

Wright, Beatrice A., *Physical Disability—A Psychological Approach.* New York: Harper & Row, 1960.

CHAPTER 13

FAMILY INFLUENCES

The influence of the teacher on the developing child is only one factor within a framework of many forces that act upon the child. The teacher is not the only one who educates the child. Indeed, the school may provide only moderate influences in the child's educative environment when compared with the significance of the home as an educational force. Thus the teacher cannot ignore the significant fact that children figuratively bring their families to school. During the first four or five years of the child's life, the family has shaped his personality in many definite ways. As a result of these early experiences the child has learned his own patterns of receiving and giving affection, of perceiving and responding to the world, of determining what is right and wrong, and of participating in the process of communication and human interaction. These learnings and the manner in which they have been presented will have laid the foundation for the kind of personality the child will possess. They will have provided him with the rudiments of his sense of self, determining whether he views himself as adequate or inadequate, confident or unsure, his level of curiosity, interest, and awareness already channeled in certain directions.

The teacher's understanding of how the family influences the child can be most helpful. At the theoretical level it can serve as a framework for understanding the teacher-pupil interaction (see Chapter 15), which is in many ways analogous to the parent-child interaction, in that both of these represent a relationship of the immature individual to a socializing adult. The understanding of how parents influence the child can serve a more direct purpose also. It enables the teacher to plan for the child so that positive home influences are reinforced and built upon, and negative influences are counteracted. It also makes possible more effective communication with the parent and can help the teacher realize the limits of the parent's ability to cooperate with the school.

In this chapter a theoretical framework for understanding the parent-child relationship is developed. A number of different kinds of parent-child interaction patterns and the possible effects of these on the personality of the child and his school performance are described. The concluding discussion of the chapter deals with the issues of home and school communication and of children's home television viewing and its impact on their development.

THE PARENT-CHILD RELATIONSHIP

The danger of overgeneralization from limited data exists in all areas of the behavioral sciences. This danger is even more evident when we attempt to analyze the very complex phenomenon called the parent-child relationship. It is only with a great deal of caution and reservation that any conclusions about the effects of certain kinds of parent attitudes and child-rearing practices can be drawn. We must be even more cautious in reasoning that certain kinds of behavior deviations in children are the result of certain kinds of parent behavior. Thus, Peterson et al. (1959), in a study that investigated the relationship of parental attitudes and child adjustment, were compelled to conclude that:

> Though certain general statistical tendencies emerged we still found families in which the parents appeared maladjusted, evidently didn't get along, and exhibited the most abhorrent kinds of attitudes toward their children, but the children appeared to be getting along beautifully. We saw parents whose attitudes and other characteristics were in nearly perfect congruence with the stereotype of the "good parent," but whose children displayed problems of the most severe order (pages 127-128).

Although all the literature on child development assumes that parental influences are crucial, it is extremely difficult to determine which aspects of parental behavior lead to definite outcomes in child behavior. There are a number of reasons for this. First, the behavior and the attitudes of parents do not remain constant over a period of time, so that if we characterize the parent as being autocratic, let us say, when the child is age five, this pattern may change to a more democratic one as the child grows older. "The developmental cycles of the parents parallel the developmental cycle of the child. . . . Some parents are able to cope with the behavior of young children beautifully, but as parents of adolescents they may be at a distinct disadvantage. The relationship between a mother and infant is a relatively poor predictor of the relationship which will exist between them at a later date" (Grams, 1960, page 32). This has been confirmed empirically in the study of patterns of child rearing by Sears et al. (1957), where the measure of warmth shown by the mother to the infant was found to be only slightly correlated with the measure of warmth shown when the child reached age five. Another reason for the difficulty in tracing parental influences on the behavior of children is the fact that much of the research in this area has concentrated on the role of maternal attitudes and behavior. Only recently has attention been given to the role of the father (Peterson et al., 1959; Eron et al., 1961). A description of parental attitudes becomes extremely complicated when it must be based on the interaction of the parents with one another, as well as the resultant effects of two adults with individual personalities and their consequent differing behaviors. Size of family, sex of children, and their age differences form a cluster of variables that are difficult to control in empirical investigation. All of these contribute to shaping the child's behavior independent of the particular type of parent behavior. In a study of the personality roles in the larger family, Bossard and Boll (1955) found that the interaction within the family produced a number of specialized roles such as the responsible child, the popular child, the socially ambitious child, the studious one, the irresponsible one, and the spoiled child. Characterizing parent attitudes tells only part of the story of family influences, because in families where there are siblings, an older child may offer support and nurturance that the parents may have failed to provide, or the presence of another child in the family may in some ways detract from the security provided by the parents.

In spite of the many variables operating within the family that make it difficult to predict the effects of parental attitudes and behavior on the child's personality, the research literature shows a surprising amount of agreement at least in reporting trends.

THE VARIABLES OF PARENT BEHAVIOR

In Figure 13.1 is a diagrammatic presentation of some of the continua that can be used to describe parent behavior. The description of any home can be extended beyond these to include such variables as degree of child-centeredness, harmony in the home, level of activity, and so on. However, the five dimensions in Figure 13.1 will suffice for our purposes inasmuch as they permit a reasonably meaningful and inclusive discussion of the topic based upon research findings.

Combining the distribution curves, one from each of the five con-

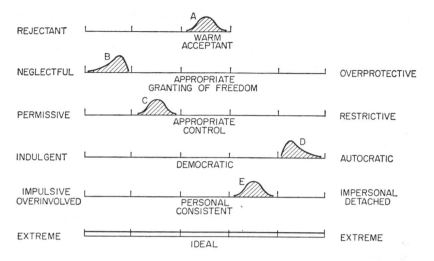

FIGURE 13.1 *Five continua of parent behavior. The distribution curves set on the horizontal lines represent the range and frequency of a particular parent's behavior with respect to one of the continua. For example, C represents the range and frequency of a particular parent's behavior on the permissive-restrictive continuum. This hypothetical parent is sometimes more permissive and sometimes less. If we were to make a number of observations of this parent's behavior in regard to control, the frequency and range would be as shown in C. Each of the distribution curves represents a distribution in regard to the various continua characterizing parent behavior. The distribution curve may be normal or skewed.*

tinua in Figure 13.1, we can arrive at a very large number of different parent behavior patterns. Almost every combination of distribution curves is possible, a few of them are, however, incompatible. For example, it is not likely that a home that is warm and acceptant, A, will also be neglectful, B, or impersonal-detached, E. A few other incompatible combinations may be discerned. It would be inappropriate here to describe every different kind of home that can result from the various combinations. The following descriptions are limited to a general consideration of each of the continua separately, showing from time to time how the description is modified when the characteristic occurs in combination with a type of parent behavior on another continuum.

Rejectant-Acceptant

The basic emotional orientation of parents is of extreme importance in determining the personality structure of the child. This characteristic of the relationship is subtle and is difficult to determine. Our culture and its mores make it difficult for parents to acknowledge that they have negative feelings toward their children. Parents tend to feel guilty when they have to admit that children deprive them of material

things, of freedom of movement, and that socializing them can sometimes be emotionally stressful. Parents differ considerably, however, in
the extent to which they have these feelings and the behavior that reflects them. Sears, Maccoby and Levin (1957) describe this continuum as
follows:

> There is an attitude that colors all the relations between the mother and
> the child. At one extreme, this dimension is defined as an *acceptance* of
> the child; at the other, as *rejection*. Acceptance means that the mother
> gives love without reservation, not necessarily with great demonstration,
> but without exacting a price of consistently "good" behavior from the
> child. He is hers and he is part of her. She loves *him* without regard for
> what he *does*. Rejection, on the other hand, is a pervasive attitude of
> witholding love, at least a little bit. It may involve a sense of contingency
> —'I'll love you *if*'—or an attitude of resentment and disappointment
> (page 170).

In a study of the appraisal of parent behavior by Baldwin et al.
(1949), *acceptance* is considered as one of five variables closely related
to warmth. The other four variables are: *Direction of Criticism* (Ap-
proval-Disapproval): The acceptant parent is able to criticize the child
without making the child feel hated and rejected. "Also, these parents,
in correcting the child, usually succeed at making it clear that it is an
isolated bit of behavior which is disapproved rather than his entire
personality" (page 6). *Affectionateness:* This variable, associated with
warmth, is a measure of the overt behavior of parents and the extent to
which it reflects love or antagonism. *Rapport:* This variable is a measure
of "the ease with which contact is established, communication between
parent and child carried on, the comfort and lack of strain in the relationship and the feeling of mutual sympathy and understanding" (page
6). *Child-centeredness:* This variable is discussed with the other continua
presented in Figure 13.1, particularly that of permissive-restrictive and indulgent-autocratic.

The Results of Acceptance and Rejection

The effects of rejection would be modified in one direction or another depending on whether this parent characteristic occurs in combination with neglect or overprotection, with an impersonal-detached
attitude, or one that is overinvolved and impulsive.

If the attitude of parents is generally one of acceptance and emotional warmth, the child's personality is likely to be socially acceptable
and one that faces the future confidently (Baldwin, 1955). If, on the
other hand, the parents are rejecting, a number of harmful effects can
result. Sears et al. (1957) found that children of rejecting parents were
more likely to be dependent than those of nonrejecting parents.

Baldwin et al. (1945) describe an actively rejecting mother who is at the same time autocratic, restrictive, somewhat detached, and inconsistent. She is reported to have said when her daughter was six months old, "I hate to sit and hold her. I don't care to hold babies . . . for some reason or other I never did." She is described as going out of her way to be frustrating, caustic, and unpleasant to her daughter. The effects of this treatment are summarized in the following paragraph.

> In reaction to this vigorous and constricting policy Betty had steadily become withdrawn, shy and stubbornly resistant, in a passive fashion, to adult authority. At school her decorous and superficially docile behavior cannot be criticized, but in any situation which demands a response she retreats into an almost inaudible, "I don't know." Her bewildered, discouraged teacher says, "I just can't get at her—nothing seems to reach her" (page 24).

Neglect-Overprotection

Human infancy and childhood is a prolonged period requiring protective care from adults. The child who fails to receive adequate protection can be seriously hurt. Many parents who neglect their children do so because of their being overburdened by large families, economic strain, and their own personal problems. The neglected child is one whose out-of-school life is largely unguided and whose parents, for one reason or another, seem incapable of fulfilling their socializing responsibility. This form of neglect occurs more frequently in the lower socioeconomic classes. The case of Linda in the next chapter is an illustration of a neglected child. Another form of neglect is the separation of the parents from the child for extended periods of time. The private school and the summer camp can provide enriched opportunities for growth, but if the child senses that such placement is an expression of parental rejection and neglect, the consequences can be detrimental.

Although overprotection may seem at first to be the antithesis of neglect, a careful exploration of the motives that sometimes result in parental overprotection, reveals some remarkable similarities. Levy (1943), in his well-known clinical description of maternal overprotection, notes that this type of behavior often masks a basically rejecting attitude. The parent cannot admit this rejection and feels unconscious guilt for having such feelings. Any mishap that might befall the child is greatly threatening. The parent then develops a pattern of overprotective behavior that is designed to protect him or her from this threat. The overprotective parent will help the child before the child has had a chance to make his own attempt to overcome an obstacle, he will shelter the child from all kinds of real and imaginary dangers, and he will show excessive anxiety about the child. Ausubel (1958) points out that overprotection can also serve as a defense for an anxiety-ridden parent personality. He states, "In some instances the predisposing anxiety is reinforced by such contributory factors as marital unhappiness, a long history of sterility or miscarriages, severe illness or injury in the child, and death of a previous child or close relative" (page 368).

The Results of Neglect and Overprotection

The effects of neglect are in many ways similar to those of rejection. It must be remembered that the child is likely to incorporate into his personality, the attitudes others show toward him and these incorporated attitudes then form the basis for future relationships. The child who has been rejected and neglected by his parents will develop self-rejecting attitudes and is likely to have difficulty in relating to others, since his low self-esteem will cause him to induce rejecting behavior from others. Jersild (1960) comments on this sequence of events as follows:

> In our schools and in the community at large we can see many persons who appear to bear the marks of having been rejected by others and who show symptoms of a rejecting attitude toward others. The child at school who is unresponsive and sullen is quite probably one who has been neglected or rejected or feels rejected . . . such a child is baffling and hard to reach. It is difficult for him to respond to a friendly approach. Such a child is exasperating, but teachers who have little feeling for other human beings will find him especially exasperating. They may respond to his rejecting attitude by rejecting him, using some of the many weapons at their command—ignoring him, giving him failing grades, making him the butt of sarcastic remarks, complaining to his parents . . . so the youngster most in need of understanding and sympathy receives the least.
>
> However, an unresponsive child may come under the influence of a teacher who is able to reach out to those whom others reject. Such a teacher can make a remarkable difference. The child who was a surly brat may soften and become friendly under the influence of a teacher who cares and seeks to understand (pages 140-141).

Neglect, as we have considered it here, is one form of parental rejection and the effects on the child are therefore similar to other forms of rejection. Another way of looking at neglect is that it is an expression of an impersonal, detached parental attitude. The effects of this attitude are considered in the discussion of the last continuum in Figure 13.1

In general, overprotection leads to infantile, withdrawing, and submissive behavior. The child is likely to show signs of insecurity and a generally difficult adjustment. The adjustment pattern of children who have been overprotected differs from that of those who have been more overtly rejected in that the former are more dependent, babyish, and fearful. In extreme cases of overprotection the parents will have conveyed to the child an impression that the world is a dangerous and hostile place and that the child is generally incapable of meeting the ordinary demands and frustrations of living. When the overprotection is associated with indulgence, the child's behavior will often be characterized by "disobedience, impudence, tantrums, excessive demands and varying degrees of tyrannical behavior" (Levy, 1943). These effects are more likely the result of indulgence rather than overprotection.

Permissive-Restrictive

In addition to protecting the child from danger, parents have the responsibility of changing the child's behavior from that which is impulse determined to more responsible forms of controlled action. They may do this by being more or less permissive or restrictive and coercive. The attitudes of parents in this dimension will be reflected in the degree of severity of toilet training, strictness with regard to noise, table manners, the care of property in the household, and in the extent to which the parents use physical punishment.

The advice given to parents as to how they should fulfill this aspect of their responsibility has changed considerably over the years. Wolfenstein (1953) studied the various *Infant Care* bulletins issued by the U. S. Children's Bureau. She found that the bulletin issued in the second decade of this century advised parents to restrain their children severely. Subsequent bulletins have been considerably more lenient in their recommendations. Experts for a while were recommending extreme permissiveness. More recently, this has changed to the suggestion that a child who lacks limits in his environment will exhibit anxiety in addition to difficulty in learning appropriate self-control. It is interesting to note that the advice that parents receive from experts is not as important in determining their behavior as their own basic attitudes toward themselves and their children. Bettleheim (1952) has pointed out that if parents who are coercive and who attempt to accelerate the child's achievement of developmental goals are advised to be more permissive, let us say in regard to toilet training, they may delay such training but they will remain coercive in regard to other aspects of development. This suggests that teachers must exercise great caution in giving parents advice about a particular practice.

The Results of Permissive-Restrictive Parent Behavior

The findings of Sears et al. (1957), referred to previously, confirmed those of an earlier study by Sears et al. (1953). In both studies severity of punishment for aggression (restrictive parent behavior) was associated with high aggression in children, particularly in boys. In the first-mentioned study, it was found that high permissiveness also led to high aggression. It seems that both extremes of this continuum lead to aggressive behavior in children.

Another study (Watson, 1957) analyzed the effects of permissive and strict discipline on the personalities of children. Watson selected homes that tended to have parents who showed reasonable warmth and protection. The parents responded to a questionnaire in which they indicated how they cope with the kind of child behavior that elicits either permissive or strict parental control. No parents in the study responded consistently with permissiveness or strictness to all of the thirty-five items on the questionnaire, but Watson was able to divide the parent population into a more permissive group and a stricter group. He found that children whose discipline had been more restrictive tended to show more hostility. Those who had experienced more freedom tended to show more initiative and independence, more cooperation, more friendly feelings toward others and a higher level of creativity, originality, and spontaneity. There were no distinct differences with respect to security-anxiety in the two groups of children; children with marked signs of anxiety were found in both groups as were children who seemed quite secure. Watson states that, "It is impressive, however, to find no clear personality advantage associated in general with strict discipline in a good home. Where differences do emerge, these are consistently to the credit of the more permissive upbringing." Watson cautions his reader not to conclude that permissiveness alone is necessarily the cause for the advantages indicated, the personality characteristics as well as the permissiveness may both grow out of a pattern of living that is quite complex. A change toward permissiveness alone might not have any effect if the total pattern remained the same.

In the study by Peterson et al. (1959), referred to earlier, it was shown that the type of adjustment problem shown by children who had been referred to a guidance clinic, was related to the kind of parental attitudes. Children who displayed adjustment difficulties characterized as *conduct problems* (truancy from home and from school, disobedience, rudeness, temper tantrums, swearing, stealing, fighting, lying, and destructiveness) were more likely to have mothers who were characterized as generally maladjusted and fathers who were evidently permissive and ineffectual in their discipline.

Indulgent-Autocratic

For the past several pages we have been considering how the parent feels toward the child and how he acts in fulfilling his obligations in regard to protecting and socializing the child. In the parent-child interaction, as in any human interaction, there inevitably arises a conflict of needs and a method for resolving this conflict must be worked out. The various modes of resolving the conflict of need in the home range between autocracy and indulgence.

In extreme cases of indulgence the parents have given up all their rights as human beings and deny the child nothing. Every whim and fancy of the child is satisfied. The indulgent parents act as abject servants of the child. This type of relationship often occurs in conjunction with overprotection and leads to a very permissive form of discipline. The indulged child is commonly referred to as spoiled.

The autocratic parents, on the other hand, do not allow any opportunity for responsible decision on the part of the child. Where the indulgent mother, in establishing infant-feeding practices, will deny herself any latitude from a self-demand schedule, the dominating, autocratic mother will not inconvenience herself one iota in establishing a firm parent-ordered schedule. In any situation where the desires of the parent and the needs of the child are in conflict, the parent's needs take precedence. The child is not likely to be consulted whenever a family decision is about to be made. The autocratic parent is likely to be restrictive and coercive in his discipline and tends to be somewhat rejectant in his attitude.

The Results of Indulgent-Autocratic Parent Behavior

The consistently indulged child is likely to be a very poor class member. He has not generally learned the process of give and take so necessary for age-mate relationships. He is frequently resentful of the teacher for he cannot offer him unlimited attention without denying the rights of other children. Both teacher and classmate will tend to resent the show-off tactics often shown by this child. The child who has been able to control his parents so easily at home desires the acceptance of the group but does not know how to compromise in order to achieve it. Although the school can provide the security so badly needed, because an indulged child is insecure without limitations, his surface behavior suggests that he resents the limitations set by the school. This child will not do assignments out of school if they interfere with TV viewing or other activities. The child will often come to school tired, because parents do not set rules for bedtime and he may even be undernourished because he is permitted very wide latitude in his nutritional choice. The teacher should attempt to establish reasonable limits on this child's behavior and to insist firmly on certain codes of conduct for all in the classroom. Movement toward maturity is likely to be slow because much of what the teacher can accomplish in school is quickly undone at home. The parents' indulgence of the child is carried to the point of supporting the child in his fight against school restrictions. The prognosis in those few cases where both parents are extremely indulgent and where there are no other siblings, is not a good one. When these children reach adolescence and adulthood they do not know how to exert constructive effort to accomplish an end and frequently dream of the good old days.

Baldwin (1948) has pointed out that the dominating autocratic "home atmosphere tends to produce quiet, non-resistant children who

are unaggressive and well-behaved, but who are also restricted in originality, curiosity and fancifulness. Some parents (and teachers, too) will
feel that conforming behavior in their children which is bought at the
price of curiosity and originality constitutes a real bargain!" Peterson
et al. (1959) found that children who were referred to a child-guidance
clinic and whose problem was described as a personality problem (se-
clusiveness, sensitivity, changeability of mood, nervousness, inferiority
feelings, absent-mindedness, day-dreaming, and inefficiency in work)
tended to come from homes where fathers displayed autocratic attitudes
or else lack of parental concern. It can be estimated that the dominated
child would remain longer in a state of *heteronomy* with regard to
moral choices where he would act as if he believed that obedience is always right and to have a will of his own is wrong (see Chapter 6). The
dominated child is likely to encounter difficulty in relating easily to
other children. Radke (1946) has noted that children from autocratic
homes were rated as more unpopular by their age-mates, they were more
inconsiderate and more likely to become involved in fights and quarrels.
Radke explains this type of behavior outcome as the result of the child's
assuming the role of his own parents when relating to other children. Because his parents have not been considerate of his needs he, having identified with his parents, cannot be considerate of others, especially children.

The child from the autocratic home functions more effectively in
the classroom where the teacher sets forth a clear-cut routine of assignments and recitations. In those situations where the teacher encourages
cooperative planning procedures the dominated child may not know
how to function without resorting to dominating or submissive behavior.
The long-range effect of the democratic classroom is more likely to help
the child achieve maturity whereas the teacher-dominated classroom may
reinforce the child's dependence and subservience. This issue of the
teacher's behavior and its effects on children will be discussed in detail
in Chapter 15.

In helping the dominated child, the teacher frequently will encounter a resentful parent attitude, for the teacher represents a threat
to parental authority. The autocratic parent may wish to exert the same
control over the teacher as he holds over the child. Before proceeding
to a discussion of the fifth and last dimension of the parent-child relationship, a description of the problems that arise in dealing with a child
from an autocratic, overdominating home will be given.

A Child from an Autocratic Home

It was customary in June for all sixth-grade teachers of the school
district to meet with the seventh-grade teachers and to briefly comment
on each of the children. This procedure is useful because it enables a

teacher who has achieved a measure of understanding of some of his pupils, to transmit this to the persons best able to use the information. The
teacher who receives this information must interpret it, however, before
making use of it. When Harriet's name was mentioned, her sixth-grade
teacher mentioned that she was a shy, quiet child with average school
ability and was no problem at all. Miss Lawrence, the seventh-grade
teacher who was to receive Harriet into her class, knew that the teacher
offering these comments about Harriet was a dominative, though kindly
person, who provided much control and direction to her students. Miss
Lawrence wondered how Harriet would fare in her classroom, which
was somewhat less structured and less teacher dominated.

After several weeks at school had passed in the seventh grade,
Miss Lawrence began to think that Harriet was too shy and quiet. The
girl was tall, thin, with a pale complexion, slightly awkward but with an
over-all impression of delicateness. Her classroom behavior was generally
that of a bewildered spectator; she seldom entered into group discussion
and hesitated in joining committees that had been organized for projects; she almost waited to be assigned without giving any indication of
preference. When the children were working alone, Harriet would seek
the teacher's help and seemed unable to move very far without continual reassurance that she was complying with the teacher's instructions.

Miss Lawrence noticed that Harriet had no friends. The girl
spent most of her free periods, such as recess and lunch time, in the classroom reading. Miss Lawrence treated her cordially and often engaged
her in conversation. Gradually Harriet seemed to be more at ease at
least in the presence of the teacher, if not yet with her peers.

During one of these sessions when Harriet was alone with the
teacher she approached the teacher's desk shyly and asked if Miss Lawrence would like to see some pictures in her wallet. She explained that
these were pictures of her real mother who had died five years previously. She went on to tell how pretty her real mother was and what
lovely red hair she had. This was the first time Miss Lawrence realized
that Harriet was living with her father and stepmother and she became curious to know more about the family conditions as a possible explanation of Harriet's withdrawing behavior.

One day in a human relations discussion (Miss Lawrence was
using *Reading Ladders in Human Relations* prepared by the American
Council on Education (1949) as a source guide in conducting this classroom activity) the topic of brothers and sisters came up. Harriet raised
her hand and volunteered a comment for the first time in these several
months. She told the group that she was not particularly fond of caring
for her younger brother. Harriet was able to express these feelings only
after she realized that others in the group had similar feelings of resentment and that these had been accepted by the teacher. The open ex-

pression of feeling helped to relieve some of the guilt associated with the feelings of hostility.

Harriet had repressed her feelings toward her brother for some time now. Had she not been provided with an opportunity to express these feelings without being condemned she might have found subtle, subconscious ways of expressing them and thus produced even stronger feelings of guilt. Excessive repression of feeling, whether in adults or children, produces an incapacity to act. It should be noted that in avoiding or counteracting repression the teacher does not give the child permission or encouragement to act out directly what is felt; the teacher rather provides an opportunity to have feelings aired in order to reduce guilt. Prohibiting the expression of feeling produces *repression,* that is, the feeling exists but a positive way of handling it does not. In avoiding repression Baruch (1955) has suggested the following as the three major tasks before the teacher: (Her points parallel the discussion of the school's role in fostering emotional maturity in Chapter 11.)

(a) She needs to help the child with *affect-identification.* (This is anger you are feeling! Or, in child terms, "You're feeling mean!")

(b) She needs to help the child with *object-identification.* (You are angry at the child who pulled away your toy, at me, at your brother or sister, at your father or mother—many times at the latter. . . . Since it is the parents primarily who have represented the big ogres of denial and demand, the others against whom anger is hurled are apt to be objects of displaced aggression.)

(c) She needs to help the child with *channel-identification.* (Here is a safe action-pathway through which you can let your feelings flow out.) (page 165).

During the course of the next several weeks the seventh-grade class was involved in a poetry contest. The teacher selected the ten best poems and read them to the class, and she then asked the children to choose the three they considered best. Some of the children wanted to know the names of the authors to help them make a choice. Miss Lawrence took a few moments to have the children consider why the names should not be divulged. They quickly grasped the idea that in making choices, decisions, or in judging a product, the rational procedure is to eliminate, insofar as possible, the intrusion of nonessential judgment factors. By being objective and by helping children achieve objectivity, the teacher contributes greatly to the child's growth toward maturity, and counteracts the inevitable subjectivity (sometimes beneficial for other reasons) that he experiences at home. The first prize in the poetry contest went to Harriet.

Harriet's relationship to the group had improved somewhat as she gained some confidence in her own abilities. Until one day in the middle of the class the door burst open and standing in the doorway was a tall, severe-looking woman with jet black hair done up in a chignon. She was extremely neat and well-dressed. In a demanding tone she asked the teacher if she were Miss Lawrence. Still surprised, Miss Lawrence nodded; Harriet's mother strode across the room, deposited 30 cents on the teacher's desk and told her to give it to Harriet for lunch because she was going away and wouldn't have time to prepare lunch. She left the room as abruptly as she had entered. All the children turned to Harriet whose face was red with embarrassment. Harriet did nothing the rest of the day and left school as quickly and unobtrusively as possible. A few days later Harriet had another setback when her mother had sent her to school after lunch with her hair done up in curlers and the children poked fun at her.

For a period of several weeks she exhibited the same kind of withdrawn behavior as she had when she first entered the group. At one point Harriet won a spelling bee and she seemed to work harder on her studies and she made one or two casual friends but most of her time seemed to be spent in reading novels about young girls. In a sense this was a flight from reality. When faced with pressures that appeared to threaten her sense of adequacy, Harriet sought gratification in fantasy and in identifying with fictional characters. Some of this kind of escape is to be expected in many adolescents, but in Harriet's case it seemed excessive.

Miss Lawrence became concerned and sent a note to the parents requesting that they come to school. A rather curt response was received from Harriet's stepmother stating that Harriet was the teacher's responsibility in school and the mother had no intention of wasting her time coming to school. Miss Lawrence felt then that she had made a mistake in sending the note. Harriet did spontaneously indicate that she was worried about her school work and when the teacher offered to help after school, Harriet said she had to hurry home to prepare supper. Miss Lawrence at first thought that this was an excuse but she soon discovered that Harriet's stepmother had a job and expected Harriet to have the house clean and supper ready for the family every night; if she did not, she received a beating. Not long after, Miss Lawrence received a note from the mother asking that Harriet's library privileges be withdrawn, because all she did nights after supper was read. The teacher's first impulse was to write a note telling her that Harriet was her problem at home, but she knew better. When parents show destructive behavior in their relationship with children, it is best for teachers to ignore or side-step issues and to avoid an open showdown, for the only result of such parent-teacher conflict is inevitably detrimental to the child. There were a few other incidents that indicated that Harriet was having a difficult time, but Miss Lawrence continued to reassure her and seemed to build a quiet strength in the girl.

In spite of the lack of communication between the teacher and the parents, Harriet's maturing and the satisfaction of some personal needs at school seemed to have enabled her to assert herself at home to some extent. For the first time, it appeared, she felt able to ask for privileges. The relative certainty she had acquired in making these requests, caused the stepmother to modify her dominating manner and she acceded more and more; this in turn gave Harriet more confidence on which to build her adjustment. A few days before the close of school, the girls in the class gave a shower for Miss Lawrence whose engagement had been announced. Each girl wore a big hoop skirt, a fad at the time, and Harriet too was dressed to conform with this fad. Her hair was attractively arranged and she participated actively with the other girls in the preparations and the enjoyment of the event. She seemed to have found a way of coping successfully with a dominating parent and it is reasonable to assume that an understanding teacher helped her in this achievement.

Overinvolved-Impersonal Parent Behavior

Becoming and being a parent is almost always one of the most meaningful experiences in a person's life. To a certain extent every parent comes to feel that the child is an extension of himself or herself, and that the child's development and his behavior are reflections of the parent's being. Thus, if the child is bright or talented the parents are proud; if the child misbehaves or doesn't measure up to expectations, the parents tend to feel anxious and ashamed. This latter condition was experimentally demonstrated by Merrill (1946). She selected thirty mothers with their respective preschool children. She observed each mother and child through a one-way vision screen as they interacted in a free-play situation for two half-hour periods. For the control group the second half-hour period was a repetition of the first. The mothers in the experimental group were informed after the first play session that their children's play performance had not been an altogether satisfactory sample of their potentialities. Observation during the second period revealed that the mothers in the experimental group showed an increase of dominating behavior "as expressed in arbitrary directing of and interference with, the child's activity." Because of the parents' involvement with the child, a teacher's seemingly innocent comments are often misinterpreted by the parents. The parent who is overinvolved in the child's development is unable to control his identification with the child and cannot permit the child to become differentiated as a personality, free to act independently at each developmental stage.

Occasionally we encounter parents who are impersonal, detached, and seemingly uninvolved in their child's development. This is more likely to be true of fathers than of mothers. There are fathers who, because of their work or because of their personalities, dissociate themselves from their families. Our data on the effects of an impersonal parent-child relationship are drawn from studies of children who spent their early years in an institution where emotional interaction with adults was largely detached.

The Results of Overinvolved-Impersonal Treatment

The effects of overinvolvement will depend upon the kind of parent personality exhibiting the behavior. The case of Shirley Ann Harper adapted from Baldwin et al. (1945), is one in which the results of the parents' possessiveness seems to have been modified by other positive features of the home.

From Shirley Ann's birth, the Harper household could be characterized as indulgent and child-centered. The parents early treatment consisted of lavish kisses, affectionate conversation, and considerable handling. The mother's references to Shirley Ann are often in terms like "Shirley is our life," "She's my little sweetheart," or "At school she's really a teacher's little helper."

The parents appear almost rapturous over the "bundle from heaven" they have produced and they are most concerned with molding this property into an utterly nice, utterly proper child. Mrs. Harper insists on such behavior as good table manners, including saying grace, and a subservient respect for her elders. The parents' approval of Shirley Ann is intense, their punishment is half-hearted and full of sympathy for "the poor little thing."

The girl's social contacts are severely limited so as to prevent "bad" influences. Very few people, outside the family are permitted more than the most casual relationship with Shirley, all being found "bad for her" in one way or another. A very select private school is selected to exert the proper guidance on Shirley and to set a high moral tone.

> An interviewer summarizing a conversation with Mrs. Harper wrote: "The general impression of the home is that Shirley is the apple of the eye; she has a secure place, but is handled with old-fashioned strictness about routines and 'niceness,' is being brought up 'properly.' I felt that Shirley was on to this and could manage her parents skillfully, crying, loving, being cute, good, independent, etc., within the well-defined discipline limits, and that she is far more dominating and sure of herself, more indulged and self-centered than her parents suspect. I had the feeling that Shirley was well in command of the situation and was keeping her parents happy" (page 39).

In this second description of an overinvolved parent we find a focusing of parental anxiety and its displacement onto the child. The results are more severe than in the previous case.

Matthew was a twelve-year-old boy who was repeating fifth grade and still failing the work. He was considered mentally deficient by parents, teachers and classmates but psychological examination showed that he actually was of superior intelligence, with an I.Q. of 133.

The boy's father had had considerable difficulty in his vocational adjustments and had often been unemployed. He displaced anxiety from himself onto worry about the boy's future, stressing success in school as a preparation for later vocational success. When the boy was in third grade, the father began to supervise his school work. Although Matthew's teachers gave him good marks in reading, his father decided that he was poor in this subject. The father came to this conclusion after asking Matthew to read matter that was far too advanced for a third grade pupil. From that time, however, the father centered his anxiety upon the boy's reading and began to tutor him in it. Invariably, he scolded and criticized the boy during these home lessons, so that they always ended with Matthew in tears and his father in a temper. It is not strange, therefore, that the boy made no further progress in reading between the third and fifth grades or that by the time he was in fifth grade, he had a serious reading disability. By then, also, he was so sensitive to criticism that he would burst into tears at the slightest reprimand from a teacher and would fight with any child who said a teasing word to him.

Neither remedial teaching nor psychotherapy helped in this case so long as the boy remained at home, for the father was unable to change in his relationship to the boy, continued to displace anxiety onto him, and could not be induced to forego tutoring him. When the boy went to a boarding school and was thus freed from his father's anxiety and criticisms, he was able to learn to read with the help of individual remedial teaching (Blanchard, 1947, page 175).

A number of studies have documented the fact that impersonal treatment, particularly during the early years of life, can be seriously harmful to development. Ribble (1944) and Spitz (1945 and 1949) have shown that infants who spend an extended period of time in institutions where physical care is adequate but where emotional interaction with a mother or mother substitute is lacking, tend to be markedly deficient in their over-all development. Goldfarb (1943a and 1943b) conducted a study in which he compared children who had experienced institutional care during the first three years of life with those who had been placed in foster homes shortly after birth. He studied these two groups from age seven to adolescence and found that on most measures of development and adjustment the institutional group was retarded and handicapped. The intelligence scores were lower, the power of integrated abstract thinking was poorer. The institutional group showed such signs of social immaturity as being unable to participate in games or to make friends, and retarded speech development. Goldfarb found more restlessness and hyperactivity in the institutional group as well as the inability to concentrate, temper displays, and poor school achievement. These findings have been generally confirmed by Bowlby (1953).

COMMUNICATING WITH PARENTS

The success of the communication process depends on the degree of mutual understanding existing between the communicators. Although teachers and parents are both concerned about the same thing, namely the development of the child, they do not have the same view of the child. The perception of the child is markedly colored by the emotional investment each may have. The parent ordinarily is much more involved in his child, whereas the teacher is more objective. The parent ordinarily lacks the developmental norm against which to assess the child, whereas the teacher with some experience with numbers of children can assess the child more realistically. In one study (del Solar, 1949) it was found that parents often made demands that were not in harmony with their child's abilities or his current stage of development. The teachers believed that this lack of coordination between parental expectations and demands and the child's ability to meet them had caused many children to lose confidence in their abilities and tended to make them apprehensive and tense. Many parents reported that it was only after their child started school that they understood what they could reasonably expect from their youngsters. They discovered that teachers are, in a sense, specialists in child development; they are likely to have a balanced and realistic view of the child's abilities and know what to expect at each age level. On the other hand, the teacher must understand that the parents know a great deal about the child and that some of this information can be useful to the teacher. Also, as we have pointed out in our previous discussion, it is important for the teacher to understand how the parent has influenced the child. The communication process is then a two-way affair.

The medium for communication between teacher and parent is often the child. Parents learn about their child's teacher through the child's comments about school, and teachers form judgments about parents by observing and listening to children. This channel frequently distorts the communication process. Children cannot always assess a situation realistically, consequently they may unintentionally exaggerate or displace blame. It was pointed out in Chapter 11 how a child with school phobia displaced her anxiety about a home situation by complaining that the teacher yells too much or that the teacher doesn't like her. During adolescence children will often complain to their teachers about their parents, hoping to gain sympathy and support as they work through their developmental task of gaining emancipation from adult authority. One teacher of this writer's acquaintance found himself in difficulty for not reporting a truancy to the office. The youngster had gained the teacher's sympathy by telling of the severe beating that his father had administered. The truancy was discovered and the teacher's dereliction of duty was exposed. Teachers must be careful not to take a position that abrogates the rights of parents. Discussion of issues with parents can do much to produce a satisfactory solution for the student's problem.

The parent-teacher contact is more successful if it grows out of routine communication rather than if it is attendant upon the development of an immediate problem. This routine communication can be difficult when teachers have to deal with parents who themselves have had unsatisfactory experiences in school. When a particular problem arises and the teacher wishes to enlist the assistance of the parents, the cooperation of the child is an important consideration. The teacher should not convey to the child that he is aligning himself with the parent against the child. If the child's cooperation and preferably his consent is not obtained, he can readily sabotage the whole communication process.

In an action-research project pertaining to the interpersonal perceptions of teachers, students, and parents, Jenkins and Lippitt (1951) found that teachers expressed a greater interest "in having parents visit and consult with them at school than is recognized by parents." This would suggest that teachers who have an interest in such parent participation must find effective means of communicating this interest to parents.

The written report to parents is the most common and regular means of communication from the teacher. It is wise to keep in mind that the report card is not designed to find fault with the child and by implication, the parent. Nor should the report card be evasive and misleading. It is more than a perfunctory way of keeping parents pacified. The report card is a means of providing parents with information about their child's progress and development. Parents are most certainly entitled to this information and they are entitled to have it presented in understandable terms. The best report card is one that indicates to the parents whether or not there is something they need to do in regard to the child's progress in school. It is not sufficient to state, "Mary needs help with her reading," or "Richard is careless in spelling." Statements such as these may prove frustrating to the parent and can well lead to action that would prove detrimental to the child. A more useful type of statement would be, "Would it be possible for you to arrange regular visits to the public library for Mary so that she can draw some books on the history of our community. A suggested list is enclosed," or "I think it would be helpful if you could review the spelling lesson with Richard each week, he seems to need a little more time with spelling; the assignments for the coming weeks are enclosed. Richard, of course, knows that I have asked you to help. If you feel you need some guidance in carrying out this recommendation, please stop by any day between three thirty and four thirty." In general, if the student's progress in a particular subject or topic is deemed inadequate and the teacher believes that the parents can be of assistance, the teacher's communication should offer the kind of guidance that will lead to constructive participation on the part of the parent. The role of parents in helping and supervising homework was discussed in Chapter 7.

There has been much discussion about the school's responsibility in reporting standardized test results such as IQ's, grade norms, and the like. The extreme positions on this issue have ranged from opening all school records to parents to that of giving no information about test results, lest this information be misinterpreted and misused. Perhaps a position between these two extremes is more reasonable. That is to say, that some information which the school might need in order to carry on its work should be kept in a confidential file while other information pertaining to the child's development and which is used to plan the educational and vocational future of the child must be communicated to the parent. However, the process of communication involves an understanding of the parents' ability to interpret the data. Therefore, it would not be wise to report exact figures such as IQ or specific grade norms. It would be better to explain what the particular score implies for predicting the student's progress. The teacher must always keep in mind, moreover, that no educational measure is perfectly reliable and that each measure has particular validity (see Chapter 9).

TELEVISION

Because television viewing is such a widespread home activity, it is important for the teacher to understand the nature of this activity and some of its effects. Much justified criticism has been leveled at commercial television programing. Too many programs represent thin plots held together by violence and crime. Much of what is offered on television represents a gross distortion of the values that responsible adults would want to inculcate in children. Our task here is not to add to this criticism but to analyze objectively the extent to which children use the medium and, insofar as possible, to determine what effects this activity has on children. The discussion is based on the excellent, comprehensive report presented in the book by Schramm et al. (1961) entitled *Television in the Lives of our Children.*

The Amount and Kind of Television Viewing

The amounts of time reported by various studies will differ, depending on the manner in which the estimate is obtained; whether by diary or memory, whether the information is obtained from the mother or the child, whether Sunday is included in the estimate or not, and so on. In general, the data supports the following statements about television viewing through the school years: In the first three grades the average time a child spends viewing television is about fifteen to sixteen hours per week. This figure increases to about the sixth or seventh grade when it reaches a peak of about twenty-two hours per week and then gradually declines through the high school years. These average figures do not reveal the fact that children differ widely in the amount of time they spend on television. When an average figure of 2½ hours a day is reported for a group of children, there will be some who viewed more than four hours and others who viewed less than one hour. However, during the school years the child spends nearly as much time viewing television as he does in school and more than in any other single activity. It would be interesting to know in what ways the activity patterns of children have changed since the advent of television. Schramm and his colleagues were able to compare the children in a community without television with those in a similar community with television. They found that the time devoted to television is taken from a variety of leisure time and other activities. "It cuts deeply into movie-going, radio-listening, comic book and pulp magazine reading. It reduces the time for play. It postpones bedtime slightly. It dominates the child's leisure" (page 169). For the most part, television has substituted for a variety of other kinds of fantasy activities that have been seriously criticized in much the same way that television has.

The content of the programs that appeal to children changes with age. When the child enters school his primary interest is in the children's variety shows and adventure programs consisting also of science fiction and children's westerns. This interest dominates through the early school years but very soon the interest includes the straight crime program and the situation comedy. As the child approaches adolescence he acquires an interest in the popular music variety shows. Public affairs programs, such as news and current events, gain a small audience in the later high school years.

Schramm and his colleagues report that the quality of the child's relationships with his family and his peers will determine the way in which he will use television. For the most part if these relationships are unsatisfactory "he tends to retreat to television where he can for a time leave the field of real-life problems and possibly reduce his tension. More conflict more television" (page 172). They found also that the child who is moved to be aggressive by frustration is likely to seek and remember the violent content of television and if his peer relationships are not satisfactory, he is likely to seek out the fantasy in television. The child who has a warm and acceptant home, who has satisfying relationships with peers, and who derives enjoyment from school will use television in such a way as not to be detrimental to him.

The Effects of Television

The effects of television can be divided into the following four categories: physical, emotional, cognitive or intellectual, and behavioral. There seems to be little or no evidence that television has harmful physical effects such as undue eyestrain, or serious loss of sleep, or energy. Although the evidence is not clear, television does seem to be a source of fear and may actually lead to a heightened state of excitement that could be deemed harmful. It may create an emotional set in children in which reality appears drab and unexciting compared to the glamour of television. The cognitive effects are beneficial only in the early years. The learning from television during this period is incidental but nevertheless significant. Children come to school with vocabularies about a grade higher than they do if they are not exposed to television. However, after the first year or so of school these effects seem to disappear and one might suspect that the intellectual effects are negative. Schramm and his associates state that: "Television has proved itself better at stimulating interest than stimulating intellectual or creative activity. . . . There is little sign that television is raising taste, and some fear has been expressed that it may be hardening in children a taste level based on its own common-denominator standards" (pages 173-174).

Many have expressed concern over television's possible harmful behavioral effects and have attributed to it such disturbances as delinquency and serious withdrawal into fantasy. This writer recently evaluated a nine-year-old boy who was seriously disturbed and who manifested a definite lack of contact with reality. Much of his behavior was imitative of television activities, he pretended (his pretense was too real) to be shooting and escaping in a fashion he had learned through television. The parents were inclined to blame television for his bizarre behavior and had restricted his viewing. Nevertheless, the disturbance continued. Careful investigation revealed that the basis for the boy's disturbance was much deeper and involved than simply his exposure to television. Beyond any doubt he would have been a seriously disturbed boy had television never been invented, he simply would have expressed his disturbance in a different manner. Freedman (1961) in a chapter contributed in the Schramm volume states the following:

> The intensity and psychic significance of the child's response to television is the reciprocal of the satisfaction he gains in the milieu of his family, school, and friends. One would predict that the less intelligent, the most disturbed youngsters, and those having the poorest relationship with their family and peers would be most likely to immerse themselves in televiewing as escape and stimulus. Intelligent, relatively stable youngsters in reasonably harmonious homes would be comparatively unaffected by it (page 192).

The factors that make for delinquency reside in the complex of the home, the neighborhood, and a personality predisposed to delinquent behavior. "The most that television can do is feed the malignant impulses that already exist."

How the Schools Can Use Television

The uses of educational television in and out of school are not our concern here. This mode of instruction must follow the general rules of teaching that were discussed in the first part of the book. It does little good for teachers to bemoan the poor quality of commercial television. This absorbing medium is here to stay for a while and the present organization of commercial television is not likely to change significantly so that little change in the quality of programing can be expected. Recognizing the limitations, the teacher would do well to consider his responsibility to his students vis-à-vis television. The teacher can encourage the selection of programs that have a reality orientation by incorporating the ideas presented into classroom learning. Some television presentations can be used for examples and even for assignments. Schramm et al. suggest that it is a good thing "to bring television into the real-life process of learning, to break down the barrier between passive fantasy experience and active use." A more important responsibility of the teacher is that of helping children develop discriminating tastes. The teacher needs to help the child learn to differentiate the good and the bad, the authentic and the superficial, in many areas of his experience. If the child could be helped to make these distinctions in television, he would at least make constructive use of this experience even if it is too much to hope that such discriminatory attitudes might ultimately improve the quality of television.

These things the school can do but the school must gain the cooperation of the parents. It will do no good if when the teacher assigns *Hamlet* the parents insist on watching a crime mystery. "The schools must take the parents into their confidence and their planning when they undertake this use of television."

SUMMARY

The child's personality and his significant attitudes are acquired in his family. In order for the school to work constructively with the child and to provide for a more complete understanding of personality development, the various ways in which parents influence their children are considered. The research literature on this topic points to certain plausible trends, yet the cause and effect relationships between a particular parent's behavior and a particular child's personality structure cannot be traced directly.

Because the parent-child relationship is such a complex phenomenon, there are many ways of describing it. The discussion is based on a consideration of five dimensions or continua of parent behavior and the general effects of the extremes of these parent behavior continua. These are:

1. *Rejectant-Acceptant.* This continuum describes the general emotional orientation of the parent to the child. An acceptant parent treats the child warmly and loves him for his own sake. A rejectant parent can at best only give love on a contingent basis. Children who feel that they are accepted by their parents will generally have a high degree of self-acceptance and self-confidence. Children who are rejected are likely to become withdrawn, resistant, and show signs of nonacceptance of self.

2. *Neglect-Overprotection.* This continuum describes the manner in which the parent fulfills his responsibility in providing protection for the child. The neglected child's behavior is similar to that of the rejected child. The overprotected child, if he is not at the same time indulged, will show signs of immature behavior and will be insecure.

3. *Permissive-Restrictive.* Parents have the responsibility of transforming the child's impulse-driven behavior to more socialized and controlled behavior. The parents' methods of accomplishing this may be placed on the permissive-restrictive continuum. Permissive parent behavior, when it is accompanied by other wholesome parent characteristics, generally leads to child behavior that is more spontaneous and original. When permissive parent behavior is ineffectual it may lead to conduct problems in children. Children reared in families where discipline is strict are likely to be hostile toward others and show less initiative and independence.

4. *Indulgent-Autocratic.* The manner in which conflict of interests between parent and child is resolved determines whether the relationship is called indulgent or autocratic. The child who has been excessively indulged is likely to be tyrranical and a poor group member. The child who has been treated autocratically will tend to be quiet, nonresistant, and restricted in originality. They may also act aggressively toward peers.

5. *Overinvolved-Impersonal.* The overinvolved parent is one who has almost completely identified with the child, while the impersonal parent is one who tends to dissociate himself from the child. The overinvolved parent does not readily permit the child's free development and this may lead to insecure and sometimes academically disabled child behavior. The data on the results of impersonal treatment are derived from studies of children who have been institutionalized during their early years. These children tend to be socially immature, restless, and

hyperactive; they are handicapped also in their intellectual development.

Teachers and parents must be very cautious as they attempt to understand each other with the child as the channel of communication. Children unintentionally provide distorted views of their environment. In communicating with parents, teachers must view a deficiency in the child's achievement as something to be corrected rather than condemned. The parents' cooperation should be enlisted with the child's consent and it should be specifically directed.

Television viewing, although a relatively new phenomenon, is a widespread and time-consuming home activity. Programs for children are designed to hold interest and to bring profit to commerical enterprises rather than to provide educative experiences. Research has shown that with the advent of television children tended to consolidate their needs for fantasy on television where before they distributed their fantasy seeking time among movies, comics, and other activities that have been subjected to the same kind of criticism as television. Where the child's home life is reasonably harmonious and satisfying, television seems to produce no significant harmful effects. On the other hand, in the type of home that tends to produce maladjustment and emotional instability in the child, the child will use television as a means of escape into fantasy life or as a source of stimulation for acting out his unhealthy impulses. Teachers can do much in cooperation with parents to foster selective viewing, the development of discriminating taste, and better use of reality-oriented television viewing.

READING REFERENCES

Miller, D. R. and G. E. Swanson, *The Changing American Parent*. New York: John Wiley & Sons, 1958.

Parsons, T. and R. F. Bales, *Family, Socialization, and Interaction Process*. New York: Free Press of Glencoe, 1955.

Schramm, W., J. Lyle and E. B. Parker, *Television in the Lives of our Children*. Stanford: Stanford University Press, 1961.

Sears, R. R., Eleanor E. Maccoby and H. Levin, *Patterns of Child Rearing*. New York: Harper & Row, 1957.

Stevenson, H. W. (Ed.), *Child Psychology*. Sixty-second Yearbook (Pt. 1) National Society for the Study of Education. Chicago: University of Chicago Press, 1963 (particularly chaps. 2 and 8-10).

Stout, I. W. and Grace Langdon, *Parent-Teacher Relationships* (What Research Says to the Teacher No. 16). Washington: National Education Association, 1958.

CHAPTER 14

SOCIAL CLASS FACTORS

Many of the individual differences discussed in the preceding chapters are conditioned by the social class status of the pupil. Families from different social classes differ not only in the economic advantages that they offer children, but also in providing consistently different learning settings. Children who come from families characterized as upper class will generally have better diets, better medical attention, better recreational opportunities than will children from lower-class families. But more important, a large number of investigations have shown that social class status determines the goals for which people strive, attitudes toward sex, cleanliness, aggression, and many other significant personality characteristics. The social class background of the pupil will influence his motivation toward school tasks, his familiarity with and interest in the concepts and content of the school curriculum, his choice of friends, his attitude toward the teacher as an authority figure and to the school as an institution. In short, the social class structure of our society is a pervasive influence in shaping individual differences. The teacher and the educator can better fulfill their responsibility if they understand the dynamics of our changing social class structure and if they understand the various ways in which individual children are affected by their membership in one or another class.

The first part of this chapter describes what is meant by social class or socioeconomic status, how it is measured, and the distribution of the classes in our society and in our schools. A larger portion of the chapter is devoted to a discussion of the various effects of social class membership upon the growing child. The third section discusses the ways in which different teachers react to social class differences. The chapter concludes with a statement of the ways in which the school as an institution can deal constructively with the problems arising from the social class structure of our society.

THE MEANING OF SOCIAL CLASS

Because the term "social class differences" is associated with the concepts of class struggle and revolution, it tends to produce negative reactions in many readers. One need not accept the proposition that the social classes are engaged in a death struggle in order to recognize that our society, as well as almost all social groups, is stratified. Even the casual observer of any community cannot fail to discern that there are slum dwellers, others who live in very modest circumstances, still others who share more fully in the affluence of our society, and a few whose social position places them in the upper classes.

Various research studies that have undertaken to investigate the social class phenomenon, have emphasized one or another dimension along which class differences operate. Kahl (1957) has reviewed the basic research on this topic and concludes that there are five basic variables that contribute to or are the product of social class differences.

PERSONAL PRESTIGE   In every community it will be found "that some people are looked up to, respected, considered people of consequence, and others are thought of as ordinary, unimportant, even lowly" (page 19). As the teacher looks around his class he will recognize here the daughter of a prominent physician, or the son of a well-known jurist, and there the child of a widowed seamstress or of the local barber. The prestige rating of a family is an important factor in social class position.

POSSESSIONS   The clearest indicators of possessions are income and type of dwelling. People with high incomes who dwell in expensive homes and in good neighborhoods "can afford an elegant style of life in consumption behavior, have contacts with people of note, are granted considerable prestige and through the workings of capital investment, can multiply their incomes" (page 9). On the other hand, the individual with an unstable income, with a poor credit rating, and who lives in a substandard dwelling will be unable to provide in the same way for the material needs of his family. There is no question but that these differences have a marked influence on children's development.

INTERACTION   Individuals differ in the range and selection of other persons with whom they interact. It was noted in Chapter 8 that through human interaction children learn to check, correct and extend their concepts of reality, and learn ways of coping with human feelings. It has been shown (as we shall detail later in this chapter) that at all ages people of similar social class level tend to have more personal and meaningful interaction with each other than with those of different levels. These patterns of differential contact both in adulthood and in childhood are influential in shaping the differing value systems found in the various classes.

CLASS CONSCIOUSNESS   The development of a stratified society in this country has followed a course different from that found in European nations. "The absence of a feudal past, the lack of a hereditary aristocracy, accounts in large part for different development which stratification has taken in the United States" (Mayer, 1955, page 29). This has meant that the signs of social class position are less defined and less clear. Class consciousness in our society is in many cases ambiguous. In spite of the ambiguity and lack of clarity of class distinctions, there is evidence that even children become aware of class differences and develop attitudes toward themselves and toward each other as a result of this awareness.

VALUE ORIENTATIONS   The members of the different classes develop different systems of value, different standards, and different beliefs about what is good, right, decent, and moral. They come to accept their own values as superior and self-evident and consider the values held by members of the other classes inferior or irrelevant. For teachers this means that children who come from the various social classes bring with them different ways of behaving and different views of life. These differing value orientations often create conflict and tension between the child and the teacher or between parents and the school and only when teachers understand the problem fully can they deal with it effectively. A later section describes the value-attitude system held by each of the social classes.

How an Individual's Social Class Is Determined

The best way to understand the meaning of a theoretical construct, such as social class status, is to ask how the scientist measures it. The variables that have been presented briefly will take on more meaning when we study how they have been employed to determine empirically the social class positions of the members of a community.

In the first two volumes of the six volume *Yankee City Series,* Warner and Lunt (1941 and 1942) have presented a detailed analysis of the social interaction and the status system of a modern community. This significant sociological contribution opened the way for an extensive literature on social class, because it provided the techniques for measuring this process. In a later volume Warner and others (1960) have spelled out more specifically the procedures for the measurement of social class. Warner's method for studying the class structure of a community is called Evaluated Participation. This method relies on information obtained from extensive interviews with selected members of the community. This method takes a great deal of time and is more appropriate for the sociologist or the cultural anthropologist than for the teacher. However, it is outlined briefly here because the simpler methods of class determination are based originally on this method.

The method of Evaluated Participation is based on the assumption that members of a community are explicitly or implicitly aware of the social organization of their community and that they evaluate the participation of other members of the community in terms of this organization. The task of the interviewer is to discover how the participation of all or nearly all the individuals of a community is evaluated by selected members of that community. The interviews are analyzed in a number of different ways. First we must determine whether the various informants agree on the social class configuration and whether they agree on the class placement of particular individuals. This part of the procedure is called matched agreements. The information in the interviews provides a basis for placing various individuals insofar as the informants identify where each should be placed through: (1) symbolic placement or simple assignment to a class, calling the person a real aristocrat, a middle-class person, or some other term of evaluation of social class position; (2) status reputation, an evaluation of the reputation of the individual as it is related to social status; (3) comparison with others whose social class has been determined; (4) institutional membership, where the institutions are ranked in terms of social status.

Using the method of Evaluated Participation, Warner concluded that there are five classes and he was able to assign most of the members of a community to one or another of these. In order to provide a shorter and simpler procedure, Warner developed an Index of Status Characteristics. The index relies on a rating from one to seven, one being the highest rating, on each of the following four factors: occupation, source of income, house type, and dwelling area. In order that the results obtained by the index be made to correspond to those obtained by the more laborious and presumably more valid method of Evaluated Participation, each of the ratings on the four factors receives different weights. Occupation has a weight of 4, source of income and house type each have a weight of 3, and dwelling area has a weight of 2. The rating number is multiplied by its assigned weight. Thus the highest class score a person can obtain would result from a rating of one on each of the four indexes multiplied by the appropriate weight, $(1 \times 4) + (1 \times 3) + (1 \times 3) + (1 \times 2)$, which gives a total of 12. The lowest class score would be the rating number 7 multiplied by the appropriate weights giving (7×4) $+ (7 \times 3) + (7 \times 3) + (7 \times 2) = 84$. The range of values is divided into the same five classes as derived from the method of Evaluated Participation. These classes are named as follows: I upper, II upper-middle, III lower-middle, IV upper-lower, V lower-lower. The reader can readily see that both methods of determining social class, the method of Evaluated Participation and the Index of Status Characteristics, are procedures for measuring various aspects of the five basic variables mentioned earlier in the chapter.

Lawson and Boek (1960) have shown that the index is a useful short measure of social class even when the individuals being assigned are from different communities. They also confirmed Warner's finding that occupation is the one status characteristic most closely related to class level.

In spite of the apparent precision with which social class status is assigned, it should be kept in mind that many individuals straddle class lines, that is, they have some of the characteristics of one social class and some of another. In addition, these individuals and others may be in the process of moving up or down across class lines, so that assignment to class position must be viewed as tentative in many cases (Havighurst and Neugarten, 1957).

The Distribution of the Classes in Our Society

Each community, depending on its size, age, and economic character, will present its own distribution of its population among the various classes. Thus a community with major industries requiring highly skilled workers will have a higher proportion of lower- and upper-middle-class people, while one in a coal-mining region will have a higher proportion of upper-lower-class families. Also the particular time at which we observe a community will determine the class distribution. In the course of as little time as one decade one community may flourish and attract to itself a certain kind of population, while another may become economically depressed losing large numbers of its middle-class group while retaining its lower-class intact. Havighurst (1961) has pointed out that with the rise of the "metropolitan complex" consisting of an industrial center and its dependent suburbs, three clearly marked types of homogeneous communities have appeared. "One is an upper-middle and upper-class suburb, with a very small number of lower-middle-class residents. Another is a working-class and lower-middle-class suburb, essentially of the 'common-man' character, with very few lower-lower-class residents. A third is a city slum, almost solid lower class, and as much as half lower-lower" (page 139).

With all of these forces making for differences in class distribution, it is noteworthy that over a long period of time the many communities that have been studied have been found to show a reasonable resemblance in regard to the relative sizes of the social classes. Table 14.1 presents the ranges of percentages found at each class level for middle-sized communities, population 5000 to 100,000.

TABLE 14.1 THE RANGE OF PERCENTAGES OF THE POPULATION FOUND AT EACH CLASS LEVEL IN DIFFERENT MIDDLE-SIZED COMMUNITIES

Class		Percentage range	Estimated percent in U.S.
I	Upper	1-3[1]	2
II	Upper-Middle	7-12	8
III	Lower-Middle	20-35	30
IV	Upper-Lower	25-40	40
V	Lower-Lower	15-25	20

[1] In some older communities the upper class is divided into two segments, upper-upper consisting of those with a tradition of family wealth and position and the lower-upper consisting of those who have more recently acquired their wealth. In metropolitan areas other distinctions among this small group can be found.

Source: R. J. Havighurst and Bernice L. Neugarten. *Society and Education,* Boston: Allyn and Bacon, 1957. Also, W. L. Warner, et al., *Social Class in America,* New York: Harper & Row, 1960.

Of greater interest to the teacher is the distribution of social classes to be expected within the school. The size of each social class and its geographic location within a community will determine the kind of social class distribution found in each school. In the case of the city elementary school, drawing as it does on a limited neighborhood, we would expect to find a fairly homogeneous student population. One elementary school will draw its students mainly from the two upper levels, another from the "common-man" level, that is, lower-middle and upper-lower class, while schools located in the slum sections of cities will draw their students from the two lower classes. In a centralized school, the elementary grades will contain a more representative cross-section of the social class distribution of the area served and the figures in Table 14.1 for the population at large would apply.

In high schools similar patterns of population distribution are to be found. However, the higher rate of drop-out among the lower classes changes the picture somewhat. Havighurst (1961) has estimated the social class distribution of students in three types of secondary schools, namely, a typical comprehensive high school, an upper-middle-class suburban high school and a city high school in an area with encroaching slums. The social class distribution of students in each of these schools is shown in Figure 14.1. In this figure the vertical dotted lines divide the graph into segments representing that portion of the nation's popula-

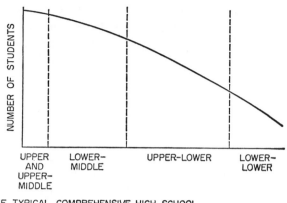

(*a*) THE TYPICAL COMPREHENSIVE HIGH SCHOOL

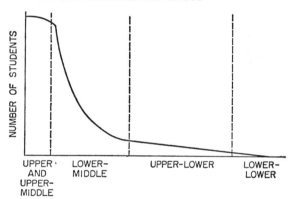

(*b*) AN UPPER-MIDDLE-CLASS SUBURBAN HIGH SCHOOL

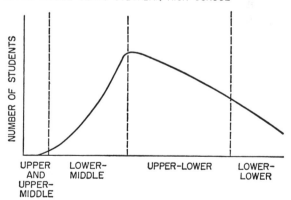

(*c*) A CITY HIGH SCHOOL IN AN AREA WITH ENCROACHING SLUMS

FIGURE 14.1 *Social class distribution of students in three types of secondary schools. From R. J. Havighurst, "Social-Class Influences on American Educa-tion," in N. B. Henry (Ed.),* Social Forces Influencing American Education, *Yearbook of the National Society for the Study of Education,* **60,** *Pt. 2, Chi-cago: University of Chicago Press, 1961, p. 141.*

tion to be found at each class level. The two upper classes would account for 10 percent, the lower-middle 30 percent, the upper-lower 40 percent, and the lower-lower 20 percent. The solid line on the graph shows that portion of each class found within each type of school. Thus in Graph A is shown a typical comprehensive high school serving all students of a given area. The curve dips downward showing the effects of the high drop-out rate in the lower classes. In Graph B is shown the distribution likely to be found in an upper-middle class suburb. It can readily be seen that the school contains very few students from the two lower classes that together make up an estimated 60 percent of the nation's high school age youth. "These are the schools which walk away with national and state scholarship contests" (page 142). Graph C shows the student population distribution in a city high school located in an area with enroaching slums. "More than half of the students are of upper-lower-class background, with lower-lower and lower-middle about evenly balanced and upper-middle-class students in a small minority. In this school it is almost impossible to maintain a college-preparatory atmosphere" (page 142).

THE EFFECTS OF SOCIAL CLASS MEMBERSHIP

Social stratification has sociological and psychological aspects. Up to this point some of the sociological dimensions have been considered. This section takes up the various psychological effects of this social process. Social class membership produces a number of effects that are relevant in a discussion of educational psychology. It was noted briefly in Chapter 10 that there exists a problem in the measurement of intelligence in that most tests currently in use appear to favor children from upper- and middle-class homes and to discriminate against those from lower-class homes—this problem is considered. The discussion will show how the child's family mediates the values and life orientation of its social class; how this life style influences the child's developing personality.

Child-Rearing Practices and Social Class

In the previous chapter some of the ways in which parents influence their children's personality were described. Most of the variables of parent behavior considered there were independent of social class membership. It was pointed out, however, that the kind of relationship that existed between the parent and the child during the first five years of the child's life was of prime importance in determining the course of personality development. The quality of this parent-child relationship manifests itself, in part, in the child-rearing practices adopted by the parent. These practices have been shown to differ along social class lines.

The findings of the various studies on social class differences in child-rearing appear, at first glance, to be contradictory. The influential study on this topic by Davis and Havighurst (1948a) showed that middle-class parents tend to train their children with more strictness and that they are more likely to frustrate the child's impulses than lower-class parents. On the other hand Sears and his associates (1957) reached the opposite conclusions: "The middle-class mothers were generally more permissive and less punitive toward their young children than were working-class mothers" (page 446). Bronfenbrenner (1958), after carefully reviewing the data of a score of studies, offers an explanation for these contradictory findings. He suggests that child-rearing practices within each of the social classes have changed over a period of time and the differences in the findings can be accounted for by the differences in the time at which the data were gathered.

Class differences in feeding, weaning, and toilet training show a clear and consistent trend. From about 1930 until the end of World War II, working-class mothers were uniformly more permissive than those of the middle-class. They were more likely to breast feed, to follow a self-demand schedule, to wean the child later both from breast and bottle, and to begin and complete both bowel and bladder training at a later age. After World War II, however, there has been a definite reversal in direction; now it is the middle-class mother who is more permissive in each of the above areas.

The studies reviewed by Bronfenbrenner further reveal that in more recent years working-class parents are more likely to use physical punishment as a technique of discipline whereas middle-class parents are more likely to use reasoning, isolation, or love-oriented techniques. Love-oriented discipline is the use of "praise for good behavior," expression of disappointment, the use of "symbolic rather than direct rewards and punishment."

These differences and others presented below are reported as statistical trends and must not be taken as definitive for any particular child from any particular home. Further, it should be emphasized again that the patterns of parent behavior that appear to be linked to class status are in a continuous process of change. This means that the descriptions of social class effects on behavior, values, school achievement, and intelligence are not inevitable or permanent. On the contrary, as we shall point out later, the school can play an important part in shaping the values of the future adult citizens of our society. This can only be done when teachers understand how forces such as social class operate in the lives of their students.

The Effects of Social Class: The Early School Years

The social class differences in child-rearing practices and parent-child relationships reported in the preceding paragraphs would suggest that the child from the middle-class home would, in general, be better prepared to make use of the school experience. This is in part due to the fact that the school as an institution is designed to achieve what some have called middle-class objectives. Also, the middle-class child can better make the transition from home to school, since teachers are for the most part middle-class oriented individuals, the child's adjustment to a new but similar adult personality will proceed more smoothly. The middle-class child is much more likely than the lower-class child to have had a nursery school or kindergarten experience (Stendler, 1951). Also, he is more likely to have received some preliminary training in communication skills and even more specific school skills such as the recognition of the letters of the alphabet, color naming, and the use of paper and pencil. The upper- and middle-class parents will more likely reflect a more favorable attitude toward scholastic achievement and success; they will reward it in their children, and they will make the child aware of the future rewards to be gained from schooling.

The lower-class child, on the other hand, is generally not as well prepared for school. He lacks much of the preliminary preparation and because the parents themselves may have negatively toned attitudes toward school, based on their own childhood experience, they transmit these to the child. For example, Stendler (1951) found that one fifth of the parents in the lower-lower class stated in an interview that the child's report card had not been received. Of some 200 parents in the other classes only one parent did not obtain the child's report card. Milner (1951) showed that a marked relationship existed between social class and language development by the first grade. Her results are shown in Table 14.2. It can be seen that the larger proportion of children whose language development is retarded come from lower-status families. Milner reports that mothers of children with low scores communicated less with their children than did mothers of high-scoring children. She found the following to be more characteristic of mothers of low-scoring children:

1. They do not eat breakfast together with the children;
2. They do not talk with the children during breakfast *or* they only give direct orders, cautions and instructions to them in a one-way communication fashion;
3. The children do not talk with anyone between the time they finish breakfast and the time they leave for school;
4. No one has any conversation with the children while they are eating their supper;
5. Neither they nor any other related adult hug, or kiss, or speak approvingly to their children (page 105).

TABLE 14.2   DISTRIBUTION OF LANGUAGE DEVELOPMENT SCORES IN
THREE SCHOOLS DIFFERING IN SOCIAL CLASS

Grade 1 class from:	Number of high scores	Number of low scores
School A (class consisting of 26 upper- and lower-middle class children).	16	1
School B (class consisting of 45 upper-lower and lower-middle class children).	5	8
School C (class consisting of 40 children from two lowest status categories).	0	12

Source: Esther Milner, "A Study of the Relationship between Reading Readiness in Grade-One Children and Patterns of Parent-Child Interaction," *Child Development,* 1951, **22,** pp. 95-112.

Hollingshead (1949) studied the impact of social class on the adolescents of a Midwest community. His findings on adolescent friendship choices will be reported later. However, his speculation on how the preparation at home for the encounter with the school influences the child's success or failure in school, is of interest to us here.

> The culture complex associated with classes I, II and III (upper- and middle-class) trains boys and girls to respond positively to competitive situations such as that presented by examination and intelligence tests. Experience imbues them with a need for personal achievement that is expressed in their constant search for success, teaching them from infancy to face each new situation aggressively and to overcome it to the best of their ability. When they take a test, whether it is arithmetic or intelligence, they normally try to do their best on it, for their ego is on trial and they must make good, and they generally do. On the other hand, the class V (lower-class) adolescent has been subjected to a family and class structure in which failure, worry and frustration are common. He has not been trained at home to do his best in school. His parents have not ingrained in him the idea that he must make good grades if he is to be a success in life. Moreover, the class system as it functions in the school does not help him overcome the poor training he has received at home and in the neighborhood (pages 175-176).

Although coming from an upper- or middle-class home gives the child a distinct advantage over his peer from the lower-class family, it is not always an unmitigated blessing. The middle-class family interaction pattern does not necessarily produce a spontaneous, creative type of child. The pressure for academic success and the parent's implied threat of withdrawal of love should the child fail, may well lead to a level of anxiety and apprehension that interferes with mental functioning. It is common in families of the middle class for the parents to view the child's ability and achievement as marks of the parents' accomplishment. The child is given a measure of love if he helps his family "keep up with the

Joneses" by means of noteworthy academic or athletic performance. Love is withdrawn and disappointment shown, if the child fails to perform as well as the parents feel he should or if the child, by doing poor work, threatens the family's social class position. This barter-type relationship exists more frequently in families that have recently acquired a higher social class position.

Since the parents' expectations of the child are set outside the child's abilities, he will often see himself as a failure. The child subjected to this pressure, experiences difficulty in developing any intrinsic motivation for school work. Even when he does well he is rewarded not for the work itself but for the advantage in the status competition stressed by the parents. The teacher, on the other hand, because he is less involved, may be able to establish a more supporting relationship with the child, enabling him to learn for his own purposes.

Social Class Effects: Later School Years

As a group upper- and middle-class children will be better prepared for school learning and, as they progress through the grades, the advantage over their lower-class age mates increases. A number of factors operate to produce this effect. These factors can be classified as those pertaining to the child's personality characteristics and his attitudes toward the school and those pertaining to the reaction of the school community. These two sets of factors interact with each other. That is to say, the attitudes of the student induce a reaction from teachers and peers that tends to reinforce the attitude, and the reaction of teachers and others to certain class characteristics tends to produce in the student other attitudes and feelings about school. It is often difficult to discern which of these comes first, the social class determined characteristic or the reaction of the school community to status characteristics. Probably, as in any interaction effect, they are inseparable.

The differentiated experiences of children from the various social classes produce different personality and behavior characteristics. Leshan (1952) has found some support for the hypothesis that there are different time orientations in the various levels of social class. The lower-lower-class individual is characterized by an orientation to the present rather than to the future. He is not inclined to frustrate himself over long periods or to postpone immediate gratification for the sake of possible future rewards. The future is perceived as indefinite and vague, and it does not have strong motivational value because its rewards and punishments are uncertain. In the classes above the lower-lower class, the individual's plans for the future play a prominent role in shaping behavior. He becomes increasingly better able to postpone immediate gratification of impulse and desire in order to reap the possible benefits of greater rewards in the future.

Schramm et al. (1961) whose study on television was referred to in the previous chapter, confirm these findings. They found, moreover, that adolescents who are high users of television and low users of print and whom they called the "fantasy group" are more likely to come from the lower socio-economic groups. "Between the sixth and the tenth grades, children of white-collar families are making a major change, decreasing their use of television, turning to reality experiences" (page 108); while the working-class children continue to rely heavily on fantasy experiences. Schramm and his colleagues demonstrate that these differences are closely related to the differing social class values of immediate versus deferred gratification.

These findings have several implications for education. Much as we may try to make the content of the curriculum currently meaningful in the lives of children, there always seems to be an implication of future use for what the child learns in school. This becomes more and more true as the child progresses through school. The lower-class youngster has difficulty in changing his time orientation. Also as he grows older he must make decisions and choices between homework and TV, between continuing in school and taking a job, between completing his studies and getting married. The lower-class person, more than the middle-class one, tends to make decisions that favor his present needs rather than more distant goals.

There is further evidence that social class differences produce differences in basic personality structure from a study by Miller and Swanson (1960). They studied a group of junior high school boys and found that social class position with its concomitant family interaction patterns was significantly related to a number of personality variables.

One part of the study deals with the mechanisms of defense. (Some of these mechanisms and their operation were described in Chapter 11.) Miller and Swanson classified the various defenses into two categories. In the first category they placed those that are simple in that they appear early in life and do not require complex learned skills, those that distort large segments of reality, those that serve almost any type of conflict, and those that are socially disruptive. An example of a defense in this first category is denial in fantasy. It is simple and like dreaming requires little training, distorts reality, can be used in almost any type of conflict, and may prevent the carrying on of normal social relationships. In the second category they placed those defense mechanisms that are complex as they depend on learned skills and distort reality less, but that are applicable only to specific types of conflict. Our illustration of aggression turned inward in Chapter 11, is an example of a defense in this category. Miller and Swanson found that their junior high school subjects who came from lower-class families where discipline was more severe, were more inclined to use defenses in the first category.

Those boys who came from middle-class families where discipline was more benign, tended to use defenses in the second category.

Another finding is related to the preferred styles of expression of the different social classes. They investigated the incidence of two expressive styles, namely, the *motoric* or the use of the voluntary, large muscles, and the *conceptual* or the preference for the manipulation of ideas. As might be expected, they found that boys from the working-class were predominantly motoric while the boys from the middle class were more conceptual.

In their final review, Miller and Swanson present the following summarizing paragraph.

> Boys in the middle class persevere; they feel that they must succeed in difficult tasks and blame themselves when they fail. If they are in conflict about aggression, they are inclined to reverse it or turn it inward. It is more difficult for working-class boys to persevere. If the task is difficult and their intelligence moderate, they may revert to denial. These children seem to have as many internalized prohibitions against direct aggression as the sons of white-collar workers, but social pressures and the internalized values of the group prompt them to fight. They are frequently plagued by problems of self-control and of guilt. When they express aggression, they tend not to blame themselves or to reverse their impulses (page 396).

In addition to the personality effects produced by social class position, a number of studies have documented the effects on reputation among peers and on peer relations. While children in the primary grades tend to ignore class lines in choosing friends at school, fifth- and sixth-grade children and high school youth take social class into account as they establish their cliques and choose their associates. Neugarten (1946) found that when children were asked to identify the person they would like best for a friend they most often chose children above them in social class; the second most frequent choices were made within the same class, and very few choices were made downward in the social scale. This resulted in lower-class children being chosen almost exclusively from among peers of their own class, if they were chosen at all.

In another study (Havighurst and Taba, 1949) it was shown that character reputations among adolescents were clearly related to class position. When adolescents are asked to rate each other on five character traits (honesty, loyalty, responsibility, moral courage, and friendliness), "the data show that subjects in the upper social classes tended to be rated above the average in all five traits; those in the lower classes, to be rated below the average" (page 49). The data of this study seem to point to the fact that character reputation is related primarily to the student's conformity to school standards and ideologies. The character ratings of the lower-class youth were more variable than those of the upper-middle class. The authors suggest that upper-middle-class homes consistently support the value orientation of the school, whereas in the lower-class homes the values of the school may be reinforced in some cases and not reinforced in others.

Hollingshead (1949) studied the actual associations of high school youth and found that in dating and in clique relations, the preponderance of choices were of equals with equals in regard to social class and only in rare instances did these associations cross more than one social class line. He summarizes his data as follows:

> The majority of clique and dating relations takes place between persons who belong to the same prestige class. When cross-class ties are established, they tend to involve persons from an adjacent class, except that persons in each class try to develop relationships with persons a class higher in the prestige structure than themselves. Conversely, the higher class person, on the average, tried to limit his contacts with persons of lower prestige than himself in order that he not be criticized for "lowering himself." This process operates in all classes, but is especially noticeable in contacts with Class V (lower-lower class). This class is so repugnant socially that adolescents in the higher classes avoid clique and dating ties with its members (page 241).

The reader is reminded of the discussion of delinquency in Chapter 6. It was pointed out there that children from lower-class homes find it difficult to achieve any mark of success or a sense of worth within the school and this frequently leads to truancy and other forms of delinquency-prone behavior. Delinquents as a group tended to express feelings of not being recognized. The discussion of peer relations documents the fact that these feelings are based on reality. However, as indicated earlier, it is difficult to tell whether the rejection by teachers and peers produces the nonconforming behavior in the lower-lower class youngster, or whether the behavior that he brings to school is objectionable and induces rejection. In either case, the task of the school is to reduce undesirable behavior traits and to develop more acceptant attitudes. This question is returned to at the conclusion of the chapter.

Intelligence Test Scores and Social Class

Of all the effects produced by social class status the most meaningful for the school and the one that has aroused the most controversial discussions is that of intelligence testing. In Chapter 10 it was pointed out that several investigators had been concerned about the finding that intelligence tests were biased in favor of the middle class. One study (Davis and Havighurst, 1948b) found that 90 percent of the items used in four tests of intelligence discriminated significantly between children of high and low socioeconomic levels. Operating on the assumption that large populations that are undifferentiated as to genetic constitution should not differ in intelligence, Davis and Eells proceeded to con-

FIGURE 14.2 *Sample practice exercise for the Davis-Eells Test. From W. A. Davis and K. Eells,* Directions for Administering and Scoring the Davis-Eells Test of General Intelligence or Problem-Solving Ability, *New York: Harcourt, Brace & World, 1953.*

struct a test of general intelligence or problem-solving ability. This is a group test for grades one to six, the items are designed to be equally interesting to all children regardless of social class, and performance is not dependent on reading skill, speed of response, or previous school instruction.

The test problems in the Davis-Eells Test consist of a series of pictures. Figure 14.2 shows a sample of the practice exercises. The child is told to look at the appropriate picture while the person administering the test tells about the picture. As an example, for picture A, the first practice exercise, the following is read:

> Now look at the *first* picture. It shows a woman; it shows a man with a bump on his head; and it shows a broken window. A boy is outside the window. Now here is the way you do this picture. I am going to say three things about this picture. Look at it and find out *the thing* that is true.
>
> No. 1: The man fell down and hit his head.
> No. 2: A ball came through the window and hit the man's head.
> No. 3: The picture *does not show how* the man got the bump on his head. Nobody can tell because the picture doesn't show how the man got the bump.
>
> Which number was true?
> Listen for wrong answers. Explain why each incorrect answer is not right. Then say:
> Yes, No. 2—A ball came through the window and hit the man's head—is true.
> (Instructions are given for marking the correct answer).
> (Sample B) Now look at the *next* picture; it is beside the one you just did. It shows a *boy* and a *girl,* waving their hands. Look at the picture while I tell you about it. Which number is right? Be sure to look at the picture.

No. 1 Box: They are waving at a *boy*.
No. 2 Box: They are waving at a *girl*.
No. 3 Box: We *cannot tell* from this picture *whom* they are waving to.
   (Davis-Eells Manual, 1953, pages 2-3)

The intent of Davis and Eells in devising their test was to avoid validating their test against the criterion of school performance. They chose rather to examine the nature of problem solving and to develop items that appear logically related to this process. The test calls to our attention that the term intelligence may be viewed as more than school performance, or verbal ability expressed only through reading. This is important to keep in mind. However, one may question the usefulness of this test, which purports to be culture-fair. Let us suppose that a child from a poor socioeconomic background scores high on this culture-fair test but low on the usual test of intelligence. The high score may help us understand that in many problem situations in life this youngster would be able to do well, it does not predict school performance one way or the other. The low score tells us that school performance is likely to be weak, but it does not predict how the youngster is likely to perform in problem situations outside of school work. School people are understandably more interested in school tasks and predictors of performance in academic subjects. They like to think of reading disability and poor number performance as deficiencies. Davis and Eells minimize these difficulties and point out that these alone are not sufficient basis for a label of low intelligence. Academic ability might be a better term for what has been called intelligence particularly as measured by group tests of intelligence, but academic ability is a most desirable quality. This high regard for academic ability may be termed a bias, however, to remain consistent with the values presented in Chapter 6 it must be asserted that the realm of ideas is an important one for the self-realization of a person. Conant (1961) quotes a knowledgeable person in the field of testing (he does not identify this person) who pointedly expresses the author's point of view.

> If a child does poorly on an aptitude test because he comes from the wrong side of the tracks, it isn't the test that is being 'unfair,' it is hard facts of social circumstances that are unfair. Anyone who is seriously interested in improving the lot of the culturally underprivileged should direct his attention not to changing tests—which would accomplish literally nothing —but to improving the quality of educational opportunity for all children (pages 14-15).

Davis and his many co-workers at the University of Chicago have pointed out a number of assumptions that were being widely overlooked in the use of intelligence-test results. An IQ score is not a measure of biological superiority or inferiority. It can be demonstrated, by choosing test items that do not favor one group or another, that genetic factors, if there are any in the makeup of the characteristic called intelligence, are not differentially distributed in our population. These investigators further drew attention to the fact that the term intelligence was being misused when it was derived from the performance on tests that related to verbal or academic success. There are many other skills and abilities that are not related to school achievement and that are not measured by the usual intelligence test, yet these skills and abilities are as much a part of intelligence as school performance.

Children from the lower socioeconomic classes are, as a group, handicapped in their school performance. This handicap is not due to any biological inferiority but rather to lack of supporting experiences in the home. The handicap, nevertheless, is one of major significance and efforts need to be made to enable those who cannot learn in our schools, to overcome this deficiency. The concluding section of this chapter offers recommendations for action that could alleviate this problem.

THE TEACHER AND SOCIAL CLASS

In order to understand the teacher's relationship to children from the different social classes, the social class orientation of the teachers themselves must be examined. Early studies of the social background of teachers showed that teachers as a rule came from white-collar and upper-middle-class backgrounds. More recently it appears that there is greater diversity in the social backgrounds of teachers, many more are currently from homes of the blue-collar or upper-lower-class homes. For these teachers, as well as for many others, the profession of teaching may be the avenue for social mobility and the method for achieving a higher social status than that held by their parents. Whatever their social origins, teachers as a group hold to most of the so-called middle-class values, and many of them, because of their recent social mobility, hold these values uncritically and intensely. Some of these middle-class values have been considered in the discussion of the effects of social class on the growing child. In the adult middle-class individual these values take on additional characteristics that are relevant to the discussion here. The following list of adult middle-class values is based in part on a presentation by McCandless (1961).

1. Most teachers, as members of the middle class, express a belief in God and they are usually active in church activities. In Chapter 6 a case is described in which a teacher's uncritical view of religious belief leads her into difficulty with a middle-class boy whose family had no avowed religious affiliation.

2. Middle-class teachers value cleanliness and order very highly

and they respond negatively to body odors, dirty hands, unkempt hair, as well as to lack of order.

3. They value thrift, ownership, and a good reputation on money matters.

4. The teacher, as a member of the middle class, has a strict code of honesty. Many middle-class people violate this code but they tend to be more surreptitious in doing so than lower-class people.

5. They view emotions and reason as being in conflict, and value the latter over the former.

6. The middle-class teacher stands strongly opposed to the expression of strong emotion, particularly those emotions that are aggressive or sexual in nature.

7. The use of clean and correct language stands fairly high on the middle-class teacher's scale of values.

8. The middle-class person is likely to operate on the premise that hard work and self-discipline will be rewarded. Along with this goes a strong sense of duty and responsibility to others as well as a sense of guilt when engaged in activities that bring satisfaction in and of themselves.

9. The middle-class teacher believes that learning and schooling are means of improving one's social position. The teacher who has used this avenue for his own social mobility is likely to believe this even more firmly.

This is not meant to be a caricature of the value system of the middle-class individual or a stereotype of the public school teacher. Members of the middle class may have many individual characteristics that would modify those listed here. Spontaneity, objectivity, warmth, and concern for the human personality are a few such characteristics that are to be found in abundance among middle-class teachers.

Teachers and children from middle-class homes share similar class derived values, hence these do not usually form a basis for tension and conflict when the teacher attempts to socialize and to teach the child. However, the parent from the lower-lower-class home, as just indicated, has often not attempted to inculcate these values and, in fact, may have transmitted values that are in direct opposition to those held by the middle class. It is with these children (more than 25 percent of our school-age population) that middle-class teachers often experience difficulty because of the clash of values. Davis (1948) has pointed out that the schools serving the children from the lower-lower class "are almost a complete failure. The staffs of these schools are aware of their basic failure, and are demoralized" (page 23). This aggravates an already serious problem, for as Conant (1961) on this same issue states, "teachers who have achieved some seniority rights often apply for transfer away from the slum neighborhoods." Teachers who are generally trained to teach children with a middle-class orientation experience serious difficulty in dealing "with slum-area children whose values run directly counter to those of the teachers" (page 68).

The following three descriptions of classroom situations illustrate some of the various ways in which this clash of values can be handled.

A Case of Unbending Middle-Class Teachers

Our first illustration takes us to a high school of the type described in Figure 14.1 as a city high school in an area with encroaching slums. This case situation of unbending middle-class teachers is adapted from Rasey (1950).

Miss Dean, a social worker in the Department of Public Welfare of a large metropolitan area, visited Hilton High School. Many children from the families she served attended this school and she had become greatly concerned with the apparent misfitting of much of the curriculum to the needs of some pupils and the consequent resentful attitudes toward school among a number of adolescents.

Thinking that the young person preparing for work would be able to see a relation between the study of English and everyday living, Miss Dean went to visit the head of the English Department. Mr. Chamberlain proved to be a curious mixture of complacency and insecurity. He reported that young folks weren't what they used to be when he was a boy. "Too much riff-raff up from the South—ought to have stayed where they were." Miss Dean asked him if he knew that many of the pupils worked more than twenty hours per week; he retorted that he did not need to know this and that school was not for them anyway—just a waste of public money and effort.

When Miss Dean asked to visit a classroom, the department head took her to the room of Miss Allen. She was a neatly-dressed woman of about forty. The class was writing, apparently answering questions from the board. Miss Allen was seated at her desk marking notebooks. She had just completed marking the last one and started to transfer the marks into a classbook full of tiny squares after each name. She used three pens. She explained that the black indicated grades received from work done on time. Green indicated excused absences made up. Red was for unexcused absences that could not be made up. Miss Dean asked about two boys whose names she recognized and whose records were red practically across the page. Miss Allen could only talk about the marks in the little squares in her record book. She quite evidently knew little or nothing about the students' lives outside of school; such as who worked, who came from broken homes or where they lived. Neither did she show much awareness or concern about how her students felt about her class or school in general.

While Miss Dean was engaged in conversation with Miss Allen,

Mr. Chamberlain had left the room and then returned with a boy whom Miss Allen had sent to the English office. He asked the boy to be seated while he spoke to Miss Allen. He commended her for maintaining high standards and encouraged her to continue her efforts in this direction so as to push the rubbish out early and to give college material a chance. Mr. Chamberlain then turned to the boy and said, "Now what was your trouble?"

The boy answered sullenly, "I couldn't git Ivanhoe." Miss Allen then joined her departmental chairman in berating the boy, pointing out that he was big, that he was lazy, and that he failed the course once before. They then sent him back to the study hall without a word of assistance.

Miss Dean asked both English teachers why they thought everyone should "git Ivanhoe." Mr. Chamberlain stated that it was important in a cultured English-speaking society and that it was implied in most college requirements. Miss Allen said that it was suggested in the state course of study. The best their corkscrew logic could muster was college requirement—for a boy they were trying to crowd out because he wasn't high school material.

A Middle-Class Teacher Accommodates to Lower-Class Children

This illustration is adapted from Havighurst and Neugarten (1957). The setting is an elementary school serving a neighborhood bordering on an industrial section of a city of about one million.

Unlike most teachers, Mrs. Gordon, who had been teaching at this school for fifteen years, had requested to teach in this neighborhood. She had previously taught in schools serving children who came from upper-middle-class homes. She had somehow resented the snobbishness and the superficial liberality of the children and the parents.

Mrs. Gordon did not mind her assignment of supervising the children as they entered the school. One November morning she stood at the girl's entrance to the grimy, red-brick school seeing that the girls formed an orderly line ready to march in when the buzzer sounded. She heard a scuffle behind her and a big eighth-grade girl landed on the pavement beside her. "Damn you!" the girl shouted, and then looking up at Mrs. Gordon she said, "Teacher, they pushed me."

Mrs. Gordon ordered the girl back into line, telling her that she was setting a bad example for the younger children. Mrs. Gordon followed the end of the line into the building and up to her own fifth-grade room on the third floor. The children were noisy and boisterous but they settled down as their teacher strode into the room and spoke out in a strong but pleasant voice, "Good morning, class."

"Good morning, teacher," several of them answered, and smiled as she smiled at them.

"Ray, will you please open the window?" Mrs. Gordon asked, and a big boy raised a window. She had to do this every morning, for the smell would become quite strong after a few short minutes. She knew that there were children in her class who came from homes where hot water for bathing and laundry was a luxury not easily afforded. Two boys wore pieces of stocking on their close-cut heads, covering a shiny ointment used to treat ringworm.

Forty boys and girls stood next to their seats in straight rows as they repeated the pledge of allegiance. Mrs. Gordon liked this ceremony. It was to her a symbol of unity in a variegated group that she sometimes called her "United Nations." Eighteen of the children were Negroes, some dark-skinned, others with lighter complexion. A few children were Mexican and four of the class were Puerto Rican children who had come into the class in the last two weeks. As she looked around the room she realized that since the beginning of the school year eight children had transferred out and ten of the present class were newcomers. There were a few children with Italian names, a few with Polish names, and twin brothers with the name of McManus, the same name as the school. The latter spoke a colloquial English having moved to the city last year from a rural Kentucky community.

Mrs. Gordon's father had been a laborer and later a labor organizer. She and her husband, an engineer, lived in a "good" residential neighborhood and her two sons, now in college, had gone to the school near her home. She never had any doubts about her ability to handle children. She ruled them kindly but firmly. Most of the children felt she was a fair teacher, although a strict one, and a number of them would return to visit years later and would thank her for having taught them how to work. Many of them had been successful in their young careers.

As she looked around her room she recognized many whom she had not reached and some whom she might never be able to help. They would drop out of school, as their parents had, at the earliest opportunity. But she would possibly teach them a little more than their parents knew. There were always one or two bad ones. She was keeping her eyes on John Washington, a tough, over-age Negro boy with a sullen expression. One day he had been annoying the boy sitting in front of him, and the boy had turned his head sharply and rammed it into Washington's open knife. The gash in his cheek had required five stitches. The principal had warned the Washington boy that if he ever came to school with a knife again he would be sent to the special school for delinquent boys. Mrs. Gordon knew that a number of the students who had been graduated from the school had spent time in correctional institutions. However, she regarded it as her job not only to reduce delinquency but also to help as many children as possible lead productive and satisfying lives.

Mrs. Gordon thought that a few of the children in her room showed clear promise of doing well. There was Maria, the girl who had the looks and possibly the talent to become a great dancer. Mrs. Gordon personally took Maria to the settlement house in the neighborhood and asked the director to place the girl in a dance group. There was also David, the Negro boy who was a good reader and good at arithmetic. She thought that he might benefit from college work. She told him this and she told it to his father and mother when they had visited during open house. She told them about Donald Matthews, the highest ranking boy in her first class at McManus, also a Negro, who had just won a fellowship for graduate work in chemistry at the state university where he had distinguished himself as an athlete as well.

Mrs. Gordon knew that the great majority of her pupils would grow up to be hard-working respectable people, and from her they needed patient teaching and firm handling.

A Third Case Involving Social Class Effects

After a decade of teaching in a moderately new elementary school midway between a very nice residential section and a slum area, Mrs. Bishop thought she had encountered every possible type of problem. Because of the school's location, she had become interested in the problem of social class differences and in summer school she had read some of the works of Warner, Davis, Hollingshead, and Havighurst.

She had ordinarily established a fine working relationship in her home economics classes between herself and the girls from the lower social classes and also among the children from various types of homes. But Linda was the most pathetic child she had ever taught. Never had Mrs. Bishop seen a girl more completely different from the group or more completely shunned by her peers.

In the homemaking classroom all the girls found seats around the tables with friends. Linda sat apart and alone. She was a girl of medium height, rather heavy, and quite dirty. Her glasses wore a thick film of grease and her hair stood out from her head in a matted tangle. Her cotton skirt and blouse were spotted and soiled and the torn folds of a slip hung below the skirt. On her feet she wore men's high sneakers and no socks.

As the teacher and the class became better acquainted, Mrs. Bishop noted that Linda did not participate in class discussion except to answer a direct question. She spoke almost in monosyllables, turning her head away and with something of a speech defect. After a few weeks the teacher consulted the guidance folder and found a record of failure throughout her school career. She had repeated first, second, and sixth grade, and was now three years over-age in seventh grade. A note in the folder indicated a reading difficulty in the second grade but no remedial measures were instituted. This fact led Mrs. Bishop to discount the group intelligence test measures that indicated IQ's from 70 to 80.

Mrs. Bishop found from the record that Linda's home had been visited by her third-grade teacher who had entered a note indicating that the girl lived with her grandmother, an older sister, and a younger brother in an area known in town as "the tunnel." This was a short street built over a railway tunnel with a livery stable and several vacant buildings on one side and a few run-down dwellings on the other. The buildings on this street had since been demolished to make way for a low-cost housing project.

Linda's father had died in an accident when her mother was pregnant with the third child. Shortly after the boy was born the mother had remarried leaving the three children in the care of the maternal grandmother. The grandmother, whom Mrs. Bishop met some months later, supported the children by cleaning offices downtown while the mother, who now had two other children, paid little attention to her first family.

The older girl was in high school and seemed to be getting along reasonably well in a commercial program. The brother, who was in the fourth grade, was slow but fairly well adjusted to the group. Mrs. Bishop wondered why these environmental circumstances seemed to affect one child so adversely, whereas the other children were affected to a much lesser degree. She could only speculate that at the time of the father's death and the mother's abandoning the family, Linda's age made her more vulnerable than the others to these experiences of rejection.

Mrs. Bishop began to make some plans for this girl. She thought that she might have her in her home economics class for this year and the next and she decided "to make haste slowly." Her main project after Christmas was the making of a cotton skirt. The teacher knew that Linda's grandmother would resent having to purchase the materials for the skirt. With the help of an understanding principal, Mrs. Bishop purchased a simple pattern, fabric, thread, and so forth, put them in a suit box such as the other girls would be using, and quietly presented them to Linda before the beginning of the project. Linda worked hard, stolidly, and stubbornly. She lacked the manipulative skill and the previous experience of the other girls, but she wanted that skirt and with the teacher's encouragement she finally managed to finish it in a quite creditable way. This was a big event in her life, since this seemed to be the first time in a long time that she had tried and had been successful. Her appearance improved just a little and she did not appear to be as withdrawn. She even managed to smile.

In the spring Mrs. Bishop heard about a project sponsored by a service organization that provided eye examinations and glasses for needy school children. It was not difficult for her to arrange to have Linda fitted with new glasses. Also, the school nurse had arranged for some much needed dental care. Linda completed the seventh grade with some noticeable improvement.

At the beginning of the eighth grade, Mrs. Bishop presented a unit entitled "Improving Our Personal Appearance." The class planned the various parts of the unit such as posture, cleanliness, shampooing hair, manicuring nails, choosing hair styles, selecting matching colors and styles of clothes, and proper methods of caring for clothes. The teacher knew that many of the girls would benefit from this unit, but she hoped that it might make a significant impact on Linda. Accordingly, she asked Linda ahead of time if she would permit the teacher to demonstrate haircutting and shampooing on her. She agreed readily. It turned out to be quite a task for a double period but Mrs. Bishop was able to thin, comb, cut, shampoo, and set the hair. She put a large mirror in front of Linda so she could watch and learn how to do her hair herself. When the job was done the teacher presented Linda with the comb, brush, and bobby pins.

After this incident, signs of changed behavior became more apparent. Her appearance improved and with it her acceptance as part of the group. This acceptance appeared to serve as a reinforcement for the improved behavior and she appeared to be developing some self-acceptance. She began to contribute occasionally to class discussion and her speech showed some improvement. Other teachers reported that they could respond more positively to the girl and they noted a gain in her academic performance, even though she was still seriously retarded.

In the spring of the eighth grade, Linda decided to make her own graduation dress. She had been able to persuade her grandmother to give her some money to purchase the material and the very simple pattern. Linda had several lapses in the course of this venture, but none of them was crucial. The dress needed to be laundered when the sewing was done and Mrs. Bishop took the dress home and laundered it for her. Linda borrowed white shoes from her sister who was earning some money and was no longer ashamed of her as she had been previously. The principal arranged for Linda to obtain a "special" diploma, which she received with some pride on graduation day.

Some three years later, Mrs. Bishop met Linda downtown. She seemed neatly and appropriately dressed. Mrs. Bishop stopped to talk to her and found that she had married, that she and her husband were working and seemed to be getting along quite well. Mrs. Bishop conveyed her feelings in stating, "I was happy and pleased, for I sincerely believed that my two years of effort had borne fruit; that I was able to give Linda some of the affection, feeling of belonging and likeness to others that she needed so badly, that I was perhaps partly responsible for helping her achieve better mental health."

Although the last two illustrations are of moderate successes in dealing with children from the lower-lower class, all is not well on this issue. On the contrary, the problem of the school in the slum area is becoming increasingly serious. It is possible that if nothing constructive is done to ameliorate the situation, it can grow to such proportions as to lead to social catastrophe. It is with this thought in mind that the following recommendations are offered.

THE IMPROVEMENT OF EDUCATION
IN THE LOWER CLASSES

Because the proper education of the children from the lower-lower class has broad social implications, the recommendations for improvement cannot be limited only to teachers and teaching procedures. They must also take into account the parents of these children and the community at large. Implementing these recommendations will in many instances involve an increase in expenditure of money. However, if our society is to approach its ideal of equal educational opportunities for all children, the present inequity in educational expenditures must be reduced. Conant (1961) has pointed out that in spite of the more complex pedagogic task of the slum school, as compared to the school in the wealthy suburb, the expenditure per pupil is in the latter more than twice that spent in the former. The contrast is further exaggerated when the school facilities are examined and the ratio of professional staff to pupil population. "In the suburb there is likely to be a spacious modern school staffed by as many as 70 professionals per 1,000 pupils; in the slum one finds a crowded often dilapidated and unattractive school staffed by 40 or fewer professionals per 1,000 pupils. The contrast challenges any complacency we may have about our method of financing public schools" (page 3).

Teachers and Teaching

Even if these financial inequities were to be corrected, the program for the education of lower-class children requires adequately trained teachers for the task. The one thing that teachers must learn is that some middle-class values to which they subscribe are something less than divinely revealed. "The prospective teacher should be taught to distinguish the basic democratic values of our society from the host of lesser class-bound values which are not a necessary part of a public educational program" (Warner et al., 1944). Even after making such a distinction the teacher may find the lower-lower class child deficient in regard to some basic values in regard to his choice of ways to achieve self-enhancement and in his consideration of the rights of others (see Chapter 6).

One area of value conflict is that of physical aggression. Common consent and voluntary cooperation are more desirable social arrangements than those that rely on physical power and violence. The slum child's environment is often one that condones and encourages physical aggression as a way of resolving differences. The teacher who reacts to this particular problem by taking an overly sympathetic, extremely charitable, and do-good attitude is likely to be quickly demoralized. Some children will interpret this attitude as a sign of weakness and will frequently taunt and provoke the teacher into retaliation or withdrawal and retreat. On the other hand, the mailed fist approach can also lead to disaster for it is not likely that the teacher will be as well schooled in methods of attack as the child has been. Moreover, it is not reasonable to expect that a child will learn to be less aggressive physically when even the teacher and the school are openly hostile and aggressive toward him.

Conant commends the strict discipline and order that seems to have worked so well in the slum school. Under present conditions of staff shortage and large classes, rigid rules of discipline must be maintained. This should be regarded as a temporary measure. With a professional staff adequate both as to number and training, it should be possible to "bring some kind of order to otherwise chaotic lives" along with a measure of self-acceptance and self-control.

It should be clear from the discussion earlier in this chapter that lower-class children as a group do not do as well in the many areas of school performance requiring verbal skills. They rely more heavily than middle-class children on motor skills. In view of this situation, some have suggested that the school place less emphasis on the development of verbal skills and more on motor skills in order to equalize the success opportunities for children from the various social classes. What this suggestion might accomplish would be to make the middle-class child more skilful in the motor area but it would also serve to exaggerate the difference in the verbal area. We must help the child who is deficient in verbal skills to overcome this deficiency. As Milner (1951) has stated a handicap in communication skills and the lack of a well-developed symbol system leads ultimately to a deficiency in the ability to carry on abstract and conceptual thinking. She submits that the solution to the problem lies in the school's recognition of the extent and nature of the lower-class child's handicap and the planning of an appropriate instructional program for the pupils who are low in linguistic skills.

The steps to be taken in planning an appropriate instructional program for the lower-class child need to be both preventive and remedial. If we admit that the lower-class home environment renders its effects before the child enters school, then something must be done before the usual age of school entry. One principal reports that in his school, which draws from a cross-section of the social classes, some children from the lower-class will hardly utter a word for a period of six months in the first grade. Preschool experiences need to be provided on a wide-spread basis particularly in the slum areas. This procedure would do much to reduce the incidence of retarded readers. Making such educational experiences available to lower-class children would also serve to facilitate the involvement of parents on a constructive basis.

Another preventive measure would be the redesigning of early reading materials to eliminate their middle-class bias. The slum child is presented with stories and word descriptions of action that are completely alien to his experience. Fathers are dressed in business suits and carry brief cases; mothers are at home or out shopping, neatly dressed and arranging for someone's birthday party; and children visit well-preserved grandparents who operate a farm with lambs, calves, and little chicks. This material is no longer even relevant to the experience of most middle-class children. New types of material, such as those developed by Richards and Gibson in their *English Through Pictures* (1960), appear to be most promising. This material relies on stick figures and line drawings that depict in a more universal form the objects or actions to be associated with the word forms and eliminates many of the distracting elements found in the traditional primer. The procedure is designed to develop a better appreciation of word use and language structure. This approach to the teaching of reading reduces the middle-class bias of early language instruction, while at the same time improving the learning of all children. Wherever possible the class-bound values and orientation of all instructional materials should be neutralized.

On a remedial level the schools must take steps to identify the slow readers early and to institute remedial instruction. Conant (1961) reports on a project designed to help the slow reader.

> In 1953 the St. Louis elementary schools organized special groups called "Rooms of Twenty." In these groups were placed third-grade pupils who showed that they would have difficulty in the fourth grade. Especially competent teachers were assigned to these rooms and were given a free hand to develop skills in reading, spelling, oral and written language, handwriting, and arithmetic. Studies show substantial progress, and, more important, pupils in these special classes more than hold their own in later schoolwork after a maximum of one year in the special class.
> For those whose reading difficulties are even more acute in grades 4 through 6, there are five reading clinics in the city. . . . Children attend these reading clinics for not more than two years, two or three times a week, while they continue to attend the elementary school (pages 57-58).

At the junior and senior high school level, the particular needs of the lower-lower-class pupil need to be considered in designing the school program. For those who in spite of their impoverished environment continue to show promise of educational growth, a program of cultural enrichment and careful counseling is most fruitful. Exactly such a program, called "Higher Horizons," has been tried in New York City with very encouraging results. These bright children in the slum neighborhood were chosen in grade seven. A more favorable teacher-pupil ratio was established and additional staff, in the nature of one counselor for 250 pupils, part-time psychologists, and social workers were assigned to the project. The educational and cultural experiences of the children were broadened to include concerts, plays, museums, and the like. Our whole society will most certainly benefit if even a small portion of these youngsters fulfill their potential, which might otherwise never be realized.

Such special programs are of interest because they serve to demonstrate what can be done for lower-lower-class children when special thought is given to their needs. On a more general level, the curriculum of the high school needs to be critically reviewed and revised so that the educational experiences prepare the students for their subsequent employment. While agreeing with Eban (1961) that the obligation of the school "is to the citizen's mind and spirit, not to his employer or labor exchange," it is necessary to recognize that the person who is unable to be productive in a technological society cannot afford to submit himself to the ennobling influences of the humanities and other refining disciplines. For that segment of our population that is struggling to achieve a productive place in our society, it would be unreasonable for the school to deny children the opportunity to acquire work-skills in the name of "ennobling influences." The school must not turn its back on those children who will make use of formal and systematized instruction *only* to acquire the specific skills for later employment. Our own recent history tells us that many immigrant parents who could accomplish little more for themselves than to earn a livelihood, were able to encourage their children to derive the fuller benefits of a broad and humanizing educational experience. The school's task of fitting youth for work is a difficult and complex one and it involves the school in the larger community in a way heretofore not done. An outline of how this might be accomplished follows after a brief discussion of the relationship of the school to the lower-class parent.

Influencing the Home

Much of the discussion in this chapter has elaborated a fundamental proposition, namely, that the differences in school performance and attitudes toward school shown by children of the different social classes are in large measure due to the differences in parental influences. If this proposition is valid, then some attention must be given to the modification of these influences. In order to do this the school must establish direct contact with the home. This is not always easy, because parents are suspicious of and sometimes hostile toward the school. It becomes necessary for the school to use specially trained social workers and visiting teachers who are skilled in overcoming the barriers of suspicion and hostility.

Once contact has been established the school can then institute parent education procedures. A parent education program for a slum district would have two purposes. The first aim is the development of the parents' own communication skills. To the extent that the parent learns to communicate verbally and to read, the child's orientation to school and academic development would be improved. A second and more difficult aim of parent education would be to provide an adult education program that would compensate for what was lacking in the parents' own education. If they never had an opportunity to develop vocational skills or if their skills have become obsolete in an increasingly automated technology, the school can do something in training or retraining of parents. If the school can convey to parents that it is seriously concerned about their own and their children's welfare, many of the negative attitudes can be overcome. This kind of adult education program was common in the schools several decades ago when this country was receiving large waves of immigrants.

School and Employment

The problem of employment opportunities, or rather the lack of them, would appear, at first glance, to be purely an economic problem and not one of educational psychology. But any condition that interferes with the effectiveness of the school and that has psychological dimensions merits our consideration. Such is the case with employment opportunities for youth. Havighurst (1953) lists among the important developmental tasks of adolescence that of achieving assurance of economic independence and that of selecting and preparing for an occupation. He has pointed out that successful achievement of developmental tasks leads to a person's happiness and to success with later tasks, "while failure leads to unhappiness in the individual, disapproval by the society, and difficulty with later tasks" (page 2). He underestimates, however, the difficulty of lower-class youth in achieving these developmental tasks pertaining to vocation and economic independence when he states, "Except in times of severe unemployment, this task is easily accomplished by lower-class youth. They quit school and start an earning career as early as they are allowed by law to do so" (page 128). Conant's (1961) treatment of the problem is more convincing and at the same time more disquieting. He points out that special studies conducted in slum areas revealed that of the male youth between the ages of sixteen and twenty-one, 48 percent of the boys who were graduated from high school and

63 percent of those who dropped out before graduation, were unemployed and were roaming the streets. This leads to "a vicious circle of lack of jobs and lack of ambition; one leads to the other."

The problem is further complicated by a number of factors. First, the number of those who do not complete high school is greatest in the lower-classes. These people can enter only the occupations that do not require special skills or training and it is in this segment of the nation's work force where there has been an enormous decline in demand (Wolfbein, 1960). A second factor is the existence of discriminatory employment practices that create great hardship for a large proportion of lower-class individuals who are Negroes or members of other discriminated groups. A third factor, which may well be the product of the total employment picture as well as other more subtle influences, is the matter of personal characteristics that determine vocational success as much as requisite skills. The middle-class employer carries into adult life his adolescent attitudes of antipathy for lower-class values and characteristics. This operates against the lower-class job applicant.

The problem of out-of-work youth is one of great magnitude. The recommendations for a course of action that will realistically confront the problem, will involve the school, particularly the urban high school, in the larger community in a manner that represents a radical departure from tradition. Although these recommendations are not directly aimed at teachers in the classroom, it is important that teachers, as responsible and directly affected citizens, understand the problem and support constructive moves for its resolution. The classroom teacher will be the first to benefit from any amelioration of the situation in that students will be less resistive and indifferent to instruction. The recommendations listed here are selected from those offered by Conant (1961).

1. The school should extend its vocational programs so that all high school students will have an opportunity to gain experience in a field of work that is likely to lead to a full-time job on leaving school. For the gifted student this will mean academic opportunities so that he can continue in a program of higher education. For the average student a school-apprentice program should be provided that will enable the student to find work in the skilled trades. For the slow learner who would not benefit from an extended period of training, a two year work-experience program beginning at age fourteen under the auspices of the school would seem desirable.

2. The school should continue to concern itself with the occupational career of all youth up to the age of twenty-one. Guidance officers will need to expand their services to assure a smooth transition from school to employment. The school will need to be involved in a close and continuing relationship with employers, labor unions, social welfare

agencies, and government employment services. Only when the school is provided with the resources to implement a conviction that all youth can and should be employed, will it fulfill its obligation.

3. The school must lend all its support to the elimination of discriminatory employment practices. Government is becoming aware of its responsibilities in this area and with the help of such institutions as the school, much should be accomplished in the next decade. The reader is referred to the discussion in Chapter 6 of institutional change as one of the means for counteracting prejudice.

4. The need for special consideration in training teachers for lower-class children has already been discussed. The adolescent who anticipates that he will not find a job and who feels that the school is not in any way concerned with this, will be a difficult problem for the teacher. Although the teacher may not be able to do anything about employment availability, he can do a great deal to sustain the student's morale and to assure him that the school is doing all that is possible on his behalf.

SUMMARY

The sociological and economic facts of social class produce significantly different psychological settings in which children grow and influence the way in which they react to the school situation. The dimensions along which social classes differ are personal prestige, access to material things, modes of social interaction, consciousness of status, and value orientations.

These dimensions are taken into account in the procedures developed for determining social class position. The most comprehensive procedure for determining social class is the method of Evaluated Participation, which requires the interviewing of different individuals in the community. A simpler and less cumbersome method is the Index of Status Characteristics, which takes into account occupation, source of income, house type, and location. Of these, occupation appears to be the most significant measure. Various studies of different communities have shown that the two upper classes comprise about 10 percent of the total population in the U.S. and the two lower classes comprise 60 percent. The lower-middle class makes up the remaining 30 percent. Schools differ markedly depending on the particular segments of the social class structure that they serve.

It appears that those qualities of the home that are related to social class position have changed over the past several decades. The middle-class parents have become more permissive and the lower-class parents have become more demanding and punitive. In general, the lower-class home does not prepare the child for school tasks as well as does the middle-class home. The lower-class home does not support the communication process and the development of verbal skills. The middle-class home, on the other hand, may apply excessive pressures on the child for achievement and may make it difficult for the child to find satisfaction in school work for its own sake. These differences, which generally favor the middle-class child, are further exaggerated in adolescence when the lower-class adolescent's inability to postpone gratification, his preference for the motoric rather than the conceptual style of expression, and the lack of acceptance by the peer-group and by a middle-class teacher, all contribute to poor school performance and more frequent school drop-out.

Various studies of intelligence-test performance have shown that social class position is a very significant variable. These findings have led to attempts to devise a culture-fair test, that is, one which does not discriminate against lower-class children. The difficulty with these tests is that they do not predict school performance. The solution to the problem of the poor performance in school of lower-class children is to cease attributing it to genetic factors and to help children who are handicapped in verbal skills and other academic prerequisites, overcome these important deficiencies.

The middle-class teacher should become conscious of his own class-based value system and recognize that on some counts it is not inherently better than that held by lower-class children. For example, the middle-class teacher tends to view emotions and reason as being in conflict and stands opposed to the overt expression of sexual and aggressive emotions. It is important to note that different middle-class teachers respond differently to the clash of values and also that as families from the different class levels change, both teachers and pupils will acquire different class-derived value systems.

Schools that serve children living in the slum areas of metropolitan areas face problems that are approaching catastrophic proportions. Part of the problem is the financial inequity, which results in schools requiring greater financial support having less than the schools serving children from the upper-classes. In addition to correcting this financial imbalance, special corrective measures must be implemented. Teachers need special training for the special requirements of teaching in the slum schools. Remedial instruction and enrichment opportunities need to be provided. Improved relationships with the home need to be established. Finally, the school must work with other agencies in the community to increase employment opportunities and to provide for the development of employable skills.

READING REFERENCES

Conant, J. B., *Slums and Suburbs: A Commentary on Schools in Metropolitan Areas.* New York: McGraw-Hill Book Company, 1961.

Davis, W. A., *Social Class Influences upon Learning.* Cambridge: Harvard University Press, 1948.

Havighurst, R. J., "Social-class influences on American education." In N. B. Henry (Ed.), *Social Forces Influencing American Education.* Sixtieth Yearbook (Pt. 2) National Society for the Study of Education. Chicago: University of Chicago Press, 1961.

———— and Bernice J. Neugarten, *Society and Education,* 2d ed. Boston: Allyn and Bacon, 1962.

Miller, D. R. and G. E. Swanson, *Inner Conflict and Defense.* New York: Holt, Rinehart and Winston, 1960.

Passow, A. H. (Ed.), *Education in Depressed Areas.* New York: Bureau of Publications, Columbia University, Teachers College, 1963.

Warner, W. L., R. J. Havighurst, and M. B. Loeb, *Who Shall be Educated?* New York: Harper & Row, 1944.

PART 4

FOCUS ON THE TEACHER

Campbell Hays from Monkmeyer

CHAPTER 15

TEACHER-PUPIL RELATIONSHIPS

The discussion in each of the preceding sections has repeatedly noted that interpersonal relations exercise a considerable influence in the total developmental process. On the development of individual differences, it was pointed out that the kinds of stimulation and socializing experiences that the child receives in his family or as a result of being a member in one or another social segment of the society, are important influences in shaping his personality and his school behavior. In discussing the problems of classroom management, some of the various patterns of peer group and pupil-pupil interaction and the possible effects of these on the child's feelings about himself and others, as well as his attitudes toward learning tasks were examined. It has been emphasized that the quality of the interpersonal relationships between the teacher and the pupil affect the process of educational and personal development.

The curriculum, school policy, buildings, and all else pertaining to the school situation are in and of themselves inert. They become operative only as the teacher proceeds to accomplish his task. The extent to which the teacher is effective in his teaching is primarily determined by the relationship existing between the teacher and his pupils and by the climate or atmosphere in the classroom. This topic has come to occupy an increasingly important place in modern educational psychology.

To understand teacher-pupil relationships an analysis in terms of the teacher's role is necessary. The concept of role is used here in a technical sense as it is defined by Spiegel (1957).

> A role is defined as a goal-directed pattern or sequence of acts tailored by the cultural process for the transactions a person may carry out in a social group or situation. It is conceived that no role exists in isolation but is always patterned to gear in with the complementary or reciprocal role of a role partner (alter). Thus all roles have to be learned by the persons who wish to occupy them in accordance with the cultural (or subcultural) values of the society in which they exist. If that society is fairly homogeneous and well integrated, then the roles will be patterned in such a way that their complementary structure is obvious and stable (page 3).

In earlier times when the teacher's role in relation to his students was clearly defined by all participants including not only the teacher and the pupil but also the parent, the school board member, and the entire community, the discussion of the teacher-pupil relationship could be disposed of in relatively simple terms. Today, because of our increased understanding of child development, because of the changing pattern of relationships between adults as socializing agents and the children they teach, and because of our increased sensitivity to the relationship of the classroom as a miniature society to the society at large, the role definitions of the teacher and the pupil have become more complex as well as more ambiguous. Complexity and ambiguity of role can produce doubt and anxiety in both the teacher and the pupil. The matter of classroom atmosphere, which grows out of the teacher-student relationship is one of recurrent concern to all teachers.

The crucial aspect of the teacher-pupil relationship is the way in which the teacher conceives and acts out his role of leadership and authority and the way the child is able to fulfill the reciprocal role of the one being influenced and led. After considering some general and structural features of the teacher-pupil relationship, the question of the use of authority is considered. In the course of this discussion various kinds of teacher authority and their effects are described. The discussion is then broadened to see how characteristics of teachers, other than that of authority, affect different kinds of pupils. The chapter is concluded by considering the special problems encountered by the student teacher and the substitute teacher in establishing constructive interpersonal relationships in the classroom.

STUDYING THE TEACHER-PUPIL INTERACTION

President James Garfield's description of the ideal educational arrangement, consisting of Mark Hopkins and himself, as the pupil, at either end of a simple bench, is incomplete. It fails to tell us what is going on between them. The relationship between any two people, if it is in the least meaningful, consists of several layers. For example, there is the manifest layer, which is the overt behavior exhibited by the parties in the relationship, and there is the intentional layer consisting of feelings, motives, and the intent of the action. This applies to the classroom situation in which the several individual pupils interact with each other as well as with the teacher.

When we speak of the teacher-pupil relationship it is generally assumed that it is the teacher who bears the primary responsibility for establishing the form of classroom interaction. Even when the interaction becomes chaotic, it is assumed that the teacher has lost control or is no longer able to maintain a structure or organization in the relationships. While it is true that it is the teacher who must decide whether or not to organize the class into committees, how much free movement and pupil initiative to allow, and so on, the teacher is not entirely a free agent in these regards. There are conditions in the teaching setting that compel certain kinds of interaction and that prohibit others. The social and cultural context in which the teaching takes place determines certain aspects of the teaching style and method. In some communities, for example, it is appropriate for the teacher to use physical punishment as a means of maintaining control, whereas in others, a teacher is forbidden by law to use physical punishment under any circumstances. The grade level and the subject matter taught also determine the pattern of teacher-pupil relationship. Obviously, the pattern that is appropriate for the primary grades would not be appropriate for the senior high school grades. Similarly, the teaching of a class in physical education lends itself to quite different arrangements from one in English composition. The intellectual and personal characteristics of the pupils and the size of the class are other factors that will determine the appropriateness of any particular method of instruction. A teacher's feelings and behavior will vary according to whether a large portion of the class consists of bright pupils or slow-learning ones, whether it consists of academically conscientious students or resistant and indifferent ones.

This type of conceptualization of the teacher-pupil relationship leads to the inevitable conclusion that the most appropriate form of teacher-pupil relationship, as is probably true of any human relationship, is determined by the specific terms of the situation. For this reason, it is impossible to offer universal prescriptions for teaching methods. Ryans (1960), whose study of the characteristics of teachers is referred to later, states that "teacher roles vary in relation to the characteristics of the pupils taught, to grade level, and to field of learning." Similarly, the Committee on Criteria of Teacher Effectiveness of the American Educational Research Association (1951) cited by Jackson (1962), agreed that it was impossible to define the effective teacher as a unitary and universal concept. The committee suggests "that there may be effective teachers

who may differ markedly among themselves. Perhaps the problem
should be studied narrowly: 'What is effective teaching in French or beginning arithmetic?' or 'What makes an effective fifth-grade teacher in a
rural community?' "

The problem of conceptualizing the teacher-pupil relationship in
terms of "good" and "bad" or "effective" and "ineffective" is further
complicated by the fact that a teaching method applied to a specific
class may be very effective for *some* students but rarely will it be the
most effective method for *all* the students. The teacher then must be
prepared to relate differently to different pupils and to vary teaching
methods so that the needs of different pupils can be met (Wispé, 1953).

In spite of these many qualifications that must be placed upon the
description of the teacher-pupil relationship, the teacher can be enlight-
ened by an analysis of the various possible structural arrangements
within the classroom, by a consideration of the issue of teacher control
and authority, and by an understanding of the patterns of teacher behavior and their possible effects on different kinds of students. These factors, structure, authority, and teacher characteristics are extremely important dimensions of effective teaching.

The Structural Aspects
of Classroom Interaction

The first thing that any visitor would observe about a classroom
would be its manifest structure. He would note whether the teacher was
working in the corner of the room with a small group of children while
the others were working quietly alone at their seats; whether the class
was divided into committees with the teacher supervising in an unobtrusive manner; or whether the teacher was leading the discussion with the
interaction being restricted to an occasional exchange between the
teacher and one or another pupil. Kerkman and Wright (1961) in an interesting investigation, using time-lapse photography in a number of
different classrooms, found that this latter type of teacher-pupil interaction produced two kinds of student response: "Attending to the teacher,
possibly with a supplicant hand upraised, and actually engaging the
teacher, often with some apparent camaraderie." These and other similar organizations make up the structural aspects of classroom interaction.

Each of these patterns of interaction can be diagrammed. The
teacher working with a small group might be doing so in an arrangement
in which all the overt stimulation and response occur between the
teacher and separate pupils. This pattern, called coaction by Olson
(1957), is diagrammed in Figure 15.1a. An organization that allows for
exchange and interaction among all the members of the group is shown
in Figure 15.1b. Enlarging the scope to include the entire class, the situation in which the teacher attempts to hold the attention of the entire

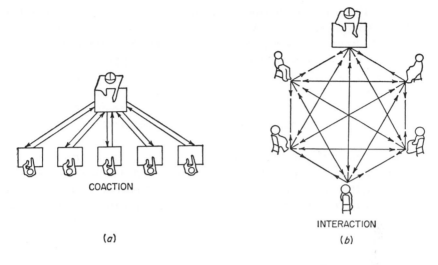

COACTION

(*a*)

INTERACTION

(*b*)

FIGURE 15.1 *Teacher-pupil relationships in small groups under conditions of coaction and interaction. From W. C. Olson,* Psychological Foundations of the Curriculum, *UNESCO Studies and Documents, no. 26, Paris, France: UNESCO, 1957.*

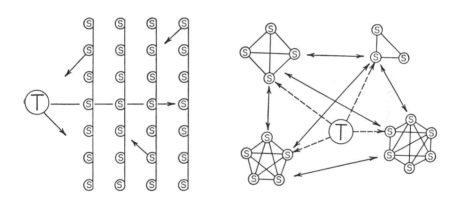

FIGURE 15.2 *Two forms of classroom structure. From N. A. Flanders, "Diagnosing and Utilizing Social Structures in Classroom Learning," in N. B. Henry (Ed.),* The Dynamics of Instructional Groups. Yearbook of the National Society for the Study of Education, 59, *Pt. 2, Chicago: University of Chicago Press, 1960, pp. 197-198.*

class group is shown in Figure 15.2a; or one in which the teacher organizes the class into work groups with interaction permitted between various subgroups is shown in Figure 15.2b. Another common pattern of classroom structure is one in which individual students work alone at their seats while the teacher supervises either actively or passively. The school day in a fifth-grade class described in Chapter 7 illustrates these and other classroom structures.

The circumstances that make one or another structural arrangement preferable are not clearly known. It would appear, however, that the consistent use of only one pattern is probably less desirable than variation of pattern. The use of the small group with a more open form of communication is likely to produce greater involvement of the learner and is likely, in the long run, to produce independent and responsible student action. In Chapter 3 it was noted that the more the learner is involved in acquiring meaning, the more effective the learning. Increasing participation by decreasing the size of the group as in Figures 15.1b and 15.2b will tend to increase involvement and hence make the learning more effective. On the other hand, the small group can become a setting for the "sharing of ignorance" and the direction and guidance of the teacher given to the group as a whole or to the entire class becomes a necessity if the student is to receive some direction for his activity.

The optimum balance of various structural patterns is still largely a matter of conjecture. Kerkman and Wright (1961) found that the proportion of children working on their own increased with age and they consider that this form of socially independent action is a more mature form. They also found that the interaction between the teacher and pupil in the classrooms of a larger community tended in the direction of the student attending to the teacher. In the classrooms of a smaller community, a town, the interaction was more likely to be one of engaging the teacher. They feel that this difference in pattern of interaction is due to the fact that "town children keep running into their teachers in the drugstore and many other settings more often than city children." It would be interesting to discover by means of the cinematographic technique developed by Kerkman and Wright, whether different subject matter areas at various grade levels lend themselves to different arrangements of classroom structure.

Classroom Control

There are two ways of viewing the issue of classroom control. One way is to consider the issue from the standpoint of reducing discipline problems or dealing with misbehavior. The other is to examine the interaction pattern that exists in the classroom and to note the extent and the means of the teacher's control and direction of all the activity in the classroom. An understanding of the latter should illuminate the matter of discipline.

Withall (1951) developed an instrument called a climate index, which provides a method for assessing the quality of the teacher's control. By analyzing and classifying the recorded statements of the teacher of an eighth-grade art class, Withall found that he could place all the statements into one or another of seven categories that comprise the climate index. The index has been shown to be applicable to a variety of classroom situations. The seven categories into which teacher statements can be placed are as follows[1]:

1. *Learner-supportive statements or questions.* These are . . . statements or questions that express agreement with the ideas, actions or opinions of the learner, or that commend or reassure the learner. . . . The *dominant intent* of these statements or questions is to *praise, encourage* or *bolster the learner.*

2. *Acceptant or clarifying statements or questions.* . . . The dominant intent of these teacher-responses is *to help the learner* to gain insight into his problem, that is, define his "real" problem and its solution in more operational terms.

3. *Problem-structuring statements or questions.* . . . [These] offer facts or ideas or opinions to the learner about a. phenomena, b. procedures, in a non-threatening and objective manner. . . . The *dominant intent* is to elucidate the problem and therefore facilitate the learner's problem solving activities.

4. *Neutral statements evidencing no supportive intent.* These statements are neither teacher-sustaining, nor learner-sustaining nor problem-centered. . . . Statements having to do with administrative procedure, the room in which the class will meet, the hour at which a conference will occur, especially after consensus has been achieved, fall into this category.

5. *Directive statements or questions.* These . . . advise the learner regarding a course of action or his future behavior and which narrowly limit his choice or offer no choice. . . . The *dominant intent* of these responses is to have the learner take up the teacher's point of view and pursue a course of action that she advocates.

6. *Reproving, disapproving or disparaging statements or questions.* By means of these statements a teacher may express complete or partial disapproval of the ideas, behavior and, to him, personality weaknesses of the learner. The teacher's internalized societal values largely enter into these responses. By means of these statements some teachers believe they are fulfilling their responsibility of inculcating in young people, society's standards of acceptable and desirable behavior and achievement. The *dominant intent* of these statements is:
   a. to represent to the learner societal values as the teacher sees them.
   b. to admonish the learner for unacceptable behavior and to deter him from repeating it in the future.
   c. to impress on the learner the fact that he has not met the criteria of successful achievement which the teacher accepts.

7. *Teacher-supportive statements or questions.* These are statements or questions in which the teacher refers to himself and expresses a defensive attitude, . . . with the purpose of reassuring himself and of confirming his position or his ideas in the eyes of those around him. The *dominant intent* of these statements is to *assert,* to *defend* or to *justify* the teacher.

[1] From J. Withall "The Development of the Climate Index," Journal of Educational Research, 1951, **45,** pp. 96-98.

Statements in categories 1, 2, and 3 are considered evidence of learner-centeredness in the classroom and those in categories 5, 6, and 7 are evidence of teacher-centeredness. By using the climate index in this way one is able to obtain a ratio of learner-centeredness to teacher-centeredness for a particular classroom.

Using Withall's climate index, Flanders (1951) studied the reactions of learners to situations that were intentionally oriented by the experimenter toward teacher-centeredness or learner-centeredness. He found that students in a teacher-centered learning situation felt under pressure, showed more negative feelings and signs of anxiety, and that their attention was directed toward interpersonal concerns rather than to the achievement problem or the subject content of the class. He found also that the teacher-centered situation tended to elicit student behaviors characterized by hostility, withdrawal, apathy, and aggressiveness; whereas the learner-centered situation tended to elicit behavior characterized by problem orientation and decreased interpersonal anxiety.

These findings by Flanders confirm those of an earlier, oft-quoted study by Lewin et al. (1939) on the effects of different leader-induced social climates. This investigation had as one of its primary aims the study of the effects upon individual and group behavior of the variations in social atmosphere created by different forms of adult social control imposed upon club groups each consisting of five ten-year-old boys. The different types of leader control were labeled "authoritarian," "democratic," and *"laissez-faire."* [2] The chief characteristics of these three forms of adult control are presented in Table 15.1. Analysis of the specific behaviors of these different kinds of leaders showed that the authoritarian leader tended to show more of the kind of behavior described in Withall's climate index as teacher-centered, while the democratic leader showed more student-centered behavior.

The implications of the findings of this study on group climate are not directly applicable to the educational setting inasmuch as the groups were small, consisted only of boys, and the activity was clearly recreational. The findings are, nevertheless, suggestive for educational practice. In the authoritarian led groups, the boys responded by showing two different kinds of reactions, one was an apathetic, dependent reaction and the other was a more hostile, aggressive reaction. In all of the autocrati-

---

[2] The choice of the term "democratic" to describe this form of leader control is an unfortunate one. In a truly democratic group the leader achieves and maintains his position by consent and agreement of a large segment of the group members. In the classroom and in the club groups described here, this is not the case. The teacher or the club leader is assigned to the group; he maintains his leadership position without regard to the group members' wishes. Roles such as these that one achieves as a result of technical competence and that one maintains at the pleasure of individuals other than those being led, fall outside the dimensions of "democratic" and "authoritarian." These terms have normative and moralistic overtones and introduce an undesirable bias into the interpretation of the research on the teacher-pupil relationship.

TABLE 15.1 DESCRIPTIONS OF THREE FORMS OF ADULT CONTROL OF CHILDREN'S GROUPS

Authoritarian	*Democratic*	*Laissez-Faire*
1. All determination of policy by the leader.	1. All policies a matter of group discussion and decision, encouraged and assisted by the leader.	1. Complete freedom for group or individual decision, with a minimum of leader participation.
2. Techniques and activity steps dictated by the authority, one at a time, so that future steps were always uncertain to a large degree.	2. Activity perspective gained during discussion period. General steps to group goal sketched, and, where technical advice was needed, the leader suggested two or more alternative procedures from which choice could be made.	2. Various materials supplied by the leader, who made it clear that he could supply information when asked. He took no other part in work discussion.
3. The leader usually dictated the particular work task and work companion of each member.	3. The members were free to work with whomever they chose, and the division of tasks was left up to the group.	3. Complete nonparticipation of the leader.
4. The dominator tended to be "personal" in his praise and criticism of the work of each member; remaining aloof from active group participation except when demonstrating.	4. The leader was "objective" or "fact minded" in his praise and criticism and tried to be a regular group member in spirit without doing too much of the work.	4. Infrequent spontaneous comments on member activities unless questioned and no attempt to appraise or regulate the course of events.

Source: R. Lippitt and R. K. White, "The 'Social Climate' of Children's Groups," *Child Behavior and Development* by Barker et al. New York: McGraw-Hill Book Company, Inc. Copyright, 1943, p. 487. Used by permission.

cally led groups the boys showed discontent with the group activity and the groups had difficulty accepting and working toward the adult-imposed group goals. When the leader was late in arriving "no group initiative to start new work or to continue with work already under way was developed" (Lippitt and White, 1958). In the *laissez-faire* group the lack of structure led to dissatisfaction with the group's inefficiency and the lack of accomplishment. The members' desires to accomplish something and to work cooperatively were frustrated by the absence of direction and leadership. Lippitt and White state: "The adult restrictiveness of the benevolent authoritarian role and the environmental unstructuredness of the *laissez-faire* situation were both found to inhibit greatly genuine 'psychological freedom' as contrasted to 'objective freedom'" (page 510). The importance of psychological freedom for the development of autonomy and the self-management capacities of children, has been forcefully delineated by Murphy (1963) and Shaftel (1963).

In the democratic groups of the Lewin et al. (1939) study, morale was higher, there were more signs of friendship, and there was a sense of continuing satisfaction in accomplishment as well as from the harmony existing within the group. The boys had experience with each of the forms of adult control and generally indicated a preference for the democratic leader. It is of practical interest to teachers to note that when the democratically led groups were without the adult leader because he was late, the group became actively productive on its own, and when the leader left the room during the activity session the group continued in a productive fashion.

After surveying a larger amount of experimental evidence, Stogdill (1959) concludes as follows about the effect of different kinds of leader control. "The exercise of a high degree of control over performance and interaction reduces satisfaction and productivity. Granting an optimum degree of freedom of action increases productivity and satisfaction but weakens co-ordination control. Under a maximum degree of freedom, co-ordination breaks down, production is reduced, and satisfaction is lowered" (page 283).

Baller and Charles (1961) in considering the implications of the Lewin et al. findings for educational practice, similarly conclude that while the classroom that is organized democratically may at times be noisier, more difficult to "oversee" or to co-ordinate, it will, however, result in more constructive and more cooperative activity and will provide more opportunity for the development of skills in self-control and group effort. They point out one further implication, namely, that one should not mistake the mere avoidance of authoritarian methods for democratic group control. A classroom situation in which adult leadership abdicates its responsibilities in extreme permissiveness, providing no direction, and disregarding standards of accomplishment, is a *laissez-faire* situation that is by no means equivalent to the democratic classroom in its effects on the participants.

Using an observational approach similar to those just described, Anderson (1943) classified teacher behavior into two large categories. He termed the form of teacher behavior that paralleled teacher-centeredness or authoritarian, dominative, and the learner-centered or democratic he termed integrative. He found that teacher behavior characterized by *domination with evidence of conflict* led to child behavior rated lower on a mental-hygiene scale than when the teacher behavior was characterized as *socially integrative with evidence of working together*. Anderson describes a dominating kindergarten teacher, demonstrating some of the effects of this kind of teacher behavior.

A group of kindergarten children were making May baskets. Terry had folded his basket on the lines which had been drawn on the material the night before by the teacher. He had pasted the flaps as he had been instructed and had the handle fastened in place. The teacher had cut out of other paper a handful of diamond-shaped pieces which she had distributed four to a child. These were to serve as decorations to be pasted horizontally on the basket. As she walked about the room she noticed Terry pasting his diamond decoration vertically.

"Oh, oh, Terry," she said," "the decorations are to be pasted on lying down and not standing up."

"But I want to paste mine this way," said Terry.

"Well, that isn't the way they are supposed to go. Here now, just paste it this way." And she turned the diamond horizontally and pasted it before Terry seemed to know what had happened. She remained while Terry at her instructions pasted two more shapes horizontally. Then she turned away, leaving Terry to paste the fourth.

At the end of the period Terry had only three decorations on his basket. When the teacher inquired about his basket, Terry, pointing to the undecorated side of his basket, said that he did not want one there.

"Oh, but every basket should have four. Here is one your color. We'll just paste it on quickly." And with Terry speechless and transfixed she pasted it on quickly.

Mary Lou had observed that at her table several handles did not stick. "I guess I don't want a handle," she remarked to the boy seated next [to] her. She cut up the handle of her basket and pasted the pieces as decorations all over the basket. The teacher's remark to this *fait accompli* was, "Oh, you've spoiled yours, Mary Lou; yours is all messy and doesn't have a handle" (page 459).

Although the research studies cited here, and others as well, report in general that morale and other feelings about being in the group are more positive in learner-centered or democratic groups than in the teacher-centered groups, the findings in regard to the amount of learning and productivity are not consistent from study to study. In a resumé of a number of studies that investigated the outcomes of authoritarian and democratic methods of leadership, Anderson (1959) states that eleven such studies report greater learning in learner-centered groups, eight studies report findings favoring teacher-centered methods, and the largest number, thirteen studies, reported no difference.

It is obvious that factors other than method of teacher control are operative in determining learning achievement or student productivity. It is also likely that the two types of classroom control produce different kinds of achievement. This has been demonstrated in a study by Crabtree (1961), summarized by Shaftel (1963). Crabtree established two different types of classroom structure. The first could be characterized as one of "emergent structure," in which the children were given opportunities to explore their own ideas. The teacher contributed subject-matter resources and other forms of teaching assistance only when the children had indicated that such contributions would be relevant. This first group was a variant of the learner-centered classroom. In the second type of classroom, the structure was predetermined by the teacher. The teacher selected the discussion topics and directed the discussion. The teacher regularly evaluated the students' responses in terms of their conceptual accuracy, that is, in terms of right and wrong. This second group was a variant of the teacher-centered classroom. The content of instruction was the same in both groups consisting of two topics in social studies, each topic lasting three weeks. Each of the two groups of children experienced both forms of group structure, thus serving as their own experimental controls. The results were measured in terms of the proportions of divergent and convergent thinking in each of the two forms of group structure. These types of thinking were defined in Chapter 10. Divergent thinking is described as thinking in which the subjects produced a large variety of responses and developed original ideas. Convergent thought "leads to the one right answer or to a recognized best or conventional answer." Crabtree found that in the learner-centered situation divergent thinking represented 48 percent of the observed thinking responses as compared to 18 percent in the teacher-centered or teacher-determined structure. Convergent thinking was more frequent (54 percent) in the teacher-centered structure than in the learner-centered organization (21 percent). The productivity level and the achievement gain of a classroom group are functions of the measures used to determine the gain, the objectives of teaching, as well as the form of teacher leadership.

The Bases of the Teacher's Control

The matter of teacher control can be further differentiated by considering the bases or the sources from which control may arise. French and Raven (1959) have defined five different bases of social power that seem applicable to the matter under discussion.

COERCIVE POWER   The coercive power of the teacher over the pupil stems from the awareness on the part of the pupil that he may be punished by the teacher if he fails to conform to the teacher's attempt to influence his behavior. The implications of the use of coercive power were discussed in Chapter 2. It was pointed out that the teacher's demands or coercive power must be used with caution. If this source of the teacher's power is improperly applied the student will abandon the adopted behavior as soon as he is no longer under the teacher's control and also the negative feelings induced by the threat of punishment can readily spread to the activity itself.

REWARD POWER   The strength of the reward power of the teacher over the pupil increases with the magnitude of the rewards that the pupil perceives the teacher can provide for him. The discussion of the influence of expectations and particularly incentives in Chapter 2, is relevant here. It is important to remember that if the reward is extrinsic, that is, it is not intrinsically related to the behavior, there is danger that the pupil may come to consider that the activity itself is not worthwhile. Also it should be noted that whether or not a reward has the power to influence depends on the perception of the pupil not that of the teacher.

LEGITIMATE POWER   This source of the teacher's power is determined by the extent to which the pupil has internalized or accepted those values that make it legitimate in his eyes for the teacher to influence him and that obligate him to accept the teacher's influence. French and Raven state that one of the bases for legitimate power is the cultural value system. The legitimate power inherent in the teacher's role has a long history in all cultures in which education is somewhat formalized. Even in those traditional cultures in which the teacher was accorded low honor in the community at large, for example the Chinese and the Eastern European Jewish cultures mentioned by Mead (1951), the legitimate power of the teacher was considerable. In those segments of society where the norms and standards of conduct are in a state of disorganization, the legitimate power of the teacher, along with that of other authority figures, is challenged and opposed. The use of legitimate power can lead to role conflict when the teacher exercising this power interacts with his pupils in another role relationship in which legitimate power is not relevant. Such role conflict is likely to reduce the legitimate power of the teacher. This would be the case when, for example, a teacher of adolescents has become a personal friend of his pupils and shares confidences with them, or where he has a family relationship with one or several of his pupils.

REFERENT POWER   The referent power of the teacher has its basis in the pupil's identification with the teacher. The process of identification value acquisition was covered in Chapter 6. The concept of reference groups in Chapter 8 takes into account the fact that the group may exercise referent power over the individual. French and Raven state that one of the factors that will determine the strength of the teacher's referent power is the extent to which the student is attracted to the teacher. It would appear that when a teacher inspires a student he is exercising referent power. In most instances the teacher and the pupil are not clearly aware of the presence of this source of power. Also, the changes in pupil behavior that occur as a result of referent power tend, after a time, to become independent of the teacher, because the pupil internalizes this type of power and his behavior is afterward guided by what has now become the pupil's own value system.

EXPERT POWER   To the extent that the teacher has some special skill or knowledge and the student is aware of and can make use of this expertness, the teacher exerts expert power. The subject-matter specialist or the technically trained shop, music, or home economics teacher are likely to exert expert power along with other forms of power. As the student grows older it is likely that the teacher's influence through referent power decreases and the influence through expert power increases; also the student's submission to the influence of expert power becomes more specific and situational and less generalized.

In an exploratory study, Rosenfeld and Zander (1961) investigated the effects of these different forms of teacher power. Using a questionnaire form administered to 400 male tenth-grade students, they were able to determine the following: the form of power that each student attributed to the teacher; the student's aspired grade (obtained by means of this question: "Considering how hard you plan to work, what final grade do you think you should get in math this year?"); and the student's perceived level of capacity (obtained by means of this question: "What final grade do you think you could get if you worked to the limit of your ability and did the best you could in mathematics for the rest of the semester?"). The aim of the study was to determine the effects of the various kinds of attributed teacher influence on the degree of congruity between perceived level of capacity and aspired grade.

The investigators found that students were inclined to accept the teacher's influence when it is based on reward, legitimate, referent, or expert power, and to ignore or oppose it when based on indiscriminate coercive power. Indiscriminate coercive power was described as teacher disapproval when the student feels that he is performing as well as he can. This type of attributed power produces negative effects on achievement aspiration, future performance, and lack of congruence between the student's aspirations and capacity. The use of other sources of power tends to be positively correlated to congruence between aspiration and capacity. They found also that the form of power affects also the student's attitudes toward the teacher and his attitudes toward the content of the course. The direction of this attitude change is negative for indiscriminate coercion and generally positive for the other kinds of power.

In another study (Alden, 1959 reported by Kounin et al., 1961) an attempt was made to experimentally manipulate two of the above-mentioned sources of teacher power, namely referent and expert power. Different classes of fifth-grade students were variously introduced to a new teacher who was to present a lesson in secret handwriting. The form of the introduction was intended to establish the new teacher's expert or referent power. To establish expert power the new teacher was introduced as an expert in secret writing; to establish referent power the teacher was introduced as someone who was very fond of children. In each class selected children were trained to act the role of misbehaving pupils and each teacher used a different kind of "desist-technique" against this planned misbehavior. Some techniques emphasized teacher disapproval, for example: "I see a boy playing with paper clips. I just don't like a boy who plays with things when he should be paying attention." Other techniques were oriented to the task and to achievement, for example: "I see a boy playing with some paper clips. Because secret writing demands concentration, I don't see how he can learn much about it when he plays with things instead of paying attention."

Although we might question the amount of referent power established merely by an introduction of the sort described, the findings of the study are interesting. The desist-techniques that emphasized the task rather than teacher disapproval were more likely to elicit positive reactions from children in the class. Children exposed to a task-oriented desist-technique increased their ratings of the teacher's skill in handling children and showed greater interest in secret writing. When a teacher who had been introduced as an expert used a task-oriented desist-technique, the children rated higher the teacher's liking for pupils and they demonstrated greater recall of the content of the presentation. It appears that the basis of the teacher's power makes a difference in how children respond to the various methods that the teacher might use to control the misbehaving pupil.

Discipline and the Control of Misbehavior

The term discipline has been defined in a number of different ways. It is used here to refer to the problem of the teacher's control and redirection of behavior that threatens to disrupt the order of the classroom group. This is the meaning of the term that most teachers appear to have in mind when they express a concern about discipline. Some use the term with a somewhat narrower reference, namely, the use of punishment or coercive power to control misbehavior. A class that has deterio-rated into chaotic misbehavior with students shouting, throwing things, and being generally unruly, though a rarity in reality, is a nightmare in the fantasy of every teacher. Most teachers feel sufficiently secure to avoid behaving in the manner of a martinet or a tyrant; yet, this con-cern about the proper use of authority and the maintenance of group order is a general source of anxiety for most teachers.

In dealing with any group, particularly groups of children who are in the process of development, the issue of discipline is an important and a complex problem. The kind of authority and restraint that a teacher imposes upon a group of children will in some measure contrib-ute to the kind of morality and character that the members of the group will develop. (See discussion on this topic in Chapter 6). In one study (Kounin and Gump, 1961) it was shown, for example, that the methods that the teacher uses to control the class will influence the children's conceptions of right and wrong. The investigators interviewed the chil-dren in six first-grade classrooms. Three of these classes were selected because their teachers had been consistently rated as highly punitive, they threatened the children and showed a constant readiness to punish. The matched classes were selected because the teachers were rated as nonpunitive. The children were asked individually what they thought was "the worst thing to do in school" and why these misbehaviors were bad. The investigators concluded the following:

> As compared with children who have nonpunitive teachers, children who have punitive teachers: manifest more aggression in their miscon-ducts, are more unsettled and conflicted about misconduct in school, are less concerned with learning and school-unique values, show some, but not consistent, indication of a reduction in rationality pertaining to school misconduct (page 49).

Presumably the nonpunitive teachers had developed methods of control other than coercive ones. All six teachers selected for the study were described "as having good organization, well-behaved classes, and as achieving the learning objectives for their grade." It is quite possible that if the nonpunitive teachers had failed to provide structure and con-structive control, the children's conceptions of school misconduct might have been even more aggressive, more conflicted and unsettled about school misconduct, and even less concerned about school unique values than were the children of the punitive teachers.

The issue of discipline is a far-reaching one because of its rela-tionship to the social philosophy of the society in which the school exists. The kind of authority that prevails generally in the classrooms is both a reflection of the social philosophy of the society and a source of that philosophy. A society with strong authoritarian overtones in its political life, as for example Nazi Germany, will tend to encourage coercive and punitive methods of classroom control. Many have argued that the democratic order in our society can best be maintained by establishing in our schools a type of control that permits children to learn how to use their critical judgment, to accept responsibility, and to exercise purposeful self-control. The teacher and the school represent to the child the formal institutions of our society. The school experience, embodied for the child in his interactions with his teachers, is an important determinant in the acquisition of the attitudes and values of democratic citizenship. If this responsibility of democratic education is to be successfully discharged, it requires that the teacher provide a learning setting in which the child can become aware of his own motives and can come to feel more and more competent and adequate. As he develops in this atmosphere he will become able to "read" his situations somewhat as a musician reads a score and adjusts his response to fit his understanding of what he sees. "This is in contrast to the expectation that a person can be required to perfect a predetermined set of responses which are honest, or polite, or respectful and engage in those responses habitually" (Woodruff, 1960, page 383). These contrasting positions on the matter of discipline parallel those taken on the issue of transfer of training (see Chapter 5). The first, which emphasizes the adjustment of response based on an understanding of the situation, is an application of the point of view that assumes that the learner transfers to new situations acquired learning sets and the ability to generalize. The second view of discipline, which suggests that the learner should be taught a predetermined set of responses, is similar to that interpretation of Thorndike's theory of transfer by identical elements that would propose that the learner be taught specific responses to specific situations

The implementation of discipline and order that is a function of an emerging situation is a difficult undertaking. All that can be done here is to offer a number of general statements about the problem of classroom control. The application of these generalizations to the actual classroom situation is infinitely more difficult than their enunciation. Nevertheless, thoughtful attention to these generalizations will serve to allay some teacher anxiety and thus help make the teacher more able to establish constructive relations with pupils.

Sheviakov and Redl (1956), whose excellent discussion of school discipline was referred to in Chapter 8, list a number of issues to be considered in establishing group order. One of these issues is the determination whether a suggested control technique will work. The position they take on this question is that a control technique cannot be considered effective *a priori*. We must understand the method of discipline in much the same terms as we understand the outcome itself, that is, the teacher must respond sensitively to the ongoing situation and not expect to come into a class with a set of predetermined disciplinary responses. The claims of so-called experts on discipline, Sheviakov and Redl rightly assert, remain meaningless until their recommended techniques are examined in relationship to the specific aspects of a teaching situation.

Another issue in regard to discipline centers on the complications arising from the teacher's attempts to maintain a balance between concern for the individual and the welfare of the group. This question was raised in the case of Mrs. Hillis and Charles in Chapter 11. Several studies (Hunter, 1957; Schrupp and Gjerde, 1953; and Stouffer, 1952) have demonstrated that in the years since 1928 when the Wickman study was reported, teachers' attitudes toward children's behavior have become similar to that of mental hygienists. However, the teacher's position can never be entirely the same as that of a therapist who ordinarily deals with an individual rather than with a group. Whatever the teacher does in relationship to one student will have an impact on the group. Kounin and Gump (1958) refer to this as the *ripple effect* in discipline. The techniques that are appropriate for helping the individual may not always coincide with the techniques that would be most effective for influencing the group and vice versa. Sheviakov and Redl (1956) suggest that:

> When there is conflict between the interests of an individual and the welfare of the group, one basic law may guide our disciplinary choice: the *law of marginal antisepsis*. By this we mean that a technique which is right for the child's problems must at least be harmless to the group. A technique which is rightly chosen for its effect upon the group must at least be harmless to the individuals involved (page 25).

Another similar problem in the use of control techniques presents itself when the teacher must decide whether or not a particular procedure that will influence the surface behavior or that will correct an immediate situation will interfere with long-range objectives in influencing basic attitudes. A corollary of this issue is to decide whether a particular disruptive act is of sufficient importance to merit control. If the teacher were to pay attention to every minor disturbance he would need to be excessively controlling and would likely induce an atmosphere in which the motivation to learn would become secondary to the student's attempts to avoid the teacher's disciplinary action. Some of the illustrations in the last chapter and others presented have dealt with this form of the principle of *marginal antisepsis:* "any technique used to bring about surface behavioral change must at least be harmless to long-range attitude changes, and any technique used to invite basic attitude changes must at least be harmless to the surface challenge we have to meet through reality pressures" (page 32).

Patterns of Teacher-Pupil Interaction

The discussion of the teacher-pupil relationship thus far has focused mainly on one dimension, namely that of control. The descriptions of the various kinds of classroom organization, for example, teacher-centered or student-centered, are essentially different uses of the teacher's control and authority. The analysis of the various sources of the teacher's power and their use further examined the nature of the teacher's control. The discussion of discipline centered on the specific issue of control of disruptive behavior. The interaction of teachers and pupils most certainly has a broader base than that of control alone. Other dimensions of the teacher-pupil interaction would include such matters as the teacher's personality, his mode of operation, the pupil's personality, and his earlier educational and developmental experiences. When the teacher-pupil interaction is regarded from this broad, inclusive perspective, our generalizations and conclusions become more speculative and tentative.

In a study of the adolescent personality, Blos (1941) suggests that certain developmental periods present personal challenges to the teacher in terms of the teacher's own developmental history. His description of the challenge of adolescence to the teacher is as follows[3]:

> For in the life of every adult the phase of adolescence has left unresolved conflicts in its wake, and final emotional stabilization has been achieved by compromise and other devices. Adolescent fantasies, strivings, and actions are covered in adulthood by an amnestic veil and do not necessarily interfere with effective adult living. The teacher, however, confronted daily with young people is apt to respond to their behavior in terms of the particular struggle he has encountered in his own adolescence. This often accounts for the teacher's sensitivity to and selective awareness of adolescent problems in his group, for his unusual understanding of one student and his complete lack of understanding of another. . . . He reacts to an extent he seldom suspects in terms of his own human needs and his own personality problems. He tends to feel close to those pupils whose interests or problems parallel his own, whose attitude toward maturation and its hazards call up the self-control which he, too, labored to achieve; similarly, he tends to be less interested or even to be unduly annoyed by others on equally personal grounds. . . .
>
> Of this the teacher may be totally unaware, recognizing only his likes and dislikes, easily rationalizing them as sound personality evaluations. He may find hostile adolescent behavior particularly hard to face; he may be repelled beyond reason by overdependent pupils, or he may be tempted to let them lean upon him too heavily; he may need the affection of his pupils too much, or be unable to accept it at all. . . .
>
> Personal reactions of this sort cannot be entirely avoided; they are part and parcel of every human being. But the more consciously such as-

[3] From P. Blos, *The Adolescent Personality*, New York: Appleton-Century-Crofts, 1941. (Copyright, 1941, D. Appleton-Century Company, Inc.)

pects in a situation can be recognized, the less they tend to distort relations and to hamper critical judgment. . . . He needs to understand not only his students' problems but his own as well and be aware of the fact that he too is at any instant operating in a total situation, a situation which among other things includes his own history and personality. It needs no further elaboration to point out that such self-awareness is an essential equipment of all who choose work with children as their primary task (pages 500-501).

It is understandable, though regrettable to some, that due to the pressure of numbers, the usual programs of teacher training have been unable to make provision for the development of the kind of self-aware-ness that Blos considers so essential for effective teaching. Even should such provisions be made, it would be useful for teachers to have some knowledge of the systematic investigations dealing with the patterns of teacher-pupil interaction, such as those to be discussed here and to partici-pate in some form of in-service training program as described in the next chapter.

In one study, using an observational technique, Baxter (1941) found certain definable and consistent patterns of teacher-pupil relation-ships. In a preliminary, intensive observation of six teachers, Baxter found that she could describe the prevailing teacher-pupil behavior in definitive terms. One classroom manifested "a relation of mutual harmonious and appreciative responsiveness." Another showed a mutu-ally intelligent understanding of the contribution of each to the class-room setting. In a third class the relationship showed a lack of under-standing of common purpose and in a fourth there was a mutual submission to dull routine. In a fifth class the relationship was one of aggressive driving in the acquisition and exhibition of facts learned. A sixth class manifested a relation of eager participation by both teacher and pupils in activities that were mutually understood and enjoyed. Baxter found that the reactions of pupils and their teachers were mark-edly similar and she concluded that the teachers tended to stimulate their pupils to the same kind of behavior that they themselves exhibited.

Using an elaborated case study approach in which he studied various facets of the teacher-pupil relationships, Bush (1954) arrived at a typology of both teachers and pupils. He attempted to answer the question whether certain types of teachers are able to establish more effective relationships with certain types of pupils. Bush was able to dis-cern three types of pupils and three types of teachers in his study of teacher-pupil relationships. The following descriptions are adapted from his report.

PUPIL TYPE A   The type A pupil is similar to the well-adjusted middle-class child described in the last chapter. His preferred mode of expression is conceptual rather than motoric. He is able to score high on tests requiring the use of abstract symbols. He exhibits few emotional problems, he is accepted by others, and is secure in his relationships with them. He finds school work challenging and is appropriately concerned about doing well. "His primary need is for intellectual stimulation, a rigorous and challenging experience that will develop the rational, knowledge-acquiring and thinking aspects of his personality." The type A pupil resembles the combination of the self-directive and adaptive adolescent personalities described by Havighurst and Taba (1949).

PUPIL TYPE B   The pupil who manifests problems of social adjustment is classified as type B. He tends to be resentful and hostile toward school and shows this by apathy or aggression. The school is usually not the primary source of this student's problem but his personal-social adjustment must be attended to before he can make satisfactory school progress. Many children from disturbed homes would be placed in this category, as would many who come from families suffering from economic privation. The type B pupil resembles a combination of the defiant and unadjusted adolescent personality types described by Havighurst and Taba (1949).

PUPIL TYPE C   The student of type C tends to be highly individualistic in his preferences and to depart from the behavior norms that teachers expect from their students. He is assertive and expresses his feelings strongly. His relationship to other people is less important than his relationship to his own thinking and feeling. His major concern is with trying to create and to express himself in terms of what he is feeling.

> This essentially restless and restive individual is chafed by the normally confining and restricting regulations and inflexible organization and routine of the school. . . . He usually needs the assistance of an artistically sensitive adult who will free him from conventional requirements and who, by encouragement and example, will enable him to express his own individuality in creative and artistic production (Bush, 1954, page 173).

TEACHER TYPE A′   The teacher classified as type A′ emphasizes the intellectual development of his pupils above all else. He is likely to view himself as one who demands high standards of performance from all his pupils. "He may approach pupils with a friendly reserve or a vitriolic, sarcastic, and abusive attitude, using whichever, in his opinion, will teach the most subject matter, or whichever his own personality drives dictate." There is a business-like atmosphere in the classroom. This teacher is usually quite competent in his field and uses his expertness as the prime focus of the relationship between himself and his students.

TEACHER TYPE B′   Whereas the teacher of Type A′ emphasizes the intellectual development of his pupils, Type B′ is more concerned with the emotional and social development of his students. This type of teacher attempts to establish a personal friendly relationship and to understand the total context of the student's life. The subject matter is organized so that it has some functional relationship to everyday life. He does not emphasize so much the teacher's expertness but rather his willingness to learn and to explore with the student. The relationship he tries to establish is of a counseling, friendly nature.

TEACHER TYPE C′   The type C′ teacher appears to have as his major purpose the release of the student's creative energies. This type of teacher believes that many pupils have a creative potential and that it is the teacher's task to discover and to nurture it. The relationships between this type of teacher and his pupils will be highly variable, because the teacher uses the emotional aspects of the relationship to produce the desired behavior in the pupil. Students are given considerable latitude in their choice of activities when they show signs of special interest or they may be driven by the teacher in order to develop the requisite skills for creative work. This teacher's insight into the subject he teaches tend to be based on intuition rather than on more careful scholarship.

Of the 650 pupils studied by Bush, 10 to 15 percent could be classified as type A, 20 to 25 percent type B and 5 percent as C. About one half of the pupils could not be classified as being predominantly one type or another. The data compiled by Havighurst and Taba (1949) on the distribution of adolescents by personality types confirm the figure of 20 to 25 percent for type B (unadjusted and defiant types); their figure for type A would probably be somewhat higher than Bush's estimate of 10 to 15 percent. Of the 27 teachers that he studied, Bush found that six could be classified as type A′, six as type B′, one as type C′, and 14, or more than half, were unclassifiable.

Although there were only a few cases in some of the categories of interaction (for example, type C pupils with type C′ teachers), Bush concludes that a more effective educational relationship is established when student types are matched to teacher types. Bush advances the proposition, similar to the one suggested in Chapter 7 in regard to class grouping, that as teachers vary in their abilities to meet the needs of different kinds of students, a more educationally effective teacher-pupil relationship would result from a program that attempted to match pupils and teachers on the basis of personality characteristics.

Spindler (1955), who has attempted to apply the generalizations of cultural anthropology to education, suggests that the teacher's classroom behavior represents in part an attempt to resolve the conflict arising from the transformations taking place in American culture. Specifically, he contends that most teachers, having been socialized in middle-class homes, have acquired a "traditional" value system. This value system (as described in Chapter 14) consists of a Puritan morality, a work-success ethic, an achievement orientation, and a future time orientation. This "traditional" value system is in the process of being transformed into an "emergent" value system. This latter value system, which Spindler claims is the orientation of most teacher-training programs, places heavy emphasis on socialibility, consideration for others, sensitivity and tolerance for other people's feelings, and conformity to group values.

The differences in the personal culture background of the teacher and the professional culture to which he is exposed in teacher-training produce conflict. Spindler hypothesizes that teachers resort to one of three types of adaptation to resolve this conflict. The first is that of ambivalence, characterized by contradictory and vacillating behavior particularly with respect to the exercise of discipline and authority. This type of conflict resolution leads to the teacher being *laissez-faire* in some situations and authoritarian in others. A second type of conflict resolution is a compensatory reaction. "The teacher overcompensates consistently either in the direction of the emergent or the tradition-centered values." In this case the teacher would take on, in an exaggerated manner, many of the characteristics of teacher type A′, B′, or C′ just described. The third type of reaction Spindler calls adapted. This type of teacher can be either emergent or traditional value-oriented. However, because he has come to terms with the value conflict he is able to act consistently and harmoniously with one or the other value system.

Ryans (1960), who directed a large-scale investigation of the characteristics of teachers, applied factor-analytic methods to a large amount of data derived from a variety of sources. He was able to identify "three major clusters of observable teacher behavior." These three dimensions are described as follows:

Pattern X—warm, friendly, understanding versus aloof, egocentric, restricted teacher behavior.

Pattern Y—responsible, businesslike, systematic versus evading, unplanned, slipshod teacher behavior.

Pattern Z—stimulating, imaginative, enthusiastic versus dull, routine teacher behavior.

Ryans found that there was a tendency for teachers who received high ratings on each of the patterns X, Y, and Z to show more of the following characteristics among others than did teachers who were rated low: (1) to appraise generously the behavior and motives of others, (2) to be interested in literature and the arts in general, (3) to enjoy social groups including relationships with pupils, (4) to prefer permissive classroom procedures.

In studying the relationship between pupil behavior and the characteristics of the teacher's behavior, Ryans (1961) found high positive correlations between ratings on each of the three patterns and what was termed "productive pupil behavior," which reflected "alertness, participation, confidence, responsibility and self-control, initiating behavior, etc." In secondary school classes the correlations between ratings of teacher behavior on these three dimensions and "productive pupil behavior," although still positive, were of a much lower order. It was found that the classroom behavior of the secondary school teacher that was stimulating and original, Pattern Z, tended more than Patterns X and Y to be related to productive pupil behavior. Why is it that pupil behavior in the elementary school seems more reactive to the teacher's behavior than in the secondary school? Probably because the older student's behavior tends to be more largely self-generated. He is more likely to have developed behavioral constancies so that his response has become more independent of the teacher's behavior. In the elementary school, on the other hand, the child looks more to the outside for cues to his behavior and while he is in the classroom the behavior of the teacher is an important source of these cues.

In addition to these developmental differences of the effects of the teacher's behavior, there is evidence that the various characteristics of teachers have different effects on different kinds of pupils. Washburne and Heil (1960), using Ryans' idea of several polar categories, classified a group of elementary school teachers into three types, the turbulent, the self-controlling, and the fearful. The turbulent teacher is described as one who places major emphasis on thinking, conjecturing, and objectivity; as one who is attracted by ideas rather than by people and as one who accepts and expresses his impulses. Also, the turbulent teacher is not greatly concerned with structure and order. The self-controlling teacher is one who focuses on order, organization and planning, and is work inclined. In human relations the self-controlling teacher is sensitive to the feelings of others and shows warmth and understanding toward his pupils. The fearful teacher is anxious and is unable to establish an orderly teaching environment. The fearful teacher is one who likes to have rules to guide his action and is anxious to have others as well as himself abide by rules. In human relations he tends to be self-protective and cautious about committing himself. When facing uncertainty his thinking becomes constricted.

> The results of the study confirmed the major hypothesis, namely, that different kinds of teachers get varying amounts of achievement from different kinds of children. The self-controlling teacher got the most achieve-

ment from the several different kinds of children; the fearful teacher got the least achievement. The turbulent teacher got almost as much achievement as the self-controlling teacher from children classified as conformers and strivers but less than half as much achievement from children classified as opposers and waverers. Although the fearful teacher got the greatest achievement with strivers, the amount of such achievement did not differ appreciably from that obtained by the self-controlling teacher and the turbulent teacher (page 425).

Using two categories of teacher behavior, namely warmth and permissiveness, and one category of pupil personality, that of need for affection, Christensen (1960) confirmed in part the findings of Washburne and Heil. He found that pupil achievement-growth in vocabulary and arithmetic was greater in those classes where pupils rated their teachers higher on a warmth scale.

It is interesting to note that although pupil liking of the teacher is a positive factor in achievement and morale, teacher warmth as expressed in the teacher's liking for the pupil is not significantly related to the pupil's liking for the teacher. Bush (1954) found these correlations to be low and he further calls into question the widespread belief that a liking for children is a universal requirement for effective teaching. In line with the position reflected above in the quote from Blos, Bush contends that too much emotional warmth may be harmful, that personal entanglement can destroy the objectivity that enables the teacher to have insight into the student's behavior. He points out that some teachers use their relationships with their students in ways that are designed to work out their personality problems, without being aware of it. He gives the following examples:

Miss Gray, an older woman living by herself and in great need of affection, considered herself to be a counseling type teacher. In trying to help children with their personal problems, she mothered them to suffocation. One pupil said of her, "I wish she wouldn't be so pokey, stick her nose into everything and find out all about us. I wish she wouldn't try to mother us." A middle-aged single man who, because of effeminate characteristics, had less than normally satisfying relationships with his fellows, sought to compensate by spending endless hours out of class in company with certain young men under his tutelage and was finally dismissed because of alleged homosexuality (pages 87-88).

Until we find more reliable means of describing the personalities of teachers and pupils as they function and interact in the classroom and until we can ascertain with more clarity the effects on various students of different kinds of teacher-pupil interaction, any conclusion about effective teacher-pupil relationships will remain highly tentative, very general, and often painfully self-evident. The teacher-pupil relationship is a complex and unique phenomenon. If these relationships are categorized and some of them are labeled effective and others ineffective we go beyond empirical evidence. Each relationship as it unfolds over time represents a conglomeration of many features, some positive and some negative, which balance out into a unique constellation in each instance. Some of these features reside initially in certain personal and professional characteristics that the teacher brings to his first teaching assignment (Medley, 1961) and that probably developed before the selection of teaching as a career. Other features of the relationship arise from characteristics of the pupil that he brings to school or to the classroom that induce different reactions in different teachers. Yet in spite of these long-standing factors that determine the quality of the relationship, when the teacher studies, analyzes, and tries to understand the processes of teaching, child growth and development, and human interaction, then the teacher-pupil relationship can become appropriately objective and hopefully increasingly effective.

THE STUDENT TEACHER

The position of the student teacher involves the working out of more complex relationships than that of the regular classroom teacher. The success of the student teaching venture depends not only on being able to establish a workable relationship with the pupils but also on being able to work with the supervising teacher or the regular classroom teacher as well as with the college supervisor. Redl and Wattenberg (1951) note that the student teaching situation has a number of "emotional traps." For example, because the pupils recognize that the student teacher lacks the authority of the "real" teacher, they may express hostility more freely and openly. On the other hand, because the student teacher lacks some of the coercive or reward power of the regular teacher, he may come to exercise more referent or possibly more expert power. The relationship between the supervising teacher and the student teacher and the feelings of the pupils toward the regular teacher will affect the student teacher's relationship to the pupils. If the pupils sense that there is a rivalrous relationship between the two adults, they may be inclined to play off one against the other. If the pupils like their regular teacher they may try to show-up the newcomer and receive some subtle encouragement in this from their teacher; if, on the other hand, they bear some resentment toward their regular teacher they may respond more positively toward the student teacher than they do toward the regular classroom teacher. If the latter situation develops the supervising teacher may become excessively critical of the student teacher in private conference or in reporting to the college supervisor. If the supervising teacher demonstrates a lack of confidence in the student teacher, the pupils may try to protect the student teacher or they may join in expressing the same lack of confidence, depending on their feelings toward their classroom teacher. Where the relationship between the supervising teacher and the student teacher is one of apparent equality, the pupils may in a short time show no difference in behavior or attitudes, whichever teacher is in charge of the class.

The ordinary difficulties encountered in student teaching are generally not of such magnitude as to interfere seriously with the success of the vast majority of the thousands of individuals who annually fulfill the requirement of student teaching and who derive from this experience a sense of confidence and mastery so essential to embarking on a teaching career. Occasionally these difficulties reach such proportions as to create doubt about the potential teaching ability of the student. The following case study adapted from Clothier and Wyatt (1952) illustrates some of the difficulties encountered in the student teaching situation.[4]

As Mrs. Forman sat in the conference room waiting for Dr. Ames from the University, she thought back to the Monday a month ago when Jan Carson first came to her room as a student teacher. She smiled ruefully as she remembered her own eagerness and confidence in her anticipation of working with a student. She had considered that being selected as a supervising teacher would give her an opportunity to fulfill more completely her professional obligations. Now she was not at all certain that she could finish the term with the student in her room. Where had she failed? She began to reconstruct mentally the events which led to her present disappointment.

"Mrs. Forman? I'm Jan Carson, your student teacher for this term. The principal pointed you out to me and suggested that I come over and introduce myself."

Mrs. Forman remembered how surprised she had been when she had turned from her work at the duplicating machine in response to Jan's introduction. Jan certainly had not fit the mental image of the typical college girl that Mrs. Forman had constructed. Jan was a slender girl of about medium height with black hair and black eyes. She wore a severe black dress and an equally severe coiffure that together with the absence of make-up accentuated the sombreness of her appearance. Mrs. Forman, expecting a typical girl of twenty-one or so, remembered having to control herself as she greeted her cordially: "Well, Jan, I'm happy to meet you. We have been looking forward to your coming. The children could hardly wait for today to arrive, and I must confess that I have been anticipating it too. Come, let's sit down and chat a little while before the children arrive. I'm sure that you have many questions to ask."

The boys and girls had been told about Miss Carson's arrival

---

[4] From G. Clothier and Nita Wyatt, *Case Studies in Student Teaching*. Cedar Falls, Iowa: The Association for Student Teaching, Bulletin no. 18, 1952, pp. 33-36.

and why she would be in their fourth-grade class until the end of the year. Mrs. Forman had engaged the children fully in planning for Miss Carson's arrival. Mrs. Forman recalled how eagerly the children had helped to move in a desk and to set it up on one side of the room. They had helped in providing a complete set of books and a seating chart. Yet in spite of all this the first day in class had not come off as anticipated. Jan said very little to anyone. Only once during the day did she manage a faint smile for a child. The children had introduced themselves each in turn but because Jan seemed to be examining each speaker sternly the children soon became ill at ease. Mrs. Forman remembered thinking that Jan's shyness and aloofness were going to present a problem.

During the days that followed Jan had frequently frowned and shaken her head to indicate that she disapproved of what was going on in the classroom. Mrs. Forman had tried to get Jan to express openly what was bothering her but somehow Jan always managed to evade the issue.

Mrs. Forman's thoughts were interrupted by the arrival of Dr. Ames, Jan's supervisor from the School of Education at the University. He greeted Mrs. Forman cordially. Mrs. Forman burst out, "Dr. Ames, am I glad you're here! I have just about given up on Jan Carson. She evidently disapproves of my teaching and I cannot help reacting to this apparent dislike. I do believe that she is an intelligent person and she could become a good teacher, but I'm just not the one to supervise her student teaching."

Dr. Ames appeared a little distressed as he declared, "Mrs. Forman, we are convinced that you are fully qualified for this job. I'm not sure what can be done about Jan but whatever the outcome I do hope that you will cooperate with us next year."

"I'm sorry, Dr. Ames," Mrs. Forman said apologetically. "I guess I've just worried about Jan until I've become a problem myself. As I told you when you were here last, I didn't like her implied criticism when she observed my teaching. I didn't become concerned, however, until she began to undertake some of the teaching herself. She has an expressionless face and her voice is a droning monotone. She loses the children's attention and then tries to regain it by repeating endlessly. She takes twice as much time as necessary to present a simple lesson. I'm worried because the children are beginning to lose the spontaneity and originality that I've worked so hard to develop. When I make suggestions for improving her teaching she listens impassively and nods assent, but she ignores them the next time around. I really don't know what to do next!"

Dr. Ames hesitated briefly before beginning to speak. "Yes, I am well aware that Jan has been very critical of your teaching methods. She indicated as much to me when I was here last. At that time Jan had not yet taught the class; she had only observed. She seemed not to understand why you conducted the class the way you did or else she misinterpreted your intentions. For example, she commented that you ridicule students by laughing at their errors and she complained also about what she interpreted as a lack of definite plans and schedules for all the subjects."

Mrs. Forman was stunned at hearing that Jan had made such comments. "She certainly rejects me as a person and a teacher, doesn't she? What do you think I can do about a problem like this?" asked Mrs. Forman.

Dr. Ames hastened to assure Mrs. Forman that Jan's comments had not influenced his own estimate of Mrs. Forman's teaching ability. He stated, "I tried to impress upon Jan that you were selected as a supervising teacher because of the fine record of teaching which you had established here and at your previous position. It could be that the trouble here is a basic personality conflict between the two of you. Or, it could be that Jan has misinterpreted what was taught her in her professional education courses and cannot reconcile what she believes to be good practice and the realities of a particular classroom situation. It could be that Jan is hypercritical because she is not as stable emotionally as she should be. I am anxious to see her teaching and to talk to her again before we decide what to do. Could we go up to the classroom now?"

"Yes," said Mrs. Forman. "She will be teaching arithmetic as soon as recess is over."

Mrs. Forman went to her desk as Dr. Ames edged into a chair at the back of the room. The first twenty minutes of the lesson seemed to go well. Jan explained the new process in arithmetic to the children. However, at the end of more than a half hour Jan was still explaining and the children had hardly had a chance to respond at all. She finally stopped and told the children to begin working on their assignment. Several of the children turned to Mrs. Forman with puzzled expressions, obviously uncertain about what they were supposed to do. Jan was so engrossed with helping one child that she did not notice their difficulties. Mrs. Forman said quietly, "Miss Carson, I believe you should write the assignment on the board for the children." Jan gave Mrs. Forman a look of defiance and went on to help another child who had raised his hand. About five minutes later, after all the children seemed to be working, Jan went to the board and wrote down the assignment.

After a few minutes during which Jan supervised the work of the children, Dr. Ames indicated to Jan that he wished to talk with her in the conference room. As they went down the hall, Mrs. Forman stepped to the door to close it after them. She could not help overhearing Jan's distraught voice saying, "Did you see what Mrs. Forman did? She has tried several times to make me look silly in front of the children. I'm sure she is jealous because some of the children are beginning to like me more than they do her and because I use more modern methods than she does. She has tried to make me look bad in the eyes of the children. She has no more tact in working with adults than she does working with children. How can she be so insensitive!" she wailed.

The authors of this case study do not present a solution to this problem. Instead they ask the reader a number of questions, such as: What evidence is there to support Dr. Ames' hypothesis of a personality conflict between the supervising teacher and the student teacher? Was Mrs. Forman at fault when she interrupted the class with her request that Jan write the assignment on the board?

Although the student teaching experience in this case presentation did not turn out happily, it should be noted that even in this case the practice teaching was being done under auspicious circumstances. This is generally true. For example, the supervising teacher is selected on the basis of experience, proven teaching skill, and a willingness to work with a student teacher. This will ordinarily mean that the pupils being taught will be reasonably controlled and directed and that the presence of the student teacher has been anticipated and planned for. Further, the student teacher is usually given an opportunity to observe the class and to become acquainted with individual pupils both through his own observation and through discussions with the regular teacher. Because the situation is somewhat protected, it is not always possible to predict teaching success from a successful student teaching performance. On the other hand, we cannot predict teaching failure from an unsuccessful experience in student teaching. The lack of success in student teaching may sometimes be due to the lack of freedom, poor relationships with the supervising teacher, or similar features of the apprentice teaching setting that are not characteristic of the usual teaching situation.

THE SUBSTITUTE TEACHER

In contrast to student teaching, substitute teaching provides little opportunity for advance planning. The substitute teacher who is on call usually receives very little advance notice and his presence is frequently a surprise to the class. There is seldom an opportunity to learn the names of the students, to know individual student characteristics and needs, to understand how the regular teacher has developed the subject matter during the school term and what structural arrangements have been found effective in a particular class. In short, most of the important supports of a continuing teaching situation are not available to the temporary substitute. Because of this, substitute teaching is frequently sadly disappointing. In the primary grades it is the students who will likely suffer disappointment in having their routine interrupted and in the uncertainty of relating to a strange adult. It is difficult for young children, who are still heteronomous with regard to many school rules, to submit to any modification of these rules. For example, the rituals of watering plants, erasing black boards, distributing supplies, going to gym, and all the rest, take on an air of sanctity and the substitute teacher just cannot know how to solemnize these sacred rites. In the more advanced grades it is the temporary substitute who is likely to suffer disappointment. Adolescents do not feel insecure in their anonymity, and some of them will use to it to act out some of their aggression against the substitute teacher who is viewed as a helpless adult. One teacher, who after her first period of substitute teaching in an eighth-grade class described herself as physically and mentally exhausted, spiritually humiliated and broken, stated that she felt that the students responded to her unexpected presence with the same excitement as finding a squirt gun in a box of cereal.

Shortly after being graduated with honors in English from a liberal arts college, Mary O'Neil had been married. Although her husband's career in engineering did not make it necessary for Mary to earn additional income, she wanted the stimulation of at least some part-time teaching. The principal in the local high school advised her to take some courses at the university in a nearby community and he agreed that when she had fulfilled the requirements for a provisional teaching certificate he would be pleased to place her name on his very short list of substitute teachers. Mary registered for some courses shortly thereafter. She studied educational psychology and educational philosophy one semester; adolescent psychology, methods of teaching English, and developmental reading in the summer term. She was able to arrange to do her practice teaching during the fall semester in the school connected with the university's school of education. Although she still needed some credits, the school principal agreed to place her name on his list for the second semester as many of his staff had been out with the flu and there were days when he was desperate just to have the classes covered.

Mary received a call late one Thursday afternoon asking her if she would be at school the next day at seven-thirty to start teaching at eight o'clock. All the secretary told her was that she would teach English in several sections of eighth grade and one of ninth and that Mr. Wilson, the regular teacher, had left lesson plans with the head of the department who would not be available until the next morning. Mary wondered what the next day would be like. Some of her fellow-students in her professional education courses had described their substitute teaching experiences in such a way as to make her anxious, but she felt confident that she would be able to handle it. At dinner her husband had been a little peeved because Mary wanted to stay home that evening when they had planned to go to the movies with another couple. Mary wanted to be rested for her adventure the next day.

The department chairman briefed Mary on her five English periods. He went over the lesson plans but had no time to place the material to be covered into some kind of understandable context. Mary later thought that it didn't make very much difference since her problem in each class was not to teach but to maintain order and to control her temper. Each class seemed to greet her in unison with what appeared to be mischievous delight, "Oh boy, Mr. Wilson's absent." In each class the students would not take their seats; in one of them paper airplanes came soaring toward the front of the room. The boys were unruly and the girls giggled. Mary found herself trying to untangle one nasty situation after another as she became angrier and angrier. It took almost half the period to gain some semblance of order and she had to exercise constant vigilance to maintain it. She used what little time she had in each class to give a written assignment and to supervise it. At the end of the day she reported to the department chairman and to the principal that the day had been wasted for the students and had been an ordeal for her. She was convinced that she would not want to repeat the experience.

After giving the matter some thought, Mary decided that she could prepare more adequately for the next occasion. She decided that if she would be called for one day of teaching she would not try to use the lesson plan prepared by the teacher but would have her own carefully worked out plan for each of the grades in which she might teach. She decided to become acquainted with the teachers of English and to find out what she could about those students in each class who could be relied upon to help maintain group control. She would try to learn a few names so that she could call on pupils directly. She thought that her anger had been too easily provoked and that she had reacted to the students' behavior as if it had been a personal affront. In reality the horseplay had been the result of the novelty of the situation and had not been truly malicious. She was sure that she could establish better relations with her students if she could get them meaningfully involved in an interesting class activity and if she avoided humiliating students, threatening them, and setting unrealistic expectations.

Mary was called in about a dozen more times that year and each time the teaching went a little better. The arrival of a baby interrupted Mary's teaching but when her mother came to live with her a few years later, Mary took on more substitute teaching in the local high school and taught some forty to fifty days each year. She enjoys her teaching; the students in many of the classes have come to know her and to respect her. She in turn has come to know some of the pupils and feels that during these occasional teaching days she has taught them some important lessons about themselves and about the world.

SUMMARY

The interaction of the teacher with his pupils is one of the important social influences that determine the direction of the pupils' personality development as well as the effectiveness of the classroom learning. The classroom organization or structure is one of the manifest aspects of the teacher-pupil relationship. Structure may be characterized as coactive or interactive. In the former all relationships are between the teacher and separate pupils; in the latter the interaction takes place among all the members of the class group. Although much of the decision as to which kind of classroom structure and control will prevail rests with the teacher, he is by no means a free agent in this matter. The type of community, the grade level, the type of student, the subject matter, and other factors all contribute to the end-product of one or another form of classroom structure and control. It is therefore impossible to describe the one effective type of teacher-student relationship. Effective and ineffective relationships will differ one from another depending on the educational setting.

The extent to which the teacher controls the activity of the classroom and the means that he employs to exercise control, are important manifestations of the teacher-student relationship. The classroom in which the teacher retains all the control has been termed teacher-centered, authoritarian, or dominative. Those classes in which the teacher has granted to the students some of the decision-making power, have been called learner-centered, democratic, or integrative. The research findings are quite consistent in pointing to the benefits of the latter form of control insofar as satisfaction with the group activity and morale are concerned. One form of classroom control does not appear to be consistently superior to another in producing greater gains in subject matter achievement. There is some suggestion, however, that if we differentiate subject-matter achievement into outcomes such as divergent and convergent thinking, we find that the learner-centered classroom is more conducive to the development of divergent forms of thinking and the teacher-centered classroom is more effective in producing convergent thinking. It is quite clear that a classroom in which the teacher does not exercise control himself and where he does not accept the responsibility of transferring control to the students (a *laissez-faire* situation) is one in which morale, subject-matter achievement, and in all probability personality development, are all adversely affected.

The teacher derives his power to determine structure and control from one or more of several sources. This power may be derived from the pupil's awareness that the teacher can punish him. This is called coercive power. The teacher may exercise control as a result of his power to reward. The teacher's role generally carries with it a certain amount of legitimate power or the power vested in the role by the cultural value system. If the student identifies with the teacher, the teacher exercises referent power; if the student turns to the teacher as one who can provide expert guidance, the teacher then exercises expert power. Each of these sources of the teacher's power has its limitations as well as its appropriate use. Some are useful in resolving a problem with short-range implications, others are more useful for long-range purposes.

The matter of discipline or the control of misbehavior is one that causes concern to most teachers. The teacher needs to be aware that the methods used to deal with disruptive behavior will have an effect on the child's view of his own aggressive impulses and will also contribute to the manner in which the child will come to fulfill his responsibilities as a citizen in society. The aim and the method of discipline must rest on a sensitivity to the situation rather than on a precoded set of responses.

The quality of the interaction between the teacher and the pupil will depend on the teacher's personality, his mode of operation, the pupil's personality, and his earlier developmental experiences. Many of these factors are complex, subtle, and hidden from conscious awareness on the part of both the teacher and the pupil. Different kinds of pupils respond differently to different kinds of teachers. Students may be characterized in terms of their competence and interest in dealing with abstract symbols, their personal-social adjustment, or their assertiveness in regard to their own feelings. Teachers, likewise, can be characterized in terms of their emphasis on intellectual development, emotional-social adjustment, or the development of creativity and self-expression. It has been suggested that matching of students with teachers, though administratively complicated, would lead to more productive instruction. The patterns of teacher characteristics have been described on various bipolar dimensions, for example, warm, friendly versus aloof, restricted; systematic, responsible versus unplanned, slipshod; enthusiastic, imaginative versus dull, routine. It has been shown that students in classes of teachers with high ratings on these dimensions show more participation, confidence, responsibility, and other forms of productive behavior. It should be noted, however, that different patterns of teacher characteristics produce varying amounts of achievement from different kinds of children.

The classroom relationships in the case of the student teacher will depend in large measure on the kind of atmosphere that the regular teacher (the supervising teacher) has established and the relationship that evolves between the student teacher and the supervising teacher. The college supervisor also plays a role here. Although there are many "emotional traps" in the student teaching situation, most prospective teachers find the experience of apprentice teaching useful, stimulating, and meaningful.

The substitute teacher usually lacks the human relations supports found in the continuing teaching situation. He is not likely to know the names of students, their particular needs, and the classroom routine. Young children may find the experience with the substitute teacher disappointing. Older students often harrass the substitute teacher and make the teaching situation a difficult one for the teacher. A teacher who knows in advance where he will do his substitute teaching would be well advised to find out all he can about the school, the particular classes in which he might teach, and to try to establish some minimal relationships with some of the students in those classes in which he is going to teach.

READING REFERENCES

Association for Supervision and Curriculum Development 1963 Yearbook, *New Insights and the Curriculum*. Washington: National Education Association (particularly chaps. 5-8).

Baruch, Dorothy W., *New Ways in Discipline*. New York: McGraw-Hill Book Company, 1949.

Bush, R. N., *The Teacher-Pupil Relationship*. Englewood Cliffs, N.J.: Prentice-Hall, 1954.

Hymes, J. C., Jr., *Behavior and Misbehavior: A Teacher's Guide to Action*. Englewood Cliffs, N.J.: Prentice-Hall, 1955.

Ryans, D. G., *Characteristics of Teachers*. Washington: American Council on Education, 1960.

Sheviakov, G. V. and F. Redl (new revision by Sybil K. Richardson), *Discipline for Today's Children and Youth*. Washington: National Education Association, 1958.

Spindler, G. D., *The Transmission of American Culture*. Cambridge: Harvard University Press, 1959.

CHAPTER 16

THE TEACHER

There have been many exaggerated descriptions of the teacher in America, his task, and his contributions to society, ranging from those that have been overly sentimental and romantic (such as Sharp, 1957), to those that have been unreasonably critical and disdainful (such as Dunn, 1955; Koerner, 1963). On the one hand, some have depicted teachers as saviors of democracy and as idealistically devoted to their pupils and to their mission. On the other hand, others have described the typical teacher as subversive, neurotic, and impractical, whose choice of teaching stems from an unwillingness or an inability to meet the demands of the more "productive" occupations. The intention here is not to add to either of these unrealistic and extreme views, nor even to mediate between them, but to increase the teacher's understanding of the work he does and of himself.

Teachers can teach more effectively and they can understand better the nature of their work if they clarify the primary, long-range objectives of teaching. The first topic here is a consideration of some of the objectives of teaching. In order to understand himself and his work, the teacher needs not only to review and to re-evaluate his objectives, he needs also to understand the social context in which he works. The discussion of the social context of teaching in the preceding three chapters has covered family influences, social class factors, and the teacher-pupil relationship. In this chapter the discussion of the social context of teaching is extended and the status of teaching as an occupation or, more commonly stated, teaching as a profession, is examined. Some of the professional relationships as well as the duties, obligations, and privileges associated with teaching are also considered.

The selection of teaching as a career and the continuation in this work involves many complex motives and arouses many strong feelings. Teaching almost always involves a commitment of a personal kind, not the same in any two instances to be sure, but a commitment nevertheless. The challenge of understanding one's motives and facing one's feelings is greater in teaching than in almost any other lifework. It is a challenge that must be met because teaching is a form of self-expression and also because teaching requires a constant personal interaction of a most difficult sort. This problem, which even evades a clear formulation, will form the basis for the closing discussion of this chapter.

THE OBJECTIVES OF TEACHING

There has been a constant attempt here to make the reader aware of the need to keep educational means and procedures carefully geared to educational aims and objectives. For example, the discussion of programmed instruction elaborated the educational objective of cognitive development. It was noted that some facets of cognitive development could be well-served by programmed instruction while others would not. Likewise, in the discussion of evaluation procedures the point that tests and test items needed to be designed differently for the different purposes of instruction was emphasized. It was maintained that the entire evaluation procedure should not interfere with the proper development of personality. In other words, each time a problem is encountered we need to re-examine our educational aims so as to understand the problem and to resolve it satisfactorily. As social conditions change, our educational problems change and consequently our understanding of educational aims must change. The issues raised here pertain to the objectives of teaching. The functions and the roles of the teacher will be examined in the light of several of the objectives previously discussed in relation to other issues. It is hoped that this further elaboration of educational aims will serve to clarify them and make them more relevant to the teaching task.

Teaching may be viewed as having a two-fold function: (1) To transmit and to conserve the cultural heritage, and (2) To initiate change and to free the learner to live in a changing world. These functions are not mutually exclusive, as many have contended, but they are, on the contrary, mutually reinforcing and interdependent. The teacher is not compelled to choose between them but should see his task as incorporating both functions as part of the integral whole of effective teaching.

Teaching to Conserve the Cultural Heritage

The layman often views the teacher's task as consisting wholly and exclusively of teaching "knowledge." This is another way of saying that the society has assigned to the teacher one responsibility, namely, that of transmitting the cultural heritage to the child. This view was expressed to this writer by a highly placed official in the department of education of a foreign country who stated that he hoped some day to be able to provide each teacher with what he called a "catechism" so that each teacher in every classroom in his country would be instructed in his work from moment to moment and from detail to detail. American teachers find such assertions offensive. However, one must be cautious in rejecting the point of view merely because of the offensive manner in which it is presented. Teachers should not object to the suggestion that culture and worthwhile tradition should be included in the curriculum. Nor should they object to the suggestion that they follow a syllabus and that they be instructed in methods of teaching. What is objectionable is the notion that the curriculum should consist *wholly* of fixed knowledge and that the teacher must follow slavishly a detailed syllabus that presumes to dispense with the teacher's judgment and intelligence.

The role of the teacher as a mediator of the cultural heritage was touched on in Chapter 3. In the discussion of the role of the learner in acquiring fixed meaning, it was pointed out that the accumulated wisdom of the society can serve to identify for the teacher the capacities and the fulfillments open to the child. The teacher mediates the culture not only because it sets a direction for his work but because the community outside the school expects him to do so. Because the teacher serves as one who conserves the values and the content of the past, certain kinds of behaviors and personal qualities are important.

Grambs (1957) in discussing the roles of the teacher states that it is expected by the community that the teacher will serve as a model for the young. "The continuous association of the teacher with young people impels the community to invoke the teacher as a standard setter. It is the wish of parents that teachers be adequate to this role. Parents actually have encouraged youngsters to use teachers as models rather than other adults" (page 81). In times past this expectation led to many restrictions on the teacher's behavior. This was particularly difficult for the teacher when there existed a marked inconsistency between the ideal behavior and actual practice in the community. The teacher was expected to live up to the ideal standard and he was not permitted to make his own decision in regard to smoking, drinking, social card playing or dancing, and the like. Although the extent to which such inconsistencies in community expectations produce role conflict for the teacher depends upon the nature of the community and upon certain personal characteristics of the teachers (Getzels and Guba, 1955), it is our impression that the over-all amount of such conflict has been considerably reduced since World War II. Community ideals and practices have come to converge on many of these minor issues. While the teacher is expected to serve as a model, many aspects of the teacher's private life are no longer evaluated as evidence of his qualifications to do so.

In considering the teacher's role as a model in mediating the culture we would refer the reader to our discussion of the process of identification in Chapter 6. The concept of identification as used there explains the general similarities between one generation and the next. Identification was defined earlier as the process of modeling oneself in behavior, thought, and feeling after another person. It is difficult to know how much a particular child identifies with a particular teacher. Yet the need of the child to identify with the adult forms the basis for the child's willingness to learn, to acquire the information that the teacher appears to have, and to behave in ways that conform to the standards of conduct accepted by the adult. If teachers are to serve as models in mediating the culture, they need to be participants in that culture to the extent that they exemplify the best of society's traditions. Participating in the culture means actively appreciating one or more of its art forms, understanding its historical roots, a familiarity with its literature, and an awareness of the basic scientific notions and the role they have played in shaping the culture. This may appear like a large order but what is suggested here is only a statement of minimal prerequisites if teachers are to fulfil their role as mediators of the culture. This attitude of expecting the teacher to be a person of "culture" is being reflected in the changing requirements for teacher certification (Conant, 1963). This change in the requirements should serve to correct the deplorable condition in which college seniors who planned to teach, regularly achieved lower average scores on tests of "general culture" and other academic abilities than did those seniors who were planning to engage in other occupations (for example, Learned and Wood, 1938, and North, 1958). It should be clear that different teachers meeting different kinds of students will mediate the cultural heritage in different ways. An appropriate expression of this role in the primary grades will not be the same as that for the high school grades, but at all levels the person who is called a teacher should have the basic resources that would make it possible for him to competently fulfill the role of transmitting the heritage of the society.

Teaching to Initiate Change

Another aspect of the teacher's function is to initiate change and to prepare the child to meet the demands of a changing world. The discussions of teaching for understanding, problem solving, and creativity in Chapter 4, as well as that of transfer of training in Chapter 5, dealt with this topic. It is the teacher's responsibility to help the student achieve more mature ways of thinking and more effective ways of solving problems. In order for the child to become capable of expressing himself creatively, the teacher needs to provide a measure of freedom and a nonthreatening classroom environment. The best way to foster useful applications of past learning to new situations is by extracting at each present moment the full meaning of each current experience. In the discussion of teaching for values (Chapter 6) it was pointed out that the primary aim of moral training is to help the child to become an autonomously moral person who seeks his own unique self-enhancement without infringing on the rights of others. In the last chapter also, in discussing the issue of classroom discipline, it was stated that the aim of discipline is to enable the child to respond in an orderly fashion to the changing situation. All of this can be summed up by stating that the function of teaching is to enable the child to discover the unknown, to express a constructive discontent with the present, and to anticipate the challenge of change with confidence.

The teacher's role of initiating change and fostering a renewal of the past, does not readily suggest a specific content in the teacher training program. It depends rather on certain qualities of character and temperament; such qualities as idealism, a willingness to tolerate uncertainty, a capacity for constructive criticism, a sense of "the nagging existence of mystery," and so on. These are not characteristics that can be inculcated or adopted by fiat or mere wish and desire. They require patient cultivation. It is not essential that *all* teachers exhibit them to a high degree. However, if our society is to produce capable leadership in science, politics, industry, and education, there must be an opportunity for most children to meet some teachers who show these characteristics to a degree where some of them will become inspired. Our society needs teachers who will lead their students to question the current emphasis on material progress, on mechanical efficiency, and on financial profit. These teachers can show that man's inventiveness can be applied in the service of mankind, to improve man's condition, and to free him to seek his fulfillment. Teachers of this sort will contribute their share to preventing society's drift toward a moral impasse that will ultimately lead to stagnation and decay.

Teaching and Understanding the Individual Child

The importance of the teacher's understanding and acceptance of the individual child has been frequently noted. It is our conviction that the child cannot grow to accept his cultural heritage nor can he become free to initiate and accept change, unless he has received a measure of understanding from significant adults during his growing years. The manner in which the teacher can come to extend this kind of understanding to children needs to be made explicit. The Commission on Teacher Education (1945) and Prescott (1957) describe a procedure called the child-study program that is designed to give teachers an opportunity to learn how to understand individual children and is based on scientific knowledge from the various disciplines that study human beings. Before presenting the salient features of the child-study program, the implications of understanding human behavior will be considered. This may also clarify what may appear to be a contradiction in previous statements that teachers should both conserve the past and initiate change.

How is one to understand the behavior of another? Is man's behavior completely determined by his history and his past experience or is it the result of his free-will and intention? This question of control versus freedom or determinism versus free choice has concerned philosophers and psychologists. If the teacher adopts a deterministic view (there is the question of whether the teacher's choice of a point of view is free or determined) he will not be able to judge the student's behavior but only hope that he can redirect the course of his unfolding history. If the teacher adopts the opposite view, he will not feel the need to understand why the student behaves as he does, having a ready-made answer, "He willed it so." Some have deduced from the study of psychology, with its attempts to establish the laws of behavior and the effects of environmental influences, that the deterministic position is the more valid one. This is not so. The following paraphrase of a statement by Ryle (1949) is a more useful view: The laws that psychologists have found and will find may, in one sense of the metaphorical verb, govern everything that happens, but they do not ordain everything that happens. Indeed they do not ordain anything that happens.

Ryle offers an illustration to elucidate this point. He proposes that we imagine a scientifically trained observer, not acquainted with chess or any other game, being allowed to examine the chess board between the moves made by the players. The observer does not see or know of the players. In time he begins to discern certain regularities in the change of position of the pieces and given enough time he will have worked out all the rules of chess. He is then allowed to see that the pieces are moved by people called "players" engaged in what is called a "game" of chess.

The observer commiserates with the players saying that every move they make is governed by unbreakable rules, that they are therefore in bondage. "The whole course of what you tragically dub your 'game' is remorselessly pre-ordained."

The players laugh and explain to the observer that though every move is governed, not one of them is ordained by the rules. While it is true that once the player begins to move a piece the rules govern the manner in which it may be moved, the rules do not say which piece shall be moved, at which stage of the game, nor how far and in which direction it will be moved. "The rules are the same for all the games of chess that have ever been played, yet nearly every game that has ever been played has taken a course for which the players can recall no close parallels. The rules are unalterable but the games are not uniform."

Freud's description of psychological processes may, at times, appear to be deterministic, but even he adopts a position similar to Ryle's in the following passage (1950):

> So long as we trace the development from its final stage backwards, the connection appears continuous, and we feel we have gained an insight which is completely satisfactory or even exhaustive. But if we proceed the reverse way, if we start from the premises inferred from the analysis and try to follow these up to the final result, then we no longer get the impression of an inevitable sequence of events which could not be otherwise determined. We notice at once that there might have been another result, and that we might have been just as well able to understand and explain the latter. The synthesis is thus not so satisfactory as the analysis; in other words, from a knowledge of the premises we could not have foretold the nature of the result (pages 226-227).

The same may be said about the teacher's understanding of the child's behavior. The principles of psychology may help him understand that if a certain course of action is adopted certain outcomes may be expected to occur. (By quantifying our terms we can use statistics to state the probability of occurence within a population of subjects). Psychological principles, however, do not tell the teacher whether the course of action will be adopted, when it will be adopted, or what the precise effects will be in the case of a particular individual.

Kelly (1955) makes the same point. In a discussion of determinism and man's free-will he states:

> Ultimately a man sets the measure of his own freedom and his own bondage by the level at which he chooses to establish his convictions. The man who orders his life in terms of many special and unflexible convictions about temporary matters makes himself the victim of circumstances. Each little prior conviction that is not open to review is a hostage he gives to fortune; it determines whether the events of tomorrow will bring happiness or misery. The man whose prior convictions encompass a broad per-

spective, and are cast in terms of principles rather than rules, has a much better chance of discovering those alternatives which will lead eventually to his emancipation (vol. 1, pages 21-22).

The teacher who short-circuits his understanding of the child by "a prior conviction that is not open to review," not only enslaves himself to this prior conviction and thus reduces his freedom of operation, but also brings unhappiness to the child by reducing his choices as well. This applies whether the teacher's premature judgment or construction about the child expresses approval or disapproval.

The Child-Study Program

Any systematic approach to the understanding of the child is subject to the dangers of overinvolvement on the part of the teacher as noted in the previous chapter. Also we should note that the empirical evidence on the effects of an organized approach for the development of such understanding is contradictory, largely because the variables involved are so complex and difficult to control. Thus, Hoyt (1955) finds no significant effects of teacher knowledge of pupil characteristics on pupil achievement and attitudes towards classwork. On the other hand, Ojemann and Wilkinson (1939) report "that the data obtained in [their] study are consistent in showing that when teachers learn to know their pupils as personalities in their respective environments teachers tend to become more effective guides for learning—the pupils achieve more in academic areas—. . . ." One such program of child-study, developed and described by Prescott (1957), is presented in detail because teachers who have participated in it have reported that this experience has been valuable for them, and also because it demonstrates how several of the topics of educational psychology are relevant to the teacher's task.

Participation in the program is voluntary on the part of teachers, administrators and supervisors. Groups of from eight to fifteen persons who agree to participate actively in the program, meet every other week during the school year, each meeting lasting for about two hours. The groups usually select their own leaders and coleaders whose task it is to convene the group and to facilitate the functioning of the group. Associated with the study group there are also a local coordinator and a consultant who serve the groups and the program in specialized ways. The standard program for each participant lasts three years, although members are free to leave whenever they wish and groups are reorganized each year.

During the first session the purposes of the child-study program are outlined. Some of the purposes are:

> To guide participants to discover the kinds of information about individual children that are necessary to understand them, and to develop skill in gathering and objectively recording this information.

To acquaint participants with the steps in reasoning that are necessary to arrive at scientifically sound judgments about the motivation, behavior, and needs of individual children; and, by group processes, to guide them in developing skill in this method of analyzing children and arriving at sound judgments about them.

To encourage and aid participants in working out, within the scope of the teacher's normal professional functions, specific plans for assisting individual children and groups of children to take their necessary next steps in development, learning, or adjustment; and to aid them in working out the implications of the insights gained through their study of children for planning and practice in the general educative process.

To assist participants to recognize children who need expert diagnosis, therapy, or remedial instruction, and to help them locate and refer the child to available agencies for diagnosis, therapy, or remedial instruction (pages 447-448).

During the first session the purposes of the program are discussed and special emphasis is given to developing and abiding by a strong code of professional ethics (see discussion below). Such a code is necessary because the participants will be gathering confidential information about one child's developmental history within the family and the community setting. The remainder of the session is devoted to the matter of determining what kinds of children to select. Each participant is urged to choose two or three children from whom one will be selected during the second session. The selections are made so that the study group will have an opportunity to examine the wide range of factors that influence learning and behavior.

After each participant has selected his child for study he proceeds to gather information about the child. The sources of information would include the following: observations of the child in school and elsewhere, the records at school, home visitation and parent conferences, descriptions of the child's life space manifested, for example, in free compositions such as autobiography, three wishes, and the like, conferences with colleagues who have taught the child in the past or are currently teaching him, examination of samples of the child's classwork, conversations with the child. Each participant learns how to gather information from these sources and how to record it objectively and without interpretation or evaluation. The members of the study group then learn to make tentative hypotheses explaining and interpreting a given behavior. According to Prescott, it usually takes about two months for a group to learn to hypothesize effectively. The next analytical experience during the first year is to recognize and list recurring situations and patterns of behavior.

The aim of the first year of study is to make each participant aware of three factors that shape the motivation of the child and that determine his readiness to learn. These factors are:

1. The developmental tasks and conscious goals that the child is striving to accomplish.

2. The adjustment problems the child faces, which occupy his mind and make it difficult for him to accomplish his developmental tasks and to meet the school's expectancies and demands.

3. The child's assets in terms of experience background, personal relationships, interests, aptitudes, and learning capacities (page 457).

With an understanding of these three factors the teacher can begin to see how the child views his world and how he anticipates the future. Having gained this understanding the teacher can help the child achieve those of his goals that are developmental and the teacher can make the learning task relevant to the child's experience background and motivation. While the focus during the first year of the program is on one child, each group member has participated in the analysis of each of the children studied by the group and in most instances the participants become aware of the importance of understanding each child as a unique developing individual.

In the second year of the child-study program new groups are formed. Each participant again selects a child and builds up a record as in the first year but, of course, he is now able to do it much more rapidly. The group, with the aid of the leader and the consultant, works out a framework for the analysis of the information contained in the record. This framework consists of the important areas of human development including the following: (1) Physical factors, such as health status, limitations, and motor skills. (The discussion in Chapter 12 elaborates this section of the framework.) (2) Socialization and family influences. (See discussion in Chapters 13 and 15.) (3) Cultural background, such as social class status, membership in nonschool agencies and groups. (See discussion in Chapter 14.) (4) Peer-groups status, student's role in peer-groups, and reaction of peers to him. (See Chapter 18.) (5) Development of self-concept and academic skills. (See Chapters 2, 9, and 10.) (6) Emotional factors and characteristic mechanisms of adjustment. (See Chapter 11.) The participants are encouraged to use this guide so that they will be able to synthesize their information about the child and also so that they will be able to relate it to more theoretical scientific discussions of concepts explaining human behavior and development. Each member of the group then receives practice in the process of relating information about the individual child to explanatory scientific concepts. By the end of the second year, after interpreting the records in terms of each developmental area just listed, each participant seeks to view the child he is studying as a functioning person.

The third year program is an extension of the second year with greater emphasis on studying the literature dealing with human development, group dynamics, and the dynamics of adjustment. The classification and the integration of the information about the child provide opportunity for the participants to understand "how the self emerges and is shaped and about how self-mediated factors, including interests, values, goals, and adjustment mechanisms influence perception, behavior, and further development." The participants are encouraged also to study the structure of the classroom group using such devices as the sociogram (see Chapter 8).

It is difficult to incorporate the equivalent of a child-study program as a part of the usual preservice professional education experience. As the discussion clearly indicates, those who participate in the child-study program need to have some ongoing contacts with school children. Nevertheless, the program as described here should enable the reader to see that psychological concepts can occupy an important place in the teacher's continuing in-service education.

A Synthesis of Teaching Objectives

As stated earlier, the teacher does not need to choose one or another of the objectives of transmitting the cultural heritage or initiating change. His task is to incorporate as much as possible of both of these in his teaching. Some writers who have expressed a strong opinion favoring one particular objective, have often made it appear that the other objectives are either not worthwhile achieving or that the school need not or should not commit itself to anything else than the one objective. Writing in this vein Hutchins (1936), whose position has been called "rational humanism" or "essentialist," states: "We may wisely leave experience to life and set about our job of intellectual training."

Those who emphasize the teacher's role in fostering social change contend that this function is primary and that the knowledge of the cultural heritage is an instrument for charting the future and not an end in itself. This philosophical position has been called "reconstructionism." Counts (1952) has expressed one form of this point of view in stating: "A democratic education must be sensitive and responsive to the changing foundations, the deep-flowing currents, and the emerging conditions and potentialities of industrial society in both its domestic and world relations." To be fair to Counts, he also holds that the school should be "a center for the nurture of intellectual virtues." Most reconstructionist views are derived from Dewey (1916) and would agree with him when he states: "Since education is a social process, and there are many kinds of societies, a criterion for educational criticism and construction implies a *particular* social ideal." This view suggests that educational activity is properly directed toward establishing an ideal society.

Another group of educators has maintained that the child's "felt needs" should guide the teacher in designing the learning activities. This group has usually contended also that the primary concern of the school should be the child's ultimate adjustment, his preparation for family responsibilities, vocation, citizenship, and the like.

If an extreme interpretation of these aims and an insistence on the exclusiveness of one or another of them is avoided, there is no inherent contradiction between them. They are in a sense different ways of saying that the well-being of the society, that is all of us, depends on the proper fulfillment of the individual. The crux of the matter is the definition of individual fulfillment. Fulfillment is a process that takes place when the individual incorporates his cultural heritage to the fullest extent that he is capable, and when he commits himself to adding to the future unfolding of that heritage so that he contributes something toward making his society correspond more closely to his ideal. This kind of individual occurs most readily when he grows in an environment that demonstrates to him that he is understood and accepted as a unique individual. Gardner (1961) has also stressed the importance of individual fulfillment as a broad educational aim not only of the schools but of the society at large.

> The chief instrument we have devised to further the ideal of individual fulfillment is the educational system. But in our understandable preoccupation with perfecting that instrument, we have tended to forget the broader objectives it was designed to serve. Most Americans honor education; few understand its larger purposes. Our thinking about the aims of education has too often been shallow, constricted and lacking in reach or perspective. Our educational purposes must be seen in the broader framework of our convictions concerning the worth of the individual and the importance of individual fulfillment.
>
> Education in the formal sense is only a part of the society's larger task of abetting the individual's intellectual, emotional and moral growth. *What we must reach for is a conception of perpetual self-discovery, perpetual reshaping to realize one's best self, to be the person one could be* (page 136).

TEACHING AS A PROFESSION

Public attitudes toward teachers and teaching appear to be contradictory. On the one hand, teaching seems to be held in high esteem if we judge from the fact that people entrust to teachers a considerable share of the responsibility in shaping their children's lives. On the other hand, the fact that teachers' salaries do not compare favorably with those of most other professions indicates a low regard for teachers. Objective surveys of the status attributed to teachers show that the grade-school teacher is ranked above the median of a representative list of occupations (Cattell, 1942) and that secondary school teachers and college professors rank higher than elementary school teachers (Deeg and Paterson, 1947). In the discussion of social class (Chapter 14) it will be recalled that occupation is an important determinant of social class placement. Centers (1949) places teachers in the professional group, which ranks second from the top in his seven-point classification of occupations. Even within a more restrictive definition of the term, teaching is generally classified as a *profession*. Becker (1962) has pointed out that when an occupation is accorded the title profession in our society it symbolizes "a morally praiseworthy kind of occupational organization."

In order to gain a better understanding of the degree to which teaching meets the characteristics of a profession, the dimensions of a profession as conceived by various social scientists will be examined. Teachers constitute an extremely numerous group and generalizations about the activities of so large and diversified a group can only be made with caution and should always be qualified.

Teaching and the Characteristics of a Profession

The discussion in this section is based in part on the comprehensive treatment of education as a profession by Lieberman (1956), and a briefer presentation on the nature of a profession by Becker (1962).

An occupational group that is considered a profession renders a service that is considered to be necessary for the continued functioning of the society. The service is unique, definite, and essential. In the opening sentences of the first chapter it was stated that the educational system is a keystone to the whole social structure, for only as it functions properly can all the other institutions continue to serve the needs of the society. That teaching renders an essential function, there can be no question. Lieberman states: "If education has made any progress toward becoming a profession in the past one hundred years, such progress is undoubtedly due in part to the growing conviction that educational services are so important to the welfare of children and of society that they must be made available to all children, rather than be limited only to those children whose parents could afford to pay for them" (page 2).

On the matter of uniqueness and definiteness of service, teaching does not measure too well. It would be stretching a point to say that the functions of the teacher, as just outlined, are fulfilled exclusively by the teacher. In fact, the school relies on other educational agencies such as the home, the church, and the mass media, to carry out its task effectively.

A second characteristic of the services rendered by a profession is that they cannot be applied routinely but require continuous adaptation to the varying situations encountered. The service thus requires intellectual techniques and a long period of specialized training. In discussing the "ideal" profession Becker states: "The body of knowledge over which the profession holds a monopoly consists not of technical skills and fruits of practical experience but, rather, of abstract principles arrived at by scientific research and logical analysis." Those who teach advanced levels of subject matter hold a monopoly, in a sense, over a body of knowledge, particularly if they keep up with the scientific advances and the scholarly work in their field. What about those who teach the more elementary levels of subject matter? They can demonstrate their professional competence by being well-versed in the knowledge dealing with the teaching of elementary subject matter. Teachers of the primary grades should know the research dealing with the teaching of reading, the place of phonics, the best procedure for teaching borrowing in subtraction, the most effective method for teaching spelling, and so on. Teachers need to become expert on topics such as these so that they feel the confidence that comes from professional competence. The field of educational psychology should certainly be considered one of those fields of knowledge in which teachers should become increasingly competent.

The training for teaching has not been particularly lengthy and the selection of candidates has not been based on the kinds of abilities that make for the intellectual competence described above. These aspects of teacher selection and training are gradually changing for the better. Butts and Cremin (1953) have noted this change:

> Another improvement was the breaking down of the tradition that elementary school teachers needed less preparation than high school teachers and thus could be trained separately in normal schools, whereas secondary school teachers needed a college or university education of longer duration. In recent years, however, the trend has been to raise the level of preparation for both elementary and secondary school teachers and to insist that they equally require a college or university type of education (page 604).

A third characteristic of a professional group is that the individual practitioner is permitted a broad range of autonomy in rendering his service. This autonomy is restricted only by a code of ethics, to be discussed below, and insures the person receiving the service that no other interests will be placed before his in the performance of the service. Among the other interests that might intrude are those of private gain for the practitioner or those related to the institutions within which the professional renders his service. Professional autonomy in the case of teaching allows the teacher to use his knowledge, skill, and judgment to serve the pupil's interests alone.

The high degree of feminization in teaching in a society where women are granted less personal autonomy than men, the great amount of nonprofessional control in such matters as certification, the manner in which salaries are set; these and other features of the teaching profession account for the fact that teachers have not achieved a high level of professional autonomy. The efforts of teachers' organizations in the maintenance of academic freedom and the establishment of protective tenure policies, have been aimed at increasing and guaranteeing the teacher's professional autonomy.

It is difficult to convince those who apply the rule of the market place to all remunerative activity, that this rule is inappropriate in a profession. In fact, the "commercial" concept of work motivation, which would have us believe that men's work activities can be completely manipulated and controlled by salary schedules and monetary reward, and which may have some measure of validity in piece work or sales occupations, denies the complexity of motive and the cooperative nature of the teaching task. Although an extended discussion of "merit" salary schedules would take us too far afield, and there has been much spoken and written in favor and in opposition to such schedules, the view of salary as reward interferes with the professional autonomy of teachers (Smith, 1955).

In addition to matters that interfere with the achievement of professional autonomy, the personality needs characteristic of teachers as a group would seem to be even more crucial. In a study by Jackson and Guba (1957) it was found that among the needs most characteristic of a group of public-school teachers were high deference, that is, a need to yield to the leadership and judgment of others, and low dominance, or little need to lead, to make decisions, and to influence others. Professional autonomy can be achieved only when selection and training produce teachers who are capable and desirous of exercising independent judgment and who can implement the type of salary schedule that eliminates the distraction of financial concern from the teacher's work.

The fourth characteristic of a professional group is its code of ethics, which is formulated and interpreted by the group itself. Violations of the code can lead to expulsion from the profession. Although what matters most in the vitality of a profession is the professional spirit and altruistic motives, it is essential that even when these are lacking in individual practitioners their behavior be made to conform to its ethical standards. A code also serves the purpose of educating the members of a profession to their duties and obligations to those they serve. The code of ethics as formulated by the National Education Association (1952)[1] is designed primarily to serve the educational purpose. The excerpts from the NEA code that follow have been selected to con-

[1] In July 1963, the NEA Representative Assembly, meeting in Detroit, Michigan, adopted a new Code of Ethics of the Education Profession. This new code differs in some particulars from the 1952 code. Like the 1952 code it is made up of principles: the first dealing with the educators commitment to the student, the second with commitment to the community, the third with commitment to the profession, and the fourth with commitment to professional employment practices.

vey the general tone of the code and to show that a knowledge of educational psychology makes many of the items of the code more meaningful.

First Principle. The primary obligation of the teaching profession is to guide children, youth and adults in the pursuit of knowledge and skills, to prepare them in the ways of democracy, and to help them become happy, useful, self-supporting citizens. . . . In fulfilling the obligations of this first principle, the teacher will— . . .

Recognize the differences among students and seek to meet their individual needs.

Encourage students to formulate and work for high individual goals in the development of their physical, intellectual, creative, and spiritual endowments. . . .

Respect the right of every student to have confidential information about himself withheld except when its release is to authorized agencies or is required by law.

Accept no remuneration for tutoring except in accordance with approved policies of the governing board.

Second Principle. The members of the teaching profession share with parents the task of shaping each student's purposes and acts toward socially acceptable ends. . . . In fulfilling the obligations of this second principle, the teacher will—

Respect the basic responsibility of parents for their children. . . . Provide parents with information that will serve the best interests of their children, and be discreet with information received from parents.

Keep parents informed about the progress of their children as interpreted in terms of the purposes of the school.

Third Principle. The teaching profession occupies a position of public trust involving not only the individual teacher's personal conduct, but also the interaction of the school and the community. . . .

Fourth Principle. The members of the teaching profession have inescapable obligations with respect to employment. These obligations are nearly always employer-employee responsibilities based upon mutual respect and good faith. . . .
The teacher will—

Conduct professional business through proper channels.

Refrain from discussing confidential and official information with unauthorized persons. . . .

Engage in no gainful employment, outside of his contract, where the employment affects adversely his professional status or impairs his standing with students, associates and the community. . . .

Fifth Principle. The teaching profession is distinguished from many other occupations by the uniqueness and quality of the professional relationships among all teachers. Community support and respect are influenced by the standards of teachers and their attitudes toward teaching and other teachers. . . . The teacher will— . . .

Maintain active membership in professional organizations and thru participation, strive to attain the objectives that justify such organized groups.

Seek to make professional growth continuous by such procedures as study, research, travel, conferences, and attendance at professional meetings (pages 371-372).

It is obvious that this code deals with more than professional ethics. It describes desirable teacher behavior rather than ethical behavior. As Lieberman points out an effective code must not confuse undesirable behavior patterns with unethical ones. A code must contemplate enforcement. For this reason this code is an educational instrument rather than a true code of professional ethics.

The fifth characteristic of a professional group is the existence of a comprehensive organization that sets the standards for entry into the profession, promotes high standards of practice, enforces the code of ethics, protects the rights of the individual practitioner, and acts on behalf of the social and economic welfare of the group. It can be seen from these many responsibilities that any professional group without a strong professional organization will have difficulty being a true profession. The organization also provides a reference function for the group, setting norms and creating values. In teaching there is presently no such organization. Neither the National Education Association with a very large membership of teachers and administrators, nor any other professional organization carries out to any adequate degree any of the functions listed above. Many reasons have been given for this condition but unless teachers can create a strong organization with which they can identify, they will experience continued difficulty in gaining the benefits derived from membership in a true profession, and society will be denied the values of truly professional teaching services.

Professional Relationships

The school as a social institution represents an organization of various roles. The observed behavior within a particular school situation is the resultant of a vast number of interrelated factors including the reciprocal roles interacting in the situation, the expectations of the various individuals directly and indirectly involved, as well as the unique personalities and the current needs of those participating in the role interaction.

Some role interactions are horizontal in nature, that is, the individuals interacting and affecting each other occupy the same role level in the institutional hierarchy. One example of such horizontal interaction is that of the peer group, students interacting with students, discussed in Chapter 8. Another example is that of teachers interacting with each other. The types of relationship and the various effects of the teacher-teacher interaction parallel those of the student peer group interaction. The relationship may be competitive or cooperative. The teacher group can serve as a reference group for the individual teacher, influencing attitudes and values, producing norms and shaping behavior. This reference effect is sometimes pronounced when a new teacher joins an established faculty with some homogeneity of opinion. The satisfactions derived by the teacher within his group of colleagues can contribute significantly to the enjoyment of the teaching career and conversely, being rejected by one's colleagues can be the cause of dissatisfaction with teaching.

Other role interactions within the school are vertical in nature, that is, the interacting role participants occupy subordinate and superordinate positions in the institutional hierarchy. The teacher-pupil relationship, discussed in the previous chapter, is one example of vertical-role interaction. Another example is the teacher-administrator interaction. In vertical-role interaction the matter of exercise of power is an issue. The various sources of power available to the teacher were described in the preceding chapter. This description, with only slight modifications, would apply to the administrator-teacher relationship.

It has been suggested that the type of relationship established by the administrator in working with his staff will be influential in determining the character of the teacher-pupil relationship. Thus, if the principal in the school uses coercive power to influence the teaching staff, teachers are more likely to rely on this kind of power in working with their pupils; if the principal works autocratically with his staff, teachers are likely to conduct their classes in this fashion. The teacher's behavior in relationship to the pupil is very much influenced by his awareness of the principal's expectations. Gordon (1955) describes how this operates in one high school.

> The extent to which the principal will support the formal expectations of the system by an exercise of authority will determine the kind of authority role the teacher may assume in the classroom. . . . Changes in the exercise of authority from the principal's office result in a greater diffusion of power throughout the school system among both teachers and pupils. In Wabash the number of classroom evictions over a three-year period were for successive years respectively 160, 81, and 50. Reduction in the number of evictions was related to the dissemination of a rumor among the teachers that "the principal has a little black book in which he records the number of students which teachers send to his office. When he gets ready to rate your teaching he looks in the little black book and decides your salary increase for the next year." It appeared that the greater the support the principal gives the teachers' authority, the more likely the formal institutional role of the teacher will be utilized to coordinate the classroom. The less willing the principal is to support the teachers' institutional authority, the more likely that the teacher will absorb conflict in the classroom role, and the more likely he will be to resort to personalized leadership, and face a situation of endemic conflict (page 25).

Three different kinds of teacher or leader control, namely, "authoritarian," "democratic," and *"laissez-faire,"* were described in the preceding chapter. On the basis of some indirect research evidence it was concluded that the democratically led group would engage in more cooperative and constructive activity and that a high degree of control by the leader would reduce satisfaction and productivity in those in subordinate positions. We would expect that these conclusions would apply also to the administrator-teacher relationship. Bidwell (1955) found, however, that the amount of satisfaction in teaching as measured by a questionnaire was not as much related to the form of leadership as it was related to the extent to which the teacher's expectations of the administrator's behavior were consistent with his perceptions of his actual behavior. That is, when the teacher expected the administrator to act autocratically and perceived his behavior as autocratic or when he expected democratic administrative behavior and perceived it as democratic, satisfaction tended to be high. When the teacher expected one form of behavior and his perceptions of the actual behavior were such as to disappoint his expectations, satisfaction tended to be lower.

The teacher's professional relationships with colleagues and with administrators are influenced by his early life history. This is so because the perceptions of various aspects of one's world that are laid down in the childhood years, form the core of the perceptions of adult life. Friend and Haggard (1948) have shown that reactions and adjustments to the work situation are in many ways determined by the feelings and perceptions once experienced in the family. Their extensive investigation of the factors associated with occupational adjustment would lead us to conclude that a teacher who is able to establish harmonious relationships with colleagues and administrators is likely to be a person who experienced feelings of belonging and acceptance in the family group. Saul (1947) has described this persistence of childhood patterns in the following terms: "Every person has his own individual emotional constellation arising out of the emotional influences and experiences of his own childhood. . . . This 'nuclear constellation' is an important part of the core of every personality. In the relatively normal individual it only colors the personality and helps determine it; in others, it forms the nucleus of the person's emotional problem, which may be mild and within normal limits or severely neurotic." Saul points out that some infantile emotional-perceptual "cores" influence some persons more than others, and in different ways. The case illustration that follows is adapted from one presented by Saul and has been modified to make it more relevant to this discussion. The illustration is aimed only to make clear the nature of the "nuclear constellation" and its expression in the professional relationships of the teacher.

Mrs. Goff had been a teacher for more than twenty years during which time she had held six positions. The pattern in each school was the same. She would start off doing very well in her teaching and making an excellent impression on her principal. Gradually her hostility to the principal would become so open and intense that it would be only a matter of time before some incident would precipitate her resignation. The perceptions that Mrs. Goff had of men who were in a dominant position, as in the case of the school principal, could be traced to the way in which she learned to perceive her father. Her father had been away a great deal while she was a child, and when he was at home he was partly indulgent toward his daughter and partly irritable and rejecting. Her childhood response was to react with longings for her father to like her and then to have a deep resentment against him. This became a fixed pattern from which she could not free herself in her relations with men. Each time she had to change positions she would find some reason for turning down any offer to teach in a school with a woman principal. It was almost as if she was compelled to reenact the painful drama of her childhood. Her competence as a teacher in the elementary grades as well as the fact that she had sufficient control not to do anything seriously damaging when her hostile feelings overwhelmed her, enabled her to obtain a new position each time.

Such a tendency to put certain men into a category results from a failure to discriminate them perceptually from the original object, in this case the girl's own father. Even though the principals with whom Mrs. Goff worked were totally different in personality, the fact that they were in a dominant position, as was her father, caused her to perceive them as the same and the feeling response was very much the same as her childhood response, so that she could not control her eventual hostility toward them. Unconscious influences of this sort, having their roots in early experience, shape the person's current perceptions and reactions, sometimes causing the individual to deal effectively with a particular situation and sometimes creating problems in his relationships with others. More will be said about these unconscious forces in our closing discussion.

MOTIVES AND FEELINGS IN TEACHING

What are the factors that determine a person's choice of teaching as a career? While there are as many different answers to this personal question as there are people who choose to teach, questionnaire and interview surveys reveal certain normative trends. Relying on data gathered in interviews and self-report techniques, McGuire and White (1957) found that the majority of the teachers in their study "seem to prefer situations which are structured, where a certain security is assured, and where the behavior of other people is predictable." They assert that the evidence in their study indicates that this basic predisposition is learned in the family and in other early socializing contexts, long before the person undertakes his training for teaching. Dutton and Keislar (1961) similarly report that attitudes toward teaching appear to be formed long before graduation from high school. They summarized the findings of a number of investigations of the attitudes of high school pupils toward teaching as follows: "Students wanted to become teachers because they felt that the work was important; they wanted to work with children or youth; there was an opportunity to improve social conditions; teaching was intellectually stimulating; they possessed competence in one or more areas; work conditions were attractive; and they sought security in a growing profession."

Studies of interests and attitudes reveal only a superficial part of the answer of why people choose teaching as a career. As Lloyd-Jones and Holman (1957) state:

> There seems to be one basic difficulty with all the studies that attempt by questionnaire to find out why people intend to become teachers or why they are teachers: They assume that the individual really knows what motivated him into teaching and that he is able to write it down briefly in the space provided for it. They assume that he can disentangle the knot of cultural and socio-economic factors from the psychological ones. They underestimate the complexity of motivation and assume that it can be broken down into a few factors such as love of teaching and of children, influence of parents, attractiveness of the profession, love of subject, or the desire for security. The limitations of the questionnaire itself require this kind of simplicity (page 237).

Jersild (1955) also points out that it is possible for a person to harbor illusions about himself. A teacher, for example, may believe that the motivation for his work springs from a desire to advance knowledge but is actually a means of expressing competitive drives, or the "need to gain recognition and to overcome a feeling that he is really not much good."

The second chapter on the determinants of behavior closed with the following statement: "The self seeks meaning in the concrete and symbolic reality and it continuously responds to its environment in such ways as to maintain and enhance its adequacy." This applies to the teacher no less than it does to the pupil. A person chooses teaching as his vocation, if he anticipates that through teaching he will satisfy his needs for achievement, prestige, and accomplishment (Super, 1948). The anticipation of the need satisfactions offered by teaching and the awareness of one's own needs, as well as the relationship between the two, may be realistic or unrealistic and they may be conscious or unconscious or both.

Certain features of teacher-training programs have been instrumental in attracting persons with certain characteristics and self-perceptions into the teaching profession. In many parts of the country teacher-training programs were less costly in money and in time than other professional training programs. They were also less selective in their admissions and had a reputation of being less demanding scholastically. These features influenced the choice of those who came from lower-economic-status homes and who chose education as an avenue for upward social mobility. Financial considerations often forced a choice between teacher training or no higher education at all. It is interesting to note in passing that individuals from lower-status background who through establishing themselves in a teaching career have been able to follow a way of life different from that of their family, retain close ties with their parents. McGuire and White (1957) point out that: "The clear break with parents which appears among socially mobile business people is not often present among teachers." Also, teaching has probably attracted people who viewed themselves as less academically able and who were more fearful of failure than those who entered other professions. This is not to suggest that those who entered teaching were only socially mobile members of the lower socioeconomic classes and those who were academically less able or less secure, but rather that teaching as a profession, because of the nature of the teacher-training programs, has attracted larger numbers of such people than other professions. One might predict that as teacher-training programs undergo extensive revision and their status in higher education in America changes, the kinds of people who will enter teaching will also change.

Perhaps of greater interest and direct concern than the motives for selecting teaching as a career, is the related topic of the feeling states associated with teaching. As noted in Chapter 12, in the preceding chapter, and in this chapter as well, the early experiences in every adult's life have left unconscious predispositions that make the individual sensitive to those aspects of his present experience that reawaken the feelings connected with unresolved childhood and adolescent conflicts. Because they deal with children and adolescents who are reacting to similar conflicts, teachers are more exposed than those in other occupations to situations that touch on those sensitive developmental perceptual-emotional constellations. In a book dealing with the implications of this issue for education, Jersild (1955) states that: "The teacher's understanding and acceptance of himself is the most important requirement in any effort he makes to help students to know themselves and to gain healthy attitudes of self-acceptance." He goes on to elaborate on the major personal concerns of teachers as revealed in an extensive empirical study. Two of these personal concerns are anxiety and meaninglessness. Consideration of these will not instruct anyone directly how to achieve self-fulfillment and self-acceptance, for this cannot be taught in the usual sense. The person must work this out in his own particular way. He can be helped by considering some of the obstacles that lie in his path. By dealing forthrightly with his own being, a person can participate more constructively with others as they struggle toward a meaningful existence. Lindgren (1962) offers a reasonable hypothesis, "that a teacher's insight into and understanding of his students is in approximate proportion to the insight and understanding he possesses regarding himself."

Only a person whose world is endlessly repetitious and unchanging will not experience anxiety. That person has been overwhelmed by life. Because anxiety is a painful emotion, we try in many different ways to reduce its impact. We try to eliminate it from our awareness. Some will try to control their anxious feelings by resisting change in their environment and by trying to keep their world compulsively ordered. They act as if they wish time would stand still for them. Others attempt to deny the presence of anxiety by resorting to a generalized denial and avoidance of their surroundings. "Resistance of this sort may take the form of not learning (not noticing, not hearing, not catching the meaning, not trying, . . . not remembering the assignment)" (Jersild, 1955). This unwillingness to face the unfolding future and the tendency of hiding from oneself has been decried by the philosopher Martin Buber (1955) in the following: "In spite of all similarities, every living situation has, like a newborn child, a new face that has never been before and will never come again. It demands of you a reaction which cannot be prepared beforehand. It demands nothing of what is past. It demands presence, responsibility; it demands you" (page 114).

Many people do not differentiate between acknowledging and being aware of the disturbing feelings of anxiety or hostility and the disruptive behavior that it is often assumed accompanies these feelings. They assume that when one suggests acknowledging what one is feeling one is condoning all sorts of socially undesirable behavior. It is difficult to understand that the feeling may arise uncontrollably and that the behavior may remain under control. It is this writer's experience in working with persons seeking help with their personal problems, that it is the denial of feeling and its suppression that produces uncontrolled behavior rather than the acknowledgment of feeling. When one is aware of his anger or his anxiety and can experience himself being angry or anxious, an appropriate and responsible course of action can more readily be adopted. At least one can inform others how one feels. "It is only by facing anxiety as it exists, as fully as we can, without putting a false gloss on the human struggle, that we can begin to deal realistically with the children we teach and with the nature of our own humanity" (Jersild, 1955).

One scientist (Wiener, 1954) has noted that:

As entropy increases, the universe, and all closed systems in the universe, tend naturally to deteriorate and lose their distinctiveness, to move . . . from a state of organization and differentiation in which distinctions and forms exist, to a state of chaos and sameness. . . . But while the universe as a whole . . . tends to run down, there are local enclaves whose direction seems opposed to that of the universe at large and in which there is a limited and temporary tendency for organization to increase. Life finds its home in some of these enclaves (page 12).

It would appear that the struggle of each of us to find meaning and purpose in life is a struggle against entropy. While the child is growing, new meanings open up for him constantly. Organization and differentiation increase and the problem of meaninglessness is for most healthy children of no great concern. In the adult, however, the problem becomes acute. Jersild (1955) found that 60 percent of his respondents (people involved in education) expressed concern about feeling that they were not sure what they wished to get from life; "some said that what they were doing or what was happening didn't seem to mean much; some said they saw little or no meaning in many of the things they had to learn or teach." This concern is not found exclusively among teachers, it is a widespread condition in our civilization. As man needs to struggle less with nature in order to secure his physical existence and as he creates a complex, impersonal, industrial society, he seems to face more poignantly the problem of the meaning of his existence. Because teaching still has retained the possibilities of warm, personal transactions, it can provide many opportunities for teachers to gain a sense of purpose in their lives and it can become the setting where children can continue to grow in their sense of meaningfulness. Teachers who have not faced and resolved the meaninglessness of their lives will not be concerned with students' growth of meaning and understanding. The communications between the teacher and the pupil "are subject to disorganization in transit. They generally come through in less coherent fashion and certainly not more coherently than they were sent" (Wiener, 1954). Where teachers are not concerned, the initial messages will be almost void of meaning and the student will experience a sense of futility in his attempt to gain understanding. If he experiences such lack of concern consistently he can only conclude that life is meaningless. The challenge for the teacher is to be concerned. Concern and commitment are counterforces to meaninglessness. They counteract entropic forces both for the teacher in providing purpose to his work and for the pupil in providing meaning in his world.

SUMMARY

The teacher in our democratic society contributes to the accomplishment of two major objectives: The conservation of the cultural heritage and the initiation of change. In order to transmit the cultural heritage effectively the teacher needs to be able to serve as an exemplar and a model for the child. To do this the teacher needs to become steeped in the cultural tradition and he needs to be a participant in its various facets; its literature and art, its history, and science. In order for the schools to produce individuals who will pioneer in science, politics, industry, and education, some teachers must be able to inspire their students to question the *status quo* in these areas and to accept the challenge of change with confidence.

The successful conservation of the heritage of the society and the initiation of change both depend on the teacher's understanding of the child. Understanding of others depends upon an awareness that the world each of us constructs is both structured and emergent or undetermined so that each of us is controlled as well as free. The study of psychology can help us see these two aspects of human behavior. One systematic approach that has been used to aid teachers in gaining such an understanding is the child-study program. The program is designed to help participants, teachers and administrators, learn how to gather and record information about pupils that will be useful in understanding them. It is designed further to help the participants use this information in such ways as to make sound judgments about pupils so as to guide their learning more effectively and to recommend special services where these are indicated.

Teaching is considered a professional activity. This means that the services teachers render are to a certain extent unique, definite, and essential to the society. The teacher, in order to function as a professional person, should have gained mastery of a body of knowledge. In some instances this mastery will be of subject matter, in other instances it will consist of the research on how certain skills are best taught. A professional activity, such as teaching, cannot be carried on routinely but needs to be constantly adapted to the changing demands of the teaching situation. The professional person needs to have a high degree of professional autonomy that insures the person being served that no other interests will be placed before his in the performance of the service. The efforts of teachers' organizations in regard to certification, tenure, and academic freedom, as well as the debate surrounding the type of salary schedule most appropriate for teachers, are all expressions of the desire to establish and maintain professional autonomy. A professional group develops and implements a code of ethics. The only such code available to teachers is the one prepared by the National Education Association. Many sections of this code describe desirable teacher behavior rather than ethical conduct. A professional group has an organization that concerns itself with the maintenance of standards and the protection of the rights of the individual practitioner. For many reasons such an organization is lacking in the teaching profession. This lack makes precarious the status of teaching as a profession.

Role interactions in the school setting may be horizontal or vertical in nature. In horizontal role interaction the participants occupy the same level within the institutional role hierarchy. In vertical interaction the participants occupy superordinate and subordinate positions. The teacher interacts horizontally with fellow teachers and vertically with students and also with administrators and supervisors. The way the teacher interacts with his colleagues and with supervisors and administrators is determined both by the atmosphere within the institution and by the early life history of those participating. The kind of relationship that the administrator establishes with his staff, whether it be cooperative, supportive, arbitrary, or indifferent, will determine how the teacher will relate to colleagues and students. The kind of early experiences that the teacher has had will determine how he will perceive and respond to each passing human interaction situation.

Teachers become and remain teachers for a variety of complex motives, which, for the most part, are unknown even to themselves. Certain features of the occupation of teaching and the training program seem to have attracted into teaching individuals with certain characteristics. The majority of teachers seem to choose teaching because they expect the work to provide a setting in which situations are structured, in which the behavior of others is predictable, and where a certain amount of security will be assured. The preference for such expectations appears to be developed long before entry into the training program. For many, teaching offers a way to achieve social mobility.

The feelings aroused in teaching are painful and hard to accept as part of one's being. The tendency to avoid facing such feelings as hostility, anxiety, meaninglessness, and loneliness can lead to a kind of self-alienation. When this occurs, the teacher is unable to contribute to the constructive resolution of the conflicts centering on these feelings experienced by students. Teachers who can experience and accept their own feelings can act responsively and they can help others achieve self-understanding and self-acceptance.

READING REFERENCES

Anderson, A. W., The teaching profession: an example of diversity in training and function. In N. B. Henry (Ed.), *Education for the Professions*. Sixty-first Yearbook (Pt. 2) National Society for the Study of Education. Chicago: University of Chicago Press, 1962.

Conant, J. B., *The Education of American Teachers*. New York: McGraw-Hill Book Company, 1963.

Henry, N. B. (Ed.), *The Integration of Educational Experiences*. Fifty-seventh Yearbook (Pt. 3) National Society for the Study of Education. Chicago: University of Chicago Press, 1958 (particularly chaps. 3-5, 9, 10).

Jersild, A. T., *When Teachers Face Themselves*. New York: Bureau of Publications, Columbia University, Teachers College, 1955.

Lieberman, M., *Education as a Profession*. Englewood Cliffs, N.J.: Prentice-Hall, 1956.

Morse, A. D., *Schools of Tomorrow—Today*. Garden City, N.Y.: Doubleday & Company, 1960.

Prescott, D. A., *The Child in the Educative Process*. New York: McGraw-Hill Book Company, 1957.

Spindler, G. D., *Education and Culture: Anthropological Approaches*. New York: Holt, Rinehart and Winston, 1963 (Part 2).

Stiles, L. J. and others, *Teacher Education in the United States*. New York: Ronald Company, 1960.

BIBLIOGRAPHY

ADORNO, T. W., ET AL., *The Authoritarian Personality.* New York: Harper & Row, 1950

ALDEN, ELIZABETH, *The Effects on Non-Target Classmates of the Teacher's Use of Expert Power and Liking Power in Controlling Deviant Behavior.* Unpublished doctoral dissertation, Wayne State University, 1959

ALLPORT, G. W., *Personality: A Psychological Interpretation.* New York: Holt, Rinehart and Winston, 1937

———, *The Nature of Prejudice.* Cambridge, Mass.: Addison-Wesley, 1954 (Anchor Books edition, 1958)

———, *Becoming: Basic Considerations for a Psychology of Personality.* New Haven: Yale University Press, 1955

———, *Pattern and Growth in Personality.* New York: Holt, Rinehart and Winston, 1961

ALPER, THELMA G., Task-orientation vs. ego-orientation in learning and retention. *American Journal of Psychology,* 1946, **59:** 236–248

AMERICAN COUNCIL ON EDUCATION, *Helping Teachers Understand Children.* Washington, D.C.: American Council on Education, 1945

AMERICAN COUNCIL ON EDUCATION, Intergroup education in cooperating schools. *Reading Ladders for Human Relations.* (rev. ed.) Washington, D.C.: American Council on Education, 1949

AMERICAN PSYCHOLOGICAL ASSOCIATION, Technical recommendations for physchological tests and diagnostic techniques. *Psychological Bulletin,* 1954, **51:** Supplement

ANASTASI, ANNE, *Differential Psychology.* (3d ed.) New York: Macmillan, 1958

————, Cultural differences. In C. W. Harris (Ed.), *Encyclopedia of Educational Research*. (3d ed.) New York: Macmillan, 1960

————, *Psychological Testing*. (2d ed.) New York: Macmillan, 1961

————, AND J. D. DRAKE, An empirical comparison of certain techniques for estimating the reliability of speeded tests. *Educational and Psychological Measurement,* 1954, **14:** 529–540

ANDERSON, H. H., Domination and socially integrative behavior. In R. G. Barker, J. S. Kounin, and H. F. Wright (Eds.), *Child Behavior and Development*. New York: McGraw-Hill, 1943

ANDERSON, J. E., *The Psychology of Development and Personality Adjustment*. New York: Holt, Rinehart and Winston, 1949

————, Dynamics of development: systems in process. In D. B. Harris (Ed.), *The Concept of Development*. Minneapolis: University of Minnesota Press, 1957

ANDERSON, R. C., Learning in discussions: a résumé of the authoritarian-democratic studies. *Harvard Educational Review,* 1959, **29:** 201–215

ANDERSON, R. H., Organizing groups for instruction. In N. B. Henry (Ed.), *Individualizing Instruction*. Yearbook of the National Society for the Study of Education, **61:** Pt. 1. Chicago: University of Chicago Press, 1962

ANDERSON, W. E., An attempt through the use of experimental technique to determine the effect of home assignments upon scholastic success. *Journal of Educational Research,* 1946, **40:** 141–143

ARNY, CLARA B., *Evaluation in Home Economics*. New York: Appleton, 1953

ASCH, S. E., Studies of independence and conformity. A minority of one against a unanimous majority. *Psychological Monographs,* 1956, **70:** No. 9 (Whole No. 416)

ASSOCIATION FOR SUPERVISION AND CURRICULUM DEVELOPMENT, 1949 Yearbook, *Toward Better Teaching*. Washington, D.C.: National Education Association, 1949

AUSUBEL, D. P., *Theory and Problems of Child Development*. New York: Grune & Stratton, 1958

————, The use of advance organizers in the learning and retention of meaningful verbal material. *Journal of Educational Psychology,* 1960, **51:** 267–272

AXLINE, VIRGINIA M., *Play Therapy*. Boston: Houghton Mifflin, 1947

BAGLEY, W. C., *Educational Values*. New York: Macmillan, 1911

BALDWIN, A. L., Socialization and the parent-child relationship. *Child Development,* 1948, **19:** 127–136

————, *Behavior and Development in Childhood*. New York: Holt, Rinehart and Winston, 1955

————, JOAN KALHORN, AND FAY H. BREESE, Patterns of parent behavior. *Psychological Monographs,* 1945, **58:** No. 3 (Whole No. 268)

————, ————, AND ————, The appraisal of parent behavior. *Psychological Monographs,* 1949, **63:** No. 4 (Whole No. 299)

BALLER, W. B. AND D. C. CHARLES, *The Psychology of Human Growth and Development*. New York: Holt, Rinehart and Winston, 1961

BANDURA, A. AND R. H. WALTERS, *Social Learning and Personality*. New York: Holt, Rinehart and Winston, 1963

BARD, H., *Homework: A Guide for Secondary School Teachers.* New York: Holt, Rinehart and Winston, 1958

BARKER, R. G., TAMARA DEMBO, AND K. LEWIN, Frustration and regression. In R. G. Barker, J. S. Kounin, and H. F. Wright (Eds.), *Child Behavior and Development.* New York: McGraw-Hill, 1943

———, ET AL., *Adjustment to Physical Handicap and Illness: A Survey of the Social Psychology of Physique and Disability.* New York: Social Science Research Council, 1953

BARUCH, DOROTHY W., Mental health practices at the preschool level. In N. B. Henry (Ed.), *Mental Health in Modern Education.* Yearbook of the National Society for the Study of Education, 54: Pt. 2. Chicago: University of Chicago Press, 1955

BARTLETT, F. C., *Remembering: A Study in Experimental and Social Psychology.* Cambridge, England: Cambridge University Press, 1950

BAXTER, BERNICE, *Teacher-Pupil Relationships.* New York: Macmillan, 1941

BAYLEY, NANCY, Consistency and variability in the growth of intelligence from birth to eighteen years. *Journal of Genetic Psychology,* 1949, **75**: 165–196

———, On the growth of intelligence. *American Psychologist,* 1955, **10**: 805–818

———, AND R. D. TUDDENHAM, Adolescent changes in body build. In N. B. Henry (Ed.), *Adolescence.* Yearbook of the National Society for the Study of Education, 43: Pt. 1. Chicago: University of Chicago Press, 1944

BECHTOLDT, H. P., Construct validity: a critique. *American Psychologist,* 1959, **14**: 619–629

BECKER, H. S., The nature of a profession. In N. B. Henry (Ed.), *Education for the Professions.* Yearbook of the National Society for the Study of Education, **61**: Pt. 2. Chicago: University of Chicago Press, 1962

BENNE, K. D., What the teacher should know about religion. Yearbook of the American Association of Colleges for Teacher Education, 1955, **8**: 213–221

BENNETT, G. K., H. G. SEASHORE, AND A. G. WESMAN, *Counseling from Profiles.* New York: Psychological Corporation, 1951

BERENDA, RUTH W., *The Influence of the Group on the Judgments of Children.* New York: King's Crown Press, Division of Columbia University Press, 1950

BERLYNE, D. E., The arousal and satiation of perceptual curiosity in the rat. *Journal of Comparative and Physiological Psychology,* 1955, **48**: 238–246

———, *Conflict, Arousal, and Curiosity.* New York: McGraw-Hill, 1960

BETTLEHEIM, B., Mental health and current mores. *American Journal of Orthopsychiatry,* 1952, **22**: 76–88

———, Segregation: new style. *School Review,* 1958, **66**: 251–272

BEXTON, W. H., W. HERON, AND T. H. SCOTT, Effects of decreased variation in the sensory environment. *Canadian Journal of Psychology,* 1954, **8**: 70–76

BIDWELL, C. E., The administrative role and satisfaction in teaching. *Journal of Educational Sociology,* 1955, **29**: 41–47

BIRCH, J. W., Early school admission for mentally advanced children. *Exceptional Children,* 1954, **21**: 84–87

BLAIR, G. M., R. S. JONES, AND R. H. SIMPSON, *Educational Psychology.* New York: Macmillan, 1954

BLANCHARD, PHYLLIS, Psychoanalytic contributions to the problems of reading disabilities. In Anna Freud et al. (Eds.), *The Psychoanalytic Study of the Child,* 2: New York: International Universities Press, 1946

BLOOM, B. S. (Ed.), *Taxonomy of Educational Objectives,* Handbook I: *Cognitive Domain.* New York: Longmans, 1956

————, AND LOIS J. BRODER, Problem-solving processes of college students. *Supplementary Educational Monographs,* 1950, No. 73

BLOS, P., *The Adolescent Personality.* New York: Appleton, 1941

BODE, B. H., *Modern Educational Theories.* New York: Macmillan, 1927

BOGARDUS, E. S., A social distance scale. *Sociology and Social Research,* 1933, **17:** 265–271

BOGUSLAVSKY, G. W., Psychological research in Soviet education. *Science,* 1957, **125:** 915–918

BOND, G. L. AND M. A. TINKER, *Reading Difficulties: Their Diagnosis and Correction.* New York: Appleton, 1957

BOND, H. M., Wasted talent. In E. Ginzberg (Ed.), *The Nation's Children.* 2: *Development and Education.* New York: Columbia University Press, 1960 (Golden Anniversary White House Conference on Children and Youth)

BOSSARD, J. H. S. AND ELEANOR S. BOLL, Personality roles in the large family. *Child Development,* 1955, **26:** 71–78

BOWLBY, J., *Child Care and the Growth of Love.* Baltimore: Penguin Books, 1953

BROLYER, C. R., E. L. THORNDIKE, AND ELLA WOODYARD, A second study of mental discipline in high school studies. *Journal of Educational Psychology,* 1927, **18:** 377–404

BRONFENBRENNER, U., Socialization and social class through time and space. In Eleanor E. Maccoby, T. M. Newcomb, and E. L. Hartley (Eds.), *Readings in Social Psychology.* (3d ed.) New York: Holt, Rinehart and Winston, 1958

————, Freudian theories of identification and their derivatives. *Child Development,* 1960, **31:** 15–40

BROWNELL, W. A., Readiness for subject-matter learning. *NEA Journal,* 1951, **40:** 445–446

————, AND G. HENDRICKSON, How children learn information, concepts, and generalizations. In N. B. Henry (Ed.), *Learning and Instruction.* Yearbook of the National Society for the Study of Education, 49: Pt. 1. Chicago: University of Chicago Press, 1950

BRUCH, HILDE, Psychological aspects of obesity. *Psychiatry,* 1947, **10:** 373–381

BRUECKNER, L. J. AND G. L. BOND, *The Diagnosis and Treatment of Learning Difficulties.* New York: Appleton, 1955

BRUNER, J. S., On perceptual readiness. *Psychological Review,* 1957, **64:** 123–152

————, *The Process of Education.* Cambridge, Mass.: Harvard University Press, 1960

————, JACQUELINE J. GOODNOW, AND G. A. AUSTIN, *A Study of Thinking.* New York: Wiley, 1956

BRYAN, W. L. AND N. HARTER, Studies in the physiology and psychology of the telegraphic language. *Psychological Review,* 1897, 4: 27–53

BUBER, M., *Between Man and Man* (Translated by R. G. Smith). Boston: Beacon Press, 1955

BUGELSKI, B. R., *The Psychology of Learning.* New York: Holt, Rinehart and Winston, 1956

BUREAU OF CHILD DEVELOPMENT AND PARENT EDUCATION, *Factors in the Learning Process.* Mimeographed, Albany, N. Y.: New York State Education Department, undated

BUREAU OF ELEMENTARY CURRICULUM DEVELOPMENT, *Handwriting.* Albany, N. Y.: New York State Education Department, 1955

BUROS, O. K. (Ed.), *The Third Mental Measurements Yearbook.* New Brunswick, N. J.: Rutgers University Press, 1949

BUSH, R. N., *The Teacher-Pupil Relationship.* Englewood Cliffs, N. J.: Prentice-Hall, 1954

BUSWELL, G. T. AND B. Y. KERSH, Patterns of thinking in solving problems. *University of California Publications in Education,* 1956, **12,** No. 2: 63–148

——, W. A. BROWNELL, AND IRENE SAUBLE, *Teaching Arithmetic We Need, Grade Five.* Boston: Ginn, 1955

BUTLER, R. A., Discrimination learning by rhesus monkeys to visual-exploration motivation. *Journal of Comparative and Physiological Psychology,* 1953, **46:** 95–98

——, Exploratory and related behavior: a new trend in animal research. *Journal of Individual Psychology,* 1958, **14:** 111–120

——, AND H. F. HARLOW, Persistence of visual exploration in monkeys. *Journal of Comparative and Physiological Psychology,* 1954, **47:** 258–263

BUTTS, R. F. AND L. A. CREMIN, *A History of Education in American Culture.* New York: Holt, Rinehart and Winston, 1953

CAMERON, D. E., Remembering. *Nervous and Mental Disease Monographs,* 1947, No. 72

CAMPBELL, D. T., Recommendations for APA test standards regarding construct, trait, and discriminant validity. *American Psychologist,* 1960, **15:** 546–553

CANNON, W. B., *The Wisdom of the Body.* New York: Norton, 1932

CARMICHAEL, L., H. P. HOGAN, AND A. A. WALTER, An experimental study of the effect of language on the reproduction of visually perceived form. *Journal of Experimental Psychology,* 1932, **15:** 73–86

CASSIRER, E., *An Essay on Man: An Introduction to a Philosophy of Human Culture.* Garden City, N. Y.: Doubleday, 1944 (Originally published by Yale University Press)

CATTELL, R. B., The concept of social status. *Journal of Social Psychology,* 1942, **15:** 293–308

——, New concepts for measuring leadership in terms of group syntality. *Human Relations,* 1951, 4: 161–184

CENTERS, R., *The Psychology of Social Classes.* Princeton, N. J.: Princeton University Press, 1949

CHILD, I. L., E. H. POTTER, AND ESTELLE M. LEVINE, Children's textbooks and personality development: an exploration in the social psychology of education. *Psychological Monographs,* 1946, **60:** No. 3 (Whole No. 279)

CHRISTENSEN, C. M., Relationships between pupil achievement, pupil affect-need, teacher warmth, and teacher permissiveness. *Journal of Educational Psychology,* 1960, **51:** 169–174

CHURCH, J., *Language and the Discovery of Reality.* New York: Random House, 1961

CLOTHIER, G. AND NITA WYATT, *Case Studies in Student Teaching.* Cedar Falls, Iowa: The Association for Student Teaching, 1952, Bulletin No. 18

COFFIELD, W. H. AND P. BLOMMERS, Effects of non-promotion on educational achievement in the elementary school. *Journal of Educational Psychology,* 1956, **47:** 235–250

COHEN, A. K., *Delinquent Boys: The Culture of the Gang.* New York: Free Press, 1955

COLEMAN, J. S., *The Adolescent Subculture.* New York: Free Press, 1961a

————, Social climates in high schools. *Cooperative Research Monograph.* Washington, D.C.: U.S. Office of Education, 1961b, No. 4

COLLINS, S. D., KATHARINE S. TRANTHAM, AND JOSEPHINE L. LEHMANN, Sickness experience in selected areas of the United States. *Public Health Service Publication* No. 390. Washington, D.C.: U.S. Public Health Service, 1955, No. 25

COMBS, A. W. AND D. SNYGG, *Individual Behavior: A Perceptual Approach to Behavior.* (2d ed.) New York: Harper & Row, 1959

COMMINS, W. D. AND B. FAGIN, *Principles of Educational Psychology.* (2d ed.) New York: Ronald, 1954

COMMISSION ON TEACHER EDUCATION, *Helping Teachers Understand Children.* Washington, D.C.: American Council on Education, 1945

COMMITTEE ON CRITERIA OF TEACHER EFFECTIVENESS, *Report of the Committee.* Mimeographed, Washington, D.C.: American Educational Research Association, 1951

CONANT, J. B., *Slums and Suburbs: A Commentary on Schools in Metropolitan Areas.* New York: McGraw-Hill, 1961

————, *The Education of American Teachers.* New York: McGraw-Hill, 1963

CONNOR, FRANCES P., The education of children with chronic medical problems. In W. M. Cruickshank and G. O. Johnson (Eds.), *Education of Exceptional Children and Youth.* Englewood Cliffs, N. J.: Prentice-Hall, 1958

COOPERATIVE TEST DIVISION, *Cooperative School and College Ability Tests.* Princeton, N. J.: Educational Testing Service, 1957

COUNTS, G. S., *Education and American Civilization.* New York: Bureau of Publications, Teachers College, Columbia University, 1952

CRABTREE, CHARLOTTE, *Effects of Structuring on Productiveness of Children's Thinking.* Unpublished doctoral dissertation, Stanford University, 1961

CRAIG, R. C., *The Transfer Value of Guided Learning.* New York: Bureau of Publications, Teachers College, Columbia University, 1953

CRONBACH, L. J., *Educational Psychology.* New York: Harcourt, 1954

————, *Essentials of Psychological Testing.* (2d ed.) New York: Harper & Row, 1960a

————, Validity. In C. W. Harris (Ed.), *Encyclopedia of Educational Research.* (3d ed.) New York: Macmillan, 1960b

————, *Educational Psychology.* (2d ed.) New York: Harcourt, 1963

————, AND P. E. MEEHL, Construct validity in psychological tests. *Psychological Bulletin*, 1955, **52**: 281–302

CROWDER, N. A., Automatic tutoring by intrinsic programming. In A. A. Lumsdaine and R. Glaser (Eds.), *Teaching Machines and Programmed Learning*. Washington, D.C.: Department of Audio-Visual Instruction, National Education Association, 1960

CRUICKSHANK, W. M. AND G. O. JOHNSON (Eds.), *Education of Exceptional Children and Youth*. Englewood Cliffs, N. J.: Prentice-Hall, 1958

CUNNINGHAM, RUTH, ET AL., *Understanding Group Behavior of Boys and Girls*. New York: Bureau of Publications, Teachers College, Columbia University, 1951

DAVIES, DOROTHY R., The effect of tuition upon the process of learning a complex motor skill. *Journal of Educational Psychology*, 1945, **36**: 352–365

DAVIS, W. A., *Social Class Influences upon Learning*. Cambridge, Mass.: Harvard University Press, 1948

————, AND K. EELLS, *Directions for Administering and Scoring Davis-Eells Test of General Intelligence or Problem-Solving Ability*. New York: Harcourt, 1953

————, AND R. J. HAVIGHURST, Social class and color differences in child rearing. *American Sociological Review*, 1948a, **11**: 698–710

————, AND ————, The measurement of mental systems (can intelligence be measured?). *Scientific Monthly*, 1948b, **66**: 301–316

DEEG, M. E. AND D. G. PATERSON, Changes in social status of occupations. *Occupations*, 1947, **25**: 205–208

DE HAAN, R. F. AND R. J. HAVIGHURST, *Educating Gifted Children*. Chicago: University of Chicago Press, 1957

DEL SOLAR, CHARLOTTE, *Parents and Teachers View the Child*. New York: Bureau of Publications, Teachers College, Columbia University, 1949

DESPERT, J. LOUISE, Factors in some young children's colds. *Medical Clinics of North America*, 1944, **28**: 603–614

DETERLINE, W. A., *An Introduction to Programed Instruction*. Englewood Cliffs, N. J.: Prentice-Hall, 1962

DEUTSCH, M., An experimental study of the effects of cooperation and competition upon group process. *Human Relations*, 1949, **2**: 199–232

————, AND MARY E. COLLINS, The effect of public policy in housing projects upon interracial attitudes. In Eleanor E. Maccoby, T. M. Newcomb, and E. L. Hartley (Eds.), *Readings in Social Psychology*. (3d ed.) New York: Holt, Rinehart and Winston, 1958

D'EVELYN, KATHERINE E., *Meeting Children's Emotional Needs: A Guide for Teachers*. Englewood Cliffs, N. J.: Prentice-Hall, 1957

DEWEY, J., *The Child and the Curriculum*. Chicago: University of Chicago Press, 1902

————, *Moral Principles in Education*. Boston: Houghton Mifflin, 1909

————, *Democracy and Education*. New York: Macmillan, 1916

————, Some aspects of modern education. *School and Society*, 1931, **34**: 579–584

————, *Experience and Education*. New York: Macmillan, 1938

DIMOCK, H. S., *Rediscovering the Adolescent*. New York: Association Press, 1941

DOLLARD, J., ET AL., *Frustration and Aggression.* New Haven: Yale University Press, 1939

DORSEY, M. F. AND L. T. HOPKINS, The influence of attitude upon transfer. *Journal of Educational Psychology,* 1930, **21**: 410–417

DRUCKER, P., *Landmarks of Tomorrow.* New York: Harper & Row, 1959

DUNCKER, K., On problem-solving (Translated by Lynne S. Lees from 1935 original). *Psychological Monographs,* 1945, **58**: (Whole No. 270)

DUNLAP, J. M., The education of children with high mental ability. In W. M. Cruickshank and G. O. Johnson (Eds.), *Education of Exceptional Children and Youth.* Englewood Cliffs, N. J.: Prentice-Hall, 1958

DUNN, JOAN, *Retreat from Learning.* New York: McKay, 1955

DUTTON, W. H. AND E. R. KEISLAR, Attitudes toward teaching. *Journal of Teacher Education,* 1961, **12**: 165–171

DYER, H. S., A psychometrician views human ability. *Teachers College Record,* 1960, **61**: 394–403

EBAN, A., Education in a new society. *The Atlantic Monthly,* 1961, **208**: No. 5, 88–91

EBBINGHAUS, H., *Memory* (Translated by H. A. Ruger and C. E. Bussenius from 1885 original). New York: Bureau of Publications, Teachers College, Columbia University, 1913

EDUCATIONAL POLICIES COMMISSION, *Education of the Gifted.* Washington, D. C.: National Education Association, 1950

———, *Moral and Spiritual Values in the Public Schools.* Washington, D.C.: National Education Association, 1951

———, *The Central Purpose of American Education.* Washington, D.C.: National Education Association, 1961

EDUCATOR'S WASHINGTON DISPATCH, *Portfolio of Teaching Techniques.* New London, Conn.: Arthur C. Croft, 1951.

EDWARDS, A. L., Political frames of reference as a factor influencing recognition. *Journal of Abnormal and Social Psychology,* 1941, **36**: 34–50

———, The retention of affective experiences—a criticism and restatement of the problem. *Psychological Review,* 1942, **49**: 43–53

EELLS, K., *Social Status and Intelligence-test Items.* Unpublished doctoral dissertation, University of Chicago, 1948

ELIAS, L. J., *High School Youth Look at Their Problems.* Pullman, Wash.: State College of Washington, 1949

ELLIS, W. D., *A Source Book of Gestalt Psychology.* New York: Harcourt, 1938

ENGLISH, H. B., *Dynamics of Child Development.* New York: Holt, Rinehart and Winston, 1961

ENSTROM, E. A., *The Extent of the Use of the Left Hand in Handwriting and the Determination of the Relative Efficiency of the Various Hand-Wrist-Arm-Paper Adjustments.* Unpublished doctoral dissertation, University of Pittsburgh, 1957.

———, The relative efficiency of the various approaches to writing with the left hand. *Journal of Educational Research,* 1962, **55**: 573–577

ERIKSON, E. H., *Childhood and Society.* New York: Norton, 1950

———, Identity and the life cycle. *Psychological Issues,* 1959, **1**: No.1

ERON, L. D., ET AL., Comparison of data obtained from mothers and fathers on child-rearing practices and their relation to child aggression. *Child Development,* 1961, **32:** 457–472

ESON, M. E., The Minnesota Teacher Attitude Inventory in evaluating the teaching of educational psychology. *Journal of Educational Psychology,* 1956, **47:** 271–275

————, AND N. GREENFELD, Life space: its content and temporal dimensions. *Journal of Genetic Psychology,* 1962, **100:** 113–128

FAIGIN, HELEN, Social behavior of young children in the kibbutz. *Journal of Abnormal and Social Psychology,* 1958, **56:** 117–129

FESTINGER, L., *A Theory of Cognitive Dissonance.* New York: Harper & Row, 1957

————, AND H. H. KELLEY, *Changing Attitudes Through Social Contact.* Ann Arbor: Research Center for Group Dynamics, University of Michigan Press, 1951

FEUER, L. S., *Psychoanalysis and Ethics.* Springfield, Ill.: Charles C. Thomas, 1955

FIEDLER, MIRIAM F., Teachers' problems with hard of hearing children. *Journal of Educational Research,* 1949, **42:** 618–622

FLANDERS, N. A., Personal-social anxiety as a factor in experimental learning situations. *Journal of Educational Research,* 1951, **45:** 100–110

————, Diagnosing and utilizing social structures in classroom learning. In N. B. Henry (Ed.), *The Dynamics of Instructional Groups.* Yearbook of the National Society for the Study of Education, **59:** Pt. 2. Chicago: University of Chicago Press, 1960

FLUGEL, J. C., *Studies in Feeling and Desire.* London: Duckworth, 1955

FORLANO, G., *School Learning with Various Methods of Practice and Rewards.* New York: Bureau of Publications, Teachers College, Columbia University, 1936

FRANK, L. K., *Feelings and Emotions.* Garden City, N. Y.: Doubleday, 1954

FRAZIER, A., AND L. K. LISONBEE, Adolescent concerns with physique. *School Review,* 1950, **58:** 397–405

FREEDMAN, L. Z., Daydream in a vacuum tube. In W. Schramm, J. Lyle, and E. B. Parker, *Television in the Lives of Our Children.* Stanford, Calif.: Stanford University Press, 1961

FREEMAN, F. N., *Teaching Handwriting* (What Research Says to the Teacher, No. 4). Washington, D.C.: Department of Classroom Teachers, American Educational Research Association, National Education Association, 1954

FREIDUS, ELIZABETH S., A teacher's view. In *The Child with Damage.* Proceedings of the 1959 Annual Meeting of the Association for the Aid of Crippled Children, New York: The Association for the Aid of Crippled Children, 1959

FRENCH, J. R. P., JR. AND B. RAVEN, The bases of social power. In D. Cartwright (Ed.), *Studies in Social Power.* Ann Arbor: Research Center for Group Dynamics, University of Michigan Press, 1959

FRENKEL-BRUNSWICK, ELSE, A study of prejudice in children. *Human Relations,* 1948, **1:** 295–306

————, Patterns of social and cognitive outlook in children and parents. *American Journal of Orthopsychiatry,* 1951, **21:** 543–558

FREUD, ANNA, *The Ego and the Mechanisms of Defense.* New York: International Universities Press, 1946 (First published in German, 1936)

FREUD, S., *New Introductory Lectures on Psychoanalysis* (Translated by W. J. H. Sprott). New York: Norton, 1933

——, *A General Introduction to Psychoanalysis.* New York: Liveright, 1935 (First published in German, 1917)

——, *Collected Papers,* 2. London: Hogarth, 1950

——, *The Future of an Illusion* (Translated by W. D. Robson-Scott from 1927 original). Garden City, N. Y.: Doubleday, 1957

FRIEND, JEANNETTE G. AND E. A. HAGGARD, Work adjustment in relation to family background. *Applied Psychology Monographs,* 1948, No. 16

FROMM, E., *Man for Himself.* New York: Holt, Rinehart and Winston, 1947

FROMM, ERIKA AND LENORE D. HARTMAN, *Intelligence: A Dynamic Approach.* Garden City, N. Y.: Doubleday, 1955

GAIER, E. L., The relationship between selected personality variables and the thinking of students in discussion classes. *School Review,* 1952, **60:** 404–411

GALANTER, E. (Ed.), *Automatic Teaching: The State of the Art.* New York: Wiley, 1959

GARDNER, J. W., *Excellence: Can We be Equal and Excellent Too?* New York: Harper & Row, 1961

GARRETT, H. E., A developmental theory of intelligence. *American Psychologist,* 1946, **1:** 372–378

——, *Statistics in Psychology and Education.* (4th ed.) New York: Longmans, 1953

GARRETT, HELEN, When shall we begin to teach reading? Albany, N. Y.: New York State Education Department, 1949, Bulletin No. 1367

GATES, A. I., ET AL., *Educational Psychology.* (3d ed.) New York: Macmillan, 1949

GESELL, A., The ontogenesis of infant behavior. In L. Carmichael (Ed.), *Manual of Child Psychology.* (2d ed.) New York: Wiley, 1954

——, AND FRANCES L. ILG, *Child Development: An Introduction to the Study of Human Growth.* New York: Harper & Row, 1949

——, ——, AND LOUISE B. AMES, *Youth: The Years from Ten to Sixteen.* New York: Harper & Row, 1956

GETZELS, J. W. AND E. G. GUBA, The structure of roles and role conflict in the teaching situation. *Journal of Educational Sociology,* 1955, **29:** 30–40

——, AND P. W. JACKSON, *Creativity and Intelligence; Explorations with Gifted Children.* New York: Wiley, 1962

——, AND H. A. THELEN, The classroom group as a unique social system. In N. B. Henry (Ed.), *The Dynamics of Instructional Groups.* Yearbook of the National Society for the Study of Education, **59:** Pt. 2. Chicago: University of Chicago Press, 1960

GHISELIN, B. (Ed.), *The Creative Process, a Symposium.* Berkeley: University of California Press, 1952

GIBB, J. R., Sociopsychological processes of group instruction. In N. B. Henry (Ed.), *The Dynamics of Instructional Groups.* Yearbook of the National Society for the Study of Education, **59:** Pt. 2. Chicago: University of Chicago Press, 1960

GLASER, R., Principles and problems in the preparation of programmed learning sequences. Mimeographed report, *Cooperative Research Project* No. 691 (9417). Washington D.C.: U.S. Office of Education, 1960

———, DORA E. DAMRIN, AND F. M. GARDNER, A technique for measurement of proficiency in diagnostic problem solving tasks. *Educational and Psychological Measurement*, 1954, 14: 283–293

GLUECK, S. AND ELEANOR GLUECK, *Unravelling Juvenile Delinquency*. New York: Commonwealth Fund, 1950

GOLDFARB, W., Infant rearing and problem behavior. *American Journal of Orthopsychiatry*, 1943a, 13: 249–265

———, The effects of early institutional care on adolescent personality. *Journal of Experimental Education,* 1943b, 12: 106–129

GOLDSTEIN, K., Concerning rigidity. *Character and Personality*, 1943, 11: 209–226

GOODLAD, J. I., Some effects of promotion and nonpromotion upon the social and personal adjustment of children. *Journal of Experimental Education*, 1954, 22: 301–328

———, The teacher selects, plans and organizes. In *Learning and the Teacher*. Yearbook of the Association for Supervision and Curriculum Development. Washington, D.C.: National Education Association, 1959

GORDON, C. W., The role of the teacher in the social structure of the high school. *Journal of Educational Sociology*, 1955, 29: 21–29

GOUGH, H. G., ET AL., Children's ethnic attitudes: I Relationship to certain personality factors. *Child Development*, 1950, 21: 83–91

GRAMBS, JEAN D., The roles of the teacher. In L. J. Stiles (Ed.), *The Teacher's Role in American Society*. New York: Harper & Row, 1957

GRAMS, A., Parent education and the behavioral sciences. *Children's Bureau Publication*. Washington, D.C.: U.S. Government Printing Office, 1960, No. 379

GRAY, W. S., *On Their Own in Reading*. Chicago: Scott, Foresman, 1948

GREEN, E. J., *The Learning Process and Programmed Instruction*. New York: Holt, Rinehart and Winston, 1962

GREENBERG, PEARL J., Competition in children: an experimental study. *American Journal of Psychology*, 1932, 44: 221–248

GRINKER, R. R. AND F. P. ROBBINS, *Psychosomatic Case Book*. New York: Blakiston, 1954

GUILFORD, J. P., Three faces of intellect. *American Psychologist*, 1959, 14: 469–479

———, ET AL., A factor-analytic study of creative thinking: I Hypotheses and description of tests. *Reports from the Psychological Laboratory of the University of Southern California*, 1951

HAGGARD, E. A., Socialization, personality, and academic achievement in gifted children. *School Review*, 1957, 65: 388–414

HALL, J. F., *Psychology of Motivation*. Philadelphia: Lippincott, 1961

HALL, W. F. AND RUTH DEMAREST, Effect on achievement scores of a change in promotional policy. *Elementary School Journal*, 1958, 58: 204–207

HANLEY, C., Physique and reputation of junior high school boys. *Child Development*, 1951, 22: 247–260

HARLOW, H. F., The formation of learning sets. *Psychological Review*, 1949, 56: 51–65

————, Analysis of discrimination learning by monkeys. *Journal of Experimental Psychology*, 1950, **40**: 26–39

————, Motivation as a factor in the acquisition of new responses. In *Current Theory and Research in Motivation: A Symposium*. Lincoln: University of Nebraska Press, 1953a

————, Mice, monkeys, men, and motives. *Psychological Review*, 1953b. **60**: 23–32

HARRIS, D. B. (Ed. and Contributor), *The Concept of Development*. Minneapolis: University of Minnesota Press, 1957

HARTFORD, E. F., *Moral Values in Public Education: Lessons from the Kentucky Experience*. New York: Harper & Row, 1958

HARTLEY, RUTH E., L. K. FRANK, AND R. M. GOLDENSON, *Understanding Children's Play*. New York: Columbia University Press, 1952

HARTMANN, G. W., *Educational Psychology*. New York: American Book, 1941

HARTSHORNE, H., M. A. MAY, AND F. K. SHUTTLEWORTH, *Studies in the Nature of Character*. 3: *Studies in the Organization of Character*. New York: Macmillan, 1930

HAVIGHURST, R. J., *Human Development and Education*. Longmans, 1953

————, Social-class influences on American education. In N. B. Henry (Ed.), *Social Forces Influencing American Education*. Yearbook of the National Society for the Study of Education, **60**: Pt. 2. Chicago: University of Chicago Press, 1961

————, AND BERNICE L. NEUGARTEN, *Society and Education*. Boston: Allyn and Bacon, 1957

————, MYRA Z. ROBINSON, AND MILDRED DORR, The development of the ideal self in childhood and adolescence. *Journal of Educational Research*, 1946, **40**: 241–257

————, E. STIVERS, AND R. F. DE HAAN, A survey of the education of gifted children. *Supplementary Educational Monographs*, 1955, No. 83

————, AND HILDA TABA, *Adolescent Character and Personality*. New York: Wiley, 1949

HEARD, IDA MAE, Our arithmetic class was a talking-thinking class. *Monograph for Elementary Teachers*. New York: Harper & Row, 1959, No. 92

HEBB, D. O., Heredity and environment in mammalian behavior. *British Journal of Animal Behavior*, 1953, **1**: 43–47

————, The motivating effects of exteroceptive stimulation. *American Psychologist*, 1958, **13**: 109–113

HEGGE, T. G., S. A. KIRK, AND WINIFRED D. KIRK, *Remedial Reading Drills*. Ann Arbor, Mich.: Wahr, 1936

HENDRICKSON, G. AND W. H. SCHROEDER, Transfer of training in learning to hit a submerged target. *Journal of Educational Psychology*, 1941, **32**: 205–213

HILDRETH, GERTRUDE, The development and training of hand dominance: I Characteristics of handedness; II Developmental tendencies in handedness; III Origins of handedness and lateral dominance. *Journal of Genetic Psychology*, 1949, **75**: 197–275

HILGARD, E. R., *Theories of Learning*. (2d ed.) New York: Appleton, 1956

————, AND D. G. MARQUIS, *Conditioning and Learning*. (2d ed. Revised by G. A. Kimble) New York: Appleton, 1961

HOLLINGSHEAD, A. DE B., *Elmtown's Youth: The Impact of Social Classes on Youth.* New York: Wiley, 1949

HOLMES, F. B., An experimental investigation of a method of overcoming children's fears. *Child Development,* 1936, **7**: 6–30

HONZIK, MARJORIE P., JEAN W. MACFARLANE, AND LUCILLE ALLEN, The stability of mental test performance between two and eighteen years. *Journal of Experimental Education,* 1948, **17**: 309–324

HOROWITZ, E. L., The development of attitude toward the Negro. *Archives of Psychology,* 1936, **28**: No. 194

HOVLAND, C. I., Human learning and retention. In S. S. Stevens (Ed.), *Handbook of Experimental Psychology.* New York: Wiley, 1951

HOWELL, W. J., Work-study skills of children in grades IV to VIII. *Elementary School Journal,* 1950, **50**: 384–389

HOYT, K. B., A study of the effects of teacher knowledge of pupil characteristics on pupil achievement and attitudes towards classwork. *Journal of Educational Psychology,* 1955, **46**: 302–310

HUNT, J. MCV., Experience and the development of motivation: some reinterpretations. *Child Development,* 1960, **31**: 489–504

———, *Intelligence and Experience.* New York: Ronald, 1961

HUNTER, E. C., Changes in teachers' attitudes towards children's behavior over the last thirty years. *Mental Hygiene,* 1957, **41**: 3–11

HUTCHINS, R. M., *The Higher Learning in America.* New Haven: Yale University Press, 1936

HUXLEY, A., *Beyond the Mexique Bay.* New York: Vintage Books, 1960 (First published in 1934)

JACKSON, P. W., The teacher and individual differences. In N. B. Henry (Ed.), *Individualizing Instruction.* Yearbook of the National Society for the Study of Education, **61**: Pt. 1. Chicago: University of Chicago Press, 1962

———, AND E. G. GUBA, The need structure of in-service teachers: an occupational analysis. *School Review,* 1957, **65**: 176–192

JAHODA, MARIE, Psychological issues in civil liberties. *American Psychologist,* 1956, **11**: 234–240

JAMES, W., *Principles of Psychology.* New York: Holt, Rinehart and Winston, 1890. 2 vols.

———, *Talks to Teachers on Psychology: And to Students on Some of Life's Ideals.* New York: Holt, Rinehart and Winston, 1902

JENKINS, D. H. AND R. LIPPITT, *Interpersonal Perceptions of Teachers, Students, and Parents.* Washington, D.C.: Division of Adult Education Service, National Education Association, 1951

JENSEN, B. T., What about transfer? *Peabody Journal of Education,* 1956, **34**: 71–77

JENSEN, GALE, The sociopsychological structure of the instructional group. In N. B. Henry (Ed.), *The Dynamics of Instructional Groups.* Yearbook of the National Society for the Study of Education, **59**: Pt. 2. Chicago: University of Chicago Press, 1960

JERSILD, A. T., Emotional development. In L. Carmichael (Ed.), *Manual of Child Psychology.* New York: Wiley, 1946

———, *In Search of Self*. New York: Bureau of Publications, Teachers College, Columbia University, 1952

———, *When Teachers Face Themselves*. New York: Bureau of Publications, Teachers College, Columbia University, 1955

———, *Child Psychology*. (5th ed.) Englewood Cliffs, N. J.: Prentice-Hall, 1960

———, B. GOLDMAN, AND J. LOFTUS, A comparative study of the worries of children in two school situations. *Journal of Experimental Education,* 1941, **9:** 323–326

JOHNSON, D. M., *The Psychology of Thought and Judgment*. New York: Harper & Row, 1955

JOHNSON, G. O., The education of mentally handicapped children. In W. M. Cruickshank and G. O. Johnson (Eds.), *Education of Exceptional Children and Youth*. Englewood Cliffs, N. J.: Prentice-Hall, 1958

JOHNSON, MARGUERITE W., The influence of verbal directions upon behavior. *Child Development,* 1935, **6:** 196–204

JONES, H. E., The adolescent growth study: I Principles and methods; II Procedures. *Journal of Consulting Psychology,* 1939, **3:** I 157–159; II 177–180

JONES, MARY C., A laboratory study of fear: the case of Peter. *Pedagogical Seminary and Journal of Genetic Psychology,* 1924, **31:** 308–315

———, The later careers of boys who were early- or late-maturing. *Child Development,* 1957, **28:** 113–128

———, AND NANCY BAYLEY, Physical maturing among boys as related to behavior. *Journal of Educational Psychology,* 1950, **41:** 129–148

JONES, V., *Character and Citizenship Training in the Public School*. Chicago: University of Chicago Press, 1936

———, Character development in children—an objective approach. In L. Carmichael (Ed.), *Manual of Child Psychology*. New York: Wiley, 1946

JUDD, C. H., The relation of special training to general intelligence. *Educational Review,* 1908, **36:** 28–42

KAHL, J. A., *The American Class Structure*. New York: Holt, Rinehart and Winston, 1957

KAWI, A. A. AND B. PASAMANICK, Prenatal and paranatal factors in the development of childhood reading disorders. *Monographs of the Society for Research in Child Development,* 1959, **24:** No. 4

KEISTER, MARY E., The behavior of young children in failure. In R. G. Barker, J. S. Kounin, and H. F. Wright (Eds.), *Child Behavior and Development*. New York: McGraw-Hill, 1943

KELLY, ELIZABETH M. AND H. A. STEVENS, Special education for the mentally handicapped. In N. B. Henry (Ed.), *The Education of Exceptional Children*. Yearbook of the National Society for the Study of Education, **49:** Pt. 2. Chicago: University of Chicago Press, 1950

KELLY, G. A., *The Psychology of Personal Constructs. 1: A Theory of Personality*. New York: Norton, 1955

———, Man's construction of his alternatives. In G. Lindzey (Ed.), *Assessment of Human Motives*. New York: Holt, Rinehart and Winston, 1958

KENDLER, H. H. AND T. S. KENDLER, Effect of verbalization on reversal shifts in children. *Science,* 1961, **134:** 1619–1620

KERKMAN, D. H. AND H. F. WRIGHT, A cinematographic study of classroom behavior patterns. Paper presented to meeting of the American Psychological Association, 1961

KINGSLEY, H. L. AND R. GARRY, *The Nature and Conditions of Learning.* (2d ed.) Englewood Cliffs, N. J.: Prentice-Hall, 1957

KINSEY, A. C., W. B. POMEROY, AND C. E. MARTIN, *Sexual Behavior in the Human Male.* Philadelphia: Saunders, 1948

KITTELL, J., An experimental study of the effect of external direction during learning on transfer and retention of principles. *Journal of Educational Psychology,* 1957, **48:** 391–405

KLEIN, E., The reluctance to go to school. In O. Fenichel et al. (Eds.), *The Psychoanalytic Study of the Child,* 1: New York: International Universities Press, 1945

KLINEBERG, O., *Race Differences.* New York: Harper & Row, 1935

KNOX, G. E., Classroom symptoms of visual difficulty. *Supplementary Educational Monographs,* 1953, No. 77, 97–101

KOERNER, J. D., *The Miseducation of American Teachers.* Cambridge, Mass.: Houghton Mifflin, 1963

KOUGH, J. AND R. F. DE HAAN, *Teacher's Guidance Handbook.* Chicago: Science Research Associates, 1955

KOUNIN, J. S., Intellectual development and rigidity. In R. G. Barker, J. S. Kounin, and H. F. Wright (Eds.), *Child Behavior and Development.* New York: McGraw-Hill, 1943

———, AND P. V. GUMP, The ripple effect in discipline. *Elementary School Journal,* 1958, **59:** 158–162

———, AND ———, The comparative influence of punitive and nonpunitive teachers upon children's concepts of school misconduct. *Journal of Educational Psychology,* 1961, **52:** 44–49

———, ———, AND J. J. RYAN, III, Explorations in classroom management. *Journal of Teacher Education,* 1961, **12:** 235–246

KUHLEN, R. G., *The Psychology of Adolescent Development.* New York: Harper & Row, 1952

———, AND BEATRICE J. LEE, Personality characteristics and social acceptability in adolescence. *Journal of Educational Psychology,* 1943, **34:** 321–340

KVARACEUS, W. C., *Juvenile Delinquency* (What Research Says to the Teacher No. 15). Washington, D.C.: Department of Classroom Teachers, American Educational Research Association, National Education Association, 1954

LANE, H. AND MARY BEAUCHAMP, *Human Relations in Teaching.* Englewood Cliffs, N. J.: Prentice-Hall, 1955

LANGDON, GRACE AND I. W. STOUT, What parents think about homework. *NEA Journal,* 1957, **46:** 370–372

LAUGHLIN, FRANCES, *The Peer Status of Sixth- and Seventh-Grade Children.* New York: Bureau of Publications, Teachers College, Columbia University, 1954

LAWSON, E. D. AND W. E. BOEK, Correlations of indexes of families' socioeconomic status. *Social Forces,* 1960, **39:** 149–152

LEARNED, W. S. AND B. D. WOOD, *The Student and His Knowledge.* New York: The Carnegie Foundation for the Advancement of Teaching, 1938, Bulletin No. 29

LEE, E. S., Negro intelligence and selective migration: a Philadelphia test of the Klineberg hypothesis. *American Sociological Review,* 1951, **16**: 227–233

LEIGHTON, A. H., *My Name is Legion: Foundations for a Theory of Man in Relation to Culture.* New York: Basic Books, 1959

LESHAN, L. L., Time orientation and social class. *Journal of Abnormal and Social Psychology,* 1952, **47**: 589–592

LESSER, A., Emotional problems associated with handicapping conditions in children. *Children's Bureau Publication.* Washington, D.C.: U.S. Government Printing Office, 1952, No. 336

LEVINE, J. M. AND G. MURPHY, The learning and forgetting of controversial material. *Journal of Abnormal and Social Psychology,* 1943, **38**: 507–517

LEVY, D. M., *Maternal Overprotection.* New York: Columbia University Press, 1943

LEWIN, K., Behavior and development as a function of the total situation. In L. Carmichael (Ed.), *Manual of Child Psychology.* New York: Wiley, 1946

———, Group decision and social change. In T. H. Newcomb and E. L. Hartley (Eds.), *Readings in Social Psychology.* New York: Holt, Rinehart and Winston, 1947

———, R. LIPPITT, AND R. K. WHITE, Patterns of aggressive behavior in experimentally created "social climates." *Journal of Social Psychology,* 1939, **10**: 271–299

LIEBERMAN, M., *Education as a Profession.* Englewood Cliffs, N. J.: Prentice-Hall, 1956

LINDGREN, H. C., *Educational Psychology in the Classroom.* (2d ed.) New York: Wiley, 1962

LIPPITT, R. AND M. GOLD, Classroom social structure as a mental health problem. *Journal of Social Issues,* 1959, **15**: 40–49

———, AND R. K. WHITE, The "social climate" of children's groups. In R. G. Barker, J. S. Kounin, and H. F. Wright (Eds.), *Child Behavior and Development.* New York: McGraw-Hill, 1943

———, AND ———, An experimental study of leadership and group life. In Eleanor E. Maccoby, T. M. Newcomb, and E. L. Hartley (Eds.), *Readings in Social Psychology.* (3d ed.) New York: Holt, Rinehart and Winston, 1958

LIVERANT, S., Intelligence: a concept in need of re-examination. *Journal of Consulting Psychology,* 1960, **24**: 101–110

LLOYD-JONES, ESTHER AND MARY V. HOLMAN, Why people become teachers. In L. J. Stiles (Ed.), *The Teacher's Role in American Society.* New York: Harper & Row, 1957

LOREE, M. R., *Educational Psychology.* New York: Ronald, 1959

LORGE, I. D., Influence of regularly interpolated time intervals upon subsequent learning. *Teachers College Contributions to Education,* 1930, No. 438

LOWENFELD, V., *Creative and Mental Growth.* (3d ed.) New York: Macmillan, 1957

————, AND K. BEITTEL, Interdisciplinary criteria of creativity in the arts and sciences: a progress report. In J. H. Hausman (Ed.), *Research in Art Education*. Yearbook of the National Art Education Association, **9**: Kutztown, Pa.: State Teachers College, 1959

LUCHINS, A. S., *The Einstellung Effect in Learning by Repetition*. Unpublished doctoral dissertation, New York University, 1939

————, Mechanization in problem solving—the effect of *Einstellung*. *Psychological Monographs*, 1942, **54**: No. 6 (Whole No. 248)

LUH, C. W., The conditions of retention. *Psychological Monographs*, 1922, **31**: (Whole No. 142)

LUMSDAINE, A. A. AND R. GLASER (Eds.), *Teaching Machines and Programmed Learning: A Source Book*. Washington, D.C.: National Education Association, 1960

MCCANDLESS, B. R., *Children and Adolescents: Behavior and Development*. New York: Holt, Rinehart and Winston, 1961

MCDONOUGH, PAT, *Better Bowling*. New York: Alumni Publications, undated

MCGEOCH, J. A. AND A. L. IRION, *The Psychology of Human Learning*. (2d ed.) New York: Longmans, 1952

MCGUIGAN, F. J., Variation of whole-part methods of learning. *Journal of Educational Psychology*, 1960, **51**: 213–216

MCGUIRE, C. AND G. D. WHITE, Social origins of teachers—in Texas. In L. J. Stiles (Ed.), *The Teacher's Role in American Society*. New York: Harper & Row, 1957

MCKIM, MARGARET G., Curriculum research in historical perspective. In *Research for Curriculum Improvement*. Yearbook of the Association for Supervision and Curriculum Development. Washington, D.C.: National Education Association, 1957

MALLER, J. B., Cooperation and competition: an experimental study in motivation. *Teachers College Contributions to Education*, 1929, No. 384

MASLOW, A. H., *Motivation and Personality*. New York: Harper & Row, 1954

MASSLER, M., AND T. SUHER, Calculation of "normal" weight in children. *Child Development*, 1951, **22**: 75–94

MAYER, K. B., *Class and Society*. Garden City, N. Y.: Doubleday, 1955

MEAD, MARGARET, *The School in American Culture*. Cambridge, Mass.: Harvard University Press, 1951

MEDLEY, D. M., Teacher personality and teacher-pupil rapport. *Journal of Teacher Education*, 1961, **12**: 152–156

MERRILL, BARBARA, A measurement of mother-child interaction. *Journal of Abnormal and Social Psychology*, 1946, **41**: 37–49

MERTON, R. K., *Social Theory and Social Structure*. New York: Free Press, 1957

MILES, M. B., *Learning to Work in Groups*. New York: Bureau of Publications, Teachers College, Columbia University, 1959

MILLER, D. R. AND G. E. SWANSON, *Inner Conflict and Defense*. New York: Holt, Rinehart and Winston, 1960

MILLER, G. A., The magical number seven, plus-or-minus two, or, some limits on our capacity for processing information. *Psychological Review*, 1956, **63**: 81–97

MILLER, H. AND DOROTHY W. BARUCH, Psychosomatic studies of children with allergic manifestations: I Maternal rejection: a study of sixty-three cases. *Psychosomatic Medicine,* 1948, **10**: 275–278

MILNER, ESTHER, A study of the relationship between reading readiness in grade-one children and patterns of parent-child interaction. *Child Development,* 1951, **22**: 95–112

MONTAGU, M. F. A., *The Direction of Human Development: Biological and Social Bases.* New York: Harper & Row, 1955

MOONEY, R. L. AND L. V. GORDON, *Mooney Problem Check List.* (rev. ed.) New York: Psychological Corporation, 1950

MORENO, J. L., Who shall survive? *Nervous and Mental Disease Monographs,* 1934, No. 58

MORSE, W. C., Diagnosing and guiding relationships between group and individual class members. In N. B. Henry (Ed.), *The Dynamics of Instructional Groups.* Yearbook of the National Society for the Study of Education, **59**: Pt. 2. Chicago: University of Chicago Press, 1960

MOWRER, O. H. AND C. KLUCKHOHN, Dynamic theory of personality. In J. McV. Hunt (Ed.), *Personality and the Behavior Disorders,* **1**: New York: Ronald, 1944

MURPHY, G., *Personality: A Biosocial Approach to Origins and Structure.* New York: Harper & Row, 1947

MURPHY, LOIS B., Self-management capacities in children. In A. Frazier (Ed.), *New Insights and the Curriculum.* Yearbook of the Association for Supervision and Curriculum Development. Washington, D.C.: National Education Association, 1963

MURSELL, J. L., ET AL., The measurement of understanding in the fine arts. In N. B. Henry (Ed.), *The Measurement of Understanding.* Yearbook of the National Society for the Study of Education, **45**: Pt. 1. Chicago: University of Chicago Press, 1946

MUSSEN, P. H. AND MARY C. JONES, Self-conceptions, motivations, and interpersonal attitudes of late- and early-maturing boys. *Child Development,* 1957, **28**: 243–256

NATIONAL EDUCATION ASSOCIATION, New NEA code of ethics. *NEA Journal,* 1952, **41**: 371–372

NATIONAL FOUNDATION FOR INFANTILE PARALYSIS AND THE CITIZENSHIP EDUCATION PROJECT, *Understanding the Disabled.* New York: Citizenship Education Project, Teachers College, Columbia University, 1956

NEUGARTEN, BERNICE L., Social class and friendship among school children. *American Journal of Sociology,* 1946, **51**: 305–313

NEWCOMB, T. M., *Personality and Social Change: Attitude Formation in a Student Community.* New York: Holt, Rinehart and Winston, 1943

NORRIS, EUGENIA AND D. A. GRANT, Eyelid conditioning as affected by verbally induced inhibitory set and counter reinforcement. *American Journal of Psychology,* 1948, **61**: 37–49

NORTH, R. D., The teacher education student: how does he compare academically with other college students? In *The Education of Teachers: New Perspectives.* Washington, D.C.: National Commission on Teacher Education and Professional Standards, National Education Association, 1958

O'CONNOR, C. D. AND ALICE STRENG, Teaching the acoustically handicapped. In

N. B. Henry (Ed.), *The Education of Exceptional Children.* Yearbook of the National Society for the Study of Education, 49: Pt. 2. Chicago: University of Chicago Press, 1950

OJEMANN, R. H. AND FRANCES R. WILKINSON, The effect on pupil growth of an increase in teachers' understanding of pupil behavior. *Journal of Experimental Education,* 1939, 8: 143–147

OLSON, W. C., *Psychological Foundations of the Curriculum* (UNESCO Educational Studies and Documents, No. 26). Paris, France: UNESCO, 1957

———, AND B. O. HUGHES, Growth of the child as a whole. In R. G. Barker, J. S. Kounin, and H. F. Wright (Eds.), *Child Behavior and Development.* New York: McGraw-Hill, 1943

———, AND ———, Concepts of growth—their significance to teachers. *Childhood Education,* 1944, 21: 2–12

OTTO, H. J. AND E. O. MELBY, An attempt to evaluate the threat of failure as a factor in achievement. *Elementary School Journal,* 1935, 35: 588–596

PARSONS, T. AND R. F. BALES, *Family, Socialization, and Interaction Process.* New York: Free Press, 1955

PASAMANICK, B. AND A. A. KAWI, A study of the association of prenatal and paranatal factors with the development of tics in children. *Journal of Pediatrics,* 1956, 48: 596–601

———, M. E. ROGERS, AND A. M. LILIENFELD, Pregnancy experience and the development of behavior disorder in children. *American Journal of Psychiatry,* 1956, 112: 613–618

PASSOW, A. H., Enrichment of education for the gifted. In N. B. Henry (Ed.), *Education for the Gifted.* Yearbook of the National Society for the Study of Education, 57: Pt. 2. Chicago: University of Chicago Press, 1958

PATRICK, J. R., Studies in rational behavior and emotional excitement: II The effect of emotional excitement on rational behavior in human subjects. *Journal of Comparative Psychology,* 1934, 18: 153–195

PATTON, D. H. AND ELEANOR M. JOHNSON, *Spelling for Word Mastery.* Columbus, Ohio: Chas. E. Merrill, 1956

PAUL, I. H., Studies in remembering: the reproduction of connected and extended verbal material. *Psychological Issues,* 1959, 1: No. 2

PEARSON, G. H. J., *Psychoanalysis and the Education of the Child.* New York: Norton, 1954

PETERSON, D. R., ET AL., Parental attitudes and child adjustment. *Child Development,* 1959, 30: 119–130

PIAGET, J., *Judgment and Reasoning in the Child* (Translated by Marjorie Warden). New York: Harcourt, 1928

———, *The Child's Conception of Physical Causality.* New York: Harcourt, 1930 (First published in French, 1927)

———, *The Moral Judgment of the Child.* New York: Harcourt, 1932.

———, *The Language and Thought of the Child.* New York: Meridian, 1955 (First published in French, 1926)

PLANT, J. S., *The Envelope, a Study of the Impact of the World upon the Child.* New York: Commonwealth Fund, 1950

POSTMAN, L., J. S. BRUNER, AND E. M. MCGINNIES, Personal values as selective factors in perception. *Journal of Abnormal and Social Psychology*, 1948, **43:** 142–154

PRESCOTT, D. A., *Emotion and the Educative Process.* Washington, D.C.: American Council on Education, 1938

———, *The Child in the Educative Process.* New York: McGraw-Hill, 1957

PRESSEY, LUELLA C., The permanent effects of training in methods of study on college success. *School and Society*, 1928, **28:** 403–404

PRESSEY, S. L., A simple apparatus which gives tests and scores—and teaches. *School and Society*, 1926, **23:** 373–376

———, A machine for automatic teaching of drill material. *School and Society*, 1927, **25:** 549–552

———, Educational acceleration: appraisals and basic problems. *Bureau of Educational Research Monographs.* Columbus: The Ohio State University, 1949, No. 31

———, AND R. G. KUHLEN, *Psychological Development through the Life Span.* New York: Harper & Row, 1957

QUILLEN, I. J., What are the basic concepts to be developed in children? *Childhood Education*, 1947, **23:** 405–409

RADKE, MARIAN J., Relation of parental authority to children's behavior and attitudes. *University of Minesota Institute of Child Welfare Monographs*, 1946, No. 22

———, HELEN G. TRAGER, AND HADASSAH DAVIS. Social perceptions and attitudes of children. *Genetic Psychology Monographs*, 1949, **40:** 327–447

RANSON, M. KATHLEEN, An evaluation of certain aspects of the reading and study program at the University of Missouri. *Journal of Educational Research*, 1955, **48:** 443–454

RAPAPORT, D., *Organization and Pathology of Thought.* New York: Columbia University Press, 1951

RASEY, MARIE, *This is Teaching.* New York: Harper & Row, 1950

RAY, W. S., Verbal compared with manipulative solution of an apparatus problem. *American Journal of Psychology*, 1957, **70:** 289–290

REDL, F., Discussion. In Helen L. Witmer and Ruth Kotinsky (Eds.), New perspectives for research on juvenile delinquency. *Children's Bureau Publication.* Washington, D.C.: U.S. Government Printing Office, 1956, No. 356

———, AND W. W. WATTENBERG, *Mental Hygiene in Teaching.* New York: Harcourt, 1951

RETHLINGSHAFER, DOROTHY, *Motivation as Related to Personality.* New York: McGraw-Hill, 1963

RIBBLE, MARGARET A., Infantile experiences in relation to personality development. In J. McV. Hunt (Ed.), *Personality and the Behavior Disorders*, 2. New York: Ronald, 1944

RICHARDS, I. A., *Principles of Literary Criticism.* (2d ed.) London: Routledge, 1926

———, *Basic English and Its Uses.* London: Routledge, 1943

———, *Literacy and Standards Via World Television.* Mimeographed lecture given at the Institute of Contemporary Arts, Fifth Annual Congress, Washington, D.C., 1963

———, AND CHRISTINE GIBSON, *English Through Pictures.* New York: Washington

Square Press, 1960. (First published as *Pocket Book of Basic English,* 1945)

RICHARDS, T. W., Mental test performance as a reflection of the child's current life situation: a methodological study. *Child Development,* 1951, **22:** 221–233

RIESMAN, D., ET AL., *The Lonely Crowd.* New Haven: Yale University Press, 1950

RIVLIN, H. N., The objectives of educational psychology in the education of teachers. *Educational Psychology in Teacher Education.* Ann Arbor, Mich.: National Society of College Teachers of Education, 1953, No. 3

ROBINSON, E. S., The "similarity" factor in retroaction. *American Journal of Psychology,* 1927, **39:** 297–312

ROBINSON, F. P., *Effective Study.* (rev. ed.) New York: Harper & Row, 1961

ROGERS, C. R., *Dealing with Social Tensions.* New York: Hinds, 1948

———, *Client-Centered Therapy.* Boston: Houghton Mifflin, 1951

———, Toward a theory of creativity. In M. Barkan and R. L. Mooney (Eds.), *Conference on Creativity: A Report to the Rockefeller Foundation.* Columbus: The Ohio State University, 1953

ROSENFELD, H. AND A. ZANDER, The influence of teachers on aspirations of students. *Journal of Educational Psychology,* 1961, **52:** 1–11

ROSENZWEIG, S., Types of reaction to frustration: a heuristic classification. *Journal of Abnormal and Social Psychology.* 1934, **29:** 298–300

RUEDIGER, W. C., The indirect improvement of mental function through ideals. *Educational Review,* 1908, **36:** 364–371

RYANS, D. G., *Characteristics of Teachers.* Washington, D.C.: American Council on Education, 1960

———, Some relationships between pupil behavior and certain teacher characteristics. *Journal of Educational Psychology,* 1961, **52:** 82–90

RYLE, G., *The Concept of Mind.* New York: Barnes & Noble (University Paperbacks), 1949

SANFORD, N. (Ed. and Contributor), *The American College.* New York: Wiley, 1962

SAUL, L. J., Physiological effects of emotional tension. In J. McV. Hunt (Ed.), *Personality and the Behavior Disorders,* 1. New York: Ronald, 1944

———, *Emotional Maturity.* Philadelphia: Lippincott, 1947

SCHLOSBERG, H., Three dimensions of emotion. *Psychological Review,* 1954, **61:** 81–88

SCHRAMM, W., J. LYLE, AND E. B. PARKER, *Television in the Lives of our Children.* Stanford, Calif.: Stanford University Press, 1961

SCHRUPP, M. H. AND C. M. GJERDE, Teacher growth in attitudes toward behavior problems of children. *Journal of Educational Psychology,* 1953, **44:** 203–214

SEAGOE, MAY V., *A Teacher's Guide to the Learning Process.* Dubuque, Iowa: W. C. Brown, 1956

SEARS, PAULINE S., Levels of aspiration in academically successful and unsuccessful children. *Journal of Abnormal and Social Psychology,* 1940, **63:** 466–492

———, Problems in the investigation of achievement and self esteem motivation. In M. R. Jones (Ed.), *Nebraska Symposium on Motivation.* Lincoln: University of Nebraska Press, 1957

SEARS, R. R., Identification as a form of behavioral development. In D. B. Harris (Ed.), *The Concept of Development*. Minneapolis: University of Minnesota Press, 1957

————, Relation of early socialization experiences to aggression in middle childhood. *Journal of Abnormal and Social Psychology*, 1961, **63**: 466–492

————, ELEANOR E. MACCOBY, AND H. LEVIN, *Patterns of Child Rearing*. New York: Harper & Row, 1957

————, ET AL., Some child-rearing antecedents of aggression and dependency in young children. *Genetic Psychology Monographs*, 1953, **47**: 135–234

SELLS, S. B., The atmosphere effect: an experimental study of reasoning. *Archives of Psychology*, 1936, No. 200

SELYE, H., *The Stress of Life*. New York: McGraw-Hill, 1956

SHAFTEL, FANNIE R., Toward more autonomy for learners. In A. Frazier (Ed.), *New Insights and the Curriculum*. Yearbook of the Association for Supervision and Curriculum Development. Washington, D.C.: National Education Association, 1963

SHARP, D. LOUISE, *Why Teach?* New York: Holt, Rinehart and Winston, 1957

SHELDON, W. H., Constitutional factors in personality. In J. McV. Hunt (Ed.), *Personality and the Behavior Disorders*, 1: New York: Ronald, 1944

————, AND S. S. STEVENS, *The Varieties of Temperament*. New York: Harper & Row, 1942

————, ————, AND W. B. TUCKER, *The Varieties of Human Physique*. New York: Harper & Row, 1940

SHERIF, M., *The Psychology of Social Norms*. New York: Harper & Row, 1936

————, AND CAROLYN W. SHERIF, *Groups in Harmony and Tension*. New York: Harper & Row, 1953

————, AND ————, *An Outline of Social Psychology*. (rev. ed.) New York: Harper & Row, 1956

SHERMAN, M. AND CORA B. KEY, The intelligence of isolated mountain children. *Child Development*, 1932, **3**: 279–290

SHEVIAKOV, G. V. AND F. REDL, *Discipline for Today's Children and Youth*. (rev. ed. Revised by Sybil K. Richardson) Washington, D.C.: Association for Supervision and Curriculum Development, National Education Association, 1956

SHUTTLEWORTH, F. K., The physical and mental growth of girls and boys age six to nineteen in relation to age at maximum growth. *Monographs of the Society for Research in Child Development*, 1939, **4**: No. 3

SIMON, MARIA D., Body configuration and school readiness. *Child Development*, 1959, **30**: 493–512

SIMPSON, G. E. AND J. M. YINGER, *Racial and Cultural Minorities: An Analysis of Prejudice and Discrimination*. New York: Harper & Row, 1953

SKINNER, B. F., *The Behavior of Organisms*. New York: Appleton, 1938

————, "Superstition" in the pigeon. *Journal of Experimental Psychology*, 1948a, **38**: 168–172

————, *Walden Two*. New York: Macmillan, 1948b

————, *Science and Human Behavior*. New York: Macmillan, 1953

————, Teaching machines. *Science*, 1958, **128**: 969–977

SLEIGHT, W. G., Memory and formal training. *British Journal of Psychology,* 1911, 4: 386–457

SMITH, C. C., *New Wine in Old Bottles.* Mimeographed, Albany, N. Y.: State University of New York at Albany, 1955

SMITH, G. M., *A Simplified Guide to Statistics for Psychology and Education.* (3d ed.) New York: Holt, Rinehart and Winston, 1962

SMITH, J. A., ET AL. (Eds.), *Independent Learning Activities.* Albany, N. Y.: Capital Area School Development Association, State University of New York at Albany, 1958

SMITH, K. U., *Delayed Sensory Feedback and Behavior.* Philadelphia: Saunders, 1962

SMITH, M. B., J. S. BRUNER, AND R. W. WHITE, *Opinions and Personality.* New York: Wiley, 1956

SMITH, S., Language and non-verbal test performance of racial groups in Honolulu before and after a 14-year interval. *Journal of General Psychology,* 1942, 26: 51–93

SONTAG, L. W., C. T. BAKER, AND VIRGINIA L. NELSON, Mental growth and personality development: a longitudinal study. *Monographs of the Society for Research in Child Development,* 1958, 23: No. 2

SORENSON, H., *Psychology in Education.* (2d ed.) New York: McGraw-Hill, 1948

SPIEGEL, J. P., The resolution of role conflict within the family. *Psychiatry,* 1957, 20: 1–16

SPINDLER, G. D., Education in a transforming American culture. *Harvard Educational Review,* 1955, 25: 145–156

SPITZ, R. A., Hospitalism: an inquiry into the genesis of psychiatric conditions in early childhood. In O. Fenichel et al. (Eds.), *Psychoanalytic Study of the Child,* 1. New York: International Universities Press, 1945

———, The role of ecological factors in the emotional development of infancy. *Child Development,* 1949, 20: 145–155

SPITZER, H. F., Learning and teaching arithmetic. In N. B. Henry (Ed.), *The Teaching of Arithmetic.* Yearbook of the National Society for the Study of Education, 50: Pt. 2. Chicago: University of Chicago Press, 1951

STAR, S. A., R. M. WILLIAMS, JR., AND S. A. STOUFFER, Negro infantry platoons in white companies. In S. A. Stouffer et al., *The American Soldier.* 1: *Adjustment During Army Life.* Princeton, N. J.: Princeton University Press, 1949

STENDLER, CELIA B., *Children of Brasstown.* Urbana, Ill.: Bureau of Research and Service, College of Education, University of Illinois, 1949

———, Social-class differences in parental attitudes toward school at grade-I level. *Child Development,* 1951, 22: 37–46

STEPHENS, J. M., Transfer of learning. In C. W. Harris (Ed.), *Encyclopedia of Educational Research.* (3d ed.) New York: Macmillan, 1960

STODDARD, G. D., *The Meaning of Intelligence.* New York: Macmillan, 1943

STOGDILL, R. M., *Individual Behavior and Group Achievement.* New York: Oxford, 1959

STOKE, S. M., An inquiry into the concept of identification. *Journal of Genetic Psychology,* 1950, 76: 163–189

STOLZ, H. R., Shorty comes to terms with himself. *Progressive Education,* 1940, **17:** 405–411

———, AND LOIS M. STOLZ, Adolescent problems related to somatic variations. In N. B. Henry (Ed.), *Adolescence.* Yearbook of the National Society for the Study of Education, 43: Pt. 1. Chicago: University of Chicago Press, 1944

STONE, A. A. AND GLORIA C. ONQUÉ, *Longitudinal Studies of Child Personality.* Cambridge, Mass.: Harvard University Press, 1959

STONE, C. P. AND R. G. BARKER, The attitudes and interests of premenarcheal and postmenarcheal girls. *Journal of Genetic Psychology,* 1939, **54:** 27–71

STOUFFER, G. A. W., JR., Behavior problems of children as viewed by teachers and mental hygienists. *Mental Hygiene,* 1952, **36:** 271–285

STRANG, RUTH, *Behavior and Background of Students in College and Secondary School.* New York: Harper & Row, 1937

———, Guidance to meet the needs of youth. In N. B. Henry (Ed.), *Adapting the Secondary-School Program to the Needs of Youth.* Yearbook of the National Society for the Study of Education, 52: Pt. 1. Chicago: University of Chicago Press, 1953

———, *The Adolescent Views Himself.* New York: McGraw-Hill, 1957

———, Homework and guided study. In C. W. Harris (Ed.), *Encyclopedia of Educational Research.* (3d ed.) New York: Macmillan, 1960

STRODTBECK, F. L., Family interaction, values, and achievement. In McClelland et al. (Eds.), *Talent and Society.* New York: Van Nostrand, 1958

SULLIVAN, E. T., W. W. CLARK, AND E. W. TIEGS, *California Test of Mental Maturity.* Los Angeles: California Test Bureau, 1957

SULLIVAN, H. S., *The Interpersonal Theory of Psychiatry.* New York: Norton, 1953

SUPER, D. E., Experience, emotion, and vocational choice. *Occupations,* 1948, **27:** 23–27

SYMONDS, P. M., *Dynamic Psychology.* New York: Appleton, 1949

———, *What Education Has to Learn from Psychology.* New York: Bureau of Publications, Teachers College, Columbia University, 1958

TANNENBAUM, A. J., *A Study of Verbal Stereotypes Associated with Brilliant and Average Students.* Unpublished doctoral dissertation, Teachers College, Columbia University, 1959

TERMAN, L. M., *The Measurement of Intelligence.* Boston: Houghton Mifflin, 1916

———, AND MAUD A. MERRILL, *Measuring Intelligence.* Boston: Houghton Mifflin, 1937

———, AND ———, *Stanford-Binet Intelligence Scale: Manual for the Third Revision, Form L-M.* Boston: Houghton Mifflin, 1960

———, AND MELITA H. ODEN, *Genetic Studies of Genius.* 4: *The Gifted Child Grows Up.* Stanford, Calif.: Stanford University Press, 1947

———, AND ———, Major issues in the education of gifted children. *Journal of Teacher Education,* 1954, **5:** 230–232

THELEN, H. A., *Dynamics of Groups at Work.* Chicago: University of Chicago Press, 1954

———, *Education and the Human Quest.* New York: Harper & Row, 1960

———, AND R. W. TYLER, Implications for improving instruction in the high school. In N. B. Henry (Ed.), *Learning and Instruction.* Yearbook of the National Society for the Study of Education, 49: Pt. 1. Chicago: University of Chicago Press, 1950

THOMPSON, G. G. AND J. E. HORROCKS, A study of friendship fluctuations of urban boys and girls. *Journal of Genetic Psychology,* 1947, **70:** 53–63

——, AND C. W. HUNNICUTT, The effect of repeated praise and blame on the work achievement of introverts and extroverts. *Journal of Educational Psychology,* 1944, **35:** 257–266

THORNDIKE, E. L., The nature, purposes, and general methods of measurement in the solution of school problems. In G. M. Whipple (Ed.), *Measurement of Educational Products.* Yearbook of the National Society for the Study of Education, 17: Pt. 2. Chicago: University of Chicago Press, 1918

——, *Educational Psychology.* 1: *The Original Nature of Man;* 2: *The Psychology of Learning;* 3: *Work and Fatigue, Individual Differences.* New York: Bureau of Publications, Teachers College, Columbia University Press, 1921

——, Mental discipline in high school studies. *Journal of Educational Psychology,* 1924, **15:** 1–22, 83–98

TINKLEMAN, S. N., *Improving the Classroom Test: A Manual of Test Construction Procedures for the Classroom Teacher.* Albany, N. Y.: Bureau of Examinations and Testing, New York State Education Department, 1958

TORRANCE, E. P., Current research on the nature of creative talent. *Journal of Counseling Psychology,* 1959, **6:** 309–316

——, Personality development in the highly creative child. Mimeographed. *Minnesota Studies of Creative Thinking in the Early School Years, Research Memorandum, Bureau of Educational Research* 60–1. Minneapolis: College of Education, University of Minnesota, 1960a

——, *A Collection of Ideas for Developing the Creative Thinking Abilities Through Language Arts in the Fourth, Fifth and Sixth Grades.* Mimeographed, Minneapolis: Bureau of Educational Research, College of Education, University of Minnesota, 1960b

TRYON, CAROLINE M., Evaluation of adolescent personality by adolescents. *Monographs of the Society for Research in Child Development,* 1939, 4: No. 4

TYLER, LEONA E., *The Psychology of Human Differences.* (2d ed.) New York: Appleton, 1956

TYLER, R. W., Achievement testing and curriculum construction. In E. G. Williamson (Ed.), *Trends in Student Personnel Work.* Minneapolis: University of Minnesota Press, 1949

UNDERWOOD, B. J., "Spontaneous recovery" of verbal associations. *Journal of Experimental Psychology,* 1948, **38:** 429–439

VANDEBERG, ETHYL, Readiness for language arts begins in the kindergarten. *Elementary School Journal,* 1953, **53:** 447–453

VERNON, P. E. (ED.), *Secondary School Selection.* London: Methuen, 1957

VIGOTSKY, L. S., *Thought and Language* (Edited and translated by Eugenia Hanfmann and Gertrude Vakar). New York: Wiley, 1962

WALKER, HELEN M., Statistical understanding every teacher needs. In *Improving Educational Research.* Washington, D.C.: American Educational Research Association, National Education Association, 1948

WALLAS, G., *The Art of Thought.* New York: Harcourt, 1926

WANDT, E. AND G. W. BROWN, *Essentials of Educational Evaluation.* New York: Holt, Rinehart and Winston, 1957

WARD, L. B., Reminiscence and rote learning. *Psychological Monographs,* 1937, 49: No. 220

WARNER, W. L., R. J. HAVIGHURST, AND M. B. LOEB, *Who Shall be Educated?* New York: Harper & Row, 1944

———, AND P. S. LUNT, *The Social Life of a Modern Community* (Yankee City Series, 1). New Haven: Yale University Press, 1941

———, AND ———, *The Status System of a Modern Community* (Yankee City Series, 2). New Haven: Yale University Press, 1942

———, MARCIA MEEKER, AND K. EELLS, *Social Class in America.* New York: Harper & Row, 1960

WARREN, J. R. AND P. A. HEIST, Personality attributes of gifted college students. *Science,* 1960, 132: 330–337

WASHBURNE, C. AND L. M. HEIL, What characteristics of teachers affect children's growth? *School Review,* 1960, 68: 420–428

WATSON, G. B., Some personality differences in children related to strict or permissive parental discipline. *Journal of Psychology,* 1957, 44: 227–249

WATSON, J. B. AND ROSALIE RAYNER, Conditioned emotional reactions. *Journal of Experimental Psychology,* 1920, 3: 1–14

WATSON, W. S. AND G. W. HARTMANN, The rigidity of a basic attitudinal frame. *Journal of Abnormal and Social Psychology,* 1939, 34: 314–335

WECHSLER, D., *The Measurement of Adult Intelligence.* (3d ed.) Baltimore: Williams & Wilkins, 1944

WEIR, M. W. AND H. W. STEVENSON, The effect of verbalization in children's learning as a function of chronological age. *Child Development,* 1959, 30: 143–149

WEISS, E. AND O. S. ENGLISH, *Psychosomatic Medicine.* (2d ed.) Philadelphia: Saunders, 1949

WERNER, H., The concept of development from a comparative and organismic point of view. In D. B. Harris (Ed.), *The Concept of Development.* Minneapolis: University of Minnesota Press, 1957

WERTHEIMER, M., *Productive Thinking.* (rev. ed.) New York: Harper & Row, 1959

WESMAN, A. G., A study of transfer from high school subjects to intelligence. *Journal of Educational Research,* 1945, 39: 254–264

WHEELER, L. R., A comparative study of the intelligence of East Tennessee mountain children. *Journal of Educational Psychology,* 1942, 33: 321–334

WHITE, R. W., *The Abnormal Personality.* (2d ed.) New York: Ronald, 1956

———, Motivation reconsidered: the concept of competence. *Psychological Review,* 1959, 66: 297–333

WICKMAN, E. K., *Children's Behavior and Teachers' Attitudes.* New York: Commonwealth Fund, 1928

WIENER, N., *The Human Use of Human Beings: Cybernetics and Society.* (rev. ed.). Garden City, N. Y.: Doubleday, 1954

WILSON, R. C., Creativity. In N. B. Henry (Ed.), *Education for the Gifted.* Yearbook of the National Society for the Study of Education, 57: Pt. 2. Chicago: University of Chicago Press, 1958

WISPÉ, L. G., Teaching methods research. *American Psychologist,* 1953, 8: 147–150

WITHALL, J., The development of the climate index. *Journal of Educational Research,* 1951, 45: 93–100

WITTY, P., Who are the gifted? In N. B. Henry (Ed.), *Education for the Gifted.* Yearbook of the National Society for the Study of Education, 57: Pt. 2. Chicago: University of Chicago Press, 1958

WOLFBEIN, S. L., Education and employment. In E. Ginzberg (Ed.), *The Nation's Children.* 2: *Development and Education.* New York: Columbia University Press, 1960 (Golden Anniversary White House Conference on Children and Youth)

WOLFENSTEIN, MARTHA, Trends in infant care. *American Journal of Orthopsychiatry,* 1953, 33: 120–130

WOOD, DOROTHY A., *Test Construction: Development and Interpretation of Achievement Tests.* Columbus, Ohio: Merrill, 1960

WOODRUFF, A. D., Discipline. In C. W. Harris (Ed.), *Encyclopedia of Educational Research.* (3d ed.) New York: Macmillan, 1960

WOODWORTH, R. S., *Dynamics of Behavior.* New York: Holt, Rinehart and Winston, 1958

WRIGHT, BEATRICE A., *Physical Disability—A Psychological Approach.* New York: Harper & Row, 1960

WRIGHTSTONE, J. W., *Class Organization for Instruction* (What Research Says to the Teacher, No. 13). Washington, D.C.: Department of Classroom Teachers, American Educational Research Association, National Education Association, 1957

WULF, F., Über die Veränderung von Vorstellungen (Gedächtnis und Gestalt). *Psychologische Forschung,* 1922, 1: 333–373 (Translated and condensed as: Tendencies in figural variation in Ellis, 1938)

YARROW, MARIAN R., J. D. CAMPBELL, AND L. J. YARROW, Acquisition of new norms: a study of racial desegregation. *Journal of Social Issues,* 1958, 14: 8–28

YOUNG, P. T., *Emotion in Man and Animal.* New York: Wiley, 1943

READINGS

COLLECTIONS IN

EDUCATIONAL PSYCHOLOGY

BALLER, W. R. (Ed), *Readings in the Psychology of Human Growth and Development*. New York: Holt, Rinehart and Winston, 1962

CHARTERS, W. W., JR., AND N. L. GAGE (Eds.), *Readings in the Social Psychology of Education*. Boston: Allyn and Bacon, 1963

COLADARCI, A. P. (Ed.), *Educational Psychology: A Book of Readings*. New York: Holt, Rinehart and Winston, 1955

DECECCO, J. P. (Ed.), *Human Learning in the School (Readings in Educational Psychology)*. New York: Holt, Rinehart and Winston, 1963

FULLAGAR, W. A., H. G. LEWIS, AND C. F. CUMBEE (Eds.), *Readings for Educational Psychology*. New York: Thomas Y. Crowell, 1956

HAIMOVITZ, M. L. AND NATALIE R. HAIMOVITZ (Eds.), *Human Development: Selected Readings*. New York: Thomas Y. Crowell, 1960

HARRIS, T. L. AND W. E. SCHWAHN (Eds.), *Selected Readings on the Learning Process*. New York: Oxford University Press, 1961

MORSE, W. C. AND G. M. WINGO (Eds.), *Readings in Educational Psychology*. Chicago: Scott, Foresman, 1962

NOLL, V. H. AND RACHEL P. NOLL (Eds.), *Readings in Educational Psychology*. New York: Macmillan, 1962

REMMERS, H. H., ET AL. (Eds.), *Growth, Teaching, and Learning: A Book of Readings*. New York: Harper & Row, 1957

ROSENBLITH, JUDY F., AND W. ALLINSMITH (Eds.), *The Causes of Behavior: Readings in Child Development and Educational Psychology*. Boston: Allyn and Bacon, 1962

SEIDMAN, J. M. (Ed.), *Readings in Educational Psychology*. Boston: Houghton Mifflin, 1955

—— (Ed.), *Educating for Mental Health: A Book of Readings*. New York: Thomas Y. Crowell, 1963

CHART OF RECOMMENDED SELECTIONS

Chapter in text	Baller (1962) Chapter nos.	Charters and Gage (1963) Page nos.	Coladarci (1955) Serial nos.	DeCecco (1963) Chapter and selection nos.
1	1		3, 4, 7, 10, 22, 37	1–2, 1–5, 8–1
2	6 14	219	9, 23, 24, 25, 26, 28	2–1, 2–2, 2–4, 4–4
3			2, 5	1–1, 1–3, 3–5, 4–6, 5–4
4			33	2–3, 4–1, 4–2, 4–5, 5–3
5			29, 30, 31, 32	4–3
6		40, 57, 107, 254	38	
7		133		3–3, 3–4, 6–2, 6–3
8	12	87, 97, 107, 114, 123, 126, 264	14, 16, 17, 18, 21, 45	9–1, 9–2
9		212	40, 41, 42, 44, 46	2–5, 10–1, 10–2, 10–4
10	10		27	7–1, 7–2, 7–3, 8–2
11	5 7	226	11, 36	
12	9		6	
13	13	235		
14	8	3, 12, 21	8, 20, 43	
15	15	141, 153, 162, 173, 181, 190, 196, 287	13, 19, 35	8–3, 9–3, 9–4
16	2	271, 278, 309	1, 12, 15, 34	1–4

CHART OF RECOMMENDED SELECTIONS

Chapter in text	Fullagar, Lewis, and Cumbee (1956)	Haimovitz and Haimovitz (1960)	Harris and Schwahn (1961)	Morse and Wingo (1962)	Noll and Noll (1962)
	Serial nos.	Serial nos.	Serial nos.	Page nos.	Serial nos.
1	14, 40			1, 3, 38, 151	2, 3, 4, 17, 18
2	15, 28, 29, 30, 42	25, 46, 50, 56, 58	25	67, 155, 251, 256, 258	20, 22, 24, 37
3	1, 3, 31, 32, 33		1, 2, 3, 13, 14, 15, 17, 18, 28	100, 115, 169, 174, 210	7, 8
4	5, 9, 10	6	5, 6, 7, 8, 10, 11, 31	183, 188, 193	
5			29	222	19
6	26	7, 29, 35, 36, 43, 80	19, 20	91, 122, 135, 198, 273	31, 43
7	6, 36, 37	61	30	144, 226, 369	21, 27, 29, 30
8	35, 46	32, 33	22, 23	269	26, 34, 49
9	48		33, 34, 35	353, 359, 364	28, 44, 45, 46, 47, 48, 49, 50, 51, 52
10	17, 19, 21, 22	64, 65		242	6, 9, 12, 13, 14, 15, 38, 41, 53
11	2, 20, 24, 38, 39	57, 59	27	129, 308, 325	33, 42
12	12, 13, 41	42, 73	26, 32		
13		5, 17, 23, 38, 51	21	70, 83, 110	
14	18, 34	28, 55, 66			36
15	43, 44, 49	30, 31	24	12, 263, 282, 286, 336	25, 35, 39, 40
16	16, 47	24		7, 25, 29, 157, 162	1, 10, 23, 32

CHART OF RECOMMENDED SELECTIONS

Chapter in text	Remmers et al., (1957) Page nos.	Rosenblith and Allinsmith (1962) Chapter and selection nos.	Seidman (1955) Serial nos.	Seidman (1963) Serial nos.
1	183, 188, 194, 520	1–2, **3**–1, **6**–8, **11**–12	8, 11, 31	17
2	122, 152, 281, 300, 357, 373	6–2, **10**–1, **10**–3, **10**–6, **10**–12	32, 33, 36, 57, 59, 60	12, 35
3	99, 107, 110, 200, 495	3–2, **10**–4, **10**–5	21, 22, 23, 24, 42	27
4	158	6–6, **11**–1	38, 40, 43	22, 32, 33
5	170, 172	**11**–2, **11**–3	39	30
6	7, 399	3–7, 4–1, 4–3, 5–4, 7–3, **10**–5	46, 48, 49	34, 37, 38
7		3–5, 3–6, **11**–11	37, 51, 54, 55	24, 29, 31, 44, 46, 48, 49
8	236, 391	9–1, 9–2	25, 26, 27, 28, 29, 61	3, 11, 13, 14, 28, 41, 42, 43
9	446, 449, 458, 490, 501, 546	**11**–6, **11**–7, **11**–8		
10	54, 63, 97, 467, 475, 478	2–1, **2**–2, **8**–2, **8**–3, **8**–4, **8**–5, **8**–6, **8**–7		20
11	246, 256, 274, 318, 336, 344, 364	3–3, **10**–7, **10**–13	16	6, 7, 10, 36
12		2–5, 2–6	1, 2, 3, 34	
13		3–4, 9–3, **10**–10	64, 65, 66	2, 4
14	77, 380, 403	4–6	9	5, 15, 55
15	17, 230, 413, 538	7–4	15, 17, 18, 67, 69	8, 9, 21, 25, 40, 47
16	27, 267, 551		20, 30, 44, 58, 71, 74	19, 23, 26

AUTHOR INDEX

SUBJECT INDEX

Ability grouping, 208–211; for gifted students, 321

Ability, intellectual, 301–303; range and altitude of, 280–282; tests, 309

Absolute zero, of measurement scale, 250

Abstraction, as quality of intelligence, 302

Acceleration, for gifted students, 320

Acceptance, by family, 400–403; by peers, 236–238

Accuracy, of performance, 279–280

Achievement, influenced by peer group, 35–36, 232; influenced by teacher characteristics, 482–484; tests, 290–291

Activity, directed, 41–43

Administrator-teacher interaction, 510–513

Adolescence, developmental tasks, 12; emotional characteristics, 335–336; heterosexual choices, 224–228; physical changes, 367–371; subculture, 35–36

Affect (see Emotion)

Aggression, 345–353; basis of, 346–347; displaced, 349–350; prosocial, 351–352; regression as, 350–352; sex differences in, 351–352

Aims of education, development of rational powers, 8–9; and differential psychology, 12–14; as enlargment of awareness, 59–60; and evaluation, 270–278; and human development, 9–12; and psychology of personality, 7–8; and social psychology, 14–15; see also Objectives of teaching

Allport-Vernon Study of Values Test, 332

Anecdotal record, 288, 501–504

Anger, 345–353; see also Aggression

Anticipation, 341

Anxiety, 336–345; of parents, 413–414

Application of learning, evaluation of, 275–276

Aptitude, 291–295; profile of, 291–292

Aspiration, level of, 48

Attitudes, change of, 221–222; and intelligence, 312–313; and social class, 425, 440–442; see also Values

Autistic thinking, 92

Autocratic relationships, in the classroom, 465–470; in the home, 406–412

Autokinetic effect, 221

Behavior, determinants of, 19–49; environmental determinants, 30–43; self as determinant of, 43–49; universal determinants of, 21–30

Body types, and personality, 361–363

Boredom, 25–26

Brain damage, 372–374

California Test of Mental Maturity, 309

Cerebrotonia (see Temperament)

Cephalo-caudal direction of physical development, 386

Character reputation, and social class, 436–437

Characteristics of teachers, 480–483

Cheating, 164–166

Childhood, body types, 362, 366; developmental tasks, 12; emotional characteristics, 334–335; moral judgment, 146–152; thought patterns, 97–104

Child-guidance clinic, 343–344

Child-rearing practices, and social class, 430–432

Child-Study Program, 501–504

Class, social (see Social class)

Classroom interaction, 460–464

Climate, classroom index, 464–466

Coaction, 462–463

Cognition (see Thinking)

Cognitive domain, evaluation, 271–276

Cognitive field, 95–96

Communication with parents, 415–417

Compensation, 352–353

Competition, 216–218

Compliance, as basis for moral behavior, 162–164

Conation (see Striving)

Concepts, 57–61; and language, 58

Concurrent validity, 266–267

Conditioning, 56–57; classical, 56; in emotions, 340; instrumental, 56–57, 191; and role of learner, 67

Conduct problems, 406

Conformance, as basis for moral behavior, 162–164

Conformity, 222

Consent, as basis for moral behavior, 163–164

Conservation of cultural heritage, 496–497

Construct validity, 268–269

Content validity, 267

Control, 464–476; see also Discipline

Convergence, as basis for moral behavior, 163–164

558